The Fragile Juggernaut

Studies in the Political Economy of Global Labor and Work

VOLUME 6

The titles published in this series are listed at *brill.com/pelw*

The Fragile Juggernaut

Marx & Engels on Capitalism, Class Struggle and Crisis

By

Harry Cleaver

BRILL

LEIDEN | BOSTON

Cover illustration: Hindu Juggernaut chariot. © Library of Congress (public domain).

The Preface was originally published in the online web journal The Commoner, Issue 05, Autumn 2002.

Appendix 1 was previously published in *Teoria kryzysu jako teoria walki klas* (Poznań: Wydawnictwo A+, 2017).

Library of Congress Cataloging-in-Publication Data

Names: Cleaver, Harry, 1944- author.
Title: The fragile juggernaut : Marx & Engels on capitalism, class struggle and crisis / by Harry Cleaver.
Description: Leiden ; Boston : Brill, [2025] | Series: Studies in political economy of global labor and work, 2667-288X ; volume 6 | Includes bibliographical references and index.
Identifiers: LCCN 2024030807 (print) | LCCN 2024030808 (ebook) | ISBN 9789004708365 (hardback) | ISBN 9789004708631 (ebook)
Subjects: LCSH: Financial crises–Philosophy. | Financial crises–Europe–History–19th century. | Capitalism–Social aspects–Europe. | Marx, Karl, 1818-1883. | Engels, Friedrich, 1820-1895. | Marxian economics.
Classification: LCC HB3714 .C58 2024 (print) | LCC HB3714 (ebook) | DDC 338.5/42–dc23/eng/20240801
LC record available at https://lccn.loc.gov/2024030807
LC ebook record available at https://lccn.loc.gov/2024030808

Typeface for the Latin, Greek, and Cyrillic scripts: "Brill". See and download: brill.com/brill-typeface.

ISSN 2667-288X
ISBN 978-90-04-70836-5 (hardback)
ISBN 978-90-04-70863-1 (e-book)
DOI 10.1163/9789004708631

This book is printed on acid-free paper and produced in a sustainable manner.

Juggernaut

Originally, a British colonial misspelling of Jagannath, one title for the Hindu God Vishu, the noun juggernaut has come to refer to "a massive inexorable force, campaign, movement, or object that crushes whatever is in its path" (Merrium-Webster Dictionary). The "object that crushes" comes from early reports that some worshipers threw themselves under the wheels of the huge Jagannath chariots towed through the streets in public Ratha Yatra ceremonies. Translated as "Lord of the World," Jagannath or Juggernaut seems a good characterization of how capitalists (and some critics) understand their system and its role in the world.

Harry Cleaver

Contents

Preface (2024)

This book presents a comprehensive analysis of Karl Marx and Friedrich Engels' writings on crisis, highlighting the key role played by the struggles of workers throughout capitalism's organization of society. Its origin is an essay, "Marx's Theory of Crisis as a Theory of Class Struggle," which I wrote in collaboration with Peter Bell, originally published in 1982. Since then, I have repeatedly revised the essay and in the process considerably amplified it. To this most recent revision I have added: this foreword, an earlier preface, and an annotated bibliography of Marx and Engels' writings on crisis which I compiled while doing the research for this book.

The original essay, intended to be the opening chapter of a book, was pared down for publication in the series *Research in Political Economy*, edited by Paul Zarembka.[1] "Paring down" involved condensing the essay – to a length compatible with its inclusion in a collection – mainly by leaving out some of the argument, some quotations from Marx and Engels' writings and a great many footnotes. In the present, revised, and amplified version of the essay I have reincorporated much of what was previously left out, including extensive footnotes to the material upon which it is based, and added new material based on my continuing research and thinking about what I have found since 1982.[2]

The two prefaces were occasioned by the publication of revisions of the essay in 2002 and 2016. I provided the 2002 preface as background to the essay's inclusion in a special issue of *The Commoner*, an online journal edited by Massimo de Angelis.[3] The 2016 preface, "Note to Polish Readers," was written for a Polish translation of the original essay published as a book.[4] That "Note" is included here as an Appendix because it adds to both the essay and the earlier preface in two ways. The first part provides considerable detail on Marx and Engels' writings on crises in Poland – thus adding to the essay's sketch in

1 Peter F. Bell and Harry Cleaver, "Marx's Crisis Theory as a Theory of Class Struggle," *Research in Political Economy* 5 (1982): 189–261.

2 A note on authorship. Although I wrote the original 1982 essay, it was the product of an active collaboration between myself and Peter Bell, so we were both cited as authors. At the time, if I remember correctly, Peter was drafting a chapter critiquing Paul Baran and Paul Sweezy's writings on crisis. We subsequently abandoned our book project in favor of directing our efforts to what seemed like more pressing matters, e.g., the neoliberal assault on the working class in the 1980s, both at home and abroad. I originally attributed the two prefaces to both of us, due to our original collaboration and on the assumption that Peter would eventually return to work on this subject. He has not done so, therefore – at his suggestion – here I take full and unique credit (and blame) for both prefaces, for the substantial amplification of the original essay and thus, for the book as a whole.

3 https://thecommoner.org/back-issues/issue-05-autumn-2002/

4 *Teoria kryzysu jako teoria walki klas* (Posnań: Wydawnictwo A+, 2017).

Chapter 2 of the evolution of their writings on crisis. The second part takes up the issue of assessing the relevance of these old writings to contemporary crises, both in general and in the specific case of Poland. In that preface I wrote:

> We have insisted, repeatedly, that our interest in Marx and Engels' writings is not philological but political. We have not intended our reinterpretation to be just another contribution to the analysis of the history of thought, but rather one that uncovers how, and in what ways, these old ideas can help us cope with new problems, especially the constraints imposed on our lives by contemporary capitalism. Today, we are two decades into the twenty-first century. Obviously, a lot has changed since our two authors wrote. Yet, despite many changes, crises of all sorts are still very much with us. Are Marx and Engels' thoughts from so long ago still relevant? Are the sorts of crises they addressed like the crises that you face today and to what degree, if any, do their analyses illuminate your present problems and can usefully inform your strategies of struggle?

These questions, I felt, would inevitably be raised by readers in Poland, long alienated from Marx due to the ways the Soviets and their local clients used his writings to justify their efforts to subordinate all of life to the very (state) capitalist imposition of work, exploitation, and alienation. So too should they be raised by all readers in evaluating the relevance and usefulness of both the original texts and the analysis set forth here. While I cannot examine the relevance of these ideas to the experiences of each reader, writing this second part of the "Notes" convinced me to compose many new footnotes to illustrate my own evaluation of the relevance of Marx and Engels' thoughts on crisis in the years since they wrote, including the present.

The extensive annotated bibliography of Marx and Engels' writings includes those on which we based our original essay and many of those referenced in my subsequent revisions. Ideally, the essay would be followed not merely by annotations on material utilized, but by the original material itself – hyperlinked for quick and easy reference. Early on, I had hopes for such linkages in a digital version of the essay. Unfortunately, such an arrangement proved impossible because much of the material has been withdrawn from our digital commons.[5] Nor is it practical in hard copy because of the large amount.

The original essay included two brief, historical sketches of Marx and Engels' writings and political activity – in so far as they related to their analyses of

5 This is primarily due to the refusal of the publishers of *Marx Engels Collected Works* (*MECW*) to allow free reproduction of the material included in those fifty volumes. Some 1,450 articles from *MECW* were digitized and made available at www.marxist.org but they were removed under threat by the publishers. Material from many other sources are still available at that site.

crisis – now Chapter 2, Section 1, "The Early Studies: 1843–1850" and Chapter 2, Section 2, "The Years of Theory: 1853–1867," ending with the publication of Volume 1 of *Capital*. By that time Marx had already completed the manuscripts that Engels would reshape into Volumes 2 and 3. Because I have drawn upon those volumes and other things they wrote after 1867, in both the original essay and this amplified version, I have extended the historical sketch to cover the period between 1867 and the end of their lives – in a new Chapter 2, Section 3, "After *Capital*, 1867–1895."

I undertook the elaboration of this new section with much the same reluctance with which Engels took on writing an extended critique of Eugen Dühring (1833-1921) in the late 1870s, albeit for different reasons. Engels was reluctant because he found Dühring's ideas largely insipid and wrong and only undertook the task because those ideas were infecting the burgeoning German Social Democratic movement for which he and Marx still had hopes. In my case, there were two factors which made writing this section burdensome. First, the eventual disappointing behavior of the social-democratic parties of that time, and second, this later period also included Engels' dive into creating a post-Hegel dialectical materialism, which provided the starting point of a version of Marxism which would reach its nadir in Stalinist Marxism-Leninism.

With respect to the first of these factors, the hopes of Marx, Engels, and many of their followers for the usefulness of political parties for workers, after swelling with the formation of the Second International, were plunged into despair when those so-called working-class parties voted support for the military mobilizations that led to World War I. Moreover, in the years that followed, those same, or similar parties, while helping workers win some gains have repeatedly participated in constraining and harnessing their struggles within capitalist development. Familiarity with this history long ago diminished my interest in studying their early formation and development, including Marx and Engels' efforts to influence their behavior.

With respect to the second of these factors, I was never sympathetic to Engels' effort to turn Marxism into an all-embracing philosophical system – which Marx himself rejected – and have downright despised its adaptation and use in the form of Marxism-Leninism.[6] Both attitudes made it painful to

6 Marx's rejection can be found in several places. One such was his dismissal of the argument by Nicolai K. Mikhailovski (1842–1904) that his analysis of primitive accumulation implied the historical necessity for all countries, including Russia, to pass through the stage of capitalism. Marx protested Mikhailovski "metamorphosizing" his "historical sketch of the genesis of capitalism in Western Europe into a historico-philosophical theory of general development, imposed by fate for all peoples, whatever the historical circumstances in which they are placed." Karl Marx, "Letter to [the editorial board of] *Otechestvenniye Zapiski*," November 1877, *MECW, Vol. 24*, p. 200.

return to a whole set of readings once set aside, even with the limited objective of recovering moments of their thinking about crises.

To be clear: these three historical sketches are by no means offered as serious biographical contributions. Their focus is narrow, on our two authors' writings on crisis, and these sketches are merely intended to help the reader situate those writings in time and circumstance. The relevant history is gleaned from the writings themselves and from a variety of histories and biographical sources – often at odds with one another. Footnotes indicate the sources used and sometimes the conflicts among them.

The various passages from Marx and Engels' writings quoted in this essay, have, for the most part, been taken from *Marx Engels Collected Works* (*MECW*), with five major exceptions. On the assumption that most readers are more likely to have access to 1) the Penguin editions of the three volumes of *Capital* and the *Grundrisse* and 2) to the new translation of *Marx's Economic Manuscript of 1864–1865* than *MECW*, I quote from the former, but in footnotes give page number references to both editions.[7] The translations in these editions are different, so fastidious readers – with enough time and inclination – might want to compare them. They might also check www.marxist.org for other translations from other sources. Those who can read German, of course, can consult the originals in Marx-Engels-Gesamtausgabe (*MEGA*). Lacking that skill, I do not provide volume or page number references to that work.[8]

7 Karl Marx, *Capital: A Critique of Political Economy, Volume 1*, trans. Ben Fowkes (New York: Pelican Books, 1976, London: Penguin Classics, 1990), *Capital: A Critique of Political Economy, Volume 2*, trans. David Fernbach (New York: Pelican Books, 1978, Penguin Classics, 1992), *Capital: A Critique of Political Economy, Volume 3*, trans. David Fernbach, (New York: Pelican Books 1981, London: Penguin Classics, 1991); *Grundrisse*, trans. Martin Nicolas (New York: Pelican Books, 1973, Baltimore: Penguin, 1993), *Marx's Economic Manuscript of 1864–65*, trans. Ben Fowkes (Chicago: Haymarket Books, 2017). All footnote references to these volumes just use their title and page number, e.g., *Capital, Vol. 2*, p. xxx. *MECW* references provide volume and page numbers.

8 *MEGA* is the largest published collection of Marx and Engels' writings and reproduces them in their original languages. The collection is still expanding, under the stewardship of the *Internationale Marx-Engels-Stiftung* (*IMES*) in Amsterdam. For more information on *MEGA* see its entry in Wikipedia. In some English translations, references are given to corresponding volumes and sections of *MEGA*, but not having access to the texts themselves and therefore unable to verify others' references, I have chosen not to reproduced them. For an account of the history of efforts to compile Marx and Engels' writings in substantial collections, see the Appendix to Kevin Anderson, *Marx at the Margins: on nationalism, ethnicity and non-western societies* (Chicago: University of Chicago Press, 2010, 2016), and the "Introduction" in Riccardo Bellofiore and Roberto Fineschi, eds., *Rereading Marx: New Perspectives After the Critical Edition* (London: Palgrave, 2009), 1–16.

Preface (2002)

Crisis theory is the Achilles heel of the left. Different views of capitalist development and breakdown have always shaped, and been shaped by, political strategies. In the early and mid-1970s the onset of a crisis of Keynesian policy, and hence theory, brought on by an international cycle of working-class struggle, led to a widespread preoccupation with "crisis theory" in both capitalist and anti-capitalist circles. This essay was written as an intervention in the debates of those times.

Throughout the Keynesian period the regulations set in place during and after the Great Depression coupled with Keynesian policies, both national and international, reduced the depth and shortened the length of business cycle downturns. As a result, the subject was largely neglected in both mainstream macroeconomic theory and among Marxists. When I took a course in business cycle theory at Stanford in the late 1960s the basic message was essentially: "we have things thoroughly in hand, in the future we will only have recessional slowdowns in growth and no depressions in aggregate output." In the wake of the engineered downturn in 1970 and the subsequent "Great Recession" of 1974–75, it became obvious that this had been a pipe dream. The search for alternatives to Keynesian theory and policy was on.

Among mainstream economists that search included the first serious re-consideration of neoliberal policies since Keynes. Among Marxists, it meant a scramble to retrieve and revitalize a variety of theories of crisis that had flourished and competed in an earlier, pre-Keynesian period. So urgent was the capitalist preoccupation with finding new theoretical solutions to the crisis that economic journals and the business press both carried assessments of what Marxists were saying, to see if any of it might be of use.

By the early and mid-1970s, when all this was happening, the anti-Vietnam war movement had born fruit, both good and bad. On the one hand, a combination of Vietnamese valor and U.S. internal protest was forcing the U.S. government out of Vietnam (final defeat and exit came in 1975). On the other, many militants were abandoning the New Left for one sect or another of the Old Left and the old sectarian theories and debates were re-emerging – picking up where they had left off years before. This was true with respect to "crisis theory" as it was with respect to other things. As a result, the arguments of that period largely repeated early debates that pitted, for example, underconsumptionist crisis theory against falling-rate-of-profit crisis theory. The political sects associated with various theories are often unpredictable, but there was considerable continuity and the "new" debates generally seemed like dusted-off versions of the old ones.

There were a few new wrinkles, but not many. The Sraffians and some American Radicals, for example Ray Boddy and James Crotty, offered a kind of neo-Ricardian "profit squeeze" crisis theory that was Marxian to the degree that it admitted class struggle over distribution but Ricardian in its neglect of class struggle in production. Other radical economists adopted strands of Marxist theory, usually drawn from the early writings, such as the "anarchy of production," or over-production.

In 1982, the only innovative rethinking of Marxian crisis theory in recent history had occurred in Italy where the Italian New Left had had to take on the very powerful and theoretically sophisticated Communist Party of Italy (CPI). There the "extraparliamentary" Left—that refused to play the CPI's game of seeking to share power via elections—undertook extensive re-evaluations both of the state of the class struggle and of Marxian theory. During those re-evaluations (that took several years and were spurred and inspired by a whole series of struggles) a number of Marxists, e.g., Romano Alquati, Raniero Panzieri, Mario Tronti, Antonio Negri, found ways to locate many of Marx's theoretical concepts within the dynamics of class struggle in ways that had never been done before. Concepts like "technology" or the "organic composition of capital," which had often been treated as either neutral (by the CPI) or purely as denoting weapons wielded by capitalists, were recast as theoretical expressions of aspects of class struggle. At the same time, at least in part because of the CPI's embrace of Keynesian "development," some of those same Marxists re-interpreted mainstream economic theory in class terms. They came to see that despite its "neutral," non-political language, it was very much a theory of the management of antagonistic class relations of struggle. Thus, for example, Negri reinterpreted Keynes as having done more than simply coming up with a new method of exploitation. He discovered a relatively progressive capitalist solution to the new power of the working class that emerged in the 1930s: harnessing wage struggles to drive accumulation. For example, in Keynes' macroeconomics, the new power of workers to achieve rising wages shifted his "consumption function" in a way that provoked capitalist investment and growth. These Marxists looked around and decided that what Antonio Gramsci (1891–1937) called "Fordism" (a particular way of organizing and managing capitalist class relations) had come to Italy from America and the Keynesian policies embraced by the CPI were its institutionalization at the level of the "social factory." What Marxist theory provided, they saw, was the means to decode such policies and provide workers with the theoretical tools for dissecting every aspect of "the economy" in class terms.[1]

---

1 A considerable body of this kind of work can be found referenced in the Texas Archives of Autonomist Marxism. A brief sketch can be found in the introduction to Harry Cleaver, *Reading* Capital *Politically*, 2nd ed. (Leeds: Anti/Theses and Edinburgh: AK Press, 2000). A much more complete survey is now available in Steve Wright, *Storming Heaven: Class Composition and Struggle in Italian Autonomist Marxism*, 2nd ed. (London: Pluto Press, 2017) and in his more recent *The Weight of the Printed Word: Text, Context and Militancy in Operaismo* (Chicago: Haymarket Books, 2021).

In a distorted manner some of these insights were taken up first in France, then in Britain and finally in the US by the "regulation" theorists. They took over the Italian New Left understanding of Fordism, for instance, and turned it into a periodization of capitalist management (or "regulation"). From a dynamic response to class struggle, the analysis was reduced to sketching a style of domination. In their lingo, "Fordism" would become more or less equivalent to "Keynesianism" and the post-Keynesian period would be seen as a "post-Fordist" one. What disappeared throughout most of their analysis was the omnipresent antagonistic class dynamics of the Italian theory on which they had drawn and, of course, the politics associated with them.

In the same period, some of those Italian reformulations of Marxist theory were imported undiluted and undistorted into those same countries by an entirely different set of actors. In France a variety of militants, including Yann Moulier-Boutang, read and translated many key Italian texts and drew on them to rethink their own situation. This led first to the journal *Camarades* and later to *Babylone* and then *Multitudes*. In Britain the same thing happened through the work of John Merrington and Ed Emery whose translations were published as a series of *Red Notes* and included both theoretical texts and extensive accounts and documentation of the political situations that had generated those texts. Eventually, that material circulated to the US, first through the movement of individuals exposed to it in Britain and then through the circulation of documents. The first results of that circulation were the appearance in the US of the Wages for Housework movement and then the journal *Zerowork* (1975, 1977). My own contributions to the elaboration of such theory began in 1978 with *Reading* Capital *Politically* – a systematic re-reading of Chapter One of Volume One of *Capital* in the light of the rest of Marx's work, incorporating insights from what I had come to call "Autonomist" Marxist theory – because of its emphasis on the ability of workers to take autonomous initiative in the class struggle.

The unsettled theoretical debate about "crisis" in capitalism and how to theorize it led Peter Bell and myself to contemplate writing a book surveying, politically decoding, and offering an alternative to the various strains of "Marxist crisis theory" that were then circulating and clashing. As a prelude to, or opening moment of, such a project we decided to undertake as systematic a study of Marx and Engels' writings on crisis as we could manage, given the texts available to us in languages we could read. While we found many of the Italian innovations inspiring and useful, including moments of analysis of the specific crisis of Keynesianism, nowhere could we find such a systematic study by those theorists. So, we undertook one. The result is the essay below that was originally published in *Research in Political Economy* in 1982. As it turned out, after undertaking this part of the study, largely my work, much of the analysis of other, more contemporary material was never written up in the form of chapters. However, samples of the kind of commentary those chapters would have contained can be found in Peter Bell, "Marxist Theory, Class Struggle and the Crisis of Capitalism," (1977), and Harry Cleaver, "Karl Marx: Economist or Revolutionary" (1986).[2] We concluded that the then current debates were not only largely sterile but also, in relation to other projects that interested us (such as dealing with Reaganomics and the onset of the international debt crisis), not worth the time it would take to demonstrate the fact in detail. So, the book was never completed.

Harry Cleaver
Austin, Texas and Boston, Massachusetts
Summer 2002

2 Peter Bell, "Marxist Theory, Class Struggle and the Crisis of Capitalism," in Jesse Schwartz, ed., *The Subtle Anatomy of Capitalism* (Santa Monica: Goodyear Publishing Company, 1977). Harry Cleaver, "Karl Marx: Economist or Revolutionary?" in Suzanne Helburn and David Bramhall, eds., *Marx, Schumpeter & Keynes* (Armonk: M. E. Sharpe, 1986).

CHAPTER 1

Introduction

> Philosophers have
> hitherto only *interpreted*
> the world in various ways;
> the point is to *change* it.
>
> KARL MARX

Every time there is an economic crisis in our capitalist system, some of those trying to understand what's going on turn back to Karl Marx, a man and political activist of the nineteenth century. This includes not only his followers – Marxists of various stripes – but economists and even the business press. With crises recurrent, and this return to Marx along with it, any number of articles and books have been written, reassessing the analysis Marx spelled out in his many writings. For Marxists, this return to Marx has involved renewing old debates, going all the way back to ones he was involved in. For economists it has meant reassessing whether there might be some aspect of his work still useful, despite their general agreement that the fundamentals of his theory were flawed and appropriately set aside long ago. For the business press, reflecting the anxiety of its readers, it has often been a desperate search for something, anything that might help explain the crisis at hand – even if it comes from their most important critic.

This book offers one more contribution to the Marxist tradition, one more reinterpretation of Marx's writings on crisis. Because his writings were often inspired by those of his friend and frequent co-author Friedrich Engels and in turn provided the latter with many theoretical underpinnings for his own work, this essay reads and interprets both of their writings and their interconnections.

My principal objectives are to show, *first*, how their theoretical work grew out of, and was integral to, their political struggles, *second*, how their theories of crisis were repeatedly formulated in terms of class conflict, *third*, how their analysis revealed not only the power but also the fragility of capitalism as a social system, precisely due to the many ways in which resistance to its rule repeatedly threw it into crisis, and *fourth*, how their analysis, based on their observation, study, and political engagement in the nineteenth century, is still relevant in the twenty-first century both to our understanding of capitalism and to coping with the crises that face us today. This exposition of their theories of crisis offers a new interpretation and demonstrates how that interpretation is internally consistent, semantically meaningful, and politically useful. In other words, in keeping with Marx's Eleventh Thesis on Feuerbach, this book offers not just another exercise in Marxian scholarship and political economy but some help in figuring out how to change the world.

1 Work, the Vulnerable Heart of Capitalism

The analysis I offer here differs from more traditional interpretations because it understands Marx and Engels' theories of accumulation and crisis as socio-political theories of the development of the antagonistic social relations of capitalist society. The antagonism, I argue, is rooted in the capitalist imposition of work and how, in response, people resist, struggling against the subordination of their lives to work – to being exploited and alienated – and often seek to craft alternatives. Therefore, I interpret all of Marx's concepts of value, surplus value, variable and constant capital, the organic composition of capital and so on, as denoting aspects of those relations of struggle. The development of capitalism is more than the evolution of capitalists, their businesses, and their economy. It is an evolving social system, which unfolds as capitalists try to reproduce their reduction of life to work on an ever-increasing scale, as people resist it, and as they try to get beyond it.

To many Marxists, the imposition of work *appears* to be merely something required by capitalists' endless search for profits, which are obtained by exploiting people's labor.[1] Profits are the motive, the objective, the "end", while work is merely the "means." I am arguing the opposite, namely that viewed socially and politically, the search for profits is merely the necessary means through which capitalists maintain and grow their peculiar social order. Investing profit expands the imposition of work on new people or in new ways.

This centrality of imposed work as the primary means of social control differentiates capitalism from previous social orders in which work has also been

1 "The sole purpose of a purchase of labor-power is production for profit." Riccardo Bellofiore and Nicola Taylor, eds., *The Constitution of Capital: Essays on Volume 1 of Marx's* Capital (New York: Palgrave Macmillan, 2004), 23.

imposed (ancient slavery, serfdom, etc.). In those other systems, the amount of work imposed was limited by particular objectives. But, as Marx argues in the second section of Chapter 10 of Volume 1 of *Capital*, it is the endless quality of the imposition which differentiates capitalism. The capitalist imposition of work is endless for two reasons. First and foremost, simply because it is the primary way capitalists organize people's lives, even their own – thus, their opposition to every effort to reduce the amount of work and the control it gives them over society. Second, while the capacity of each individual unit of capital to impose work is limited by its size, there is no theoretical limit to the ever-renewed conversion of objects and human activities into commodities whose production provides the opportunity to impose more work. That alone makes the possibilities for capitalists as a class to impose the work of producing commodities endless.

Although, in their own search for profits, merchants also impose work over and over again on those who handle and transport their goods, as long as they merely traded in surpluses produced by those beyond their control (other people's serfs, independent peasants, craftspeople, hunters and gatherers, etc.), their ability to put people to work was limited. Industrial capitalists overcome this limit by taking over production and imposing work not only on those who transport goods but on those producing them. Unlike merchants, by expropriating everyone else's means of production and hence their independence, capitalists can force everyone to seek income by working for them – even the merchants whose business has become dependent on the capitalist control over production.

Resistance to this endless creation of commodities and the imposition of the work of producing and transporting them has forced capitalists to intervene ever more actively and ever more thoroughly in people's lives outside the waged workplace. Workers' success in eventually forcing down the hours of their labor and then liberating their children from waged labor, forced capitalists to organize the re-incarceration of children into schools and to intervene in family life to ensure the reproduction of the willingness and ability to work, i.e., of life as the commodity labor-power. In the process, it has turned society into a "social factory," a whole social order modeled on the capitalist imposition of commodity-producing work. In this social order, Marx and Engels argued, one finds two different and antagonistic classes: one of capitalists and one of workers, a working class. How exactly those classes are defined and understood has, unsurprisingly, been a key issue among Marxists who have accepted the idea but differed on how they understand it.

2 "Class" and Class Struggle

My interpretation of Marx's theory of crisis as one of "class struggle" is based on the following understanding of the "classes" in capitalism. I mean, on one side, those "functionaries" of capitalism, who seek to impose or maintain the subordination of life to work,[2] and, on the other side, those upon whom it is imposed, who often resist and struggle to create alternatives. By differentiating class-in-itself and class-for-itself, Marx distinguished between one's *class status* and one's *class behavior*.[3] People find themselves part of the working class-in-itself simply by suffering the imposition of work. Those who resist that imposition and fight for what they need and want, often for life beyond work, become part of the working class-for-itself.[4] Both resistance to work

---

2 When ownership of the means of production (capital, narrowly defined) was generally personal, when owners managed or oversaw the management of their own businesses, it made sense to call such owners "capitalists." However, with the development of "joint stock" or "limited liability" corporations, in which ownership is diffused among myriad stockholders, Marx saw that the imposition, organization, and policing of work on the job devolved primarily to managers (from CEO's and Boards of Directors down the administrative hierarchy), who he called "functionaries" of capital. Thus, the key relationship of *ownership* was replaced by that of *managerial control*. Eventually, some non-Marxists recognized the same phenomenon and called it "managerial capitalism." See, for example, Adolph Berle and Gardiner Means, *The Modern Corporation and Private Property* (1932), John Kenneth Galbraith, *The New Industrial State* (1967) and Alfred Chandler, "The Emergence of Managerial Capitalism," *The Business History Review* 58, no. 4 (Winter 1984) 473–503.

3 Marx's most famous delineation of this distinction is in his analysis of the French peasantry in "The Eighteenth Brumaire of Louis Bonaparte" (1852), *MECW, Vol. 11*, p. 187. I have elaborated this conception of class against the all-too-common practice of seeing individuals as simply belonging to one rigidly defined class or another – what I call the "Madame Defarge theory of class," after the character in Charles Dickens' novel *Tale of Two Cities* (1859) set during the French Revolution. Once Madame Defarge had incorporated the name of a noble into her knitting, they were doomed to the guillotine regardless of their behavior. Similar practices were followed by Stalinists in the USSR with their lists of "kulaks" and Maoists in China with their lists of "rich peasants." Such "classification" has also been all too common among sociologists, political scientists, journalists, and political pundits. As I have argued elsewhere, ultimately working-class struggle for-itself involves not merely improvements in its condition but escaping capital's dialectic by creating alternatives, first as experiments then in crafting entirely new worlds in which the class distinction between the "functionaries" of capitalism and a separate working-class no longer exists. See, Harry Cleaver, *Reading* Capital *Politically*, 2nd ed. (Leeds: Anti/Theses and Edinburgh: AK Press, 2000), Chapter 2: The Commodity Form.

4 In the case of the capitalist class, the parallel dichotomy of class-in-itself and class-for-itself was clearly of less interest to Marx. While he was aware that individual "functionaries of capital" – like members of earlier ruling classes – might resist their role, even drop out of their class, becoming *déclassé* and choose to be workers, even struggle alongside workers, such behavior was uncommon. One example, of which he was well aware, was Robert Owen (1771–1858), a textile manufacturing capitalist who became so frustrated with his inability to convince other capitalists of his reformist ideas that he defected from

and the fight for alternative ways of organizing life can obviously take many forms, from the open-ended struggle for time and energy liberated from work to concrete experiments in new ways of being.

This dual concept of class recognizes how the behavior of individuals is often contradictory. Within the hierarchies of income, wealth and power characteristic of capitalism, individuals may both suffer the subordination of their lives to work yet be involved in imposing it on others. In other words, individuals may, to varying degrees, act as both workers and as functionaries of capital. An individual's position in the hierarchies largely determines the degree to which one suffers the imposition of work and the degree to which one imposes it on others. Greater willingness and ability to impose work is rewarded by more income, power and status, a higher position in those hierarchies. Greater resistance to that imposition is penalized by lower income, lower status, a lower position.

This book, by emphasizing workers' struggles and their role in creating crises for capitalism, privileges Marx's concept of working class for-itself. We can recognize how many workers, at a given moment, may not be struggling against their exploitation or even be complicit with it. Complicity can be either passive, simply getting through the job without resisting, or active, as typified by those lucky enough to have jobs where they can exercise an unusual degree of control over their work and thus actually enjoy it, e.g., creative artists, research scientists, teachers, and, as a result, work enthusiastically. This amounts to imposing work on themselves, quite independently of whether they have any supervisory role vis-à-vis other workers. Within conflicts over this social order, I call those who work "workers" or participants in the "working class" and those who seek to maintain it "capitalists" or "functionaries of capital," while keeping in mind the possible contradictions in the behavior of individuals or groups.[5] Recognizing this contradiction also helps in understanding how individuals

---

his class, becoming first a campaigner for worker-owned cooperatives and then tried to set up utopian communities.

5 Marx recognized this phenomenon of the self-imposition of work even for those who did not like their jobs, e.g., in the case of piece work where low piece-wages encourage hard work to the point where the "superintendence of labour becomes to a great extent superfluous." *Capital, Vol. 1*, p. 695, or *MECW*, *Vol. 35*, p. 552. While he saw this in factories, it also operates beyond the domain of waged and salaried labor, in places like schools where many students who have accepted the framework of competing for grades, impose long hours of homework on themselves, or in homes where unwaged housewives labor to repair and procreate labor-power, driven by hopes and expectations fostered by capitalist-shaped culture and advertising.

and groups of individuals sometimes shift from imposing work to resisting it or vice versa.[6]

Recognizing the centrality of pitting people against each other to capitalists' ability to impose work allows us to understand how all kinds of differences – gender, race, ethnicity, nationality – have been preserved or created and instrumentalized to undermine resistance and gain complicity with life-as-work. Therefore, as Marx clearly understood, "class" has never designated a homogeneous mass, but has always been highly differentiated by 1) being organized hierarchically, with some accorded more power, e.g., men over women, whites over blacks, English over Irish, local over immigrant, skilled over unskilled, salaried over waged, waged over unwaged and so on, and 2) by the inevitably different characteristics of struggles by those in different positions within the hierarchy. As it has been designed to do, this organization of power inevitably involves conflicts among workers, among capitalists, and between workers and capitalists. How those conflicts play out – aggravating differences or overcoming them – results in changes in the distribution and composition of power among workers, among capitalists and thus between workers and capitalists.[7]

What have been called the "laws of motion" or the "objective historical movement" of capitalist development I understand to be regularities in the unplanned outcomes of the conflicts between antagonistic subjects. As in physics where two vector forces create a resultant force whose direction and magnitude are distinct from either of the two, so too in the class struggles that constitute capitalist development, the "laws" of accumulation and of crisis are the unplanned outcomes of confrontation. Those outcomes are the result of myriad "vectors" of struggle, both within each class and between them. Therefore, analyzing the composition and dynamics of class struggle at any

6 A common example of such a shift in the behavior of individuals comes with promotion to a managerial position in which the "job" becomes imposing work on those who were once co-workers but are now subordinates. This can happen either within the existing hierarchy of jobs or even within unions where "promotion" means becoming a shop steward or union enforcer. Distaste for doing to one's comrades what one has suffered is one reason why many workers refuse such promotions. An example of such a shift among a whole section of the workforce has been that in the behavior of teachers. As supervision by school administrators and even state legislators has become onerous micro-management trying to control not only what they teach, but also the materials they use, and what they are allowed to say to their students, we have seen teachers rise from compliance with mandated work rules to resistance, a resistance that has included both individual exodus from such jobs and the collective formation of unions and the organization of strikes.

7 Although in his theoretical essays Marx mostly focuses on conflicts between workers and capitalists, with no further differentiation, his studies of actual struggles demonstrate a lively awareness of divisions and conflicts among workers and among capitalists.

point in time and place is no simple matter – as Marx and Engels' own essays make clear.

Building from an such an understanding of the fundamental Marxian concept of the antagonistic social nature of capital, I offer a reinterpretation and synthesis of such traditional themes of "crisis theory" as the tendency of the rate of profit to fall, underconsumption, disproportionality, and the "contradiction between the forces and relations of production."

3 Capitalism, the Fragile Juggernaut

The mere fact that capitalism has progressively dominated the history of our society and planet over the last few hundred years – despite repeated revolts – has given it an air of invulnerability, of being an unstoppable juggernaut. Added to that lamentable fact have been the myriad ideologies conjured up by its apologists that have not only treated its existence as historically inevitable but portrayed it as the culmination of social evolution. With capitalism, have we not, asked the neoconservative Francis Fukuyama, reached the "end of history"?[8] It may not be the best of worlds, but is it not the best we are capable of creating? Whatever its flaws, we are told, they can be remedied by piecemeal reforms and there is no point in looking beyond it for some other way of organizing society. In the infamous words of British Prime Minister Margaret Thatcher, "There is no real alternative." She was arguing for acceptance of her policies, but the phrase became a slogan justifying capitalism in general.

Even among the critics of capitalism, including Marx and Engels, the vast majority of words inscribed or uttered have been dedicated to describing not only how successful capitalism has been but also how its power has allowed it to crush, absorb, or instrumentalize all alternatives. Often, books on capitalism by its critics, including Marxists, read as virtual paeans to that power, leaving the impression of capitalism as an evil but almost invincible impersonal force. As a result, proposals about how to organize working class struggle have often rung hollow. Hollow because in their analyses of an all-powerful capitalism workers appear overwhelmingly as victims. If, on the contrary, we recognize how pervasive workers' struggles have been and how their repeated success at rupturing capitalist plans have revealed its fragility, analyses of those struggles can provide the basis for imaging how we can not only rupture capitalist plans but shatter the juggernaut and bring it down.

8 Francis Fukuyama, "The End of History?" *The National Interest* 16 (Summer 1989): 3–18.

The central thrust of my interpretation of Marxian theory sees *accumulation* as the expanded reproduction of a fabric of capitalist control that is always tenuous, repeatedly threatened, and often torn by workers' struggles. The most serious crises are working-class produced rips in that fabric and a consequence of workers either directly undermining some aspect of capitalist control or elaborating a positive alternative which indirectly threatens escape from that control. Sometimes the rips are partial and limited, which capitalists can patch over. Sometimes, the rips spread, opening seams, and exploding in overt, revolutionary uprisings, threatening to shred the fabric as a whole. Where capitalists can crush or even harness such threats, whether limited or explosive, those crises are successfully "internalized"; they remain *within* capitalism and can even accelerate accumulation. Marxian analysis, however, reveals how resistance, struggle, and crisis inevitably reappear because of how capitalism organizes the world, including ever more exploitation and alienation.[9]

This is not to deny that there are many influences within the complex pattern of accumulation which are only indirectly related to workers' struggles. Many of these are discussed below. Struggle always takes place in a concrete setting, at a given level of development, and within a particular *class composition* that shapes the direction and outcome of the conflict.[10] But I contend that from the viewpoint of the working class, every factor related to crisis must be evaluated in terms of the development of sufficient power to overthrow the system. Marx and Engels' work is most useful to those of us opposed to capitalism when we interpret it within the framework of our struggles.

Such a "political reading" of crisis theory eschews reading Marx and Engels' writings as philosophy, as political economy, or simply as criticism of capitalism. It insists on reading them from an anti-capitalist, working-class perspective as providing ideas which can be appropriated as strategic and tactical weapons for workers within the class struggle.

---

9 This reverses the traditional view of revolution as one working class response to crises generated by contradictions internal to capital and independent of workers' struggles.

10 The concept of *class composition*, which denotes the dynamics of the power relationships within and between the working class and capital at a point in time, along with those of *political recomposition* (changes achieved by workers' struggles that increase their power) and *decomposition* (changes achieved by capitalist efforts that undermine workers' power) was developed by the Italian Marxists discussed in my Preface of 2002. For a detailed analysis of the development of these concepts see Steve Wright, *Storming Heaven: Class Composition and Struggle in Italian Autonomist Marxism*, 2nd ed. (London: Pluto Press, 2017).

4 What Constitutes a Crisis?

This reading leads directly to the question of the very meaning of "crisis." The concept is ambivalent and has been subject to many interpretations. Its conventional meaning among Marxists has been the denotation of a breakdown in the expanded reproduction of the system. With the concept originating in medicine as a turning point, life or death, in a disease, most Marxists have focused only on "crises" that they believe bring the system as a whole to its knees, with the threat, of course, not merely of collapse but of revolutionary overthrow. The historical sketch in Chapter 2 shows that this was how Marx and Engels saw the situation in 1847–48, where a large-scale, international crisis in capitalist reproduction gave way to a whole series of revolutionary uprisings in Europe. Typical of the dismissal of less dramatic crises, is the Polish Marxist economist Henryk Grossman (1881–1950): "According to Marx, crises can result from changes in prices. As such, they do not interest him; they are special cases. Marx takes 'capital in general' as the object of his analysis, i.e., he is only interested in those crises that necessarily arise from the nature of capital as such, from the essence of capitalist production, 'which are peculiar to it as capital'."[11] On the contrary, this essay shows how Marx and Engels were very much interested in all kinds of crises, not least because they lead to others, building towards a possible "final" crisis to which capitalists can find no adequate response.

In their writings, they use the term "crisis" to characterize not only many kinds of breakdowns in capitalist reproduction, but also situations facing workers. Most obviously, in the frequent fluctuations that economists call "business cycles" and Marx and Engels called periodic crises, there have been two very different kinds of "crisis." The first being *a crisis for capitalists*, often brought on during an upturn in accumulation by workers' struggles, e.g., wage increases that outstrip productivity growth and undermine profits, leading to a downturn when capitalists respond by cutting investment, laying off workers, shutting down plants and reducing wages. But those acts create an immediate *crisis for workers* by stripping them of income and throwing their survival and wellbeing onto whatever savings they may have set aside or onto community networks of mutual aid. Where unemployment is general and alternative jobs are scarce, wages and salaries are low and savings few or non-existent, in communities lacking networks of mutual support, the lack of income quickly

11 Rick Kuhn, ed., *Henryk Grossman Works: Volume 3: The Law of Accumulation and Breakdown of the Capitalist System, being also a Theory of Crises* (Chicago: Haymarket Books, 2021), 119.

begats absolute penury and impoverishment and all the woes that accompany them: increased anxiety, loss of dignity, inability to take care of children and other family members.

When such responses are accompanied by important organizational changes in the structure of the class relations, such as the introduction of labor-displacing machinery, or the displacement of production operations from areas where workers' struggles have been strong enough to throw local capitalists into crisis to other areas where workers are weaker, the crisis for workers is even more profound and long-lasting, often undermining their existing forms of self-organization and ability to fight for what they need and want.

Such crises – for both capitalists and workers – may be small or large, temporary ruptures in the rhythm of accumulation or those critical moments when the continued existence of the system is a stake. This complexity is why Chapters 4 and 5 of this essay, on the possibilities and predispositions to crisis, make up the bulk of this essay. Exploration of Marx and Engels' writings have revealed analyses of a great many possibilities and predispositions, some small, some great, some transitory and some long-term secular tendencies.

One result of that exploration, which motivated the original version of this essay, was dissatisfaction with existing interpretations of Marxist crisis theory in a number of respects; these interpretations variously: (1) see only theories of the development of capital and capitalists, but not of the class relation, (2) focus on the centrality of capitalist competition, which is conceptualized in terms of relations among units of capital separate from the class relation, (3) sever the unity of the spheres of production and circulation by privileging the former (falling rate of profit/rising organic composition of capital) or the latter (underconsumption or neo-Ricardianism), (4) assign the dominant role to the so-called "forces of production," often understood simply as technology, (5) fetishize Marxian categories including crisis theory, such that it becomes a theory of investment behavior or mechanical breakdown,[12] or (6) destroy the unity within Marxist crisis theories by asserting the existence of many different strands, or separate theories.[13] In this essay, however, I mostly set aside critical evaluations of other interpretations, in favor of spelling out an alternative.

12 Despite the association of the term "breakdown" with such theories, I choose to use the term more broadly to signify a *rupture* in some aspect of the organization of accumulation. A "breakdown" is also a *failure* in some planned moment of accumulation. Because the causes of a breakdown vary, they must be identified to explain any particular *rupture/failure*. But the term's very lack of specificity as to cause makes it a useful synonym for crisis in some moments of expanded reproduction.

13 Peter Bell, "Marxist Theory, Class Struggle and the Crisis of Capitalism," in *The Subtle Anatomy of Capitalism*, ed. Jesse Schwartz (Santa Monica: Godyear Publishing Company, 1977), 170–94.

Here, I read Marx and Engels' texts for what I can learn about struggles in the period in which they were written – to discover, in turn, the degree to which their insights still apply in the present.

I argue that the basic analytical framework worked out by Marx and Engels is still valid and accurately describes many of the fundamental features of contemporary capitalist society. Clearly much has changed since they wrote. A concrete analysis of contemporary capitalist society obviously requires an adaptation and extension of Marxist theory to take these developments into account. Having participated in such efforts elsewhere, this essay eschews the temptation of "up-dating" Marx and Engels' writings and grounds understanding of the original analysis directly in the texts themselves. It is not enough, but I have found it to be one useful step.

Let me show you where we're going. I've organized my analysis of Marx and Engels' widely scattered discussions of crisis in seven chapters.

Chapter 2. Marx & Engels' Studies of Crises. These two men's writings on crisis are scattered from early on in their lives throughout the decades that followed. As their engagement in political struggles and their studies of capitalism, class struggle and crises evolved, so did their analysis, often in response to new developments, always as interventions into on-going struggles. This chapter provides a sketch of that evolution to provide historical context for the more detailed dissection of their theory of crisis which follows.

Chapter 3. Marx's Theory of Accumulation. This chapter frames my synthesis of Marx and Engels' writings on crisis in their major published books, their journal articles, and their correspondence. It does so by providing an interpretation of Marx's analysis of the nature and functioning of capitalist accumulation when it is *not* in crisis.

Chapter 4. Possibilities of crisis. This part brings together the passages where Marx and Engels point out the various moments at which it is *possible* that the processes of production and circulation can be interrupted. I organize their comments first by sketching their analysis of how the possibility of crisis is inherent in markets – which predate but become an essential, albeit subordinate, dimension of capitalism – and then by examining the possibilities of crisis in each stage of the circuit of industrial capital.

Chapter 5. Predispositions to crisis. The existence of possibilities of interruption does not mean that rupture will in fact occur. So, Marx and Engels also examine the forces within accumulation that may lead to the actualization of those possibilities; in other words, the forces which establish various predispositions to crisis. Here I situate their analyses of many frequently discussed "causes" of crisis, for example, the tendency of the rate of profit to fall or tendencies to underconsumption, among a great many other forces at work.

Chapter 6. Offsetting Tendencies. Although Marx and Engels frame their analyses of crisis in terms of the forces that tend to undermine accumulation, they also recognize and analyze some of the strategies and tactics that capital uses to offset those tendencies. A few of those are laid out in Chapter 14 of Volume 3 of *Capital*; many more are scattered through their writings.

Chapter 7. Crisis as Solution. Marx and Engels have highlighted how capital often tries use the crisis itself to overcome interruptions and ruptures in accumulation and to restore the conditions of reproduction. The capitalist use of crisis often involves countering ruptures caused by workers' struggles by imposing new constraints on them, new crises-for-workers. When they are successful, crisis becomes an equilibrating moment in a secular process, overcoming predispositions to disequilibrium – effectively an offsetting tendency, but one that is unique and important enough to deserve separate treatment.

Chapter 8. Crisis and Revolution. Crisis becomes revolution when capital fails to realize the second moment of crisis, when it fails to turn the crisis against the working class and restore control. In other words, when the workers' struggles threaten the overthrow of the system as a whole. To date, revolutionary threats have been both local and temporary; retaining control elsewhere, capital has been able to contain and reverse such defeats, reestablishing accumulation. The optimism of Marx and Engels' analysis lies in their perceptions that first, because the reestablishment of accumulation inevitably recreates, on an expanded scale, of all the antagonistic contradictions of the system, and second, so too does it recreate the possibilities of ruptures so great, so widespread and thoroughgoing that capitalists are unable to cope as revolutionary uprisings overthrow the system and people free themselves from being "mere workers" by changing every part of society more to their liking.

CHAPTER 2

Marx & Engels' Studies of Crises, 1843–1895

Karl Marx and Frederick Engels were men of the nineteenth century and their understanding of economic and political crises was based on both observation of the events of their time and the theories they developed to understand them. They lived, fought, and wrote during a period of recurrent economic crises marked by several major political upheavals in some of which they participated as militant revolutionaries.

Dedicated to active political organizing against an expanding capitalism that was subordinating more and more people to endless work, in cruel, often murderous ways, Marx and Engels studied economic crisis, not as academic theorists but as militants. They studied the periodical crises of capitalist accumulation while helping organize and expand: first, the Communist League in the period of the Revolutions of 1848, and then the First International in the period surrounding the Commune of Paris in 1871. As working-class political parties began to be formed, they contributed both critique and positive input into the formulation of the politics of such parties. In every case, they were dedicated to the unification of workers' struggles across national borders and the transcendence of capitalism.

Given the importance Marx and Engels attached to workers' struggles not only in causing crises in capitalist accumulation but also in their potential to overthrow capitalism completely, their interest in discovering the dynamics of capitalist growth aimed at showing workers two things: first, the sources of the frequent crises of their time, and second, how the interests of some workers were inevitably bound up with those of others elsewhere. The path towards greater power for workers lay in strengthening connections and developing ways to collaborate.

In their writing and in their political activity, we can discover both their understanding of the ways in which workers' struggles circulate and their own efforts to accelerate that circulation. Their efforts included:

1. the serious study of languages relevant both to their studies and to their ability to communicate politically,
2. writing up and giving verbal accounts of struggles in one place to convey stories of those struggles to workers elsewhere,
3. translating their writings, by themselves or through others, to increase the likelihood of their accounts of workers' actions in one place having an impact on workers elsewhere,

DOI:10.1163/9789004708631_003

4. helping organizations in one place create or strengthen links with organizations elsewhere,
5. by supporting emigrants like themselves, they facilitated the international circulation of the experience of struggle and the spreading of lessons learned

Educated in both the gymnasium and university in German, Latin, and Ancient Greek, Marx and Engels repeatedly studied those modern languages they found relevant to understanding capitalist development and workers' struggles. Moreover, as they became more and more deeply involved in politics, they worked hard at learning the languages they needed to communicate their ideas – in both writing and conversation – to others struggling for change.[1]

Obviously, neither man was a member of the factory proletariat that they saw as the increasingly dominant sector of the working class and whose struggles they were dedicated to circulating. When he wasn't fighting the system, Engels worked as what Marx eventually called a "functionary of capital" for his father's business. Marx made his living as a writer of books and as a journalist. Income from both sources was highly irregular. Although he dismissed writers who worked for capitalist employers as an insignificantly small part of the working class, he did just such work. Despite their anti-capitalist content and objective, his books were printed and sold as commodities – earning him income, either as advances or as royalties, while earning profits for his publishers. His journalism, first for the *New York Herald Tribune*, and then as a contributor to *New American Cyclopaedia* made him, in effect, an intellectual gig worker, unsalaried and paid by the piece, per article by the *Tribune*, per page by the *Cyclopedia* editors.[2] For both men, their primary modes of political action were writing and organizing. Both drew on skills learned in school and continued to study, write, and organize, learning through participation, first

1 Most good biographies of Marx and Engels contain accounts of their language learning. A recent survey, drawing on both biographies and now available letters, is Kaan Kangal, "Marx and Engels as Polyglots" *Monthly Review* 75, no. 9 (February 2024): 22-35.

2 Although the payment went to Marx, like Tom Sawyer in Mark Twain's novel, who got a friend to do his work of painting a fence, Marx often talked Engels into writing some of these pieces published under his name – especially those for which he thought Engels was more qualified, e.g., on military matters. His personal annoyance with the piecework character of his journalism certainly contributed to his detailed analysis of piece-wages in Chapter 21 of Volume 1 of *Capital*. One complaint to Engels: "It's truly nauseating that one should be condemned to count it a blessing when taken aboard by a blotting paper vendor such as this [the Tribune]. To crush up bones, grind them and make them into soup like PAUPERS in the WORKHOUSE – that's what the political work to which one is condemned in such large measure in a CONCERN like this boils down to. I am aware I have been an ass in giving these ladies more than their money's worth – not just recently but for years past." Marx to Engels, January 23, 1857, *MECW*, *Vol. 40*, p. 98.

in reform circles and later among worker organizations. As I point out below in my historical sketch, they developed these skills within the context of rapid socio-economic change in which a whole array of reformers and revolutionaries were already active.

In their now collected works, one can easily see how Marx and Engels' writing took two forms: writing to and for comrades in struggle and writing for public consumption. In the absence of telephones or email, most correspondence with others was either face to face or epistolary, handwritten letters to share ideas and to organize. Their written correspondence was voluminous as they shared experience, discussed organizational strategies, critiqued others' ideas, offered early formulations of their own ideas, which later appeared in their published works, or recaps of points already made in print designed to highlight their political implications. Their correspondence with each other and with comrades illuminates our understanding of both the evolution of their analysis of crisis and their perception of its importance for political action. Until finally being published in *MECW* and *MEGA*, most of their letters were unknown and unavailable outside the archives that contained them. But among those that were, perhaps the best known was Marx's letter to Engels telling him about slaving night after night to pull together his analysis during the crisis of 1857 in anticipation of possible revolutionary upheaval. (See, Section 2.1.) Today, hundreds of such letters are readily available, although mostly studied only by their biographers.[3]

In their public political writing, one can find exhortations to collaboration across differences, e.g., the famous call in the *Communist Manifesto* for "workers of the world" to unite, but almost all their efforts, both theoretical and political, were designed as interventions aimed at bringing about or speeding up the circulation of struggles – the only path they could see to the overthrow of capitalism. Those interventions included a) writing articles in the language appropriate to the targeted group of workers, e.g., in German for the *Rheinische Zeitung* or *Neue Rheinische Zeitung*, but in English for Chartist and American newspapers, b) the creation of new publishing efforts to overcome linguistic barriers, e.g., the *Deutsch-Französische Jahrbücher* aimed at linking Germans and French struggles by publishing articles by revolutionary intellectuals in both languages, and c) efforts to get their major works published in as many languages as possible, e.g., Marx's efforts to recraft the French translation of *Capital* to increase its accessibility to workers in France. Whether they were directly involved in struggles, e.g., the 1848 Revolution in Germany, or observing

3 I include myself among those who have, so far, failed to study this correspondence in detail. While for this book I scoured the many volumes of *MECW* for discussions of crisis, I largely ignored everything else.

them from afar, e.g., the Paris Commune, they wrote about them to circulate the lessons they drew from those experiences to other workers in other places.

Not only their writing but also most of their political organizing aimed to bring workers together across linguistic and cultural differences –in the League of the Just, in the formation of the Communist Correspondence Committee, in the Communist League and in the International Working Men's Association, or First International. And, for Engels, who outlived Marx, in the Second International.[4] Part of this work was writing up position papers and manifestos for the various groups, e.g., Engels' "Draft of a Communist Confession of Faith" and Marx and Engels' *Communist Manifesto* for the League of the Just. This kind of writing was integral to their political work throughout their lives.

But like other organizers of their day, they didn't just write. In the absence of any form of audio-visual recording and reproduction, they also took the time and devoted considerable energy to public speaking to groups of workers and to potential supporters among the middle classes. We know about such efforts from letters, lecture notes eventually published and from contemporary accounts. Early examples include the speeches Engels gave in Elberfeld and later prepared for publication.[5] In a letter, he recounts to Marx:

> Here in Elberfeld wondrous things are afoot. Yesterday we held our third communist meeting in the town's largest hall and leading inn. The first meeting was forty strong, the second 130 and the third at least 200. All Elberfeld and Barmen, from the monied aristocracy to épicerie (small shopkeepers) was represented, only the proletariat being excluded."[6]

Among the better-known examples of speeches to workers, also cited below in Section 2.2, is Marx's report to the Central Council of the First International

4 In terms of organization, this emphasis on circulating struggles across differences in the working class has been a central part of Marx and Engels' legacy. The Second International (1889–1916) was followed by the Third International – the "Communist International" or "Comitern" – (1919–1943) created by the Bolsheviks in the wake of the Russian Revolution and the Fourth International formed by Leon Trotsky and his followers in 1938 after his exile from the USSR and in opposition to Stalin's domination of the Comitern. It can also be seen in Marxist support for anti-colonial or national liberation struggles in the post-WWII period and in the alter-globalization efforts of recent years undertaken by all sorts of opponents of capitalism.

5 These February speeches were written up by Engels and published in August in the *Rheinische Jahrbücher zur gesellshaftlichen Reform*. See endnote 91, MECW, *Vol. 4*, p. 697. "Speeches in Elberfeld," February 8, 1845, MECW, *Vol. 4*, pp. 243–251. "Speeches in Elberfeld," February 15, 1845, MECW, *Vol. 4*, pp. 256–64.

6 Engels to Marx, February 22 – March 7, 1845, MECW, *Vol. 38*, pp. 22-23.

presented on June 20 and 27, 1865, eventually published posthumously in 1898 as *Value, Price and Profit*.[7]

Beyond researching, writing about, and telling tales of distant struggles to local audiences, Marx and Engels – like so many workers, moved from place to place and carried their experience of struggle with them. Engels moved from Germany to England; Marx moved from Germany to France (Paris) to Belgium (Brussels) to England (London). In each place, they not only lived within communities of émigrés and refugee revolutionaries like themselves but also welcomed others from afar to share their experiences and learn from them. Among them were Poles and Russians from the Eastern European front of the struggle for democracy, worker, and peasant rights. These included Joachim Lelewel, who collaborated with Marx and Engels in Brussels, Walery Wróblewski, a general in the Paris Commune and later a member of the General Council of the First International,[8] and Mikhail Bakunin who also joined the First International after opposing Czarist occupation of Poland, participating in the Czech Rebellion of 1948, being imprisoned in Russia but escaping exile to Siberia. Influenced by Proudhon and destined to become a major figure in the anarchist tradition, Bakunin sparred with Marx and Engels over revolutionary strategy.[9]

These prominent individuals, however, were just visible representatives of vast numbers of lesser or unknown workers on the move, carrying their experience of struggle with them to new terrains. With the rapid development of capitalism came massive movements of workers. Some were moved forcibly, e.g., slaves, press-ganged seamen and those arrested, jailed, and transported to the peripheries of the expanding capitalist world. For far more, geographical displacement was either part of their work, e.g., sailors and soldiers, or a form of struggle, e.g., pirates or immigrants seeking freedom from exploitation. Marxists have tended to emphasize the role of capitalists in all this movement, from merchant capitalists seeking new markets to industrial capitalists seeking new pools of labor and sources of raw materials. Their roles in conquest, the creation of colonies and empire were obvious. Less obvious has been the autonomous mobility of many workers either making use of capitalist circuits or breaking free of them. Yes, some capitalists profited from providing transportation to

7 See endnote 87, *MECW*, *Vol. 20*, pp. 466–67.

8 See the mentions of Lelewel and Wróblewski in "Notes to Polish Readers" included in this volume.

9 Their differences in strategy, which eventually led to Bakunin's expulsion from the International, are well-known and were based on differing analyses of how workers should deal with the state. Whereas Bakunin argued for revolutionaries to immediately abolish the state, Marx argued for taking it over – to prevent counter-revolution – and then gradually abolishing it as people developed alternative institutions. More on this in Chapter 8: Crises and Revolution.

workers on the move, e.g., German companies selling immigration (tickets to the US) to workers in the wake of the 1848 uprisings. But many of those who moved had participated in the revolution and were escaping the subsequent repression to pursue their struggles elsewhere, e.g., those who moved to Texas and founded communist communities.[10] Yes, sailors were workers on the commercial fleets of the expanding empire, but they often mutinied, becoming pirates, or jumped ship leaving the sea altogether, becoming immigrants in new lands. As Linebaugh and Rediker have demonstrated, capitalist expansion in the Atlantic (and beyond) not only included the formation of a polyglot working class – on land and on the sea – but also the movement of those workers circulating their experience and struggles throughout that world.[11]

I divide my account of Marx and Engels' studies and writings on crisis into three periods.

The *first period* is the decade of 1842 to 1852, during which Marx and Engels elaborated their critiques of Hegel's philosophy, plunged into the study of political economy, and began to become seriously involved in political struggles. I end this period when both Marx and Engels had completed their major works analyzing the forces involved in the Revolutions of 1848 and with the dissolution of the Communist League in 1852.

The *second period* includes the 1850s and 1860s, encompasses the long lull in their political activity and the most intense development of their theories of capitalism and its crises. It was during this interim that Marx composed the fullest elaboration of his theories of capitalism and class struggle in a series of notebooks and manuscripts. I date the end of this period as 1867, the year he published Volume 1 of *Capital.*

The *third period,* 1867 to 1895, encompasses the rest of Marx and Engels' lives – Marx died in his 65th year in 1883 and Engels in his 75th in 1895. During these years both men continued to think, write, and participate in various political efforts, including the First International and the formation of the first working-class political parties to enter the terrain of electoral politics.

Comparing their early writings on crisis with later ones reveals both continuities and important changes. The most important continuity is the central concern with the relationship between crisis and workers' struggles. The most important changes result from Marx's elaboration of his theories of value, surplus value and accumulation. Those concepts allow Marx and Engels to understand crisis in terms of class struggle with much greater clarity and in more detail than hitherto possible.

---

10 Ernest Fischer, *Marxists and Utopias in Texas* (Burnet, TX: Eakin Press, 1980).

11 Peter Linebaugh and Marcus Rediker, *Many-headed Hydra: Sailors, Slaves, Commoners, and the Hidden History of the Revolutionary Atlantic* (Boston: Beacon Press, 2000).

1 The Early Studies: 1842–1852

In 1839, while working at his family's textile business in his hometown of Barmen, Engels published – in vivid detail and from direct observation – a series of letters reporting on the exploitation and suffering of industrial workers.[12] But while juxtaposing the condition of workers with "the wholesome, vigorous life" of people elsewhere, his condemnation was general and not related to any critique of capitalism or any idea of crisis. That would come later. Instead of such analysis, he berated the local bigotry, religious extremism, and anti-intellectualism that he associated with the hypocritical Lutheran pietism of property owners and the desperation of workers. He seems to have only begun the serious study of political economy and of capitalist crisis after meeting Marx in the fall of 1842.[13]

In November of 1842, while on his way to his father's cotton mill in Manchester, England, Engels took time to visit the offices of the *Rheinische Zeitung* in Cologne, Prussia, a liberal journal founded by Rhenish industrialists with an editorial staff that included Marx.[14] Despite some differences, they agreed that Engels would write for the journal about the situation in England.[15]

---

12 At the time, Barmen and the adjacent town of Elberfeld (see below) were part of Prussia, an independent Kingdom until forming the North German Confederation in 1867, a step toward the unification of Germany in 1871. Engels' "Letters from Wuppertal" were published in a progressive Hamburg journal, the *Telegraph für Deutschland*, in March and April 1839, *MECW*, *Vol. 2*, pp. 7–25. Wuppertal = Wupper Valley = valley of the Wupper river, a tributary of the Rhine. The water of the Wupper powered the industries of the valley in that period. Eventually, with the substitution of the steam engine for waterpower, demand for coal by Wuppertal industry would drive the development of mining in the nearby Ruhrgebiet or Ruhr Valley.

13 Many may identify with Engels's reaction in this period when so many Christians have been proving themselves hypocritical bigots in their embrace of white supremacy and Christian nationalism and so many workers have been suffering the consequences of unconstrained neoliberalism.

14 The business backers of the paper were seeking greater freedom and a roll in government – something they would only get with the Constitution and Parliament created by the Prussian king Frederick William IV in the wake of the Revolution of 1848. Biographers differ on Marx's position at the paper. McLellan claims that in October 1842, Marx was made editor-in-chief. Sperber, on the other hand, claims that Marx only received "an employment contract." Whatever his formal position, all agree his coming on board strengthened the paper's critique of the Prussian government and dramatically increased its circulation. See David McLellan, *Karl Marx: A Biography* (New York: MacMillan, 1973), 43, and Jonathan Sperber, *Karl Marx: A Nineteenth Century Life* (New York: Liveright, 2013), 91.

15 Engels tells of his first "distinctly chilly" meeting with Marx, in an 1895 letter to Franz Mehring (1846–1919). See, Engels to Mehring, London, End of April 1895, *MECW*, *Vol. 50*, p. 503.

In Manchester, amidst its infamous "satanic mills," Engels found himself in the heart of British industrialization and in the midst of the English working class and its major political movement of the time: Chartism. With English workers suffering much the same exploitation as their German counterparts, the Chartists had organized peacefully the previous May and presented a petition to the House of Commons – with over 3 million signatures – demanding democratic reforms, including universal adult male suffrage, giving propertyless workers as well as property owners the right to vote. It was overwhelmingly rejected.[16] That rejection, coupled with rising unemployment, led to a wave of strikes throughout much of industrial England. Engels wrote stories for the *Rheinische Zeitung* on the economic situation and the angry reaction of workers plunged into poverty through the loss of their jobs and with no hope from Parliament.[17]

His reports contain elements of an analysis of crisis – and its relation to revolution – that he would soon systematize: the necessity of industry to expand, the resulting need for markets, inevitable limitations on those markets, fluctuations in trade and crises of overproduction or glutted markets, at home or abroad. But crisis for the capitalists also means crisis for workers: overproduction means layoffs, rising unemployment and hunger. The more severe the downturn, the greater the suffering. He predicted that when a "large-scale trade crisis" creates "general lack of food among the workers," then "fear of death from starvation will be stronger than fear of the law" and, with peaceful petitions having failed, revolution will result.[18]

In this period "trade" refers to both domestic commerce and international trade. As capitalists' command over production expanded, they required profitable markets for their products. In his analysis of primitive accumulation, Marx would later show, in *Capital, Vol. 1*, Chapter 30, how capitalists' theft of locals' land and tools and their imposition of wage labor creates a "home" or domestic market. Then in Chapter 31, he would show how they repeated the process abroad via colonialism. In both cases, capitalist success required victory over the resistance of those being expropriated. At home, the repression required was justified, when anyone bothered, by such claims as the need for more "efficiency" in production, despite the way increasing mechanization

16 It was neither the first, nor the last Chartist petition. For a brief history see the Wikipedia article "Chartism".

17 "The English View of the Internal Crisis," Nov. 29, 1842, *MECW, Vol. 2*, pp. 368–69, "The Internal Crises," Nov. 30, 1842, *MECW, Vol. 2*, pp. 370–74, and "The Condition of the Working Class in England," December 20, 1842, *MECW, Vol 2*, pp. 378–79.

18 "The Internal Crises," *MECW, Vol. 2*, p. 373.

displaced workers and threw them into poverty. Abroad, colonialism, after crushing local resistance via military conquest of some and the co-optation of others, developed foreign markets and extracted cheap resources via exploited cheap labor, while rationalizing these actions with the racist rhetoric of "white man's burden" to "civilize" the supposedly backward and racially inferior natives.

Early on, international trade was justified in Britain by merchants arguing the need for trade surpluses to bring gold and silver into the country.[19] Their "mercantilist" arguments were soon replaced by those of British political economists such as Adam Smith (1723–1790) and David Ricardo (1772–1823) in favor of "free trade," which would supposedly benefit all trading partners. Although British imperialists touted that the sun never set upon the Union Jack, the same could be said of the banner of "free trade" carried by political economists and policy makers alike. These arguments supported an aggressive expansionism, while typically ignoring how all colonial powers, including the British, denied the markets they seized to others – so they really weren't "free" at all.[20]

Against such hypocrisy, capitalists operating in weaker nation states pitted arguments for the "protection of infant industries" against aggressive British expansionism. Capitalists in countries such as Germany and the United States sought bigger profits by getting tariffs and other barriers erected to keep out

19 This was an argument specific to Britain, whose colonies turned out to lack precious metals, unlike those of Spain in Mexico and Peru. Although later mercantilists replaced the crude arguments of "bullionists" by more sophisticated ones, they all argued – while asking for support from the government – that trade was the main path to increasing the local stock of precious metals and national wealth.

20 "Free markets" are a capitalist myth; both supply and demand have always been the object of manipulation by all concerned: capitalists, governments and customers (both other capitalists and workers). This is true for both input markets (for labor-power and the means of production) and output markets (for the final product). Domestic trade has been shaped by all sorts of government policies, from legal regulation and tax policies to direct subsidies. Foreign trade has also been manipulated through such means as tariffs, customs duties, and colonialism. This is even more obvious today, where governments regularly negotiate trade arrangements, codifying both domestic and international trade in laws, treaties and institutions, e.g., the Federal Trade Commission in the US, the General Agreement on Tariffs and Trade (GATT) and the World Trade Organization (WTO) at the global level. Lurking in the shadows behind those governments are generally intense capitalist efforts to shape agreements in their particular interests. Out front in broad daylight are often masses of consumers and workers protesting that influence and results inimical to *their* interests. Recent examples include cross-border opposition in Canada, the United States and Mexico to the North American Free Trade Agreement (NAFTA) and recurrent protests and disruptions of the WTO. The "Battle of Seattle" was only one of many such protests.

cheaper foreign (often British) imports. They too had their political economists as apologists. For example, George Friedrich List (1789–1846) sharpened the arguments of Adolphe Thiers (1797–1877) and Alexander Hamilton (1755–1804) into advice to both Prussian and American policy makers and laid out his arguments systematically in his book *The National System of Political Economy* (1841). All these proceedings and debates formed the backdrop to first Engels' and then Marx's turn to the study of political economy.

Marx's interest in political economy was stimulated, in part, from his efforts, as editor of the *Rheinische Zeitung*, to critique on-going legal debates over the laws dealing with peasants caught appropriating fallen wood in once common but now enclosed forests.[21] He also took up the economic problems of vintners in his native Moselle Valley. They were suffering a decline in the value of their wines and the absence of any helpful government action, such as a compensatory reduction of taxes. The situation seems to have been a byproduct of the creation of the *Zollverein*, a customs union that removed barriers to trade among several German states. As a result, the vintners were subject to competition from growers elsewhere in Germany. In addressing the conflict, Marx neither analyzed this background nor took up the ongoing debates over "free trade" and "protectionism" – as he would a few years later.[22] At this point, he only attacked government press censorship that inhibited open discussion.[23] With respect to these problems of peasants and vintners, years later he explained how he found himself "in the embarrassing position" of having to discuss them in print with no background knowledge.[24] Only in critiquing the

21 "Proceedings of the Sixth Rhine Province Assembly, Third Article, Debates on the Law on Thefts of Wood," *Rheinische Zeitung*, October and November 1842, *MECW*, *Vol. 1*, pp. 224–63. Such laws against direct appropriation on privately owned lands have been widespread and long predate capitalism. One thinks of the iconic tale of Robin Hood, who, in at least one version, was outlawed for poaching the "King's" deer. See, Chapter One of Howard Pyle, *The Merry Adventures of Robin Hood* (Racine: Whitman Publishing Company, 1883). Capitalists continued such practice, to criminalize appropriation, whether of wood, edible plants, or animals. On some laws against poaching see, Douglas Hay, "Poaching and the Game Laws on Cannock Chase," in Douglas Hay, et al., *Albion's Fatal Tree: Crime and Society in Eighteen Century England* (New York: Pantheon Books, 1975). On Marx's critique of the Law on Thefts of Wood, see Peter Linebaugh, "Karl Marx, the Theft of Wood, and Working-Class Composition: A Contribution to the Current Debate," *Crime and Social Justice* 6, (fall-winter, 1976): 5–16.

22 See below, Chapter 4, p. 208.

23 See his response to government complaints about treatments of these problems in the *Rheinische Zeitung*, "Justification of the Correspondent from the Mosel," *MECW*, *Vol. 1*, pp. 332–58.

24 "In the year 1842–43, as editor of the *Rheinische Zeitung*, I first found myself in the embarrassing position of having to discuss what is known as material interests." Karl Marx,

debate over the appropriation of fallen wood did he deal directly with workers' struggles. He sided with the peasants, pointing out how the Provincial Assembly permitted the forest owners to usurp the law in their own interest.

Regularly harassed by a government censor who rejected article after article, Marx nevertheless succeeded in publishing several essays by Moses Hess (1812–1875) discussing socialist and communist ideas.[25] Attacked for these articles by a more conservative newspaper, Marx responded by arguing not for communist ideas but for submitting "these ideas to thorough criticism ... to long and profound study."[26] Indeed, he was soon engaged in just such careful reading of writers such as Étienne Cabet (1788–1856), Charles Fourier (1772–1837), and Pierre-Joseph Proudhon (1809–1865), all of whom inevitably raised issues of political economy.[27] Because Marx published article after article critical not only of oppression and poverty in Prussia but also of the injustice of legal reforms proposed by King Frederick William IV, all while demanding open public debate and complete freedom of the press from censorship, the government moved to suppress the *Rheinische Zeitung*, ordering its closing by the end of March 1843.[28]

"Preface" to *A Contribution to the Critique of Political Economy* (1859), MECW, *Vol. 29*, p. 262. Many years later, Engels affirmed that "Marx always used to tell me that it was precisely his preoccupation with the law on thefts of wood and the condition of the Mosel winegrowers that led him from politics pure and simple to economic conditions and thus to socialism." Engels to Richard Fischer, April 15, 1895, MECW, *Vol. 50*, p. 497.

25 Sometimes said to have been the individual who introduced communist ideas into Germany, Hess claimed to have influenced Engels during the latter's visit to Cologne earlier in 1842. "Engels, who was revolutionary to the core when he met me, left as a passionate revolutionary." Quoted in David McLellan, *Friedrich Engels* (Harmondsworth, UK: Penguin Books, 1977), 21.

26 See "Communism and the Augsburg *Allgemeine Zeitung*," MECW, *Vol. 1*, p. 220.

27 See Saul Padover, *Karl Marx: An Intimate Biography* (New York: McGraw-Hill, 1978), Chapter VIII.

28 Two things are worth noting. First, the suppression of the *Rheinische Zeitung* was part of a broader wave of repression that forced the closure of several papers that had dared to question or challenge the government. Second, not only was the Prussian government upset about public criticism, but it was, in turn, under pressure from the Czarist government in Russia for permitting the publication of articles critical of *its* policies. See, McLellan, *Karl Marx: A Biography*, 50. Throughout his life, Marx would single out the Czarist regime as being a primary bulwark of absolutism and reaction on the continent. Such repression of the press and criticism, along with the refusal of any form of democratic input into its decision making, illustrates why these regimes were called "absolutist." The monarchs demanded absolute power and tolerated no challenge. Such a regime was rejected during the American Revolutionary war, 1775–1783, and overthrown in France in 1789. Both capitalists and working-class revolutionaries sought the overthrow of such centralized power. In some cases, monarchies have survived by accepting constitutions,

1.1 *Paris and Manchester*

Following the shutting down of the *Rheinische Zeitung* in March and his marriage to Jenny von Westphalen (1814–1881) in June, Marx and his wife moved to Paris in October 1843. Once settled, he began to 1) make up for his ignorance of political economy by studying both English and French political economists[29] and 2) collaborate with Arnold Ruge (1802–1880) to launch a new paper. Their *Deutsch-Französische Jahrbücher* aimed at linking struggles in Germany and France by publishing articles by revolutionary intellectuals in both languages and developing contacts with workers. Although he was unable to attract contributions from those French socialists whose writings he had been studying, Marx did establish connections with both immigrant German and local French workers in Paris – often unable to speak each other's languages, organized separately, and often in conflict. These difficulties, caused by differing ideas and languages, undoubtedly contributed to Marx's life-long search for organizational ways to overcome them and unite workers' struggles across national, ethnic, and linguistic differences.[30]

In this situation, it is not surprising that Marx's studies of political economy were thoroughly mixed with the philosophical, legal, and political debates of the time. Engels, on the other hand, living and working in the midst of England's burgeoning manufacturing industry, was drawn to examine closely, and analyze carefully, the capitalism that surrounded him, first in Germany, then in

---

a small degree of democracy (originally, in nineteenth century Britain, only those with property could vote for members of parliament) and limits on its power. In a few cases, e.g., Islamic monarchies such as Saudi Arabia, royal families still cling to power – while others, such as Donald Trump and his followers, aspire to such status, admiring others who seem to have achieved it, such as Vladimir Putin (1952–), Xi Jinping (1953–), Kim Jong Un (1982–), and Viktor Orbán (1963–).

29 Among those he studied, according to Padover, were Adam Smith, James Mill (1773–1836), David Ricardo, his follower John Ramsey McCulloch (1789–1864), Jean-Baptiste Say (1767–1832), and Michel Chevalier (1806–1879), op. cit., p. 189. At the beginning of his *Economic and Philosophical Manuscript of 1844* (see below) he also recounted studying the German socialists Wilhelm Weitling (1808–1871), Moses Hess, and Frederich Engels (his *Outline*), *MECW*, *Vol. 3*, p. 232.

30 This problem continues to plague anti-capitalists world-wide. In these first decades of the twenty-first century, although English has, to some extent, become the common language of Empire for intellectuals, the bulk of material written about local struggles and assessing broader trends continue to be written in local languages and thus inaccessible to those unfamiliar with those languages. The arrival of the Internet and the creation of translation programs have ameliorated this situation somewhat, but the problem persists. As noted in the preface to the Polish translation of this essay, my inability to access Polish language materials on both Marx and Engels' writings and on contemporary conditions in Poland was frustrating because it limited my knowledge of both past and present.

England.[31] While Marx was still struggling with his Hegelian roots and writing "Contribution to the Critique of Hegel's Philosophy of Law" (1843–44),[32] Engels followed up his 1839 "Letters" and his 1842 reports from England by composing a systematic "Outline of a Critique of Political Economy" (1844), his first effort to set out elements of an understanding of crisis that they would soon share.[33]

In the "*Outline*", after first developing a critique of some of the economic categories of classical political economy (including private property, trade, value, price, rent, labor, and capital), Engels turns to a discussion of competition (between capitalists, between workers, and between classes), monopoly and trade crises. He establishes what would remain as some (but not all) of the basic tenets of Marxian crisis theory:

1. Crises are caused by production outstripping available markets. This he analyzes in terms of fluctuations in supply and demand and the impact of price changes on production:

   > If demand is greater than supply the price rises and, as a result, supply is to a certain degree stimulated. As soon as it comes on the market, prices fall; and if it becomes greater than demand, then the fall in prices is so significant that demand is once again stimulated. So it goes on unendingly ...[34]

2. This overproduction is the result of there being no plan to equalize aggregate production and aggregate demand, but only the frenzied efforts of

---

31 Engels was by no means unaware or had lost interest in either philosophical or political debates. He wrote a number of articles for local radical newspapers – the Owenites' *The New Moral World* and the Chartists' *The Northern Star* – about events, debates and political movements on the continent. See Volume 3 of *MECW*.

32 There are two parts to this text. The first is the main body of existing manuscript, *MECW*, *Vol. 3*, pp. 3–129. The second is an "Introduction," *MECW*, *Vol. 3*, pp. 175–87. Both the first and the second are available, in a different translation, at https://www.marxists.org/, under the title "Critique of Hegel's Philosophy of Right".

33 "Outline," (October - November 1843) (*Deutsch-Franzosische Jahrbucher*, 1844), *MECW*, *Vol. 3*, pp. 433–43.

34 Frederick Engels, "Outline of a Critique of Political Economy" (1843), first published in the *Deutsch-Französische Jahrbüicher*, 1844, *MECW*, *Vol. 3*, p. 433. Keep in mind that here, as elsewhere in Engels and Marx's analyses of supply and demand, they are NOT thinking in terms of the supply and demand *curves* familiar to modern microeconomics, but simply of the quantities of commodities being supplied to or demanded in markets. With the exception of a little-known French philosopher and mathematician, Antoine Augustin Cournot (1801–1877), who wrote a book on *Recherches sur les principes mathématiques de la théorie des richesses* in 1838, such curves were unknown until late in the nineteenth century.

different capitalists to keep ahead of both workers and other capitalists.[35] The implication, he argues, is that were workers to take over, they would produce only what they needed and thereby avoid crises.

> The law of competition is that demand and supply always strive to complement each other, and therefore never do so ...[36]
>
> The struggle of capital against capital, of labor against labor, of land against land ... drives production to a fever pitch ...[37]
>
> If the producers as such knew how much the consumers required, if they were to organize production, if they were to share it out amongst themselves, then the fluctuations of competition and its tendency to crisis would be impossible.[38]

Beyond this Engels does not explain why, with no plan, production must outstrip demand *enough* to cause a crisis.[39]

3. The pattern of expansion, overproduction, crisis and recovery is a recurrent one:

> ... trade crises, which reappear as regularly as the comets, and of which we have now on the average one every five to seven years. For the last eighty years these trade crises have arrived just as regularly as the great plagues did in the past ...[40]

---

35 "Aggregate" in Keynesian macroeconomics is a synonym for total. In the case of production, it means the amount that all businesses will supply at a given price level. In the case of demand, it means the sum of all expenditures by consumers, business and government, plus net exports, also at various prices levels. In both cases, the aggregation is achieved by summing the *monetary* value of production and of expenditures.

36 Ibid., p. 433.

37 Ibid., p. 435.

38 Ibid., p. 434. This claim, of the possibility of planning supply as to properly meet demand, neither more nor less, was one side of a debate that has raged ever since. Soviet 5-Year plans quickly became the object of critique by those skeptical of the possibility of comprehensive planning. Classic theoretical arguments against the possibility were laid out by Ludwig von Mises (1881–1973) and Friedrich Hayek (1899–1992).

39 Economists and their models generally assume that capitalists will make small marginal adjustments in production in response to small changes in price and inventory and by so doing eliminate any kind of dramatic crisis of overproduction. The actual extent of crises, such as that of 1842 followed by the Chartist-led strikes, led Engels to foresee far more drama than imagined by economists.

40 "Outline of a Critique of Political Economy," MECW, *Vol. 3*, p. 433. Engels was by no means the first to recognize recurring patterns of general crisis. Malthus had argued for their existence against Ricardo, who believed that only single-market overproduction was

4. The crises get progressively worse over time as capitalism develops:

> ... each successive crisis is bound to become more universal and therefore worse than the preceding one.[41]

5. Finally, crisis accentuates conflict between classes and will lead ultimately to revolution:

> ... and finally causing a social revolution such as has never been dreamt of in the philosophy of the economists.[42]

Engels sees in this pattern a strange contradiction within capitalism that he and Marx would refer to repeatedly in the years ahead:

> A stage must be reached in the development of production wherein there is so much superfluous productive power that the great mass of the nation has nothing to live on ... that the people starve from sheer abundance.[43]

Yet he also sees in this growth of productivity the basis of a possible social order in which increased social wealth and less work would go together:

> This immeasurable productive capacity, handled consciously and in the interest of all, would soon reduce to a minimum the labor falling to the share of mankind.[44]

---

possible. Both the Welsh industrialist and reformer Robert Owen – whose ideas and followers Engels and then Marx would soon critique – and the Swiss socialist Jean Charles Leonard de Sismondi (1773–1842) both observed and analyzed what economists would eventually call "business cycles." See, Owen's *Report to the Committee of the Association for the Relief of the Manufacturing Poor* (1817) and Sismondi's *Nouveaux principes d'économie politique, ou de la richesse dans ses rapports avec la population* (1819). Observations of such regularity became so common as to eventually provoke 1) economists to construct mathematical models that generate cycles, including the kind of ever-worsening fluctuations that Engels predicted, e.g., William Baumol, *Economic Dynamics* (1951, 1959) and 2) government and private agencies to collect data to keep track of and help predict business cycles, e.g., the US Department of Commerce, the National Bureau of Economic Research, and a host of private "forecasting" efforts.

41 Ibid., p. 434.

42 Ibid., p. 434.

43 Ibid., p. 435.

44 Ibid., p. 436.

Thus, he offers the beginnings of a vision of post-capitalist society based not on utopian speculation of the sort then popular among English and French socialists, but rather on an analysis of the actual pattern of development of capitalism and the possibilities created.

Two years later, in speeches at Elberfeld, Engels argues how this vision of less work could begin to be realized through the elimination of huge amounts of unproductive work. A businessman himself, it was easy for him to look around and identify numerous sources of wasted human time and energy in trade, i.e., speculators, swindlers, superfluous middlemen, exporters, commission agents, forwarding agents, wholesalers and retailers, all of which, he judges, "contribute nothing to the commodity itself."[45] But he goes on to identify many other areas where people are employed in jobs that exist only because of the inequities of capitalism, e.g., the police and those in the judicial system, primarily deployed against crimes provoked by unjustly distributed property, and standing armies used against workers at home and in colonies abroad and against other capitalist powers. Freeing all these millions from unproductive activities so that they could participate alongside those already employed in truly socially productive activities could reduce the labor required of each individual.

> Given a just distribution of social activity ... the present customary labor time of the individual will be reduced by half simply by making use of the labor which is either not used at all or used disadvantageously.
>
> However, the benefits which communist organization offers through the utilization of wasted labour power are not yet the most significant. The greatest saving of labour power lies in the fusing of the individual powers into social collective power ...[46]

45 Frederick Engels, "Speeches in Elberfeld," (on February 8 and 15, 1945) first published in *Rheinische Jahrbücher zur gesellshaftlichen Reform*, 1845, MECW, *Vol. 4*, pp. 246–47.

46 Ibid., pp. 251–2. Although Engels made no effort to actually count the number of people engaged in unproductive work or calculate by how much each individual's workload might be reduced by shifting such people's labor to more productive activities, odds have it that by his definitions the percentage of "unproductive" workers today is much higher than his speculations in 1845. Here too, Engels had his forerunners, from Aristotle, whom Marx would cite in *Capital* as dreaming of replacing slaves with robots, through William Godwin (1756–1836) who not only hoped for less work and more leisure but also argued that only capitalism stood in the way of progressively freeing people completely from work. See his *Enquiry Concerning Political Justice and its Influence on Morals and Happiness* (1793), (Harmondsworth, UK: Penguin Classics, 1985), especially Vol. II, Book VIII, Chapter VI: "Objections to this System from the Allurements of Sloth." The parallels between their arguments are striking. Godwin wrote. "What is this quantity of labour that a state of equality will require . . . ? It is so light as rather to assume the guise of agreeable

Beyond the sphere of production, Engels goes on to make a similar argument about the labor savings that could be gained by reorganizing the sphere of reproduction, i.e., housing and family life. As one possible step, he recommends the proposals by Robert Owen to replace separate individual houses by communal palaces where both resources and labor could be saved through collective heating, cooking, etc.[47]

Thus, Engels' concern with crisis and class struggle is directly connected with his vision of a world beyond capitalism, which workers can construct. No mere academic concern, but that of a revolutionary grappling with the present to change the future.

Marx read Engels' "Outline", made a short, two-page summary of it in his notebooks and published it in the first (and only) issue of the *Deutsch-Französische Jahrbücher*. The failure of his summary to make any mention of Engels' discussion of crises suggests that he was not yet focused on the issue.[48]

His own first effort at synthesizing his previous study of philosophy and his more recent study of economics, were the *Economic and Philosophical Manuscripts of 1844*, which he wrote during the summer before he met Engels in Paris and began to work closely with him. In that text, Marx draws from his reading of Adam Smith and other classical political economists the same conclusion as

---

relaxation and gentle exercise than of labour … There will be no persons devoted to the manufacture of trinkets and luxuries; and none whose office it should keep in motion the complicated machinery of government, tax-gatherers, beadles, excise-men, tide-waiters, clerks and secretaries. There will be neither fleets nor armies, neither courtiers nor lacqueys. It is the unnecessary employments that, at present, occupy the great mass of every civilized nation … From the sketch which has been given, it seems by no means impossible that the labour of every twentieth man in the community would be sufficient to supply to the rest all the absolute necessities of life. If then this labour, … were amicably divided among the whole, it would occupy the twentieth part of every man's time … half an hour a day employed in manual labour by every member of the community would sufficiently supply the whole with necessaries." pp. 745–46.

47 Ibid., pp. 252–53. Some of these ideas were put into practice in "Red Vienna" in the late 1920s when the city was governed by the Social Democratic Workers' Party of Austria. While passing through that city in 2012, I had the pleasure of being taken to explore the most famous of such housing, the Karl-Marx-Hof, built for about 5,000 residents. It is worth keeping in mind that in many indigenous communities around the world the kind of collective cooking, clothes washing, etc., that Engels envisioned are common, albeit not in modern public housing. I've observed such in both Mexico and India. The breaking up of such collective behavior is typical of capitalist tendency to divide and conquer in the sphere of the reproduction of labor-power – a process that has probably reached its nadir in American suburbs full of single-family dwellings, famously parodied (along with the kinds of people such division tends to produce) in the song *Little Boxes* written and sung by Malvina Reynolds (1900–1978) in 1962. Available on YouTube.

48 "Summary of Frederick Engels' Article," MECW, *Vol. 3*, pp. 375–76.

Engels, namely that crisis in the overall economy results from overproduction driven by competition – between capitalists, between capitalists and workers, and between workers. He writes:

> Finally, as the amassing of capital increases the amount of industry and therefore the number of workers, it causes the same amount of industry to manufacture a larger amount of products, which leads to over-production ...[49]

And:

> Whilst labour brings about the accumulation of capital and with this the increasing prosperity of society, it renders the worker ever more dependent on the capitalist, leads him into competition of a new intensity, and drives him into the headlong rush of over-production, with its subsequent slump.[50]

Like Engels, he also emphasizes how the growth in the division of labor, while crippling workers within capitalism, does raise productivity, making possible the liberation of workers' time from work and the flowering of human being beyond work. In parallel to Engels' speeches at Elberfeld, Marx cites Friedrich Wilhelm Schulz (1797–1860):

> In France it has been calculated that at the present stage in the development of production an average working period of five hours a day by every person capable of work could suffice for the satisfaction of all the material interests of society ...[51]

Finally, in these long-unpublished pages, Marx directly confronts the class antagonisms that underly all the competition leading to crisis: the capitalist imposition of alienating work, exploitation, and workers' resistance. His analysis in these pages does not yet have the precision that his later theoretical work would make possible, but it does reveal the heart of the phenomenon of crisis – the antagonism between classes – and how revolution is the only path beyond it to communism.

---

49 "Economic and Philosophical Manuscripts of 1844," *MECW*, *Vol. 3*, p. 238.

50 Ibid., p. 240.

51 Ibid., p. 242. The passage is from Schultz, *Die Bewegung der Production* (Movement of Production), Zurich und Winterthur, 1843.

When political pressures from the Prussian and French governments killed the *Deutsch-Französische Jahrbücher*, Marx joined the staff and wrote for the journal *Vorwärts! Pariser Deutsche Zeitschrift*, a liberal German language journal published in Paris, made more radical by Marx's contributions. In them, he both critiqued others' ideas and politics, which he felt were erroneous and dangerous – like those of Ruge with whom he had parted ways – and began to analyze those workers' struggles he had found at the heart of crisis.

In a long article – published in two issues of *Vorwarts!* – Marx attacks Ruge's dismissive response to the June 1844 uprising of weavers in Silesia, then a province of Prussia.[52] Like the vintners in the Moselle Valley, the weavers were suffering from competition resulting from trade. Unlike them, they were also suffering from the very capitalist introduction of labor-displacing machinery. Against Ruge's dismissal, Marx hails the character of the weavers' rising as social, as a true proletarian revolt – however limited – against not just the political system but against capitalism. Indeed, he compares their rising favorably with the recent worker strikes reported by Engels from England and those by weavers in Lyons, France a decade earlier. Citing a song sung by the weavers, he argues that the lyrics aimed not only at the machines that were displacing them but also at the "ledgers, titles to property" of their employers and the bankers, the "hidden enemy" behind those employers.[53] His celebration of the revolt of Silesian weavers and condemnation of their repression so enraged the Prussian government that it successfully pressured the French government to close *Vorwarts!* and expel Marx from France in January 1845.

Prior to that expulsion, a visit by Engels to Paris in late August and a meeting with Marx resulted in ten days of intense discussion and the beginning of their first joint project – an attack on the Young Hegelians. Conceived as a short pamphlet, Marx amplified the attack into a 300-page manuscript, published in February 1845 as *The Holy Family: The Critique of Critical Criticism, Against Bruno Bauer and Company*. In the course of *his* critique, Marx dissects and demolishes *their* critique of Proudhon, praising him both as the first to recognize the negative effects of changing property relationships on human society and as having his analysis firmly anchored in the real concrete life of social struggle.

52 "Critical Marginal Notes on the Article 'The King of Prussia and Social Reform. By a Prussian," *Vorwärts!*, August 7, 10, 1844, *MECW*, *Vol. 3*, pp. 189–206. Engels had mentioned the turmoil in Silesia in two articles written for *The Northern Star*, No. 346, June 29, 1844, *MECW*, *Vol 3*, pp. 530–31 and pp. 532–34.

53 His attention to these workers' own words, can be seen as a forerunner to his later "Worker's' Inquiry" (1880), aimed at a systematic study of workers' own perspective on their work, exploitation, and alienation.

While Marx was finishing that project, Engels proceeded on his own to research the conditions of life and struggles of workers within the accumulation of capital in Britain. Based on his study of official reports and his personal observations, he then wrote a detailed analysis of his findings. His research covered both working conditions in factories and the lives of workers outside those satanic mills: their poverty, horrible living conditions, inadequate nutrition and susceptibility to disease, all worsened by periodic losses of jobs and income during commercial and industrial crises.[54] The result was his authoritative *The Condition of the Working Class in England* (1845), dedicated to "the working classes of Great Britain."[55]

In two chapters, Engels develops his analysis of crisis and class struggle. The capitalists' pitting of Irish workers against English ones, he argues, "has deepened the chasm between workers and the bourgeoisie, and hastened the approaching crisis." He draws upon the medical notion of crisis and applies it to capitalist society.

> The course of the social disease from which England is suffering is the same as the course of a physical disease; it develops according to certain laws, which has its own crises, the last and most violent of which determines the fate of the patient. And as the English nation cannot succumb under the final crisis, but must go forth from it, born again, rejuvenated, we can but rejoice over everything which accelerates the course of the disease.[56]

At the same time, as before, he focuses on crisis as a necessary outcome of the "unregulated production," the outcome of industrial competition, and insists on the "perpetual" periodicity of the cycle. Once more, he attributes the onset of crisis to the problem of overproduction, or the glutting of the market. He

---

54 On the devastations of disease due to low income, execrable living conditions and lack of medical care, see, *MECW*, *Vol. 4*, pp. 364–65, 396–400. Perhaps the most notable parallels during the current pandemic of Covid-19 are Engels' descriptions of the grossly overcrowded living conditions of workers and their families – the universal prescription for the spread of disease. Much the same problem persists today among those at the bottom of the income hierarchy: those who can barely afford to rent a roof over their heads, much less multiroom dwellings where intra-family "distancing" is possible and among those with no roof at all, homeless and living in the street, often huddled in little clusters of tents under overpasses or in abandoned buildings.

55 *MECW*, *Vol. 4*, pp. 295–583.

56 *MECW*, *Vol. 4*, p. 419. Engels rejoicing at "everything which accelerates the course of the disease" would become a recurrent theme among not only Marxists but also reactionaries in the form of "accelerationism."

implicitly supposes that all markets for particular goods would eventually be glutted, and that the problem arises because capitalist producers cannot judge when that will happen. In this work, he details the phases of the crisis more systematically than he had done in the "Outline".[57] He also describes more completely the process through which speculation and credit act both to stimulate investment and production and to accelerate collapse.[58]

Engels' major innovation, however, dealt with the relation between crisis and the class struggle. He formulated more clearly how the maintenance of competition among workers, e.g., between the English and the Irish, constituted the key to capitalist control and how the generation of an unwaged "reserve army" increased that competition. The rapid growth of the reserve army, which occurs during crises as workers are laid off, has two effects. First, it weakens those who retain their jobs, making it easier for capitalists to force down wages. Second, this very process contributes to the growth in class tensions, especially anger among those who lost their jobs. As a result, those workers ....

> ... begged, not cringing like ordinary beggars, but threatening by their numbers, their gestures and their words ... Here and there disturbances arose ... The most frightful excitement prevailed among the workers until the general insurrection broke out throughout the manufacturing districts.[59]

In his chapter on "labor movements" Engels traces how these tensions grew and were transformed by workers into combinations and trade unions, escalating their struggles into an intense conflict between the classes. In his political analysis of these workers' struggles, his theory of crisis plays a critical

57 Ibid., pp. 381–82.

58 Although all investment is a kind of speculation on uncertain future profits, here Engels is referring to money spent buying either commodities or securities in anticipation of either an increase or decrease in their value. In such speculative expenditures profit is sought, not by employing workers and the means of production to produce new commodities – what many economists call "*real* investment" – but rather by gambling on the future prices of the items purchased. Speculation can stimulate the economy to the degree that the excitement stimulated by the influx of money actually results in more real investment. But to the degree that it merely contributes to unsustainable overproduction of commodities or to a "bubble" in asset prices, the inevitable sudden fall in prices or devaluation of assets creates a crisis.

59 *MECW*, *Vol. 4*, p. 387.

role. On the one hand, he argues that the laws of supply and demand would always conquer the unions:

> All these efforts naturally cannot alter the economic law according to which wages are determined by the relation between supply and demand in the labor market. Hence the Unions remain powerless against all great forces which influence the relation.[60]

However, he also argues forcefully that these struggles are by no means hopeless but are indeed essential. They prevent capitalists from lowering wages as quickly as they otherwise would during a downturn and "then too, the unions often bring about a more rapid increase of wages after crisis than would otherwise follow."[61] In this way, "the active resistance of the English working-men has its effect in holding the money greed of the bourgeoisie within certain limits."[62] But more than this, these short-term struggles over wages point beyond the trades unions whose power is limited by the institutional framework. Trade union struggles, Engels writes, constitute "schools of war" for workers preparing them for revolution:

> These strikes, at first skirmishes, sometimes result in weighty struggles; they decide nothing, it is true, but they are the strongest proof that the decisive battle between bourgeoisie and proletariat is approaching. They are the military school of the workingmen in which they prepare themselves for the great struggle, which cannot be avoided.[63]

Because the crisis reappears; the struggles reappear:

> Stagnation in business and the want consequent upon it engendered the revolt at Lyons in 1834 … in 1842 at Manchester, a similar cause gave rise to a universal turnout for the Charter and higher wages.[64]

60 Ibid., p. 505. Eventually, Engels and Marx would demonstrate how some of those "great forces" are not exogenous but are shaped by workers' struggles.

61 Ibid., p. 506.

62 Ibid., p. 507.

63 Ibid., p. 512. The gist of these arguments would be reiterated in Marx's lectures in 1865. See below, p. 40.

64 Ibid.

> The crisis of 1842 came on. Agitation was once more as vigorous as in 1839.[65]

Based on this pattern Engels accurately predicts not only the subsequent crisis of 1847 but also a renewal of struggle—albeit not as successful as he hoped.

> The approach to Socialism cannot fail, especially when the next crisis directs the workingmen by force of sheer want to social instead of political (parliamentary action) remedies. And a crisis must follow the present active state of industry and commerce in 1847 at the latest ... The working men will carry their Charter ...[66]

As the crisis of 1847 unfolded, Engels narrates how as cotton textile factories laid off workers and announced a reduction in wages for those still employed, a meeting of worker delegates "from all over the country" threatened to strike:

> This strike, together with the strike of the Birmingham iron-workers and miners which has already started, would not fail to assume the same alarming dimensions which signaled the last general strike, that of 1842.[67]

At the same time, Engels saw how the "liberal" bourgeoisie tried to use the crisis against both workers and landlords by fomenting protest against the Corn Laws, e.g., tariffs against imported grain. Passed in 1815 in the wake of the Napoleonic Wars (1803–1815) at the behest of landlords, the Corn Laws (1815–1846) kept up the price of grain and by so doing also kept up landlords' rents. Inevitably, the high price of grain also made bread more expensive, forcing capitalists to pay higher wages and obtain lower profits than they would like. Thus, their opposition.

In support of their condemnation of the Corn Laws, capitalists drew on the political economist David Ricardo who argued that rising wages (due to the higher price of bread) and increased rents, which financed only the luxurious lifestyles of the landed aristocracy, squeezed industrial profits, which were

65 Ibid., p. 520.

66 Ibid., p. 524. While time proved Engels right about how crisis engenders uprisings, it proved his optimism overblown about "the working men ... carrying their Charter." They never did. It wasn't until the Reform Act of 1867 that substantial numbers of working *men* gained suffrage – itself only one of the Chartist demands. Women would only gain equal suffrage in 1928 – as the result of decades of struggle.

67 Frederick Engels, "The Commercial Crisis in England – The Chartist Movement – Ireland," October 23, 1847, (*La Reforme*, Oct. 26, 1847) MECW, *Vol. 6*, pp. 308–9.

vital to investment and growth.[68] So, they organized against those laws, forming a nation-wide Anti-Corn Law League in 1839. When the crisis of 1842 came on, they saw an opportunity to incite workers in their cause, appealing to the latter's need for cheaper bread. In his chapter on labor movements, Engels describes how some capitalists provoked workers into action in the hope workers would turn their frustration and rage against the landlords.

> The bourgeoisie was determined to carry the repeal of the Corn Laws with the help of the crisis, the want it entailed, and the general excitement [worker protests] ... the Liberal bourgeoisie half abandoned their law-abiding habits; they wished to bring about a revolution with the help of the workers ...

But how to provoke that help? With the crisis causing capitalists to lay off workers and unemployment rising, those workers who still had their jobs were loath to walk off them in protest.

> it was not the working-men who wished to quit work, but the manufacturers who wished to close their mills and send the operatives into the country parishes upon the property of the aristocracy, thus forcing the Tory Parliament and the Tory Ministry to repeal the Corn Laws.[69]

---

68 Against this support for Anti-Corn Law legislation, the landlords had Thomas Malthus (1766–1834) who defended the laws, basically arguing that given the recent wars, England needed to be self-sufficient in food production and keeping tariffs on grain high would help achieve that. See his *The Corn Laws* (1814) and his *Grounds of an Opinion on the Policy of restricting the Importation of Foreign Corn* (1815).

To this Ricardo responded first, that once large scale exports of grain to England became normal and expected, no country could shut off such exports without disastrous consequences to their own agriculture and the danger of popular revolt (he cited the results of Bonaparte's cutting off of Russian grain exports as an example), second, England could, as in the past, obtain grain from other countries especially once the free opening of British markets led producers in other countries to expand production expressly for the purposes of exporting to England, and third, that any decline in English agricultural production due to cheap grain could be softened by an gradual freeing of trade and at any rate capital withdrawn from agriculture would be invested in manufacturing to good effect and any decline in landlord consumption due to the fall in rents would be compensated for by a rise in the expenditure of profits and wages. See his *An Essay on the Influence of a Low Price of Corn on the Profits of Stock* (1815).

69 Ibid., p. 520. Engels drew upon this chapter for an article on "The History of the Corn Laws" for the *Telegraph für Deutchland*, December 1845, MECW, *Vol. 4*, pp. 656–61.

Unfortunately for the capitalists, as Engels details, instead of going after the landlords, thousands of workers, who were outraged at having their wages cut, instead mobilized against the capitalists demanding "a fair day's wages for a fair day's work" and spread their strikes quickly from mill to mill and town to town. At which point, as Engels relates "the bourgeoisie ... resumed its law-abiding attitude, and placed itself upon the side of the government as against the working-men."[70]

Beyond his descriptions and theory of crises and class struggle, Engels also used his analysis as the basis for an explicit critique of the bourgeois socialists of his day (such as the English Owenites and the French Utopians). His support for strikes and wage struggles included support for the Chartists whose cause he openly endorsed. This was a position that he and Marx would continue to hold through the forties as they broadened their writings to develop these views in *The German Ideology* (1844–45),[71] in the *Poverty of Philosophy* (1847),[72] and in the *Communist Manifesto* (1948).

As Marx and Engels' first joint work, *The Holy Family* (1845) was primarily concerned with their critique of the Young Hegelian socialists, so too was their second, *The German Ideology*. Although *The German Ideology* represented a distinct advance in the development of their perspective, especially the first section on Ludwig Feuerbach (1804–1872) where they set out their view of history, it had virtually nothing to add to the work Engels had already done on crises *within* capitalism. Rather, the major thrust was to set out their views on the centrality of class conflict in the evolution of social orders and to distinguish the class struggles of capitalism from those in earlier class societies. They distinguished between the "productive forces" and the "forms of social intercourse" or, as they would later say, the "relations of production." The development of the former, they argued, is at first stimulated by, but then constrained by the latter. This situation they saw as key to the collapse of one social order and the transition to the next. In this sense, their work did contribute to the theory of crisis, at least with respect to the fundamental forces acting to undermine capitalism as a system:

> Thus, all collisions in history have their origin, according to our view, in the contradiction between the productive forces and the form of intercourse.[73]

---

70 Ibid., p. 521.

71 *MECW, Vol. 5*, pp. 19–537.

72 *MECW, Vol. 6*, pp. 105–212.

73 *MECW, Vol. 5*, p. 74.

The concrete specificity of this development, however, remains even less clear in *The German Ideology* than it was in Engels' works, where the periodical contradiction between the productive forces (as production/output) and the forms of intercourse (the market) was defined in terms of an overproduction crisis and accentuated working-class struggle on the path to revolution. Much of Marx and Engels' subsequent work on crisis in which the forces and dynamics of this process are more fully developed, can be seen as the elaboration of the concept of the "forms of intercourse" acting as fetters on the productive forces. As spelled out in Chapter 3 below, this reaches its fullest development in Marx's "mature" works where the "forms of intercourse" are grasped in terms of the necessary imposition of – and worker resistance to – labor, value and the surplus value; all of which become harder and harder to impose as production and productivity expand.

1.2 *Brussels*

Based on their experiences in France and England, and the analysis in the "Outline" and in *The Condition of the Working Class in England,* Marx and Engels decided to begin political organizing in 1846–47. Expelled from Paris by the Guizot government in January 1845, Marx moved to Brussels. There, after working with Engels on *The German Ideology* and joining the newly formed International Democratic Association, they decided to launch a Communist Correspondence Committee to broaden their contacts and expand the number of adherents to their analysis before engaging directly in any existing political movement. Through exchanges of letters and meetings they sought to link together, through themselves, working class militants in Germany, France, and England. Their major effort in his project was directed toward the League of the Just, a clandestine organization based in London among German émigrés, with a public German Workers' Educational Union. The League's members had left behind the insurrectionism of Louis Auguste Blanqui (1805–1881), turning first to the utopianism of Fourier and Cabet in France but then moving towards the Chartists.[74] As already mentioned, Engels had established close ties with the Chartists and written several articles for their journal. When the League of the Just convened a congress in 1847, members adopted many of Marx and Engels' ideas and changed the name of their organization to the Communist League. At that point, Marx "turned the Brussels Corresponding Committee into a branch" of the renamed organization.

74 See McLellan, Chapter III, Section III on "The Founding of the Communist League," pp. 154-76.

Failing to attract Proudhon to their Committee, Marx and Engels complemented their support for the Chartists with attacks on the French socialist movements. Although he had praised Proudhon in *The Holy Family*, in his polemical *Poverty of Philosophy* (1846–47) Marx excoriates the man's economic analysis, his method, and his politics. Here, as they would do in the *Communist Manifesto* (1848), the theory of crisis bolstered their advocacy of working-class wage struggle and revolution against utopians, bourgeois socialists and others. He used arguments similar to those laid out earlier by Engels in *The Condition of the English Working Class*[75] to attack Proudhon's opposition to wage struggles. Proudhon had argued against them on the grounds that wage increases could only lead to higher prices and hence scarcity.

Against that argument, Marx points out that wage struggles lead not only to price increases, but also to the development of production as capitalists are forced to introduce new machines to replace troublesome workers. (This important point is taken up in detail in Chapter 4, Section 4.3 below.) Again, like Engels, he points out that worker combinations and strikes had been growing constantly:

> In spite of both of them [economists and socialists], in spite of manuals and utopias, combination has not ceased for an instant to go forward and grow with the development and growth of modern industry.[76]

Why was this? Because, Marx writes, of the very dynamic of industrial organization and the exploitation of workers:

> Large-scale industry concentrates in one place a crowd of people unknown to each other. Competition [between workers] divides their interests. But the maintenance of wages, this common interest which they have against their boss, unites them in a common thought of resistance-combination.[77]

---

75 *MECW, Vol. 4*, pp. 375–388, 397–99, 501–29; 579–83.

76 Karl Marx, "The Poverty of Philosophy" (1847), *MECW, Vol. 6*, pp. 105–210.

77 Ibid. Eventually, in the late 1970s, the high development of workers' self-organization and struggle in large factories and offices led to a reversal of the tendency to concentrate workers that Marx identifies. Some capitalists began to consciously disperse their labor force – a sort of return to something like the early putting out system in which employees work at home on machines and raw materials provided by their employers – whether material or digital – and once transformed/produced into output returned to them. When this reversal began to be noticed in Italy, it led to a national conference on the "Diffused Factory" in June of 1978, at the Università degli Studi di Milano, Milan, Italy. Much of the

This transformation of resistance into permanent combinations spreads, Marx notes, until it assumes the general character of a struggle in which the workers affirm themselves as a class.

> If the first aim of resistance was merely the maintenance of wages, combinations, at first isolated, constitute themselves into groups as the capitalists in their turn unite for the purposes of repression, and in face of always united capital, the maintenance of the association become more necessary ... In this struggle—a veritable civil war—all the elements necessary ... for a coming battle unite and develop. Once it has reached this point, association takes on a political character ... In the struggle, of which we have pointed out only a few phases, this mass becomes united, and constitutes itself as a class for itself, the interests it defends become class interests.[78]

As in Engels' "schools of war," Marx argues that only through combinations and strikes does the working class really become a class capable of overthrowing the bourgeoisie. He said little about the relation between crises and the class struggle, but where he did mention it, he implied that the struggles were often less intense during periods of prosperity, thus agreeing with Engels' linking of more intense class struggle with periods of crisis.

> If in 1844 and 1845 strikes drew less attention than before, it was because 1844 and 1845 were the first two years of prosperity that English industry

---

discussion at that conference, which I attended, focused on the role of this "diffusion" of workplaces in the evolution of class struggle in Italy – given how the spatial dispersal of workers makes their autonomous interaction and coordination difficult. For a sample of the issues, see *Quaderni del territorio: ristrutturazione produttiva e nuova geografia della forza-lavoro* (anno I, n. 1, 1976). Since then, "work at home" has become fairly common, both among regular employees, especially but not uniquely among those who work on computers and whose work is easily monitored by their employers, and precarious workers hired for one task at a time. In the wake of the student movements of the 1960s, there was some experimentation in the US with the "diffusion" of campuses that would make it hard for students to organize. Such "diffusion" of labor expanded considerably during the Covid-19 pandemic in both industry and in schools. Since then, the discovery by stay-at-home workers of the advantages of managing your own work without direct oversight has prompted some business to try get them back in the office and under immediate supervision. The long-term impact on the organization of work remains to be seen – and will, undoubtedly, be determined by struggle between workers and their bosses.

78 "The Poverty of Philosophy", *MECW*, *Vol. 6*, pp. 210–11.

> had had since 1837. Nevertheless, none of the trades unions had been dissolved.[79]

When the Communist League decided a "confession of [their] faith" should be drafted and discussed, Engels set to work, eventually coming up with a text titled "The Principles of Communism."[80] In that text, which amounted in many ways to a first draft of the *Communist Manifesto,*[81] he reiterates his earlier analysis of crises within capitalism and how they would lead to revolutionary "ferment." With the rapid growth of capitalist industry, he writes,

> very soon more was being produced than could be used. The result was that the goods manufactured could not be sold, and a so-called trade crisis ensued. Factories had to stand idle, factory owners went bankrupt, and the workers lost their bread ... After a while the surplus products were sold, the factories started working again, wages went up, and gradually business was more brisk than ever ... the state of industry has continuously fluctuated between periods of prosperity and periods of crisis ... and every time it has entailed the greatest misery for the workers, general revolutionary ferment, and the greatest danger to the entire existing system.[82]

The gist of this account was applied by Marx to fluctuations in wages in lectures given in December of 1847, but not published until later (see below).[83]

Written primarily by Marx but drawing on Engels' "Principles" draft, the *Communist Manifesto* announced the political credo of the Communist League. The *Manifesto* was written during the crisis of 1847, just before the revolutions that swept Europe in 1848. The *Manifesto* provided both an analysis of the development of capitalism—including its crises—and a prescription for action in the forthcoming social conflict.

At last, Engels' analysis of crisis began to be integrated in an important way into their joint works in support of their political position. Beyond *The German Ideology*, where crisis was conceived in the very general terms of "the history of the revolt of modern productive forces against modern conditions

79 Ibid., p. 208.

80 MECW, *Vol. 6*, pp. 341–357.

81 Terrell Carver does a side-by-side comparison of passages in the two texts in his *Marx & Engels: The Intellectual Relationship* (Bloomington: Indiana University Press, 1983), 87–94.

82 MECW, *Vol. 6*, p. 347.

83 Karl Marx, "Wages," MECW, *Vol. 6*, pp. 424–25, 429–30, 432.

of production," or against forms of "social intercourse," in the specific case of capitalism, the "productive forces" are the machines, workers, and their organization while the "conditions of production" are, above all, the need to sell the commodities produced in markets. They see crises emerging from the inability to coordinate the two phenomena.

> It is enough to mention the commercial crises that by their periodical return put on trial, each time more threateningly, the existence of the entire bourgeois society.[84]

So, the contradiction between the forces and relations of production lead to revolution via the path of Engels' recurrent, worsening crises. What is the origin of these crises? What exactly is meant by the inability to control the productive forces? The meaning lies in the tendency for production to outstrip the bourgeois ability to handle it:

> In these crises there breaks out an epidemic that, in all earlier epochs, would have seemed an absurdity—the epidemic of over-production ... there is too much civilization, too much means of subsistence, too much industry, too much commerce ... The conditions of bourgeois society are too narrow to comprise the wealth created by them.[85]

But if Marx means more by the phrase "too narrow to comprise the wealth" than commercial breakdowns, he does not specify it here. Nor would he set out a systematic explanation for some years. But if he does not explain the forces involved in this loss of control, he does see clearly how capital deals with the problem:

> And how does the bourgeoisie get over these crises? On the one hand by enforced destruction of a mass of productive forces; on the other by the conquest of new markets, and by the more thorough exploitation of the old ones.[86]

And yet, these measures cannot solve the problem permanently because the same forces that have led to the development of the productive forces will do so again with the same result:

---

84 Karl Marx & Frederick Engels, "The Communist Manifesto" (1848), *MECW*, *Vol. 6*, p. 489.
85 Ibid., pp. 489–90.
86 Ibid., p. 490.

> That is to say, by paving the way for more extensive and more destructive crises, and by diminishing the means whereby crises are prevented.[87]

These crises of capitalism are linked to the rise of the proletariat and to the class struggle by the growth of industry and trade which tend to unite the working class secularly in their struggles with capital. As they become "concentrated in greater masses," crises aggravate those struggles by increasing the fluctuations of wages:

> The growing competition among the bourgeois, and the resulting commercial crises, make the wages of the workers even more fluctuating ... the collisions between individual workmen and individual bourgeois take more and more the character of collisions between two classes. There upon the workers begin to form combinations (Trade Unions) against the bourgeois; they club together in order to keep up the rate of wages.[88]

Although he was not very clear, Marx again seems to be arguing that working class struggles—aimed at "keeping up" wages in the face of fluctuations—would be particularly intense during periods of downturn and crisis. Certainly, this was consistent with his and Engels' observations on the rise of the Chartists after the crisis of 1836, their experience in 1846 to 1848 and Marx's critique of Proudhon.

But if the *Communist Manifesto* primarily presents an analysis of the class struggles of a rapidly developing capitalism, it was also written in a period in which that development on the continent was constrained and hindered by governments not yet under the control of capitalists. Both France and Prussia were ruled by authoritarian monarchies. Thus, the support of Rhineland industrialists for the *Rheinische Zeitung* whose pages regularly carried articles critical of those constraints. Thus too, the government censorship, harassment, and ultimate banning of the paper, complemented by driving its most acerbic critic, Marx, out of the country. The same drama was repeated in Paris, by the French and German governments closing down the *Deutsch-Französische Jahrbücher* and then, *Vorwärts!* while forcing Marx to leave France for Belgium.[89]

---

87 Ibid.

88 Ibid., pp. 492–93.

89 The contemporary, early twenty-first century, return of authoritarian behavior among neo-fascist governments in Europe and the US, has brought a return to attacks on independent criticism in the press quite like what Marx and comrades were experiencing in

Beyond these general observations and endorsements of wage struggles, Marx and Engels also focus on the historical specificity of the crisis of 1846–48 that they see leading toward inevitable uprisings against the established orders. They argue – against the views of petty-bourgeois, "true" bourgeois, and critical utopian socialists – that working-class struggle is absolutely necessary. They see these upheavals in Europe as crises, not of capitalism but of the existing monarchies, which claimed absolute power, unchecked by either the emerging capitalist class or by workers. Thus, they view these uprisings as bourgeois revolutions aimed at replacing the power of monarchs with elections, some form of democracy. Through these means capitalists seek control of the state, civil liberties, and freedom of the press, which would provide both vehicles to spread bourgeois ideology and better flows of information about problems facing their ability to govern.[90] Such changes, Marx and Engels judged, would improve the terrain of struggle for workers. Therefore, they called for the

---

the 1840s. Trump-the-pathological-liar's unsubstantiated branding of all critical reports as "fake news" has been adopted by several authoritarian governments in Europe. (At last check, the *Washington Post* had cataloged over 30,000 Trump lies.) These attacks have been aimed at obscuring stepped up repression of a wide variety of hard-earned rights, through legislative action and vicious rhetoric which has encouraged violence – against both individuals and democracy itself, e.g., voter repression and the January 6, 2021 effort to block the peaceful transfer of power through a physical assault on the US Capitol. Along with the attacks on women's reproductive rights, by SCOTUS' overturning of Roe and the passage of anti-abortion legislation in all too many states, we are also seeing a new wave of attacks on LGBT+ rights. In June 2021, Hungarian lawmakers passed legislation banning any mention of LGBT+ in schools or any media available to minors – in direct violation of EU rules. https://www.pinknews.co.uk/2021/06/15/hungary-anti-lgbt-homophobia-propaganda-law-ban-fidesz-viktor-orban-section-28/ This anti-LGBT+ crackdown is being repeated in the US by neo-fascist state governments such as DeSantis' in Florida with his "Don't Say 'Gay'" law.

90 Although Marxists, for obvious reasons, have generally emphasized the ideological role played by the capitalist press – which has never been as "free" as it has pretended – just as important has always been the interclass intelligence provided to capitalist policy makers by reporters' stories about conflicts within the system. A "free press" dramatically multiplies ruling classes' sources of intelligence. These sources of information often arrive sooner, and sometimes are more reliable, than more "serious" studies of such conflicts by academics and government bureaucrats commissioned to study them. One of the great weaknesses of authoritarian governments that suppress such information flows is how they rarely know what is going on before conflicts explode. This weakness of nineteenth century pre-capitalist authoritarian governments was replicated in the twentieth century in the USSR and its client states – as was plainly revealed in upheavals such as those in East Germany in 1953, in Hungary in 1956, in Czechoslovakia in 1968, in the food protests in the USSR in the 1970s, in the emergence of *Solidarność* in Poland in 1980 and ultimately in the collapse of those regimes. In case after case, the suppression of the press and of revelatory dissent resulted in uprisings for which the regimes were totally unprepared,

working class to support such revolutions as a necessary step – one that would dramatically improve political conditions – before turning against the bourgeoisie itself. This position, they would later decide, in the light of subsequent events, was ill-advised.

When the continental upheavals of 1848–49 exploded with the February Revolution against King Louis Philippe in France, the March Revolution against King Frederick William IV in Germany and uprisings in Italy, Austria, and so on, Marx and Engels found themselves no longer theorizing about crisis and revolution but face-to-face with the reality. They immediately joined the fray, supporting both demands for democracy against feudal and monarchical power and insurrectionary actions. When the Democratic Association in Brussels demanded that the Belgian government arm workers, several of its members, including Marx and his wife were arrested, briefly jailed and deported.

1.3 *Paris*

From Belgium they travelled to Paris where Marx's previous expulsion was rescinded by friends in the new Second Republic government who invited him back. There, Marx took part in the political meetings of the Society of the Rights of Man and sought out militant groups of German workers. Once joined by Engels, they set up a German Workers' Club and created a new Central Committee of the Communist League. As events unfolded, they opposed the formation of a militia of armed German workers to overthrow the Prussian government from the outside. When others did form a "German Democratic Legion", it was quickly crushed. On the other hand, when news came of mass demonstrations in Berlin and of King William conceding parliamentary elections, a constitution and freedom of the press, Marx and Engels returned to Cologne – with copies of the *Communist Manifesto* in hand – to join the revolution. They also brought with them leaflets containing "The Demands of the Communist Party in Germany" calling for such things as the unification of Germany, universal suffrage, arming of the people, land reform to free peasants of feudal obligations, nationalization of transport and making it free to

having lost the potential for preventive measures that better information might have made possible.

The flip side, the vulnerability to capitalist rule created by a "free press" are the ways workers have found to use it for their own purposes, from using reports in capitalist media to circulate their analyses and even their struggles (more efficient than illegal efforts like *samizdat* in the USSR and Eastern Europe), to the creation of their own above-ground press media, from handbills and flyers to newspapers and journals to circulate their ideas more effectively – as Marx and Engels repeatedly sought to do through their journalism.

"the impecunious classes," a progressive income tax, state guaranteed employment – to offset the negative effects on workers of capitalist crises – and free education.[91]

1.4 *Cologne*

In Cologne, they created a *"Neue" Rheinische Zeitung* through which they carried on their propaganda work. When conflicts in the Communist League led to the dissolution of its Central Committee in May of 1848, the *Zeitung* became the focal point for their organizational work as well as their propaganda. During this period of almost a year, Marx and Engels worked, through their paper and political co-workers, to influence the direction of the struggle. Everywhere in Europe, the old order was being challenged, in national assemblies by bourgeois democrats and in the streets by workers demanding both democracy and improvements in their wages, working conditions and standards of living. In the beginning, Marx and Engels argued forcefully for the strategy developed in the *Manifesto*: support for working-class struggles, but also for the bourgeois revolt against absolutism. They argued against those who would confine workers' struggles to "economic" issues, e.g., wages, arguing the need for both workers and peasants to join the fight to change the political system to gain more latitude for struggle, e.g., freedom of the press, which in those moments made their *Zeitung* possible.

But, as events unfolded in 1848, Marx and Engels were forced to modify their position by overwhelming evidence that the bourgeoisie was not taking sufficient action or leadership to ensure the success of what they viewed as its own revolution – one spearheaded by workers, but in support of capitalist priorities. In France, they saw the National Assembly turn against the workers by moving to abolish the National Workshops that provided wages. That action brought on the "June Days" of revolt, viciously repressed by the new government. In country after country, they saw liberal capitalists joining with conservatives to compromise with absolutism and betray the very workers and peasants who had been in the streets fighting for their demands. In "The June Revolution", Marx analyzed the betrayal in France, which led to Cavaignac's slaughter of thousands and the deportation of thousands more.[92] That betrayal, he argued, outlined a pattern repeated elsewhere on the continent. In his analysis, he directly addressed the relationship between class struggle and industrial crisis.

Unemployed workers had risen in February against the regime of King Louis Philippe during a crisis, demanding the creation of public employment

91 MECW, *Vol. 7*, pp. 3–5.

92 "The June Revolution," *Neue Rheinische Zeitung*, June 28, 1848, MECW, *Vol. 7*, pp. 144–49.

(the National Workshops) to ward off poverty and starvation, as well as participation in government, the Second Republic and National Assembly. But that government, with only two members representing workers' interests, not only canceled the workshops but also proved unable to deal with crisis. It was not, Marx writes, "within the power of any assembly any more than of a king to tell a universal industrial crisis – *advance up to this point and no further*."[93] All it did do was abandon any effort to alleviate worker suffering and by so doing bring on greater revolt.

If, during most of 1848, the *Neue Rheinische Zeitung* had played down the class conflict between workers and capital, the abandonment of leadership by the bourgeoisie caused them to re-emphasize the autonomy of the working class and support independent action on its part as the only way to avoid catastrophe. To spell out their analysis of this abdication by the Prussian bourgeoisie of its role, Marx wrote a series of articles: "The Bourgeoisie and the Counter-Revolution" in December.[94] To bring the working class-capital conflict back to the center of discussion by showing how the interests of workers and capitalists were opposed, Marx published another series of articles in the *Zeitung* under the title "Wage Labor and Capital" (1849) – essentially the lectures he had prepared the previous year.[95]

As was to become his wont, in these articles, Marx roots his analysis of wages in that of commodities in general because workers sell their labor-power to capitalists as a commodity. In his exposition, crisis is presented, once again, as the result of overproduction. First, crises for capital:

> These fluctuations, which, looked at more closely, bring with them the most fearful devastations and, like earthquakes, cause bourgeois society to tremble to its foundations ... [96]

And then crises for workers. As capital and its command over labor is accumulated, he explains,

> there is a corresponding increase in earthquakes ... in a word, crises increase. They become more frequent and more violent ... A lord, at once aristocratic and barbarous, [capital] drags with it into the grave

93 Ibid., p. 148.
94 *MECW*, *Vol. 8*, pp. 154–78.
95 *MECW*, *Vol. 9*, pp. 197–228.
96 Ibid., p. 208,

> the corpses of its slaves, whole hecatombs of workers who perish in the crises.[97]

Besides demonstrating the unavoidable opposition between workers and capitalists, Marx also countered reactionary arguments that blamed the depressed economy and high unemployment on the continent on social unrest. A *Zeitung* editorial on the "The State of Trade," published in March 1848, demonstrated with historical data how downturns were the result of overproduction exacerbated by speculation and accentuated by financial collapse and how the crisis of 1847 that originated in England circulated to the continent. He did not, however, entirely ignore the contribution of workers' struggles to crises, while maintaining that capitalist behavior could lead to crises. "The revolutions," he argues, "contributed to the fact that now and then trade stagnated ... [but] In Southern Germany, on the Rhine, in Hamburg and in Berlin, with or without the revolution we would have had our bankruptcies."[98]

As revolutionary efforts in Europe – by both timid bourgeois liberals and insurgent workers – were defeated by the old regimes, conflicts broke out among the factions fighting for change, financing for the *Zeitung* dried up and individuals suffered increased police and military repression. In September 1848, a state of siege was declared in Cologne and on October 4th an arrest warrant was issued for Engels and another editor of the paper.[99] Engels and Marx were forced to leave the city. Marx went to Paris where he was again expelled and then moved on to London. Engels also left Cologne but joined the insurrection in Baden to give the popular army whatever advice he could, based on his own military training. He stayed until the revolt collapsed in July when he fled to Switzerland and eventually back to London.

1.5 *London*

In London, Marx and Engels set about two urgent tasks. The first was rebuilding the Communist League. They felt that the defeats on the Continent would soon be followed by a new round of revolution, and they wanted to be

97 Ibid., p. 228.

98 *MECW*, *Vol. 9*, p. 7. Eventually, this vision of crisis as occurring independently of workers' struggles would be abandoned as Marx discovered more and more of the "internal" dynamics of capitalist development to be aspects of class struggle. Such passages, however, have provided some Marxists with grounds for their belief that overproduction as a cause of crisis is a phenomenon driven by forces autonomous of workers' actions and the latter are mere reactions to the former. I return to this issue in Chapter 5 on "Predispositions to Crisis."

99 The other editor was not Marx, but Heinrich Bürgers (1820–1878). *MECW*, *Vol. 7*, p. 593.

organizationally prepared. This new upheaval they expected to envelope both England and the Continent, as the end of British prosperity of 1848–49 would coincide with crisis across the channel:

> ... as this crisis will inevitably coincide with great clashes on the Continent, it will bear fruit of a very different type from all preceding crises. Whereas hitherto every crisis has been the signal for further progress, for new victories by the industrial bourgeoisie over the landowners and financial bourgeoisie, this crisis will mark the beginning of the modern English revolution.[100]
>
> The effects of the trade crisis now breaking will be more significant than those of any crisis hitherto. It coincides with the agricultural crisis which already began with the repeal of the Corn Laws in England and was intensified with the recent good harvests. For the first time England is simultaneously experiencing an industrial crisis and an agricultural crisis. This double crisis in England is being hastened and extended and made more inflammable by the simultaneously impending convulsions on the Continent, and the continental revolutions will assume an incomparably more pronounced socialist character through the recoil of the English crisis on the world market.[101]
>
> Political developments on the Continent are likewise pressing daily more urgently towards a showdown, and the coincidence of trade crisis and revolution, which has already been mentioned several times in this Revue, is becoming more and more certain.[102]

These comments, written in the spring of 1850, reflected both a continuing optimism that all was not lost and analytical links among prosperity, crisis, and the pattern of working-class revolt.

Their autocritique and planning involved two thrusts. First, they reaffirmed their new belief in the necessity of autonomous working-class action even within an essentially bourgeois revolution. In the discussion and debate within the re-established Communist League, Marx and Engels emphasized this autonomy as a prerequisite for the inevitable conflict between workers and capital that would follow bourgeois success in overthrowing absolutist

100 "Review: January–February 1850," *MECW*, *Vol. 10*, pp. 264–65.

101 "Review: March–April 1850," *MECW*, *Vol. 10*, p. 340.

102 Ibid., p. 341.

regimes. They argued for maximizing working-class strength in the struggle against absolutism, including the maintenance of its own ability with arms after victory and the creation of working-class organizations and alternative state functions, as the only possible way to avoid subsequent defeat.[103]

Second, they undertook an extensive analysis of the experience of their own activity (in the Communist League) and of the course of the Revolution in general. Removed from the heat of the conflict for the first time in a year, they had time to reflect and to try to grasp the general forces that had shaped the Revolutions and that would shape the future. In this reflection, they leaned heavily on their analysis of economic crisis and its relation to the class struggle.

Their initial optimism, however, did not last. As the counter-revolution was secured across Europe, Marx returned to his studies of political economy and a closer examination of the pre-1848 economic crises and their relation to the 1848 revolutions. The results of these studies were published as articles in the *New Rheinische Zeitung Revue* in 1848 and 1849. The most important of these articles, for their evolving theory of crisis and class struggle, was the "Review (of international economic and political development): May-October 1850," which appeared in the last issue of the *Revue*.[104]

In this article Marx and Engels traced both the emergence of crisis in England as a product of the industrial and commercial expansion of 1843–45 and the spread of that crisis to the Continent. There is no major change in their interpretation of the causes and nature of crisis. They attribute its source to the emergence of overproduction despite the opening of new Far Eastern markets and new trade and investment outlets in the New World. There is no new explanation as to the reason why this overproduction is inevitable, but there is considerable analysis of the role played by speculation in accentuating its developments and impact. They analyze the development of speculation in railways, cotton, corn, and foreign trade – the expansion of credit and the creation of false ventures, e.g., those designed purely to make quick profits through stock issues on non-existent assets – one of those things that Marx would later analyze under the title "fictitious capital." (See Chapter 5, Section 3.3.)

> Based on the real expansion of the British and continental railway systems and the speculation which was bound up with it, there gradually arose during this period a superstructure of fraud reminiscent of the time

103 History has demonstrated, again and again, that one of the first signs that a new post-revolutionary regime is turning against workers and peasants is the demand for the surrender of arms by everyone except the official police and military.

104 "Review: May–October 1850," *MECW*, *Vol. 10*, pp. 490–532.

> of Law and the South Sea Company. There were projects for hundreds of lines which had not the slightest chance of success, which their very authors never had any intention of really carrying out and whose sole purpose indeed was to enable the directors to squander the deposits and to make fraudulent profits from the sale of stocks."[105]

When this superstructure of speculation and fraud collapsed, it led quickly to the restriction of the production on which it had been based:

> Speculation regularly occurs at times when over-production is already in full swing. It provides channels by which this over-production may temporarily be diverted, whilst by this very process hastening the onset of the crisis and magnifying its impact. The crisis itself first breaks out in the field of speculation and only seizes hold of production later. Not over-production but over-speculation, itself only a symptom of over-production.[106]

It was from this capitalist crisis at the English heart of the European economy that subsequent crises on the Continent sprang. "The first repercussions of the crisis appeared on the continent as early as October (1847) … As the crisis abated in intensity in Great Britain, so it increased on the Continent and affected places that it had not hitherto reached."[107] By the time the Revolutions broke out in France in February 1848 and in Germany in March, the crisis in England was over, but the crisis in those countries well under way. Marx and Engels grappled with the problem of trying to sort out the direction of

105 Ibid., pp. 491–92. The "Law" referred to here is John Law (1671–1729), a banker and ex-con from Scotland, who founded the Banque Générale Privée in 1716, nationalized a year later, at Law's request, to become the Banque Royale or first central bank of France. He used it to create the *Compagnie d'Occident* (The Mississippi Company) in 1717 and obtain for it a government-sanctioned monopoly on trade in Louisiana and the West Indies. Law encouraged speculation on the Company's shares, which resulted in the Mississippi Bubble that burst in 1720 and bankrupted the Banque. See, James Narron and David Skeie, "Crisis Chronicles: The Mississippi Bubble of 1720 and the European Debt Crisis," New York Fed, *Liberty Street Economics* (January 10, 2014). https://libertystreeteconomics.newyorkfed.org/2014/01/crisis-chronicles-the-mississippi-bubble-of-1720-and-the-european-debt-crisis/ The South Sea Company was a British joint-stock company, founded in 1711 and like the Mississippi Company was granted a monopoly to trade in the Americas – mainly in slaves. Here too speculation resulted in a dramatic rise in the value of the Company's stock, the South Sea Bubble, which also burst in 1720.

106 Ibid., p. 490.

107 Ibid., p. 496.

causality between this economic crisis and the political upheavals that swept Europe, and they found causes running each way. With respect to, "The Panic which broke out in Paris after February and spread throughout the continent at the same time as the revolutions …"[108], they find the causes indeterminate:

> In the case of failures of bankers and traders in other places on the Continent, it is impossible to decide to what extent they arose from the continuation and gradual spread of the commercial crisis … or to what extent they were really consequences of losses resulting from the revolution panic.[109]

Nevertheless, they offer the general reflection that:

> However, this much at least is certain, that the commercial crisis contributed infinitely more to the revolution of 1848 than the revolution to the commercial crisis.[110]

They used this same reasoning to understand how returning prosperity cut short class conflicts in England. They trace the numerous beneficial effects of the Continental upheaval on the economies of England and the United States. In both cases, new prosperity was partly built on the capital that flowed out of the Continent during the upheaval, and partly on the elimination of outlets for speculation, which forced capital into productive enterprise. They argued, that although the crisis had begun in England, its circulation to Europe had contributed to English prosperity, thereby helping to undercut all revolutionary movement there (that is, the Chartists), "The French Revolution of 1848 saved the English middle class,"[111] where capital's power and thus its ability to cope was greatest:

> While, therefore, the crises first produce revolutions on the Continent, the foundation for these is, nevertheless, always laid in England. Violent outbreaks must naturally occur rather in the extremities of the bourgeois

108 Ibid., p. 497.

109 Ibid., p. 497.

110 Ibid.

111 "Preface" to the 1892 English edition of *Condition of the Working Class in England in 1844*, *MECW*, *Vol. 27*, p. 263.

> body than in its heart, since the possibility of adjustment is greater here than there.[112]

The return of prosperity to England, they went on to show, was soon followed by the defeat of the revolutions and the spread of prosperity to the Continent in its turn – lagging in recovery as in crisis. Faced with this widespread recovery during the summer of 1850, Marx and Engels were forced to conclude that this development would undermine any quick return of a revolutionary situation.

At the same time, they began to look at the European situation within the framework of their analysis of the contradiction between the forces of production and forms of social intercourse. They began to think that perhaps the development of the forces was not as advanced as they had previously thought — that there was still room for further development before the crisis. The new soberness in their assessment of the situation was accompanied by the conviction that crisis must eventually return and through it the revolution.

> With this general prosperity, in which the productive forces of bourgeois society develop as luxuriantly as is at all possible within bourgeois relationships, there can be no talk of revolution. Such a revolution is only possible in the periods when *both these factors*, the *modern* productive *forces* and the *bourgeois forms of production*, come in *collision* with each other ... A new revolution is possible only in consequence of a new crisis. It is, however, just as certain as this crisis.[113]

The upshot of this analysis was the conviction on the part of Marx and Engels that the revolutionary possibilities, which they had expected to re-emerge soon, would be much longer in coming. They gave reasons in the Review to think that a crisis might recur as early as 1852, but they apparently did not put much faith in this prediction. They were soon embroiled in political infighting within the Communist League over the proper course of action.

The change in their views was evidenced in their opposition to others who desired to continue to organize as if a new revolutionary surge was imminent. As a result of this conflict, the League split. With the continuing success of reaction on the continent, especially the successful destruction by Prussian police

112 Karl Marx, "Class Struggles in France," January – November 1, 1850, *MECW*, *Vol. 10*, p. 134.

113 Ibid., p. 135.

of the League's organization in Germany in 1851, Marx and Engels decided to officially terminate the organization in 1852.[114]

This brought to a close their active participation in the political struggles of the period, as they both turned to research, writing, and making a living. For the next decade they would think, study and write in more or less complete isolation from active political movement. In this, they were not simply abandoning the field of action, but following the only realistic course open to them in the light of the defeat suffered by the working classes in England and Europe, and their belief that major political movement would only be generated by another round of major crises. Their return to research was part of the general movement of the working class in this period to relinquish the initiative in the class struggle and heal its wounds in preparation for struggles to come.

It was during this long decade of relative working-class quiescence that Marx was able to return to his studies of political economy and work on the development of the basic theoretical framework necessary to a more precise understanding of the class relations of capitalism. Here he went back to the early efforts of Engels' "Outline" and of his own *Poverty of Philosophy* to critique the categories and theories of political economy and construct a meaningful and consistent analysis of capitalism as a social system. It was during this period that his conceptualization of how the labor theory of value could be used as the key to a quantitative and qualitative analysis of capitalist relations took shape. This was a work of many years for Marx and interspersed with his job as a journalist for the *New York Herald* and other papers, all carried out under conditions of much personal poverty and ill health.

When the crisis of 1851–52, which Marx and Engels had predicted, finally arrived, it was of considerably less amplitude—a "minor trade crisis"—and was accompanied by no significant resurgence of working-class struggle. In the continuing atmosphere of industrial prosperity and the rapid growth of European capitalism, which characterized the next five or six years, Marx and Engels carried on their solitary efforts. It was only slowly that they came to recognize that the crisis of the late 1840s was not a prelude to a final massive upheaval of capital and the revolution that they had expected, but rather a prelude to a long period of capitalist expansion. "The revival of trade, after the crisis of 1847," Engels would later write "was the dawn of a new industrial epoch."[115]

114 Biographers debate whether Marx officially dissolved the Communist League, or it just fell apart. David McClellan, for example, suggests "It seems probable that Marx exercised the power granted him in Brussels ... to declare a formal dissolution ...," McClellan, *Karl Marx: A Biography*, 183.

115 "Preface," op. cit., *MECW*, *Vol. 27*, p. 258.

2 Years of Theory, 1857–1867

The first few years of the 1850s, after the split in the Communist League, were politically quiet ones for Marx. His endless studies in the British Museum, reading, copying excerpts, and making notes, were interrupted only by his work as a journalist. Those studies bore theoretical fruit in 1857 when the outbreak of a major crisis provoked him to pull his thoughts together. Despite the crisis causing the *New-York* [*Daily*] *Tribune* to reduce his already low payments by half, making his financial situation even more dismal,[116] he was nevertheless excited by the revolutionary potential of a crisis he had been anticipating since the beginning of the decade. "Though my own financial distress may be dire indeed, never, since 1849, have I felt as cozy as during this outbreak," he wrote to Engels.[117]

2.1 *From Notes to Weighty Tomes*

In a tremendous burst of energy Marx worked night after night for months, pulling together his notes and synthesizing the new ideas that he had been developing over the past several years. As he wrote to Engels, "I am working like mad all night and every night collating my economic studies so that I at least get the outlines clear before the déluge." The *déluge* was an expected revolutionary upheaval – such as the Revolutions of 1848, which had followed the crisis of 1847.[118]

The result was a series of notebooks – published long after his death as the *Grundrisse*,[119] which many consider not only the first moment in the production of Marx's so-called "mature" works, but also the first "draft" of what would become *Capital*.[120] Although unpolished, they embodied a tremendous leap

---

116 Franz Mehring, *Karl Marx, The Story of His Life* (Ann Arbor: University of Michigan Press, 1918, 1962), Chap 9, 255. Mehring uses the title *New York Tribune*, which was correct except for the years from 1842 to 1866 when it bore the title *New-York Daily Tribune*.

117 Marx to Engels, November 13, 1857, *MECW*, *Vol. 40*, p. 199.

118 Marx to Engels, December 8, 1857, *MECW*, *Vol. 40*, p. 217.

119 The *Grundrisse der Kritik der Politischen Ökonomie*, or *Fundamentals* (or *Outlines*) *of the Critique of Political Economy*, remained unpublished in full in German until 1939–41 and in English until 1973.

120 This is the position of the editors of *MECW*, who sometimes call it "the original rough version of *Capital*." See Vol. 28, p. XI, and sometimes "the first version of *Capital*," Vol. 30, p. X, of Enrique Dussell in his "The Four Drafts of Capital: Towards a New Interpretation of the Dialectical Thought of Marx," *Rethinking Marxism* 13, no. 1 (2001): 10–26 and of Fred Moseley in his Introduction to *Marx's Economic Manuscript of 1864–1865*. It was not the position of either David McLellan or Antonio Negri who saw in the *Grundrisse* manuscripts a much greater synthesis of ideas only some of which would eventually appear

forward in Marx's theoretical work. Despite his excitement and fervent wish, the crisis of 1857 did not result in another explosion of revolutionary activity, neither in England nor on the Continent, as had happened in 1848. In that absence, Marx continued his theoretical efforts.

To polish, sharpen, reorganize, and clarify in his own mind and for publication, Marx repeatedly reworked the ideas in these notebooks in three more manuscripts leading up to *Capital*. The first, which he published in German in 1859, was his *Zur Kritik der Politischen Ökonomie,* or *A Contribution to the Critique of Political Economy* – largely a rewrite of the first part of the *Grundrisse*, which dealt with value and money.[121] The second, intended as a continuation of *Zur Kritik* was the huge "Manuscript of 1861–63" – comprised of 23 notebooks and 1,472 pages.[122] The entire manuscript has only recently become available in English in *MECW* (Vols 30–34), published from 1988 to 1994.[123] The third was the "Manuscript of 1864–65," supposedly a complete draft of *Capital*, although the part corresponding to Volume 1 has been lost. The parts containing the material which Engels prepared as Volumes 2 and 3 have just recently been published in English.[124] All these texts contain analyses of the possibilities of crisis and various forces at work tending to bring them about.[125]

in *Capital*. See McLellan's *Karl Marx: A Biography* (1973), pp. 275–284 and Negri's much more elaborated interpretation in his *Marx Oltre Marx: Quaderno di Lavoro sui Grundrisse* (Milano: Feltrinelli, 1979). In English as: *Marx Beyond Marx, Lessons on the Grundrisse* (New York: Autonomedia, 1991).

121 *Zur Kritik* was published in Berlin in June 1859. An English translation by N. I. Stone was published in English by Charles Kerr & Co. in Chicago in 1904. A different translation by Salo Ryazanskaya was published in 1970 by the troika of Progress Publishers in Moscow, Lawrence Wishart in London and International Publishers in New York. That translation was also the basis of the one provided in *MECW*, *Vol. 29*, pp. 257–417.

122 A big chunk of the manuscript would be edited by Karl Kautsky (1854–1938) and published in three volumes as *Theories of Surplus Value*. That material was re-edited and translated into English and the three volumes were published sequentially by Progress Publishers (Moscow) as *Theories of Surplus Value: Volume 4 of Capital,* Pt. I in 1963, Pt. II in 1968 and Pt. III in 1971.

123 The "Manuscript of 1861–63" was published for the first time, in German, in the *MEGA* in 1976–82.

124 The section corresponding to Vol. II of *Capital* was published in German in *MEGA* in 1988 and the rest was published in 1992. The first English translation was published as *Marx's Economic Manuscript of 1864–1865*, (Brill, 2015, Haymarket Books, 2017). The chronology is from Fred Moseley's introduction.

125 The availability in 2015 of an English translation of the original *Manuscript of 1864–1865*, out of which Engels crafted Volume 3, now makes it possible for those of us without knowledge of German to compare the original manuscript with Engel's edited version. Unfortunately, the editor – Fred Mosely – by only linking the new translation to *MEGA* and not to the Penguin edition of Volume 3, which is the version most easily available,

All this work of theoretical thinking and writing elaborated a whole series of concepts in an increasingly clarified manner. This allowed Marx and Engels to dissect a wide variety of phenomena they had been studying in the development of the class struggle more clearly than ever before. As sketched below in Chapters 3–8, these concepts allowed them both to more clearly grasp the conditions of capitalist development and to analyze those conditions, both their realization and their crises, in terms of the ongoing struggle between workers and their exploiters.

Devoted to thinking through these things with the ever-present goal of helping workers both understand what their class enemies were up to and their possibilities of rupturing those plans, their theories were unclassifiable in terms of contemporary scholarly "disciplines." Yes, they studied some philosophers and drew upon some of their concepts to enrich their own insights, yet they were not philosophers, per se. Yes, they studied the political economists of their time – ever apologists, strategists and tacticians for capital – but they were not political economists, much less the even more narrowly focused economists of the twentieth century and today. So, reading their theory as philosophy or as an alternative economic theory of capitalism fails to see how they drew upon every theoretical effort they found useful to understand

---

has made finding a familiar passage from Volume 3 within the *Manuscript* a tedious, time-consuming business. Similarly, because he bracketed the material Engels left out merely with the karats > and <, I highly recommend reading the text with a highlighter to more clearly identify those words and passages.

The earlier publication of the manuscript in German gave rise to considerable debate among Marxologists about the importance of what Engels included, what he left out and what he changed, and the importance of the differences. See for example: Martha Campbell and Geert Reuten, eds., *The Culmination of* Capital: *Essays on Volume III of Marx's* Capital (New York: Palgrave, 2002). Unfortunately, the theoretical perspectives of those engaged in the debates and their resulting preoccupations are so different from my own as to make most of the debate irrelevant to this project. The same situation obtains with regard to similar volumes written in reaction to the availability of original manuscripts which Marx wrote in crafting Volume 1 and from which Engels extracted and compiled Volume 2, e.g., Riccardo Bellofiore and Roberto Fineschi, eds., *Re-reading Marx: New Perspectives after the Critical Edition* (New York: Palgrave, 2019), Michael Heinrich, *How to Read Marx's* Capital*: Commentary and Explanations on the Beginning Chapters* (New York: Monthly Review Press, 2021), Fred Moseley, *Marx's Theory of Value in Chapter I of* Capital: *A Critique of Heinrich's Value-Form Interpretation* (Palgrave Macmillan, 2023), Christopher Arthur and Geert Reuten. eds., *The Circulation of Capital: Essays on Volume Two of Marx's Capital* (London: Macmillan Press, 1998). To the degree that I have found any of this new source material useful in clarifying Marx and Engels' thinking on crisis beyond the material in the Penguin editions of Volumes 1 - 3, I have included references and appropriate footnotes.

capitalism and get beyond it – from philosophy and political economy through the kinds of approaches that today are classified as sociological, or anthropological, or political science or radical critical social theories, e.g., those of the radical social critics of their time, utopian socialists like Robert Owen, Charles Fourier or Saint Simon and anarchists such as Proudhon and Bakunin. They even drew inspiration from the analyses of the scientists of their day who were developing new theories and understanding of mathematics, thermodynamics, chemistry, and biology both in the abstract and in application to industry, in both commodity production and consumption. They examined not only how things were made but also the consequences of industrial processes for the safety or dangers of the commodities produced. One example: adulteration of foods, which sometimes merely lessened their nutritional value and sometimes made them quite poisonous to their consumers.[126]

Another result of their theoretical development was to facilitate recognition of how many phenomena, often seen as exogenous factors (intervening from the "outside,") could be grasped as quite internal to the overall dynamics of the class struggles of capitalism. To take just a couple of examples, both "natural disasters," such as epidemics or pandemics or floods or droughts, and wars, ranging from those between nation states through civil wars and colonial conquest, not only turn out to be moments of the more general class war constituted by ever-present struggles between workers and capitalists but also to play quite contradictory roles. For example, those "natural disasters" may cause crises in various moments of capitalist reproduction but how capitalist policy makers respond may turn them into weapons against workers aimed at counteracting workers' struggles. Wars, say between nation states, may cause crises in some moments of capitalist reproduction, e.g., cutting off trade, killing off workers drafted into military service (mostly working-class men), but those conflicts may also include surges in investment and production, deployed in such a way as to counter worker struggles at home. Or, however, "productive" a war may initially appear, in terms of one national government seizing territory and resources, stimulating growth and providing a "nationalist" excuse to repress dissent at home, its negative effects on workers, both within the armed forces and in civilian life may be so great as to trigger a revolutionary uprising

126 With bread being the most basic consumption commodity of European workers in those days, it was fitting that Marx focused on how capitalists adulterated bread to cut costs and maximize profits, reducing its nutritional value to workers. See his discussion in Chapter 10, Section 3 of Volume 1 of *Capital*. Such practices continue to this day, despite the rise of workers' awareness of such practices and the formation of specialized groups dedicated to ferreting out and exposing them, e.g., the private, non-profit Consumer Reports, founded in 1936, and government agencies such as the Food and Drug Administration.

disrupting capitalist accumulation far more than the war itself.[127] Marx and Engels recognized these contradictory aspects and analyzed them in the different stages of activity which capitalists must realize in order to reproduce their system on an expanded scale.[128]

By the time the first volume of *Capital* appeared in 1867, Marx and Engels had re-entered the political arena.

2.2 *The First International (1864–1876)*

Their return to active political life came after a decade (1852–62) of rapid capitalist expansion, a multiplication of the industrial proletariat and a resurgence of workers' struggles that included the formation in 1864 of the International Working Men's Association (the First International). This Association was initially formed by an assortment of British unionists, Owenites, French workers, Proudhonists and even a professor or two. They were all men and aimed at coordinating activities in supporting strikes and preventing the international use of

127 This was clearly the case when the Franco-Prussian War (1870–71) triggered the revolutionary rising that created the Paris Commune. (See below) A more recent and well-known example was the Russian revolution in 1917 – partly spurred by the effects of Czarist participation in WWI.

128 Both Marx and Engels grew up in a nineteenth century plagued by all kinds of war. Some examples: wars among pre-capitalist groups, e.g., the Ashanti-Akim-Akwapim War in West Africa (1814–16), wars of colonial conquest e.g., the First Anglo-Ashanti war in the Gold Coast (1823–31), the First Anglo-Burmese War (1824–26) in South Asia, the French conquest of Algeria (1830–1903), national liberation from colonialism, e.g., the wars of independence in South America (Brazil 1820–22), in Southeast Asia (Java War 1825–30) and in the Caribbean (Haitian Revolution 1791–1804, the Cuban War of Independence 1895–1898), civil wars, some short, e.g., the June Uprising in France (1848), some long, the American Civil War (1861–65), the First Central American Civil War (1826–29), wars among the major European powers, e.g., the Crimean War (1853–56) and revolutions, e.g., the July Revolution in France (1830), and, of course, the Revolutions of 1848 in which both Marx and Engels took part in Germany. Marx was born two years before the end of the Napoleonic Wars in 1815, which were soon followed by wars of liberation e.g., of Greece against the Ottoman Empire (1821–32). Engels, born two years later, received military training in the Prussia Army shortly before he met Marx in 1842. Although he attended some university classes, and reportedly preferred beer hall debates among Young Hegelians to the parade ground, something stuck such that over the years he contributed more to the study and writing about war than his more university-educated comrade. See, Tristram Hunt, *The Frock-Coated Communist: The Life and Times of the Original Champagne Socialist* (New York: Penguin Books, 2009). For both, however, wars constituted crises in structures of social power, increasingly of capitalist power to structure the world according to its own rules.

scab labor.[129] Marx and Engels were invited to join the Association and quickly moved to prominence. Marx wound up preparing the final versions of the Inaugural Address and Provisional Rules – not easy given the conflicts among the different groups of workers involved: British Chartists, French Proudhonists, Italian Mazzinites, and so forth. Indeed, Giuseppe Mazzini (1805–1872), whose followers had prepared the first draft of the Inaugural address, was furious at Marx's rewrite.[130] In that address, despite acknowledging some success in extending the scope of the 1847 Ten Hours' Bill and the creation of some industrial cooperatives, Marx recapped the history of class struggle since the defeats of 1848 emphasizing the contradiction between industrial growth and persistent poverty, periodically worsened by "the quickened return, the widening compass, and the deadlier effects of the social pest called a commercial and industrial crisis."[131] The objective of the International, at least from Marx and Engels' point of view, was stated cleanly by the latter, years later: "Its aim was to weld together into one huge army the whole militant working class of Europe and America."[132]

Once the International was launched, Marx and Engels set to work, as they had in the Communist League, spreading their own views among the membership and critiquing opposing tendencies. Although the organization had been founded on the principle of organizing across borders and there was general agreement to demand a universal working day of eight hours (adopted at their congress in Geneva in 1868), there were also important disagreements.

One concerned the wisdom of struggles to increase, or prevent the decrease, of wages. It was within this debate that Marx delivered the two lectures that were later published as *Value, Price and Profit*.[133] These lectures, which set out in capsule form the theory and arguments that would appear in *Capital* two years later, were written during the "real epidemic of strikes, and a general

---

129 The all-male character of the organization was challenged by Harriet Law (1831–1897), a prominent secularist and feminist speaker who wrote a letter to the organization on women's rights. As a result, she was asked to join the General Council of the International. Although she played a role for five years, she remained the sole woman on the Council.

130 McLellan, *Karl Marx: A Biography*, 347.

131 *MECW*, *Vol.* 20, pp. 10–11.

132 Frederick Engels, "Preface to the Fourth German Edition of the *Manifesto*," London, May 1, 1890, *MECW*, *Vol.* 27, p. 58. In this Preface Engels goes on to explain how that couldn't happen at that time. But in 1890, the birth of the *Second* International encouraged him to write, optimistically, "today, as I write these lines, the European and American proletariat is reviewing its fighting forces, mobilized for the first time, mobilized as *one* army, under *one* flag, for *one* immediate aim: the standard eight-hour working day to be established by legal enactment ... today the working men of all countries are united indeed.," p. 60.

133 *MECW*, *Vol.* 20, pp. 101–149.

clamor for a rise of wages," that swept Europe shortly before the crash of 1866. Their political purpose was to refute the arguments of another member of the International, the Owenite John Weston, who had argued that workers should abandon wage struggles because inflation and recession would always undermine any gains made. Marx vehemently attacked this position arguing that it would have disastrous economic and political consequences for the working class. Drawing on his studies of crises, he argued that while it was true that crises would limit the gains workers could make, their situation would be even worse without those struggles. Basically, he was repeating the arguments Engels had used a decade earlier in his *Condition of the Working Class in England*.

Wages (the price of labor-power) fluctuate over the course of business expansions and crises like the prices of other commodities. But, Marx argued, precisely because capitalists tend to get away with *reducing* wages during crises, – by laying off workers – it is important that workers struggle to force them *up* during periods of expansion:

> If during the phases of prosperity, when extra profits are made, he did not battle for a rise of wages, he [the worker] would, taking the average of one industrial cycle, not even receive his *average* wages, or the *value* of his labour[-power]. It is the utmost height of folly to demand that while his wages are necessarily affected by the adverse phases of the cycle, he should exclude himself from compensation during the prosperous phases of the cycle.[134]

Marx's advocacy that the International strongly support workers' wage struggles was based not only on the need of workers to protect their average income, but again, like Engels before him, he also saw those struggles as constituting indispensable opportunities for the workers to organize themselves as a class, a preparation necessary to the ultimate overthrow of the system as a whole:

> By cowardly giving way in their every-day conflict with capital, they would certainly disqualify themselves for the initiating of any larger movement.[135]

These lectures, it must be remembered, were written toward the end of Marx's vast work on *Capital* and thus founded its politics on that basis. Although in

134 Ibid., p. 143.
135 Ibid., p. 148.

these writings, he did not bring in the many causes of crisis[136] explored in his theoretical writings, he maintained the same overall political conclusions and strategies that he had held in the earlier period of the 1840s. He again supported wage struggles as a necessary step in working-class development and as a prelude to the abolition of the wage system itself, i.e., the revolutionary overthrow of capital.

3 After Capital, 1867–1895

I date this third and last period of Marx and Engels' writings from the first publication of Volume 1 of *Capital* in September 1867 through Marx's death in March 1883 to Engels', twelve years later in August 1895.

Despite his last years being plagued with poor health and the all-too-frequent deaths of both children and grandchildren, which frequently interrupted his efforts to write, Marx did manage to turn out a number of important contributions. They included 1) his analysis of the Franco-Prussian war and the Paris Commune, 2) his revisions of Volume 1 of *Capital*, 3) his commentaries on political developments and conflicts in the budding socialist political movement, e.g., *Critique of the Gotha Programme* (1875), 4) his program for the deep study of the workplace, i.e., *A Workers' Inquiry* (1880), and 5) his conclusions from his study of pre-capitalist societies and of Russia, e.g., his letters to Zasulich (1881).

For Engels, his most substantial writings during this period were, 1) his critique of Dühring on science and economics: *Anti-Dühring* (1878), 2) his main effort to popularize their ideas: *Socialism: Utopian and Scientific* (1880), 3) his re-do of Hegel's comprehensive view of dialectics: *The Dialectics of Nature* (1883), 4) his exploration of some hitherto undeveloped themes: *The Origin of the Family, Private Property and the State* (1884), 5) his recap of German philosophy: *Ludwig Feuerbach and the End of Classical German Philosophy* (1886) and 6) his work sorting, sifting and organizing Marx's manuscripts into Volume 2 (1885) and Volume 3 (1894) of *Capital*.

These last thirty years were ones of many sorts of crises: wars, financial panics, epidemics, worker strikes and popular uprisings all ruptured accumulation, both at home and abroad. The renewed colonial expansion by capitalists seeking profitable sources of cheap labor, raw materials and markets in Asia, Africa, and Oceania and by the US government in the Western territories all caused

136 On the other hand, in Chapter 5 of this book, I explore those causes and in Chapter 6 those countervailing forces he identified.

crises for the indigenous populations – who repeatedly fought back, rupturing and delaying plans of conquest. Finally, capitalist states warred among themselves both disrupting and, like colonialism, providing new opportunities for investment and profit making. Throughout this period, Marx and Engels continued to follow and analyze these events and their relation to workers' struggles both at home and abroad. Always with the primary aim of influencing the evolving forms and content of workers' political self-organization, they continued both to publish the results of their research and to intervene directly in debates about the best ways for workers to proceed.

3.1 *A New Terrain of Struggle: Electoral Politics*

The year 1867 was an important one – not only because the first volume of *Capital* came off the presses, but also because of two other events. The first was the financial crisis of 1866–67. Marx closely followed the crisis, as with those in 1847 and 1857, filling several notebooks with information and reflections – despite being preoccupied with getting the manuscript and proof sheets of *Capital* to the printer.[137] The second was the passage of the Reform Act of 1867 by the British Parliament – prompted by mass demonstrations against the rising unemployment and falling wages caused by the crisis. The Act profoundly changed the dynamics of class struggle within Britain by allowing at least some propertyless workers to participate in elections.

Although the Chartist Movement and its demand for the enfranchisement of workers had long faded from the scene, two new organizations had been carrying on the struggle for working class suffrage: the Reform Union, founded in 1864, and the Reform League, founded in 1865. The League, created by middle class radicals and workers associated with the First International, was supported by Marx.[138] It was partly through their efforts, mobilizing hundreds of thousands of workers in huge public meetings, that the enfranchisement of many adult male workers was achieved with the passage of a new Reform Act in 1867.

Although the short-term effects merely tilted elections in favor of Liberals against Conservatives, the more profound and long-lasting effect – especially after the Ballot Act of 1872 that made ballots secret, and thus safer for workers who voted against the wishes of their employers – was to open a new political option for workers' struggles that would lead to the rise of social democratic

---

137 It was too late for him to incorporate all this into the first volume of *Capital* but not for Engels to eventually incorporate some of it into his preparation of Volume 3 (see below).

138 "The great achievement of the 'International Association' is this: The Reform League," Marx wrote to Engels, "is our doing." Marx to Engels, May 3, 1865, *MECW*, *Vol. 42*, p. 150.

political parties. This changed the formal sphere of electoral politics from being an object out of reach of workers, something to be pressured from the outside, into a new terrain of struggle, first to get candidates elected who represented workers' interests and second, to draft and fight for new laws beneficial to workers.[139] The appeal of these new parties lay not only in being vehicles to struggle for laws benefiting workers but also in their apparent potential for a peaceful transition out of capitalism. It was this potential that led Marx, according to Engels, to believe that "England is the only country where the inevitable social revolution might be effected entirely by peaceful and legal means."[140]

This access to direct influence on legislation was an objective for which Marx & Engels had fought back in Germany, by supporting liberal demands for royal power to accept the formation of a parliament based on elections. Then, upon the failure of those efforts, they joined the rising of 1848 to force such a change. The eventual formation by Frederick William IV of a bicameral parliament, with the lower house made up of elected representatives, was similar to the English Parliament but with voting based on the amount of taxes paid rather than property as such. In both cases, workers were excluded. The success, in England, of workers finally winning participation in elections meant, inevitably, the formation of formally institutionalized political parties claiming to represent the interests of workers through electoral politics. Marx and Engels' political activities drew them progressively into debates over the programs of such parties and into debates over whether those programs would either facilitate or hinder transitioning beyond capitalism.

3.2 *Continuing Conflicts within the First International*

In the years immediately following all these events, Marx and Engels' political activities were preoccupied with trying to build the First International, an organization created, not to contest elections but to unite the struggles of

139 Over time, it would become apparent that the same dynamics of outside pressure, which had previously forced the passage of the Factory Acts and then these acts giving some workers the vote, would be the primary source of power for their elected representatives. While their representatives within governments found a new public platform for articulating worker demands, it has been recurrent mass movements outside the electoral arena that have provided those representatives with leverage to achieve changes benefiting workers.

140 Engels, "Preface to the English Edition" (November 5, 1886) in *Capital, Vol. 1*, p. 113, or MECW *Vol. 35*, p. 36. Least this be misinterpreted as overly optimistic, Engels also added "He certainly never forgot to add that he hardly expected the English ruling classes to submit, without a 'pro-slavery rebellion', to this peaceful and legal revolution."

workers across borders. Their efforts to expand various national sections and coordinate among them included, inevitably, setting forth their own views and their critiques of others' ideas.

For example, Marx and Engels disagreed with the Proudhonists over a variety of issues. The one closest to my concern with crisis was the Proudhonists' idea that reforming the financial system – where speculation and instability constituted important sources of crisis – could pave the path to transcending capitalism. Back in 1857, Marx had begun the *Grundrisse* notebooks with an attack on the Proudonist Alfred Darimon (1819–1902) and just that idea. While their proposal remained essentially the same, Marx's study of the financial sector and of financial crises, which made up a large part of his *Economic Manuscript of 1864–1865* and would eventually be published as part of Volume 3 of *Capital*, confirmed his critique of such Proudhonist projects as futile and the conflict was fought out both between and during the International's various Congresses.

In the case of the anarchist Mikhail Bakunin (1814–1876), Engels and Marx's attitudes varied, from praise to condemnation. In the wake of the 1848–49 revolution in Germany, Engels praised Bakunin's role in an uprising in Dresden. "The working men … found *an able and cool-headed commander in the Russian refugee Michael Bakunin* …"[141] In 1864, Marx met with Bakunin and invited him to join the First International, remarking to Engels, "Bakunin sends his regards … I saw him yesterday for the first time in 16 years. I must say I liked him very much, more so than previously … On the whole, he is one of the few people whom after 16 years I find to have moved forwards and not backwards."[142] Bakunin, for his part, recognized how Marx and Engels had delved into "political economy" far more profoundly than he had, writing "Marx was, and still is, incomparably more advanced than I … I greatly respected him for his learning and for his passionate devotion … to the cause of the proletariat."[143] Indeed,

141 Frederick Engels, "Revolution and Counter-Revolution in Germany: XVIII: Petty Traders," *New-York Daily Tribune*, No. 3576, October 2, 1852, *MECW*, *Vol. 11*, p. 90. Because the *Tribune* attributed the authorship of this series of articles to Marx, they appeared under his name. Engels' authorship was only discovered in 1913 in correspondence between himself and Marx. It was therefore unknown to James Guillaume (1844–1916) whose 1907 biographical sketch of Bakunin (in Volume 2 of the French edition of the six volumes of Bakunin's *Oeuvres*) is included in Sam Dolgoff, ed., *Bakunin on Anarchism* (Montreal: Black Rose Books, 1980).

142 Marx to Engels, November 4, 1864, *MECW*, *Vol. 42*, pp. 18–19.

143 Quoted by Guillaume in his Biographical Sketch of Bakunin in Dolgoff, p. 25.

despite subsequent differences, he found Marx's analysis of capitalism so useful that he went so far as to begin translating *Capital* into Russian in 1869.[144]

Those differences, however, made a split inevitable. Unlike their differences with Proudhon over finance within capitalist development and crisis, those with Bakunin primarily concerned political strategy. Although Bakunin became a member of the Geneva section of the First International in 1868, he fought all of Marx and Engels' efforts to achieve unity of principle and action among its various sections. Demanding only agreement on the principle of cross-border solidarity for membership in the International, he advocated instead for autonomy of ideas and actions. For him, the class struggle was real but simple: capitalists exploit, workers resist. And because the state (mainly the government) is controlled by capitalists and wields its armed might against workers, the only reasonable objective of class struggle is the overthrow of the state. As a result, Bakunin rejected Marx and Engels' embrace of workers' struggles for democracy, access to the vote and the possibility of influencing government policy on their behalf, e.g., the Factory Acts or laws against child labor, objectives long sought by workers. For Bakunin, such participation by workers in the formal political system, designed and structured by capitalists, was a trap, one that would inevitably result in the diversion of energy for revolution into negotiations with capitalists over changes that would not challenge the system as a whole. So, whereas Marx and Engels saw the Reform Act of 1867 opening a new terrain for workers' struggles, on which they could win victories that would increase their ability to struggle further, Bakunin saw only a hapless illusion.[145] The vociferousness with which each came to attack the other

---

144 Diverted by Sergey Nechayev (1847–1882) into participation in organizing in Russia, Bakunin abandoned his translating, and the task was taken up first by Lopatin and then by Danielson (see below). Just how much of *Capital* Bakunin actually studied, I have been unable to determine. To date I have found no writings of his reflecting on Marx's theories of crisis, nor its relation to class struggle.

145 For Bakunin's views on his differences with Marx and Engels see his essay "The International and Karl Marx" (1872) in Dolgoff, op. cit., pp. 286–320. The subsequent history of social democratic parties' participation in electoral politics has demonstrated precisely the contradictory forces that Marx and Bakunin debated. While those parties have sometimes facilitated workers winning some protections and rights, they have also often replaced revolutionary aims with reformist ones, which have strengthened rather than undermined capitalism. The result has been the repeated formation of movements and groups with more revolutionary goals acting autonomously from and often against the programs of "official" working class parties and labor unions. Besides the United States which saw in the 1960s the rise of Civil Rights, New Left and Black Power movements, all of which operated outside existing political parties, another country in which such autonomous grassroots activity has been well-documented is Italy, where the collaboration of the supposedly pro-worker Communist Party of Italy (CPI) with Post-WWII

has continued to divide many anarchists and Marxists ever since. Bakunin was finally expelled from the International in 1872.

3.3 *War and the Paris Commune*

These conflicts unfolded within the context of an ongoing series of crises and revolts in Europe, the first of which to draw Marx and Engel's close attention was the onset of the Franco-Prussian War (July 19, 1870 to January 28, 1871) and one of its unforeseen consequences: the Paris Commune (1871).[146] When France, under the rule of French Emperor Napoleon III declared war and invaded Germany, Marx, Engels, the International's General Council and its sections in both France and Germany condemned it. The war, they argued, was one between ruling elites, in which workers qua soldiers were pitted against each other on the battlefield, while being repressed at home; only the ruling class of one side or another would benefit.

The International's First Address about the war, drafted by Marx at the direction of the General Council, not only blasted Napoleon's aggression but also pointed out his practice of using war abroad to attack workers at home, including their organizations, such as the International.[147] The International's sections in France had opposed Napoleon's "plebiscite" – designed to demonstrate popular support for his policies – and issued a manifesto against the war, which led directly to arrests of members. Nor did Marx judge Napoleon alone in his desire to use foreign wars to justify repression at home. He also condemned Prussian chancellor Otto Von Bismarck (1815–1898) who had, during the Austro-Prussian War (1866), "conspired with that very same Louis

---

capitalist development provoked the rise of a substantial "extra-parliamentary" movement. It both critiqued that collaboration and organized rank & file worker struggles against the subordination of their needs to capitalist development. More recently, the indigenous Zapatista movement in Chiapas, Mexico, arising outside the existing political party politics of that country, has refused to be suborned to either the "leftist" Partido de la Revolución Democrática or, more recently, to its one-time candidate but now President Andrés Manuel López Obrador (1953-). They have, instead, pursued collaboration with other indigenous and autonomous movements both within Mexico and around the world.

146 Another fruit of the war was the unification of Germany under Prussian leadership. Bismarck began the war leading the North German Confederation, formed in 1867, but by its end had drawn in several South German states and in 1871 formed a unified German Empire.

147 K. Marx, "To the Members of the International Working Men's Association in Europe and the United States," *MECW*, *Vol. 22*, p. 3. This usage of foreign wars for conquest of new land, new resources and potential workers included colonialism, in which Napoleon indulged freely, expanding the French empire in places such as New Caledonia, Cochinchina, and Africa.

Bonaparte for the purpose of crushing popular opposition at home." In both cases, war formed a crisis for workers, both on the battlefield and on the home front.[148]

The Address condemned the war as aimed at increasing Napoleon's power in Europe as well as "a source of fresh speculations." This last charge was consistent with Marx's analysis of the entire Second Empire (1852 – 1870) as fostering and propping up a capitalism run amuck, rife with stock jobbing and speculation. Following and analyzing the chaotic development of industry, finance and speculation in France was an important source for Marx's analysis of capitalist crisis, much of which would eventually be included in Volume 3 of *Capital* by Engels pulling together Marx's voluminous notes and material in the *Manuscript of 1864–65*. Sharing Marx's condemnation of the capitalism of the Second Empire, Engels also portrayed the war as birthed by "a set of adventurers who turned administration, government, army, navy – in fact, all France – into a source of pecuniary profit to themselves."[149]

Because Napoleon was the aggressor, the International initially, reluctantly, accepted the participation of German workers in the name of self-defense, but only so long as the conflict did not "degenerate into a war against the French people."[150] But as the coalition of German states, put together by Bismarck, not

148 This dual character of capitalist war continued into the twentieth century. American involvement in WWI provided a pretext for anti-German and anti-immigrant propaganda that contributed to the Red Scare and wholesale repression of workers in the late teens and twenties. Anti-Japanese racism and internment during WWII echoed the anti-immigrant actions from WWI. After securing a no-strike pledge from workers during WWII, capitalists tried to use their quietude to increase their war profiteering at workers' expense. See Martin Glaberman, *Wartime Strikes: The Struggle Against the No-Strike Pledge in the UAW During W.W. II* (Detroit: Bewick Editions, 1980). The racist vilification of the Vietnamese as "gooks," etc., during the war on Vietnamese independence, made the lives of Vietnamese refugees in the US difficult after the loss of the war in 1975. Something similar is happening today with Muslim refugees from the US government's wars in the Middle East (Gulf Wars I & II) and Central Asia (Afghanistan).

149 *MECW*, *Vol.* 22, p. 77. The parallels with the Trump family of grifters could not be more obvious as not only Donald but Ivanka and Jared used their White House positions to enrich themselves.

150 K. Marx, "To the Members of the International Working Men's Association," op. cit., *MECW*, *Vol.* 22, p. 6. One legacy of this support has been widespread Marxist opposition to all obviously aggressive wars, from those of colonial conquest, through World Wars I & II to more recent invasions of other countries, e.g., the Korean War, the French colonialist return to Vietnam after WWII followed by the US government's neocolonial efforts to replace the French after their defeat, the Bush/Cheney invasions of Afghanistan and Iraq, and, most recently, the Russian invasion of the Ukraine. On the other hand, supposedly Marxist parties allied with the Soviet Union, largely turned a blind eye to its replacement of the Czarist empire with a new Soviet one and then its replacement of German control

only defeated the French army but then invaded France, that "degeneration" did take place and their opposition became much stronger.[151]

The capture of Napoleon and the defeat of his army led to the creation in Paris of a provisional Government of National Defence, its mobilization against the advancing German army and the announcement of a Third French Republic.[152] As the German army fought its way across northern France winning battle after battle, its progress was followed closely by Engels. He wrote some 59 articles recounting and analyzing these military clashes, while also pointing out war profiteering among capitalists and how Napoleon had weakened his army by keeping troops in Paris – for the control of its workers.[153]

The German army's advance ended with the surrounding and siege of Paris. The failure of the new government to break the siege, coupled with a revolutionary rising (crushed) led to its surrender and to the signing of a humiliating armistice and final treaty.[154] That agreement disarmed the French army, ceded Alsace and Lorraine to the Germans and promised both indemnity and heavy reparations – to the tune of 5 billion francs.[155] A new government was formed, with its seat outside of Paris at Versailles, which quickly passed new legislation to raise the funds necessary to pay the Germans and get them to withdraw from France. The costs of raising those funds fell heavily on the French people. Their reaction was outrage and uprisings in several French cities including Paris. The uprising in Paris led to Parisians not only forming their own government, separate from the one in Versailles, but also forming a

---

over Central Europe with its own domination and subsequent repression of local uprisings, such as those in East Germany in 1953, Hungary in 1956 and Czechoslovakia in 1968.

151 This evolution can be seen in Marx's two "Addresses" to the Central Council of the International. These, along with other documents tracing the activities of the International in various countries, can be found in *MECW, Vol. 22*.

152 In one form or another the Third Republic would govern France until its defeat by the Nazis in 1940. During the last two decades of the nineteenth century, France under that government would expand what Napoleon III had called the Second French Empire into a much more extensive empire by creating new colonies in Indochina, Africa and the South Pacific.

153 The 59 articles on the war written by Engels in 1870 and 1871, can be found in *MECW, Vol. 22*. Napoleon, Engels wrote, did not intend "to send the mass of the troops now in Paris to the front. Paris must be kept down." "Notes on the War – X," August 19, 1870, *MECW, Vol. 22*, p. 55.

154 These were the Traité préliminaire de paix du 26 février 1871 and the Traité de Francfort.

155 Traité préliminaire de paix, "ART. 2. - La France paiera à S.M. l'Empereur d'Allemagne la somme de 5 milliards de francs. Le paiement d'au moins 1 milliard de francs aura lieu dans le courant de l'année 1871, et celui de tout le reste de la dette dans un espace de trois années, à partir de la ratification des présentes."

government of a new kind, an actually democratic one, which Marx and many others would celebrate as the first workers' government in history – the Paris Commune.

The Parisians were not alone; communes were declared in several cities. These included the short-lived Commune of Lyon, where Bakunin, then in the First International, was active and the Commune of Marseille. There was even a Commune in Algiers, capitol of the French colony of Algeria – a place to which many of the revolutionaries of 1848 had been deported. Unfortunately, THAT Commune, organized by settler-colonialists, did not link up with the near simultaneous indigenous Mokrani/Kabyle revolt against the French occupation of the country – not until surviving revolutionaries of both camps were packed off to the same prison island in New Caladonia. Although Marx and Engels celebrated the ethnic and national diversity of the Communards of Paris, as I noted in my "Note to Polish Readers" (below), it found its limits in the colonies.[156]

Marx and Engels, following these events from London, participated only indirectly through their First International contacts in Paris. Once the Commune was formed, they provided advice to those directly involved on the ground, while mobilizing solidarity with the Communards everywhere they could. Marx's involvement was so well-known that he was attacked in newspapers – quite wrongly – as being the "eminence grise" behind the rising.[157] The

156 See, Niklas Plaetzer, "Decolonizing the 'Universal Republic': The Paris Commune and the French Empire," *Nineteenth Century French Studies* 49, nos. 3 & 4 (Spring-Summer 2021), 585–603. Upon the signing of this armistice, Napoleon and his entourage were released. Blamed for the war, its loss and the siege of Paris, with too little support in France for any hope of a comeback, he and his family went into exile in England where he died in 1873.

157 Such efforts to blame – and often persecute – Marxist intellectuals for the actions of others can be seen as either a projection of ruling class modes of top-down structures of power onto opponents or as a merely convenient justification for the repression of outspoken critics. The absence of such leadership within horizontal rhizomes of distributed power and decision making hasn't stopped capitalists from pretending top-down structures exist as part of more general repression. One notable example was the Italian government's blaming – and attempt to arrest – Antonio Negri as the brains behind the Red Brigades in April 1979. Although Negri escaped to France, many other intellectuals were caught up in the governments' dragnet to repress dissent – a repression actively pushed by the Italian Communist Party against its extra-parliamentary critics. In this case, Negri eventually returned to Italy, stood trial, and was exonerated of the charges. More recently, some of those who also escaped to France and have lived in exile for decades were arrested and deported by a more complicit Macron administration. On this latest case, see the interview with Enzo Traverso "On the Arrests of Italian Militants in France," Verso Books Blog, June 25, 2021. https://www.versobooks.com/blogs/news/5115-on-the-arrests-of-italian-militants-in-france

International was also attacked, mostly based on lies cranked out by the French police and repeated uncritically in capitalist newspapers. He eventually laid out his analysis of the Commune in *The Civil War in France* (1871).[158]

Much of Marx's analysis in that essay consists of identifying and lambasting those responsible for the war, for the selling out of France in defeat and for the crushing of the Commune, especially Adolphe Thiers who organized the massacre of the Communards and became President of the Republic.[159] My interest here, however, is limited to what little he had to say about crisis. Unlike the revolutions of 1848, birthed in part by the crisis of 1847, the Commune was born in the midst of war, in a Paris surrounded by German troops – a crisis for sure but of a quite different kind. Within this context, his comments about crisis are of two sorts. The first concerns the economic situation faced by France *and* the Commune as a result of the policies of the Second Empire. The second concerns the steps taken by the Commune in the face of the situation in which it found itself.

The war-as-crisis revealed another – dramatically worsened by the surrendering government granting massive reparations to the victorious Germans – namely a fiscal crisis. That, Marx argued, was the inevitable result in a country bankrupted by years of speculation and ever-growing mountains of debt. Marx wrote about how under the sway of the Second Empire, "bourgeois society freed from political cares, attained a development unexpected even by itself. Its industry and commerce expanded to colossal dimensions, financial swindling celebrated cosmopolitan orgies, the misery of the masses was set off by a shameless display of gorgeous, meretricious and debased luxury,"

Another example was the attempt by the Mexican government to blame the 1994 indigenous uprising in Chiapas on its intellectual spokesperson Subcomandante Marcos, although it was actually an array of community councils which had ordered its Zapatista Army of National Liberation into action. The repression which followed was quite general and aimed at permanently crippling the ability of the Zapatista communities to resist exploitation. Whereas in Italy the government launched a *police* roundup of intellectuals, in Mexico it dispatched tens of thousands of *army* troops and, when that effort was stymied politically, it financed and armed *paramilitary* violence against the communities.

158 K. Marx, "The Civil War in France," *MECW*, *Vol. 22*, First Draft, pp. 437–514, Second Draft, pp. 515–551, Final, published version, pp. 307–355.

159 This and similar historical essays provide antidotes to the common complaint that Marx's use of the terms "capital" or "capitalists" to denote the class as a whole – as in Chapter 10 of Volume 1 on class struggles over the length of the working day – oversimplifies and wrongly depicts the class as a homogenous whole. They illustrate how while that practice is associated with analyzing overall trends, in his close examination of real historical moments Marx recognizes and analyzes the heterogeneity and internal conflicts within the capitalist class. His and Engels' manifold analyses of the working class and of struggles between factions demonstrate the same differentiated approach.

this "rottenness ... [was] laid bare by the bayonet of Prussia."[160] "The Second Empire had more than doubled the national debt and plunged the large towns into heavy municipal debts. The war had fearfully swelled the liabilities and mercilessly ravaged the resources of the nation."[161]

For those who formed the Third Republic off at Versailles, the solution was obvious. In the short term: borrow, take on more debt, but as soon as possible shift the cost of the war and reparations from the "appropriators of wealth" to the "shoulders of the producers." This had been done after the revolution of 1848, where concessions to workers were paid for by raising taxes on the peasantry – a ploy successful in turning the latter against the former. But to borrow, the Versailles government had to meet the demands of the bankers who insisted that before any new loans would be forthcoming, the Commune must be crushed. "Thus, the immense ruin of France spurred on these patriotic representatives of land and capital, under the very eyes and patronage of the invader, to graft upon the foreign war a civil war – a slaveholders' rebellion."[162] True to their word, once the Commune was crushed, a new loan was forthcoming.[163]

This insistence by the bankers, agreed upon and executed by the Versailles government, derived not merely from a distaste for Parisians taking control of their own city, but from the policies being set forth by the Communards. Not only did the Commune declare that "the true originators of the war would be made to pay its cost," but it also enacted a series of other measures which struck

160 "The Civil War in France," *MECW*, *Vol. 22*, p. 330.

161 Ibid., p. 319.

162 Ibid., p.219, "No money was to be paid down until after the 'pacification' of Paris", p. 320.

163 Editors' note, *MECW*, *Vol. 22*, p. 669, note 182. Similar were the demands of New York City banks in the mid-1970s as conditions for rolling over that city's debt: cut welfare payments and cut the wages and benefits of city workers. See, Donna Demac & Philip Mattera, "Developing and Underdeveloping New York: The 'Fiscal Crisis' and the Imposition of Austerity", *Zerowork* 2, (1977), 113–139. Under the same rubric of "austerity," making workers and the poor pay became a central element in the conditions set by the International Monetary Fund for rolling over the debt of country after country during the international debt crisis of the 1980s and 1990s. See, H. Cleaver, "Close the IMF, Abolish Debt and End Development: a Class Analysis of the International Debt Crisis," *Capital & Class* 39, (Vol. 13, Issue 3, Winter 1989): 17–50. Where resistance flared, the banks demanded more, as illustrated by the case of the Zapatista uprising in Chiapas, Mexico in 1994. In that case, just like the Parisian bankers who wanted the Commune crushed, Chase Manhattan Bank, in the person of Riordan Roett, writing for Chase investors in emerging markets, demanded the "elimination" of the Zapatistas. See Roett's essay and the follow-up story by *Counterpunch*, which originally obtained and wrote about it, Ken Silverstein and Alexander Cockburn, "Chase Memo Tumult: Come Blow Our Horn," *Counterpunch* 2, no. 4 (February 15, 1995): 3.

at the heart of capitalist power. These included: no prosecutions for delayed repayment of debt, the abolition of interest on debt, ending nightwork at bakeries, no more fines on waged workers, closed factories handed over to their workers, the suppression of the army – traditionally used to control workers and peasants as much as for foreign wars – and its replacement by arming the people, a parallel change in the police making it responsible to the people and a "revocable agent of the Commune," public servants to be paid workers' wages, magistrates and judges to be elected and revocable, secularization of science and education to be made free to all, the Commune form of government to be extended throughout the country, formed at each level through universal suffrage and revocable. In short, "the merely repressive organs of government were to be amputated, its legitimate functions were to be wrested from an authority usurping pre-eminence over society itself, and restored to the responsible agents of society." "Yes, gentlemen," Marx wrote, "the Commune intended to abolish the class-property which makes the labour of the many the wealth of the few. It aimed at the expropriation of the expropriator. It wanted to make individual property a truth by transforming the means of production, land and capital, now chiefly the means of enslaving and exploiting labour, into mere instruments of free and associated labour."[164] That reorganized, co-operative labor would put an end "to the constant anarchy and periodical convulsions which are the fatality of Capitalist production."[165] Of all this, Marx argued, the Commune only had time to take the first revolutionary steps towards replacing capitalism with communism. But in doing so it constituted a threat not only to bankers but to all capitalists. The great fear of capitalists and great hope of revolutionaries, that a capitalist crisis could be turned into the overthrow of the system and the building of an alternative seemed to be unfolding inside Paris. These were the things that excited Marx and terrified those at Versailles – provoking vicious massacres to put down the threat, the taking on of more debt. This last contributed to France suffering participation in a new banking crisis in 1873 and in the Trans-Atlantic depression of 1873–1896.

164 "The Civil War in France," *MECW*, *Vol. 22*, 331–341. Despite these rhetorical flourishes that treat the Commune as a unified subject, both Marx's essay and subsequent studies of the Commune have made clear that its existence and its evolution was the product of diverse, often conflicting interests – more united in what they no longer wanted than in the character of what would replace it. Marx was excited by what he saw, especially how universal suffrage would give great weight to the power of workers and peasants to determine that path and how those elected were subject to recall if they failed those who had elected them. But to what degree the Commune and its offspring would have followed the path to communism that Marx projected would never be known.

165 Ibid., p. 335.

3.4 *Revisions and Translations*

Despite the demands for keeping abreast of conflicts within the First International and analyzing workers' struggles in England and abroad, Marx continued his theoretical work. He wanted to finish his promised second volume of *Capital* on the circulation of capital, a third on "the various forms of the process of capital in its totality" and a fourth on the history of the theory.[166] All this he had already studied and spelled out in voluminous notebooks but not yet prepared for publication. His attempts to finish this work, however, were repeatedly interrupted, not only by ill health in his family,[167] his involvement in politics and his efforts to keep up with various crises and revolts, but also by preoccupation with the second German edition of *Capital* and various translations of the book.

His own dissatisfaction with the first edition led Marx to undertake some serious revisions in both structure and content in the Second German Edition. He indicates some of these in his 1873 Postface, especially his revisions of the analysis of value in the opening chapter where he combined the original with the supplemental material previously attached as an appendix. After reviewing critiques of the First Edition, after denouncing the descent of political economics from efforts to understand capitalism to efforts to apologize for it, and after analyzing the development of political economy in Germany, he ends the Postface by discussing the differences between his dialectical method and Hegel's. He argues that capital itself, through its crises and recoveries will eventually teach doubters the reality of dialectics.

> The fact that the movement of capitalist society is full of contradictions impresses itself most strikingly on the practical bourgeois in the changes of the periodic cycle through which modern industry passes, the summit of which is the general crisis. That crisis is once again approaching, although as yet it is only in its preliminary stages, and by the universality of its field of action and the intensity of its impact it will drum dialectics even into the heads of the upstarts in charge of the new Holy Prussian-German Empire.[168]

---

166 Promised in his Preface to the first edition. *Capital, Vol. 1*, p. 93, or *MECW*, *Vol. 35*, p. 11.

167 Ill-health would not only repeatedly prevent Marx himself from writing but would kill several members of his family including his wife Jenny who died of liver cancer in 1881. For an account of these tribulations see, Marcello Musto, *The Last Years of Karl Marx: An Intellectual Biography*, (Stanford: Stanford University Press, 2020).

168 *Capital, Vol. 1*, p. 103, or *MECW*, *Vol. 35*, p. 20. This essentially foregrounds a similar statement in Chapter 25: "When this periodicity has once become consolidated, even political economy sees that the production of a relative surplus population … is a necessary condition

By 1882, the publisher of the Second Edition was running out of copies, so Marx, who at the time was working on Volume 2, began to make notes for the changes he wanted for a Third Edition. He died before he could complete either project.

The first translation of Volume 1 was into Russian. Marx – who had studied the language in order to understand the struggles unfolding in that land – closely supervised the initial efforts by a young Russian, German Lopatin (1845–1918)) who came to London in 1870 to begin translating and corresponded with another, Nikolai Danielson (1844–1918) who completed the process (and later also translated Volumes II and III). The translation slipped by Czarist censors and appeared in 1872 – quickly selling more copies than the German and fueling debates between Russian "Marxists" and Russian populists.[169]

The second translation was into French and here again, Marx was intimately involved, editing, revising and adding to the translation. His deep involvement was undoubtedly spurred by the advantage he saw in how it was to be published: serially, in bite-sized morsels. He wrote to the publisher: "I applaud your idea of publishing the translation of *Das Kapital* in periodic instalments. In this form the work will be more accessible to the working class and for me that consideration outweighs any other."[170] He changed so much that in his Postface to the translation he wrote that "this French edition ... possesses a scientific value independent of the original and should be consulted even by readers familiar with German."[171] The most significant passage concerning crisis that

for modern industry." Ibid., p. 786, or *MECW*, *Vol. 35*, pp. 627–8. In the French edition Marx replaced "political economy" with "économistes."

169 See McLellan, *Karl Marx: A Biography*, 394. The debates – into which Marx was drawn – included one over whether revolution had to wait for the full development of capitalism and the rise of an industrial proletariat in Russia or could unfold successfully on the basis of peasant struggles. The dominant view of Marxists, in Russia and elsewhere, has been the former interpretation of Marx and Engels' writings. They were dismissive of peasant struggles arguing their inevitable disappearance via the "proletarianization" with the development of capitalism. Once drawn in, however, and after studying the social situation in Russia, Marx took the side of the populists hypothesizing that in the case of revolution the peasant "mir" or village commune had the possibility of providing an alternative path for the "social regeneration" of Russia beyond capitalism. With the emergence of a world-wide indigenous renaissance, made visible and energized by the Zapatista uprising, this hopeful view of the potentialities of one kind of traditional peasant organization has received new attention. See, Theodore Shanin, ed., *Late Marx and the Russian Road: Marx and the Peripheries of Capitalism* (New York: Monthly Review Press, 1983).

170 Marx to Maurice La Châtre, March 18, 1872, *MECW*, *Vol. 44*, p. 344.

171 *Capital, Vol. 1*, p. 105, or *MECW*, *Vol. 35*, p.24. The failure of first Engels and then other editors of various English editions of *Capital* to include all of Marx's changes has been repeatedly lamented by various commentators, including Kevin Anderson, "The 'Unknown' Marx's *Capital*, Volume 1: The French Edition of 1872–75, 100 Years Later," *Review of Radical*

he added to the French translation was the following, in which he argued that crisis only becomes endemic as capitalism becomes fully developed.

> But only after mechanical industry had struck root so deeply that it exerted a preponderant influence on the whole of national production; only after foreign trade began to predominate over internal trade, thanks to mechanical industry; only after the world market had successively annexed extensive areas of the new World, Asia and Australia; and finally only after a sufficient number of industrial nations had entered the arena – only after all this had happened can one date the repeated self-perpetuating cycles, whose successive phases embrace years, and always culminate in a general crisis, which is the end of one cycle and the starting point of another. Until now the duration of these cycles has been ten or eleven years but there is no reason to consider this duration as constant. On the contrary, we ought to conclude, on the basis of the laws of capitalist production as we have just expounded them, that the duration is variable, and that the length of the cycles will gradually diminish.[172]

Because Marx was unable to finish preparing Volumes II and III of *Capital* before he died in 1883, Engels undertook to do so, publishing the first two years later in 1885 and the second in 1894. He also oversaw and edited the translation from the Third German Edition into English by Samuel Moore and Edward Aveling (Eleanor Marx's partner), published in 1887.

3.5 *Working Class Parties and Debates*

As workers were able to win the goal that had eluded the Chartists: laws giving propertyless workers access to participation in elections, this allowed many to abandon covert and illegal secret groups in favor of an overt and legal political terrain. They came onto a terrain, however, already shaped by the existence of formal political "parties," i.e., institutions created by various political factions among capitalists, landowners and other property owners, e.g., the so-called "middle class." Those parties organized the selection of candidates for public office; they drafted programs laying out their policy goals and they mobilized supporters to vote in elections. In England, such formal parties were created in the wake of the Exclusion Crisis (1679–1681), with the Whigs and the Tories contesting elections to Parliament. In the United States political

Political Economics 15, no. 4 (December 1983): 71–80 and Paul Zarembka, *Key Elements of Social Theory Revolutionized by Marx* (Boston: Brill, 2020).

172 *Capital, Vol. 1*, p. 786 and *Le Capital: Livre I*, (Paris: Garnier-Flammarion, 1969), 462.

parties were created not long after the signing of the Constitution. The first American parties, formed in the late 1700s, emerged out of policy differences among advisors in the first presidential administration: the Federalist and Democratic-Republican Parties. By the time male British workers began to win the right to participate in elections, electoral politics in England were dominated by the Liberal (once Whig) and Conservative (once Tory) Parties, while in the US they were dominated by the Democratic and Republican Parties. In Germany, there were several parties representing various political interests, several of which dated from before that country's unification in 1871.

Faced with a terrain already well organized by their class enemies, militants in various workers' movements had to decide whether to participate or refuse. For those who chose to participate, the question was how? Should they join existing parties – created by and in the interests of their exploiters – and organize within, pushing policies supporting workers' struggles as some reformists had done in the past, or should they organize autonomously, forming their own *working-class* parties? Some workers, along with many middle-class reformers, chose to work within existing parties. Others, believing that the interests of those in existing parties were unlikely to be swayed by marginal worker participation, chose to organize independently. Yet those forming their own working-class parties, did so with the aim of winning public office, through which they hoped to lobby for and win legal and institutional changes of benefit to workers. In their most optimistic imagination, workers could gain enough positions to win ever greater reforms, transforming capitalism into something else, something better. As mentioned, others, such as Bakunin and his followers, refused to be drawn onto this terrain, preferring to continue organizing for the overthrow of the whole capitalist system, including its electoral infrastructure. Still others would attempt to organize both inside and outside the formal electoral system.

Emerging working-class parties – like their predecessors – followed the common practice of drawing up and issuing public programs, laying out their principles and objectives for the world to see and assess – much as Marx and Engels did when they drafted the *Communist Manifesto* for the Communist League in 1848. Such programs commonly had some theoretical underpinning, either made explicit or implied, as well as indications of the kinds of policies and actions the issuing party intended to pursue. As parties contended or sought to collaborate, Marx and Engels continued to push their own perspective in working class circles and much of their writing was done as interventions into the resulting political battles within and between such parties. Without trying to cover the full extent of their efforts, I do want to comment on three famous efforts to influence the directions being taken by working-class parties: their critique of the Gotha program (1875), Engel's essay *Anti-Dühring* (1878) and his *Socialism: Utopian and Scientific* (1880), extracted from *Anti-Dühring*.

3.6 *Marx: Critique of the Gotha Program*

The Gotha program was drafted by leaders of the Social-Democratic Workers' Party (S-DWP) of Germany in preparation for a joint conference in Gotha, Germany with the General Association of German Workers (GAGW). The conference was aimed at unifying the two groups.[173] The GAGW, the first political party in Europe to present itself as representing the interests of workers, was founded in 1863 by Ferdinand Lassalle (1825–1864) and continued, after his death, to be dominated by his followers. The S-DWP was founded in 1869, led by August Bebel (1840–1913) and Wilhelm Liebknecht (1826–1900) and based on the principles of the First International. With the objective of the conference being to achieve a unification of the two parties, the draft program, although written by the leaders of the S-DWP, sought to include ideas acceptable to the GAGW.

Upon studying the draft program, both Marx and Engels felt their comrades in the S-DWP had conceded far too much to the Lassaleans. Like those who refused this terrain altogether, e.g., Bakunin, they clearly saw the danger of working-class parties' effectiveness as organs of struggle being undermined by accepting to restrict their demands to those entirely compatible with capitalist development. Therefore, several of their critiques were aimed at avoiding such a fate. However, the sole aspect of crisis touched on in the draft and addressed in Marx's letter of critique was the theoretical question of the proper working-class role in the *final* crisis – the end of capitalism.[174] Of the many forces that tend to create ruptures and crises in capitalism, analyzed by them in other works (and sketched below in Chapters 4–8), he says nothing. What he does protest is the Lasallean substitution of "*the* social *question*" for class struggle and its faith, written into the program, that it is through aid from the government, especially in the form of support for worker cooperatives and education

173 The draft program was printed in *Der Voksstaat*, (S-DWP) No. 27, and the *Neuer Social-Demokrat* (GAGW) on March 7, 1875, according to footnote 95 of *MECW, Vol. 24*, pp. 602–603. It was from the former source that Marx lifted passages in his "Marginal Notes" mentioned below.

174 They spelled out their critique of the draft program, in advance of the meeting, in a letter from Engels to August Bebel in late March, *MECW, Vol. 24, pp. 67–73*, and a letter from Marx to Wilhelm Bracke on May 5th, that included Marx's "Marginal Notes on the Programme of the German Workers' Party," written in April-Early May 1875, *MECW, Vol. 24*, pp. 77–78, 81–99.

that capitalism can be brought to its end and replaced.[175] Of cooperative societies, Marx writes,

> But as far as the present co-operative societies are concerned, they are of value only insofar as they are the independent creations of the workers and not protégés either of the governments or of the bourgeois.[176]

And of education,

> "*Education of the people by the state*" is altogether objectionable ... Government and Church should rather be excluded from any influence on the school. Particularly, indeed, in the Prusso-German Empire ... the state has need, on the contrary, of a very stern education by the people.[177]

In other words, he argues that it is only through their own, autonomous struggles, whether in dealing with capitalists or in creating new social institutions, that workers can end and replace the capitalist system. The state within capitalism was designed for its propagation and cannot be expected to become the vehicle of its supersession. He attacks neither the project of a unified party nor the participation of its members in elections nor the participation of any elected delegates in parliament, and thus within the German state. What he does protest is the abandonment of class struggle on other terrains and reformist demands that fail to lay the groundwork for further struggle.

It is essential, he argues, to begin with the class struggles that the Lassaleans ignore and to recognize the important role of trade union actions, not only within each country but also coordinated (like capital itself) across borders, internationally (the objective of the First International).

> Fifthly, there is absolutely no mention [in the draft] of the organization of the working class as a class through the medium of trade unions. And that is a point of the utmost importance, this being the proletariat's true class organization in which it fights its daily battles with capital, in which it trains itself ...[178]

---

175 "In the place of the existing class struggle appears a newspaper scribbler's phrase: '*the* social *question*', for the '*solution*' of which one 'paves the way'," *MECW*, *Vol 24*, p. 93.

176 "Marginal Notes," *MECW*, *Vol. 24*, p. 94.

177 Ibid., p. 97.

178 Engels to Bebel, London, March 18–28, 1875, *MECW*, *Vol. 24*, p. 70.

> It is altogether self-evident that, to be able to fight at all, the working class must organize itself at home as a class … To this extent its class struggle is national, not in substance, but, as the *Communist Manifesto* says, "in form". But the "framework of the present-day national state, for instance, the German Empire, is itself in turn economically 'within the framework of the world market'," politically "within the framework of the system of states".[179]

In other words, workers' *self-organization*, not just its consciousness, must match that of capital and be international. In short, the draft program is retrograde vis-à-vis the *Communist Manifesto*, written almost thirty years earlier! In its shift from recognizing how workers' struggles could throw capitalism into crisis and how workers' own initiatives could craft new alternatives, the program sketched principles of a social-democratic organization, which not only accepts to work within a political system organized by capital, but which also relies on a key element of that system – the government – to engineer its end. Marx was having none of it. No class struggle, no real crisis, no real change. Workers had to take over and *dictate* both the end of capitalist exploitation and the crafting of a post-capitalist order.[180]

Despite these and many other critiques, the joint conference adopted the draft program with only minor changes and the two parties merged to form a new Socialist Workers Party of Germany (*Sozialistische Arbeiterpartei Deutschlands* or SPD). United, it rapidly became the largest social-democratic party in Europe, participating in elections and winning seats in the German parliament.

3.7 *Engels: Anti-Dühring*

Behind this abandonment of any mention of class struggle in the program of the SPD lay not only Lassalle's ideas but also those of Eugen Dühring. A lawyer turned lecturer in philosophy and political science at the University of Berlin, Dühring had been the first person outside of Marx and Engels' circle to write a review of *Capital* when it was published in 1867.[181] Despite what he judged to be the review's deficiencies, Marx appreciated the effort because it was better to be critiqued than ignored – which had been the general response of the German press. "I must be grateful to the man," he wrote, "since he is the first

---

179 "Marginal Notes," *MECW*, *Vol. 24*, pp. 89–90.

180 This is my interpretation of Marx's evocation of the "dictatorship of the proletariat" during the transition from capitalism to communism, as explained in my *Rupturing the Dialectic*, 238–240.

181 E. Dühring, "Marx, Das Kapital, Kritik der politischen Oekonomie, 1. Band, Hamburg, 1867," *Erganzungsblatter zur Kenntngi der Gegenwart,* Bd. 3, Heft 3, 1867, pp. 182–6. Engels published his own review in *Die Zukunft*, No. 254, October 30, 1867.

expert who has said anything at all."[182] That gratitude, however, was short-lived as Dühring repeatedly denigrated Marx's ideas, while, to use the latter's words, setting "himself up as a revolutionary in political economy" in such writings as: *Capital and Labor: New Answers to Old Questions,* Fragen: Berlin, 1865 and *Critical Foundation of Political Economy*, Berlin, 1866.[183] He was also "setting himself up" by offering to those in the social-democratic movement alternatives to Marx and Engels' analyses of capitalism, of its class struggles and of political strategy and tactics, in, for example, his *Critical History of Economics and Socialism* (1871, 1875).[184]

As Marx and Engels perceived important personages in the social-democratic movement, including Bebel, Liebknecht and Edward Bernstein (1850–1932) falling under Dühring's spell, it became clear to them how Dühring's ideas had contributed to the poor reception of their critiques of the Gotha program. Bebel, for instance, had already published in *Der Vokssstaat* – the primary organ of the Social-Democratic Party – two articles praising Dühring in 1874, prior to the Gotha conference. In them, he declared Dühring's latest publication "the best book on economics produced in the recent period since Marx's *Kapital* and we may strongly recommend the study of the book."[185] In these circumstances, Marx decided that Dühring's ideas needed to be critiqued "without compunction."[186] Under complaint, Engels quite reluctantly undertook to "break a lance with the tedious Dühring."[187] Albeit in consultation with Marx, he wrote and published a series of polemical articles in *Vorwärts* in 1877 and

182 Marx to Kugelmann, March 6, 1868, *MECW*, *Vol. 42*, p. 544.

183 Ibid. The relationship between Dühring, Marx and Engels was usefully sketched by Gunter Krause in "Dühring in the perspective of Karl Marx and Engels," *Journal of Economic Studies*, Vol. 29, no. 4/5, (2002): 345–363. These translated titles are from Krause; the originals are: *Capital and Arbeit. Neue Antworten auf alte Fragen* (Berlin: Verlag von Alb. Eichhoff , 1865) and *Kritische Gnmdlegung der Volkswirthschafskhre* (Berlin: Verlag von Alb. Eichhoff, 1866). Having been unable to discover any English translation of these works, I am forced to rely – with the usual amount of salt – on those who have read them in the original and given accounts in English. I am, therefore, not able to judge the degree to which Engels' representations of Dühring's ideas are accurate, or mere assertions, as Adamiak claims, "in its rendition of certain of Dühring' ideas, marked distortion is evident." Richard Adamiak, "Marx, Engels, and Dühring," *Journal of the History of Ideas* 35, no. 1 (January – March 1974): 109 - 911.

184 *Kritische Geschichte der Nationalokonomie und des Socialismus,* 1 Auflage, Leipzig, 1871, Berlin, 1875.

185 "Ein neuer 'Communist'," *Der Volksstaat*, Leipzig, No. 30, Marz 13, 1874 and No. 33, Marz 20, 1874, cited and quoted in Adamiak, "Marx, Engels, and Dühring," p. 106.

186 Marx to Engels, May 25, 1876, *MECW*, *Vol. 45*, p.119.

187 Engels to Marx, May 28, 1876, *MECW*, *Vol. 45*, p. 122. Besides finding Dühring "tedious," Engels also complained about having to put aside his work on the dialectics of nature, a project upon which he had been working since 1873.

1878. He then combined these articles into a substantial book in 1878 – *Herr Eugen Dühring's Revolution in Science* – one chapter was based on a draft written by Marx.[188]

Anti-Dühring consists of three parts: the first part covers Dühring's writings on science and his "new" philosophical system. Here Engels draws on his own research on the "dialectics of nature." The second part dissects Dühring's supposed "revolution" in political economy and the third part challenges his analysis of the road to socialism. In so doing, however, Engels seizes the opportunity to not only critique Dühring but also to spell out many of his and Marx's perspectives on these topics, exercises which make the book an important source on their views as well as their understanding of his. Given the focus here on their analyses of class struggle and crisis, I only highlight those of their views which touch on these subjects and leave aside all the rest.[189]

Although like Marx and Engels, Dühring critiqued capitalism and called for struggles for material gains via unions, strikes, etc., paving a road to socialism, unlike them he apparently argued that capitalism, like other oppressive systems before it, was based primarily on "force" rather than on economic relationships. Thus, for him, the "force state" became the primary object to be replaced and in its place, he offered a utopian vision of a decentralized socialist system of autonomous communes.[190] Engels disparaged this vision, even more than he and Marx had done of earlier utopians, because Dühring didn't have the excuse of writing *before* the struggles of industrial workers had really gotten organized, not only nationally but also internationally, e.g., the First International.

Against Dühring's analysis, Engels posed his and Marx's understanding of how in the history of "civilization" the role of "force" was based on the mode of exploitation that underlay and defined both classes and their antagonisms. This view was worked out back in the 1840s and spelled out in writings such as the *Economic and Philosophical Manuscripts of 1844*, the *German Ideology* in 1846, and the *Communist Manifesto* in 1848. In *Anti-Dühring* this perspective is reiterated several times, in various chapters of the book. Sometimes it is in the same words found in those earlier texts, sometimes explained in later

188 Frederick Engels, *Herr Eugen Dühring's Revolution in Science*, MECW, *Vol. 25*, pp. 1–309. That chapter was "X: From the *Critical History*" in Part II: Political Economy, MECW, *Vol. 25*, pp. 211–243.

189 It will be obvious to any reader of *Anti-Dühring* that a whole range of issues taken up in Engels' essay *indirectly* bare on their analyses of crisis and class struggle, e.g., his discussions of method, but I have chosen to limit myself here to only his *direct* comments on crisis.

190 According to Adamiak, p. 103.

language, such as that of the Preface to the *Contribution to the Critique of Political Economy* or of *Capital*. For example, in the Introduction, Engels writes:

> Then it was seen that *all* past history was the history of class struggles; that these warring classes of society are always the products of the modes of production and of exchange – in a word, of the *economic* conditions of their time ...[191]

Although Engels illustrates this interpretation with examples from various periods of history, my concern here is with capitalism and the crises experienced by its "warring classes," i.e., capitalists and workers. What is striking in Engels' treatment of crisis is his almost total reliance on the contradiction between the development of production and the limits on the size of the market.

> We have seen that the ever increasing perfectibility of modern machinery is, by the anarchy of production, turned into a compulsory law that forces the individual industrial capitalist always to improve his machinery, always to increase its productive force ... [However,] resistance is offered by consumption, by sales, by the markets for the products of modern industry ... The extension of the markets cannot keep pace with the extension of production. The collision becomes inevitable ... collisions become periodic ... since 1825, when the first general crisis broke out, the whole industrial and commercial world, production and exchange among all civilized people and their more or less barbaric hangers-on, are thrown out of joint about once every ten years ... the productive forces are in rebellion against the mode of exchange ...[192]

Within this scenario – familiar since their earliest writings – Engels does mention elements developed later, such as "hard cash" disappearing, credit now exploding, now vanishing, bankruptcy proliferating, big capitalists squeezing out little ones, but nowhere does he bring in the kind of detailed analysis of these things worked out by Marx in either Volume 1 of *Capital* or in his unfinished manuscripts. Least the reference to limits of consumption in the above quotation be miss-read as privileging "underconsumption" by workers, note

191 *MECW*, *Vol. 25*, p. 26. In a later formulation, Engels clarified by inserting "with the exception of its primitive stages," ibid., p. 649, fn27.

192 Ibid., pp. 262–263.

that the "products of modern industry" whose production is seen to repeatedly outstrip markets include *both* consumer goods and producer goods.[193]

Engels does add to Marx's analysis of the increasing socialization of production. Marx laid out in *Capital* how the ever-increasing scale of capitalist production, through both concentration (investment) and centralization (mergers and takeovers) gave rise to the joint-stock or limited liability corporation, in which the diversification of ownership through the sale of corporate stocks and bonds results in the actual management of capital being passed to salaried corporate managers, whom he called "functionaries of capital" and Engels called "salaried employees." Eventually, Engels argues, the scale of production and distribution outgrows the joint-stock company form of management, and, when "this form also becomes insufficient: the official representative of capitalist society – the state – will ultimately have to undertake the direction of production."[194] A takeover, he notes, already begun under Bismarck.[195] He duly points out, however, that these transformations in the form of management "either into joint-stock companies, or into state ownership, does not do away with the capitalistic nature of the productive forces ... The more [the state] proceeds to taking over the productive forces, the more does it actually become the national capitalist, the more citizens does it exploit. The workers remain wage-workers – proletarians. The capitalist relation is not done away with."[196]

Unfortunately, when Engels forecasts that the proletarian seizure of state power would immediately transform "the means of production into state property," he fails to specify exactly how those proletarians can then make sure that

193 Despite Marx's dismissal of such narrowing, the "underconsumptionist" theory of crisis embraced by many of his followers in the history of Marxism has always turned on the production of consumer goods and the limits on markets for them caused by workers' low wages. This was also true among some non-Marxists, such as John A. Hobson (1858–1940) whose theories of both crisis and imperialism was founded on this perspective. The error of such analysis, clearly seen by Marx, was the failure to recognize how industrial products included both consumer and producer goods, so that inadequacies in aggregate demand might be traceable to either a shortage of expenditures by workers or of investment by capitalists. See Chapter 5.3. below. This error by Hobson was pointed out by John Maynard Keynes in his *General Theory* (1938), while ignoring how Marx had made the same point decades earlier.

194 Ibid., p. 265.

195 Ibid., fn *.

196 Ibid., pp. 265–266. In this manner, Engels not only explains the emerging character of state capitalism in Germany but foretells the fate of socialism in Russia after 1917 as the result of Lenin and the Bolsheviks adapting the German model for the new Soviet economy.

the "capitalist relation" is, in fact, "done away with" and actually achieve the abolition of "all class distinctions and class antagonism," and, in the process do away with "the state as state."[197] While Dühring's projection of capitalism being replaced by a network of autonomous communes resembled earlier utopian projects, Engels' under-specified alternative, echoing Marx's affirmations in his critique of the Gotha Program of how workers would use state power to end and replace capitalism, left both of them open to the old Bakuninist charges of embracing a statist centralization of power. This Engels and Marx had long denied, yet their on-going refusal to imagine how the projected "dictatorship of the proletariat" could transcend the form of the state, meant that the charge continued to reappear, not only among their opponents in German social-democracy but throughout the history of "Marxism," beginning with the "revisionism" of Edward Bernstein and Karl Kautsky (1854–1938) in the period of the Second International (1889–1916).

Published in Leipzig in early July 1878, the circulation of Engels' book was suddenly curtailed in October when Bismarck succeeded in getting an Exceptional Law against the Socialists passed, making the SPD illegal and banning its literature, including *Anti-Dühring*. Its underground circulation nevertheless succeeded in shifting some minds from Lassalean and Dühring's views to ones more in line with those of Marx and Engels. Moreover, the law, which would remain in force until 1890, had the effects of both increasing support for the repressed party and stirring further debate within it.[198]

---

197 Ibid., p. 267. Lenin's explanation of how these things would come about, of course, was through the actions of the Communist Party representing the interests of the workers. Unfortunately, despite claims that the CP organization was "democratic centralism," no mechanism ever provided workers with the ability to counter the failure of the Party to act in their interest. As a result, workers within the USSR, like workers elsewhere, were thrown back on traditional methods of protest, including covert actions when the CPUSSR followed the German model of state capitalism in repressing overt dissent.

198 The debates continued to reflect differences within the SPD over political strategy and tactics, including their manifestation in Party publications. One such debate unfolded during the planning of a Party paper to be published in Switzerland, to avoid the repression within Germany. In an internal "Circular Letter," written by Engels in response to a proposal by Bernstein, Hochberg and Schramm, he blasted the "Zurich Trio" for arguing that the Party and its new publication should eschew overt support for working-class demands and struggle and seek instead to woe "supporters from the ranks of the educated and propertied classes"! Why? Because the Party needs "men (sic!) who are fit to represent it in the Reichstag." This amounted, Engels argued, to abandoning the basic idea – laid out years ago in the *Communist Manifesto* – that ending capitalism and creating a new society must be done by workers themselves. There was nothing, however, in either document about any other aspect of crisis.

3.8 *Engels: Socialism: Utopian & Scientific*

Paul Lafargue (1842–1911), an activist in the First International and husband to Marx's daughter Laura, urged Engels to extract some chapters from *Anti-Dühring* into smaller publications to achieve a wider circulation in France of its ideas and analysis. Engels did so, revising and publishing three chapters, first in three issues of *La Revue socialiste* in March-May 1880 and then in a pamphlet titled *Socialisme utopique et socialism scientifique* that same year. A German version would follow in 1882 and an English one in 1891 under the title *Socialism: Utopian and Scientific*.[199]

With respect to crises, Engels' only significant revision to his original essay is in Section II. In *Anti-Dühring*, his account of the progressive socialization of production included the formation of joint stock companies, an intermediary stage that would give way to the takeover of production by the state. But here, in his revised text, he inserts yet another intermediary stage: that of "trusts." To wit:

> The producers on a large scale in a particular branch of industry in a particular country unite in a "Trust," a union for the purpose of regulating production. They determine the total amount to be produced, parcel it out among themselves, and thus enforce the selling price beforehand ... The whole of the particular industry is turned into one gigantic joint-stock company; internal competition gives place to the internal monopoly of one company ... In trusts, ... production without any definite plan of capitalist society capitulates to the production upon a definite plan of the invading socialistic society.[200]

199 Friedrich Engels, *Socialism: Utopian and Scientific*, MECW, *Vol. 24*, pp. 281–325.

200 Ibid., pp. 317–318, also *MECW, Vol. 25*, pp. 639–640. In his Preface to the Fourth Edition, Engels explains he added these words to the text of *Anti-Dühring* because "the new form of production, the 'trusts' ... have "become important." May 12, 1891, *MECW, Vol. 27*, p. 202. Decades later, this theme of expanding capitalist planning laying the groundwork for workers' control in a socialist society, was taken up by a dissident Trotskyist faction of the American Socialist Workers Party (SWP) known as the Johnson-Forest Tendency. In a pamphlet, Tendency members expanded the idea, drawing attention to workers – as well as capitalists – crafting new elements of a post-capitalist, socialist society in the present, J. R. Johnson (C. L. R. James, 1901–1989), F. Forest (Raya Dunayevskaya, 1910–1987) and Ria Stone (Grace Lee, 1915–2015), *The Invading Socialist Society* (1947). After breaking with the SWP and forming their own organization they further explored the idea in *Facing Reality: The New Society ... Where to Look for it, How to Bring it Closer. A Statement for Our Time* (1958).

In other words, the dynamics of capitalist development results in ever more planning by bigger and bigger firms, effectively laying the groundwork for socialist planning. Unfortunately for the capitalists, however, Engels argues that "trusts of this kind, as soon as business becomes bad, are generally liable to break up …"[201] The result of capitalist development, they may be; but they provide no solution to crisis.[202]

3.9 *Engels: the Dialectics of Nature*

Upon completion of his book and pamphlet, Engels returned to his work on the dialectics of nature from 1878 to 1882. However, once again his research was cut short, this time by Marx's death in 1883. Feeling compelled to finish the job of editing Marx's manuscripts into Volumes 2 (completed in 1885) and 3 (completed in 1894) of *Capital*, he once again set aside his own research. As a result, he never did complete his work, leaving behind, as Marx had, only an incomplete manuscript and fragmentary notes. Nevertheless, the coherence of what he had already written did result in his manuscript and notes eventually being published in 1925 in the USSR. So, although it was published posthumously, the text does give us further insight into Engels' thinking about crises in the period surrounding *Anti-Dühring* and *Socialism: Utopian and Scientific*.

Because this project was focused on demonstrating how dialectics are as relevant to understanding nature as for understanding human society, the vast majority of his manuscripts and notes involve re-interpreting available scientific evidence and the evolution of science itself from the point of view

201 Engels, *Socialism: Utopian and Scientific*, MECW, *Vol. 24*, p. 317.

202 Engels was not alone among Marxists in viewing the emergence of trusts as a new stage in capitalist development, with implications for crises. At the turn of the century, perhaps the most important study of this phenomenon was by the Austrian Marxist Rudolf Hilferding (1877–1941) who published his *Finance Capital: A Study of the Latest Phase of Capitalist Development* in 1910. Hilferding not only highlighted the rise of trusts and monopoly power but also showed how their formation in the field of finance increased the leverage of financial institutions such as banks over industrial firms to the point where the latter became dependent on the former and subject to their dictates with respect to decisions about investment, etc. Nor were Marxists alone in recognizing the rise of trusts. Muckraking (investigative) journalists reported on the power of Robber Barons and neoclassical economists' theories of monopoly and oligopoly provided theories of how they limit output and raise prices – to the detriment of consumers. Both contributed to the rise of "anti-trust" legislation to curb such practices. Three decades later, the American Marxist Paul Sweezy (1910–2004) in his book *The Theory of Capitalist Development* (1942), while retaining Hilferding's focus on monopoly, argued that the internal retained earnings of multinational, conglomerate, industrial corporations had grown to the point of freeing them from the kind of control by financial corporations that preoccupied Hilferding.

of materialist dialectics.[203] There are only a few passages in these texts tying developments in science to crises within capitalism. They deploy basically the same concepts of crisis that are in the two works he did bring to completion, namely an emphasis on the tendency of production (supply) to outstrip available markets (demand).

Engels also denounces the way *Social* Darwinists appropriated Charles Darwin's analysis of evolution by reducing it to nothing but a "struggle for existence." This amounted, he argued, to nothing but a "transference from society to organic nature of [Thomas] Hobbes' theory of *bellum omnium contra omnes* and of the theory of competition."[204] This reduction completely ignored how "The interactions of bodies in non-living nature include both harmony and collisions, that of living bodies conscious and unconscious co-operation as well as conscious and unconscious struggle."[205] Engels was certainly thinking about how the capitalist organization of competition, both among themselves and among workers, was their way of managing networks of co-operation both within units of production and across industries.[206] Moreover, he insists that where capitalism has developed, "where the means of development are socially produced – the categories taken from the animal kingdom are already totally inapplicable."

203 This effort to demonstrate that everything develops in a dialectical manner lay the foundation for the emergence of *dialectical materialism* understood as a philosophy, indeed as a cosmology, one in which *historical materialism* is a subset. This perspective was reduced to a dogma under Stalin, one that had a crippling influence on the development of science in the Soviet Union and led to their being caricaturized as "diamat" and "histomat." In less dogmatic forms they live on among some Marxists in journals such as *Historical Materialism*.

204 "A war of all against all." *MECW*, *Vol.* 25, p. 584.

205 These passages were taken almost verbatim from a letter from Engels to Lavrov, November 12–17, 1875, *MECW*, *Vol.* 45, pp. 107–109.

206 Remember how in Volume 1 of *Capital*, Marx immediately follows Chapter 12 on technological change being circulated by competition with Chapter 13 on Co-operation. Engels' critique of the one-sided appropriation of Darwin's ideas would find a more fully developed echo in Piotr Kropotkin's book *Mutual Aid* (1902), also aimed against Social Darwinists, which demonstrated through numerous examples how among both non-human animals and throughout human history co-operation has been as essential to evolution as competition. Although Kropotkin (1842–1921) is generally viewed as one of the fathers of anarcho-communism, there is a considerable overlap between his analysis and that of Marx and Engels. See, H. Cleaver, "Kropotkin, Self-valorization and the Crisis of Marxism" (1992), *Anarchist Studies* (February 1993).

> Finally, under the capitalist mode of production, production reaches such a high level that society can no longer consume the means of subsistence, enjoyment and development that have been produced, because the great mass of producers' access to these means is artificially and forcibly barred; and therefore every ten years a crisis restores the equilibrium by destroying not only the means of subsistence, enjoyment and development that have been produced, but also a great part of the productive forces themselves.[207]

It is this wasteful character, he argues, that give the "struggle for existence" a whole new meaning. Namely:

> To protect the products and productive forces produced by bourgeois capitalist society against the destructive, ravaging effect of this capitalist social order, by taking control of social production and distribution out of the hands of the ruling capitalist class, which has become incapable of this function, and transferring it to the producing masses – and that is the socialist revolution.[208]

In other words, for the struggle for existence within capitalism to be successful, capital's destructive methods must be replaced by non-destructive, careful planning by workers.

3.10 *Periodical Crisis Becomes Permanent Stagnation?*

As part of his efforts to circulate Marx's writings, besides editing and publishing the second and third volumes of *Capital*, Engels published two pieces in 1885 in which he raised what appeared to him to be a possible fundamental change in the pattern of capitalist crisis. The first was a preface he wrote for the first-time publication in German of Marx's *Poverty of Philosophy* (1847), which had hitherto only been available in the original French. Prior to its publication with the new translation, Engels published his preface as an independent article "Marx and Rodbertus" in *Die Neue Zeit*, No. 1.[209] In that preface, in the

207 *MECW*, *Vol 25*, pp. 584–585.

208 Ibid.

209 See the editors' note 141 on the composition and publication of this piece of writing, *MECW*, *Vol. 26*, p. 647. This was not the only time Engels found it desirable to critique Rodbertus; most of his 1884 Preface to Volume 2 of *Capital* is devoted to showing the falsity of Rodbertus' claims that Marx had plagiarized his own theory of surplus value. *Capital*, *Vol. 2*, pp. 83–102.

course of deploying Marx's critique of Proudhon to counter attacks by Johan Karl Rodbertus (1805–1875) on Marx and *Capital*, Engels writes the following in a footnote:

> Since England's monopoly of the world market is being increasingly shattered by the participation of France, Germany and, above all, of America in world trade, a *new* form of evening-out appears to have come into operation. The period of general prosperity preceding the crisis still fails to appear. If it should remain absent altogether, then *chronic stagnation* must necessarily become the normal condition of modern industry, with only insignificant fluctuations.[210] [my emphasis]

The old form of "evening-out," of course, was the kind of crisis he had hitherto emphasized: periodic industrial overproduction, cutbacks in production and layoffs, accompanied by crises in finance from speculative busts, bank failures, etc., followed by a rapid recovery with expanding production, rising employment, new speculations, etc.

His second discussion of such a possible failure of recovery came in an article, "England in 1845 and in 1885," published in *The Commonweal* in March of 1885 in which he contrasts crises in those two periods.[211] His analysis of the crisis of 1846 was basically the same as he and Marx had given at the time.

> Forty years ago England stood face to face with a crisis, solvable to all appearances by force only. The immense and rapid development of manufactures had outstripped the extension of foreign markets and the increase of demand. Every ten years the march of industry was violently interrupted by a general commercial crash, followed, after a long period of chronic depression, by a few short years of prosperity, and always ending in feverish overproduction and consequent collapse.[212]

Engels then sketches how, to avoid this pattern, English manufacturers pushed for free trade, succeeded in repealing the Corn Laws in 1846 and successfully

---

210 Friedrich Engels, "Marx and Rodbertus," October 23, 1884, *MECW*, *Vol. 26*, p. 288, fn*.

211 Friedrich Engels, "England in 1845 and in 1885," *MECW*, *Vol. 26*, pp. 295–301. Engels attached this article as an Appendix to the first English edition of his *The Condition of the Working Class in England*, published in New York in 1887 to update the analysis, at least partially. He later integrated it into a new Preface to both English and German editions in 1892. So, the same passages, quoted here from the original article, can also be found in *MECW*, *Vol. 26*, pp. 399–405 and *Vol. 27*, pp. 257–69 and pp. 307–23.

212 Ibid., p. 295.

expanded trade. They then credited "free trade" with "the revival of commercial prosperity" after the crisis of 1846–1847. To solidify their political power, they also took advantage of the resulting rapid growth to accept a restructuring of their relationships with workers.

> The Factory Acts, once the bugbear of all manufacturers, were not only willingly submitted to, but their expansion into acts regulating almost all trades, was tolerated. Trades Unions, lately considered inventions of the devil himself, were now petted and patronized as perfectly legitimate institutions and as useful means of spreading sound economical doctrines amongst the workers.[213]

The success of such education in pacifying labor, Engels argued, was in those "great Trades Unions," where "the labor of *grown-up men* predominates" and whose leaders came to collaborate with their employers. There, the condition of workers "has remarkably improved since 1848" – to the point of forming "an aristocracy among the working class." However, for the "great mass of the working people," he cautioned, "the state of misery and insecurity in which they live now is as low as ever, if not lower."[214] In short, by accepting the demands of some workers, capitalists were able to strengthen the hierarchy in their labor force by dividing the working class as a whole, leaving most no better off than before. These changes at home, Engels argues, combined with the dominance of English manufactures in world trade to form a kind of hay-day for British capitalism, albeit one periodically plunged into crisis. All this, he argued, could continue only so long as British manufacturers dominated world markets.

So, as in his critique of Rodbertus, Engels argued that as other countries gained ever larger percentages of markets the pattern of crisis would also change, a change already perceptible.

> We did not, indeed, pass through the full crisis at the time it was due, in 1877 or 1878; but we have had, ever since 1876, *a chronic state of stagnation* in all dominant branches of industry. Neither will the full crash come; nor will the period of longed for prosperity to which we used to be entitled

213 Ibid., p. 297.

214 Ibid., pp. 298–299. Positing the income/wealth hierarchy imposed on the working-class as a simple dichotomy of a better paid aristocracy and a large mass of much less well-paid workers would haunt Marxist thinking about that hierarchy for decades. In the worst cases, the entire working class of more industrialized countries would be treated as a sold-out aristocracy vis-à-vis the workers of countries capitalists had turned in exporters of raw materials.

> before and after it. A dull depression, a chronic glut of all markets for all trades, that is what we have been living in for nearly ten years.[215] [my emphasis]

Engels repeated this same argument in both letters and publications over the next years. For example, in a letter to Danielson, in November 1885, we find:

> But the principal cause is undoubtedly the totally changed state of the *Welmarkt* [world market]. Since 1870, Germany and especially America have become England's rivals in modern industry, while most other European countries have so far developed their own manufactures as to cease being dependent on England. The consequence has been the spreading of the process of overproduction over a far larger area than when it was mainly confined to England, and has taken – up to now – a chronic instead of an acute character. By thus delaying the thunderstorm which formerly cleared the atmosphere every ten years, this continued chronic depression must prepare a crash of a violence and extend such as we have never known before.[216]

And then, in a letter to Bebel the following year, he wrote,

> This is already the eighth year in which overproduction has exerted pressure on the markets and, instead of improving, the situation is getting steadily worse nor can there be any doubt that it is essentially different from what it used to be. Since the appearance of serious rivals to Britain on the world market, the era of crises, in the old sense of the term, has come to an end. If, from being acute, the crises become chronic yet lose nothing of their intensity, what is likely to happen?[217]

In his 1886 Preface to the English edition of Volume 1 of *Capital*, to explain why he judged that the "The working of the industrial system of [England] ... is coming to a dead stop," he wrote:

215 Ibid., p. 299.

216 Engels to Danielson, November 13, 1886, *MECW*, *Vol. 47*, p. 349.

217 Engels to Bebel, January 20–23, 1886, *MECW*, *Vol. 47*, p. 390. See also this follow-up letter, Engels to Bebel, March 18, 1886, where he agrees "with your view that periods of prosperity of over 6 months will cease to occur," *MECW*, *Vol. 47*, p. 428.

> Foreign industry, rapidly developing, stares English production in the face everywhere … While the productive power increases in geometric ratio, the extension of markets proceeds at best in an arithmetic one. The decennial cycle of stagnation, prosperity, overproduction and crisis, ever recurrent from 1825 to 1867, seems to have run its course, but only to land us in the slough of despond of a permanent and chronic depression.[218]

Projecting that this "present dreary period of stagnation shall not only become intensified, but that its intensified condition shall become the permanent and normal state of English trade," he prophesizes that the resulting negative impact on workers, will bring about a renewal of workers' struggles, up and down the hierarchy. When, he writes, the English working class loses "its privileged position; it will find itself generally – the privileged and leading minority not excepted – on a level with its fellow-workers abroad. And that is the reason why there will be Socialism again in England."[219] By "Socialism again in England," Engels meant the revival of the socialist movement in that country.

3.11 *The Second International*

Although during his last decade, from 1885 to 1895, Engels saw neither permanent stagnation nor the reduction of the standard of living of the English working class to that of their "fellow-workers abroad," in 1889 he did see both a dramatic uptick in workers' self-organization and strikes and the coalescence of an International Socialist Workers' Congress in Paris in July. That Congress, which was attended by almost 400 delegates from workers' and socialist parties in 20 countries, constituted the beginning of the "Second International" (1889–1916). It's first action was to organize an international celebration of a workers' May Day.[220]

The celebration of May Day in London, pushed back to May 4, was a dual affair: a huge gathering organized mainly by representatives of new trade unions of mostly unskilled workers, involving over 200,000 workers and a smaller one organized by conservative trade unions of mostly skilled workers – that "aristocracy" Engels argued had been collaborating with their capitalist employers and eschewing socialism and any kind of fundamental critique of

218 Friedrich Engels, "Preface to the English Edition" (November 5, 1886) in *Capital, Vol. 1*, pp. 109–113, or *MECW*, Vol. 35, p. 35.

219 Friedrich Engels, "England in 1845 and in 1885," *MECW*, *Vol. 26*, p. 301.

220 Although May Day has since been associated with workers' struggles, May celebrations long predated the rise of capitalism, the formation of the working-class and its struggles. See Peter Linebaugh, *The Incomplete, True, Authentic and Wonderful History of May Day*, (Oakland: PM Press, 2016). Originally a pamphlet published in 1986.

the system. It was the former, the great mass of newly activated unskilled workers whose rising led him to declare that "the *English proletariat*, rousing itself from forty years of hibernation, *rejoined the movement of its class*."[221] Those forty years he attributed to "the failure of the Chartist movement of 1836–50 and … the colossal rise of industry between 1848 and 1880," during which time skilled workers had shared in the increased creation of wealth by collaborating with their employers. That period of quietude, he declared, "has come to an end."[222]

During the five years that followed (1891–1895) Engels was mostly involved in contributing to the development of the socialist movement, especially in Germany but also in strengthening ties among the various socialist parties of different countries, partly through correspondence, partly through trips abroad, both to the continent and to the United States. That development, of course, involved plenty of debate over theory, strategy, and tactics.

3.12 *Engels: Sources and Circulation of Crises*

With respect to theory, Engels often found his efforts to circulate his and Marx's ideas frustrated by what he viewed as misinterpretations, including those about crises within capitalism. In an 1890 letter to Conrad Schmidt (1863–1932), Engels argues against the tendency to oversimplify the sources of crises by overestimating one source while ignoring others. As capitalism develops, he argues, crises can occur in quite different moments of its circuits because those moments become complex and generate their own internal dynamics. For example, despite reaffirming his and Marx's longstanding position that "Production is, in the final analysis, the decisive factor," he also recognizes how,

> … as soon as trade in products becomes independent of actual production, the former follows a trend of its own … does in turn obey laws of its own, laws inherent in the nature of this new factor; it is a trend having its own phases and reacting in turn on the trend of production[223]

Further,

> Once trade in money becomes divorced from trade in commodities, it will – under certain circumstances determined by production and by the

221 Friedrich Engels, "May 4 in London," May 5–21, 1890, *MECW*, *Vol. 27*, p. 61.
222 Ibid., p. 66.
223 Engels to Schmidt, October 27, 1890, *MECW*, *Vol. 49*, p. 58.

> trade in commodities and within those limits – develop in its own way subject to the special law and distinctive phases determined by its own nature.[224]
>
> ... it is, moreover, a fact that the money market may also have its own crises in which actual industrial disturbances play only a subordinate role, if any at all, and in this sphere there is much to be investigated, particularly in regard to the last 20 years.[225]

Moreover,

> If in addition and in the course of this further development, the trade in money expands to comprise trade in securities, the said securities being not simply government paper, but also the shares of industrial and commercial concerns, i.e., if the trade in money gains direct control of a section of the production by which it is largely dominated, then the reaction of the trade in money on production will be even stronger, and more complex.[226]

Not only is Engels recognizing how crises can break out in various parts of the circuits of capital for separate reasons, in production, commerce, money and financial markets, but also how these different sources of crisis then "react upon" or circulate to other moments of the circuits. I address such circulation in Chapter 5, Section 4 on the "Circulation of Breakdown".

---

224 Ibid.

225 Ibid.

226 Engels' "most striking" example of such financial control is "the North American railroads, the running of which is entirely dependent on the day-to-day stock market operations of a Jay Gould, Vanderbilt, etc., which have nothing whatever to do with any particular railroad or its interest qua means of transport." Ibid., 59. This line of argument about financial control of industry will be taken up a decade later by Hilferding in his *Finance Capital* (1910) (see footnote 202).

CHAPTER 3

Marx's Theory of Accumulation

Although, as we have seen in Chapter 2, Marx's thinking was often inspired by Engels, it was Marx who developed a new theory of accumulation and spelled it out in theoretical detail in his major works, including the three volumes of *Capital*. Therefore, I treat this theory as Marx's despite Engels' acceptance of it and his many contributions to its elaboration, especially with regard to crises.

Marx's theory of accumulation can be thought of in two ways: first, as a theory of how capital tries to organize and reproduce society on an ever-larger scale, and second, as a working-class perspective on that society. Capital's ideologs have their own theories – embodied in economics, sociology, industrial engineering and so on – designed to help solve the problems capitalists face, including those of crisis. Marx's theory, on the contrary, although also a theory of capitalist society, is formulated to reveal what is most important for workers in their struggles, including a vision of the fragility and potential mortality of capitalism.

In the Introduction to this book, I explained that "The central thrust of my interpretation of Marxian theory sees accumulation as the expanded reproduction of a fabric of capitalist control that is always tenuous, repeatedly threatened and often ruptured by workers' struggles." Marx's theory of accumulation is thus a theory of what capitalists must succeed in doing to reproduce their kind of society on an expanded scale. His theory analyzes how capitalists attempt to expand their dominance by imposing ever more commodity-producing work, subordinating most of life to that work and by so doing exercising control over society. Yet, from its origins, people have resisted having their lives subordinated to work and struggled to avoid or escape it. As a result, accumulation, socially and materially speaking, is the expanded reproduction of antagonistic relations of struggle.

> accumulation reproduces the capital-relation on an expanded scale, with more capitalists, or bigger capitalists, at one pole, and more wage laborers at the other pole … Accumulation of capital is therefore multiplication of the proletariat.[1]

1 *Capital, Vol. 1*, pp. 763–4, or *MECW, Vol. 35*, p. 609. NB: Marx's "proletariat" is made up of those workers who are paid money wages, either time-wages or piece-wages. However, payment for labor-power has come in many forms, some, also paid in money, are familiar, e.g., salaries

© HARRY CLEAVER, 2025 | DOI:10.1163/9789004708631_004

Following in the footsteps of the political economists of the eighteenth and nineteenth centuries, Marx identifies and provides a detailed dissection of the material elements involved in accumulation – money, commodities, production, means of production, and labor. As a result, many have seen Marx as just one more political economist, have read *Capital* and his other writings as an alternative political economic analysis of capitalism, one that has corrected some errors of his predecessors (or not) but remains basically on the same ground. This view, however, ignores not only how Marx explicitly identifies his project as a "critique" of political economy[2] but also how his focus and objectives were entirely different from those of political economists. Political economy emerged from preoccupations of merchants, capitalists, and rulers with the generation of material wealth and the best ways to achieve it, while maintaining order in society. Whereas the two groups of thinkers who preceded the political economists, the mercantilists, who thought that trade was the main source of wealth (especially when it brings in more gold and silver money) and the physiocrats, who thought that only agricultural labor produced wealth,[3] the political economists argued that not just agricultural labor, but all commodity-producing labor produces wealth. In all three cases, their writings address the needs of those who were putting people to work, whether in trade, manufacturing, or agriculture.

Marx, on the other hand, appalled at the costs to humans and the rest of nature of this endless imposition of commodity-producing work, formulated his theory as a critique of the exploitation and alienation that results from the capitalist mode of generating wealth and as a contribution to resistance to it. Whereas political economists (and the economists who followed them) have

---

or commissions, others, not paid in money, are less so, e.g., scraps of raw materials, housing, payment in kind (a small portion of a harvest), a bit of coal to heat company-owned cottages rented to miners, and so on. In general, in my exposition of Marx's theory, "wages" can be understood in the general sense of payment for labor-power, unless otherwise more specifically indicated.

2 Both titles of his first two published books laying out his analysis of capitalism made this explicit: *A Contribution to the Critique of Political Economy* (1859) and *Capital: A Critique of Political Economy* (1867). In other works, such as *Theories of Surplus Value*, he spelled out his differences with political economists in great detail.

3 Political economy originated in the writings of the Mercantilists, most of whom were merchants and whose writings were almost always making the case for how their recommended policies would increase the wealth of both the nation and the crown. See, for example, Thomas Mun (1571–1641), *Englands Treasure by Forraign Trade. or The Ballance of our Forraign Trade is The Rule of our Treasure* (1664). Although critiquing the Mercantilists, Smith was careful to title his book in the same spirit *An Inquiry into the Nature and Causes of the Wealth of Nations* (1776).

always deployed their theories to meet the needs of capitalists, e.g., how to maximize profits, how to grow their system, Marx on the contrary deployed his in the interests of the exploited. His analysis is framed, in the language of Thomas Kuhn (1922–1996), by an entirely different *paradigm*.[4] The theory Marx deploys, the questions he asks, the phenomena he chooses to examine in depth and his methods of analysis all differ fundamentally from those of political economists.

1 A "Labor" Theory of Value?

Yet, at first glance Marx's theory and that of his political economy predecessors seem identical in their common deployment of a "labor theory of value" – a theory later abandoned by economists. Upon closer examination, however, his theory turns out to be quite different. Whereas for political economists, labor creates "value" through its contribution to the production of wealth, for Marx the real "value" created for capitalists is the social role of labor in providing capitalists with its primary mode of social control, of organizing society. From the point of view of engineers, economists and some capitalists, labor is just one input or "factor of production" among others, alongside tools, machines, and raw materials.[5] But for Marx, of all the elements of accumulation, *labor stands out as the key social relationship through which capitalists organize,*

4 See his books, *The Copernican Revolution: Planetary Astronomy in the Development of Western Thought* (1957) and *The Structure of Scientific Revolutions* (1962). Although his preoccupation was with grasping dramatic disjunctions in the evolution of science, as opposed to the common view of science developing in a smooth process of ever greater marginal understanding, the concept's application to the social sciences has been widespread (and debated).

5 Although there are capitalists who view workers much as they view their machines, there are also capitalists who see the bigger picture, namely that in their kind of society it is their collective responsibility to put people to work so that society remains well ordered. An example of the former is quoted by Norman Ware, "I regard my work-people just as I regard my machinery . . . When my machines get old and useless, I reject them and get new, and these people are part of my machinery." *The Industrial Worker: 1840–1860*, (Chicago: Quadrangle Books, 1964), 77. Examples of the latter can be seen in the capitalist diversion of profits from money-making into various foundations set up not merely as public relations (PR) ploys but dedicated to social engineering, e.g., promulgating public schooling and public health to create a healthier (and of course exploitable) labor force. The latest manifestation of this awareness – albeit in some cases undoubtedly pure PR – is "conscious" or "socially responsible" capitalism aimed at complementing the search for profits by concern with ESG issues (environmental, social and governance). Both kinds of capitalists – those with the narrow focus on profit-making and those with broader views of their social responsibility as managers of society – can also be found rotating in and out of government.

control and burden their world. Therefore, every element of accumulation must be interpreted in terms of its embodiment of that relationship. Tools, machines and raw materials have value not just because they are the products of human labor but because people can be put to work producing them. The more work it takes to produce them, the more "valuable" they are to the process of putting people to work and controlling them.

Once this is understood, Marx's labor theory of value can be read as providing a theoretical tool for analyzing the most important relations between the classes, how capitalists seek to reproduce those relations and why resistance arises. Marx locates the core of the class relation in the way the capitalist class monopolizes the means of producing the necessities of life and *compels* – through either direct force or the threat of poverty and starvation – the rest of society to work for it to live. What economists call a "labor force" – defined narrowly as the array of individuals either formally employed or looking for jobs – Marx calls a "working class" – defined more broadly to also include those reproducing that labor force. The distinctive features of this working class, as opposed to earlier forms of forced labor are two-fold.

First, whereas in earlier societies how much those forced to work had to do was limited by the particular, concrete, and limited needs of those doing the imposing, in capitalism workers suffer an endless imposition of work because it is not just one method of control among others, but the primary mode of social control, one to be maintained and extended as much as possible and forever. As such it is accompanied and justified by ideologies that define humans (even their relationship to God) by their work.

> Capital did not invent surplus labour ... where use-value rather than exchange-value of the product predominates, surplus labor will be restricted by more or less confined set of needs ... in the capitalist the appetite for surplus labour appears in the drive for an unlimited extension of the working day ...[6]

And not merely of the formal, contracted, working day, as he goes on to show, but of every dimension of life. As workers succeeded in limiting the hours of hired labor, capital moved to colonize time outside of waged or salaried jobs turning such mundane human activities such as children's learning or taking

6 Ibid., 344–346, or *MECW*, *Vol. 35*, pp. 243–245.

care of families into the work of producing "labor-power," the ability and willingness to work for capitalist employers.[7]

While the imposition of surplus labor, the extraction of surplus value (profit), may enrich individual capitalists, Marx's analysis is focused instead on its social role. His interest in surplus value or profit is not in what capitalists siphon off for their own luxurious lifestyles but in how they invest it, putting more people to work, both directly and indirectly, and thus extending their control over society. The investment of money in obtaining labor-power, *M – LP*, is for putting people to work. So is the money spent on required means of production, *M – MP*. Producing the needed *MP* results in even more people being put to work. Therefore, investment, *M – C*(*LP, MP*), both initiates and continues the endless subordination of life to work. Any breakdown in investment, by undermining that subordination, threatens capitalist control over society.

Second, in capitalism the *dominant* form of coercion is indirect. Those separated from any access to independent means of production (such as land and tools) are forced to sell their ability and willingness to work in exchange for wages or salaries, to obtain money which provides the only legal access to consumer goods and services. Where labor-power is sold like other goods, it is itself a commodity. Thus, the dominant social relations of classes in capitalist society may be defined as (1) the endless imposition of work through the commodity form, and (2) the struggle of people against that imposition and for their own ends.[8]

Capital *establishes* this dependency through processes of "primitive" accumulation in which people are stripped of their means of autonomous life and are forced to seek employment with the capitalist owners of the means of production.[9] It *maintains* this dependency by continuing to monopolize the

7 Marx's usual definition of labor-power is "the capacity to work." Because work involves not just the strength and acuity to exercise various skills but mental control over that exercise, I disaggregate "capacity" into "ability and willingness." Workers may have abilities they exercise enthusiastically, only reluctantly or not at all – as I discuss in Chapter 4, Section 4 on the possibilities of disruption in the sphere of production.

8 This analysis was first laid out in Harry Cleaver, *Reading* Capital *Politically*, 2nd ed. (Leeds: Anti/Theses and Edinburgh: AK Press, 2000).

9 The discussion of "primitive" accumulation appears in Volume 1 of *Capital* at the end, as Part Eight. In my courses on *Capital*, we started with that part, instead of the much more abstract theory of value in Part I. Why? Two reasons: 1) It provides a dramatic and easy to read historical narrative, and 2) it makes clear why the theory in Part 1 is a *labor* theory of value. The stripping of land and tools described in Part Eight is the precondition for the development of capitalism. Although Marx's presentation is largely historical, the processes he analyzes have never ended, but continue right up to the present. This is true not only in remote areas where

means of production and by reorganizing social life to herd people into the labor market. In Marx and Engel's time, capitalists used extremely low wages and hunger to drive everyone, men, women and children, into the search for waged employment.[10]

Although in Marx's *theory* of capitalist accumulation the dominant, antagonistic social relationships which capitalists impose on the world are those between themselves and waged or salaried workers, for a very long time in the *history* of capitalism slavery played a hugely important role in early capitalist industrialization. Moreover, despite chattel slavery being eventually outlawed and illegal slavery being marginalized into the shadows, in many industries around the world capitalists have continued to force people to work against their will to generate surplus value and profit. What is commonly called "forced labor" today is really a euphemism for slavery. According to a joint report of the International Labor Organization, the Walk Free Foundation and the UN Migration Agency, "on any given day" in 2021 "there are 50 million people in conditions of modern slavery."[11] Marginal though slavery may be today, it continues to be an integral part of capitalism's global work machine and one more source of widespread suffering.

---

people are not yet thoroughly integrated into the labor force – because they still have access to some common resources – but even in highly industrialized countries where capitalism has long been established. There too the theft of lands from the commons and the destitution of craftspeople continues. Some of this was analyzed in the 1980s, under the rubric of "The New Enclosures" by Midnight Notes. More recently the theft of land in the US from National Parks and other natural areas by the Trump administration, which then handed them over for capitalist exploitation, e.g., mining, opened a new phase of this very old process. As before, this attack on the commons is being resisted by environmental groups, Native Americans, and workers in general, loath to lose what little remains unspoiled by the ravages of capitalism.

10 This imposed penury was, of course, complemented by severe punishment for evading the labor market and appropriating goods and services directly ("theft"). See Peter Linebaugh's discussion of capital's "thanotocracy" in his *The London Hanged: Crime and Civil Society in the Eighteenth Century* (London: Allen Lane, 1991).

Then, in the wake of child labor laws restricting the exploitation of children and other laws restricting women's access to jobs, it cultivated the nuclear family where women/wives do the housework of gestating and rearing children while also taking care of the reproductive needs of employed husbands and helping force children into legally mandated unwaged schoolwork, conditioning them for later entry into the labor market. It has also limited any access to the means of subsistence outside the labor market, by keeping all legal forms of unwaged income very low, from parish relief in Marx's time, to welfare and unemployment benefits in ours. All of these various forms of imposed work, waged and unwaged, have been resisted, often refused or sabotaged.

11 See, The ILO, et.al., Global Estimates of Modern Slavery: Forced Labor and Forced Marriage, Geneva, (September 2022).

Despite writing quite a bit about slavery, both ancient slavery and that in the nineteenth century, Marx never included this form of imposed work in his formal theorization of capitalist social relations and their crises. However, because of both its historical significance *and* its persistence in the world today, I feel obligated to indicate, at least to some degree, in my sketch of his theory of capitalist accumulation and its crises, how the use of slaves fits into accumulation and the parallels and relationships Marx saw between the struggles of slaves and those of "wage-slaves."

In what follows, I first treat the concrete, material relationships that capitalists must create and maintain in order to reproduce their kind of society on an expanded scale and then, second, I explain how Marx analyzes those relationships in terms of value.

2 The *Material* Circuits of Accumulation

I begin with the various material elements over which capitalists must gain control and organize so that their control can be perpetuated, preferably on an ever-larger scale:

M — *money*, the universal equivalent of all commodities, which capitalists invest by obtaining labor-power, *LP*, and the means of production, *MP*, and used by workers to purchase means of subsistence, *MS*.[12]

MP — the *means of production*, which the capitalists monopolize as a class, use to put workers to work, and have workers produce to sell to other capitalists. These include raw materials extracted from the earth and fabricated tools, machinery, factories, means of transportation and communication.

LP — *labor-power*, or the ability and willingness to work, which capital obtains either by hiring workers in labor markets or by extracting it through the direct coercion of slavery.

P — *production*, or the processes in which capitalists put their workers to work with the means of production at their disposal.

C — *commodities*, which are produced by workers, but are owned by capitalists and then sold to workers as means of subsistence, *MS*, or to other capitalists as *MP*. Although eventually proving to be marginal in capitalism, among the commodities produced and sold in capitalism have been slaves, human beings (and other animals) forced to work and thus a source of *LP*, even as they are treated as means of production.

12 I ignore here the many cases in which workers are paid in other forms, e.g., part of a harvest, or other products of their work.

MS — means of subsistence (or means of consumption): the commodities (food, clothing, housing, and so on) necessary for the production and reproduction of *LP*, bought by hired workers with money obtained in exchange for their *LP*, or in the case of slavery, either produced for themselves or supplied by their owners.[13]

Each of these elements has to be employed successfully and in a certain order to achieve accumulation. Marx represented that order, which capital seeks to achieve and then to constantly repeat on an expanded scale, in two ways.

The first, simplest representation, in Part 2 of Volume 1 of *Capital*, is the "general formula for capital," $M - C - M'$, where $M' > M$, in which capitalists spend money to make more money. But in this representation, as he points out, the source of the excess of M' over M remains a mystery.[14] The solution to the mystery, of course, is the labor expended in production.

In his second representation, that labor is portrayed as the vital part of production, ...*P*..., in what he calls the "circuit of capital." In Part 1 of Volume 2 of *Capital*, the circuit is analyzed in terms of the reproduction of three of its elements: *M* (the circuit of money capital), *P* (the circuit of productive capital), and *C* (the circuit of commodity capital). In the representations of these circuits, dashes are used to represent market exchanges and dots to represent non-exchange relations. I use the circuit of money capital as the template for

13 Marx and Engels regularly used the term "subsistence" because in their time wages were so low that what workers could buy with their wages barely allowed them to scrape by. These days the term is usually only applied to peasants and farmers who are living off the land with little or no recourse to the labor market for income. The term "subsistence agriculture," however, can also refer to the activities of waged or salaried workers who supplement their money income by gardening, canning, and raising animals. In times of high food prices, many workers, both waged and salaried, have been known to have increased recourse to these methods. An example was during the food crisis of the early 1970s when the US government engineered a dramatic rise in food prices by paying farmers to reduce production while negotiating a huge grain deal with the USSR. The expansion of gardening was so great it caused such an increased demand for canning jars as to result in a serious shortage. A similar run occurred more recently during the Covid pandemic when the loss of jobs and/or obligated home stays increased gardening. But in this case the shortage of jars was as much due to a series of takeovers that resulted in such a near monopoly of production that the main corporation producing canning equipment could reduce both production and sales, driving up prices (and, presumably, profits). On the 1970s case see, H. Cleaver, "Food, Famine and International Crisis," *Zerowork* 2, (Fall 1977). On the recent shortage See, Debbie Stroud, "Where Are the Canning Jars? Is It 1975 All Over Again?," North Carolina State University Extension Service, (August 21, 2020), who raises the issue, and Lois Thielen, who gives a better answer, "Why is there a shortage of canning jars and lids?," Yahoo News, (April 6, 2022).

14 For the mystery see Chapter V: "The Contradictions of the General Formula of Capital" in Volume 1 of *Capital*.

much of my exposition of Marx's theory of accumulation (and crisis) because it makes it easy to follow Marx's own analysis. Here is the circuit in two iterations through two time periods of accumulation. The *M'* achieved in the first period makes possible in the second period the employment of more *LP* (*LP'* > *LP*) and more *MP* (*MP'* > *MP*), expanded production, more commodities, *C"*, and hence more revenue, *M"*.

$$\begin{array}{ccccccccccccc} & & LP & & & & & & LP' & & & & \\ & & / & & & & & & / & & & & \\ M & — & C & \ldots\ldots & P & \ldots\ldots & C' & — & M'.\,M' & — & C' \ldots\ldots P \ldots\ldots & C'' & — M'' \text{ and so on.} \\ & & \backslash & & & & & & \backslash & & & & \\ & & MP & & & & & & MP' & & & & \end{array}$$

The meaning of this sequence is simple enough. Capitalists (if in the individual case),[15] or capital in general, invest money to obtain labor-power, *M* – *LP*,[16] and whatever means of production, *M* – *MP*, are required for the employment of workers, i.e., the tools, machinery and raw materials necessary to produce the intended new product, *C'*. The workers, both waged and slave, are then put to work, ...*P*..., using the means of production, to produce new commodities, *C'*.[17] Finally, those commodities, *C'*, must be successfully sold for money, *C'* – *M'*,

15 NB: throughout this essay, I usually follow Marx's habit of treating the behavior of individual capitalists only in so far as their actions are typical of capitalism in general. In other words, for my purposes I am not interested in their behavior as individuals per se. Folks with personal histories that lead them to take actions at variance with Marx's theory would be in violation of capitalism's "rules of the game." I recognize that that both incompetent and well-meaning capitalists exist. The international debt crisis of the 1980s and 1990s revealed how bankers sometimes ignored their own internal warnings of dangerously high risk and suffered the consequences. The bursting of the dot.com speculative bubble of the 1990s revealed how greed and self-indulgence often overcame good capitalist practices and led to bankruptcy. It is also possible to identify individual capitalists who have adopted measures that benefit workers, or society at large, which in no way bolster their bottom line.

16 Please note: this representation works regardless of whether the money, *M*, buys *LP* from workers who sell their labor-power, *LP* – *M*, piece-meal, or buys slaves, with whatever *LP* they possess, from other capitalists who produce them as *C*(*LP*) by either capture or breeding.

17 So, if all goes as planned, they succeed, in the words of Cambridge economist Piero Sraffa (1898–1983), in achieving the "production of commodities by commodities." See, Pierro Sraffa, *Production of Commodities by Means of Commodities, Prelude to a Critique of Economic Theory* (Cambridge, UK: Cambridge University Press, 1960). For economists more generally, what they succeed in achieving is the growth of output, in both material and monetary forms. For Marx and Engels, on the contrary, the main thing they succeed in reproducing are the antagonistic social relations of capitalism.

either to workers as means of subsistence or to other capitalists as means of production (or in the case of slaves, as sources of labor-power).

While marketed *C*(*MP*)' re-enter the circuit as new *MP*', what of *C*(*MS*)', consumer goods and services? They reinter the circuit, not as *MS*', but as *LP*'. But how? Obviously via various forms of consumption. But unlike ...*P*..., which designates the combining of *LP* and *MP* in the production of *C*', Marx provides no parallel representation for the conversion of *MS* into *LP*. His "little circuit," *LP* – *M* – *C*(*MS*), which represents waged workers obtaining and then spending their wages to purchase the means of subsistence, *C*(*MS*), ends with that purchase. There is no representation of either the work involved in finding jobs (job search), or that in the consumption of *C*(*MS*), e.g., shopping, cooking.[18] Yet those are obviously essential elements in the reproduction of labor-power, including its reproduction on an expanded scale, i.e., the *LP*' in the next circuit. As a representation of waged workers' point of view, who sell their labor-power to obtain the means of life, *LP* – *M* – *C*(*MS*) is adequate; but as a representation of a moment of capital's expanded reproduction, it leaves something to be desired.[19] Only in the case of slavery might "...*P*..." be reasonably interpreted as

---

18 An example of Marx failing to analyze the *work* of shopping can be found in this comment: "The time that a worker needs to buy his means of subsistence," he writes, "is lost time for him." *Capital, Vol. 2*, p. 226, or *MECW, Vol. 36*, p. 153. While the time (and energy) spent shopping may be lost to other pursuits, to the degree that it contributes to the reproduction of labor-power it must be counted as unwaged work – regardless of whether the shopper enjoys or despises it. While theorists of 'consumerism" point to middle-class enjoyment of shopping, the view of shopping-as-work is manifest in how the wealthy pay for the service of having others shop for them. "Personal shoppers", who hire out by the hour, are today complemented by waged workers in big chain grocery stores providing the same service.

Please note: Marx also fails to provide any representation of the work of looking for work, *LP* – *M*, which mostly falls on the unwaged.

19 To include the reproduction of *LP*, the only element of the circuit unaccounted for in Marx's representations, I have offered a parallel formulation of a "circuit of the reproduction of labor-power," for the case of waged or salaried workers, i.e., *LP* – *M* – *C*(*MS*) . . . P_c . . . *LP** where the P_c represents all the work – housework, schoolwork, subsistence agriculture, etc., required for consumption and reproducing the ability and willingness to work. See the appendix to H. Cleaver, "Malaria, the Politics of Public Health and the International Crisis," *Review of Radical Political Economics* 9, (Issue 1, April 1977): 96–100. The reproduction of slave *LP* generally also requires the work of the slaves, e.g., producing food for themselves, taking care of clothes, shoes, etc., bought for them by their owners. This proposed fourth circuit is entirely different from the fourth circuit toyed with by Marx, discovered by Christopher Authur in a manuscript available only in German and in MEGA and analyzed in his article "Marx's Fourth Capital Circuit," *Capital & Class*, 59, Vol. 20, Issue 2 (Summer 1996): 31–36, and at greater detail in his "The Fluidity of Capital and the Logic of the Concept" in Arthur and Reuten, eds., *The Circulation of Capital*,

including the production of *LP*, where $C' = C(LP)'$ = the slaves themselves, bred and then sold like *MP* but bought for their embodied *LP*.

Marx does, however, discuss some of the work of consumption in his analysis of simple reproduction in Chapter 23 of Volume 1 of *Capital* and again in his analysis of expanded reproduction in Chapter 25 by calling our attention to the conditions of life suffered by workers outside the terrain of their employment. Those conditions, after all, shape the primary domains of reproducing labor-power. Although *some* of the reproduction of labor-power is often an "incidental part of the production process," occurring on the job, such as learning skills, or eating or sleeping in worker dormitories on the job site, *most* of the work of reproduction occurs elsewhere, where "the capitalist may safely leave this [reproduction] to the worker's drive for self-preservation and propagation."[20] This is also true in cases of slavery where the places they live are set apart and they can devote some time and energy to meeting their own needs and desires.[21] The sites of that self-preservation and propagation by waged workers, which Marx has in mind, are homes and working-class neighborhoods.

From the capitalist point of view, workers' consumption is only about reproducing life as labor-power.

> The individual consumption of the worker, whether it occurs inside or outside the workshop, inside or outside the labour process, remains an aspect of the production and reproduction of capital, just as the cleaning of machinery does, whether it is done during the labour process, or when intervals in that process permit. The fact that the worker performs acts of individual consumption in his own interest, and not to please the capitalist, is something entirely irrelevant to the matter.[22]

Irrelevant, however, only to the degree that workers' consumption of *MS* is limited to reproducing their labor-power and doesn't fuel resistance to their exploitation or the elaboration of alternatives – whether individual or collective. However, given the antagonistic character of capitalist-worker

95–128. In all cases, these representations of reproduction leave out workers' autonomous consumption, i.e., consumption that creates and supports life beyond, and often against, the reproduction of labor-power.

20 *Capital, Vol. 1*, p. 718, or MECW, *Vol. 35*, p. 572.

21 One breakthrough study of such self-activity among plantation slaves in the United States was George Rawick's compilation of slave narratives and his prefatory volume *From Sundown to Sunup: The Making of the Black Community* (New York: Praeger, 1973).

22 *Capital, Vol. 1*, p. 718, or MECW, *Vol. 35*, p. 572.

relationships, workers' consumption has indeed often provided the energy to rebel, either on site or through flight.

Elsewhere, Marx does recognize that capital doesn't always "leave it to the worker's drive for self-preservation" but actively intervenes in some domains of reproduction, e.g., workhouses, prisons and schools to obtain and shape the reproduction of labor-power, precisely to minimize the chance of them becoming sites of resistance and struggle.[23] All of these, therefore, become – like the labor market and production – terrains of work, of class struggle and potential sites of crises in the capitalist ordering of society and its endless reproduction.

It is this effort to achieve eternal return that justifies the metaphors of "circulation" and "circuit". In Marx's writings the representation of the circuit is linear. A better illustration of what capitalists are aiming for is a circular spiral in which both return and expansion are more obvious (Figure 3.1).[24]

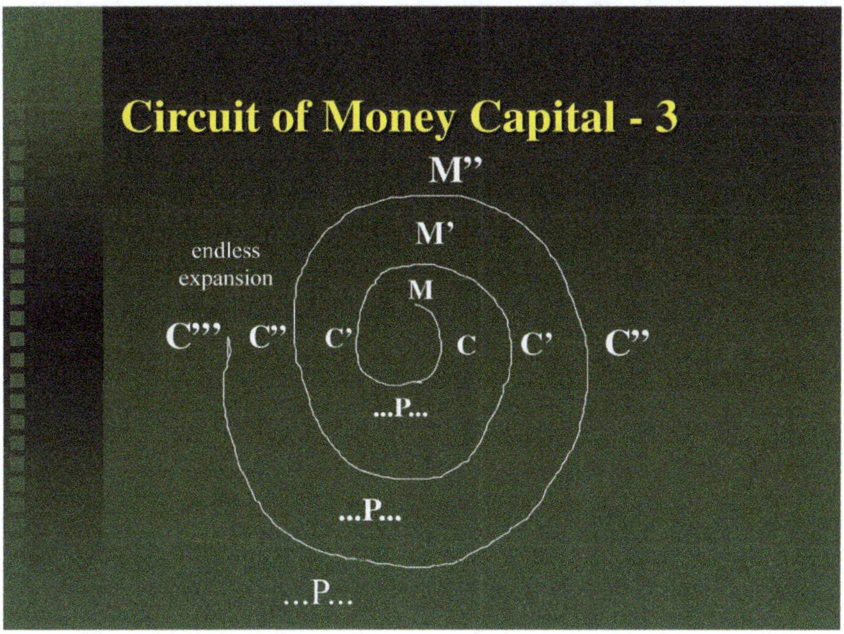

FIGURE 3.1 Circuit as expanding spiral.

23 Interventions in modern times have been far more extensive, reaching into every domain of the reproduction of labor-power.

24 The metaphors of circulation and circuit originated in the analysis of the circular flow of blood, out from the heart through arteries and back to the heart through veins, by William Harvey (1578–1657), first spelled out in his *De Mortu Cortis* (1628). That understanding was taken up by the French physician turned economist, François Quesnay (1694–1774) and applied in his *Tableau Économique* that analyzed the circular flow of value from

At the end of a successful circuit, there are no *qualitative* changes in the basic conditions of the classes – capitalists still control the means of production and most workers still have their labor-power to be exploited. Thus, the class relation is reproduced, society is maintained in the same form, and the capitalists can deploy their surplus value to set the whole machine in motion, once again.

What *does* change (hopefully, from the capitalist point of view) is the *quantity* of money in the hands of capitalists and thus their ability to expand their operations. Successful management results in extra or surplus work being performed in production, ...*P*..., beyond that required to replace used up *LP* + *MP*. If all goes well, so much labor is extracted from the workers employed in the production of the final product, *C'*, that its value, and the money, *M'*, obtained from its sale, is *greater* than the value originally invested, such that *C'* > *C* and *M'*> *M*. The excess labor embodied in *M'* thus constitutes surplus value, or profit in money terms. Then by investing that surplus, capital can reproduce or grow the whole circuit on an *expanded* scale.[25] More *M* means more *LP* and

agricultural labor to manufacturing and back again. Quesnay's *Tableau* inspired both Adam Smith and Marx, both of whom argued that the source of value was not just agricultural labor but also that deployed in other commodity-producing industries.

The long-lasting influence of this perception of circularity can be seen in the "circular flow" diagrams of virtually every introductory economics textbook. Those diagrams, of course, hide class relations by replacing the "workers" or the "working class" with "households" and capitalists or the "capitalist class" with "business." The circularity, moreover, is also confined to markets with the only "value" in circulation being money whose amount is determined by the market prices of goods and services sold. The imposition of work in commodity production is buried inside "business" and the reproduction of labor-power is buried inside "households."

25 A fundamental difference between Marx's theory of accumulation and economists' theories of "growth" is how the former is formulated in terms of the social relations of labor while the latter have been – at least since the rise of neoclassical economics – formulated such that the only measure of value that matters are money prices. For example, economists' measures of economic output, e.g., Gross National Product (GNP), and growth, e.g., percentage change in GNP, only count the monetary value of things and services sold. In Marx's theory, the most important value to capitalists is the labor they are able to impose. Money merely embodies the exchange form of labor value, so money prices are grounded – although not uniquely determined – in that value. In his theoretical representations of the relationships involved in the accumulation of capital, Marx always assumes that (labor) value = (money) price and that all exchange is of equal values. Because he knows this is rarely the case, these are simplifying assumptions; there are causes of market fluctuations that raise and lower prices quite independent of any change in the value of commodities. (These assumptions are also basic to his theory of exploitation – which he demonstrates to exist even when there is equality in exchange.) He maintains this assumption as he analyzes the potential sources of crisis in accumulation and the forces

MP can be purchased, the scale of ...*P*... can be increased and, if all goes well, an even greater value of commodities *C'* can be produced and sold. Socially and politically speaking, the most important aspect of capitalist success in achieving an expansion of their system is the imposition of more work and more capitalist control. Yet, that also means the expanded system continues to be rife with all its antagonisms and conflicts.

3 Three Observations

First, in Marx's theoretical analysis, *C' – M'*, like *M – LP* and *M – MP*, is defined as falling within the sphere of *exchange*, or of *circulation*. Yet, he recognizes that key elements involved in *actual C' – M'*, such as "both transport proper and ... and the transmission of mere information,"[26] constitute moments of *production*, not exchange. Therefore, the work done by workers in those activities contribute to the value of *C'*.

> What the transport industry sells is the actual change of place itself ... this journeying, the spatial movement of the means of transport, is precisely the production process accomplished by the transport industry ... the exchange value of this useful effect is still determined, like that of any other commodity, by the value of the elements of production used up in it (labour-power and means of production), plus the surplus-value

that predispose the system to enter into crisis. However, when he analyses how things actually unfold in history, while the theory provides a guide, he drops this assumption and takes into account precisely those changes in price – and the roles they play in crisis – that have sources other than labor value. In this essay, I adhere to this practice, exploring both his theories of crisis in terms of value and his analyses of actual crises that recognize the influence of historical contingencies.

26 *Capital, Vol. 2*, p. 134, or *MECW, Vol. 36*, p. 61. A certain amount of both transportation and communication naturally takes place directly within manufacturing, mining and agriculture as partially manufactured or partially processed product is moved from one site of production to another. Two examples: "for instance, cotton ... moved from the carding shop into the spinning shed" or "coal lifted from the pit to the surface." *Capital, Vol. 2*, p. 227, or *MECW, Vol. 36*, p. 154. Each also requires coordination via communication among workers and between managers and workers. Multinational, conglomerate corporations, with production organized over several countries, have often found it useful to externalize these productive relations of transportation and communication by having subsidiaries buy them as services while selling intermediate products to each other. This allows, for example, the minimization of taxes by managing transfer prices between subsidiaries so that most "value added" occurs in low tax, rather than high tax countries.

> created by the surplus labour of the workers occupied in the transport industry.[27]

> [the transport industry] is distinguished by its appearance as the continuation of a production process *within* the circulation process and *for* the circulation process.[28]

I point this out because in my presentation of the possibilities of, predispositions to, and capitalist strategies to offset crisis, I organize my presentation according to the three stages of the circuit, 1) *M – C(MP, LP)*, 2) ...*P*...*C'*, and 3) *C' – M'*. But, recognizing the productive function of the work done in transportation and in communication leads me to include their analysis within the second stage, ...*P*..., rather than the third, even though they are material to the accomplishment of *C' – M'*.

Second, although most of Marx and Engels' examples of commodities being produced in their time were *things* – whether *C(MS)'* or *C(MP)'*, e.g., linen, coats, corn, iron, Marx did explicitly recognize that both *services* and *slaves* could also be produced and sold for a profit by capitalists.[29]

With respect to services, despite Marx not paying them much attention beyond transportation and communication – because he thought they constituted only a tiny part of capitalist commodity production – their steady growth in the nineteenth century (and since) warrants their explicit inclusion in the analysis of accumulation and its crises.[30] We must, therefore, examine services, the work that produces them and the struggles of those doing that work, just as Marx studied those of workers producing things. Recognizing how transportation constitutes the service of moving commodities from here to there, and by so doing changes their use-values and thus adds value to them, implies that *all work that transforms commodities by changing their use-values* adds value to them. This includes a whole domain of labor long ignored by Marx's followers: the work of selling involved in *C' – M'*.

There is a long-standing tradition among Marxists, derived from Marx's *assumption* "that commodities are bought and sold at their value", that all work

27 Ibid., p. 135, or *MECW*, *Vol. 36*, p. 62.

28 Ibid., p. 229, or *MECW*, *Vol. 36*, p. 155.

29 With respect to services, see Marx's discussion of writers, artists, teachers, musicians, dancers and other performers in *Capital*, *Vol. 1*, pp. 1044–1048, or *MECW*, *Vol. 34*, pp. 448–452. He also noted the rise in intentional breeding of slaves once the international slave trade was outlawed and stopped.

30 By the mid-twentieth century, the "service sector" was well on its way to becoming the largest part of capitalist commodity production.

involved in selling, *C' – M'* is deemed unproductive and involve costs that bear no fruit, a "faux frais" of commerce.[31] Indeed, Marx wrote:

> all that is involved in these acts is the conversion of the same value from one form to another – from the commodity form [*C'*] into the money form [*M'*] ...[32]

> The general law is that *all circulation costs that arise simply from a change in form of the commodity cannot add any value to it*. They are simply costs involved in realizing the value or transferring it from one form [*C'*] to another [*M'*]. The capital expended in these costs (including the labour it commands) belongs to the *faux frais* of capitalist production.[33]

When applied to *M – LP / LP – M*, this assumption grounds his analysis of exploitation. By assuming workers are not cheated but paid the value of their labor power, he can locate exploitation in the surplus labor they do beyond what is necessary to produce their means of subsistence. But when this assumption is carried over to the analysis of *C' – M'* it leads to a certain blindness. To what?

To how the "change in the form of a commodity" can be the result of all work which changes its *use-value*, as in transportation, which by bringing goods and services to buyers makes them immediately available. Such work adds value, possibly surplus value and by so doing meets Marx's definition of "productive" labor. Although missing in Volumes 2 and 3 of *Capital*, Marx recognized this a decade earlier while writing the *Grundrisse*. There, he approvingly cited Heinrich von Storch (1766–1835)[34] about the essential role of labor in making commodities available to buyers:

> [Trade] gives the product a new use value (and this holds right down to and including the retail grocer, who weighs, measures, wraps the product and thus gives it a form for consumption), and this new use value costs

31 One example of this tradition is the chapter on "the sales effort" in Paul Baran and Paul Sweezy's book *Monopoly Capital* (New York: Monthly Review Press, 1964).

32 *Capital, Vol. 2*, p. 207, or *MECW, Vol. 36*, p. 133.

33 Ibid., pp. 225–226, or *MECW, Vol. 36*, pp. 152–153.

34 On Storch, see Mark Blaug's short bio in *The New Palgrave Dictionary of Economics* (London: Palgrave Macmillan, 2018), Jochen Schumann, "Heinrich von Storch's innovative contributions to economics," *The European Journal of the History of Economic Thought* 25, no. 2 (May 2018): 388–400, and Storch himself in *Cours d'Économie Politique, ou Exposition des Principes qui Déterminent la Prospérité des Nations*, 1815.

> labour time, is therefore at the same time exchange value. The bringing to market is part of the production process itself.[35]

Moreover, we know that what constitutes the use-value of commodities lies not only in their intrinsic properties and in their *availability* but also in potential buyers' perceptions. Many goods and services are often bought primarily for their *symbolic* use-value, e.g., as signaling status (social, sexual, political, etc.). Status, of course, in capitalism depends on one's position in its hierarchies of income, power and celebrity. In Marx and Engels' time this was obvious in the case of "luxury" goods purchased by capitalists or others high up the income hierarchy. It was also obvious to most of those nineteenth century novelists, from Jane Austen (1775–1817) to Henry James (1843–1916), who took on the changing class structure of the time, and how one's array of luxury goods continued to differentiate social status.[36] But even among low-waged workers and peasants, something as simple as meat bought and served on special occasions can be symbolic of care and affection, e.g., birthdays or marriages, or of appreciation of some special act, e.g., thanking neighbors who have helped in a harvest or donors who have helped rebuild after a disaster.[37]

Therefore, many of those Marx dismissed as "mere agents"[38] of circulation turn out to be workers employed in changing the use-value of commodities, e.g., in market research to discover (or invent) such symbolic use-values, in advertising to design strategies to convince potential buyers that a given commodity can provide those use-values, still others to materially create the resulting advertising (mostly print in the nineteenth century) and, finally, some are employed in face-to-face encounters with potential buyers to convince them of the reality of the touted use-values. To sell machines to capitalists or food to workers requires the buyers be convinced that commodities do what

35 *Grundrisse*, p. 635, or MECW, *Vol. 29*, p. 24.

36 In Jane Austen's most famous novel *Pride and Prejudice* (1813), although trying to persuade Lizzy not to accept Darcy's proposal of marriage, her father concedes that if she does, because he is rich she "may have more fine clothes and fine carriages than [her sister] Jane. But will they make you happy?"

37 Still true. While visiting a poor peasant village in Guerrero, Mexico, after the earthquake of 1985, with Mexican activist Gustavo Esteva and representatives of the Swiss Red Cross, I saw just such a gesture: the pit-cooking of an entire goat to show appreciation of money donated by that agency to help locals rebuild their heavily damaged homes. These were peasants who usually subsisted on beans and corn tortillas, for whom eating meat was a rarity, a luxury reserved for special occasions.

38 *Capital, Vol. 2*, pp. 208–209, or MECW, *Vol. 36*, pp. 134–135.

their sellers claim they do – which is often not the case.[39] All these are part of the work of "sales" and to the degree such workers effectively change (or add to) the use-values of commodities, their work falls within the sphere of production and, like transportation, "is distinguished by its appearance as the continuation of a production process *within* the circulation process and *for* the circulation process."

Third, accumulation, the expanded reproduction of capitalist social relations, via investment, has been a process involving the annexation of ever greater swaths of humanity, first through colonialism and then through neo-colonialism (what we now call globalization). This historical drama requires more of an explanation than being a mere by-product of the individual capitalists' lust for self-enrichment and their competition with one another to see who can get the bigger share of the pie. The origins of this expansion that interest me most are in the dynamics of class struggle.

Growth, it turns out, has often been the only way capitalists have been able to maintain control over those already working for them. Why? As Marx, Engels and several subsequent theorists of imperialism have pointed out, *successful struggle for more income* by already waged workers has driven capital to offset the resulting increase in costs by annexing cheaper sources of labor-power and raw materials. A parallel dynamic has resulted from workers' *successful struggles against work*. Both successes, by reducing absolute surplus value have forced capitalists to invest in means of production that raise productivity to gain a compensatory increase in relative surplus value. But, raising productivity to lower per unit costs of production tends to drive expansion of production because increased productivity makes greater production possible and greater production requires expanded markets. In all these cases, it's the successful self-organization of workers in their struggles, based on the existing concrete division of labor, which drives new investment and growth. Within this class

39 Marx and Engels both repeatedly cited and blasted poor quality consumer goods sold to workers. From Marx's analysis of adulterated bread in Chapter 10 of Volume 1 of *Capital* to today's worries about the proliferation of toxics and plastics in our food supplies, the cost cutting, profit maximizing practices of capitalists have continued despite the harm to consumers. Consumer awareness of those costs, thanks to the struggles of consumerists and environmentalists to reveal them, has forced capitalists to employ workers to convince consumers of the wholesomeness (use-value) of their commodities. The same has been true vis-à-vis the selling of means of production. There is a funny scene in Chaplin's film *Modern Times* of one capitalist trying to convince another that his worker-feeding machine can be used to keep workers on the assembly line during lunch time. It repeatedly fails and is rejected by the potential buyer. These days the media of advertising differ markedly for *C*(*MS*) and *C*(*MP*), with the former dominant in television and popular newspapers and magazines and the latter largely restricted to trade publications.

dynamic, competition among capitalists merely decides which are more successful in adapting and which are less so. To successfully develop higher productivity technologies requires the harnessing of workers' imagination and creativity to come up with newer, more productive machines or other technologies.[40] Moreover, the adoption of more productive technologies requires control over workers who must adapt to the new rhythms of work – which are often organized to undercut their existing modes of self-organization.

4 Omnipresent Conflict; Omnipresent Struggle

Under these circumstances, reproduction on an expanded scale is no smooth, simple matter, and much of Marx and Engels' writing consists of analyzing how each of these steps involves an often-arduous struggle between the classes. The enclosures that have forced peasants off their land and stolen or destroyed artisans' tools, forcing both into the labor market, have often been met with intense resistance. Faced with that resistance, capital has been willing to impose its new order through violence and bloodshed. But even where the separation has been made and capital has monopolized the means of production, the struggle has continued. The enforcement of "bloody legislation" has been required to force many of the dispossessed to actually enter the labor market – as opposed to opting for lives as vagabonds, highway robbers or revolutionaries. Branding irons, whips, chains and guns have been required to impose work, both slave and waged. Thus, the "rosy dawn" of capitalism.

> If money, according to Augier, "comes into the world with a congenital blood-stain on one cheek," capital comes dripping from head to toe, from every pore, with blood and dirt.[41]

Accumulation involves capitalists' efforts not only to establish their kind of society but to reproduce it on an expanded scale. And what they are trying to reproduce is the exploitative relationship between classes.

---

40 See, H. Cleaver, "Competition? Or Cooperation?" *Common Sense* 9 (April 1990): 20–22. Although the bulk of Marx's analysis focuses on the development of machines and manufacturing technology, he also recognizes parallel productivity-raising developments in other realms of production, such as agriculture, transportation and communication.

41 *Capital, Vol. 1*, pp. 925–926, or *MECW, Vol. 35*, p. 748.

> Capitalist production, therefore, seen as a total, connected process, i.e., a process of reproduction, produces not only commodities, not only surplus value, but it also produces and reproduces the capital-relation itself; on the one hand the capitalist, on the other the wage laborer.[42]

In the labor market, capital and labor contend, over the terms of sale – how much money for how much work, under what conditions, and so on.[43] The exchange concluded, the struggle continues during work itself – between the efforts of capitalists to obtain the maximum amount of work – whether manual or intellectual – from their workers and the latter's struggle to give up as little of their life energy as possible. The same goes for slaves; they also struggle against the work imposed on them. Finally, not even the disposition of the final product, *C' – M'*, necessarily runs smoothly. Rather, there is a wide variety of struggles ranging from workers' direct appropriation of the goods they, or other workers, have produced, to struggles and wars over international trade – over what can be sold, where and at what price. In this way, each moment of the circuit, whether in the sphere of production (work) or in the sphere of exchange (labor and final goods markets), is not only a moment of the class relation but also carries the fundamental character of that relation: antagonistic conflict. Thus, each of the variables: *LP, M, C, MP, P* are elements, or moments, of the class relation of antagonistic struggle. Class struggle for Marx and Engels was not something outside the labor-capital exchange and work relations (neither a cause nor a consequence of it). *Class struggle is rather the very subject of* Capital *itself*. The self-reproduction or accumulation of society as a set of class relations involves the reproduction and accumulation of *all* these antagonistic elements of that relation, including the crises that result.

42 *Capital, Vol. 1*, p. 724, or *MECW, Vol. 35*, p. 577.

43 The "microeconomics" analysis of the "labor market," is usually framed with a function indicating the supply of labor – how much work workers are willing to do at various wages – and another function indicating the demand for labor – how much labor capitalists are willing to hire at various wages – the interaction of which determine actual wages and the level of employment. Excluded from this simplified vision are the complex issues actually negotiated between workers and employers, e.g., such as working conditions, collective bargaining, etc. Excluded too is any recognition of the difference between labor-power hired and actual work performed – a central issue for Marx but only belatedly (mid-twentieth century) recognized by economists in their analysis of "efficiency wages."

5 Conditions of Reproduction

Of the many conditions of this reproduction that Marx analyzed, beyond the question of control over its labor force, one of the most discussed has been the criteria of "proportionality." To *simply reproduce* the existing situation, the means of production, *MP*, and means of subsistence, *MS*, must be produced in the proportions required to replace depleted means of production *and* the means of subsistence consumed by workers, whether they be waged or slave. While production *P* brings together *LP* and *MP*, this always occurs in a certain proportionate relation determined by the technology employed.[44] *Labor intensive* production methods, using a lot of labor but few tools, will require greater replacement of the means of subsistence than of means of production. *Capital intensive* production methods where few workers are employed will require the reverse. Therefore, production must not be lopsided or disproportionate in such a way that either too little or too much *MP* or *MS* are produced.[45] Marx formulated this by dividing production into two basic departments: one including all production of *MP*, and the other including all production of the means of subsistence *MS*.[46]

---

44 Neoclassical economics represents rough approximations of technology with production functions of the sort Q = f(K, L), where Q = total output, K = "capital," understood as means of production and L = the labor expended by workers on the job (NOT labor-power). Such mathematical functions generally assume the factors of production, K & L, are infinitely divisible and can be combined, unproblematically, in all possible combinations defined by the functions. They are obviously gross simplifications of real technical relations. Although work can be performed in infinitely varying amounts, many means of production, e.g., machinery, factories, vehicles for transportation, are obviously "lumpy" and NOT smoothly divisible. These functions, however, serve the objectives of economists by providing tools to derive general principles capitalists can follow in order to maximize profits, respond to changes in the relative prices of labor and capital, etc. A theory quite different from Marx's but designed for a different purpose.

45 Economists generally assume that that failures in this regard will be easily corrected by capitalist adjustments in production. Excess production will be reduced in reaction to either a fall in price or a buildup of excess inventories. Inadequate production will be increased in reaction to rising prices or depleted inventories. The resistance to recognizing how such failures can occur on a very large scale and constitute crises goes back to David Ricardo and Jean-Baptiste Say, a failure denounced by Malthus at the time and later not only by Marx and Engels but also by John Maynard Keynes. The latter's focus on correction in response to changes in inventory did not prevent him from seeing, as Marx and Engels had, how aggregate demand could not only fall so low as to cause a crisis but how it could also persist, threatening extended stagnation.

46 *Capital, Vol. 2*, Part Three, Chapter 20, or *MECW, Vol. 36*, Part III, Chapter XX. This representation assumes that the labor-power hired in both departments, LP_1 and LP_2, are actually expended in utilizing MP_1 and MP_2 in the production of MP^* and MS^*.

$$\text{Department I: } LP_1 + MP_1 \textit{ produces } MP^*$$
$$\text{Department II: } LP_2 + MP_2 \textit{ produces } MS^*$$

In these circumstances, the necessary conditions of proportionality are that the total *MP* produced, MP^*, must be sufficient to replace the *MP* used up in each department, while the total *MS* produced, MS^*, must be enough to feed, clothe, house, etc., workers and thus support the reproduction of the labor-power in each department:

$$MP^* = MP_1 + MP_2$$
$$MS^* = LP_1 + LP_2$$

If this is achieved, then the system will have produced the necessary means of reproducing the class relation.

Once again, these relations are not simple technical ones but are an intrinsic part of the struggle between the classes. Clearly workers are interested in the output of *MS* meeting their needs, whereas capitalists' major concern is having enough *MP* in order to keep control of the workers engaged in slave, waged or salaried employment – hence there is a class conflict over the allocation of resources between departments. The workers want to see Department I production geared to support Department II production, while capital must try to restrict the availability of wealth to workers (Department II production) to maintain control and force workers to work. If Department II production was such as to supply workers with vast quantities of means of subsistence their need to sell their labor-power to capital would be much lessened, and scarcity no longer a contrived and universal coercive force.[47]

47 Capital's economists assume "scarcity" as a universal human condition. Indeed, they often define economics as the study of the allocation of scarce resources among competing ends. What Marx shows us, however, is how capitalists have created and maintain scarcity as a coercive force that gives them control over people's lives. For an historical analysis of how this has been done over time see, Fredrik Jonsson and Carl Wennerlind, *Scarcity: A History from the Origins of Capitalism to the Climate Crisis* (Cambridge: Harvard University Press, 2023).

Where state capitalists have engaged in active aggregate planning of investment, as in the Soviet Union or China, the preference for investment in Department I over Department II has been obvious in the drive to "industrialize," to catch up to "Western" capitalist economies. The result, eventually, was rebellion on the part of workers against the failure to enhance production meeting their needs. That rebellion successfully forced a change in the planned allocation of investment among departments. Some of this history is analyzed with respect to food production in H. Cleaver, "Food, Famine and International Crisis," *Zerowork* #2, 1977, pp. 7–69. A looser form of such planning can be found in so-called

But accumulation is more than simple reproduction – it is expansion. Accumulation is *expanded reproduction* of the social relations of society and involves the *growth* of its components. As in the case of simple reproduction, certain conditions must be met; in this case, overall expansion requires *increases* in production in each of the Departments. Investment must buy appropriate amounts of *new MP* and hire appropriate numbers of *new* workers, *LP*, so that their expansion in each Department proceeds in proportions which allow continued expanded reproduction.

In simple reproduction, investment recreates the *same* amount of *MP* and *MS*. In expanded reproduction investment buys *more MP* and mobilizes *more LP*, so *MP* and *MS* must be expanded to *MP** and *MS** to meet the needs of each Department.[48]

$$\text{Department I: } MP^* = MP_1 + MP_2 + new\ MP_1 + new\ MP_2$$
$$\text{Department II: } MS^* = LP_1 + LP_2 + new\ LP_1 + new\ LP_2$$

A final point: While Marx spends a great deal of time analyzing and illustrating the production of *MP* and *MS*, he does not forget that while the production of *MP* involves the consumption of other *MP*, e.g., raw materials and depreciating fixed assets, the *production* of *MS* and its *consumption* by workers are two quite different moments of accumulation. Although, as he points out, a certain amount of the work of reproducing labor-power occurs on-the-job, most of it takes place elsewhere, during whatever time workers and their families have free of direct work for capital. After all, while *M – LP* for capital is a prelude to putting *LP* to work in *…P…*, *LP – M* for waged and salaried workers is a prelude to *M – C*(*MS*) and the subsequent consumption of *MS*. In the case of slavery, enough *MS* must also be available, either from the slaves' own efforts or through purchase by their owners. Therefore, he points out, "for a full elucidation of the law of accumulation, [the worker's] condition outside the workshop must also be looked at, his condition as to food and accommodation."[49] I already noted in Chapter 2 how Engels had reported, in part from personal observation, on these matters in *The Condition of the Working Class in England*

"supply-side" economic policies, which have been designed to shift resources in the opposite direction, from consumption of *MS* to investment in *MP*. See, H. Cleaver, "Supply Side Economics: The New Phase of Capitalist Strategy in the Crisis," in French in *Babylone*, no. 0 (Hiver 1981–1982): 79-123, https://la.utexas.edu/users/hcleaver/304L/304Lsupplyside.html.

48 *Capital, Vol. 2*, Part 3, Chapter 21, or *MECW*, *Vol. 36*, Part III, Chapter XXI. This is assuming increased *MP* does not result is such a displacement of *LP* as to reduce the amount of *MS* required.

49 *Capital, Vol. 1*, p. 807, or *MECW*, *Vol. 35*, p. 647.

(1845) and later in his update "England in 1845 and in 1885." Marx's "looking" at those conditions appears to have taken place primarily through examination of the reports of public health inspectors, a method paralleling his manner of looking inside the sphere of production through the reports of factory inspectors. He was well aware of the limitations of his research into workers' consumption and even apologized for it: "The limits of this book [*Capital*] compel us to concern ourselves chiefly with the worst paid part of the industrial proletariat and the agricultural labourers ..."[50] Nevertheless, as shown below in Chapters 4 and 5, what research he did perform contributed to his analysis not only of accumulation but also of the possibilities and predispositions to crisis.

6 Accumulation in Terms of "Value"

Let us now turn from sketching the material circuits capitalists must successfully manage to achieve accumulation, to Marx's analysis of those circuits and all their elements in terms of labor/value. Whereas capitalists measure the *value* of all the material elements of the circuits in terms of money, Marx follows Adam Smith and David Ricardo in providing a theory of the value of

50 Ibid. Much has been made in recent years of these limitations. Even in his "Workers' Inquiry," his 1880 list of 100 questions designed to reveal, from the workers themselves, "an *exact* and *definite* knowledge of the conditions in which the working class . . . works and begins to move." very few of the questions address, even indirectly, conditions of life outside of waged labor. *MECW*, *Vol. 24*, pp. 328–334. One multipart question, #69, asks about the prices of the various commodities, *C*(*MS*), workers and their families consume, but not about the work of consumption itself. He doesn't even replicate the kinds of questions asked by the British health inspectors whose reports he references in *Capital*. But since Mario Tronti's analysis reminding us how Marx's theory of accumulation includes the sphere of the reproduction of labor-power and since the main theorists of the Wages for Housework movement elaborated an analysis of the centrality to accumulation of the work of reproducing labor-power off-the-job, e.g., in the home through housework, Marx's limited research and exposition of his findings have been amplified by an ever growing body of writing not only about that work but also about the struggle against it and the implications for class struggle more generally. See Mario Tronti, *Operai e Capitale* (Turin: Einaudi, 1966, 1971), now available as *Workers and Capital* (London: Verso, 2019), and Mariarosa Dalla Costa, "Women and the Subversion of the Community" (1971), in Mariarosa Dalla Costa and Camille Barbagallo, eds., *Women and the Subversion of the Community: A Mariarosa Dalla Costa Reader* (Brooklyn: PM Press, 2019). This work provoked first a widespread debate about "domestic labor" and its political implications and, more recently, a burgeoning derivative literature on "social reproduction theory" – that all too often ignores the earlier work that spawned it. Also See, Alisa Del Re, "Workers' Inquiry and Reproductive Labor" in *Viewpoint Magazine*, 3, (September 25, 2013) and the rest of the issue.

money itself – and all the other elements – in terms of labor. But what does that mean? For Smith and Ricardo, it means that human labor creates wealth, first material wealth in the form of commodities and then, through sale, monetary wealth. In the Hegel-Marx tradition, labor input in production gives commodities their value, in the sense of their meaning, simply by being products of human action. In that tradition, use-values (and hence commodities) are the objectivization of human activity and because that activity has value – in the sense of being judged valuable by us humans – so too do its results. This view, clearly a-historical and applicable to all human history, is derived from the view that labor is the essence of humanity as a species. We are understood as *homo faber* – "'man' who makes," a quality which both Hegel and Marx thought differentiated us from other animals. Use-values, including those sold as commodities, embody this human essence and as such are valuable.

This view is also associated with the belief that the labor incorporated in individual commodities underlies and ultimately determines their *monetary* value and thus their *prices*. But, as Marx readily admits – even though he usually assumes it away – prices rarely reflect labor value because of the endless fluctuations in supply and demand, which are caused by all sorts of things, many of which have nothing to do with any variation in the labor input.

By the late nineteenth century, economists – working for capitalists for whom the prices of the commodities they buy and sell are all important because they determine their monetary profit – abandoned this privileging of labor and treated labor as simply one "factor of production" among others. The only value left was either the "utility" – the usefulness of commodities to those who buy them – or their monetary value, their price. Because usefulness varies from individual to individual, they were able to do away with any common notion of "utility" and replace it with the "preferences" of individuals as the basis for "price theory" or "microeconomics," focused on the determinants of supply and demand in the formation of prices. Their dismissal of any special role for labor in determining monetary value has led to the long-standing debate with and among Marxists over the so-called "transformation problem" of whether it is possible to demonstrate some convincing connection between the array of labor values and the array of prices.[51]

---

51 Participation in this debate requires acceptance of economists' preoccupation with price formation and a belief that Marx's theory, as an alternative political economy, should be able to explain the array of relative prices as effectively as mainstream economics. If, in Kuhn's language, both approaches shared the same foundational paradigm, or if the acceptance of a new paradigm depends on its ability to answer all the same questions posed by the previous one, then this demand would be reasonable. But, I argue on the contrary that: first, Marx's labor theory of value has quite different purposes, namely

While accepting the view that the things people make and the services they provide are objectifications of human activity, I don't see how that automatically makes them "valuable," even to humans. After all, humans (especially within capitalism) create all kinds of things which are detrimental to humans as well as to the rest of nature. I see the "value" in Marx's labor theory of value not as an a-historical judgement on what makes humans human and therefore on the worthiness of their activity and its results, but as an historically specific *theory of the role of labor/work within* capitalism, *or, of the social/political value of labor/work to* capital(ists). Unlike economists, I argue that Marx judged value to lie not *just* in labor's contribution to the capitalist production of commodities but in its even more essential socio-political function as capitalists' primary mode of *social control*. Therefore, the *substance* of the value of labor to capital is just this quality of providing its most fundamental means of organizing and controlling society.[52]

6.1 *The* Substance *of Value*

Marx uses the term "abstract labor" to characterize the *substance* of value because it expresses how the kind of useful labor being imposed is – for capitalists – entirely secondary to the mere fact of controlling people by putting them to work. As long as the work it imposes produces a use-value which can be sold and upon which a profit can be realized, both the use-value of the commodity and the usefulness of the labor which produces it are secondary to the control established.

Essential to maintaining that control are capitalists' abilities to put workers to work first in this job and then in that job, depending on which kind of work produces the most profitable commodities. This amounts to achieving a malleability of labor – among jobs producing a single commodity or among jobs producing different commodities. Being able to use all sorts of imposed work to organize society requires being able to manage the allocation of work, being able to shift workers from one kind of production to another.

> *Indifference* towards specific labors corresponds to a form of society in which individuals can with ease transfer from one labor to another. and

---

revealing the nature of the antagonistic social relations of capitalism, and second, that when he addressed fluctuations in monetary prices he did so using the concepts of supply and demand available at the time.

52 This is the contention laid out in my *Reading* Capital *Politically* (1979), amplified in *Rupturing the Dialectic: The Struggle against Work, Money and Financialization* (Oakland: AK Press, 2017) and detailed in Harry Cleaver, *33 Lessons on Capital: Reading Marx Politically* (London: Pluto, 2019).

> where the specific kind of labor is a matter of *chance*, hence of indifference. Not only the category, labour, but labour in reality has here become the means of creating wealth in general, and has ceased to be organically linked with particular individuals in any specific form.[53] (my emphasis)

The "indifference," of course, is that of the capitalist, not of the workers who have no control over the tasks they are set, or the tools they are given, or the methods they are told to employ, and thus of the degree of exploitation and alienation to which they are subjected. The "chance" is the outcome of the vagaries of the market and thus of profitability.

> labor is not this or another labor, but *labor pure and simple*, abstract labor; absolutely indifferent to its particular *specificity*, but capable of all specificities ... capital as such is indifferent to every particularity of its substance, and exists not only as the totality of the same but also as the abstraction from all its particularities, the labour which confronts it likewise subjectively has the same totality and abstraction in itself.[54]

An *imposed* abstraction and therefore alienating in all the ways Marx laid out in the *Manuscripts of 1844*, and therefore hostile!

To achieve this, capital must keep workers divided. In other words, all specific labors turn out to be but moments in the process of controlling the working population – and thus the population as a whole, the unwaged as well as the waged or salaried. By imposing both a complicated division of labor and repeatedly re-dividing it, capital manages the vast system of "cooperation" that has sustained society in ways that pit workers against each other insuring its control over them all.[55]

6.2 *The* Measure *of Value*

Under these circumstances the *measure* of the value of labor, or work, is simply the time imposed, more precisely, the "socially necessary" or average labor time imposed. The value of a commodity to capital is the average amount of time labor that can be imposed in its production. If productivity rises in the production of a commodity so that it takes less time to produce each unit,

---

53 *Grundrisse*, p. 104, or MECW, *Vol. 28*, p. 41.

54 *Grundrisse*, p. 296, or MECW, *Vol. 28*, p. 223.

55 And, to the degree that it is under its control, unruptured by workers' resistance, it pretends to be the source of the productive power of cooperation – as Marx argues in Chapter 13 of Volume 1 of *Capital*.

then the value of that commodity falls because producing it provides less of an opportunity for putting people to work.[56]

Finally, as illustrated in the circuit of capital above, work is organized by capital to produce commodities, *C'*, i.e., *MS*, *MP*, and even *C*(*LP*) and thus, when sold, takes the commodity-form of exchange-value.[57] By abstracting from the concrete characteristics of the different kinds of work that produce different kinds of commodities, Marx can theoretically *measure* each of the variables in terms of social necessary labor time (the measure of value). This makes possible *quantitative* comparisons, such as total sales, *M'* compared with initial investment, *M*. If $M' > M$, a surplus value is achieved in the form of money profits, which permit increased investment and growth in the entire circuit.

When money is, itself, a commodity, e.g., gold or silver, its value is determined by the socially necessary labor time required to produce it. When it is merely symbolic, e.g., paper or digital money, the value of each unit is

56 Recognition of this consequence caused much worry among capitalists and their economists in three relatively recent situations. First, during the rapid increase in labor-displacing automation in manufacturing in the 1950s and 1960s, they worried about where the jobs would come from to keep most people employed. Second, in the post-colonial era, continued expropriation of peasants and their forced exodus into cities led economists to worry about whether imported technologies were "appropriate" to absorbing the population no longer employed in agriculture. Capital-intensive technologies were critiqued as inappropriate, whereas labor-intensive ones were deemed more appropriate for solving this need to keep the displaced population busy and under control. Third, the onset of the computer revolution was feared to initiate such a rapid rise in automation as to, once again, create worry about where jobs might be found. The onset of global high unemployment in the early 1980s led critics of capitalism to suggestions that if capital couldn't provide income thru jobs, income should no longer depend on jobs. This touched off demands for guaranteed minimum income for all citizens.

In the first case, the problem was solved by the rise of the service sector, largely labor-intensive. In the second case, the problem was "solved" only partly by economists but mostly by the rural-urban migrants themselves, as they invented myriad ways of staying alive in the so-called "informal sector." Grassroots activist and advisor to the Zapatistas, Gustavo Esteva (1936–2022) pointed out, long ago, that the so-called "marginals" in the Global South actually constitute a "social majority." See his "Los 'Tradifas' O el Fin de la Marginación," *El Trimestre Economico*, Vol. L(2), Núm. 198 (Abril-Junio de 1983): 733–769. The third case – accentuated by the rapid development of artificial intelligence – is still playing out amidst neoliberal attacks on good jobs and all forms of income not based on work.

57 In the original version of this article this line read "... work is organized by capital into the production of commodities, either *LP* or *C* ..." Although true, only the waged work that produces *C*(*MS*) is accounted for in Marx's circuit of capital. Although recognized elsewhere, as I have indicated, none of the *unwaged* work of producing *LP*, e.g., housework or schoolwork, is included in his circuits.

determined by the value of commodities it circulates. In this second case, an aliquot portion of money *represents* a given amount of value.

6.3 *The* Form *of Value*

The *substance* of value, work abstracted from its particularities, can only be extracted after labor-power is obtained and put to work, either purchased in the labor market (most cases) or in the form of slaves. In turn, the products of that imposed labor can only contribute to accumulation by being sold in commodity markets for money. With markets, or exchange, being essential to the realization of the substance of value, the harnessing of potential labor-power as actual labor, etc., Marx calls the *form* of value, exchange-value. On the simplifying assumption, which Marx almost always uses, that exchange is equal, value for value, we can see that in investment the total value represented by *M* is converted into an equal value of *LP* + *MP* in some proportion, depending on the value per unit of *LP* and of *MP* and the technology used in *P*, which determines the "technical composition" of capital, which Marx expresses as *MP*/*LP*. Because the substance of value is work (abstract labor), the aim of capital, if it is to expand, is to obtain more work (value), and this is exactly what it seeks when extracting living labor from the purchased *LP* in the production process. The object is to impose enough additional work so that the labor incorporated in the product *C'* has a greater value than the original value *M* and the purchased commodities *C*(*LP* + *MP*). In order to be able to continue putting people to work, this commodity *C'* (with expanded value) must then be sold and converted into money (*M'*), the universal equivalent, or most general form of value, which can then be expended on new *LP* and *MP* and so forth.

Marx calls the value (*M*) invested in labor-power (*LP*) "variable capital," or "*v*," and that invested in the means of production, *MP*, "constant capital," or "*c*". So, in value terms, capitalist success in expanding value (getting more work) requires investing *M* in $c + v$ and then managing production, …*P*…, such that the newly employed labor-power utilizes the constant capital productively, i.e., in such a way that the labor that previously created the constant capital effectively contributes to the value of the final product (*C'*). It must also cover its own cost (*v*). Then, if the capitalists succeed in getting workers to do more work than required for these two purposes, the extra work constitutes *surplus* labor and thus *surplus* value, or "*s*".

In short, to survive and reproduce on an expanded scale, the value of the original investment, $c + v$, must be expanded such that the value of the new *C'* is $c + v + s$. The surplus labor imposed, or surplus value, *s*, is thus one *measure of success* as well as the means of future expansion.[58] This surplus value, when it takes the money form through *C' – M'* can be used to purchase new *LP* and *MP*. We can re-represent this whole sequence as follows, beginning in time period t_1:

$$\begin{array}{ll} & LP \\ & / \\ M — C & \qquad\qquad \text{(the } M \text{ expended on } C(LP + MP) = c + v) \\ & \backslash \\ & MP \end{array}$$

$$\ldots P \ldots C' \text{ (in production workers preserve } c \text{ and add } v + s, \text{ so, } C' = c + v + s)$$

In the next period (t_2), the *s* is reinvested in new *c* and new *v*, so the increased amounts of *MP* and *LP* produce *s* + *s'*.

at t_1 $C' = c + v + s$
and at t_2 $C' = c + v + \text{new } c + \text{new } v + s + s'$.

Integral to this process is the expenditure by workers of the value of their wages, *v*, on the means of subsistence/consumption portrayed in the second half Marx's "little circuit," i.e., *M* (wages) – *C*(*MS*) and, by implication, the actual consumption of the workers which reproduces their labor-power, *LP*. That consumption, whether of waged workers or slaves, also often provides them with the ability to struggle against their exploitation by capitalists and to experiment with alternative, non-capitalist activities.

The result of continual successful reinvestment is a growth in each of the variables – all of which are elements of the class relation.[59] Socially speaking,

---

58 Besides the surplus value, *s*, itself, Marx offers two other "measures of success," namely the "rate of profit," *s*/(*c*+*v*), and the "rate of exploitation," *s*/*v*, with the former expressing capitalists' calculation (surplus/investment) and the latter the ratio of surplus labor extracted to the labor required for workers' consumption, i.e., the degree to which they have been forced to work beyond meeting their own needs.

59 "Growth in each of the variables" *unless* new machines, introduced to increase productivity, displace so many workers (raising MP/LP) that despite new investment expanding production fewer workers are employed. Some displacement has always been a part of capital's strategy of relative surplus value, one which has contributed to the generation of a "reserve army" of the unemployed – useful in holding down wage growth and providing labor-power for new investments.

accumulation is the accumulation of the working class and capital, and includes the accumulation of money, of commodities and of the means of production. At each stage in this process, each element and relation is an object of struggle, and *because everything is growing, accumulation is also class struggle on an ever larger scale.* As capital expands, bringing more and more of the world's population under its control and converting more and more of Nature into mere resources for commodity production, the class confrontation becomes global and every element/moment is a site of struggle.

Now if these are the basic processes of accumulation, and if this accumulation reaches world dimensions, the further development of the theory of accumulation is a detailed study of the way in which these various moments of expanded reproduction are organized and of how that reproduction is often ruptured. This latter is the theory of crisis. It includes (1) the repeated collapse and recovery that we know as cycles, (2) the deeper historical crises that have characterized major turning points in the organization of capitalist reproduction, and, if it can be accomplished, (3) the ultimate crisis through which the system is abolished.[60]

60 Although some Marxists and many critics of Marx have read a teleological necessity into his theory of crisis indicating the inevitability of a final crisis of capitalism, others of us see no such necessity but rather a theory designed to facilitate workers' struggles to bring on such a crisis and the revolutionary transcendence of capitalism.

CHAPTER 4

The Possibilities of Crisis

The possibilities of crisis mean possible interruptions in the cycle of expanded reproduction. With the cycle or circuit as a whole made up of several different processes, often separate in time and place, there is the possibility of failure in each process, which must be successfully realized and in proper relation to the others, for the whole circuit to be completed. This contingency reveals that just as there are possibilities of crisis within capitalist efforts at expanded reproduction, so too is the expanded reproduction of capital itself *merely a possibility,* by no means guaranteed! Indeed, as they proceed, trying to complete each stage of their circuits – while trying to manage all the other institutions of society that they have reshaped for their own purposes – they are repeatedly confronted with the very real possibility of failure at each point. So, what some see as an almost unstoppable juggernaut turns out to be a rather fragile affair, tenuously held together and needing to be repeatedly patched up. Capitalists, of course, have always known this, which is one reason why they have frequently argued that they deserve profits for having hazarded their money in risky investments!

Returning to the metaphor of the circulation of blood, which – through Quesnay – inspired Marx's theory of circuits, the counterpart to a crisis in capitalist reproduction would be some rupture in the flow of blood, e.g., a blood clot that blocks the flow, or a wound out of which the blood flows instead of through the body. Failures in the various moments of capitalist reproduction, like blood clots or wounds, can be small or large, cause temporary problems or threaten the life of the system. This suggests that examination of the possibilities of crises must involve not only their identification but also some evaluation as to the degree of risk that they pose to accumulation as a whole. Traditionally, focused as they have been on their hopes for the death of capitalism, many Marxists have looked only at those possibilities they have felt might result in the collapse of the system. However, as I show below, such major crises do not arise out of the blue but tend to be the product of an accumulation of smaller, less noticeable crises. Therefore, in what follows I pay attention to all the possibilities that Marx & Engels identified, both large and small.

1 Markets & Crisis

In his exposition of his theory of crisis, before turning to the possibilities of crisis in the circuits of *capital*, Marx first points out the potential for crisis in the character of *markets*. It exists because in commodity exchange, $C - M - C$, the two acts of sale, $C - M$, and purchase, $M - C$, are separate. Here, as in his analysis of accumulation, he measures these variables by labor value and to simplify things he assumes equality in exchange. He writes of this in the *Grundrisse*, then in his *Contribution to the Critique of Political Economy* (1859), again in the section of the "Manuscript of 1861–63" that became *Theories of Surplus Value* (TSV) and finally in *Capital, Vol. 1* (1867).

In the *Grundrisse*, he points out how crisis lurks in the very nature of commodities and the contingency of $C - M$.

> The simple fact that the commodity exists doubly, in one aspect as a specific product ... and in the other aspect as manifest exchange value (money) ... this double, differentiated existence must develop into a difference, and the difference into antithesis and contradiction ... this contradiction ... contains the possibility that these two separated forms in which the commodity exists are not convertible into one another ... the exchangeability of the commodity for money ... may or may not be present.[1]

Then:

> Just as the exchange value of a commodity leads a double existence ... so does the act of exchange split into two mutually independent acts ... purchase and sale. Since these have now achieved spatially and temporally separate and mutually indifferent forms of existence, their immediate identity ceases. They may correspond or not ... consonance may be reached only by passing through the most extreme dissonance.[2]

A little further on, against political economists such as Jean-Baptiste Say who argued "supply creates its own demand," i.e., every sale results in a purchase, he counters,

> There are contradictions which are unpleasant for the apologists of bourgeois common sense, and must hence be covered up. In so far as purchase and sale ... are indifferent to each other and separated in time and space,

1 *Grundrisse*, p. 147, or MECW, *Vol. 28*, pp. 84–85.

2 Ibid., p. 148, or MECW, *Vol. 28*, pp. 85–86.

> they by no means need to coincide ... But in so far as they are both essential moments of the whole, there must come a moment when the independent form is violently broken and when the inner unity is established externally through a violent explosion ... in the splitting of exchange into two acts, there lies the germ of crises, or at least their possibility"[3]

In the *Contribution to the Critique*, he writes,

> The division of exchange into purchase and sale ... contains the general possibility of commercial crises, because the contradiction of commodity and money is the abstract and general form of all contradictions inherent in the bourgeois mode of labour.[4]

This is true regarding both cash money, which may or may not be used to purchase directly, and with credit money. Whether credit money serving as a means of payment will be forthcoming after commodities have already been delivered is always an open question.

> The difference between means of purchase and means of payment becomes very conspicuous and unpleasantly so, at times of commercial crises.[5]

> Where chains of payments ... have been developed, any upheaval that forcibly interrupts the flow of payments and upsets the mechanism for balancing them against one another suddenly turns money from the nebulous chimerical form it assumed as measure of value into hard cash or means of payment ... The *summum bonum*, the sole form of wealth for which people clamour at such times, is money, hard cash ...[6]

In the "Manuscript of 1861–63", he writes, "The possibility of crisis lies solely in the separation of sale from purchase."[7] And then:

> The general, abstract possibility of crisis denotes no more than the *most abstract form* of crisis, without content, without a compelling motivating factor [predisposition] ... The most abstract form of crisis (and therefore

3 Ibid., p. 198, or *MECW*, *Vol. 28*, p. 133.

4 *MECW*, *Vol. 29*, p. 332.

5 *IBID.*, p. 374.

6 Ibid., p. 378.

7 *MECW*, *Vol. 32*, p. 138.

> the formal possibility of crisis) is thus the metamorphosis of the commodity itself."[8]

In *Capital*, Chapter 3, he once again examines how, despite their independence, the "unity" of purchase and sale, "violently makes itself felt by producing – a crisis." However: "These forms [of motion of this immanent contradiction] therefore imply the possibility of crisis, though no more than the possibility."[9]

He also reformulates his thesis in the *Contribution* about the possibility of crisis with *credit money*: "There is," he writes, "a contradiction immanent in the function of money as means of payment" between money as account or measure of value and money as means of payment. "When actual payments have to be made, money [serves] "as the individual incarnation of social labour, the independent presence of exchange value, the universal commodity."[10] Moreover,

> This contradiction bursts forth in that aspect of an industrial and commercial crisis which is known as a monetary crisis. Such a crisis occurs only where the ongoing chain of payments has been fully developed, along with an artificial system for settling them. Whenever there is a general disturbance of the mechanism, no matter what its cause, money suddenly and immediately changes over from its merely nominal shape, money of account, into hard cash.[11]

Assuming money, once obtained, could be easily spent ($M - C$), the main problem, he argues, lies in $C - M$. "Crisis results from the impossibility to sell."[12] Why might that occur? He mentions two reasons. First, a commodity may no longer find buyers, "Today, the product satisfies a social need. Tomorrow it may perhaps be expelled partly or completely from its place by a similar product."[13] Second, the person who has effected a sale and acquired money is not

---

8 Ibid., p. 140.

9 *Capital, Vol. 1*, p. 209, or *MECW*, *Vol. 35*, p. 124.

10 Capital, *Vol. 1*, p. 235, or *MECW*, *Vol. 35*, p. 148.

11 Ibid., p. 236, or *MECW*, *Vol. 35*, pp. 148–149. Although focused, at this point in the text, on commercial crises, which can predate capitalism, he throws in "industrial crises," which for him are only characteristic of capitalism. He's getting a little ahead of the logical order of his exposition.

12 *MECW*, *Vol. 32*, p. 139.

13 *Capital, Vol. 1*, p. 201, or *MECW*, *Vol. 35*, p. 116. This is the death knell of what economists and business later called the "life cycle" of a commodity. See, Anne Sraders, "What is the Product Life Cycle? Stages and Examples," *The Street*, March 4, 2019.

compelled to buy again at once. "The outcome ... [of $C - M$] may to begin with involve a pause ... The golden chrysalis state [M] forms an independent phase in the life of the commodity, in which it can remain for a shorter or longer period."[14] In other words, individuals often opt to hold onto their money – whether from the sale of goods or of their labor-power – instead of spending it.[15]

2 And in Capitalism *Per Se*

Marx then goes on to point out how capitalists face exactly the same problems as merchants because those two aspects of commodity exchange, buying, in their case $M - C\ (LP + MP)$, and selling, $C' - M'$, both required for capitalists to successfully gain the surplus value necessary to reproduce their operations on an expanded level, are separate in time and in space. Returning to Marx's diagrammatic representation of the *circuit of capital*, we can identify three distinct stages:

$$\begin{array}{ccc} M \text{—} LP & & \\ M \text{—} MP & \ldots P \ldots C' & C' \text{—} M' \\ (1) & (2) & (3) \end{array}$$

14 *MECW*, *Vol.* 29, p. 328.

15 Marx is writing about holding money in the form of cash, "larger or smaller amounts in reserve funds of coin," or "suspended coin." If unspent money is placed in interest earning assets, he assumes that that money will be loaned out and spent by someone else. "$M - C$, the second member of the circuit $C - M - C$, splits up into a series of purchases, which are not effected all at once but successively over a period of time, so that one part of M circulates as coin, while the other part remains at rest as money" or "hoard." *MECW*, *Vol.* 29, pp. 360–1. And in the case of credit money: "Money has to be gradually accumulated so as to be available at definite dates in the future when payments become due." Ibid., 379. With the development of world trade, the possibility of trade deficits, in which exports (which bring in money) are less than imports (for which money must be paid), requires the holding of money in the form of some accepted world money, e.g., the pound sterling or US dollar, or in the form of bullion or in the form of other reserves of foreign exchange.

In Keynes' analysis of the "demand for [cash] money," he calls such holdings "transactions demand," or the holding of money for near-term spending. He also identifies a precautionary demand (holding against risk) and a speculative demand (holding against improvements in future rates of return on available financial assets). These motives hold for both businesses and individuals – at least for those with enough income to be able to hold on to some of it, a rarity among workers in the nineteenth century. See, John Maynard Keynes, *The General Theory of Employment, Interest and Money* (New York: Harbinger, 1965), Chapter 15 "The Psychological and Business Incentives to Liquidity."

The first stage involving two processes, the buying of *LP* and *MP*, must obviously take place *prior* to the second stage, production, in which *LP* and *MP* must be combined to produce the new product *C'*. The third stage, the sale of that product, can equally obviously only take place *after* it has been created. Thus, there is an unavoidable *temporal separation* between the different moments.[16] Each process must be carried out successfully and in the proper order for the entire circuit to be completed.

Other temporal separations have also been identified in the "life of the commodity," or product life cycles, i.e., successful new products are first conceived (born in the mind), then produced (born concretely), then sold for a profit. But if demand dwindles – say because of changing fashion or new competing products – capitalists will cut back their production. When their profitability declines enough, capitalists cease producing them at all and consign their corpses to the graveyards of the commodity world (neglected in attics, garages and closets, an exemplar or two in museums, or rusting or rotting, neglected in abandoned warehouses or landfills).[17]

There are also often *geographical separations* whose overcoming creates further possibilities of rupture. When *M* – *LP* took the form of buying the source of *LP*, i.e., slaves, they had to be successfully captured or bought and transported to wherever their *LP* could be exploited. The indenture of workers in Britain for employment in colonies generally included their passage abroad. Today's labor market continues to include the hiring of workers in one location and their transportation to another. Raw materials produced in one location must often be successfully transported to another for processing. Finally, more generally, many commodities produced in one location are commonly sold in many other locations – which again necessitates various kinds of transportation and all the possibilities of interruption to which they are susceptible, from

16 The case of "futures" markets, where payment may be made before production to guarantee availability, merely reverses the temporal separation.

17 This life cycle parallels that of both machines and employees, both of which eventually wear out and are discarded by capitalists. In Eastern Europe, after the "fall of the wall" and the opening of ex-Soviet economies to Western competition, much manufacturing machinery was left to rust in largely abandoned, uncompetitive factories. I visited one such factory in Poland, one that had built engines for big ships. Two-thirds of the place, including the machinery, stood unused and unlikely to be used in the future. Almost visible in their absence were the ghosts of all those workers hitherto employed on those machines, workers now discarded and gone from that factory. In recent years, the persistence of such attitudes helps account for employer prejudice against older workers and the latter's charges of "agism" when 1) they are fired upon reaching a certain age and 2) when their job applications are perceived to be rejected because of their age.

ship or train wrecks to strikes or other job actions by workers.[18] Possibilities of interruption exist in all these spatial displacements of *LP*, *MP* and *C'*. When you realize that for Marx, transportation was a domain of production as well as essential to exchange and the functioning of markets, then such disruptions must be seen as occurring not only in *M – LP*, *M – MP* and *C' – M'*, but in ...*P*...*C'* as well.[19]

Two of these processes are in the sphere of circulation and exchange: *M – C*, *C' – M'*, and one in the sphere of production, ... *P* ... *C'*. Marx examined each of these different moments of the circuit of capital to determine possibilities of failure. Because capitalism came to maturity within a world of increasing foreign trade, these problems regularly had an international as well as local, regional and national dimensions.

Given how I have argued in Chapter 3 on accumulation that the social relationships in each of these stages are those of class conflict and have insisted on the centrality of *our* struggles in those conflicts, in my further explorations of the possibilities of crisis in each of these three stages of the capitalist circuit, and in each element of those stages, I foreground the role of our struggles in potentially creating crisis. Certainly, Marx makes clear that workers' struggles are not the only source of potential rupture, but from my point of view (and I believe of his too) they are ultimately the most important because they alone have the possibility not only of creating crisis but also of overthrowing the system as a whole.

Please note: Marx's theory reveals possibilities of rupture, of failure, of crisis. In what follows, I point to many of those possibilities, some of which Marx analyzed at length, some of which he ignored. Which deserve notice and how much treatment is appropriate? While his theory tells us where to look, my choices about *which* to include here are based on historical experiences that have revealed these possibilities to be not merely theoretical but to exist in

---

18 Shipwreck and the loss of *C'*, and thus *M'*, plays a central role in Shakespeare's play *The Merchant of Venice* (1590s). In Act Three, Scene One, one of Antonio's ships "of rich lading" is reported wrecked on the Goodwin Sands off the coast of England. Strikes by Thames lightermen in London, workers "employed in the transit of goods between wharfs and ships in the river," caught Marx's attention during the summer of 1853. So too did "the most important incident in this history of strikes" the declaration of the 'Seamen's United Friendly Association' of the 'Anglo-Saxon Sailor's Bill of Rights' against the repeal in the Navigation Acts of the requirement that at least three quarters of the seamen hired by British shippers be British. In other words, protest against the use of cheap foreign labor on British ships. See, "Rise in the Price of Corn – Cholera – Strikes – Sailors' Movement," August 30, 1853, *MECW*, *Vol. 12*, pp. 287–289.

19 *Capital, Vol. 2*, Part I, Chapter 1, Section 1, or *MECW*, *Vol. 36*, Book II, Part I, Chapter I, Section I.

the world. My choices about how many words to write about them are based, partly on the extent of my knowledge and partly on my perception of their real-world importance. In footnotes, I offer many examples to convince the reader of the continuing relevance of Marx's theory. As indicated earlier, historical examples from his time are included in the body of the text; contemporary counterparts are confined to footnotes.

3 Possibilities of Crisis in the First Stage of the Circuit: Investment

As I spelled out in Chapter 3, capitalists begin their investments by gathering enough money to buy what their plans require. If successful, they must then find and enslave or hire the labor-power they need and purchase the means of production upon which their workers will be set to work. Let's examine possible crises in each of these necessary steps.

3.1 *Possible Crises in Gathering Enough Money, M*

With respect to the first stage of the circuit of money capital, *M – C(LP, MP)*, the very first possibility of crisis lies in difficulties of amassing the money, *M*, necessary to begin the process. Marx usually *assumes* the availability of enough money to finance intended investment, i.e., to purchase both *LP* and *MP*. However, every capitalist faces the possibility of *not* being able to obtain a sufficient quantity of money and thus, a crisis *avant la lettre,* so to speak. In *Capital,* Marx gives an illustration of such a possibility from far-off Russia, where landowners, no longer able to command serfs, complain that "before the harvest is sold, the wage-labourers have to be paid a considerable amount, and the basic condition for this, a supply of ready cash, is lacking."[20] Although most workers are usually not paid until after they have worked for a week or a month, the same problem can exist for any capitalist. Without enough anticipated cash coming in to pay their workers, there is no point in hiring them.[21] The same problem

---

20 *Capital*, Vol. 2, p. 117, or *MECW*, *Vol. 36*, p. 39.

21 Unless, of course, the capitalist can get away with not paying them. In the nineteenth century that often happened during downturns when workers were laid off and factories closed. Today, unfortunately, within the multinational network of ever-changing patterns of capitalist investment, it still happens that plants are closed without workers being paid their most recent wages – often in response to workers organizing to form unions, but also because of the unprofitability of a particular operation due to all sorts of problems in the circuit of capital. See, Kate Bronfenbrenner, *Final Report: The Effects of Plant Closing or Threat of Plant Closing on the Right of Workers to Organize*, International Publications, 1, Cornell University, 1996. http://digitalcommons.ilr.cornell.edu/intl/1 Where workers are

obtains about finding enough money to purchase the means of production, whether to get things going or to cover expected upkeep on fixed capital or to replace raw materials as they are used up. If money comes up short, investment stalls, whether it's an initial investment by a new start-up capitalist or an investment in expansion by an existing capitalist.

In his analysis of primitive accumulation in Volume 1 of *Capital*, Marx points out how this possibility, which had long plagued merchants, also faces would-be industrial capitalists. Both kinds of investors face the same problem of putting together enough money to buy in order to sell – for merchants to buy goods, for industrial capitalists to buy labor-power and means of production.

Within on-going accumulation the availability of money for investment generally depends upon 1) retaining past surplus value in the form of money reserves, i.e., suspended coin, hoard or highly liquid assets, and 2) the ability to borrow if such savings are insufficient for the intended investment.[22] Therefore, the possibility of investing and exploiting workers tomorrow is dependent on the success of investing and exploiting workers today and on access to *commercial* or *industrial credit*, i.e., the ability to convince other capitalists, banks, buyers of stocks and bonds or the government to loan money to help

organized and have achieved laws covering this bit of capitalist cheating, they take legal action to obtain their unpaid wages. See, https://www.workplacefairness.org/

22 Borrowing here should be understood broadly, not only loans from individuals or banks, but also new stock and bond offerings and loans from governments. Government financing of industrial production has sometimes taken the form of state-owned enterprises, which operate like private enterprise – seeking to maximize profits – but subject to government regulation and manipulation, e.g., having their profits drawn off through taxes to finance other state expenditures. Although rare in the US, the Tennessee Valley Authority (TVA) that produces and sells electricity is one well-known example, state enterprises have been much more common elsewhere. The most obvious cases were in Soviet-style "socialist," or more properly "state-capitalist" countries. But they have also been created in Western Europe, e.g. Renault, the automobile company nationalized by the French government in 1945 and owned by it until privatized in 1996, in the Middle East where the governments of most OPEC countries own and manage their oil production and marketing, and elsewhere. Many such enterprises were created in ex-colonial countries where managerial talent was thought to be concentrated in the state. (Many have been privatized under neoliberal policies adopted by governments since the 1980s.) Governments have also provided outright subsidies to private industry that do not need to be repaid, either direct monetary payments or through the financing (via taxation) of infrastructure (roads, ports, dams, etc.) that reduce costs to industry and by so doing raise profits. Although relatively uncommon in the mid-nineteenth century, the more active intervention of governments in fostering investment in the twentieth century has led to the creation of all sorts of governmental agencies charged with promulgating either a particular industry or regional development. (The TVA was designed to provide such regional support as well as to produce electricity.)

(or entirely) finance proposed investment.[23] The failure of current efforts at exploitation would not only mean less retained money for future investment, but would also negatively influence the willingness of others to lend in the future.

Having argued the importance of foregrounding workers' struggles in each of these stages and in each element of each stage, my first question is "how might workers' struggles impede the ability of capitalists to muster sufficient funds for desired investment?" The most obvious response derives from how successful worker struggles can reduce work, raise wages and salaries or force their employers to spend money on other expenditures of interest to workers, such as safety equipment (e.g., guard rails around dangerous machinery or ventilation fans in textile factories and mines).[24] Less work and all such expenditures raise costs and, ceteris paribus, reduce profits and thus the availability of retained earnings for investment. The second response is that such successful struggles by workers inevitably affect expectations about the *future* rate of profit from planned investment. Anything that lowers expected rates of profit undermines investment, both out of whatever retained earnings are available and the possibilities of borrowing money.[25]

Banks are notoriously averse to loaning money in risky circumstances. With rates of interest charged on loans contingent on estimations of risk, the higher those estimates, the more expensive potential credit, and the less profitable prospective investment. Indeed, opportunities can be rendered moot by rates of interest exceeding expected rates of return. The same effects can be seen in the ability of capitalists to raise money by issuing stocks or bonds: buyer perceptions of increased risk will reduce their purchases of securities and raise less money for investment. Reporting on crises of their time, Marx and Engels repeatedly pointed to the negative effects of increases in interest rates

---

23 See, *Capital, Vol. 1*, Chapter 31, or MECW, *Vol. 35*, Chapter XXXI.

24 Since workers have become aware of how capitalist industries have poisoned both their workplaces and the communities in which they live, and since they have forced up wages and reduced working time to the point where they look beyond mere survival, they have also demanded expenditures on equipment to stem environmental pollution. Consistent with its past behavior, business has systematically resisted all such expenditures, complaining of reduced profits and demanding government subsidies – at taxpayer/worker expense.

25 Years after Marx, Keynes formalized this relationship in his analysis of the effects of prospective rates of return on investment. Any decline in expected rates of return would reduce the "marginal efficiency of capital," with the effect of reducing investment at each rate of interest; conversely, any rise in expected rates of return would likely increase investment. See, *The General Theory*, Chapter 11.

on investment and thus on the usefulness of financial markets to raise money for investment.

Similar considerations are taken into account by government policy makers, be they kings or legislators, in deciding whether to subsidize investment, either by the state itself or through loans or subsidies to private investors. Here again the reaction to upsurges in worker struggles, especially if on a large scale and affecting expectations across industries, may be to spend money on police and military repression while putting off expenditures on investment.[26]

Workers' struggles, however, are by no means the only determinant of interest rates and thus the availability of credit for investment, be it from private money markets or government. Despite holding a theory that the supply of money is *ultimately* determined endogenously by the value of commodities in circulation, Marx nevertheless recognized how central banks repeatedly changed the interest rates they charged to influence the amount of money in circulation. For example, central banks would raise interest rates to maintain ties between their issuance of notes and their bullion reserves. With gold and silver the basis of money throughout Europe and Asia, the transference of bullion and thus the flow of investable money capital were sensitive to differences in interest rates – flowing away from lower rates and towards higher rates. Recognition of this sensitivity repeatedly led central banks to raise their rates in competition with one another to stem capital export and had the result of circulating crisis.[27] In 1856, Marx analyzed such competition between the Bank of England, the Bank of France, German banks and those elsewhere on the continent. Complicating those relationships were the increasing drains

---

26 In extreme situations, however, we see both, designed to complement each other. Such was the US reaction to the upsurge in workers struggles during and after WWII in Europe where communists and their political parties played a major role in resistance to fascism. That gave them credibility and electoral strength in the post-war period. So, the Marshall Plan subsidized reinvestment in Europe, supporting capitalists, while more covert methods were used to counter communist party efforts to strengthen their influence in unions and to gain political power in France and Italy. Such complementary methods became frequent during various post-war counterinsurgency campaigns in Southeast Asia and elsewhere in the Global South where "civic action," including investment, was designed to complement the military repression of insurgents. It continues to this day in places such as Chiapas, Mexico where government military and paramilitary methods of repressing indigenous autonomy have been complemented by various "mega [investment] projects" such as government subsidized rail lines and tourist development.

27 Marx, K., "The Vienna Note – The US and Europe – Letters from Shumla – Peel's Bank Act," (Sept. 9, 1953) *MECW*, *Vol. 12*, pp. 292–300. Marx to Engels, 3 Feb. 1851, *MECW*, *Vol. 38*, pp. 273–278,

of silver to China and India.[28] He saw all these monetary problems aggravating the emerging crisis whose seriousness was already predictable for other reasons.

> Whatever may be the temporary cause of the monetary panic, and the drain of bullion which appears as its immediate occasion, all the elements of commercial and industrial revulsion were ripe in Europe ..."[29]

One locus of such "ripeness" upon which Marx dwelt at length was France, where huge speculations in railroads were complemented by disasters in, and new taxes on, agriculture, "the dearth of lodgings and provisions in Paris, the pressure on the retail trade of the capital, [and] the strikes in different branches of Parisian industry ..."[30]

In the case of both private banks and public lenders the cost of borrowing may entail not only interest but also all sorts of conditions that the borrowers much meet. In the case of private banks, the most obvious conditions are those for collateral, specified patterns of repayment and fines for failure to meet those obligations. In the case of public lenders, you have conditions placed on central banks by governments, e.g., Peel's Bank Act of 1844, and by central banks on other banks, e.g., reserve requirements, and on foreign central banks and governments.[31] Whatever the source, the terms of borrowing must

28 See "The Causes of the Monetary Crisis in Europe," (circa October 14, 1856) MECW, *Vol. 15*, pp. 117–122, "The Monetary Crisis in Europe -- From the History of Money Circulation," (circa October 17, 1856) MECW, *Vol. 15*, pp. 123–129, and "The Economic Crisis in France," (circa November 7, 1856) MECW, *Vol. 15*, pp. 130–135. Today, "hot money" investors in liquid financial assets are known to flee open capital markets in response to perceptions of increased risk. One of many modern examples was the 1994 currency crisis in Mexico when increasing political instability in the wake of the Zapatista uprising in January of that year let to flight from the peso and its dramatic devaluation. (More on this in Chapter 5, footnote 5.) Not only did that flight reduce the available funds for investment, but the subsequent imposition of high interest rates to stem the outflow undermined availability even more, bringing on a broader crisis – and more political turmoil.

29 MECW, *Vol. 15*, p. 122.

30 "The Economic Crisis in France," MECW, *Vol. 15*, pp. 134–5.

31 Over time Marxist studies of relationships between banks and non-financial industry have evolved considerably. I have already mentioned Hilferding's *Finance Capital* and Sweezy' counter argument. In more recent years, the spread of financialization has renewed interest in the relative power of financial institutions versus industrial, agricultural or service industries – including the intellectual followers of Sweezy who make up the "Monthly Review" school of neo-Marxism. See, "Decoding Financialization" in Cleaver, *Rupturing the Dialectic*, for a sketch of this evolution. In the case of modern, supranational lenders to governments, e.g., the World Bank or International Monetary Fund, conditions

be weighed by the potential investor and creditors against anticipated profits – which must be great enough to repay the costs of borrowing and leave a net profit sufficient to make the investment worthwhile. Any increase in the costs of borrowing reduces net profits and the willingness of the investor to borrow.

The possibility of being unable either to earn or to borrow sufficient funds to finance a desired investment increases dramatically amid an economic crisis. Potential investors' possibilities of *earning* the money they need to invest may be reduced by their own inability to sell. More generally, *commercial* crises (involving generalized ruptures in *C' – M'*) bring on *monetary* crises in which the rate of interest charged by lenders rises rapidly as all kinds of firms – industrial, commercial, and financial – become desperate for cash and loath to loan in anticipation of their own needs, thus aggravating *industrial* crises.

Moreover, there are a number of possibilities of crisis for would-be investors associated with changes in the value of their money holdings. First, money in the hands of investors may become *debased* to the point of being unacceptable to those from whom they desire to buy, e.g., raw materials. Besides inevitable wear and abrasion of coin in circulation, the debasement of metal money generally had three sources: (1) governments reducing the percentage of gold or silver in coins to stretch the "value" of precious metal on hand, (2) the private clipping of coins that reduced the amount of metal (and thus their value) and (3) out and out counterfeiting. In the *Contribution to the Critique*, Marx points to the "little shilling men," who advocated repayment of government debt in debased shillings as a solution to currency problems.[32] John Locke, while serving in the Mint, took the threat to British trade of debasement of the pound sterling so seriously that he called for recoinage – despite fears that it might result in deflation at a time when the country could ill afford it.[33]

Two, somewhat similar, problems may arise with metal-based monies from reductions in the value of the metal serving as money or from bimetallism in those periods in which gold and silver both serve as money. In the first case, the resulting price increases would reduce the buying power of whatever money is available for investment. In the second case, if the value of one metal falls in

---

for their loans and for signing off on the roll-over of private international debt, have included devaluations of local currencies, reductions in subsidies for basic consumption, privatization of state enterprises, etc. See Cleaver, "Close the IMF, Abolish Debt and End Development," op. cit.

32 *MECW*, *Vol. 29*, p. 319. The British pound sterling coin was divided into 20 shillings (smaller coins) – a monetary unit which was abandoned in 1991 in the UK but continues to be used in several countries in East Africa.

33 See, George Caffentzis, *Clipped Coins, Abused Words and Civil Government: John Locke's Philosophy of Money* (New York: Autonomedia, 1989).

relation to the other, it is less able to serve its owner as money and is likely to be driven from circulation. In both cases, would-be capitalist investors unfortunate enough to be holding their money in the devalued metal would discover their ability to purchase labor-power and the means of production impaired.

A final problem, one of increasing importance in the nineteenth century with the rise of joint-stock companies, was the diversion of money from *real investment*, i.e., spending money on *LP* and *MP* to increase production, to *speculation*. i.e., money spent by individuals or firms that does nothing to increase production. Unfortunately, the word "investment" is commonly used to refer both to real investment and to speculative expenditures of money on existing assets whose prices are expected (or hoped) to rise, assets such as already issued stocks and bonds or existing supplies of housing or raw materials.[34] We must differentiate speculative spending on existing stocks and bonds from purchases of new offerings of stocks and bonds being issued to raise money for actual real investment. Investing in new production involves speculation but only in the limited sense that future outcomes cannot be known with certainty.

Let us now turn from the problem of having enough money to those potential crises that can emerge as capitalists try to obtain the *LP* and *MP* required in their investments. Assuming enough money has been found to fund the intended investment, there can still be crises associated with the availability of *LP* in labor markets and the availability of *MP* from other capitalists. In their economic models, economists treat scarcity as easily resolvable through changes in prices with changes determined by supply and demand. In the case of *LP*, they assume excess demand will raise the price of slaves or the wages of hired workers with the result that slavers will capture more workers or waged workers will have a greater willingness to sacrifice leisure and work more, or more workers will be drawn into the labor market from the "reserve army."[35] If more *MP* is needed than is currently available, i.e., the amount

34 The likelihood of money being diverted into speculation depends on a host of factors, although in recent decades the primary one has been financial deregulation which has made it easier to divert all sorts of money into speculation, most notably in housing and in financial assets.

35 Thus, contemporary microeconomists' general assumption of upward sloping supply curves of labor derived from personal preferences about mixes of income (and what it buys) and work (a loss of leisure). Not being completely oblivious to the implications of recognizing leisure as desirable and work as undesirable, economists sometimes remember that if wages rise high enough the supply curve of labor curves back to the left reflecting the choice (when available) to work less to take advantage of the opportunities provided by higher income! In typical introductory microeconomic textbooks, however, such "backward bending" labor supply curves are ignored, despite the way they provide one explanation for why capitalists try to keep wages below the point at which less work

demanded exceeds the amount supplied, they assume the excess demand will raise prices and more will be forthcoming from producers of *MP* in response to higher prices. Such corrections, economists reason, will happen quickly and smoothly so any marginal difficulty in obtaining enough *LP* or *MP* will be quickly corrected.

Marx and Engels, on the other hand, saw lots of cases where no such smooth, marginal adjustments took place, but instead corrections came in the form of serious disruptions and crises. After all, from the point of view of investors, when scarcity results in higher prices, their money buys less *LP* and/or *MP*. Given existing financing, in the short-term rising costs of *LP* and *MP* will immediately reduce the amount of investment and accumulation. If the prices of either labor-power or the means of production, or both, rise so high as to make earning an acceptable rate of profit unfeasible, capitalists will not invest at all. The result is, effectively, the same as a total *un*availability of the required resources and the resulting impossibility of either beginning or renewing circuits. If this unfolds on a large scale the results can be dramatic.

3.2 *Possible Crises in Obtaining Labor-Power*

Because within capitalism, labor is imposed, whether by slavery or through the not so "free" labor market, people resist and often revolt causing crises in the supply of labor-power. As a result, its availability is never guaranteed. Both slaves and waged workers, whom Marx often referred to as "wage-slaves", drawing a parallel with their enslaved counterparts, have struggled against that imposition and the resulting alienation. The mechanisms of coercion differed but the objective was the same – control and exploitation – and both kinds of workers have fought back.

3.2.1 Possible Crises in Obtaining Slaves

Since the rise of capitalism, capitalists have deployed several methods to obtain slaves, either as chattel property or as forced labor. Thanks to the resistance of those enslaved, each method has been subject to crises.

The first, historically dominant method, when chattel property in people was legal, was capture and sale – "the slave trade." This included the Atlantic

---

will be desired and chosen (when possible) to maintain adequate supplies of labor. The backward bend (becoming downward sloped) was first recognized by economists studying colonial labor markets where the colonized did NOT want to work for their colonizers and did so only to pay required taxes in colonial monies that could only be earned by working for the invading foreign capitalists. THEIR labor supply curves were thus downward sloped from the get-go. The lower the wages the more they had to work to pay taxes.

slave trade that furnished enslaved Africans to slave markets in Europe and the Western Hemisphere.[36] It was called "the slave *trade*" because it was mostly carried on by private capitalists, albeit often with the help and protection of governments. Against this trade, not only did people resist slavers, but those who failed and found themselves enslaved continued to resist, sometimes passively, denying their energy and creativity to their owners, sometimes through revolt or the organization of escape, e.g., the flight to freedom either in hidden Maroon colonies in the hinterland or through underground railroads to places where slavery was illegal.[37] Success in such endeavors increased the difficulty of obtaining as well as retaining slaves.

Slave resistance has also been supported by many abolitionists who have opposed slavery on various ethical or moral grounds. The revolt of the former directly deprived their owners of their *LP*; opposition of the latter demanded an end to both the slave trade, which would reduce the number of slaves, and to chattel slavery *tout court*, which would eliminate the ability of capitalists to employ slaves legally.

The second method has been the imposition of forced labor on workers found guilty of crimes and either put to work by the managers of governments' prison systems or farmed out to private capitalists. In Marx and Engels' time, Britain was notorious for "transporting" prisoners – especially condemned militants – to places like Australia and New Zealand for forced labor. Within the US, penal forced labor persisted thanks to the Thirteenth Amendment to the US Constitution that made chattel slavery illegal but legalized forced labor in prisons "as a punishment for crime whereof the party shall have been

36 The capture and trade in slaves in the nineteenth century was by no means limited to the Atlantic. Non-Muslim Europeans captured by pirates were enslaved, sold and bought along the North African "Barbary Coast." The slave trade was also rampant within Africa and in many parts of Asia.

37 Escaped slaves formed Maroon colonies throughout the Americas, from those in the swamps of Florida to the forests and plains of South America. These colonies often interacted with and sometimes merged with indigenous communities. Underground railroads, on the other hand, usually led to the relative freedom of waged labor markets. See, Richard Price, *Maroon Societies: Rebel Slave Communities in the Americas*, 3rd edn. (Baltimore, MD: Johns Hopkins University Press, 1996), Robert Schwaller, *African Maroons in the Sixteenth Century Panama: A History in Documents* (Norman: University of Oklahoma Press, 2021) and *Maroon Comix: Origins and Destinies* (Oakland: PM Press, 2018). On the underground railroad, see, Eric Foner, *Gateway to Freedom: The Hidden History of the Underground Railroad* (New York: W.W. Norton & Company, 2015) and the film *Harriet* (2019) about the struggles of escaped slave and abolitionist Harriet Tubman (1822–1913). In today's world, "underground railroads" consist mostly of organizations that help escaping slaves by providing temporary refuge and then legal support.

duly convicted." Here too, many of those forced to work have resisted, either passively or actively by striking or escaping. As in the opposition to chattel slavery, resisting prisoners have received help from outside groups opposed to this form of legal quasi-slavery.

The third method of obtaining slaves has been to breed them, i.e., enslave the children of existing slaves. This became the sole remaining method after the slave trade was made illegal, ending only with the outlawing of chattel slavery. Here too, there was resistance, especially by enslaved women who secretly used home remedies to avoid pregnancy or to abort, denying new slaves to their owners. (See, Chapter 5, Section 1.2.3.3.)

3.2.2 Possible Crises of Hiring in the Labor Market, *M – LP*

Of these two markets, *M – LP* and *M – MP*, I begin with *M – LP*, rather than *M – MP*, because the labor market is the first of the two moments of the capitalist circuit where capitalists and waged workers come face to face and where the intrinsic antagonism of the class relationship is clearly manifested. (The second moment of confrontation, of course, is production, …*P*….) In Volume 2 of *Capital*, Marx was quite explicit about the centrality of *M – LP*.

> *M – L* is the characteristic moment of the transformation of money capital into productive capital, for it is the essential condition without which the value advanced in the money form cannot readily be transformed into capital, into value-producing surplus value. *M - mp* is necessary only in order to realize the mass of labour bought by way of *M – L*.[38]

The "essentiality" of *M – LP* is not only because workers are required to generate surplus value, but also because this subordination of people to work is the fundamental basis of capitalism as a functioning social system. The "means of production" are, socially speaking, merely the means of imposing work. This is true whether in the case of the dominant form of imposing work – the wage relation – or in the secondary form of slavery. Marx writes,

> The class relation between capitalist and wage-labourer is thus already present, already presupposed, the moment that the two confront each other in the act *M – L* (*L – M* from the side of the worker).[39]

38 *Capital, Vol. 2*, p. 113, or *MECW, Vol. 36*, p. 35.

39 Ibid., p. 115, or *MECW, Vol. 36*, p. 37.

But the same is true in the case of slavery within capitalism. In both cases, the class relation being imposed involved peoples' lives being subordinated to the production of commodities. And that "class relation" is one of struggle between those whose control of *MP* gives them the power to impose work and those whose lack of such control puts pressure on them to submit to it.

In the case of *M – LP*, the possible sources of crisis faced by capitalists are first, not being able to buy *enough LP* and second, not being able to buy it *at a price* that will make putting it to work profitable. This holds whether the *LP* being purchased is "free" (waged) or slave.[40] In other words, there are too few workers to hire or slaves to be bought or the wages of the one or the cost of the other might be too high. This possibility has existed in every labor market where capitalists buy *LP*.

In Marx's theory we speak of *the* labor market, but there have always been many segmented labor markets, differentiated by industry and skill, but also by gender, ethnicity and race and corresponding pay scales. Women have been treated differently than men, relegated to particular jobs and generally paid less. There have been Men's jobs and Women's jobs. The same has been true with ethnic and racial minorities. Not only were the Irish pitted against the English (and vice versa) in nineteenth century Britain but the Irish were admitted only to labor markets for the worst, lowest paying jobs.[41] The "payment" of slaves, of course, generally in kind, room and board, has generally been much less than waged and salaried workers.[42] Once chattel slavery was abolished in the United States, Jim Crow laws created segregated labor markets in which Blacks could only apply (with any reasonable expectation of being seriously considered) for some jobs, generally low paid, but not others. There have been White jobs and Black jobs.[43] This segmentation was recreated throughout

40 In the case of chattel slavery, capitalists buy humans for their *LP*, extracted by force or manipulation. In the case of human trafficking, some capitalists pretend to hire workers but then force them to work as slaves, e.g., in the case of immigrants, withholding passports, whether in homes and brothels, agricultural fields, sweat shops, fishing boats or prisons. I take up the problems of capitalists trying to *sell LP* in the form of slaves in Section 5.1.

41 The same, of course, was true when millions of them emigrated to the United States.

42 The same was true in those cases where slave owners put their slaves out to work in waged jobs. Not only were they paid less but most of their pay went to their owners. On waged slaves in pre-Civil War southern industrialization, see: Robert Starobin, *Industrial Slavery in the Old South* (Oxford: Oxford University Press, 1970) and Klas Rönnbäck, "Were slaves cheap laborers? A Comparative study of labor costs in the antebellum U.S. South", *Labor History* 62 (2021): 721–741.

43 For a vivid contemporary example, see Charlie LeDuff, "At a Slaughterhouse, Some Things Never Die: Who Kills, Who Cuts, Who Bosses Can Depend on Race", *The New York Times*, (June 16, 2000): A1-A24.

society – in the segregation of schools by race, and in the redlining of urban spaces, which confined minorities to specific ghettos. In the world of colonialism, such discrimination among local ethnic and linguistic groups was rampant – and one source of the struggle for national liberation.

Within all of these carefully constructed, segmented markets for waged and salaried workers, employers have been able to fire their employees "at will" – just as slave owners can sell their slaves whenever they have needed to do so. Firing has often been done unceremoniously, by company goons forcibly escorting workers off the grounds of their job.[44] This has been the fate of individuals or, sometimes, of all workers when companies have shut down operations for whatever reason – from cutbacks in production or bankruptcies during crises to lockouts during contract negotiations (once workers achieved the power to impose collective bargaining).[45]

The problem of finding enough workers in any of these differentiated labor markets and at profitable cost has been endemic to capitalism for a variety of reasons. In the case of potentially waged workers, their availability depends on a number of factors: their willingness to enter the labor market at all, flight from labor markets, disease and starvation, military drains and reduced or slowed population growth.

3.2.2.1 *Avoidance of the Labor Market*

Because waged and salaried jobs are shaped by capitalism's efforts control life, making them exploitative and alienating, folks of all ages often try to avoid them. And avoiding jobs means avoiding the labor market – that portal to the heart of capitalism's hell-on-earth. When young, still curious about the world, well-fed, and left on their own, kids are often more into exploring the world than accepting the difficulties and discipline with which they see their parents and older people struggling. When older, a surprisingly large number of adults still opt out of the labor market and choose some alternative way to survive. Eventually, for those who have chosen to work for wages or salaries,

44 The word "goon" comes from South Asia and the Hindu word *guṇḍā* or *goonda* – defined in both the vernacular and law (Goonda Acts) as a hired criminal, or a hired hand who engages in criminal behavior. They can be found in the hire of large landlords, merchants and industrial capitalists and the term with its derogatory connotations has been widely applied by workers to company thugs.

45 Today, in the United States, the "pink slip," the surprise order to leave everything behind except personal items, followed by the escort to the front door (or gate) have been so common as to constitute despised ceremonies of termination. In some European countries, better organized workers have won protection from such arbitrary termination with employers obligated to notify their workers ahead of time and, in a few cases, provide assistance in finding new jobs.

accumulated fatigue, ill-health or a sense of justice after a lifetime of work drive those who can afford it to retire from whatever jobs have dominated their adult lives and eschew any further engagement with the labor market. Let's survey such avoidance in various situations and stages of life during Marx and Engels' lifetimes.

Avoidance among not-yet-disciplined youth seems endemic and can be found in every segment of the income hierarchy, from its upper echelons down to its most poverty-stricken segments. In the nineteenth century, well-to-do families in capital's new income hierarchy often emulated earlier practices of the landed gentry by allowing their children to put off entering the job market, first by "schooling", usually by tutors for boys and governesses for girls, then by taking parent-financed tours abroad (mostly boys), for fun, to widen their horizons, to improve their language skills and to prepare them for future leadership roles in capitalist society. Among the emerging middle-class, where family income has allowed, their youth often followed the same path, partly emulating their upper-class counterparts, partly just avoiding the job market and work.[46] In both cases, young adults have indulged their natural propensity to avoid knuckling down to the discipline of doing what someone else tells them to do.

The situation for the children of working-class families, in both countryside and cities, and those born into circumstances that Marx and Engels would classify as lumpenproletariat, faced more dire futures and much greater pressure to set aside their natural propensity to explore life and instead find some kind of work to supplement family income. Thus, that "selling into slavery" of children by some working-class families struggling to survive. Where even that proved impossible, children and young adults have often organized themselves into collectives (gangs) – operating within the "informal economy", frequently in ways disruptive of the usual operations of businesses. A few, among children of all sorts, have formed politically active, militant groups, some to challenge

46 The poets and writers of the Beat Generation in the 1950s inspired many to follow Jack Kerouac *On the Road* (1957) but only as a temporary escape from the labor market. I became personally familiar with many such students in the early 1960s because while an undergraduate studying in France, I spent some time sleeping under the bridges of Paris, eating at soup kitchens, and hanging out with other students taking time away from both studies and the job market. A decade later, the 1960s saw an explosion of youthful resistance to the job market by a generation of "hippies" and "radicals", critical of capital's subordination of life to work with the accumulation of stuff as the only consolation.

the structures of their society, some to organize countermeasures to the poverty and repression of their communities.[47]

But for adults, avoiding the labor market, refusing to hire out to some employer, has never been easy because of the way capitalists have monopolized the means of livelihood, land, tools, etc. Nevertheless, many have avoided and have found alternative ways to survive. Here, I'll highlight two common alternatives. First, among the expropriated, those with either no interest in regaining access to land or judging it impossible, have often chosen to move outside both traditional norms and capitalist laws doing whatever they could to live. Second, where enclosure has not been complete, both during the rise of capitalism or later, on its not-yet-enclosed margins, many have fought to either retain their access to land for subsistence agriculture or, having lost it in one place sought it elsewhere. Thus, the resistance to enclosure and later efforts to reverse it. (See below, Chapter 4, Section 5.2.2.1.)

Among those who, once deprived of land, abandoned any effort to regain it, were the beggars, vagabonds and robbers cited by Marx on the first page of Chapter 28 of *Capital.* With his emphasis on the cruelty of expropriation, his account emphasizes how they were *forced* out of their traditional roles and livelihoods. Studies by bottom-up historians provide examples of adaptation, such as Edward Thompson's *Whigs and Hunters: the Origin of the Black Act* (1975) that sketches the complex modes of survival via squatting, farming and poaching of displaced yet creative people in and around the forests of England, and Peter Linebaugh's *London Hanged* that shows how, as capitalism took over the slaughter of animals, many displaced butchers who lost their livelihood turned to robbery.[48] Many other accounts have studied how some *chose* to continue living outside the labor markets capital sought to impose. The book *London Labor and the London Poor* (1851) by Henry Mayhew (1812–1887), based on interviews with vagrants, contains lots of stories of how and why they chose uncertain lives on the streets, highways, and byways of England rather than submit to the discipline of the job, any job. For those unacquainted with life on

47 The decision by some middleclass students to avoid entering the labor market by spending some time on the streets or traveling has been common enough but hardly a cause of crisis. In the 1960s, in the context of the Civil Rights Movement at home and of the Vietnam war, we saw the emergence of radical militants among both students and non-students. These included anti-war groups such as Students for a Democratic Society and militant groups such as the Black Panthers and the Brown Berets. In all these cases, participation in the labor force was minimal and designed to support struggles outside it.

48 Edward Thompson, *Whigs and Hunters: the Origin of the Black Act* (, 1975), Peter Linebaugh, *The London Hanged,* Chapter Six: 'Going upon the Accompt: Highway Robbery under the Reigns of the Georges."

the streets, who tend to see only the hardships, such stories provide insight not only into the variety of ways vagabonds have foraged both society and nature but also, though it may seem strange, the pleasures of freedom they sometimes enjoy. Those who were once peasants used their agrarian skills to live off the land – foraging plants and poaching game – as well as begging and pilfering in towns. Although those accounts, especially fictionalized ones, often focus on individuals, such *deracinés* have often united to form collectives, such as the seventeenth century kingdom of vagabonds in Paris, which Marx mentions in *Capital*.[49]

Success at staying free from the labor market and from being exploited by some capitalist, despite being criminalized and harshly punished, has long had an appeal to those less successful at avoidance. John Garraty has reported on how French workers harassed cops arresting beggars; Eric Hobsbawm has suggested how exploits of unwaged "social bandits" appeal to the exploited and explain the persistent popularity of the frequently sympathetic portrayals not only of beggars and vagabonds but also of robbers.[50] Think, for example, of the many tales of the English outlaw Robin Hood, or the orphan Oliver Twist in Charles Dicken's novel of that title (1837–1839), or the hero of Victor Hugo's *Les Miserables* (1862), who wends his way through much of the story as a vagabond. Or, the 1901 novel *If I Were King,* its 1925 adaption as an operetta *The Vagabond King*, and subsequent film versions, all based on the romanticized adventures of the fifteenth century outlaw and poet Francois Villon.[51]

Although bottom-up historians have sometimes retrieved stories of how communities of exploited workers have formed networks of mutual aid and collaboration to better cope with their situations, less study has been done on collectivities among the "lumpenproletariat", frequently dismissed as irrelevant to class struggle, even by Marx and Engels who perceived a lack of class consciousness and how the lumpen had sometimes been used against waged workers. In the *Communist Manifesto*, they write:

> The "dangerous class" [lumpen proletariat], the social scum, that passively rotting mass thrown off by the lowest layers of old society may, here and there, be swept into the movement by a proletarian revolution;

49 *Capital, Vol. 1*, p. 899, or MECW, *Vol. 35*, p. 726.

50 John Garraty, *Unemployment in History* (New York: Harper Colophon, 1978) 25. Eric Hobsbawm, *Primitive Rebels: Studies in Archaic Forms of Social Movements in the 19th and 20th Century* (New York: W. W. Norton, 1959) Chapter 11.

51 Films based on adaptations of the original novel were made in 1920 (silent), 1930 (musical), 1938 (historical), and 1956 (1930 remake), this recurrence a testimony to the appeal of the story.

> its conditions of life, however, prepare it far more for the part of a bribed tool of reactionary intrigue.[52]

This view was reinforced by observing how some of the lumpen were mobilized to help put down workers' revolts in 1848. Still seeing the lumpen as disorganized "social scum", in the *Eighteenth Brumaire* (1851–2), Marx and Engels failed to study any of those they lumped into the lumpen other than those at the highest levels of capitalist power and corruption, e.g., Napoleon III, who Marx deemed the "Chief of the Paris Lumpenproletariat", or those organized by them, e.g., the Society of December 10.[53]

Yet, the "lumpen" were not always a chaotic assembly of isolated, self-serving individuals, easily manipulated by the powers that be. Beggars, vagabonds and robbers often grouped and struggled collectively. Robin Hood, after all, had his band of "merry men" operating out of Sherwood Forest. The later deer-stealing "Blacks" (Thompson's "hunters") of Windsor Forest were also often well organized, albeit with guns rather than bows and arrows. Oliver Twist hooked up with a gang of pickpockets working the streets of London and the "vagabond king" was king of a well-organized underground of all sorts of "lumpen." Exceptions to this neglect among historians who have studied the period leading up to and including Marx and Engel's nineteenth century are Eric Hobsbawm in his *Primitive Rebels* (1959), the authors of *Albion's Fatal Tree: Crime and Society in Eighteenth-Century England* (1975), including E. P. Thompson and Peter Linebaugh, also author of *The London Hanged: Crime and Civil Society in the Eighteenth Century* (1991), based on biographies of workers executed at the Tyburn gallows, Marcus Rediker, who has analyzed pirate communities on ships and on shore in *Villains of All Nations: Atlantic Pirates in the Golden Age* (2004) and Linebaugh and Rediker, who collaborated to write *The Many-Headed Hydra: Sailors, Slaves, Commoners, and the Hidden History of the Revolutionary Atlantic* (2000).[54]

---

52 "MECW, Vol. 6, p. 494. Marx and Engels' dismissal differed radically from the view of contemporary anarchists, such as Max Stirner or Mikhail Bakunin whose embrace of lumpen rebellion earned him Engels' nickname "the lumpen prince."

53 MECW, *Vol. 11*, pp. 148–149, 155.

54 In the post-WWII period, some Marxists turned their backs on what they took to be a sold-out, consumerist, industrial proletariat, modern versions of what Engels had called the "labor aristocracy" of better paid, unionized workers. They turned their attention at home to re-evaluating the revolutionary potential of the lumpen and abroad to struggles on what they often called the Third World "periphery" of global capitalism. The result was both a failure to thoroughly analyze the hierarchy within the former countries – as Marx had done in *Capital* – and a tendency to glorify workers struggles in the latter – a

Turning from those who abandoned the land, we enter the diverse world of farmers and peasants, often dislocated but often equally engaged in fierce struggle to hang on to or regain land and the subsistence it makes possible. Just as local farmers located near developing capitalism were threatened by enclosure, like those in Great Britain analyzed by Marx, so too were agriculturalists in colonized areas, who saw their best lands taken over by invading foreigners, and indigenous peoples on the frontiers of capitalist expansion, who had lived by hunting, gathering, and agriculture for thousands of years. Whereas agriculturalists were often familiar with exploitation by local precapitalist or emerging capitalist elites, indigenous peoples often had neither familiarity with nor understanding of labor markets. Nor did they – initially – have any need for wages.[55] Like gauchos who fled the labor market and often lived with them, indigenous peoples mostly continued apart from this new institution and refused to have anything to do with it.

The attachment of peasants to the land and their struggles to maintain their access to it has limited their availability to capitalists seeking to hire.[56] In discussing this problem, Marx cited the complaint of Russian landowners about difficulties in obtaining sufficient and timely wage-labor. Despite being freed from serfdom, he writes:

> the Russian agricultural worker, owing to the common ownership of the soil by the village community, is not yet fully separated from his means of production and is thus still not a 'free wage-labourer' in the full sense of the term.[57]

---

tendency sometimes called "Third Worldism." Among those fascinated with the former were Herbert Marcuse and among those who revived the concept in Global South was Franz Fanon. The formation of groups such as the Black Panthers and the Young Lords whose militance included organizing in their communities gave some credence to such preoccupations in the US. The widespread rebellions in Asia, Latin America and Africa, against which the US and European powers mustered counterinsurgency wars, gave hope and prompted solidarity among those dismissing the "labor aristocracy" of the North.

55 Eventually, barter trade with European colonizers would create enough of a demand for industrialized goods to induce some indigenous to enter the labor market to obtain money to buy them. See Section 3.4.1 below.

56 The degree of unavailability has varied according to circumstances. Under normal growing conditions, sufficient subsistence renders recourse to the labor market for income unnecessary. Although, in peasant communities, some may temporarily hire out to neighbors during harvests. Drought, flood, and famine, however, often drive reluctant but desperate peasants to seek employment and wages.

57 *Capital, Vol. 2*, p. 117, or *MECW*, *Vol. 36*, p. 40. This failure to totally separate workers from the means of subsistence persists in the recourse of even regularly employed waged or salaried workers to gardening or some subsistence farming. This is common in the Global South

"Not yet separated" means they still had access to lands they knew full well how to cultivate and on the basis of which they could live their lives independently of big landowners. The same problem confronted Jamaican plantation owners once their slaves were freed. Marx writes:

> They have ceased to be slaves, but not in order to become wage labourers, but instead, self-sustaining peasants working for their own consumption.[58]

It is worth remembering that in the nineteenth century, many peasants, even when forced off the land carried living memories of different and often preferred lives in agricultural communities (such as the Russian *mir*, or peasant commune) and yearned after restitution or some new access to land, somewhere else.[59]

After the American Civil War, the situation of ex-slaves paralleled that of the Jamaican and Russian cases. Mostly agriculturists by skill, however forced it had been, many wanted "forty acres and a mule" to continue working the

---

where even those driven from their rural lands make use of any unbuilt ground in cities to grow food, e.g., the common *milpa* or corn patch in Mexico. The practice has been spreading in cities in the Global North, often in immigrant communities and with the blessings of ecologists. See, Chris Carlsson, *Nowtopia: How Pirate Programmers, Outlaw Bicyclists, and Vacant-Lot Gardeners are Inventing the Future Today!* (Oakland: AK Press, 2008) and Gabriel Valle, "Food Values: Urban Kitchen Gardens and Working-Class Subjectivity," in *Mexican-Origin Foods, Foodways and Social Movements: Decolonial Perspectives*, Devon Peña et al., eds., (Fayetteville: University of Arkansas Press, 2017), 41–61.

Where collectivization has been imposed, as in the USSR, to maximize grain production for export to finance rapid industrialization, the intentional allocation of small subsistence plots of ground to workers on collective and state farms proved a serious mistake. With production on state-organized farms of no use to them, workers tended to plow much of their effort into their private plots. This not only provided subsistence but often produced a surplus which was traded in the countryside or sold in cities. The higher productivity of labor on these private plots was well-known and was the direct result of the withdrawal of efficiency from state exploitation and its application to self-valorization.

58 *Grundrisse*, p. 326, or *MECW*, *Vol 28*, p. 251.

59 Teodor Shanin argues that first generation rural-urban migrants in Russia were responsible for setting up the soviets during the Russian revolution. They were, he argues, replicating in their factories and cities organizations akin to the communes they had known in the countryside.

Over time, emigrants' children constitute a "second generation" with no memories of the land and with an entirely different set of desires and, often, with much less willingness to put up with low wages and lousy jobs. Such children, of whatever age, have often spearheaded uprisings in immigrant communities. See, Yann Moulier-Boutang, *La Révolte des Banlieues ou Les Habits Nus de la République* (Paris: Éditions Amsterdam, 2005).

land – preferably taken from the plantations where they had been working. When Reconstruction (1865–1877) failed to expropriate and redistribute the land of treasonous plantation owners, their one-time slaves resisted returning to the plantations under the low wage, near-slave conditions on offer. Some hit the road forming a mass of unemployed workers – a mass so threatening that the white supremacists who retook power passed and enforced anti-vagrancy laws to control them. Some succeeded in collectively obtaining land to found Freedmen's or Black Towns. Others negotiated sharecropping contracts to get access to land. While sharecropping turned out to involve other forms of un-waged exploitation, including debt peonage, it did provide an alternative to the labor market and reduced the availability of potential waged workers.[60]

The ability to avoid the labor market in old age depends on sources of income. Those higher up the waged/salaried hierarchy could save, either in banks or by buying bonds that generate income, independent of current salaries. The further down that hierarchy, the lower the income, the harder to save – to the point of impossibility. For the low-paid workers whose struggles were the focus of Marx and Engels' studies and political organizing, almost the only source of support in old age was the extended family – where the no-longer employed old lived with and helped their children and grandchildren – and community networks of mutual aid. But both the extended family and community networks have been repeatedly torn apart by the exodus of those following, rather than avoiding the job market. The closing of a mill or mine could mean not only the loss of jobs, but the need of the newly jobless to move elsewhere to find new ones. While such movement was sometimes from one local job to another, it also, all too often involved major geographic displacement, including immigration to other countries, e.g., those repeated waves of European immigration that populated the Western Hemisphere, while displacing the indigenous. That malleability of labor supply so vital to capitalist repeated self-reorganization has always undermined the ability of

60 C. Vann Woodward, *Origins of the New South, 1817–1913* (Baton Rouge: Louisiana State University Press, 1951). The "Freedmen's Towns" were not the hidden maroon colonies founded by escaped slaves, but simply communities of African-Americans with similar background. Often originally on the edge of cities, which have eventually expanded around them, many of those living in such Black communities sought, to the degree that persistent racism allowed, integration into the waged labor force. Over time, such communities have often been at least partially destroyed by the land being usurped through "eminent domain" for such "public improvements" as highways or eroded through gentrification.

families and communities to hold together and provide security for both those no longer able to work and those fed up with it wanting to retire permanently.[61]

3.2.2.2 *Flight from the Labor Market*

Many are the ways waged workers have fled the labor market and working for some employer. For example, many landless laborers, fed up with low and irregular seasonal wages, have tried to flee the labor market by seizing and occupying land, to obtain independent means of obtaining subsistence. (See, Chapter 4, Section 5.2.2.1 below on efforts to reverse enclosure.) Other waged workers, no longer willing to put up with their conditions of work and wages, have fled both labor market and waged labor in what have often appeared as sudden exoduses, short or long term. Short term flight has included: walking off the job, absenteeism, play, or sabotage. Marx and Engels' familiarity with such actions began with the Chartists' short-term strikes and protests, witnessed by Engels in 1842 upon his arrival in England. It continued through their observation of European workers' long-term flight to the New World, often in the wake of armed uprisings, such as those of 1848. For example, many of the German immigrants who came to Texas after the failure of the Revolution of 1848 proceeded to set up utopian communities intended to be free not only of labor markets but of all capitalist exploitation and alienation.[62] By reducing the size of the working labor force, or markedly slowing its growth below capitalist needs, all such actions can cause crises for investors.[63]

As in 1842, strikes and protests have generally been intended to be short, with workers soon returning to work, win or lose. They cause immediate crises for the struck employers, who can no longer produce, much less invest in expansion.[64] The longer such actions last, the greater the disruption to both production and planned investment.

---

61 Because these disruptive displacements have been recurrent and on a mass scale, not surprisingly, both families and communities have often tried to reconstitute themselves in new lands, whether in cities or countryside. Individuals would move, then bring other family members. In many cases, friends and neighbors would move together trying to hold together remnants of their community of origin. Thus, the establishment by immigrants of a "Little Italy" in New York City, a "Chinatown" in San Francisco, a Greektown in Chicago, a Turkish neighborhood in Berlin or an Algerian banlieue in Paris. As I mentioned in Chapter 2, Marx and his family tended to find lodging in just such communities of exiles and immigrants as they moved or were driven from one country to the next.

62 See, Ernest Fischer, *Marxists and Utopias in Texas* (Burnet, TX: Eakin Press, 1980).

63 On all kinds of flight, by all kinds of workers, see Marcus Rediker, Titas Chakraborty and Matthias Van Rossum, *A Global History of Runaways: Workers, Mobility, and Capitalism, 1600–1850* (Oakland: University of California Press, 2019).

64 On the counter use of scabs, see Chapter 6 below.

Flight from one labor market to another is – fleeing workers hope – also temporary and from a greater to a lesser evil. Beyond its universal effort to subordinate life to work, every concrete aspect of work in capitalism varies, from place to place, from employer to employer. Workers know this and frequently look for better paying, safer, less obnoxious jobs, even if it requires moving to obtain them – sometimes not far, sometimes across borders, oceans and continents.[65] Flight is particularly appealing to workers who possess special skills or knowledge acquired in one job that they can take to another. However short term for the workers, the flight of a large numbers, or the repeated flight of smaller numbers, can create a longer-term dearth of labor and a serious crisis for multiple employers.[66]

Exodus from labor markets through flight to distant shores, such as emigration from British and European labor markets to the fabled free lands of the Western Hemisphere can also be short or long-term, depending on whether those fleeing are actually able to obtain land. When successful, their attachment to the land can be as fierce as that of peasants who have resisted enclosure.[67] If such immigrants fail to obtain land, however, their flight may be

65 I first saw this in action in a Paris post office chatting with a North African worker, while waiting in line. I asked him about his job and it turned out he was considering getting a new one. He proceeded to list a whole series of alternatives across Europe, complete with wage scales, benefits, and the degree of unionization. I was impressed!

66 On capitalist responses to such flight see Chapter 6 below. Since the spread of schooling in the twentieth century, such flight undertaken by more educated workers has been labeled a "brain drain" from the countries of origin – an obvious ideological slur on the so-called "uneducated."

67 Such flight has been portrayed in many films about the American West. Examples: Jan Troell's *The Emigrants* (1971) and *The New Land* (1972) about Swedish immigrants who settle in the forests of Minnesota in the mid-nineteenth century and Ron Howard's *Far and Away* (1992) about immigrants fleeing burning crofts in Ireland and seeking free land in Oklahoma during the Land Run of 1893. In both areas "free" land was being taken from Native Americans, in the first case from the *Očhéthi Šakówiŋ* or Dekota Sioux and in the second from the repeatedly-betrayed *Tsalagi* or Cherokee (ᏣᎳᎩ), a people already dispossessed in Georgia, Tennessee, Alabama and North Carolina and forced into the 1838 Trail of Tears trek to Oklahoma.

Although such flight to land for farming has largely disappeared, along with the dwindling of available land (e.g., the "closure" of the North American frontier), difficulties for small farmers, such as foreclosure and enclosure, have continued and the increasing urbanization of society generates ever fewer interested in moving to rural areas. There are still examples of such flight, such as that which has devastated the Amazon cutting down and burning its ecologically complex jungles for conversion to farmland. Unsuited for crop cultivation, most such land has wound up as ecologically impoverished grasslands used for grazing cattle – much of whose meat is exported to wealthy consumers in the

short-lived as they are forced to re-enter the labor market. Even if they do, eventually, seek new waged jobs, their exodus from old ones remains a problem for the employers in the lands from which they fled.

The Europeans who fled to the Americas and moved west to the frontier seeking land included peasants and farmers who had lost their land, those who had worked for wages and those who gained passage across the Atlantic by accepting indenture for several years.[68] Eric Williams argues that the ease of escape for *white* workers, whether waged or indentured, was a prime motivation behind the recourse to *black* slavery by capitalists in North America and the Caribbean.[69] Those who fled exploitation in cities and towns, pushing the "frontier' westward – destroying native American communities in the process – included frontiersmen, pioneers, miners and homesteaders in North America and similar groups in South America.

North American frontiersmen who went west generally hunted for hides or trapped for furs – intruding into the lands previously occupied by Native Americans. (See, Section 3.3.1.) Gauchos went west from the cities on the east coast of South America into the Pampas, the great plains of Argentina, Uruguay and Southern Brazil. Like their counterparts up north, gauchos subordinated their work to their needs. Like many subsistence peasants, they refused to enter the labor market, killed wild cattle for food and hides, which they then sold, but only to obtain what little money they needed to buy what they could not make or trade for.[70] As I once argued to historian George Rawick, for the most part such persons escaped working-class status by subordinating their

---

Global North. Although some countries, such as Canada and Australia continued to offer free land to settlers well into the twentieth century, fewer and fewer have taken advantage of the offer. Today, some small towns offer small plots of free land for house building in the hopes of bolstering their population, but takers are quite different from workers seeking the independence of farmland.

68 Indenture was a legal contract binding a person to work for another for some period of time, during which the person holding the contract tried to extract as much labor as possible. This kind of arrangement has since been banned as a form of slavery.

69 See, Eric Williams, *Capitalism and Slavery* (Richmond, VA: University of North Carolina Press, 1944). There was a similar problem with Native American slaves who could escape and return to their communities. See, Linford Fisher, "'Why shall wee have peace to bee made slaves': Indian Surrenderers during and after King Philip's War" *Ethnohistory* 64, no. 1 (January 2017): 91–114.

70 See, the classic epic poem *El Gaucho Martin Fierro* by José Hernández (1872).

marginal relations to the market, i.e., $C - M$ and $M - C(MS)$, to their own autonomous ends.[71]

The frequent comparison of South American gauchos with North American cowboys – because of their independence, equestrian skills and relationship to cattle – rarely differentiates between those successful at avoiding the labor market and those caught up and corralled by settlers, especially ranchers, into hiring out their labor-power.[72]

Humans, it turns out, were not the only species to flee exploitation. In their own ways, many horses and cattle, imported by the Spanish conquistadors, also fled their enslavers. Almost as soon as horses and cattle reached the mainland in the sixteenth century, they began to escape and multiply, especially in the open grasslands and plains of both North and South America.[73] The rapid multiplication of wild horses provided some Europeans the possibility of living free of the exploitation organized by the colonizers. They also provided Native Americans both a physical and a spiritual resource for resistance to European invasion. Both horses and cattle provided meat and hides, while horses also provided mounts. The result was a proliferation of mounted Native Americans and unwaged Europeans roaming free, hunting wild animals, horses and cattle as a way of life.

---

71 Like some surplus agricultural products sold by subsistence peasants, the hides gauchos stripped from free cattle and sold did enter an international market for hides, the raw material for the production of shoes, boots, saddlery, and machinery drive belts. Both the agricultural products and hides did embody their labor and as with many farmers, odds have it that they were exploited by unequal trade, but the hunting and stripping was a very minor part of their lives, unlike those whose lives were clearly subordinated to working for capital in either wage labor or production purely for commerce. See, "Some Notes on Argentine Gauchos in the nineteenth century on the Question of 'Class'" from a letter to George Rawick (1987) in *Common Sense* 10 (May 1991): 58–61. Besides the *gauchos* in Argentina and Paraguay, there were *vaqueiros* and *gaúchos* in Southern Brazil, *llaneros* in west-central Venezuela and eastern Colombia, *huassos* in Chile and *vaqueros* in Mexico, whether independent or as working as hired hands for ranchers.

72 For analysis of the difficulties for capitalists in turning gauchos into waged workers see, Ricardo Salvatore, "Class Struggle and International Trade: Rio de la Plata's Commerce and the Atlantic Proletariat, 1790–1850" (PhD Diss., University of Texas at Austin, 1987). For some comparison between cowboys, gauchos and similar "equestrian cultures," see Richard Slatta, *Cowboys of the Americas: The Realities of Life as a Cowboy* (London: Lume Books, 2019).

73 Some Native Americans claim that some of these wild horses were indigenous and not descendants of Spanish breeds and have devoted themselves to preserving them and are trying to prove it through genetic testing.

Hard on the heels of such individual escapees from capitalism came pioneers and settlers, mostly in family units, often by river flatboats or overland by wagon trains, to homestead land. Along with them came artisans to build smithies, saddleries and sawmills – the nuclei of future towns, some of which would become cities. All of this flight from capitalist labor markets, although rarely recognized as such, has been honored and romanticized throughout the Americas. Myriad American pioneer and western novels and films have celebrated both waves – the early loners and the later community builders, while frequently interpreting and instrumentalizing the latter as prototypical would-be entrepreneurs, so central to capitalist ideology. This interpretation confuses all those seeking autonomy from capitalist markets with the very real, self-conscious money-makers who came to build stores, open saloons, hotels and eventually banks – which would play a central role in eventually dispossessing those working the land. And of course, all this accelerated with the coming of the highly subsidized railroads,[74] which brought ever more industrial products – means of both production (plows, then machinery) and consumption (cloth, guns, crockery, etc.) – from the East and provided access to distant markets for agricultural products, especially grain, cattle and later sheep, wool, and cotton. Against all this, those who were successful at obtaining land have fiercely resisted its loss.[75]

The flip side of flight has been *the refusal of waged workers to move* away from their communities, to labor markets where they are needed by capitalist employers. While some workers move, many others have resisted migrating to jobs. Indeed, whole communities have responded collectively by sending the few willing to go to distant labor markets while everyone else remains behind and the wages of the former help sustain the latter. So, for instance, in Marx's time male Irish workers went to England for jobs, but their wages – to the extent possible at their low level – would often be used to support their

74 Part of the subsidies received by the railroads was land, so much land as to contribute substantially to the enclosure of the frontier. See the maps showing the extent of the grants in the Library of Congress, e.g., that to the Union Pacific Railroad in Nebraska.

75 This continues to be true throughout the capitalist world, in both the Global North and Global South. Despite sporadic enclosure that has depleted the numbers of family farms and peasant holdings, resistance has continued, e.g., in the US, there was the Farmers' Alliance and the Populist Party of the nineteenth century, which included millions of farmers and more recently the National Farm Family Coalition. In the Global South, Via Campesina, is made up of farmers' movements around the world.

families and communities back in Ireland.[76] This pattern has been repeated around the world.[77]

3.2.2.3 *Other Sources of a Shortage of Labor-Power*

Beyond these refusals on the part of potential workers, other factors with the possibility of disrupting *M – LP* by reducing the availability of workers and increasing the cost of labor, have included *famine, disease and starvation, wartime conscription*, and any slow-down in population growth due to *women's struggles*.[78] The first three possibilities were realized frequently enough in the nineteenth century to seriously reduce the availability of labor. The fourth, although not yet having observable effects on population as a whole, was

---

76 Sometimes these have been individual choices, sometimes communal. Examples of the former were discovered by Karen Palazini in a Brazilian favela where she found women who chose to prepare and sell food out of their houses where they could stay in their community and with their children rather than take jobs on the other side of São Paulo, travel to which would cost part of their paycheck and require hours of time. See, "Women's Work in Lauro de Freitas, Bahia, Brazil: Marginalization or Autonomous Development" (PhD Diss., University of Texas at Austin, 1997). Another example, both within and across borders, was Italy where young, mostly male workers from the South went North to work in factories as capitalists rebuilt after WWII but sent part of their paychecks back down south to support their families and communities. Later, like other North European countries, Italian capitalists welcomed an influx of workers, again mostly male, from North Africa, as their demand for labor-power continued to grow and as women's struggles reduced the domestic birth rate and slowed the growth of the indigenous labor force. See, Mariarosa Dalla Costa, "Reproduction and Immigration," originally written and published in A. Serafini, et al., *L'Operaio multinazionale in Europa* (Milan: Feltrinelli, 1974) 207–242. Translated, in part, for *Zerowork 3*. A modern example of communal choices – that nevertheless accommodates individual ones – has been documented by Néstor Rodríguez who has identified over fifteen distinct, stable communities of Mexicans in Houston, Texas that are extensions of communities back in Mexico. Those who come north change over time but wages of those who do support both portions of what Rodríguez calls "transnational" communities. See, his "The Battle for the Border: Notes on Autonomous Migration, Transnational Communities, and the State" *Social Justice* 23, no.3 (Fall 1996): 21–37. This is quite distinct from emigrants sending money home to pay for family members to follow them, as was the case of the Irish in the wake of the great famine, as Marx reports in *Capital, Vol. 1*, p. 862, or *MECW*, *Vol 35*, p. 695.

77 It seems to be a universal trait of many racist xenophobes to believe that every immigrant worker wants to bring all of his or her family and friends to live in (and threaten the cultural integrity of) their superior country. Whether they believe it or not, they wield it to foment anti-immigrant sentiment, which helps keep immigrant workers terrorized and locals less likely to accept them into a common struggle against capitalist bosses. This belief or pretense is belied by the existence of these transnational communities and the frequent permanent return of successful immigrant workers to their points of origin.

78 In microeconomic terms, all these cause a leftward shift in the supply curve of labor.

understood by capitalists as a very real threat that had to be nipped in the bud before it could cause serious problems.

3.2.2.3.1 Disease and Starvation

Besides flight, by far the most obvious dramatic reductions in the labor force, in Marx and Engels' time, were those caused by famine, disease, and starvation. In the British Isles, the most serious famine of the nineteenth century was undoubtedly the *Gorta Mór* or Great Irish Famine of 1845 to 1859 that killed a million people.[79] In that case, although the root cause of the deaths was a disease that hit potatoes, it resulted in famine because the English colonization of Ireland had forced the conversion of most food cultivation to that of commercial crops, especially flax to pay taxes and feed the British textile industry. As a result of this manner of exploitation, potatoes had become the staple food of peasants in Ireland and when the potato blight hit, the drop in food supplies soon produced malnutrition, disease, and starvation on a massive scale. The deaths, coupled with the flight of over two million emigrants, caused a huge drop in the supply of Irish laborers. This drop and the subsequent series of revolts by Irish workers against their exploitation by the British caused recurring crises for employers.

Although on a much smaller scale, the same blight caused crises elsewhere in northern Europe and contributed to the Revolutions of 1848.[80] Marx writes of the effects in France:

> The potato blight and the crop failures of 1845 and 1846 increased the general ferment among the people. The dearth of 1847 called forth bloody conflicts in France as well as on the rest of the continent... the struggles of the people for the prime necessities of life.[81]

The great famine in Ireland was both preceded and followed by many others, especially in British-colonized South Asia where the yields of most crops depended on adequate but not excessive monsoon rains. In 1837–1838 drought and famine struck Agra in the East India Company-ruled North-Western Provinces and killed roughly 800,000 people. In 1866 drought, famine and then a cholera epidemic killed a third of the population in Orissa (Odisha). The Great

---

79 See, David Ross, *Ireland: History of a Nation* (New Lanark: Geddes & Grosset, 2002).

80 See, the introduction to Eric Vanhaute, Richard Paping and Cormac Ó Gráda, eds., *When the potato failed. Causes and effects of the "last" European subsistence crisis, 1845–1850* (Turnhout: Brepols Publishers, 2007) 1–31.

81 K. Marx, "Class Struggles in France" *MECW, Vol. 10*, p. 52.

Famine of 1876–1878 unfolded in south and southwestern India but spread north into the North-Western Provinces and the Punjab. The death toll has been estimated from 5.5 to 10.3 million people. In each such case, the degree of hunger, starvation, disease, and death depended, not only on the weather but also on colonial policies, preceding, during and following the droughts.[82] Although each of these events appeared, and was often portrayed as "natural" disasters, the truth was quite different.

The colonial replacement of food production for local consumption by the cultivation of commercial crops for export, imposed on Ireland and other colonies, not only makes workers' health more susceptible to crop failures but has often involved gathering workers into shanty housing, where the presence of disease and sickness spread quickly. Where sick workers are easily replaceable, the cost is relatively low. Where not, money has to be spent on housing and feeding those who, for the time being, can't work and the costs to employers are higher.[83]

Because capital organizes workers in an unwaged/wage/salary hierarchy, disease always hits the poorest the hardest. Given their highly contagious nature, some diseases, such as influenza, can spread throughout the income hierarchy. But those with higher incomes are better able to avoid the disease, say by moving away, or to cope with disease, once acquired, by having access to the best available health care.[84] Poor workers have no such options. Engels'

82 This was true not only in British South Asia but throughout the world of European colonialism. After WWII, as the US and the USSR vied for influence in the ex-colonial Third World, rivalry and self-interest produced a certain amount of "foreign aid" to devastated areas, e.g., the provision of famine relief aid from US food surpluses conditioned on repayment with policy changes beneficial to US corporations. An example was the demand by US diplomats for India to open its fertilizer industry to US corporate investment in exchange for food aid in coping with the drought and famine of 1965–67. See, H. Cleaver, "Food, Famine, and International Crisis," *Zerowork* 2 (Fall 1977): 7–69.

83 Such was the lament of United Fruit Company executives about the costs involved in maintaining an adequate labor force to work their banana plantations in Central America. See, the report of United Fruit's medical director, Edward Salisbury, "Costs and Returns of Industrial Health Services," in *Industry and Tropical Health* 1 (1950): 172–173. Victor Heiser, in his *An American Doctor's Odyssey* (New York: Norton, 1936) describes many such situations where disease and illness proved costly to US companies abroad.

84 Thomas Mann in his novel *Death in Venice* (1912), based on extensive research into the history of a cholera epidemic, describes just such flight from the disease-ravaged city by those able to do so, e.g., tourists and locals with enough money. It is the failure of the main character in the novel to join in that flight that results in his death from the disease. This differential continues today. Flight to distant cities, or retreat to country homes are only available to the wealthy. Access to good medical care, especially in countries without universal health care, such as the United States, is also reserved for those able to meet its

analysis of the *Condition of the English Working Class* and Marx's of the reports filed by government inspectors of workplaces and worker housing provide ample evidence of the vulnerability of low-waged workers to disease both on-the-job and off.[85]

For the most part, the negative impact of disease and starvation is localized. Hurricanes which churn up in the Atlantic and the Gulf of Mexico and cyclones and typhoons in the Pacific and Indian oceans hit low-lying coastal areas hardest. Flooding occurs mostly on coasts and in river valleys and deltas. Fires rage mainly in drought-struck brush and forested areas or among poorly constructed houses in working-class neighborhoods. When the winds die down, the flood waters recede and the fires burn out, the locals left most devastated are usually workers and their families – those living in shanty towns or poor neighborhoods – because they don't have the resources to escape, cope or rebuild.[86] Their suffering costs money to those who employ them, either in caring for them or replacing them.

The obvious exceptions to such localization have been *pandemics* in which disease has spread across much of the world, carried from country to country by some vector. In the case of the Black Death (bubonic plague) of the fourteenth century, the vectors were rats and rat fleas, carried from Asia to Europe on ships engaged in international trade and imperialism. In the case

---

high cost. The rich can also afford guardians for children kept home from school during epidemics; poorly paid workers cannot. We have seen this play out amidst the Covid-19 epidemic. In the wake of Covid-19, an analysis of cellphone data showed that *40 percent* of the people in the richest neighborhoods in New York City fled the city! See, Kevin Quealy, "The Richest Neighborhoods Emptied Out Most as Coronavirus Hit New York City," *New York Times*, May 15, 2020, "Hundreds of thousands of New York City residents, in particular those from the city's wealthiest neighborhoods, left…"

85 See, Marx's analysis in *Capital, Vol. 1*, Chapter 25, Section 5, Subsections (b) and (c), and Engels' analysis in his later essay "The Housing Question," *MECW*, *Vol. 23*, pp. 317–391.

86 In recent times, such differential impacts have been experienced from the slums of cyclone-battered Philippines or Bangladesh to the 9th Ward in New Orleans, devastated by the Hurricane Katrina (2005). Despite the promises of President George W. Bush, most working-class housing there has never been rebuilt. The same pattern was repeated with Hurricane Maria (2017) that wrecked Puerto Rico. President Donald Trump infamously tossed paper towels to the victims but denied the extent of death attributable to the hurricane and refused to provide adequate aid to rebuild. While urban fires may be more likely to destroy city slums, forest fires in California and grass fires in Hawaii have demonstrated how this is not always the case. Workers' homes built far from city centers and ever deeper into surrounding woodlands have been burned in California. So have homes in Maui in 2018 and the entire town of Lahaina in the summer of 2023 as wildfires swept through the dry grass and abandoned sugar cane of now closed plantations. See, Cost of Government Commission, *Report on Wildfire Prevention and Cost of Recovery on Maui*, July 2021.

of smallpox, cholera and every influenza pandemic, the vectors have been humans, traveling from place to place, from the Spanish invaders of the Western Hemisphere in the sixteenth century to merchants, armies and tourists in the nineteenth. In the cholera epidemics of 1817–1823 and 1826–37, the disease spread from India to other parts of Asia, the Middle East, East Africa, the coasts of the Mediterranean Sea, Northern Europe and eventually to North America and south into Mexico and the Caribbean.[87] All of these waves of disease have revealed the vulnerability of working-class populations and the continuing possibilities of crisis in labor supply. The differential results typical of local epidemics, i.e., hitting lowest-paid workers and their families hardest, have been largely the same with pandemics.[88] In all historical cases, millions of workers

87 Unfortunately, despite the discovery by modern medicine of the nature of these diseases and of effective methods of treatment, new or mutated bacteria and viruses, often spread by thoughtless capitalist practices, have caused repeated pandemics, each requiring new research and new discoveries in order to cope with each outbreak. The cholera pandemic in Latin America (1991–1995) is thought to have begun with a ship from Asia dumping its human wastes or ballast water in the harbor of Lima, Peru. It reached Chiapas, Mexico in 1995 in the midst of the Zapatista struggle for indigenous rights and democracy. At that time, I posted a series of interventions on one solidarity listserv about cholera and the political history of disease.

88 More recent pandemics have included those of cholera (a whole series, including 1961–75) spread by water contaminated by human feces, of HIV/AIDS that started in the 1980s, spread by humans, and of a whole series of influenza pandemics, e.g., the Spanish Flu (1918–1919), spread by humans, Swine Flu (2009), spread by animals and humans, SARS and MERS, and today, Covid-19. For an overview of the history see the Wikipedia entries for pandemics in general and for particular cases. We are currently seeing this differential impact play out as Covid-19 sweeps across the globe. As schools, businesses, sports arenas and other meeting places have been emptied and people ordered to stay home, "social distancing" and "self-quarantining" to slow the spread of the virus. Clearly those who can best afford to do these things are those higher up the income hierarchy and those least able to do so are those lower down. Those with savings can draw on them; for those dependent on current wages for food, rent or mortgage payments, the loss of a job immediately undermines their ability to pay bills and buy necessities. When schools are closed, children from low-waged households dependent on school breakfasts and lunches can be in serious trouble. When their only access to classes is via computer and they have none, they are left out of school-from-home. All of this played out before our eyes in 2020–21 during the Covid-18 pandemic. See, Lizzie Wade, "An Unequal Blow: In past pandemics people on the margins suffered the most," *Science* 368, no. 6492 (May 15, 2020): 700–703, and Liliana Dávalos, et. al., "Pandemics' historical role in creating inequality," *Science* 368, no. 6497 (June 19, 2020): 1322–3.

Another exception to localization, only recently recognized, has been human-accelerated global warming with its ever increasing effects on a wide variety of disasters, including flooding, fires and species extinction. (More on this in Chapter 5 on predispositions).

have suffered and been unable to work, through sickness and often death, dramatically reducing the availability of labor-power in both labor markets and production.

As capitalist circuits have become ever more entwined on a global scale, creating far-flung networks of production and sales, local disruptions can quickly circulate to cripple reproduction. Where the production in one place provides inputs into production in another place, the reduction in production due to disease ripples along the supply chain. Where disease disrupts the transportation of commodities, shutting down ports or dramatically raising the costs of transport, costs rise and profits fall.[89] (More on this in Chapter 5, Section 4.) The connections between class struggle and these pandemics that disrupt capitalist reproduction deserve far more attention than they have received. While the differential negative impact on workers has derived from exploitation and workers' failure to successfully win higher wages, better housing and access to medical care, their reaction has sometimes been outrage and uprising against the neglect of measures to protect them – actions which can further disrupt production.[90]

3.2.2.3.2 Military Poaching of Workers

Even without the contribution of imperialist armies to the spread of disease and its negative effect on the supply of labor, the simple drain of workers from the labor force into the military reduces labor supply at home and can cause

89 The global character of the current Covid-19 pandemic has caused such widespread ruptures in supply chains that the business press regularly reports on such ruptures, providing estimates of their severity, their consequences and expected duration. See, the daily email bulletins of the Bloomberg group. For example, "The cost of shipping a 40-foot container from Shanghai to L.A. reached $11,569 in the past week, almost eight times higher than pre-pandemic levels, according to the Drewry World Container Index. One illustration of the strained system is the queue of ships outside the twin ports of L.A. and Long Beach, which jumped to a record 49 vessels as of late yesterday." (9/10/2021)

90 An obvious example was how government neglect and capitalist discrimination against victims during the HIV/AIDS pandemic led to massive and ultimately successful mobilization demanding resources for both research and treatment for victims. Our most recent experience of such outrage and uprising exploded in June 2020 in the US. Although triggered by videos of police murdering an unarmed black man, the event came amidst the Covid-19 pandemic in which growing numbers of reports pointed to the differential effect of the disease on those minorities continuing to work in "essential jobs" or suffering from being laid off with inadequate unemployment compensation and having the least health insurance to help cope with the disease. Sadly, efforts by right-wing politicians to utilize the pandemic for their own political ends, has also resulted in the confounding phenomenon of conservatives raging against masks, vaccines, and social distancing – measures designed to protect them!

a crisis for employers. The "military revolution" that accompanied the rise of capitalism and its nation states involved a vast expansion in the size of armies and a resulting shift from the use of mercenaries and volunteers to large scale conscription. The most notable exemplar of this expansion occurred with Napoleon Bonaparte's conscription of a gigantic army to conquer much of continental Europe.[91] Other countries followed suit. For example, Marx mentions how reductions in the numbers of agricultural workers during the Crimean War of 1853 to 1856 contributed to such an increase in wages as to cause employing farmers to protest and introduce machinery.[92]

Military forces were recruited among both waged and unwaged workers. Among the waged workers impressed into military service were sailors from commercial vessels, either in port or at sea. This immediately reduced the number of workers available to those merchant capitalist ships, and their captains had to find replacements on their own. Among the unwaged taken into the military were conscripts from peasant villages, which immediately reduced the size of the agricultural labor force. Others were taken from taverns or prisons reducing the size of the latent reserve army of labor and its availability to employers, either as a threat to the currently employed or as replacements.[93] Both at home and abroad Black slaves and indentured "coolie" laborers from India and China were diverted from more productive labor to the work of building fortifications, etc.[94] Although local recruiting of the colonized, e.g., Sepoys in India, helped limit the drain at home, it reproduced it in the colonies.

Whatever the source, the scale of extraction of workers from the labor force available to capitalists is determined by the scale of military mobilizations and by the degree of resistance to recruitment and conscription. Conscription, after all, involves *forced* participation in the military and that in turn produces widespread avoidance and desertion from the ranks. The drain and associated conflict swelled in periods of war, either of conquest or between imperialist powers. The greater the resistance to colonialization or the bigger the war, the more workers are conscripted and the greater the problem for capitalists trying

91 See, Isser Woloch, "Napoleonic Conscription: State Power and Civil Society" *Past & Present* 111 (May 1986): 101–129 and Louis Rouanet and Ennio Piano, "Drafting the Great Army: The Political Economy of Conscription in Napoleonic France," *The Journal of Economic History* 83, no. 4 (December 2023): 1057-1100.

92 *Capital, Vol. 1*, p. 791, or *MECW*, *Vol. 35*, p. 632.

93 In modern times, where youths have been subjected to conscription, the unwaged have also been plucked from schools.

94 On the use of "coolie" laborers as late as WWI, see, Guoqi Xu, *Strangers on the Western Front: Chinese Workers in the Great War* (Cambridge, MA: Harvard University Press, 2011).

to maintain or recruit workers.[95] It's worth noting that the degree to which draft dodging resistance reduced this drain on the labor force has depended on the strategies of the dodgers. Some sought waged employment elsewhere and remained available to capitalist employers. But others disappeared from the labor force entirely by becoming bandits or by escaping to settle in remote areas.[96]

3.2.2.3.3 Reductions in Family Size

Here, I feel obliged to point to an important phenomenon that Marx and Engels *should* have taken into account in their analysis of crisis but did not – as far as I have been able to find. When they analyzed internal family dynamics, they focused on power relationships, but failed to study how those relationships affected birth rates, population growth and the availability of workers for hiring. I find this surprising considering their familiarity with what the English political economist Thomas Malthus had to say on the subject in his book *An Essay on the Principle of Population* (1793) – a man whom Marx and Engels criticized again and again on other topics related to crisis.

Malthus argued theoretically that population, and hence the supply of labor, tends to grow exponentially because workers tend to breed like rabbits, unlike the bourgeois who sometimes exercise "moral restraint" and limit the size of their families. At the same time, he saw agriculture and the supply of food tending to expand more slowly than population. As a result, population growth and the supply of labor, he argued, is mostly only checked by external factors, such as famine or war. Among the lessons he drew from this analysis were that 1) the poor had only themselves to blame for their situation and 2) feeding the poor, i.e., those with no wages, should be abandoned because with more food they would just breed faster and create more poverty. This argument appealed to capitalists and was wielded by them against the Poor Laws or any other form of relief. Eventually, in the second edition of his book (1803), after studying actual population dynamics in Europe, he admitted workers did appear to be able to

95 This problem of labor shortages caused by wars that draw off men became familiar during World Wars I and then II as it became difficult to "man" factories and even farms for plantings and harvest. Special efforts had to be made by capitalists and governments to replace absent male workers – sometimes with prisoners or immigrants, but often with local women. The problem persisted after WWI, and to a lesser degree after WWII, especially in Europe, because of the high death rate in the war. Governments also formulated pro-natalist policies to encourage women to have more children to replace those who had been killed.

96 For a wide-ranging survey of worker flight from work, which includes multiple examples of workers absconding from armies and navies, see *A Global History of Runaways*, op. cit.

exercise restraint and choose to have fewer children. But this admission had no effect upon the embrace of his theoretical argument by those opposed to any help for the poor.[97]

Instead of addressing these issues, Marx and Engels' emphasis on the internal power structures within the family focuses on the inequities of men dominating both women and children. As early as the *Manuscripts of 1844*, the *German Ideology* (1846), and the *Communist Manifesto* (1848), they argue that property relationships shape family relationships.[98] They juxtapose the *bourgeois family*, in which, they argue, the possession of property results in relationships being reduced "to a mere money relation", to the *proletarian family*, which lacks property and therefore the relation of husband "to his wife and children has no longer anything in common with bourgeois family relations."[99] They condemn the former, "the bourgeois sees in his wife a mere instrument of production [of progeny]" to maintain the continuity of family property, and mock the bourgeois pretense of a "hallowed co-relation of parent and child."[100] They call, therefore, for the liberation of women from the servitude of the bourgeois family and stopping "the exploitation of children by their parents."[101]

Yet, by the time Marx writes *Capital*, he also recognizes how – under the pressure of poverty – desperate proletarians are willing to allow their children to be exploited by capitalists.

> We find in the most recent years of the Children's Employment Commission [1850s-60s] that in relation to this traffic in children, working-class parents have assumed characteristics that are truly revolting and thoroughly like slave-dealing.[102]

Decades later, Marx and Engels' discovery of the writings of the anthropologist Lewis Morgan (1818–1881) spurred both to new thinking about the origin, nature and destiny of families. Although Marx died before he could do more

97 True then, true ever since. This kind of Malthusian argument has been reformulated and trotted out again and again in opposition to all forms of "social safety net" expenditures, right up to recent opposition to those designed to offset the effects of the Covid pandemic.

98 Marx, "Economic and Philosophic Manuscripts of 1844", MECW, *Vol. 3*, pp. 294–296, Marx and Engels, "The German Ideology," MECW, *Vol. 5*, p. 44, 180–181.

99 Marx and Engels, "Manifesto of the Communist Party", MECW, *Vol. 6*, p. 494.

100 Ibid., p. 502.

101 Ibid., pp. 501–502.

102 *Capital, Vol. 1*, p. 519, fn 40, or MECW, *Vol. 35*, p. 399.

than take notes on Morgan, Engels picked up where he left off, writing and publishing *The Origin of the Family, Private Property and the State* in 1884.[103]

In that essay, he sketches the historical evolution of the family from prehistoric times to contemporary capitalism. In doing so, he elaborates their previous assertion about the dominance of men over women in the bourgeois family. While anchoring the rise of the patriarchal family and "the subjugation of one sex by another" in pre-capitalist times, his main concern is the "final outcome of three thousand years of monogamy"[104]:

> The modern individual family is based on the overt or covert domestic slavery of the woman ... the man has to be the earner, the bread-winner of the family, at least among the propertied classes, and this gives him a dominating position ... In the family, he is the bourgeois; the wife represents the proletarian.[105]

And, as in the case of those two classes, there is a struggle in which the wife/proletarian often rebels against her servitude.

As in the *Manifesto*, Engels juxtaposes this situation to that of working-class families where, because industrialization "has moved the woman from the house to the labor market and the factory, and made her often enough the bread-winner of the family, the last remnants of male domination ... have lost all foundation ... the woman has regained, in fact, the right of dissolution of marriage ..."[106] So, if wives' traditional servitude to their husbands includes their role as brood-mares, one might expect women to use the power conveyed by the wage, in ways that would result in a decrease in birth rates. Yet, Engels says nothing about this. His only solution to women's struggles is their complete integration into the waged labor force. "... the first precondition for the emancipation of women is the reintroduction of the entire female sex into public industry."[107]

In short, neither Marx nor Engels provide any analysis of intra-family struggles around procreation and child rearing that could provide an alternative to Malthus' simple-minded vision of working-class homes as "bunny hutches" where only the food supply determines birth rates. Despite recognizing that

---

103 Friedrich Engels, "*The Origin of the Family, Private Property and the State*" (1884), MECW, Vol. 26, pp. 129–276.

104 Ibid., p. 175.

105 Ibid., p. 181.

106 Ibid., p. 179.

107 Ibid., p. 182.

women's work in the home produces labor-power, they never bring to bear on that work the kind of detailed analysis they elaborate with regard to the production of all other commodities.[108] For this to happen, several generations of Marxist feminists have had to do what those two men did not, and in so doing help us understand the sharp declines in birth rates which would eventually create crises for capitalists' ability to meet their needs for labor-power.[109]

This absence is all the more striking because not long after Marx and Engels passed from the scene demographers came to recognize how rising income produces a "demographic transition", with eventual falling birth rates and slower population growth.[110] Rising incomes free parents from the need to peddle their children to capitalists for a wage that supplements their own. Rising income also reduces the need for children's labor at home, e.g., on farms. Moreover, for both waged and unwaged families, it reduces the need for children as ultimate care providers for their parents – for many the only form of social security for old age. All these factors help explain fewer births and slower growth of the labor force. Finally, we also now know that the speed of this demographic transition has been determined by that to which Marx and Engels paid little attention: the degree to which women's struggles have given them control over their bodies, including their ability to control the number of their children. Everywhere women have gained more control, birth rates have fallen, often dramatically, causing a reduction in the growth of the population and hence of the labor force – sometimes reducing it well below the needs of capital and therefore causing a crisis in $M - LP$.[111]

3.2.3 Overzealous Investment

The most obvious possible problem on the demand side of the labor market I have already discussed in the first section of this chapter, i.e., possible problems in raising sufficient money to hire enough workers for planned investment. All the possible impediments discussed there could be repeated here, including: (1) workers past struggles causing a shortage of retained earnings and (2) problems in access to credit due to perceived risks, or to central bank

108 *Capital, Vol. I.*, pp. 519–520 fn. 40, or *MECW, Vol. 35*, p. 399, fn. 2).

109 See, Silvia Federici, *Patriarchy of the Wage: Notes on Marx, Gender, and Feminism* (Oakland: PM Press, 2021) Chapter Three: Gender and Reproduction in Marx's *Capital*, pp. 32–50.

110 Mikko Myrskyla, et. al., "Advances in development reverse fertility declines," *Nature* 460, no. 7256 (August 2009): 741–743. Although this source is modern, rising income was decreasing fertility long before.

111 In the post-WWII decades, women's gains and the slower growth of the labor force contributed to rising wages, forcing capitalists to have recourse to immigrant labor. See, Dalla Costa's "Reproduction and Immigration", op. cit.

policies, both of which can raise interest rates, undercutting expected profits. Even in the absence of such problems, however, there is another all-too-common possible source of crisis.

That source, to which both Marx and Engels return repeatedly, is how the demand for labor often outstrips supply. This commonly occurs in boom periods when capitalists are zealously investing, as quickly as money and available *MP* allow, to expand production to take advantage of apparently expanding markets and record profits. In such periods, real investment in expanding production capacity is often taking place in an atmosphere of rabid speculation, hardly an environment for careful calculations of risk. Enthusiastic investment can cause soaring demands for labor that can outstrip a depleted, stagnant, or more slowly growing supply. This increases workers' bargaining power and their ability to win increases in wages and other benefits (including less work) large enough to undercut profits. Any serious reduction in profits, or the rate of profit, constitutes a crisis for capitalists. Substantial reductions in investment can bring the boom to an end and contribute to a downturn, not only in individual industries but in economic activity as a whole. Marx writes:

> If the quantity of unpaid labour supplied by the working class and accumulated by the capitalist class increases so rapidly that its transformation into capital requires an extraordinary addition of paid labour, then wages rise and, all other circumstances remaining equal, the unpaid labour diminishes in proportion. But as soon as this diminution touches the point at which the surplus labour that nourishes capital is no longer supplied in the normal quantity, a reaction sets in: a smaller part of revenue is capitalized, accumulation slows down … [112]

Against Malthus' reasoning that fluctuations in wages are caused by fluctuations in labor supply, Marx argued the contrary, that fluctuations in capitalists' demand for labor – over the course of booms and busts – was the primary explanation for increases or decreases in wages and the effects on profits, the willingness to invest and to hire. How capitalist reductions in investment during downturns can help overcome the power of workers to raise wages, I take up in Chapter 7.

Also, on the "demand side," it is worth noting how more often than not when capitalists hire workers it has been common to put them to work and *then* pay them – a situation in which it is the workers who are effectively extending

112 *Capital, Vol. 1*, Section 1, p. 771, or *MECW*, *Vol. 35*, p. 616.

credit to the capitalists. It is an organization of $M - LP$ in which workers effectively work for free for some period until capitalists have money on hand to pay them. Marx writes, the "money of the buyer in this exchange mostly functions as *means of payment* ... it can be said that everywhere the worker gives credit to the capitalist."[113] Given the low level of wages and narrow limits of workers' savings, such credit must be short lived – a day or a week at most in Marx's time – albeit repeated regularly. Because of this, it is often the case that "In times of crisis, and even with isolated bankruptcies, it is then revealed that this credit given by the workers is no mere phrase since they do not get paid."[114] In such circumstances, failure to pay must very quickly lead to worker protests, slowdowns in labor or even work stoppages and strikes. In the nineteenth century such sequences often played out when capitalists, short of funds and unable to borrow as credit became too expensive, reduced or shut down production, laying off workers and not paying them.

3.3 *Possible Crises for Buyers of the Means of Production, M – MP*

This section deals with crises faced by capitalists who need to *buy* means of production. The flip side: crises facing capitalists *selling* means of production are dealt with in Section 5.2.2. Because capitalist purchases of *MP* are acts of investment, *willingness* to buy depends upon everything I discussed in Chapter 3 above, including both investor estimations of the potential profitability of the investment, and their *ability* to mobilize the resources necessary, not only to purchase *MP* but also to hire *LP*. That ability depends on their accumulated surplus value and, if necessary, their access to loanable funds, i.e., their ability to borrow from the monetary commons pooled and managed by various financial intermediaries. Given these conditions, the most obvious source of crisis

113 Marx points this out in the "Manuscript of 1861–63," *MECW, Vol. 30*, pp. 52–53 and in *Capital, Vol. 1*, pp. 278 and 1066, or *MECW, Vol. 35*, pp. 184–5. This situation still obtains, even with salaried workers, who are usually paid at the end of a month's labor. In isolated mining or mill towns, it has also often been the case that the local company extends consumer credit to the workers in the period running up to the day they are paid – at which point they pay back the company with their just received wages. There's a revealing scene in the film *Coal Miner's Daughter* (1980) where Loretta Lynn, still a little girl, is with her father who comes out of the company office with his pay and says "Let's go give the company its money back" as they head for the company store where they had been buying on credit. Besides low pay and high interest on "store credit," Marx also writes of a third opportunity for exploitation used by such companies with isolated and dependent labor forces: rent on ill-built and unhealthy housing. See, *Capital*, Vol. 1, pp. 585–6, 820–2, 837–842, *MECW, Vol. 35*, pp. 460, 659–660, 673–677. Some years later, in 1872–4, Engels wrote a series of articles addressing such housing issues. See, *MECW, Vol. 23*, pp. 317–391.

114 *MECW, Vol. 30*, pp. 52–53.

for buyers of the means of production are unexpected increases in their price, which would increase their costs of production and thus reduce expected profits. If the reduction is large enough, planned investment may be abandoned. The most likely sources of such unexpected increases in prices are problems in the production, transportation, or markets for needed *MP*.

In his *theory*, because it is a theory of a fully developed capitalism, Marx generally assumes capitalists buy *MP* from other capitalists with money. However, as his analysis of primitive accumulation, colonialism and the gradual transition from traditional agriculture and artisanal handicraft to capitalist industry shows, he was fully aware that capitalism first emerged and developed within a non-capitalist world. As capitalists have expanded their operations across the face of the earth, they have repeatedly faced peoples who have not yet had any use for money but have had things to trade usable as means of production for various industries. In such situations, capitalists have often resorted to one of the oldest methods of merchants: barter.

3.3.1 Barter and Crisis

As an early example of the acquisition of *MP* via barter was the fur trade with Native Americans, beginning in the 1600s. This barter was soon undercut by the acquisition of furs from European trappers, who would sometimes barter furs for things they needed but often wanted to be paid in cash. Both the barter trade in furs and that for cash were integral to the rise of capitalism, both local and international. European *merchants* were bent on acquiring furs to resell and created elaborate networks to cultivate fur trapping and trade with both Native American and European trappers. *Industrial* capitalists sought furs, instead, as means of production. These Europeans learned that they could trade use-values for furs. In so doing, they were both acquiring what they wanted and, effectively, annexing and exploiting the labor and skills of trappers for their own purposes.[115]

115 Given the refusal of most Native Americans to submit to the labor market, trade was one of the few ways their labor could be annexed. Another, notoriously practiced by early European invaders, was slavery. See, the entire issue of *Ethnohistory* 64, no. 1 (January 2017) on "New Directions in the History of Native American Slavery Studies." Assuming far more labor was involved in trapping and preparing pelts for sale than in manufacturing the items for which they were traded, Native Americans and trappers were being exploited through unequal exchange.

This form of annexation of labor-power was akin to that employed by merchants in the "putting-out system" wherein capitalists bought raw materials such as flax, wool or cotton from both capitalist and non-capitalist peasants, then "put the materials out" to spinning and weaving artisans, and then bought the resulting thread, yarn, and cloth from

On the East Coast of North America European settlers learned early on they could trade *wampum* or beads made from shells for furs from Native Americans. Originally, the invading colonists wanted furs for immediate consumption, for the same immediate use-values as the indigenous, e.g., warm coats. Oblivious to the myriad use-values of *wampum* to native Americans, the Europeans looked at *wampum* as a kind of primitive money and set about producing the beads themselves, purely for barter trade.

This pattern of trading industrial goods for Native American use-values was repeated as the European invasion moved West, with what they offered in trade varying according to the practices of the people encountered. More notorious than the trading of industrially produced use-values such as wampum, steel knives or cloth was the trading of alcohol or guns in exchange for whatever the merchants or capitalists sought to obtain.

Although an anomaly in capitalism, barter trade, like trade using money, was also susceptible to crises. The sources of such crises could be found both in the supply of use-values and in the demand for them.

Supply was subject to short-run disruptions among trappers due to conflicts over who could trap what and where. Conflicts raged not only between European and Native American trappers but also between tribes of Native Americans. Such conflicts were aggravated by those among competing European colonialists, e.g., the French-Indian War (1754–1763), in which both the French and the British allied with different tribes and pitted them against each other for their own competing imperialist interests. As the variety of manufactured trade goods and Native American desires for them grew, so did conflicts among suppliers, both Native American and European.

Supply was also subject to the long-run problem of the depletion of animal populations being trapped or hunted. As trade expanded, the earlier *limited* indigenous trapping for furs or hides, which involved a sustainable relationship between people and their environment, fell victim to their subordination to the *much greater* demand driven by the capitalists selling to European producer and consumer markets. With activities such as fur-trapping and trade the only way for indigenous peoples to obtain the goods churned out by capitalist industry, trapping for trade eventually depleted the trapped populations,

---

them as MP. Both cases deserve Marx's characterization of such annexation of labor as a purely *formal* one in the sense that capitalists had not yet enclosed and taken over either the fur industry or textile manufacturing. When takeovers involved a reshaping of the production process, he called the process a *real* subordination of people's labor. The same kind of transition took place in $C' - M'$ but I deal with that in my analysis of the third stage of the circuit.

upset local ecological balances, and caused a drop/crisis in the supply of furs and thus a rise in price and fall in profits. Similar dynamics obtained everywhere in the world as capitalists penetrated new areas populated by peoples without money.

The demand for indigenous use-values as *MP*, was, in turn, dependent on the demand for the goods being manufactured with them. In the North American fur trade, the demand for furs was dependent on the demand for various kinds of clothing made from furs, e.g., fur coats, or hats made from the felt extracted from beaver hides. So, when such hats fell out of fashion, or felt was made from cheaper rabbit fur, the result was a crisis in the trade for beaver hides.[116]

Although important in processes of primitive accumulation, as capitalist trade expanded in the nineteenth century, barter tended to be progressively replaced by the trading of goods and services for money (or the precious metals from which many monies were made).[117] On the basis of their usual assumptions of both monetary exchange and the availability of sufficient money to purchase required *MP*, Marx and Engels pointed to a number of possible sources of crisis in *M – MP*, including those resulting from the *struggles of workers*, *time lags*, *natural disturbances* and *political blockades* of trade.

3.3.2 Possible Crises for Buyers Caused by Workers' Struggles

When capitalists purchase *MP* from other capitalists, the relationship *M – MP* falls within the sphere of exchange and circulation and unlike *M – LP* involves no *direct* relationship with workers. However, the quality, supply and price of *MP* does depend on the relationships between capitalists and workers within the industry producing *MP* – be it in fields, mines, factories or offices – *and* in their transportation to wherever the capitalists buying them intend to put them to use in production.[118] In criticizing Ricardo on crisis, Marx writes,

116 The market for beaver fur eventually rebounded with the demand for new kinds of hats, e.g., cowboy hats, providing some income for remaining trappers. More recently, long after capitalist industrialization came to dominate hide and fur production, strong animal rights campaigns against the use of animal hides and fur and for the substitution of synthetics have begun to reduce the demand for such products in some markets, by both fashion houses and final consumers.

117 That said, barter, as one form of "countertrade", has never disappeared from capitalism. In the post-WWII period, the destruction in those parts of Eastern Europe taken over by the USSR resulted in most trade between Soviet state-capitalism and its clients taking the form of barter. Even today dozens of countries and businesses organize their exchanges through barter. See the Wikipedia entries on barter and countertrade.

118 As previously indicated transportation of *MP* is also a process of production – a spatial displacement – but because it involves different workers, often managed by different

> The same hold up [in investment] could occur for the opposite reasons, if the *real prerequisites* of reproduction were missing (for instance, if grain became more expensive or because not enough constant capital had been accumulated in kind). There occurs a stoppage in reproduction and thus in the flow of circulation.[119]

> Violent fluctuations in price [of raw materials] thus lead to interruptions, major upsets and even catastrophes in the reproduction process.[120]

Clearly, grain (and other *MP*) can "become more expensive" due to workers' struggles in their production and transportation (more in Section 4.2 on crises in ...*P*...) that reduce quality and cause shortages. When workers go on strike and shut down production, crops rot in the fields, nothing is added to inventory, ships are neither loaded nor unloaded and undelivered *C*(*MP*)' deteriorates. With their production shut down, enough raw materials, intermediary goods, tools, or machinery might not be accumulated. The more complex the "supply chains" of production and exchange, the more points of class struggle and the more numerous the possibilities of breakdown in both the production and shipping of *MP*.

Similarly, even in the absence of shortages, when such actions by workers producing *MP* are successful in raising wages and the increased cost of production is passed on through higher prices of *C*(*MP*)', this increases costs, c, for buyers of *MP* and reduces the rate of profit, $s/(c + v)$ undermining investment and planned expanded reproduction.[121]

3.3.3 Crises for Buyers Caused by the Appropriation of *MP*

Another source of problems in the availability of *MP*, has been their direct appropriation by workers or their theft by other capitalists. In this essay, and more generally, I differentiate between "direct appropriation", i.e., the taking of either *MS* or *MP* by workers and "theft", i.e., the theft of *MP* by capitalists. The former term amounts to a refusal of the legitimacy of laws, generally written by

---

capitalists, it constitutes a different sphere of production. Sometimes the sale of *MP* takes place before their transportation, sometimes after.

119 *MECW*, *Vol.* 32, p. 125–126.

120 *Manuscript of 1864–65*, p. 226, *Capital*, *Vol.* 3, p. 213. *MECW*, *Vol.* 37, p. 119.

121 Marx almost always assumes that the minimum acceptable level of profits is the "average," but clearly this is not always so. Capitalists attempting to penetrate new markets and carve out a share for themselves have often accepted below average profits in the short term. So-called "loss leaders" are commodities sold at below profit prices in order to draw customers into buying other items being sold at profitable prices.

capitalists or their apologists, whose definition of "theft" ignores the difference between the taking of personal private property and that of capitalist-owned means of production.[122] Wherever they occur, all such acts reduce the supply of either *MS* or *MP*, cause shortages and increase prices, reducing the real wages of buyers of *MS* and profits for buyers of *MP*. Let's examine the behavior of these two very different sorts of actors in turn.

3.3.3.1 *Direct Appropriation of MP by Workers*

Just as workers have tended to directly appropriate *MS* for their own consumption or for resale to augment their income, discussed in Section 5.2.2.2 below, so too have they appropriated some means of production, e.g., food, raw materials, fuel, or tools, for the same purposes. The peasant direct appropriation of wood in forests, which caught Marx's attention in the 1840s, was an appropriation of means of production only to the degree they cut trees that were to be harvested as lumber; fallen wood was of use only to their personal consumption, e.g., firewood for heating or cooking. An example from the eighteenth century, analyzed in fascinating detail by Peter Linebaugh in *The London Hanged*, was the repeated appropriation of tobacco throughout its transportation from drying barns in America to British wharfs, warehouses and retail outlets by slaves, waggoneers, lightermen and porters, sailors on ships, warehouse carters and even government inspectors.[123] Although some of the tobacco was clearly a consumption good, some was raw material destined to be transformed into cigars, snuff, etc. Obviously, the more tobacco that disappeared into worker pockets along the way, the less was available as *MP* and the higher the price for industrial buyers. *The London Hanged* also details such appropriation by shipyard, silk and leather workers, who would take "scraps" from their workplaces for their own use, or to work up and sell.[124] Their appropriation increased the cost of *MP* by forcing their employers to spend more on raw materials.

In agricultural zones, where foodstuffs are grown commercially as *C*(*MP*), workers, both small holding peasants and landless laborers, sometimes directly appropriate food from the fields of agrarian capitalists, effectively converting *MP* into *MS* and increasing their income.[125] This is especially common

122 The same distinction holds between the capitalist "theft" of workers' time and energy by imposing work, and their "direct (re)appropriation" of their time. Capitalists, of course, call the former legitimate work time and the latter "time theft."

123 See, Chapter Five: Socking, the Hogshead and Excise, pp. 153–183.

124 Ibid., Chapters Eight and Eleven.

125 When working as a landless laborer on a fruit farm in France, I observed and took part in such direct appropriation during harvests. In the case of cherries, "Une pour le boss, une pour la bouche" was an unspoken but common mantra among workers harvesting fruits

in periods of food shortages and famine but can take place at any time.[126] The appropriation reduces production, revenues and profits of those owning the fields from which foodstuffs have been appropriated. If widespread, it reduces supplies to the market, increases the cost of *MP*, lowering the profits of the relevant food processing industry. And to the degree that these increased costs are passed along to workers through increased food prices, they lower the real wage of consumers, reducing consumer demand.

Because many raw materials – tobacco, cotton and other fibers, ores – were produced in colonies far from the handicraft and factory workers who processed them, their transportation to distant factories was subject to all kinds of disruption by all the workers involved, on both land and sea, including mutiny and piracy.[127] In the case of mutineers turned pirates, of course, not only the cargo being carried was appropriated but often the ship itself – the most important means of production in the long-distance transportation of both *MS* and *MP*.[128]

3.3.3.2 *Theft of MP by Capitalists*

In the case of *capitalists* stealing from other capitalists, when the means of production, *MP*, are stolen merely to resell them, via hijacking or piracy, the thieves are effectively acting as agents of rogue merchant capitalists engaged in illegal activity. When the *MP* are stolen to be covertly integrated into another

that could be easily consumed. For other fruits, e.g., peaches, such appropriation for consumption was virtually impossible to conceal and therefore not practiced.

126 Peasants in Bihar Sharif, Bihar, India, described to me in 1976 at length how, after their legal public protests were violently repressed by the Indira Gandhi regime, in the middle of the night during harvest season they directly appropriated crops from the better irrigated and more heavily fertilized land of the local rich landlord – despite the threat of his armed goondas.

127 Piracy of *MP* has by no means disappeared in the twenty-first century, e.g., Somali pirates taking oil tankers in the Gulf of Aiden and holding them for ransom. Both the ransom and increases in insurance raise the price of this energy *MP*, c, lowering profits $s/(c + v)$. As in earlier periods, their actions provoked both the arming of crew and support from military forces deployed to protect such commercial shipping. The films *The Highjacking* (2012), by Tobias Lindholm, *Stolen Seas* (2012), by Thymaya Payne, and *Captain Philips* (2013), by Paul Greengrass, all portray the conflicts between pirates and commercial capitalists. Two other films show the situation of the poor Somali fisherfolk whose circumstances led to their turn to piracy: *The Pirates of Somalia: The Untold Story* (2011), by Neil Bell, and *Fishing without Nets* (2014), by Cutter Hodierne.

128 See, Marcus Rediker, *Villains of All Nations: Atlantic Pirates in the Golden Age* (Boston: Beacon Press, 2005).

firm's supply chain, the thieves are agents of industrial capitalists.[129] An example of such integration familiar in the United States from myriad Western films and TV shows has been the theft of cattle by one rancher from another.[130]

One important kind of intra-capitalist theft is industrial espionage to obtain secret information about production methods or products.[131] Marx's analysis of the diffusion of technological change – often implemented, as we have seen, in response to workers' struggles – focuses on how any development by one capitalist firm, which gives it a competitive advantage and a larger share of surplus value, is desired by others.[132] Where the new technology is easily available, diffusion takes place simply through adapting old plant and equipment or setting up new ones. But the international diffusion of new technology has often come through the migration of skilled workers and entrepreneurs who simply import or build new production facilities. In such a manner, for example, did the silk industry become established in the United States where sericulture had never been successful. Originally protected by tariffs on finished silk goods, the development of the industry was based on imported European technology and Far Eastern raw silk.[133] But where the technology has not been freely available, nor skilled workers willing to move, copying was sometimes done by reverse-engineering means of production but often by stealing

129 Modern examples include the criminal activities of the Coal Mafia in the Indian coal belt that buys stolen coal from the poor and resells it to power companies. See, Frank Daniel and Matthias Williams, *Special Report: The 'Coal Mafia" plunders India*, Thomson Reuters, (May 14, 2013). "Corruption and crime: How coal mafias fuel India's power crisis," Reuters, (December 20, 2014).

130 Such rustling has been portrayed not only in movies about the American West but also in those about Australia and other places where ranching is big business. Examples in the US include *Conagher* (1991), *Open Range* (2003), or others cited in the Wikipedia entry on range wars. In Australia, the operations of modern cattle "duffers" (rustlers) are seen in "Dirty Pool," Season 1, episode 14, in the TV series *McLeod's Daughters* (2001–2009). Another kind of theft has been practiced by oil and gas companies who used horizonal drilling to tap resources under an adjacent property.

131 Examples abound from the beginnings of industrialization to today. One story, from the nineteenth century is told in Daniel Gross's article "Industrial Espionage and Cutthroat Competition Fueled the Rise of the Humble Harmonica: How a shrewd salesman revolutionized the instrument industry", *Smithsonian Magazine*, September 17, 2014.

132 *Capital, Vol. 1*, Chapter 12, or *MECW*, *Vol. 35*, Chapter 12.

133 See, Debin Ma, "The Modern Silk Road: The Global Raw-Silk Market, 1850–1930," *Journal of Economic History* 56, no. 2 (June 1996): 335. On how technologies developed in England were diffused to France, see, Alessandro Nuvolari, et. al., "British-French Technology Transfer from the Revolution to Louis Philippe (1791–1844): Evidence from Patent Data" *The Journal of Economic History* 83, no. 3 (September 2023): 833–873.

information about new products, closely guarded mechanical methods, or chemical processes of production. The more effective such industrial espionage, the faster the diffusion.

Such espionage has always been an essential part of "competition" among capitalists. Writing about such methods in the eighteenth century, with a major focus on French spying on British industry, John Harris writes, "Espionage was a major means by which important new technology was actually transferred or attempted to be transferred … It was practiced on a very wide scale by all western countries of any industrial significance."[134] Methods included observation as "tourists" and stealing actual tools, machines, models, plans or formulae. Often essential, however, was enticing those with knowledge to "defect" to another company, either at home or abroad. Industrialists, it seems, either recognized or discovered that without the knowledge of skilled operatives about how to make a new technology work efficiently, stolen tech could be much less productive or even useless.[135] This inseparability of technology from labor points to the inherent relationship between the two. It is creative labor, after all, that first invents new technology and then brings it alive in action. So, the separation of *MP* and *LP*, e.g., of machines from humans, of "dead" labor from "living" labor is much less clear in actual production processes than it appears in the abstraction of theory.

At an international level all these methods, including espionage, have been natural complements to protectionist laws designed to keep foreign competitors out of a country while local late-comer capitalists are investing and trying to "catch up" to the methods and standards of their more able foreign competitors. The degree to which the success of these methods causes a crisis for the company or industry from which the technology is stolen depends upon how much of a market share the newly more competitive production is able to carve out. The logic of the "infant industry" argument for protection explicitly assumes that success in augmenting industrial efficiency will enhance competitiveness and the ability to steal market share and cause a crisis for competitors.

---

134 John Harris, "The Rolt Memorial Lecture, 1984, Industrial Espionage in the Eighteenth Century," *Industrial Archaeology Review* 7, no. 2 (1984–1985): 127. Also, John Harris, *Industrial Espionage and Technology Transfer. Britain and France in the Eighteenth Century* (London: Routledge, 1998).

135 John Harris provides abundant examples.

3.3.4 Crises Caused by Time Lags

As Marx's two-department model of expanded reproduction makes clear, the appropriate amounts of *MP* (and *MS* for that matter) need to be produced – and available at profitable cost – for both departments. Marx and Engels argued, as early as the 1840s, that such availability is never guaranteed – despite economists' quasi-religious belief that market dynamics would almost always bring this about. The absence of intersectoral planning and time lags in flows of information sometimes meant *overproduction* and sometimes *underproduction*, which produced either excessive or inadequate inventories of available *C*(*MP*)', thus price swings and possible interruptions in expanded reproduction.[136] As capitalists extended their operations across oceans, increases in distance lengthened the time lag between production and sale and multiplied the possibilities of interruptions.

> Further: since the circulation process of capital is not completed in one day but extends over a fairly long period until capital returns to its original form ... great upheavals and changes take place in the market ... it is quite clear, that between the starting point, the prerequisite capital, and the time of its return at the end of one of these periods, great catastrophes must occur and elements of crises must have gathered and developed.[137]

Remember, Marx was writing during the period of rapid imperialist expansion in which conquest and colonialism were beating down foreign production, creating markets for goods produced in the imperialists' homelands and opening up new sources of raw materials for processing at home. Means of production were being shipped home on voyages that could take months to complete – months during which buyers could only hope for the timely arrival of the raw materials they needed to continue or expand production. Improvements in transport technology, from horse-drawn carts to railroads, from sailing to steam vessels shortened delivery times and improvements in communication from physical mail to the telegraph shortened lags in knowledge about market conditions, but not enough to remove the problem. The crises of overproduction and over speculation that Marx identified in 1855 applied to

---

136 And sometimes these situations have unfurled in close temporal proximity, see the example of the Cotton Famine below.

137 *MECW*, *Vol. 32*, p. 126.

both finished goods being sold abroad, and raw materials being imported for processing. He wrote:

> the commercial cycle has again reached the point where overproduction and over speculation turn into a crisis ... glutting of the world market has been achieved in spite of ... the electric telegraph which has transformed the whole of Europe into one big commodity exchange, in spite of railways and steamships which have improved communication and therefore commerce to an incredible degree.[138]

The same problem of time lags could produce *under*production, the collapse of speculation and a crisis in supply from raw material importers.

3.3.5 Crises Caused by Nature

Crises caused by Nature in the ability of investors to obtain the *MP* they require result from shortages that either drive up the prices of *MP* to levels that undermine their profitable use or cause such absolute scarcity as to bring those production processes that require them to a halt. Such shortages occur because of catastrophes in either their original production or in their transportation. Dramatic changes in Nature such as drought, tornadoes, hurricanes, cyclones, flood, tsunamis, earthquakes, volcanic eruptions, wildfires, and disease can all have the effect of dramatically reducing either the quality or the quantity of *MP*, or both. On such crises in the production of *MP*, see Section 4.2.2.2 below.

3.3.6 Crises Caused by Blockades of Trade

Unlike natural disasters, the imposition of blockades on flows of *MP* have been entirely the result of capitalist and government decisions. Using government-sanctioned patents and copyrights, capitalists have prevented or slowed the flow of new technologies. Governments, using laws, protective tariffs, and force have slowed or prevented flows of actual goods. Yet, these are parallel to natural disasters in their effects: reducing availability and raising prices – increasing costs to firms requiring blockaded *MP* for their operations.

One well-known nineteenth century example of governments intentionally intervening to cut off imports of raw materials were the blockades of imports from the continent to England during the Napoleonic Wars, caused by both

138 Karl Marx, "The Crisis in Trade and Industry," (Jan. 8–22, 1855) *MECW*, *Vol. 13*, pp. 571–578. On the impact of the telegraph and transoceanic cables on international trade in grain see, A. J. H. Latham and Larry Neal, "The International Market in Rice and Wheat, 1868–1914," *The Economic History Review*, New Series, 36, no. 2 (May 1983): 273–274.

Napoleon's interdiction of trade with Britain and the British blockade of French ports.[139] The cut-off drove up the price of grain, hence of bread, undermining real wages and causing worker unrest. A parallel blockade was enacted by Thomas Jefferson with the Embargo Act of 1807 that outlawed trade with either Britain or France – partly in response to the impressment of American sailors by the British Royal Navy, partly as another protectionist measure to favor the development of domestic industries. At the end of the wars, against the expected resumption of grain imports, landlord lobbying in Britain led to the Corn Laws that restricted imports, kept local grain prices and rents high and prompted further conflict.[140] Despite continued opposition from manufacturers and workers, they were only repealed in response to the disastrous collapse in food production in Ireland that brought on the Great Irish Famine, mass starvation and emigration from Ireland.[141]

---

139 Revealing fiction, because based on real historical sources, including the Naval Digest, that tell stories of these blockades can be found in the Aubrey/Maturin novels of Patrick O'Brian. The story line of the 2003 film *Master and Commander: The Far Side of the World* was extracted from the novels' stories.

140 Such government-imposed blockages of imports predated the Corn Laws and have been repeatedly used in the years since. The motives behind such blockages have often been mixed, sometimes economic, e.g., to benefit domestic producers, and sometimes political, e.g., aimed at wartime enemies or to punish other governments for some reason. Raising prices for domestic producers were behind not only the Corn Laws but the many protectionist measures discussed in Section 4.3.3.2. below. Napoleon's interdiction of trade with England was a political act of war. Obviously, the distinction has limited meaning when embargoing trade is both an economic act and a political one. In recent decades, we have seen the US impose a whole series of overtly political embargos although they have often served economic interests as well. An obvious case has been the embargo of all trade with Cuba. Because Cuba was a major sugar producer and exporter, this has obviously been of great benefit to sugar producers in the US. The embargos of Vietnam and Iran after their revolutions, of arms with Argentina and South Africa over human rights abuses, of grain to Russia after its invasion of Afghanistan in 1980, of exports to some oil importers by OPEC in 1973–4, of Iran by the US and European governments after its revolution in 1978, and of Russia again after its invasions of Ukraine in 2014 and 2022, are all examples of actions that have been explicitly politically motivated but with substantial economic effects.

141 Although beyond the scope of this treatment, and despite being ignored by many Marxist treatments of wars between capitalist nation states, class struggle always plays a role in their genesis, evolution and ends. This is obvious in the case of Napoleon's empire building in the wake of the French Revolution (1789). It's also obvious in the runup to the Civil War in the US, which was preceded by slave revolts in Haiti (1791–1804) and the slave states. In the twentieth century it was obvious as the Russian Revolution of 1917 extricated that country from WWI and throughout the anti-colonial, independence struggles that dominated much of the century. Class struggle was also a determining factor during the Cold War as the specter of nuclear holocaust was wielded by both the Soviet and US

Another example of blockade in $M - MP$ that Marx traced, in part through Factory Inspector Reports, one which contributed to a crisis in the English textile industry was the Cotton Famine (1861–1865) during the U.S. Civil War. First the Confederate states embargoed cotton exports in 1861 and then the North blockaded southern ports – much as the English had blockaded French ones sixty years earlier. The crisis actually began with excessive, speculative stockpiling of raw cotton, a previous overproduction of cotton yarn and cloth that had glutted markets and caused cutbacks in production and growing unemployment among mill workers. This was soon followed by the cutoff in supplies from America and a dramatic rise in the cost of cotton, reduced production and even greater unemployment – nearly 500,000 workers laid off.[142] When desired cotton became either unavailable or too expensive, then regardless of how much money was available, prior investments could not be renewed, nor new ones undertaken until alternative sources could be tapped, e.g., cotton from India or Egypt.[143] I return to this case in Chapter 6 on offsetting strategies.

That historical experience reveals a further problem: reduced *quality* of *MP* caused by being forced to switch from preferred sources to secondary ones. The cotton obtained from India turned out to be of a much lower quality than that from the United States – which raised the costs of production and undermined both the quality of the product and profitability.[144]

4 Possibilities of Crisis in the Second Stage of the Circuit: Production

In the second, production stage of the circuit (… *P* … *C′*), the possibility exists that despite having acquired and purchased the two elements of production,

---

governments as a means of domestic social control. Orwell's novel *1984* (1949) captured, among other things, the usefulness of endless foreign conflicts for domestic control.

142 Eugene Brady (1930–1991) argued that because of previous stockpiling the cutoff caused no dearth of cotton for the mills, rather the fear of future dearth, combined with previous overproduction, caused a dramatic increase in the cost of cotton, a decrease of production and an increase of unemployment. See, Eugene Brady, "A Reconsideration of the Lancashire 'Cotton Famine'," *Agricultural History*, Vol. 37, no. 3 (July 1963): 156–162.

143 See, Marx's journal articles of 1861 on the "Cotton Crisis" in MECW, *Vol. 19* and his analyses in Volume 1 of *Capital*, Chapter 15, Section 7, pp. 575–588, or MECW, *Vol. 35*, pp. 450–462, *Manuscript of 1864–65*, pp. 232–236, *Capital, Vol. 3*, Chapter 6, Section 3, pp. 219–225, or MECW, *Vol. 37*, pp. 125–130.

144 Besides being more expensive, working shorter, dirtier Egyptian and Indian cotton slowed down machinery, further reducing productivity, wages and profits. *Capital, Vol. 1*, p. 585, or MECW, *Vol. 35*, pp. 459–460, *Manuscript of 1864–65*, pp. 237–238, *Capital, Vol. 3*, pp. 228–233, or MECW, *Vol. 37*, pp. 132–136.

LP and *MP*, capitalists may fail to achieve their transformation into the final product *C′* in a way that the value of *C′* is sufficient to provide, if sold at its value, at least an average rate of surplus value or profit. This is true whether we are dealing with the production of *C*(*MP*)*′* or that of *C*(*MS*)*′*. This possibility of crisis at the point of production must involve either a failure to extract enough work from enslaved or hired labor-power or some breakdown in the means of production. Possible causes of such failures can be either internal to the dynamics of production or external, e.g., disruptions due to "natural" disasters.

4.1 *Possible Crises with Labor-Power, LP* in … *P* …

For reasons, which I analyze in Chapter 5 on predispositions to crisis, the labor processes of capitalist production are rife with conflicts between workers and capital – conflicts that can evolve from sporadic individual resistance to collective organization and action – and have the potential to disrupt and precipitate crisis.

4.1.1 Enslaved or Hired, But Will They Work? Resistance to Work

In both cases, of slavery and waged labor, obtaining workers is only the first step in obtaining the labor necessary for the production of commodities. In the case of slaves, force or the eminent threat of force is usually required in an ongoing manner to get slaves to do the work desired. From reports from America, Marx and Engels were aware of the resistance of slaves that made that force necessary. In the case of waged or salaried labor, in principle, the only force required is the threat of everything that can be lost through the loss of a job.

However, every capitalist discovers it is one thing to hire workers' capacity to work, *LP*, but it is quite another to extract sufficient living labor, … *P* …, not only to preserve the original value invested, $v + c$, but also to extract surplus labor and generate surplus value, *s*.[145] For the capitalist, success in production appears "totally identical with the production of surplus labor …"[146] Therefore,

145 Although this has always been clear to capitalist managers, it took a remarkably long time for economists to recognize that "labor" was no simple input, such as the "L" hypothesized in production functions of the sort Q=f(K, L). It was not until the recognition of how "efficiency wages" (those intentionally higher than market clearing rates) could result in more work and higher productivity that they effectively acknowledged the difference Marx had noted long before, between the "ability and willingness" to work (*LP*) and actual work. Sociologists and psychologists were studying this issue much earlier – paid by capitalists to help manage discontented workers – creating specialized fields such as "industrial sociology" and "industrial and organizational psychology."

146 *Grundrisse*, p. 404, or *MECW*, *Vol. 28*, p. 331.

the central issue for both capitalists and the workers they hire is just how much work will actually be forthcoming.

In other words, will capitalists succeed in *exploiting* their workers? And, will they succeed in exploiting them *enough* to be competitive with other capitalists trying to do the same? Will their s/v and $s/(v + c)$ reach at least average levels (and preferably exceed them)? It all depends on just *how much work* they can get their workers to do.

Although capitalists do their best to hire workers who seem both *able* and *willing* to do the work they need done, the degree of both are only truly revealed on the job and may disappoint capitalists' hopes and expectations.[147] No matter prior conditioning and training, there is much truth in the well-known maxim that "most of what you need to know, you learn on the job." (This is true about both how to do the job, and how to resist it!) Much the same is true with respect to *willingness*.

Not only do workers often hide their resistance to work while seeking jobs and agreeing to terms of employment, but because conditions on the job vary, both by task and over time, so may *willingness*. Regardless of agreements concluded in *M – LP*, more often than not in *...P...* capitalists try to squeeze out a bit more labor, even at the cost of the workers' safety and health, while workers try to limit their work, to make it safer and to conserve energy for their own personal lives off the job.[148] This will be especially true if, once on the job, they find their work unsafe. Such discovery can undermine initial willingness and provoke varying degrees of resistance.

In value terms, all worker resistance that takes the form of less work undermines the total amount of value added, $v + s$, to the means of production, c. In what follows, I examine some of the ways workers work less, reducing $v + s$. Here I look only at *possible* ways of working less – albeit demonstrated in history – reserving analysis of *why* they resist for Chapter 5, Section 2 on predispositions to crisis within the sphere of production.

Given that the *amount* of work is determined primarily by the *time* of labor (how long workers work) and by the *intensity* of that labor (how hard they

147 See, George Caffentzis' insightful analysis of capitalist efforts to choose those workers most willing to channel their energy into work, i.e., those with the lowest entropy, in his, "The Work/Energy Crisis and the Apocalypse," *Midnight Notes II*, Vol. 1 (1980). See too any of the numerous business publications on "personnel" selection written to guide the evaluation of potential hires.

148 See, Marx's analysis of capitalist "nibbling and cribbling" to increase work in Chapter 10 of Volume 1 of *Capital* and my highlighting of workers' methods of achieving the opposite in my commentary on that chapter. *Capital, Vol. 1*, p. 352, or *MECW, Vol. 35*, p. 250. Cleaver, *33 Lessons on Capital*, 235–236.

work), the most obvious possibilities of crises caused by less work and less $v + s$, are workers spending less time working or working less intensely than their employers' desire. In terms of time, the most obvious potential (and historically very real) source of conflict was over the length of the working day – to which Marx devotes Chapter 10 of Volume 1 of *Capital*, one of the longest in the book. As he shows, this wasn't just a possibility, but a source of repeated crises in accumulation as capitalists, their workers and social reformers battled repeatedly over what should constitute a "normal" working day.

Although at any point in those battles, the length of a working day was often formally determined – by verbal agreement or by law – the actual number of hours, minutes and seconds of work could vary enormously. When and where craftworkers controlled their tools, e.g., where the subordination of labor was only formal, they could start and stop work at will, opening what Marx sometimes called "pores" of non-work in the working day and thus reducing its actual length. Early examples were spinners and weavers who controlled the speed of their spinning wheels and hand looms. Later examples were skilled machine tool operators, those who used machines to make machines or machine parts, and steel workers who long acted as both as engineers, designing tools and processes, and as manual workers, putting them to use.

A parallel dynamic existed with respect to intensity. Just as workers who controlled their tools could take breaks, stop and start as they pleased, so too could they control the intensity of their work; they could modulate the rhythm of work, sometimes working hard and fast, sometimes taking it easy, depending on circumstances (such as how much they could earn for a given amount of labor or how much they *needed* to earn).[149] But even where workers were assigned to merely tend machines that capitalists tried to run continuously to minimize down time and costs while maximizing output, workers were not without recourse.

One obvious way of achieving down time for workers tending machines whose speed is controlled by their bosses is sabotage. Sabotage sometimes has taken the form of machine breaking, overt in cases such as the Luddites, covert in many others. Those who work with machines, hour after hour, day after day, often come to know them even better than their designers. That knowledge

149 Thanks to the United Farm Workers providing almost daily postings on Twitter, we have plenty of illustrations, with videos, of how, under varying circumstances, farm workers – who are often paid piece-wages – vary the rhythm of their work. When conditions warrant, e.g., low piece rates and bad weather, they are forced to work faster and harder to earn enough to live. When conditions are better, either higher piece rates, better weather or hourly wages, they can earn enough with less intense work.

makes it possible for them to either make the machines safer and more productive or utilize them in ways that cause them to break or otherwise stop functioning and require unscheduled repair and maintenance – a break in the rhythm of work, whether workers repair their own machines or someone else must be called in to do it.

Other possibilities of rupture in work time include various forms of intentionally working less, e.g., workers sleeping, playing or organizing on the job instead of working, absenteeism (coming in late and/or leaving early), slow-downs, strikes, protests and uprisings. Sleeping or playing on the job has sometimes involved sabotage, sometimes merely carefully planned diversions of energy.[150]

Examples of collective slow-downs are often found in cases of piecework, where wages depend on how many "pieces" are produced, be they pounds of yarn spun by spinners, yards of cloth woven by weavers, crates of fruit picked by farm workers, or tons of ore extracted by miners. In such cases, workers sometimes collaborate to limit the number of "pieces" each produce – effectively slowing down production. One of my favorite short stories by Jack London is "South of the Slot" (1909) which recounts how a new employee is called out by a veteran for working too hard and messing up the piece rate. By producing more than the others, he risks giving the boss an excuse to lower their piece rates, forcing everyone to work harder.[151] In such a manner do workers often refuse competition among themselves and collectively set upper limits to how many pieces each will produce and thus just how much work they will do.

Shopfloor organizing – organizers talking with other workers about problems and possible actions – clearly takes time away from work and often involve preparation for taking more time, e.g., strikes.[152] Strikes may be officially sanctioned by law, e.g., pre-contract contestation between unions and employers, or unsanctioned wildcat actions by rank & file workers. They may involve walking off the job, occupying plants and preventing the replacement

150 See, the examples in Bill Watkin's "Counterplanning on the Shopfloor," *Radical America*, May-June 1971, pp. 77–85.

151 See, Donald Pizer (ed.), *Jack London: Novels & Stories* (New York: Library of America, 1982) 817–833. A more recent story of learning [to work less]-on-the-job, in a different setting, is told in Patti Smith's autobiographical song "Piss Factory" (1974) on *New Wave*, Vertigo Records, 1977.

152 Eventually, long after Marx and Engels time, workers in some industries won time for such organizing on the part of shop stewards or union reps with no loss of pay. When reaction to the Japanese "invasion" of the US auto industry in the 1970s resulted in "quality circles" to improve labor productivity, they were often used by workers as breaktime, rather than just another form of work.

of striking workers by scabs – all of which bring work and production to a halt, rupturing circuits and reproduction.

The same is true with widespread protests and uprisings, e.g., Chartist protests against Parliament inaction on their petitions or the Revolutions of 1848. Workers walking off the job and into the streets in large scale actions – especially general strikes and revolutions – may rupture not only production but other moments of the circuit as well – such as $M - C(MP, LP)$, discussed in Section 1 above, or $C' - M$," discussed in Section 3 below.

Whatever the cause, workers do get fed up with the work and even with the struggle over work, declare "Take This Job and Shove It!"!" and quit. Walking away obviously means less work by those who walk and the diversion of managerial time into replacing workers who quit.

4.1.2 "Nature" Can Kill

In Section 3.3.5 on possible problems in buying the means of production, I discussed how drought or flood could decimate crops used as *MP*, reducing supply, driving up prices, reducing capitalist profits and causing a crisis. Obviously, drought or flood can also reduce food crops (*MS*), also driving up retail prices and undermining the value of workers' wages. Where wages are already low, reductions in what they can buy brings deeper malnutrition, greater susceptibility to disease, loss of housing, even starvation – all reducing the ability of workers to work and, in the worst cases, killing them outright. The disease that blighted potatoes in Ireland, also resulted in some workers starving and others fleeing the workforce through emigration to escape the same fate. Any natural disruption – whether by flood, drought, or disease – of any crop that feeds local workers can have much the same effect of reducing available labor-power – as demonstrated dramatically in the multiple nineteenth century famines of South Asia.[153]

Severe storms, tornadoes, fires, and flooding can also damage or destroy manufacturing factories and in the process harm the workers who work in them, regardless of the nature of their final product. Earthquakes that crumble factories or whole towns crush workers as well as machinery and other means of production.

153 These natural devastations have continued to plague the labor force in the twentieth and twenty-first centuries, especially in South Asia and Sub-Saharan Africa, e.g., famine in India in 1967, drought throughout the Sahel in the early 1970s and most recently – augmented by global warming – drought and famine have been driving massive displacements of population in Africa.

Similarly, hurricanes, cyclones or dangerous coasts that sink or wreak ships can also kill their sailors. Or, if they keep ships confined to ports, they keep sailors on shore and dock workers idle, reducing their work and the production of transportation.

Clearly, the recurrent epidemics and pandemics of the nineteenth century sickened and often killed workers removing them either temporarily or permanently from working and by so doing disrupted production. With working-class wages so often at or near bare subsistence, the ravages of disease simply worsened the health of workers already weakened by chronic malnutrition, killing more quickly than slower deaths by starvation. Not only were such sufferers removed from labor markets as I discussed in Section 4.1.2.3.1., but their deaths removed them from the labor force entirely.

4.2 *Possible Crises with Means of Production, MP in … P …*

Keeping in mind that the means of production are determined by the technology of production, embodied in tools, machinery and raw materials, there are several possibilities of crises in production associated with some breakdown in these. They include workers' actions, e.g., sabotage and direct appropriation, natural disasters and, for individual capitalists, the inability to cope with inevitable depreciation or keep up with technological changes introduced by competitors.

4.2.1 Crises in *MP* Caused by Workers' Actions

The most immediate and obvious possibilities of crisis in production associated with the means of production are those caused by workers in their conflicts with capitalists over priorities. Whereas for capitalists the maximization of profit involves minimizing not only wages but also other costs, including expenditures on worker safety, workers demand measures to protect themselves on the job and laws to mandate protections. In Section 2 on "Saving on the Conditions of Work at the Workers' Expense" of Chapter 5 on "Economy in the Use of Constant Capital" in the *Manuscript of 1864–65* and in Volume 3 of *Capital*, Marx provides many examples of such cost cutting – or refusal to spend – often at the expense of worker safety.[154] During conflicts over these opposed sets of priorities, workers sometimes resort to sabotage: the breakage of tools and machinery, the destruction or contamination of raw materials, the burning down of factories. While capitalists try to forbid "… all wasteful consumption of raw material or instruments of labor … because what is wasted

---

154 *Manuscript of 1864–65*, pp. 156–179, *Capital, Vol. 3*, pp. 181–190, or MECW, *Vol. 37*, pp. 80–106.

in this way represents a superfluous expenditure of quantities of objectified labour, labour that does not count in the product or enter into its value,"[155] Marx was well aware that this aim was often thwarted by workers. In a footnote to this description, he draws on writings by John Cairnes (1823–1875) and Frederick Olmstead (1822–1903) to describe how capitalists in the slave states of the US were forced to give their workers crude tools because of the workers so frequently broke them.[156] Although they partly attributed this to what they considered slaves' racial inferiority, they also recognized resistance. Cairnes takes the following from Olmstead's *Seaboard Slave States*:

> In working niggers, we must always calculate that they will not labour at all except to avoid punishment, and they will never do more than just enough to save themselves from being punished, and no amount of punishment will prevent their working carelessly and indifferently. It always seems on the plantation as if they took pains to break all the tools and spoil all the cattle that they possibly can, even when they know they'll be punished for it.[157]

---

155 *Capital, Vol. 1*, p. 303. When Marx writes "does not count in the product or enter into its value," he is telling us the real meaning of a failure to "transfer" or "preserve" value in a way that demystifies the usual interpretation of these terms. See, the commentary on Chapter 8 in H. Cleaver, *33 Lessons on Capital.*

156 Ibid., fn 18, pp. 303–304. It seems likely slaves played on white racism, which would attribute breakage to the stupidity of their black slaves. As with machine breakage, tool breakage results in work stoppages and perhaps the diversion of energy into more interesting repair work.

157 John Cairnes, *The Slave Power: Its Character, Career, and Probable Designs: Being An Attempt to Explain the Real Issues Involved In the American Contest,* 2nd ed. (New York: Carleton, Publisher, 1862) 40, fn*. Omstead and Cairnes' and hence Marx's perception of how slave resistance prevented the use of the best tools, has been countered by a considerable literature demonstrating that this was not always so. Moreover, it is noticeable that Marx did not share their judgement of slave innate inferiority but clearly saw tool breakage purely in terms of resistance by exploited workers. Indeed, it has been shown that in some places slaves worked as artisans rather than field labor and, moreover, seem to have contributed to developing new, more efficient technologies. See, Veront Satchell, "Innovations in sugar-cane mill technology in Jamaica, 1760--1830" in Verene Shepherd, *Working Slavery, Pricing Freedom: Perspectives from the Caribbean, Africa and the African Diaspora* (New York: Palgrave, 2001) 93–111 and Jenny Bulstrode, "Black metallurgists and the making of the industrial revolution," *History and Technology* 39, no. 1 (June 2023): 1-41. Regardless, given how frequent the resort to sabotage has been throughout capital's labor force, including wage labor, it seems likely that some slaves also mistreated their owner's tools in acts of resistance.

To the degree that Cairnes was correct that the "maxim of slave management, in slave importing countries [is] that the most effective economy is that which takes out of human chattel in the shortest space of time the utmost amount of exertion it is capable of putting forth" sabotage of the means of production would seem one natural response by workers.[158] Such conflicts were widespread in the nineteenth century not only among slaves but also among wage-slaves.

Turning to industrializing Britain, where slave-produced cotton was being processed into cloth with ever-more sophisticated machinery, Marx observed the same conflict between workers' desire to work less and capitalists' desire to extract the most work possible. As early as 1846, while critiquing Proudhon, he wrote, "Since 1825, the invention and use of machinery resulted solely from the war between masters and workmen."[159] On the basis of his worked out theory of relative surplus value, he reiterated this theme in *Capital*, explaining how the introduction of machines, which held the technical possibility of *reducing* work was used by capitalists to *increase* work and undermine workers' power to resist.

> Hence too the economic paradox that the most powerful instrument for reducing labor-time [machines] suffers a dialectical inversion and becomes the most unfailing means for turning the whole lifetime of the worker and his family into labor-time at capital's disposal for its own valorization.[160]

Simultaneously, machinery, he wrote, serves employers as

> The most powerful weapon for suppressing strikes, those periodic revolts of the working class against the autocracy of capital … It would be possible to write a whole history of the inventions made since 1830 for the sole purpose of providing capital with weapons against working class revolt.[161]

Not surprisingly, workers resented these capitalist uses of machinery. Although the best known acts of sabotage were those of the Luddites (1811–1816), English

158 Quoted in *Capital, Vol. 1*, p. 377, from Cairnes, *The Slave Power*, p. 73.

159 Marx to P. V. Annenkov, December 28, 1846, MECW, *Vol. 38*, p. 99.

160 *Capital, Vol. 1*, p. 532, MECW, *Vol. 35*, p. 411.

161 Ibid., p. 563, MECW, *Vol. 35*, p. 439. Also: "Since 1825, the invention and use of machinery resulted solely from the war between masters and workmen." Marx to P. V. Annenkov, December, 28 1846, MECW, *Vol. 38*, p. 99.

handloom weavers and textile workers who destroyed machinery that displaced their labor and drove down wages, Marx recounts many such acts dating back to the seventeenth century.[162] Among which: "... nearly all of Europe experienced workers' revolts against the ribbon-loom, a machine for weaving ribbons and lace trimmings ..." And then "No sooner had Everett constructed the first wool-shearing machine to be driven by water-power (1758) than it was set on fire by 100,000 people who had been thrown out of work."[163]

Similar actions against machines have been undertaken by agricultural workers. These included the widespread "Swing Riots" in 1830 against mechanization in agriculture and involved the destruction of labor-displacing threshing machines.[164] Machines were not the only objects of anger and attack but unfolded alongside "the underground of the poaching war, the anonymous letter and the flaming corn rick."[165] By fits and starts such rebellion would become gradually better organized, leading eventually from the struggles and subsequent repression of the Tolpuddle Martyrs in 1834 to the "formation since the end of 1865 of a trade union among the agricultural labourers ... in March 1867, the labourers carried through a general strike ..."[166]

---

162 On the Luddites see Charles Poulsen, *The English Rebels* (London: Journeyman, 1984), David Noble, *Progress Without People: In Defense of Luddism* (New York: Charles Kerr, 1993) and Peter Linebaugh, *Ned Ludd & Queen Mab: Machine-Breaking, Romanticism and the Several Commons of 1811–12* (Brooklyn: PM Press, 2012). One literary portrayal of such actions is in Charlotte Brontë's novel *Shirley* (1849) where both sides are represented in a dialog, where the workers argue for saving their jobs and the capitalist argues he has no choice, given the competition of other capitalists – the very dynamic of inter-capitalist competition Marx analyzes in Chapter 12 of *Capital* as one vehicle for the spread of technological innovations. It also illustrates how the relative ability to compete depends on a capitalist's relative control over his workers.

163 *Capital, Vol. 1*, p. 554, *MECW, Vol. 35*, pp. 430–431.

164 On the Swing Riots see Eric Hobsbawm and George Rudé, *Captain Swing* (London: Lawrence & Wishart, 1969). For a broader view, see E. P. Thompson, *The Making of the English Working Class* (New York: Vintage Books, 1963), Chapter Seven, "The Field Labourers." The development and adoption of labor-displacing machinery in agriculture has continued, often in response not merely to the rise in wages but the anticipation of a rise in wages. An example of the former was the mechanical reaper in the American Mid-West. See, Paul David, "The Mechanization of Reaping in the Anti-Bellum Midwest" in Henry Rosovsky, ed., *Industrialization in Two Systems* (New York: John Wiley & Sons, 1966) 3–39. An example of the latter was the development of tomato picking machines in the 1960s in response to the successful formation of farm worker organizations. See, Jim Hightower, *Hard Tomatoes, Hard Times: A Report of the Agribusiness Accountability Project on the Failure of America's Land Grant College Complex* (New York: HarperCollins Publishers, 1978).

165 Thompson, *The Making of the English Working Class*, 225–226.

166 *Capital, Vol. 1*, p. 363, fn 54, *MECW, Vol. 35*, p. 260, fn 1.

As capitalist accumulation extended its reach beyond national borders through colonialism, one basic objective was the acquisition of raw materials at a lower cost than could be produced domestically. From the British annexation of Ireland as a source of first wool and later flax through the colonization of India facilitating the acquisition of cotton to Belgium's conquest of the Congo for its mineral wealth, the international spread of raw material sourcing simultaneously involved the creation of new sites of workers' struggles over their production.[167]

Another terrain of the production of *MP* that proved highly susceptible to worker sabotage was mining. As coal-fed steam engines replaced water-powered machinery in factories and transportation, the power of coal miners to disrupt accumulation, not only in the mines but also downstream in the industries dependent on their product, grew steadily. Given the dangerous character of the work, mine owner reluctance to invest in safety measures, and the support of isolated mining communities, the struggles of coal miners, all over the world, are legendary, from the Molly Maguires in Britain and the United States to miners in France, Silesia and India.[168] Miners, with easy access to mining equipment, including explosives, have the means not only to shut down mines but also to interrupt the transportation of ore from pit to where it would be employed. Such power forced mine owners to draw upon both private police, e.g., the Coal and Iron Police, and government military force to repress miner struggles. Those same conditions obtained in many other kinds of mines.[169]

167 Although the English economist John Hobson in his *Imperialism: A Study* (1902) emphasized underconsumption and the consequent need for new markets as the "taproot" of colonial expansion, he recognized that the search for both cheap raw materials and new, more profitable investment opportunities were also prime motivations. So did Vladimir Lenin (1870–1924) in his *Imperialism, the Highest Stage of Capitalism* (1917) and Nicholai Bukharin (1888–1938) in his *Imperialism and World Economy* (1917).

168 Among the many expressions of mining struggles in literature see Emile Zola, *Germinal* (1884–1885) based on the author's investigative reporting in the coal mines of Northern France – frequently adapted to film. Twentieth century miners' struggles exploded in the US in the 1920s, as illustrated in John Sayles' magnificent film *Matewan* (1987) and continued in the decades that followed. See, William Blizzard, *When Miners March* (edited by Wess Harris) (Oakland: PM Press, 2010), Wess Harris, *Truth be Told: Perspectives on the Great West Virginia Mine War: 1890 to Present* (Gay, WV: Appalachian Community Services, 2015), William Cleaver, "Wildcats in the Appalachian Coal Fields" *Zerowork 1* (1975): 113–127, and the documentary *Harlan County, USA* (1976) about a 1973 strike by Kentucky coal miners.

169 In recent years, the rise of struggles to protect the environment has resulted in miners gaining three new sources of support in their struggles. Ecological and human rights activists have joined with indigenous people, whose lands have been threatened or

Alongside such possible *destruction* of the means of production, workers also often threaten capitalists' organization of production by *directly appropriating* – on-the-job – the raw materials with which they have been working, the tools they have been using and the wealth they have been producing. (See, Chapter 4, Section 3.3.3.1) Where workers have had some control over the disposition of their raw material, e.g., silk or leather workers in the eighteenth century, who were supplied with fabric or leather by merchant capitalists, they could cut the material in ways designed to leave usable scraps that they could shape into objects for their own use or for sale to supplement their income. Such direct appropriation, or "wasteful consumption," obviously raised costs and reduced profits for employers.[170] Of course, workers have not only appropriated scraps, but have often appropriated directly usable elements from fields, offices and factories, e.g., food, office supplies or means of production (from raw materials to intermediary parts).[171] Such worker appropriation of *things* parallels the appropriation of their *time* previously discussed.

4.2.2 Crises in the Production of *MP* Caused by Nature

I have already noted how interruptions due to exogenous changes in Nature may hurt workers and reduce the availability and efficacy of their labor-power. Such changes can also undermine the production and quality of the means of production. This is probably most obvious in extractive industries such as agriculture and mining. In Marx and Engels' accounts, the example of crises in the production of *MP* that shows up most often is that of agricultural raw material production – especially crops – being disrupted by bad weather. Drought can reduce yields, even completely wipe out harvests. When prolonged, drought can undermine irrigation systems by drying up their sources of water, be it from reservoirs or aquifers. Its counterpart, storms, heavy rains and flooding, can disrupt the growth of crops (via "lodging" or drowning), their harvesting,

destroyed by mining, to resist and disrupt production. Critical focus on this particularly destructive area of capitalist activity has given new prominence to the term *extractivism*, i.e., exploitation of both miners and the earth in the mining industry. See, for example, Michael Becerril, *Resisting Extractivism: Peruvian Gold, Everyday Violence, and the Politics of Attention* (Nashville: Vanderbuilt University Press, 2021).

170 See, Peter Linebaugh's analysis of such methods in his *The London Hanged*, Part Three: Industry and Idleness in the Period of Manufacture, 1750–1776, especially Chapters Seven and Eight. Until criminalized, such scraps complemented money wages as part of workers' income. The appropriation of machines for personal use is described in great detail in Miklós Haraszti, *A Worker in a Worker's State* (New York: Penguin, 1977) about how Hungarian workers use the machines in their bosses' factory to make "homers."

171 An amusing hymn to such appropriation in the age of the automobile is Johnny Cash's song "One Piece at a Time" (1976).

and their irrigation systems.[172] Both animal and plant populations can also be decimated by disease, either local or pandemic, as was amply demonstrated by the "potato blight" discussed in 1.2.3.1.[173]

In January of 1853, Marx speculates that poor winter crops will bring on crisis.[174] When poor spring crops followed, Engels suggested that "the present prosperity cannot last beyond the autumn."[175] Again in 1856, discussing factors underlying the monetary crisis of the time, Marx points to crop failures, floods, and the failure of European silk crops.[176] And in his *Grundrisse* notes against Darimon, who recognizes grain crop failures but attributes crisis to the drain of bullion, Marx not only complains that "he forgets the failure of the silk harvest" but goes on to argue

> The replacement of a sudden or chronic shortage of (grain, tea, cotton, flax, etc.) in the case of a domestic crop failure deprives the nation doubly. A part of its invested capital or labour is not reproduced – real loss of production. A part of that capital which has been reproduced has to be shifted to fill this gap ... A crisis caused by a failure in the grain crop is therefore not at all created by the drain of bullion ... Exports of gold are not the cause of the grain crisis, but the grain crisis is the cause of gold exports.[177]

In the case of mining, veins of ore can dwindle, or the percentage of useable metal in ore drop below levels worth extracting and processing, given the

172 Appearing random to observers in the nineteenth century, the extent and frequency of drought and flooding, like wildfires and hurricanes, are now understood to be influenced by human practices. "Human-caused" (i.e., capitalist caused) climate change is now recognized as causing many of these "natural" phenomena to occur more frequently and to be more severe.

173 Although I have yet to come across any reference in Marx and Engels' writings, a similar blight devastated European viticulture in the late 1850s to the mid-1870s, especially but not uniquely in France.

174 Marx to Engels, 29 Jan. 1853, *MECW*, *Vol.* 39, pp. 274–277.

175 Engels to Weydemeyer, 12 Apr. 1853, *MECW*, *Vol.* 39, pp. 303–311.

176 Marx, K. "The Causes of the Monetary Crisis in Europe," (circa October 14, 1856) *MECW*, *Vol.* 15, pp.117–122, and "The Monetary Crisis in Europe -- From the History of Money Circulation," (circa October 17, 1856) *MECW*, *Vol.* 15, pp. 123–129.

177 *Grundrisse*, pp. 120, 127–130, or *MECW*, *Vol.* 28, pp. 58–59, 65–68

current technology and value of material being mined.[178] The same holds with oil and gas wells as reservoirs are drained and extraction costs increase.[179]

Finally, severe storms and flooding can also wreak havoc on factory production as well as on agriculture, thus disrupting the production of both intermediary, manufactured means of production and final products. Storms can also disrupt shipping, especially transoceanic shipping where bad weather and other natural hazards, e.g., dangerous coasts or rogue waves can sink ships, pandemic human disease can shut down ports, and disrupt supplies of *MP*.[180]

4.2.3 Depreciation and Competition

While raw materials must be replaced regularly so too, eventually, must machinery and other elements of "fixed capital," e.g., factories, barns, grain silos, irrigation systems, oil and gas drilling and refinery equipment, trucks, trains and ships. They all wear out or "depreciate" over longer periods of time and must be replaced (in part or in whole) in a timely manner to avoid ruptures in the production process. Marx discusses depreciation, both physical and in terms of value in his analysis of machines and industry in Volume 1 of *Capital*.[181] In Volume 2, Section 3, his reproduction schemes explicitly include the replacement of *MP* due to depreciation (and any other losses).

Leaving aside unforeseeable accidents, in which mine tunnels, bridges or roads collapse, refinery equipment or storage facilities explode, trucks and

178 While technological advances in ore mining have sometimes involved the machinery of direct extraction, e.g., the replacement of pickaxes in deep coal mining by Continuous Mining Machines and in open pit surface mining of hand tools by giant electric shovels and draglines, just as important have been the development of new technologies in metallurgical engineering or ore processing which have made it possible to profitably extract valuable metals from ores with ever lower proportions of metals to mineral deposit.

179 Here too, technological advances in discovery, drilling, pumping, transporting, and refining have made ever greater mining and recovery of petroleum and natural gas possible. Controversy over the most recent innovation – hydraulic fracturing or "fracking" – has added to growing opposition to the use of hydrocarbon fuels because of their contribution to global warming.

180 As in the recent case of the Covid pandemic that seriously disrupted global shipping and supply chains.

181 Depreciation in terms of value involves not only wearing out but drops in the value of existing machines in the presence of newer, more efficient ones – a common phenomenon that undermines the competitive profitability of those stuck with the old machines. Marx analyses this in his discussion of how competition results in the diffusion of new technology – when capitalists can afford it, they replace the old with the new – to maintain their share of relative surplus value. See, *Capital, Vol. 1*, Chapter 12, or *MECW*, *Vol. 35*, Chapter XII.

trains crash, ships sink, or factories and other equipment are destroyed by the kinds of natural disasters mentioned above, rates of depreciation and therefore of replacement once learned by experience are largely predictable and are incorporated into investment plans. But in this, as with all capitalist investment, things do not always pan out as planned. The timely replacement of fixed capital can fail, disrupt reproduction, and cause a crisis. One well-known cause of the failure to replace failing fixed capital has been the simple refusal of capitalists to spend the money necessary. Simply putting off such investment can have catastrophic consequences, as when factories collapse or blow up due to postponed repairs.[182]

But beyond the failure to replace existing fixed capital, can be an inability to match technological innovations introduced by competitors who are able to raise productivity, reduce costs and gain a larger share of total surplus value. What may be true of an individual capitalist enterprise may also be true of large numbers, indeed, of whole industries. Marx and Engels watched this unfold as English industrialization surged ahead of that on the European mainland and further afield. They wrote of it lyrically in the *Communist Manifesto,* calling the "cheap prices" of commodities (because produced with more productive technology) "the heavy artillery" which "batters down all Chinese walls."[183] It is true that such metaphorical artillery was often accompanied by quite material artillery and other machinery of war carried by armies and gunboats, but the failure of some producers to match the innovations of others, for whatever reason, meant crisis for them. Marx set out essentially the same argument in his opening chapter (12) on relative surplus value and how innovation by one capitalist "forces his competitors to adopt the new methods."[184] Unfortunately for many competitors, anywhere in the world, they may find that adoption impossible – creating such a crisis for them that their businesses go bankrupt and fail completely.

4.3 *Possible Crises Caused by a Rising Organic Composition of Capital*

In previous writings, but especially in *Capital,* Volume 1, Part 4 on the "Production of Relative Surplus Value", Marx lays out both the history and the logic of the tendency for capitalists to raise both the technical (*MP/LP*)

182 A contemporary example – as I write – has been the failure of Southwest Airlines to update its computer equipment, which failed to cope with the severe winter weather in December 2022, resulting in large numbers of canceled flights and stranded passengers. "Southwest put investors ahead of its customers and employees," *Washington Post,* December 28, 2022.

183 MECW, *Vol. 6,* p. 488.

184 *Capital, Vol. 1,* p. 436, or MECW, *Vol. 35,* p. 312.

and organic (c_d/v_0) compositions of capital. He analyzes the shifting of capitalist investment to increase *MP* relative to *LP*, e.g., by buying and deploying machines, within two frameworks. The first is that of the search for profits and competition. If successful in such investment, by raising productivity (and often by intensifying work) individual capitalists can cut their costs and increase their profits. If this proves true for one capitalist, those who can follow suit to be able to compete. But what, beyond simple greed, motivates investment in new – hopefully more productive – technology? The obvious answer is anything that reduces the existing rate of profit by raising the costs of production or by reducing the rate of surplus value. Leaving aside temporary increases in costs due to external causes, the most obvious candidate for raising costs is worker success at winning higher wages or other benefits, e.g., safety equipment.[185] The most obvious candidate for reducing *s/v* is any reduction in work time with no change in *v*. In *Capital,* Marx places his emphasis on the latter.[186]

This emphasis is clear in the number of words Marx devotes in *Capital* to the historical success of workers (and their reformist supporters) in obtaining reductions in work time. After sketching capitalist efforts to impose ever longer hours of labor, he describes how workers and their reformist supporters fought back, stemmed that capitalist offensive, and eventually succeeded in getting laws passed reducing the number of hours in a working day. In retrospect, his emphasis seems well placed because after his time workers have gone on to win further reductions in the number of working days in a week, the number of working weeks in a year and the number of working years in a workers' lifetime. All such reductions undermine absolute surplus value, both as a phenomenon (successful extraction of surplus labor) and as a strategy (increasing work time). Although these successes have never been complete, not then, not now, in the sense of covering all workers in all jobs, the overall effect of each such victory has been a reduction in the ability of capital as a whole to extract surplus value and profits. As a result, more and more capitalists have been forced to change their strategy of exploitation.

185 And, eventually, things like health care, paid leave, etc.

186 For this he has been reproached by some Marxists for not devoting as much time and words to wage struggles as to those to reduce work time. Among those lamenting the "absence of a chapter on wage struggles" are Michael Lebovitz and Toni Negri. See: Lebowitz, *Beyond Capital: Marx's Political Economy of the Working Class* (New York: Palgrave MacMillan, 2003) and Negri, *Marx Beyond Marx*, op. cit. Nevertheless, it is clear enough in Marx's analysis that not only can increases in wages undermine profits, but that increasing productivity makes it possible for employers to make concessions to workers while maintaining profits.

> As soon as the gradual upsurge of working-class revolt had compelled Parliament compulsorily to shorten the hours of labor, and to begin by imposing a normal working day on factories properly so called, i.e., from the moment that it was made impossible once and for all to increase the production of surplus value by prolonging the working day, capital threw itself with all its might, and in full awareness of the situation, into the production of relative surplus value, by speeding up the development of the machine system.[187]

Whether the motivation is to offset wage and benefit concessions or shorter hours, successfully "speeding up the development of the machine system" to raise productivity requires control over workers – getting them to cooperate with the change or repressing their resistance.

As the Luddites and many subsequent struggles have demonstrated, this is not always easy because such changes often cause crises for workers, e.g., layoffs, loss of wages and all the stark consequences. So, the first, most immediate possibility of crisis is the reaction of workers who may strike, destroy machines, or even burn down factories. Successfully increasing *MP/LP* requires successfully managing one's labor force. Those who are better at it have a shot at winning the competitive battle. As this dynamic has played out, the result has been a secular rise in average *MP/LP* and c_o/v_o, albeit a rise marked by repeated crises in capital's ability to manage the class struggle.

Beyond such immediate problems, by far the most profound possibility of crisis in response to increases in the technical and organic compositions of capital lies in the unintended "tendential fall in the rate of profit", which Marx analyzes at length in Part Three of Volume 3. Because he calls this tendency "the most important in the capitalist process of accumulation", I treat it separately in the next section.

4.4 *Possible Crises Due to a Tendency for the Rate of Profit to Fall*

Marx first worked out how this tendency of capitalists to raise the organic composition could have contradictory effects on profits and predispose to crisis in the *Grundrisse*, then in the *Manuscript of 1864–1865*, distilled by Engels into *Capital*, Volume 3, Part Three. How it can *raise* profits, he showed in Volume I. How it can *lower* them is less immediately obvious, but simple and with the most profound consequences. Let me outline it briefly in mathematical terms:

187 *Capital, Vol. 1*, pp. 533–534, or MECW, *Vol. 35*, pp. 412–413.

First, Marx expresses the rate of profit in terms of *value,* $s/(c + v)$, *not* in terms of money. The ratio is surplus *value* over *value* invested in c and v, *not* monetary profit over money costs.

Second, increases of productivity can lower v. Because there is no limit to this reduction, in theory complete robotization (complete elimination of human labor) could reduce v to zero. As v is reduced towards zero, s/v would seem to rise toward infinity and $s/(v + c)$ to s/c. *However,* there is an upper limit on the possible value of s given by the number of workers, the length of the working day (which cannot even approach 24 hours), and the upper limit on intensity of physical and mental endurance. Therefore, with a rise in s/v brought on by an extension of the working day, rising intensity, and mainly by rising productivity, profits, $s/(c + v)$, will tend, not to infinity, but to s^*/c where s^* is the upper limit on the possible value of s, and v has gone to zero.

Third, the relative surplus value strategy that raises productivity and lowers v is based on a rise in the organic composition of capital, c_o/v_o, which, being based on *MP/LP,* knows no theoretical limits. Therefore, the c in s^*/c can rise continuously or repeatedly, without limit. Since s^* is limited, s^*/c will tend to fall. (Note: the distinction between the organic and value compositions of capital is critical here. Rising productivity in production of *MP* could lower the *value* composition, but not the *organic* composition that is tied to *MP/LP*. Indeed, lowering the value of *MP* encourages its substitution for *LP* and thus a rise in the technical and organic compositions.) In short, the outcome of the tendency of the organic composition of capital to rise is an increasing difficulty in extracting surplus value. It takes a larger and larger investment in c to impose/extract a given amount of surplus labor.

This tendency, which Marx called the most important in the capitalist process of accumulation, is not simply a mathematical formalism, but a social process inherent in the class relation of developing capitalism. There has been so much confusion about this that I want to bring out aspects of this social process more clearly. In the *Manuscript of 1864–1865* and *Capital,* Volume 3, where the most rigorous exposition of the tendency is given, Marx gives some indication of the dimension of the problem. He insists repeatedly that:

> The progressive tendency of the general rate of profit to fall is, thus simply the expression, peculiar to the capitalist mode of production, of the progressive development of the social productivity of labor.[188]

188 *Manuscript of 1864–1865,* pp. 321–322. *Capital, Vol. 3,* p. 319; MECW, *Vol. 37,* p. 211.

Writing of the source of this movement, i.e., the tendency for the organic composition of capital to rise:

> This progressive decline in the variable capital in relation to the constant capital, … is just another expression of the progressive development of the social productivity of labor, which is shown by the way that the growing use of machinery and fixed capital generally enables more raw and ancillary materials to be transformed into products in the same time by the same number of workers, i.e., with less labor.[189]

Behind the movement of the value relations is the movement of the material relations of production. This is why the *organic* composition must never be confused with the *value* composition because it alone reflects the real moment represented by the technical composition.

The most detailed and profound discussion of the real processes involved in the tendency of the organic composition to rise is contained in the *Grundrisse*. There we find two points that are very relevant here.

The first, which he makes just about everywhere, is capital's "general tendency to drive beyond every barrier to production"[190]; its "tendency to expand them [labor and value creation] boundlessly"[191]; "the necessary tendency to raise it [the productive force] to the utmost."[192] This emphasis on the endless expansion of capital, its quest for infinitude, is inherent in the class relations. It is neither an a priori assumption nor a crude observation. It is the product of capital's need to raise productivity and expand production in the face of workers' struggles.

Second, the relative surplus value strategy necessarily becomes central; the ever-greater investment in constant capital, especially labor-replacing machinery, becomes a measure of the development of capital. Symbolically we can see that the technical composition and thus the organic composition of capital, c_o/v_o, become virtual indexes of the degree of development of capital, which is to say of the class relation:

> … the quantitative extent and the effectiveness (intensity) to which capital is developed as fixed capital indicate the general degree to which capital is developed as capital, as power over living labor …[193]

189 *Manuscript of 1864–1865*, p. 321. *Capital, Vol. 3*, p. 318; *MECW, Vol. 37*, p. 210.
190 *Grundrisse*, p. 415; *MECW, Vol. 28*, p. 342.
191 Ibid., p. 421; *MECW, Vol. 28*, p. 350.
192 Ibid., p. 422; *MECW, Vol. 28*, p. 351.
193 Ibid., p. 699; *MECW, Vol. 29*, p. 85.

But if the development of science and machinery measure the development of capital, how does the ever-greater employment of these elements of constant capital lead to crisis? Formally, the crisis, in the form of a tendency for the rate of profit to fall, grew out of the inability to compensate for a rising organic composition, c/v, by a sufficiently rising s/v. But the real meaning of this formalism is simple enough. The only way you can get the s in $s/(c + v)$ to rise with a limited rate of exploitation s/v is to *increase* the number of workers; and it is for that reason that capital must expand the mass of s to compensate for the fall in $s/(c + v)$. Yet, the result of the tendency of the organic composition of capital to rise is that the number of laborers tends to be *reduced* as they are replaced by machines. Certainly, workers thrown off in one sector, e.g., manufacturing, may be absorbed in another, e.g., services, but the overall tendency remains active in all sectors. Therefore, even the rise in the mass of s is undermined by this process. What Marx is getting at here is the very observable tendency of capital to create ever larger, more complex production processes, controlled by relatively smaller numbers of ancillary workers:

> Labor no longer appears so much to be included with the production process; rather, the human being comes to relate more as watchman and regulator to the production process itself ... No longer does the worker insert a modified natural thing as middle link between the object and himself; rather he inserts the process of nature, transformed into an industrial process, as a means between himself and inorganic nature, mastering it. He steps to the side of the production process instead of being its chief actor.[194]

In its efforts to control workers by replacing some with machinery, capital is simultaneously undermining its fundamental control mechanism: work itself. If the tendency is for every production process to be automated in response to inevitable worker resistance to exploitation and alienation, human work is decreasingly needed and becomes decreasingly important in the production of social wealth:

> But to the degree that large industry develops, the creation of real wealth comes to depend less on labor time and on the amount of labor employed than on the power of the agencies set in motion during labor time, whose 'powerful effectiveness' is itself in turn out of all proportion to the direct labor time spent on their production, but depends rather on the general

194 Ibid., p.705; *MECW*, *Vol. 28*, p. 91.

> state of science and on the progress of technology, or the application of this science to production.[195]

In this discussion in the *Grundrisse*, in this famous "Fragment on Machines," Marx is clearly talking about the reduction in *manual* labor – by far the primary sort of labor toiling for capital in his time. But it is also clear in his analysis of the labor process, in Chapter 7 of Volume 1 of *Capital*, that "the general state of science" and its application to industry – the usual definition of technology – are also the products of living labor, of mental labor.

> What distinguishes the worst architect from the best of bees is that the architect builds the cell in his mind before he constructs it in wax. At the end of every labour process, a result emerges which had already been conceived by the worker at the beginning, hence already existed ideally.[196]

Among those things "conceived by the worker" are scientific theories. But as with every other labor process, they are only the beginning; they must be tested and their consequences discovered. Both scientific and technological research involve a mixture of mental and skilled manual labor.[197] The performance of basic scientific research has always involved myriad steps requiring careful manual manipulation of equipment by scientists and their technical assistants. The application of science to industry has also always involved scientists, engineers, and their technicians in a complex array of manual tasks in crafting new machines and production processes as well as the mental labor involved in their conceptualization, evaluation of progress, etc. While this increasing importance of mental labor certainly increases the demand for such labor – offsetting to some degree the decline in the demand for manual labor – it is also subject to the same dynamic as manual labor, namely the tendency of capital, over time, to substitute the use of machines for the mental labor of individuals, thus reproducing in these fields of endeavor the same dynamic of a rising organic composition of capital as experienced elsewhere.[198]

---

195 Ibid., pp. 704–705; *MECW*, *Vol. 28*, p. 90.

196 *Capital*, *Vol. 1*, p. 284.

197 This very material mixture is often overlooked in contemporary discussions of so-called "immaterial labor."

198 While not yet obvious in Marx's time, it certainly is in ours, e.g., computers, computer-controlled equipment and artificial intelligence programs (AI).

But if the production of social wealth is increasingly independent of labor, then capital is undermining its ability to impose work as a condition of social wealth and thus as value:

> In this transformation, it is neither the direct human labor he himself performs, nor the time during which he works, but rather the appropriation of his own general productive power, his understanding of nature and his mastery over it by virtue of his presence as a social body – it is, in a word, the development of the social individual which appears as the great foundation-stone of production and of wealth. The *theft of alien labor time on which the present wealth is based* appears as a miserable foundation in face of this new one, created by large-scale industry itself. As soon as labor in the direct form has ceased to be the great wellspring of wealth, labor time ceases and must cease to be its measure and hence exchange value (must cease to be the measure) of use value ... With that, production based on exchange value breaks down.[199]

This is a vivid exposition of the concrete processes expressed by and producing the rise in the organic composition of capital and the tendency for the rate of profit to fall, and also a vision of how this tendency works to undermine the fundamental basis of capitalism, as a system based on the imposition of work through the commodity form.

5 Possibilities of Crisis in the Third Stage of the Circuit: Sales

The third moment of the circuit, $C' - M'$, like the first, is in the sphere of exchange or circulation. Its completion depends upon the successful production of the commodity C' being followed by the discovery of those both *able* and *willing* to buy it with an equivalent M'. In usual Marxist parlance, this is the *realization problem*. Only if buyers can be found do capitalists stand a chance of earning at least the average rate of profit, $s/(c + v)$. This is the flip side of two processes whose susceptibility to crisis I have already discussed in 4.1 the purchase of labor power, $M - LP$, and commodities $C(MS)$ and $C(MP)$.

However, although Marx considered slavery an anomaly within capitalism, people are still enslaved, sold and bought, by among others, traffickers of sex workers and domestic servants. Therefore, just as I included possible crises in

199 Ibid., p. 705; *MECW*, *Vol.* 29, p. 91.

obtaining slaves in Section 3.2.1, I include possible crises in *selling* labor-power in the form of slaves i.e., *C*(*LP*) – *M*.

5.1 *Possible Crises in Selling Slaves, C*(*LP*) *– M′*

The most obvious sources of crisis for both capitalists trying obtain slaves – as a substitute or complement to waged workers – and those selling slaves have been the revolts of the slaves themselves and interventions by others helping them break free. The successful flight of slaves to maroon colonies or to areas where slavery is outlawed obviously deprives slavers of their "property"/ commodities. So too, does the escape of modern slaves from sweat shops, fishing boats or illegal brothels. Slaves rising up in violent rebellion do the same, temporarily if revolt is put down, permanently when successful, as in the rising on Santa Domingue that overthrew slavery on the island. Beyond the slaves themselves, anti-slavery reformers (including ex-slaves) have joined the fight, ranging from sporadic individual action through the collective organization of flight to the ultimately successful public battle for the criminalization of chattel slavery.

As with all laws, however, success in outlawing both chattel slavery and human trafficking has only been effective to the degree that the laws have been enforced. It took the deployment of naval military forces to enforce the criminalization of the transoceanic slave trade and it took a civil war in the United States to enforce Lincoln's Emancipation Proclamation of 1862.[200]

5.2 *Possible Crises in Selling C*(*MS*)*′ or C*(*MP*)*′*

As capitalism developed, the search for and creation of markets expanded steadily – both domestically and internationally. Capitalists trying to sell both *C*(*MS*)*′* and *C*(*MP*)*′* share the problem of properly gauging the amount of their production to the size of the market and thus avoiding either underproduction

200 Still true today. In principle, wherever slavery, of one sort or another, has been outlawed, various police forces, both local and national, are supposed to shut it down. But given their neglect, corrupt complicity, or failure, it has persisted. Therefore, contemporary opponents of slavery have organized to pressure governments into more effectively enforcing existing laws against human trafficking and enacting new laws against other forms of forced labor, e.g., the de facto slavery of children in factories, of adults in prisons, and of forced marriages. See, the work of the Anti-Slavery International, Freedom United, the Anti-Slavery Society, and the list at https://www.endslaverynow.org/connect (accessed 2024). Current conservative efforts to weaken or revoke laws prohibiting child labor have been making it harder for these efforts to succeed. See, Jennifer Sherer and Nina Mast, "Child labor laws are under attack in states across the country," Economic Policy Institute, March 14, 2023.

(depleted inventories, lost sales as customers to turn to competitors) or overproduction (glutted markets, expensive inventory buildup or selling at prices below value).

5.2.1 Possible Crises of Overproduction/Underconsumption

For capitalists to be able to sell the goods and services produced by their workers, they require customers with both money and readiness to spend it on what they need or desire. Any limit to the availability of money, or to a willingness to spend it, limits demand and the ability of capitalists to sell and make profits. "New value and as value as such," Marx writes, must have the proper "magnitude of available equivalents, primarily money ... the surplus value ... requires a surplus equivalent."[201] In order to realize surplus value in the accumulation process there must be expansion at several points. "The surplus value created at one point requires other points: creation of surplus value at another point, for which it may be exchanged; if only, initially the production of more gold and silver, more money ..."[202]

Will all those other points be realized – that is, come into existence? Although there are some reasons to think they will, there is also the possibility that there will not be enough of them and aggregate demand will be less than aggregate supply.

Discussing absolute surplus value, Marx indicated how the realization of surplus value requires an expansion of the market – the "sphere of circulation" – and, to some degree, the expansion of production produces that:

> The creation by capital of absolute *surplus value* – more objectified labor – is conditional upon an expansion, specifically a constant expansion of the sphere of circulation ... A precondition of production based on capital is therefore the *production of a constantly widening sphere of circulation*, whether the sphere itself is directly *expanded or whether more points within it are created as points of production* ... to create more points of exchange; i.e., here seen from the stand point of *absolute* surplus value or surplus labor, to summon up more surplus labor ... The tendency to create the world market is directly given in the concept of capital itself ... to subjugate every movement of production itself to exchange.[203]

201 *Grundrisse*, p. 405, or *MECW*, *Vol. 28*, p. 332.

202 *Grundrisse*, p. 407, or *MECW*, *Vol. 28*, p. 334.

203 *Grundrisse*, p. 407–408, or *MECW*, *Vol. 28*, pp. 334–335.

The expansion of capital, which begins with investment *M – C(LP, MP)*, immediately creates new points of exchange for final products, namely workers who can exchange their wages, *M*, for *C*(*MS*)', and other capitalists who can invest the *M'* obtained from selling *C*(*MP*) to the investor. The growing number of wage workers are themselves "independent centers of circulation."[204]

He made the same kind of observation concerning the need for an expansion in the case of relative surplus value. "The production of *relative surplus value* … requires the production of new consumption; requires that the consuming circle within circulation expands as did the productive circle previously."[205]

However, just because the expansion of capital based on absolute and relative surplus value strategies results in the multiplication of points of exchange, and in an expansion of the money *available* to buy the output, it remains possible that the amount buyers want to buy will be less than the commodities to be sold. This possibility, Marx and Engels recognized because they saw it repeatedly.

Therefore, in the absence of a plan to coordinate the amount produced with the amount demanded, the possibilities of differences in the two amounts were inherent in the system. Capitalists can control the amount their own workers produce (based on their expectations) but they cannot control either the amount produced by their competitors or the demand for their product. For the most part, both are in the hands of others. How they cope with these problems, I discuss in Chapter 6.

In the world around them, Marx and Engels saw how production sometimes continues even though previously produced commodities have not yet been sold, either by the producing firm or by wholesalers who bought them to sell or by retailers who bought them from wholesalers.

> The production of surplus value … and the whole reproduction process finds itself in the most flourishing condition, while in fact a great part of the commodities have only apparently gone into consumption, and are actually lying unsold in the hands of retail traders, thus being still on the market. One stream of commodities now follows another, and it finally emerges that the earlier stream had only seemed to be swallowed up by consumption. Commodity capitals now vie with each other for space on the market. The late-comers sell below the price in order to sell at all. The earlier streams have not yet been converted into ready money, while payment for them is falling due … At this point the crisis breaks out.[206]

204 *Grundrisse*, p. 419, or MECW, *Vol. 28*, p. 345.

205 *Grundrisse*, p. 408, or MECW, *Vol. 28*, p. 335.

206 *Capital, Vol. 2*, p. 156, or MECW, *Vol. 36*, pp. 82–83.

In reading this passage, we must remember that "consumption" includes sale and subsequent using up of raw materials and fixed capital as well as that of final consumer goods. Although Marx and Engels mostly associate the term consumption with workers' consumption of *MS*, of food, clothing, housing, etc., they also recognized how this is what capitalists do with the *MP* they purchase.[207] They effectively "consume" *MP* in production.[208] So Marx approves this application of the term by Heinrich von Storch in critiquing Jean-Baptiste Say:

> Storch, for example, remarked quite correctly against Say that a great part of consumption is not consumption for immediate use, but consumption in the production process, e.g., consumption of machines, coal, oil. required building etc.[209]

Marx's comments on the production of, and demand for, the means of production are similar to his treatment of consumer goods:

> It is quite the same [to be points of centers of circulation] with the demand created by production itself for raw material, semi-finished goods, machinery, means of communication, and for auxiliary materials ... In so far as one capitalist *buys* from others, buys commodities, or sells, they are within the simple exchange relation; they do not relate to one another as capital. The *correct* (imaginary) proportion in which they

207 The other common meaning of consumption in the nineteenth century was "the lung disease" or tuberculosis, so-called because the disease appeared to consume or waste away the body.

208 Completely in the case of raw materials, partially in the case of fixed capital such as machines or factories.

209 *Grundrisse*, pp. 412–413; MECW, *Vol. 28*, p. 339. This recognition by Marx (and Storch) made it impossible for him to fall into the trap of those who saw in the "underconsumption" of *MS the* source of crisis in capitalist reproduction. This has included both Marxists and non-Marxists, such as John Hobson, who have based their theory of crisis on the idea that workers could not buy back all that they produced, but failed to recognize how inadequate aggregate demand could also be due to a lack of markets for *MP* due to a lack of capitalist investment. See Hobson's *The Physiology of Industry* (1889), written with Albert Mummery, and his *Imperialism: A Study* (1906). The latter would influence the two Bolsheviks, Nicolai Bukharin and Vladimir Lenin whose books *Imperialism and the World Economy* and *Imperialism: The Highest Stage of Capitalism*, both published in 1917, have been foundational for many subsequent Marxists.

> must exchange with one another in order to realize themselves at the end as capital lies *outside* their relation to one another.[210]

This means, as with the production of consumption goods, that capitalists cannot, as individual buyers and sellers, see the overall picture, cannot know in advance exactly how much buyers will want or be able to buy. Therefore, the proportions *can* be wrong.

As I pointed out in Chapter 2, Marx first encountered capitalists beset with these problems in the 1840s while studying the problems of the Moselle vintners (1843) who were producing wine (a consumer good) and Silesian weavers (1844) who were producing cloth (a means of production for the clothing industry). Both found themselves overproducing because of the influx of (cheaper) goods from elsewhere in Germany because of the *Zollverein*. Eventually, in 1848, after much study, Marx took on the issue of trade policy and the debates over it directly in a "Speech on the Question of Free Trade."[211] He laid out and examined both the arguments for "free trade" and those for "protection," coming down on the side of "free trade" – but only because he believed it increased the frequency of crisis and "hastens the Social Revolution."[212]

In Volume 1 of *Capital*, the theoretical possibility of overproduction is first analyzed by Marx in the case of individual producers, e.g., farmers or crafts persons, selling some use-values to obtain the money they require to obtain other use-values, i.e., *C* – *M* – *C*, often for their personal consumption. In Chapter 3 "Money, or the Circulation of Commodities," he points out one source of overproduction, namely that even in a world with many buyers "no one directly needs to purchase because he has just sold."[213] Just because the sellers of *C* find buyers willing to part with their *M*, those sellers can then hold onto the money they receive instead of spending it. They may, for example, *save* to accumulate enough money for future, larger purchases. The possibility of *C* – *M* with no follow up *M* – *C* implies, he argues "the possibility of crises, though no more than the possibility."[214] All this is framed in terms of the selling and purchasing behavior of individuals in particular markets.

Marx and Engels' primary interest, however, in both their journalism and their theoretical work, were the possibilities of *widespread* failure in which

---

210 *Grundrisse*, p. 421, fn *; *MECW*, *Vol. 28*, p. 349.

211 *MECW*, *Vol. 6*, pp. 450–465.

212 Ibid., p. 465. Compare with Engels' treatment of this same issue in his second "Speech at Elberfeld," February 15, 1845, *MECW*, *Vol. 4*, pp. 256–264.

213 *Capital*, *Vol. 1*, pp. 208–209, or *MECW*, *Vol. 35*, p. 123.

214 *Capital*, *Vol. 1*, p. 209, or *MECW*, *Vol. 35*, p. 124.

many capitalist producers faced many glutted or saturated markets, found they had *overproduced* and suffered a general commercial crisis. For them too, the possibility of failure to sell also lies in the separation of sale, $C(MS)'$ or $C(MP)' - M'$ (*supply*) from *consumer demand* $M - C(MS)$ and from *investment demand*, $M - C(MP)$.

Marx argued that because production was carried on by independent capitalists making their own decisions about investment and production (reaching separate deals with workers and suppliers, negotiating separate sales agreements with intermediaries, consumers, or other capitalists), there is no *overall* plan to coordinate supply and demand.[215] Thus, the proportionate division of capital investment in c and in v required for reproduction might well be incompatible with the actual amounts of *MP* and *MS* produced. From this perspective the possible inability to realize the sale, $C' - M'$, of either *MS* or *MP*, is part of the larger problem implicit in Marx's scheme of expanded reproduction analyzed in Volume 2 of *Capital*, namely the requirement that smooth accumulation requires:

$$\text{Dept I} \quad MP^* = MP_1 + MP_2 + new\,MP_1 + new\,MP_2$$
$$\text{Dept II} \quad MS^* = LP_1 + LP_2 + new\,LP_1 + new\,LP_2$$

In the absence of planning, imperfect market mechanisms, i.e., producer/seller and buyer behavior based on often flawed perceptions, erratic expectations and unexpected disruptions, provides only crisis-ridden paths to achieving these required proportions.[216]

Among the possible causes of "flawed perceptions" are the often-serious lags in information flows sketched in Section 3.3.4. There I was concerned with the problem posed by time lags in information about the availability of means of production to buyers, those who need them in order to begin, continue, or expand production. But the same problem confronts sellers of both *MP* and *MS*. Each capitalist wonders whether there will be enough buyers to purchase everything their firm is sending to this or that market. If not, they will have "overproduced" $C(MP)'$ and $C(MS)'$ *and* suffer the consequence of "underconsumption" in the case of $C(MS)'$.

215 The exception, recognized by political economists as well as by Marx and Engels, were small, local markets where capitalists producing the same commodities could form an oligopoly, set common prices, and divide up the market.

216 The inevitable problems in meeting these requirements provided Rosa Luxemburg the foundation for theories of both crisis and imperialism. See, her "The Accumulation of Capital," now included in *The Complete Works of Rosa Luxemburg, Vol. II: Economic Writings 2* (New York: Verso, 2015).

Such questions of proportionality are not simply technical or planning problems. As mentioned in Chapter 3, there is a class struggle over the proportionate allocation of resources to the two departments, and the struggles within other parts of the circuit can impinge on both the production of *MP* and *MS*, and on the allocation of *v* and *c*, in ways that undermine proper proportionality.

The opposite case – when producers crank out *less* than buyers want, signaled by an unexpected drawdown of inventories – Marx and Engels seem to have seen as simply an inducement to firms to increase production, sales, and total profits but not as any kind of crisis.

Nevertheless, despite these common problems, there are distinct differences in the problems facing those trying to sell means of subsistence and those trying to sell means of production.

5.2.2 Possible Crises in Selling the Means of Subsistence, *C*(*MS*)' – *M*'

For capitalists to sell consumer goods, workers must be both willing and able to buy.[217] Anything which substantially undermines either of those two conditions reduces demand and can cause a crisis for sellers of *C*(*MS*)'. Historically, capitalists have done their best to *force* people to buy consumer commodities by stealing and then monopolizing the means by which they might produce for themselves. The result: the only *legal* way to obtain the means of consumption has been by selling one's labor-power in exchange for the money required to buy what is needed.[218] As Marx points out in *Capital, Vol. 1*, Chapter 30, capitalist success in imposing these conditions created the "home market" for *C*(*MS*)'. The same methods were deployed in colonies abroad to create "foreign markets." Although mistakenly thought by some to be a thing of the past, such theft has been ongoing, along with all the struggle it has provoked.

217 For a long time and for obvious historical reasons, *MS* was considered to take two distinct forms, literal means of subsistence consumed by workers and luxury goods consumed by capitalists. The development of a continuous income hierarchy encompassing everyone who works for capital, from the unwaged in the reserve army through blue and white collar waged and salaried workers up to highly paid managers – those Marx called the "functionaries" of capital – has made that simple dichotomy obsolete. I assume, as Marx did most of the time, that the vast bulk of the consumption of *MS* is by workers and ignore the tiny pool of those whose only contribution to the expanded reproduction of capital is buying commodities out of surplus value, i.e., the leisured rich who, like the landed aristocracy who preceded them, live entirely off unearned income derived from financial assets and rent.

218 *Capital, Vol. 1*, Chapters 27 and 28 analyze the expropriation of land and tools and the violence with which capitalists have forced people into the labor market in search of the money they need to purchase *C*(*MS*).

Not surprisingly, many of those who have been expropriated have struggled to reclaim their stolen means of production, e.g., peasants and small farmers left landless have fought to regain their access to land and tools. To the degree such efforts succeed, they undermine the "home market" for consumer goods.

5.2.2.1 *Possible Crises due to Reversing Enclosure*

Both enclosures and efforts to reverse them predated capitalism but were renewed by the emerging capitalist class grabbing land and destroying homes and handicraft tools during that "primitive accumulation" of capital which Marx analyzed in Part Eight of Volume 1 of *Capital*. Clearly, every peasant success at seizing and then cultivating land, has made it possible for them to withdraw, to some degree, from capitalist markets for *MS*.

In his book on *The Peasant War in Germany* (1850), Engels looked back at the history of such struggles, focusing on peasant revolts in the 1500s. German peasants and their supporters demanded, among other things, the abolition of serfdom and guaranteed rights to land. They tried negotiations, appeals to courts and finally armed struggle. His analysis repeatedly compares and contrasts the struggles of German peasants with others in Britain and elsewhere.[219]

One well-known effort by the landless to seize land took place during the English Revolution of the mid-1600s. One part of the many diverse efforts by the dispossessed in that period to "turn the world upside down" was occupying, cultivating and building houses on previously stolen commons, often uncultivated "wasteland."[220] Such were the struggles of the "True Levellers," or "Diggers", one of whose leaders was Gerard Winstanley (1609–76) – who wrote both a manifesto explaining their demands and objectives and a song for them.[221]

Struggles for land continued in the 1700s and 1800s, taking place piece-meal, locally or through immigration, or as one motivation of those involved in various revolutions, e.g., the American (1775–1783), French (1789–1799), Haitian (1791–1804), French and the Dutch in 1830, the Revolutions of 1848 and the Paris Commune of 1870. To such momentary upheavals we must add the long history of resistance to colonial dispossession that involved both settler efforts

---

219 MECW, *Vol. 10*, pp. 397–482. Marx and Engels also followed such struggles in other countries, e.g., Russia and Poland. See, "Note to Polish Readers" in this volume.

220 See, Christopher Hill, *The World Turned Upside Down: Radical Ideas During the English Revolution* (London: Penguin, 1984) 107–124, and listen to Leon Rosselson's songs resurrecting and celebrating their struggles.

221 See, Winstanley, The New Law of Righteousness (1649). Hill's book recounts many events of the momentous year of 1649 when the Diggers seized land, Cromwell invaded Ireland and the king was beheaded.

to expand enclosure and those by the indigenous to stop or reverse it, throughout the Western Hemisphere, Asia, Africa and Oceania.[222]

5.2.2.2 *Possible Crises due to the Direct Appropriation of MS*

Inevitably, because capitalists maintain a "reserve army" of unwaged workers to pit against the employed, many of those dispossessed from the land, and unable to regain access, do not find jobs, cannot earn a wage and therefore are *unable* to buy, regardless of their willingness or need to do so. They either depend on those who can find jobs and wages to support them, e.g., waged spouses or other extended family members, or they find some other way to obtain what they need, or they die. In this predicament, they find themselves in the same plight as other workers who participated in the labor market but subsequently lost their jobs and been dumped into the reserve army. In both cases, one obvious alternative to dying has been to bypass markets for *MS* and *directly appropriate* what is needed.

The direct appropriation of *C*(*MS*) by workers, before they can be sold, has disrupted capitalist management of markets throughout its history. I have already pointed to such appropriation in the sphere of production – including in the transportation of *C*(*MS*) to markets. The direct appropriation of finished goods for purposes of consumption is very much like that of raw materials or intermediary goods in production discussed previously. In both cases, workers reject capitalist claims to the ownership of products they themselves, or other workers, have produced, ignore sellers' prices and, when successful, reduce *C*(*MS*)' to *MS*, destroying their exchange value to capitalists.[223]

---

222 Such struggles were renewed in the twentieth century. They included not merely small-scale land occupations but widespread revolutionary risings by peasants, including their central roles in the Mexican, Russian, and Chinese revolutions. In all these three great revolutions peasants and landless laborers seized land. See, Eric Wolf, *Peasant Wars of the Twentieth Century* (New York: Harper & Row, 1969). To a considerable degree this was also the motivation of peasants supporting anti-colonial, "national liberation" movements, such as the Vietnamese revolt that retook land stolen by French colonialists (who had converted the land from subsistence to production for export, e.g., rice and rubber). Then, in the wake of independence from colonialism, the failure of new elites in country after country to redistribute land led to widespread seizures and aggressive legal demands for land reform. Such efforts have continued by, among others, the Zapatistas in Mexico, the *Movimento dos Trabalhadores Sem Terra* (MST, or Landless Workers' Movement) in Brazil and other wings of Via Campesina.

223 But not necessarily their use-value. Not only does consumption of directly appropriated *MS* sustain the unwaged as part of capital's necessary reserve army, but because so many *MS* are designed for social control, e.g., to divert energy from struggle by entertaining buyers, such use-values to capital persist.

To all the appropriations along the supply chain from producer through transport to wholesalers and retail outlets, here I am adding the widespread direct appropriation of final consumer products from those outlets. With robbery usually defined as the taking of another's property, shoplifting and burglary are merely covert forms of robbery. Both forms of appropriation bypass price and refuse payment as the appropriator walks away with the unsold product.

Here, we must distinguish robbery-for-resale from robbery-for-consumption. Those who rob a business then re-sell their stolen goods, e.g., individuals, criminal gangs, pirates or privateers, also cause losses to their original owners – be they industrial or merchant capitalists – but the value of the goods is merely redistributed from the original owners to their thieves, rather than destroyed. The thieves effectively assume the role of rogue merchant capitalists, inserting themselves illegally into the circuit. In selling the stolen *C'*, they re-establish *C' – M'*, although the *M'* they gain is often less than the original value of the goods stolen and resold.[224] NB: I am concerned here only with the direct appropriation of commodities *from businesses*, which would otherwise sell them. I am *not* concerned with the robbery of individuals' property. Such theft either transfers property from one person to another, or, if the stolen property is sold, re-establishes *C' – M'*, albeit only to the benefit of the thief and buyer.

Methods of direct appropriation vary, from covert acts such as individual shoplifting and burglary to overt ones such as armed robbery in stores, the hijacking of trucks or ships or massive protests. The costs of small-scale robbery to capitalists may be marginal and factored into their "costs of production." Large-scale, direct appropriations, on the contrary, carried out by those with either little or no money or facing prices which have been raised beyond their ability to pay, can and have caused crises – both for those trying to sell, through the immediate rupture of *C(MS)' – M* and through the longer-term delegitimization of prices and capitalist control over them.[225] The most frequent of such uprisings, and the best documented, have been those in which

224 Whether selling to a "fence" or selling on the black market, they re-insert their purloined goods into the sphere of circulation and like legal merchant capitalists take a cut of the value.

225 The imposition of price-fixing and rationing in periods of crisis, e.g., wartime, also removed *some C(MS)* from circuits of profit making or reduced their value and hence profits. On the other hand, the spread of food stamps and other forms of income in the wake of uprisings have subsidized both workers' income and sales of *C(MS)*. Dissatisfaction and protests against capitalist price gauging have been among the forces leading to the removal of unhindered capitalist control over the production and distribution of a few *C(MS)*, e.g., electrical power and water, and their transfer to public utilities, regulated

people have seized food, the most basic of necessities.[226] Starvation is a powerful goad to action. Remember Engels's forecast in 1842, about workers faced with "a general lack of food", "then fear of death from starvation will be stronger than fear of the law." Given how capitalists have continued to wield poverty against workers, recurrent worker revolt must be expected.[227]

5.2.3 Possible Crises in Selling the Means of Production, *C(MP)' – M'*

Here we have the flip side of *M – MP* discussed in 1. There I discussed potential crises for those trying to *buy MP*, here I am concerned with potential crises for those trying to *sell MP*. However, many of the possible crises that I noted facing *buyers* of *MP* simultaneously face *sellers*, e.g., any reduction in the quantity produced. For buyers of *MP* that means a likely increase in price, higher costs of production, and less profit. For sellers that means less to sell and the danger of any increase in price being offset by reduced sales, revenue and profit – depending on the behavior of buyers.[228]

5.2.3.1 *Possible Crises with Barter*

In the example of the fur trade in Chapter 4, Section 3.3.1, the emphasis was on crises for buyers focused on reductions in supply, either short-term (local conflict) or long-term (exhaustion of species). For sellers, assuming constant demand, any substantial reduction in the supply of furs means less to sell. The long-term depletion of species whose fur can be sold, however, means the eventual reduction in the quantity available to sell, less revenue and profit, even with higher prices. It also meant a reduction in the number of trappers as trapping was largely replaced by industrialized fur farming – the breeding and murder

by the government. Since the rise of neoliberalism in the early 1980s, the push for the privatization has been aimed at restoring capitalist control.

226 For examples from the nineteenth century see, John Bohstedt, *The Politics of Provisions: Food Riots, Moral Economy, and Market Transition in England, c. 1550–1850* (London: Routledge, 2010). For our times see, David Seddon, *Riot and Rebellion: Political Responses to Economic Crisis in North Africa* (*Tunisa, Morocco and Sudan*) Discussion Paper No. 196, School of Development Studies, University of East Anglia, October 1986.

227 Although, to all appearances, most urban uprisings involving direct appropriation have been more or less spontaneous actions, some have taken the form of organized protests involving the "self-reduction" of prices. See, Bruno Ramirez, "The Working Class Struggle Against the Crisis: Self-Reduction of Prices in Italy", *Zerowork* 1 (December 1975): 142–150.

228 In neoclassical microeconomic theory, different reactions are approximated by the "elasticity of demand." With "inelastic demand", variations in price will have little impact on sales and profits, but with more elasticity, reduced sales will offset higher prices leaving the seller worse off.

of animals such as mink or foxes on a mass scale.[229] Such industrialization, requiring less labor and more investment in plant and equipment also meant a drastic reduction of the role of barter in the trade.

Serious drops in demand, however, could end the trade much sooner, as in the case of the demand for beaver fur to be processed into felt to make hats. The reduction in the demand for hats made of such fur meant a drop in the market for beaver pelts. So even if there were still plenty of beavers to be trapped, with less demand, beaver trapping became a less viable way to make a living.[230]

Other examples of dramatic drops in the demand for sellers' goods have originated in the reduction of protection for their markets, reductions which cause producers and sellers to find themselves unable to compete with competitors who can produce more cheaply and sell at lower prices. The abandonment of protectionist measures have sometimes been forced, e.g., by colonialism or war, and have sometimes been the result of economic pressures or negotiation.[231]

5.2.3.2 *Possible Crises due to Workers' Struggles*

Clearly, all struggles by workers which reduce the amount of *MP* produced and transported undermine sales and profits for those selling *MP*. This includes struggles during initial production and during transportation and sales. (See, Section 4.2.1) So, the same struggles against work, sabotage, strikes, protests, and upheavals that result in shortages and higher prices for *buyers* of *MP*, also undermine production, increase costs and prices, reduce sales, and potentially undermine profits for producers and *sellers* of *MP*.

5.2.3.3 *Possible Crises due to Deterioration of Quality*

Among the problems facing sellers of both *MS* and *MP* are those of convincing potential buyers of their useful qualities. Because both *MS* and many *MP* are sometimes produced far from where workers or capitalists will either consume

229 According to the Fur Institute of Canada, 65–75 percent of the furs produced in that country come from fur farms (and 85 per cent worldwide).

230 In our contemporary world, too many people trap (torture) and kill animals such as beavers just for the fun of it! That vicious past-time is currently fought by those trying to protect trapped species from all trapping because of its cruelty. See, for example, NH Citizens Against Recreational Trapping.

231 Widespread examples of such crises for producers and sellers happened in the wake of the collapse of the USSR and the regimes of its client states in Eastern Europe and the subsequent imposition of austerity. In Poland I visited the factory of a major producer of ship engines that had to almost completely shut down because it could no longer sell its wares. Similar problems beset businesses in countries where IMF debt-rollover packages of "structural adjustment" required the reduction or elimination of protectionist measures during the international debt crisis of the 1980s-1990s.

or process them, buyers' evaluation of quality often takes place at points of sale, e.g., ports of arrival, rather than where they were produced. For example, cotton produced in the Americas or in India for the textile factories of Britain was shipped across oceans and then evaluated and sold at their ports of discharge – to either intermediating merchants or textile producers. The same was true with all the cotton cloth or clothes produced in Britain with that imported cotton and then shipped to foreign ports as exports of *MS*.

While some means of production were unlikely to suffer any deterioration during either transportation or storage, e.g., coal or metal ores, many other means of production faced the very real possibility of serious deterioration in their quality between their production as *C*(*MP*)' and their utilization as *MP*. How serious depends on their intrinsic properties, perishability, and modes of transportation and storage. Marx discusses this while discussing turnover time in Volume 2 of *Capital*:

> The more perishable a commodity, the more directly after its production it must be consumed and therefore sold, the smaller the distance it can move from its place of production, the narrower therefore its sphere of spatial circulation, the more local the character of its market.[232]

Good examples of such limits were means of production subject to water damage during transportation in wooden ships, such as colonial exports like tobacco and rice. In the TV film series *Hornblower* (1998–2003) based on C. S. Forester's novels about the fictional career of Horatio Hornblower during the Napoleonic Wars, the episode "An Even Chance" includes a vivid illustration of the dangers of both war and deterioration. A ship smuggling bags of rice through the English blockade of French ports is attacked and taken by an English ship of war. In the taking, the smuggler's ship is holed below the water line. Before the hole can be plugged, water leaks in, the rice begins to swell and widens cracks in the ship's frame, which lets in more water. Unable to unload the rice fast enough, the swelling eventually breaks the ship apart and both cargo and ship are lost. Given how all wooden sailing ships were so vulnerable to sea water leaking in through their caulked joints, the war damage portrayed in this TV episode merely accelerated an ongoing danger to vulnerable cargos.

Much less dramatic but having a greater impact on the international trade in rice was the tendency of soft-grained rice, e.g., from Siam (Thailand) or

232 *Capital, Vol. 2*, p. 206, MECW, *Vol. 36*, p. 132.

Burma (Myanmar), to deteriorate so quickly that it could only be shipped short distances without considerable loss.[233]

The same could be true for other consumer goods subject to deterioration, such as tobacco or cotton, where sales prices are partly determined by their innate qualities and partly by their condition, a function of both their production and whatever deterioration they suffer during their long transportation from country of origin to country of utilization.

5.2.3.4 *Possible Crises due to the Direct Appropriation of C(MP)'*

Just as problems of direct appropriation face *buyers* of *MP*, as sketched in Section 3.4, so too do they also face *sellers,* albeit somewhat differently. Clearly, every direct appropriation by workers or theft of produced *MP* by capitalists reduces sales, revenue and profits for sellers. If the losses are marginal and foreseeable, sellers often try to compensate by passing the cost of lost *MP* on to buyers by raising their price, but possibly lowering sales. The net impact on profits of higher prices and lower sales will depend on the behavior of buyers.[234] If the losses are unforeseeable and massive – as with a sudden invasion by groups engaged in "self-reduction" (of prices) struggles, e.g., "food riots", or by bad weather, mutineers or pirates sinking or seizing ships at sea, the costs will be much greater, and the likelihood of crisis increased.

5.3 *Credit, Debt, and Commercial Crisis*

Temporal and geographic distances between the production of *C'* and its realization as *M'* has long made the availability of credit a major issue for capitalists engaged in commerce. This is true whether the possessor of *C'* is an industrial capitalist who has overseen production and now undertakes to sell, or a commercial intermediary who has bought *C'* to resell it. Indeed, historically, the extension of credit and the debt to which it gives rise were developed long before capitalism as a social system and played a major role in commerce.[235]

233 See, H. J. S. Cotton, "The Rice Trade of the World," *Calcutta Review*, Vol. 58, Issue 116 April 1874, pp. 288–9.

234 Given variations in the elasticity of demand, mentioned above, sellers must judge whether and to what degree to pass along increases in costs to buyers, sellers guestimate customers' likely responses.

235 Credit and debt, of course, also existed in relationships between individuals or between individuals and banks or between governments and banks. Individuals have borrowed from others to meet temporary unusual costs, say a marriage or a medical bill. The wealthy, with collateral in the form of property or dependable income from land rents or

From ancient times, banks (and others with surplus funds, e.g., governments and temples) played a vital role in financing long distance trade. That role expanded dramatically with the rapid development of international trade during the Renaissance.[236] All those engaged in long distance trade, and facing the kinds of perils already mentioned, often had recourse to credit to finance their operations with the expectation of gaining enough money through trade to cover their debts.[237]

While obtaining credit in the form of loans solves the immediate need for cash to finance the transportation, storage and selling of *C'*, holding such

---

financial assets, have long been able to borrow from moneylenders and banks. Probably the best-known example in literature of a person borrowing from a moneylender is Bassanio borrowing from Shylock in Shakespeare's *Merchant of Venice* (1596–99).

In the post-colonial era of the mid-twentieth century, a major concern of "development" economists was the concentration of surplus money in the hands of moneylenders rather than banks. The "modernization" of finance – and of the economy more generally – required such surplus be channeled through banks, whether private or governmental. The argument was that moneylenders (like Shylock) tended to make loans for "unproductive" activities (such as Bassanio's courtship of Portia), whereas banks were more likely to make loans to capitalists who would employ their borrowings "productively." See, for example, Frank Moore, "A Note on Rural Debt and Control of Ceremonial Expenditure in India," *Economic Development and Cultural Change*, Vol. 2, 1954, pp. 408–415. For many years, the literature of economic development included critical evaluations of inadequate financial institutions in the Global South and policy proposals for improving them, especially for the creation of new credit instruments for financing both manufacturing and agricultural investment. Focusing on accessing land rent and giving credit to Adam Smith, Walt Rostow (1916–2003) expressed this idea as clearly as other essays focused on finance per se, "surplus income ... must, somehow, be transferred out of the hands of those who would sterilize it in prodigal living into the hands of the productive men who will invest it in the modern sector and then regularly plow back their profits as output and productivity rise." *Stages of Economic Growth: A Non-Communist Manifesto* (Cambridge: Cambridge University Press, 1960) 24. See also: Hugh Patrick, "Financial Development and Economic Growth in Underdeveloped Countries," *Economic Development and Cultural Change* 14, no. 2 (January 1966): 174–189.

Governments have also used bank loans to finance various expenditures, from palaces to wars. Their ability to impose taxes and create money mostly guaranteed their ability to repay. The "sovereign" character of their debt increased the appeal of lending to them by banks. In *Capital, Vol. 1*, Chapter 31 on the rise of industrial capitalism, Marx presents this use of the state by banks as an important vehicle for the primitive accumulation of investable funds. Books on the history of credit and debt are numberless, but a recent one of interest providing an historical and anthropological perspective is David Graeber's *Debt: The First 5,000 Years* (New York: Melville House, 2014).

236 Wikipedia has a nice intro to "The History of Banking" but also see Graeber's book on debt.

237 As one form of money, "means of payment" is analyzed in *Capital, Vol. 1*, Chapter 3, but most of Marx's analysis of credit and its role in capitalism can be found in the *Manuscript of 1864–65*, in *Capital, Vol. 3* and in his journalism and notebooks.

debt also creates a new possibility of crisis, namely potential difficulties in repayment, in coming up with "means of payment." Marx's exposition of this difficulty begins in *Capital* with a discussion of the separation (in non-barter markets) of the acts of purchase and sale. His analysis, abstracted from the history of commerce, is organized around commodity exchange *C – M – C*, where the two acts of sale, *C – M*, and purchase, M – C, are separate. In the case of merchant capital, the two are reversed in the sequence *M – C – M'*, goods are first purchased, *M – C*, then later, if all goes well, sold, *C – M'*, at a higher price. Within the context of capitalism, Marx assumes that if the industrial capitalist sells to a merchant capitalist, the latter buys *C'* at less than its value, such that when those goods are sold at their value, *C' – M'*, the merchant capitalist shares in the surplus value generated by the workers who produced *C'*.[238]

In the 1840s, as Engels and Marx began to study these relationships, both old financial institutions such as banks and newer "financial intermediaries," such as stock and bond markets, were progressively channeling money to capitalist industry. Where Italian banking had dominated commercial trade in the Renaissance, British banking grew to dominance with industrial development in the eighteenth and nineteenth centuries. Other countries, including major ones on the continent, lagged behind Britain in the degree to which banks were making their monies available to capitalists and not just to governments and the simply wealthy.[239] So, for example, in a series of articles in 1846 and 1847, Engels describes the various means – some illegal – by which Frederick William IV of Prussia was borrowing money, at home and abroad, eventually trying to trick the United Diet into approving a new loan – despite the backdrop of crisis in which "there is comparatively little capital in Prussia," i.e., little money available for industrial investment and what was available was being

238 Although ignored at this point in his exposition, I have already indicated how Marx points out in Vol. 2 of *Capital*, how transportation – almost always an integral part of commercial operations – is another source of surplus value, extracted from the transport workers employed by merchant capitalists. See, *Capital, Vol. 2*, pp. 134–135, or MECW, *Vol. 36*, pp. 61–62.

239 By "simply wealthy" I refer mainly to "old money," individuals and families rich from inherited wealth and pre-capitalist sources of income, such as land rents and purely merchant buying and selling. As primitive accumulation progressed and landowners either became capitalists or hired others to manage their estates as agribusiness enterprises, such differentiation faded and as commerce became an integral part of capitalist operations meaningful distinctions between "old" and "new" money blurred and came to refer more to the chronological order of the acquisition of wealth than to that between pre-capitalist and capitalist sources.

diverted away from industry into speculation – one of the uses of credit most prone to crisis.[240]

Everywhere capitalism has developed, sooner or later, in response to difficulties and possible crises, new credit relationships have been developed among industrialists, merchants and specialized financial institutions such as banks at every point of the reproduction of capital where exchange occurs.[241] By the mid-1850s, Marx's studies of finance included following efforts in France – one of those countries where capitalist finance lagged – to reorient banking toward industry. He tracked the doings of the Société Générale du Crédit Mobilier, a joint stock company backed by Napoleon III that raised money by issuing stock to the wealthy and the emerging middle class.[242] While loaning money to the government – to finance, among other things the Crimean War – and to merchant capitalists engaged in commerce, the Crédit Mobilier's claim to fame was its financing of large-scale industry, such as railroads, both in France and abroad. Marx reported that the actual business practices of the company involved as much speculation with other people's money as they did investment in industry.[243]

Commercial credit can be extended either to the producing capitalist or to a commercial intermediary. A producer may borrow to cover the costs of

240 Friedrich Engels, "Violation of the Prussian Constitution," "The Prussian Bank Question" and "The Prussian Constitution" *MECW, Vol. 6,* pp. 52–53, 57 and 64–71, respectively. See his and Marx's analyses of speculation and its roles in the crises of the 1840s in Chapter 2.1. above.

241 Among the many new credit instruments created were government ones both for local financing and for international loans, supposedly guaranteed sovereign debt but revealed during the international financial crisis of the 1980s and 1990s to be far more vulnerable to collapse than anticipated. In this neoliberal period of the deregulation of finance, there has been a veritable explosion in the varieties of credit instruments, a great many of which provide platforms for speculation. The speculative housing booms of 1980s brought on the collapse of 1987 and that of the early 2000s brought on that of 2006, generating a general economic crisis in 2007–2008.

242 Whereas institutions of crédit *foncier*, e.g., land banks, base loans on the security of landed, immovable property, those of crédit *moblier* base loans on movable property, i.e., financial assets such as shares in both public and private companies available to both wealthy and middle classes with enough money to save and invest. On the development of capitalist finance in France that takes Marx's analysis into account, see Joseph Ricciardi, "*Essays on the Role of Money and Finance in Economic Development*" (PhD Diss., University of Texas at Austin, 1985). Some of his analysis has been made more readily available in Joseph Ricciardi, "Marx on Financial Intermediation: Lessons from the French Crédit Mobilier in the *New York Daily Tribune*," *Science and Society* 79, no. 4 (October 2015): 497–526.

243 See, the three articles "The French Crédit Mobilier," in *MECW, Vol. 15,* pp. 8–13, 14–18, and 19–24.

the sales effort, e.g., transporting goods and finding buyers, with repayment dependent on successful sale. Or, an intermediary (a wholesaler or retailer) may borrow to buy C' from producers, or from another intermediary, e.g., retailers buying from wholesalers. Where intermediaries have borrowed from anyone other than the producer, if their sales fall short, the producers lose nothing; they have already been paid and are able to pay off any borrowing they might have done to finance their operations. On the other hand, a chain of intermediaries based on credit may collapse, bankrupting all those involved. In such a case, the producer may suffer eventual repercussions if future sales are impaired. In all cases, immediate problems in repaying debt may be handled temporarily by rolling it over, i.e., obtaining new loans to cover repayment of existing ones, assuming the funds necessary are available at interest rates sufficiently below the expected rate of profit. But that only puts off the need for an ultimate reckoning.[244]

All these relations of credit, like the other aspects of accumulation, are elements of, and shaped by, class relations and their antagonisms. In *Capital*, Marx was quick to point this out by drawing attention to the class conflicts around credit and debt in earlier societies.

> The class struggles in the ancient world took the form mainly of a contest between debtors and creditors, and ended in Rome with the ruin of the plebian debtors. In the Middle Ages the contest ended with the ruin of the feudal debtors, who lost their political power together with its economic basis ... Here indeed, the money-form – and the relation between creditor and debtor does have the form of a money-relation – was only the reflection of an antagonism which lay deeper, at the level of the economic conditions of existence.[245]

Within capitalism, that deeper antagonism "at the level of the economic conditions of existence" is between capitalists and workers. With the availability of industrial credit dependent on capitalist control over workers, the effect on profits and the ability to repay, this is obvious. In the case of commercial credit, class struggle is integral in two ways. First, the capital-labor antagonism exists

244 This was how international banks, backed by the International Monetary Fund, handled the international debt crisis of the 1980s and 1990s, created by the Fed's dramatic increase in interest rates which plunged the world into depression. Those unable to repay their international debts could – IF they met IMF conditions to impose austerity on workers – borrow to finance repayment, thus accumulating even more debt.

245 *Capital, Vol. 1*, Chap. 3, p. 233, or *MECW, Vol. 35*, p. 146.

wherever workers are hired to transport and sell commodities, e.g., on commercial vessels, always at risk of direct appropriation, mutiny and or piracy. Second, the existence and maintenance of markets often depends on the more general stability of class relations. Where workers are in revolt markets are disrupted and may disappear completely.

In general, credit is a vehicle for overcoming barriers (potential ruptures) by buying time, but the allocation of credit depends on relative "credit worthiness" among capitalists, industrial or commercial. The most important measure of "credit worthiness" is the ability of capitalists to control their workers so that they can make the profits required for repayment. The so-called "prime (interest) rate" to large corporate borrowers is accorded to those firms that earn the highest rate of profit, often produced by a high rate of exploitation, *s/v*. The greater the perceived risk that capitalist borrowers may lose control over their labor force, the higher the "risk premium" and the higher the interest rate charged by creditors. In this way, from the viewpoint of the capitalist class as a whole, loanable funds are allocated efficiently, by providing the most support to those who appear most capable of controlling their workers.

In all these cases, where commodities are transferred from seller to buyer first and payment is only made later, credit allows the exchange to occur where it otherwise might not. But there is a sharp separation and opposition between the exchange of goods and the exchange of money, between the creditor and the debtor. In each case, because the debtor may fail to secure the necessary means of payment, that is, fail to sell *C'* at high enough prices to be able to repay loans, the possibility of crisis persists. When such a breakdown in sales occurs, Marx calls it a *commercial crisis*. When the major aspect is the collapse of a set of monetary (credit) relations, he speaks of a *monetary crisis*. These two often go together, but are differentiated from *industrial crisis*, in which the breakdown occurs in the sphere of production. I discuss the interrelation of these crises below when I examine Marx's analysis of how crisis can circulate from one aspect of accumulation to another.

5.4 *Summarizing*

Early in this chapter on the possibilities of crisis, I emphasized how the possibilities that interest me the most are the direct and indirect results of workers' struggles, of how they can impose an interruption at any of the many points in the circuits of capital, whether in *M – LP*, *M – MP*, *LP – M – C(MS)*, ... *P* ... *C'*, *C(MS)'* or *C(MP)' – M'*. Here's a brief summary of the possibilities of crisis in each of these moments caused by workers' struggles.

1. Workers' struggles can, in the past, in the present and we can anticipate in the future, reduce the availability of M – without which there is no

investment at all. Those in the past may have reduced the available surplus value below what is necessary for investment. All of them, past, present and anticipated, can undermine the willingness of creditors to loan money for investment and raise interest rates to unacceptable levels, given that interest must be paid out of surplus value. Both borrowers and lenders will estimate the consequences of any rise in interest rates resulting from the risks they anticipate.[246]

2. Workers may cause a crisis in the labor market, $M - LP/LP - M$, by refusing to enter it or by withdrawing from it. Without *LP* no production can take place, no matter how much *MP* may be on hand. Factories that can't attract workers stand empty. During strikes, the inevitable cry of capitalists is "Our machinery lies idle! Our raw materials are rotting (or rusting) in warehouses!" If workers have won higher wages, raising v, either through the initial deal or in added expenditures necessary to make *LP* function, with a given total added value of $v + s$, surplus value will be reduced.[247] Any rise in v means a fall in the rate of exploitation, s/v, and a fall in the rate of profit, $s/(c + v)$. If the fall is great enough, it's a crisis for the investor.
3. Because the value expended on the means of production, $M - MP$, the investment in constant capital (c), is counted in the value of the final product, workers' struggles that force an increased expenditure on c, lower the rate of profit, $s/(v + c)$, (*ceteris paribus*). If workers' struggles in the production or transport of *MP* raise its costs or render it unavailable, profit will be reduced or eliminated.
4. While capitalists generally seek a low v, by holding down M in $M - LP - C(MS)$, because it means a higher rate of profit $s/(c + v)$, workers resist the resultant low level of $C(MS)$ available to them. Because of the low wages of his time, Marx emphasized how reduced v often undermined the reproduction of labor-power by decreasing the size of the labor force through starvation or reducing the productivity of labor due to illness, but he and Engels also pointed out how workers revolted against such reductions in their well-being, rising up violently, directly appropriating

246 This is true whether interest is interpreted – as Marx does – as a sharing of surplus value generated by industrial capital *or* as payment for a service. In the latter case, it forms a part of the costs of production and thus has the same relation to surplus value as other components of c. For one argument in favor of the latter interpretation, see "The Source of Financial Profit – Revising Marx" in Cleaver, *Rupturing the Dialectic*, 165–180.

247 Assuming constant rates of productivity and of the intensity of labor.

commodities or fleeing when that seems fruitless. All of which can cause a crisis in simple reproduction.[248]

5. At the point of production, … *P* … *C'*, all forms of worker struggle can interrupt the circuit by effecting the value components *c*, *v*, and *s*. Inefficient production (including sabotage) can greatly increase the cost of *c* through waste, etc., reducing the rate of profit. Absenteeism, loafing, and so on, can increase the costs of labor (*v*) by increasing the costs of labor turnover, supervision, etc. All reductions of work time or intensity can cut into surplus value, as can reductions of productivity by raising costs per unit, and even globally raising *v*. All lengthening of production time can raise finance costs of borrowing, etc., increase interest payments and reduce industrial net profit, and thus the rate of profit. When successful, strikes over wages, salaries or benefits have similar effects by raising *v* directly, thus cutting *s*, either immediately, or through a rise of *v* during the next contract of *M* – *LP*.
6. Any worker unwillingness or refusal to spend money on consumer goods reduces *C*(*MS*)' – *M'*, whether the cause be attachment to subsistence farming, reduced income, uncertainty, solidarity with the workers producing them, a conscious minimization of dependence on store-bought goods or a revulsion against the endless advertising of supposedly desirable but actually completely dispensable "goods", reduces *C*(*MS*)' and thus *M'*. All direct appropriation by workers ruptures *C'* — *M'*, whether of *C*(*MS*)' or of *C*(*MP*)', undermines the sale of the final product, reduces total value, $c + v + s$, and thus surplus value, *s*, the rate of surplus value, s/v, and the rate of profit, $s/(c + v)$. This will be true, whether the appropriation takes place at the point of production, during transportation or at retail outlets. Capitalist willingness to purchase *C*(*MP*)', as with every other aspect of investment, may be undermined by worker struggles, either in-house or during the production or transportation of *MP*, that raises their price enough to undermine prospective profitability.
7. Not only do workers' struggles increase the possibilities of crisis along the circuit but they also undermine the availability of credit and loans by risk-conscious creditors to capitalists they see threatened by disruption. This is true for both industrial capitalists and merchant capital

248 Of course, capitalists are not always blind to such effects and sometimes raise *v* in the expectation of raising productivity and *s*. An example referenced by Marx was mine owners forcing their workers to eat beans. See, *Capital, Vol. 1*, p. 718, fn 9, *MECW*, *Vol. 35*, p. 572, fn 1. When planned by capital, such increases in *v* are known today as investments in "human capital."

> when their managers are forced to turn to financial intermediaries for the wherewithal necessary to keep their businesses running.[249] As the cost of credit rises, net industrial and commercial profit falls and with them future investment and future profit.

We now turn to an analysis of the forces that predispose all of these theoretical possibilities to become actualized causing actual crises for capitalists and their system.

249 As workers have forced up wages sufficiently to acquire wealth and gain access to credit from banks, the primary uses of loans has been to finance consumption, thus "consumer" credit and debt, whether the consumption be immediate or long term as in the case of consumer durables and housing. Although businesses have come to understand the advantage to them of increased purchasing power, as with business debtors, any reduction of income threatens the ability to repay, the inadequacy of "means of payment" and the threat of default. During periods of widespread rising unemployment and disappearing or falling wages, defaults can be equally widespread, terminating the income to creditors, causing a financial crisis and eliminating those consumption expenditures based on credit. Thus, a crisis for Department II businesses producing *C*(*MS*) can have a negative ripple effect on those in Department I. (More on this in the section on the circulation of crisis.)

CHAPTER 5

Predispositions to Crisis

Just as Marx and Engels saw many points at which there was a *possibility* of interruption and crisis in the reproduction process, so too did they see many reasons why those possibilities might be realized through various *causes* or *forces* that tend to produce interruption and whose existence, therefore, *predisposes* the system to crisis. They often speak of "tendencies"; a "predisposition" is a tendency. A predisposition to crisis is a force pushing in that direction; it may cause a crisis or it may be so weak or so offset by other forces that no crisis breaks out. Thus, to identify such predispositions is not to say that crises will in fact occur.[1] Because Marx and Engels' comments on such predispositions are scattered throughout their writings, deal with virtually every moment of capital's expanded reproduction, but are in no way integrated into a reasoned whole, I divide their comments into three groups. (1) Those dealing with the predisposition to interruption at various points *within individual units or circuits of capital.* (2) Those dealing with the way interruptions in one point within a circuit can *circulate* within a circuit or to other circuits, thus generalizing the crisis. (3) Those dealing with forces acting *at the level of capital as a whole.*[2]

Let us begin with a review of the sequence of processes that must be successfully completed to achieve the expanded reproduction of capital.

$$
\begin{array}{ccccc}
 & LP & & & LP' & & \\
 & / & & & / & & \\
M — & C\ldots\ldots P\ldots\ldots C' — M'.\ M' — & & & C'\ldots\ldots P\ldots\ldots C'' — M'' & \text{and so on.} \\
 & \backslash & & & \backslash & & \\
 & MP & & & MP' & &
\end{array}
$$

1 This essay rejects the many Marxist interpretations that have conceived predispositions in terms of "iron laws", which not only predispose but also predestine the system to inevitable "breakdown" and crisis. No teleology here.

2 Remember, capital as a whole consists of more than the sum of the individual circuits; it also includes the reproduction of labor-power. So, despite the way the behavior of forces at the level of the whole includes those within individual circuits, it exceeds them. Because of this, the circulation of rupture between industrial circuits does not necessarily lead directly to the totality despite being a part of it. If we treat the reproduction of labor-power in terms of the "little" circuit *LP – M –C(MS)* and treat the sum of those circuits as the sum of all reproduction processes, the behavior of the total social capital is more closely approximated by the behavior of $\Sigma k_i + \Sigma h_i$, where k_i = industrial circuits i; h_i = reproduction circuits i. The same is true if we extend Marx's little circuit to *LP – M – C(MS) ...P... LP**, which makes the reproduction of labor-power more explicit.

 | DOI:10.1163/9789004708631_006

The smooth, expanded reproduction of the circuit involves growth in each element of the circuit – albeit often at different rates, e.g., a rise in the organic composition of capital will involve *MP* growing faster than *LP*.[3] In the above representation, the second whole circuit (*M′* to *M″*) involves increased quantities of money capital, labor-power and means of production as well as more final product and more sales revenue than in the first circuit (*M* to *M′*). My organization of Marx and Engels' comments on the predispositions to breakdown follow the same outline as those on possibilities; I examine their analysis as it pertains to each stage of the circuit.

In the introduction to this essay, I state that "the central thrust of my interpretation … sees accumulation as the expanded reproduction of a fabric of capitalist control that is always tenuous, repeatedly threatened and often ruptured by workers' struggles. Crisis is thus, most basically, a 'working-class produced' tearing of that fabric and a positive consequence of workers either undermining some aspect of capitalist control or elaborating a positive alternative which also threatens that control." A corollary of this interpretation sees the most fundamental "predisposition" to crisis to be workers' (our) resistance to subordination to the capitalist organization of production, of consumption, of life. Therefore, as I examine each moment of capital's organization, I suggest the origins of that resistance, why we resist, what predisposes us to resist, how we go about it and the problems we create for our would-be overlords in doing so.

1 Predispositions in the First Stage of the Circuit: Investment

As with possibilities, I begin with the issue of whether enough money can be amassed by capitalists to launch or renew their investments. What forces predispose capitalists to crisis in gaining enough money for desired investment? Then, assuming they do get access, what predisposes failure in markets for labor-power and for means of production?

3 The displacement of workers by machines (capital's relative surplus value strategy, an increase in the technical and therefore organic composition of capital, *c/v*) tends to *slow the growth* of the *employed* (waged or salaried) labor force. On a large enough scale, it can *reduce* the number of employed, but this does not reduce the size of the entire labor force, which includes the already unwaged, augmented by displaced workers. Locally, an overall shrinkage can happen if large numbers of the unwaged die off or emigrate, such as during and after the Great Irish Famine or the more recent devastating wars in the Middle East, or as a result of genocide as in Myanmar, Palestine, and the Congo, but even then, the impact on the totality of capital is marginal as world population continues to grow.

1.1 *Forces Limiting Access to Money for Investment, M*

We have seen how difficulties in amassing the money, *M*, required for investment have the potential to thwart this first stage of the circuit before it even gets started. Workers' struggles can create difficulties in two obvious ways.

First, any past struggles by workers that reduced profits can undermine new investment by reducing the surplus value available. Worker success in raising wages faster than capitalists could raise productivity – thus undermining relative surplus value – would do just that. So would direct appropriation of the means of production or final product that undermines profits by raising costs, or success at imposing laws – such as limits to the working day – that reduce the ability to extract absolute surplus value. *Why* workers are often predisposed to create these problems for their employers I leave to each of the following sections.

Second, to the degree that retained earnings are insufficient for planned investment and capitalists have to borrow, I have argued that past struggles can undermine the ability to borrow by increasing both the investing capitalists' and creditors' perceptions of risk. Clearly, a past failure to realize at least the average profit can mean not only inadequate retained earnings for new investment but also that creditors are more likely to refuse to loan or charge such high rates of interest as to impede borrowing sufficient funds to launch a new or expand an existing circuit.[4] Failure breeds failure. (More on this when I turn to the circulation of crisis in Section 5.4)

If we assume, instead, that the previous circuit was completed successfully, rendering at least some investable retained surplus value, then if that surplus value is enough to launch the planned investment there is no problem. If not enough and would-be investors require borrowing, potential creditors will be reassured by their past success. Success breeds success.

However, as I discussed previously, another key issue of concern to investors and creditors, is the expected *future* rate of profit on any proposed new investment – which few are willing to assume to be a simple projection of past experience. Clearly, any perceptible forces at work tending to reduce expectations of future profits will not only reduce the inclination of some capitalists to invest, but also that of financial capitalists to extend new loans. Creditors, as I have mentioned, express their estimations of risk by the conditions they set

4 This is true whether the attempt to borrow is from domestic financial intermediaries or foreign ones. Already in the mid-nineteenth century both banks and stock markets operated internationally, loaning money, or offering shares to foreigners or extending operations into other countries. Just as capitalist commerce included international trade, so too were financial institutions increasingly operating across borders. Industrial firms were seeking raw materials abroad whether to buy or produce themselves through direct investment – wherever profit seemed likely, whether in protected colonies or elsewhere.

and the rate of interest they charge on loans. The greater the estimated risk, the more severe the conditions and the higher the rate of interest and thus the cost of borrowing. Interest rates high enough to reduce the expected rate of profit below the average can cancel investors' willingness to borrow and, as a result, their planned investment.

While all kinds of factors influence estimates of risk, most are contingent upon particular historical circumstances, e.g., weather and its effects on harvests of raw materials, their price, etc., or the state of foreign relations and the likelihood of an outbreak of war and military hostilities that would disrupt trade, or, less dramatically, potential changes in legislation, both at home and abroad, affecting trade and immigration, or, central bank monetary policy in response to excessive inflows or outflows of money, etc. The one factor that is built-in to every stage of the capitalist circuit, indeed in every aspect of society reshaped by capital for its own purposes, albeit variable in its intensity and effect on calculations of risk, is *class struggle*. The only question is how intense and how disruptive. All capitalists contemplating investment and all creditors contemplating loans to such capitalists know this and, as a result, their estimations of risk and the implications for future rates of profit are based, in part, on their assessment of the current state of class struggle and its future prospects.[5]

---

5 With the development of capitalism, the estimation of risk has come to be done both *internally*, within corporations, both industrial and financial, and *externally* by independent businesses. The most obvious traditional businesses preoccupied with risk assessment were insurance companies and banks. For example, banks acting as financial intermediaries between investors and their investments have employees devoted entirely to risk assessment, who share their results with both management and investing clients. I discovered an example of this in the wake of the Zapatista uprising in 1994. That many investors thought that their risks had risen was manifest in how they were pulling their "hot" money out of the Mexican stock market and repatriating it across the border to the US. Chase Manhattan Bank's newsletter to "emerging market investors" was soon giving its own assessment of risk to its clients as well as advising the Mexican government – then being run by the PRI – to "eliminate" the Zapatistas to stabilize the investment climate and, if necessary, to cheat in forthcoming elections to retain control of the government to the same purpose! Despite this advice, military action against the Zapatistas and familiar cheating in the 1994 elections, capital flight continued. Because the Salinas government ran down foreign reserves trying to defend the peso, the new government under Zedillo was forced to marginally devalue the peso. But this triggered even more massive capital flight and a dramatic devaluation, i.e., the "Peso Crisis." These were modern versions of the "money drains" Marx noticed and analyzed in the nineteenth century. See International Monetary Fund, "Factors behind the Financial Crisis in Mexico," *World Economic Outlook*, May 1995, pp. 90–97. The Peso Crisis was serious enough to ripple across other "emerging markets." Unfortunately for capitalists, so did the indigenous uprising that caused it. See, H. Cleaver, The Zapatista Effect: The Internet and the Rise of an Alternative Political Fabric, *Journal of International Affairs* 51, no. 2 (Spring 1998): 621–640.

Such assessments examine, first and foremost, the immediate pool of labor – both active and reserve armies of labor. Are those workers available and exploitable? Will they accept currently profitable wages and working conditions? Or, are they organizing and resisting, posing potential threats? Beyond the immediate pool, to what degree is the wider situation promising or threatening? Potential employers and creditors also take into account even distant class struggles that might influence local struggles. Some examples, in chronological order.

Fear ran through investors in Britain in the wake of the French Revolution in 1789. As inspired workers organized in Britain and the state tried to whip up patriotic opposition to the revolution, intellectuals debated, penning either denunciations, such as Edmund Burke's (1729–1797) pamphlet *Reflections on the Revolution in France* (1790), or support, by the Welsh Dissenter Richard Price's (1723 – 1791) *Discourse on the Love of Country* (1789), the poet William Wordsworth's (1770–1850) *Letter to the Bishop of Llandaff* (1793), and radicals Thomas Paine (1737–1809) and Mary Wollstonecraft (1759–1797) in his *Rights of Man* (1790) and her *A Vindication of the Rights of Men* (1790).[6]

Slavers and their creditors throughout the Western Hemisphere trembled in 1791 when revolution exploded in the French colony of Saint Domingue and succeeded by 1804 in throwing the slave owners off the island and establishing Haiti as the first independent, free nation of ex-slaves in the world.

Estimates of risk in Britain obviously rose considerably with the growth of the Chartist Movement and experience with its protests, petitions and strikes in 1839, 1842, and even more so in 1848, given the revolutions on the continent. Worries about workers' rebellion circulating from the continent to the British Isles was palpable and manifest in both parliament and daily journalism. Estimated changes in worker struggles, whether based on purely local circumstances or on potential foreign influences, certainly affect estimates of risk, interest rates on loans and thus the availability of money for investment. The threat, and the estimate of risk, varies, but the autonomous power of workers to disrupt the circuit guarantees a predisposition to crisis within the system. As I move through the various stages of the circuit this will become ever clearer.

Assuming the problem of coming up with required investment funds is solved, the first stage of the circuit involves hiring labor-power and buying means of production. As I have mentioned, among the possible difficulties are (1) that *LP* and *MP* might not be available with the proper characteristics, or

6 See, Ruth Mather's illustrated "The Impact of the French Revolution in Britain" (2014). For a recent, insightful re-examination of Thomas Paine, see Peter Linebaugh's introduction to *Thomas Paine: Rights of Man and Common Sense* (New York: Verso, 2009).

(2) that they might not be available in the necessary amounts for *expanded* reproduction.

1.2 *Forces Interfering with the Supply of Labor-Power, LP*

In the first investment of their capital, or in any subsequent investment, capitalists are confronted with the problem of *whether* they can hire workers in sufficient numbers, with the necessary skill mix, who can be expected to work for a wage on terms and in a manner, which will, when combined with the cost of means of production and the revenues of the sale of C' at expected prices, achieve at least an average profit. As I noted in Chapter 4 on "possibilities," this can be a problem because both those not yet hired and those already hired may resist.

1.2.1 Avoidance of the Labor Market

Why do so many, from the children of waged or salaried workers to adult unenclosed peasants avoid entering the labor market, an obvious source of income in capitalism? For one thing, they are often made aware – from stories told by others, from anti-work songs, or from observation – of the violent, alienating, and exploitative character of work-for-capital and of its uncertainty. Given how obvious it is that children have a natural predisposition to play, to explore the world, what's the likely effect then on their attitudes toward waged labor of observing their parents coming home each day from the violence of hard labor in waged jobs or from the emotionally exhausting work of salaried employees, coping with annoying bosses or recalcitrant underlings? What effect too of frustrated parents all too often bringing their frustrations home and then taking them out on their kids and spouses?[7] The factory inspectors, upon whose reports Marx and Engels drew so often, provide plenty of accounts of the horrors of waged work in that period and evidence of how only poverty drove many into the labor market and the jobs to which they gave access. The "industrial novels" of the nineteenth century often portrayed the frustrations of middle-class managers, torn between the demands of profit-maximization and those of workers. Most workers, whether waged or salaried, had little job security and with the ups and down of investment and crisis were often hired today, and fired tomorrow.[8] Childrens' awareness of all this alone produces a resistance to entering the labor market.

---

7 In modern times, little has changed. Bruce Springsteen's song *Factory* (1978) comes to mind, about his father coming home from working in a factory "with death in his eyes" and "Somebody's gonna get hurt tonight."

8 An uncertainty which has grown in recent years with the proliferation of precarious "gig" jobs of short duration, with no opportunity for advancement and few or no benefits. See George Caffentzis, "Throwing away the [Job] Ladder: The Universities in the Crisis," *Zerowork* 1 (December 1975): 128-142.

Those young people lucky enough to have alternatives, e.g., schooling or travel, were clearly inclined to seize the opportunities to delay entering the labor market. This was especially true for those whose parents' income could pay for private tutors for their children and eventual access to better jobs. Those less lucky – and that included most working-class children – found themselves under the same pressures of poverty as their parents. Whether farmed out by parents to capitalist employers or simply urged to help find a way to supplement family income at very early ages, they found avoidance of the labor market extremely difficult. With even reluctant children easier to control than adults, before the enactment of child labor laws capitalists were anxious to put them to work as young as possible at whatever jobs they could be trained to handle. So whatever satisfaction children and their parents might gain from bringing home some small contribution to family income was certainly offset by long hours working in dust-filled mines or "fluff" polluted textile mills.

Once workers and reformers were successful at getting child labor laws passed, children began to be incarcerated in schools rather than mines and mills. Whereas workhouses were generally made as obnoxious as possible, with the objective of driving the unemployed back into the labor market, schools were pitched as being better alternatives because they provided the possibility of some learning, learning that was good for its own sake and might also open the way to better jobs. But precisely because they were, like labor markets, bootcamp-gateways to jobs, discipline was higher on the agenda of schoolmasters than learning. While economists like Adam Smith or Jevons saw schools as opportunities for the ideological brainwashing of children into accepting capitalism and its economic "laws" as natural, the primary day-to-day challenge facing those managing the schools was turning energetic, excitable, curious children into potential workers who will do as they are told, the way they are told by their teachers today, in preparation for their employers tomorrow. And, to enforce discipline, schoolmasters were not loath to use the coercion of corporal punishment (and often sexual harassment) to obtain these results.[9] It's easy enough to see how this character of schools has predisposed some children subjected to such regimes to reject both the immediate discipline of school and the anticipated discipline of waged jobs. Such refusals make up the story of "drop out culture", "juvenile delinquency" and "gangs", whether in

9 As late as the early 1960s, when I was still in high school, corporal punishment ("whacks" with fraternity-like boards) was still being meted out to those of us who chaffed at arbitrary rules. It was, I gather, worse in Britain where punishment was administered with canes. Watch Lindsay Anderson's film *If ...* (1968), which includes both such punishment and student revolt against it. American "teenage movies" rarely depict such punishment, and merely mock school disciplinarians, e.g., *Ferris Bueller's Day Off* (1986).

schools or in the streets where children have sought fellowship where the rules of adherence have been much looser.

Given both the frequent dearth of available jobs – due to recurrent crises – and the characteristics of the work involved when jobs were available, many adults as well as young people have opted to find ways to survive outside the frameworks offered by capitalism. Despite capitalist ideology preaching that "growing up" involves accepting its rules, especially the rule that wages or salaries provide the only legitimate access to consumer goods and other "private property", the same urge to freedom born naturally in children persists in many adults who refuse those rules and make their own or join with others with the same predisposition. Thus, adult beggars who ask for (and sometimes demand) others to share, robbers who directly appropriate what they need or want, and vagabonds who may engage in either activity while also living off the land.

The predisposition of peasants and small farmers to cling to their land has clearly been based on the self-determination and independence it affords. The ability of agriculturalists to grow enough crops, raise enough animals and forage the commons allows them to weather all but extreme natural and human-made disasters (epidemics, destructive floods, drought, earthquakes) – including the vagaries of capitalist markets. These abilities have provided them an alternative to the deadly long hours of labor capitalists have imposed – until curbed by workers' struggles. Many traditional farming practices have often involved much less work. In some areas, winter weather alone ends much farm work.[10] In both northern and southern climes, slash-and-burn agriculture has been common and entails leaving planted areas alone during growing seasons.[11] The same has been true for hunters and gatherers. Long thought to barely scratch out a living, modern research has revealed their methods to leave plenty of time for cultural activities.[12] Given the difficult living conditions afforded waged workers, whether in mill towns, mining camps or cities, why move from a well-known countryside with all its resources

---

10 As for modern family farmers, having grown up in the Ohio portion of the "corn belt", I long saw how frozen fields basically gave my neighbors most of the winter free of work. Years later, I spent many hours playing an online game (MMO) with a farmer in Michigan, whose fields were buried under two feet of snow, giving him far more time to play than I had. Obviously, this was less true for those whose primary occupation was husbandry because animals require year-round maintenance.

11 On the limited work of agriculturalists who regularly shift their plantings, see Harold Conklin, "The Study of Shifting Cultivation" *Current Anthropology* 2, no. 1 (February 1961): 27–61.

12 On the limited work of hunter-gatherers, see "The Original Affluent Society" in Marshall Sahlins, *Stone Age Economics* (London: Routledge, 2017).

(farmland, game, medicinal plants, and spiritual connection) or from equally well-known communities where one is part of a social network of mutual aid?[13] This is the flip side of Marx's analysis of "primitive accumulation" – to which that city-boy paid little attention, notoriously dismissing (until late in life) agriculturalists as dumb local yokels unable to organize in collective self-interest.[14] Yet, many are the sources of farmer and peasant resistance to enclosure and colonialist attempts to impose capitalist social relations on whole populations.

As for the predisposition of older folks to avoid the labor market and waged or salaried jobs, it depends on how they have been living. In agricultural and hunting and gathering communities, quitting previous adult activities may come naturally from age putting limits on what one can contribute. Where extended families and close social networks prevail, mostly it just means changing the nature of one's participation, e.g., switching from fieldwork or hunting to childcare or other more sedentary activities. But for waged and salaried workers, retirement from working for capitalists means leaving an artificially constructed, authoritarian workplace of commodity-producing workers for what? As capitalists gradually urbanized their world, concentrating factories in cities to minimize costs, their practices of creating or ending jobs according to their own needs, of moving them from less profitable areas to more profitable ones, increasingly imposed high mobility on workers. That mobility has made the formation or reproduction of both extended families and coherent communities outside of work more and more difficult. Yet, waged and salaried workers have clearly fought for laws mandating retirement at ages where age-related disabilities are not a factor. They just want out. But they have also fought for income to sustain them when they are no longer working. They first won such laws and such income support in Germany in 1889 as Bismark sought to ward off greater concessions to the burgeoning workers movement.

---

13 In capitalist cities, wealth in connections to the land has largely disappeared. Yet, such connections have long existed and continue to exist in many rural communities of small farmers or indigenous peasants. One example: for the indigenous Maya of Chiapas, Mexico, who call themselves "the people of the corn", both the cultivation of maize (*milpa*) and its consumption (*comida*) are vital elements of their spiritual connections to both the land and each other. See: Gustavo Esteva and Madhu Prakash, *Grassroots Post-Modernism: Remaking the Soil of Cultures* (New York: Zed Books, 1998) Chapter Three, "Beyond the Individual Self: Regenerating Ourselves."

14 That view, expressed in the *Eighteenth Brumaire* and in his analysis of "proletarianization", was eventually modified by his studies during his final years, of the Russian peasant *mir* and other agricultural societies. It poisoned generations of Marxist attitudes towards farmers and peasants, only recently modified by the discovery of his later notes and writings *and* by the resurgence of very well-organized movements of peasants and indigenous peoples.

(See, Chapter 2, Section 3.11.) Where they have won it, retirement means answering the question "Now what?"

For those who have successfully stolen or wrested enough time away from jobs to build other networks of connection, the answer may be obvious: increased time and energy for whatever activities constitute those networks. Those whose lives have been totally eaten up by their jobs, either because they have been endless and exhausting or because they have bought into the workaholism pushed by capitalist ideology, the answer is often anything but obvious. The results for them, alas, are often rather pathetic: taking up some "hobby", searching for some kind of social life, maybe volunteer work, maybe (alas and alack) a return to the labor market, and all too often early death.

1.2.2 Flight from the Labor Market

I already discussed in Chapter 4, Section 3.2.2.2 the *possibility* of flight, either from the labor market to open lands or from one labor market to another. Both kinds of flight, if large enough, can cause a crisis for those trying to hire in the labor market being abandoned. But what *predisposes* workers to flee or walk away from a labor market in which they have already participated? The obvious reasons are 1) conditions in both the labor market and in the work lying beyond that portal and 2) the options available. When taking a job through the labor market leads to the discovery that instead of that market being a rosy moment of equal exchange leading to friendly collaboration between capitalists and workers, it's more akin to Dante's gateway to Hell with a similar welcome "All Hope Abandon Ye Who Enter Here," many workers will go elsewhere if they can. For Marx and Engels, among the obvious conditions which drove workers away were the early capitalist efforts to reduce wages as low as possible and the horrible conditions of work (long and often dangerous hours). Such conditions result in death for some but flight by others. The extremely long hours – effectively reducing wages below subsistence – and unsafe working conditions shorten lives, killing slowly or quickly, reducing the labor force, or slowing its growth. Chapter 10, in Volume 1 of *Capital*, on the struggle over the working day provides abundant evidence of how capital's "orgies" of exploitation undermined the very reproduction of the working class.[15] Who would not flee such conditions if they could?

15 Contemporary refugees from wars – the worst of working conditions – and those fleeing exploitation continue to cross borders, not in the hope of free land, but to find better labor markets and working conditions. Such movement is better understood as one strategy of those in the temporary but still active (floating) reserve army of labor. Among the many films about such folks see, *Il Norte* (1983) about Guatemalans fleeing exploitation

Another whole set of conditions, which might also provoke flight, were the miserable living conditions of workers when not at work in mines, fields, or factories – as sketched in Chapter 25 of *Capital* and described in detail by Engels, conditions conducive of daily misery, disease, and contagion. Lastly, it should be obvious that for legally enslaved workers, escape and flight was always desirable, when possible. This had to have been especially true in the period of the slave trade, which, Marx argued, made their replacement relatively cheap, so they were often worked to death.[16]

1.2.3 Other Sources of a Shortage of Labor-Power

As I outlined in Chapter 4, in addition to the reluctance of some workers to enter the labor market and the flight from it by others, disease and starvation often took a heavy toll on the number of workers available to capitalists for hire as did military recruitment in the Age of Imperialism. Finally, in spite of

---

and repression to the US. (A byproduct, we should note, of US interventions in Central America and the deportation of criminals.) Indeed, despite the recurrent effort to pit locals against recent immigrant workers, most of the US labor force is composed of immigrants or descendants of immigrants who have successfully found new jobs.

16 See, especially, Chapter 10, Section 3: "Branches of English Industry Without Legal Limits to Exploitation." That "vampire" thirst for more work, no matter the cost to workers, was curbed by struggle, but capitalists for a very long time continued to believe (or pretend) that the relationship of wages and profits was zero-sum, i.e., any increase in wages would diminish profits. As capitalists shifted from absolute to relative surplus value strategies, they and their economists eventually figured out (or admitted) not only that increases in wages were not necessarily a threat – IF they were offset by increases in productivity – but that as the source of consumer demand, rising wages could, by raising aggregate demand, induce more investment, more employment, more output and more profits. This recognition came with the late nineteenth century marginalist revolution in economic theory. (For more on this see Chapter 6) The main economist who elevated business perception of wages and consumer demand from onerous burdens to engines of capitalist growth was John Maynard Keynes in his *General Theory*. Zero-sum thinking came to be replaced, but the idea of a "normal" labor market being one in which wages didn't undermine profits remained. For the last several decades, we have witnessed neoliberal efforts to undo all the safeguards won by workers since Marx and Engel's time, including health safeguards, e.g., attacks on Social Security, on Medicare, the refusal of Medicaid by state governments, Trump's dismantling of pandemic response team and his more general disinvestment in preparedness for pandemics, despite SARS and MERS, as well as his criminally negligent response to the Covid-19 pandemic. Added to that have been the attacks on women's health, especially reproductive health, e.g., abortion, accelerated by the recent Supreme Court overturn of Roe vs Wade. All these are now taking their toll on workers' lives, up and down the wage and salary hierarchy. Leaving aside completely their moral degeneracy, the capitalists responsible have forgotten how dramatic reductions in the working-class population, e.g., during the Black Death, have led directly to major gains in wages by the reduced number of workers.

overwhelming patriarchal structures of power, women's struggles to free themselves from the role of broodmare have been seen by capitalists as predisposing the labor force to reduction, potentially higher wages and lower profits.

1.2.3.1 *Disease and Starvation*

The possibilities of serious epidemics, starvation and dramatic increases in death rates and consequent collapses in population and labor supply, mentioned in Chapter 4, turned into reality again and again, in place after place in the nineteenth century. Why? The most obvious cause lay in the character of capitalist development. The vicious exploitation of workers and the resulting poverty and living conditions made them vulnerable to hunger, malnutrition, and disease. The enclosure of the best land and its conversion to the cultivation of commercial, export crops, made food production on marginal land for local consumption vulnerable to erratic fluctuations in weather. Couple these vulnerabilities with the increased circulation of disease brought on by overseas colonization, the steady growth of long-distance trade and the associated movements of armies and navies, and you have an emerging world system predisposed to local instability, the circulation of illness or food shortages and, frequently, social uprisings in response.

1.2.3.2 *Military Poaching of Workers*

The need for military forces within capitalism parallels that for police forces. Both follow from the antagonistic character of capitalist social relationships in which exploitation and resistance to it can be small scale and frequent, requiring police action, or large scale in violent uprisings which require not only police but also military forces to preserve or restore capitalist control. The latter has been true both in the case of local conflicts, e.g., Luddite attacks on particular factories, and in the massive Chartist strikes and protests against government policies. By requiring ever more people to be put to work and ever more land and raw materials for them to work up into profitable commodities, so too has capitalism required the expansion in the size of its police and military forces, on both land and sea. Throughout the nineteenth century's "Age of Imperialism", capitalist and military expansion went hand in hand in the subordination of new lands, new resources and new people to capitalist modes of organization.

But this expansion, radiating outward from every country where capitalism has become dominant, has also led to conflicts among capitalists from different countries as they have competed for resources, labor supplies and markets. Again and again, capitalist influence on governments has resulted in military conflicts, from marginal skirmishes to full scale wars. And wars require additional cannon fodder, which can only be drawn from either the waged labor force or the reserve army of unwaged.

As I showed in my historical sketch, essential to Marx and Engels' understanding of these conflicts, including wars between competing blocs of capitalists and their associated governments were the dynamics of class conflicts, both in terms of the capitalist motivations and the responses of workers. Remember their analysis of the Franco-Prussian War in which they denounced both the French government's unprovoked attack on Prussia and then the Prussian counter-invasion of France. In both cases, they supported resistance to what amounted to capitalists trying to enhance their own power by pitting some workers against other workers to the detriment of both and they drew conclusions about appropriate worker strategies in the light of their analysis of the class conflicts at the heart of both phases of that war.

Given that soldiers and sailors always suffer in wars, and wars have always been launched for capitalist purposes, not those of workers, there has always been resistance. Individuals and small groups dodge recruitment, desert from the ranks, or organize opposition such as that of the First International to the Franco-Prussian War. That resistance, of course, has been why capitalists have had to use force to coerce workers into the military and then to keep them there. As a result of these class antagonisms, every war has had two fronts: the one facing the declared enemy and the home front of resistance and repression.

While those from better off families have often bought their way out of conscription, or bought commissions as officers rather than serving as enlisted grunts, those from peasant families in the countryside and from working class families in cities have been more likely to refuse conscription (draft dodgers in Britain or the U.S., *insoumis* in France) or collectively protest in "draft riots" – such as the one in New York City in 1863 – or go underground, resorting to criminal activities to survive while on the run.[17] To obtain voluntary recruits, the military has used the typical capitalist method of offering wages, complemented by ideological appeals to patriotism and the vilification of the enemy of the day, for their behavior, for their inferior culture, for their language, for their religion, or even for their physical appearance.[18]

17 See the analysis in Rouanet and Piano "Drafting the Great Army", op. cit. Although, where criminal activity involved joining organized crime families one can argue they were simply moving from the legal labor force into the illegal one but still available to capitalists. In modern times, while old methods have persisted, e.g., Trump buying his way out of service, we've also seen substantial draft resistance based on anti-war principles with resistors willing to go to prison if not excused or accepted as "conscientious objectors."

18 See, Ananya Ravishankar, "Linguistic Imperialism: Colonial Violence through Language", *The Trinity Papers*, 2011-Present (2020). From cartoons in newspapers to

The generalized poverty in the nineteenth century made the pay offered for joining either local militias or standing military forces often appear higher than that available in civilian jobs. "Appear" because after "taking the King's Shilling," recruits into the British army often found themselves forced to spend their pay on their equipment and subsistence. This exploitation of soldiers doing the work of imposing discipline on other workers has contributed, not surprisingly, to chronic problems with desertion in every army based on conscription.

Voluntary recruitment for wages was less effective for the naval forces because 1) wages were always higher on merchant ships and 2) navies were notorious for their shipboard discipline (floggings, hangings) and horrible working conditions (brutal work rotations, poor food, scurvy). As a result, navies were forced to have much greater recourse to legal impressment – the forcible kidnapping of sailors or civilians for military "duty." Some were rounded up by "press-gangs" in cities, others were appropriated from merchant vessels, in dock or at sea. The impressment of Americans by the British navy to crew its warships was one of the "colonial grievances" that led to the American Revolution (1775–1783) and contributed to a second war with the British in 1812.[19]

1.2.3.3 *Reductions in Family Size*

The most obvious internal predispositions to reduce the size of families are rising income and women's struggles. With respect to rising income, while the best efforts by workers to raise wages – always supported by Marx and Engels – sometimes had sufficient success to cut into profits enough to be judged a crisis by capitalists, there's little evidence, despite Malthus' claims, that such short-term increases were sufficient to warrant much change in the size of families. With respect to women's struggles, given how the work of childbearing and rearing always fell to them, they often took what measures they could to have fewer children.

---

government-produced posters designed to foster support for war, the imagery deployed has often been racist, e.g., against the Japanese in WWII or Vietnamese during the US war in Indochina, or portraying the enemy as inhumanly vicious, e.g., against the German "huns" in WWI, "krauts" in WWII, and "commies" during the Cold War.

19 More generally, see, Christopher Magra, "Anti-Impressment Riots and the Origins of the Age of Revolution," *International Review of Social History* 58, Special Issue 21 (December 2013): 131–151. Herman Melville's novel *Billy Budd: Sailor* (1891), which narrates such impressment in 1797 and the fate of one impressed American sailor, certainly provided popular support for resistance.

Successes in getting laws passed which limited the working hours of waged children and women, to the degree they were actually enforced, were more likely to have had some bearing on attitudes toward family size. The fewer hours of work for a wage, the more hours of the work of reproducing labor-power, more housework for women and schoolwork for children as capitalists engineered the "nuclear family" and widespread public schooling, consigning women and children to the work of reproducing labor-power.

Precisely because of their lack of attention to internal family dynamics – beyond its patriarchal character defined by the husband/father's domination – Marx and Engels failed to analyze the struggles of women to reduce their workloads in the home by having fewer children. Yet, we know that women throughout the income hierarchy, from unwaged slaves, through waged "proletarians", to "bourgeois" women have had recourse to various methods of contraception and abortion to do just that.[20] Had Marx broadened his "Worker's Inquiry" to include housework and schoolwork as well as the work of producing profitable commodities, he would certainly have queried women on their struggles to limit childbearing. But he did not. So we must have recourse to other authors to recognize the existence of such struggles, how they developed and how both men and capital responded.[21] Of the predisposition among many women to have fewer children, there can be no doubt, only access to knowledge, opportunity and resources varied, and the pattern of that variation was determined both by the struggles of women and by the efforts of those who sought to control them. (On efforts at control, see Chapter 6, Section 7.2.3.3)

1.2.4 Overzealous Investment

Another predisposition Marx and Engels both recognized, lay in the tendency for capital to invest and expand as rapidly as the degree of exploitation allows,

20 See, for example, Andrea Tone, *Devices and Desires: a history of contraceptives in America* (New York: Hill and Wang, 2001). Our knowledge of the use of contraception by enslaved women to subvert being used to breed more slaves is largely thanks to George Rawick's work assembling/editing slave testimonies in *The American Slave: A Composite Autobiography* (Westport, CT: Greenwood Publishing Co., 1972–76). See his overview of slave after-work activities in *From Sundown to Sunup: The Making of the Black Community* in Volume 1, and Liese Perrin, "Resisting Reproduction: Reconsidering Slave Contraception in the Old South" *Journal of American Studies* 35, no. 2 (August 2001): 255–274, which tells of how women slaves chewed the roots of their owners' cotton to avoid having children.

21 For a modern effort to do just this, see Alisa Del Re, "Workers' Inquiry and Reproductive Labor" *Viewpoint Magazine* 3 (September 25, 2013) https://viewpointmag.com/2013/09/25/workers-inquiry-and-reproductive-labor/ accessed 8-23-2024.

a propensity that predisposes the demand for labor-power to outpace supply. The frequent realization of this possibility (discussed in Chapter 4, Section 3.2.3) derives from both capitalists and speculators trying to take as much advantage as they can from expanding markets. In such boom periods, the slower growth of the labor force compels capitalists to compete for workers, by offering higher wages, potentially to unprofitable levels. The degree to which this affects individual capitalist firms depends on contingent factors, but the tendency will be there, as it will be for capital as a whole. Thus, a general expansion may lead to a rise in v, a fall in s/v and a reduction in $s/(c + v)$ (*ceteris paribus*). A substantial fall in the rate of profit, of course, tends to cause a crisis – if capitalists judge that fall to be sufficient to withdraw from investing. What Marx doesn't discuss at this point in *Capital*, but which he does make clear in his debate with Weston is how during such periods of rapid accumulation workers' self-organization and militant actions can take advantage of tight labor markets to drive wages up higher than they might otherwise rise if left purely to competition among capitalist employers.

1.3 *Forces Causing a Shortage in the Supply of the Means of Production, MP*

In the case of means of production, buyers confront supply crises in either low quality or shortages, which increase prices and costs that undermine their profits. These can be the result of either a disruption in the production of *MP* (including its transportation), *...P...C(MP)'*, or one in its sale, *C(MP)' – M*. In Chapter 4, I discussed several possibilities in both cases. The question is what forces predispose those possibilities to realization? Forces that disrupt *production of MP*, I discuss in the next Section; disruptions in *availability* of *MP* in markets, I discuss in Section 3.

2 Predispositions in the Second Stage: Production

Turning to the *second stage of the circuit*: let's examine the forces tending to interrupt capitalist production. Failure to complete the transformation of the two elements of production *LP* and *MP* into the final product *C'*, must involve either the failure of labor-power to become living labor or the means of production breaking down. Breakdowns in the means of production may be the result of 1) their inherent characteristics, e.g., the tendency of fixed capital to wear out, or the poor quality of raw material, or 2) exterior forces, e.g., worker sabotage or natural disasters. While natural disasters are episodic, because workers set the means of production in motion, they have the most continuous power to create a crisis in production. The question is: what forces are at work that predispose them to do so?

2.1 *Predispositions to Breakdowns in Labor-Power, LP*

We must recognize disruptions in the conversion of labor-power into actual labor, as with those of $M - LP$, as a fundamental dimension of class struggle. The negotiation of a contract, formal or informal, between employers and workers by no means guarantees, as Marx shows repeatedly in Volume 1 of *Capital* and as managers have always known, to what degree workers will convert their labor-power into work. And this is true both of the production of use-values and of the generation of value and surplus value. Besides workers' struggles that reduce the amount of work being done, I've also noted how the vagaries of nature may also reduce the ability of workers to work, irrespective of worker inclinations. Nature can debilitate or kill. But is there anything which predisposes those results?

2.1.1 Predispositions of Workers to Work Less

The class war over the amount of work that actually gets done, Marx shows, in Volume 1 of *Capital*, is one in which each side has certain aims about how long, how intensely and under what conditions work will be performed. Capitalists seek more work, regardless of conditions, while workers seek less work (shorter, less intense), safer, and less alienating work. There is thus a struggle that takes many forms. Against capital's techniques of control such as the wage hierarchy, despotic oversight, using differences such as race and ethnicity to turn worker against worker, or piece-wages designed to foster greater intensity and competition, workers pit absenteeism, collaboration, sabotage, loafing on the job, strikes, and so on. Why? What predisposes workers to such actions, whether they take them or not?

The general answer is the way of life capitalists seek to impose harms people and confines their activities to those that benefit its harmful system. How does it harm? Marx's answer is that the amount and kind of work capitalists impose both exploits and alienates. It *exploits* by imposing more work than necessary to reproduce workers' labor-power.[22] It *alienates* because

22 In Marx's writings, the term "exploitation" is reserved for the extraction of surplus labor and surplus value from waged or salaried workers producing profitable commodities, *C′*, with "surplus labor" defined as labor in excess of that required to produce the means of subsistence required for the reproduction of workers' labor-power, i.e., "necessary labor." Therefore, he does not use the term "exploitation" in reference to all the labor done by workers in their homes, schools and elsewhere that contributes to creating or repairing labor-power. Yet, clearly, to the degree that such labor reduces the amount of necessary

capitalists organize work and ownership so that they, not workers, control what is done, how it is done, for what purpose, and the disposition of the products of that labor, which they use to impose more work and acquiescence to the system. It is in the pursuit of maximum possible exploitation – to maximize surplus value and profits – that capitalists organize work so as to minimize their costs, often at workers' expense. As Marx's illustrates in *Capital* and elsewhere, that effort to minimize costs often leads capitalists to refuse to alleviate dangerous working conditions with resulting harm to workers both physical and psychological.[23] Because capitalists tend to discard old or injured workers, as they do with broken machinery, this alone has been enough to provoke struggle and revolt by workers.[24] Being forced to work in dangerous circumstances adds to the alienation associated with having no control over your workplace. This is why Marx's analyses of exploitation and alienation are germane to the issue of crisis: because they predispose those forced to work for capital to resist and to seek alternatives in ways that can disrupt capitalist planning.

2.1.1.1 *Predispositions to Resist Exploitation*

Exploitation = the extraction of surplus value = the extraction of surplus labor in the production of profitable commodities, i.e., labor over and beyond the labor necessary to reproduce workers' labor-power. But labor-power = the willingness and ability to work for capital, so capitalists try to confine "necessary labor" to that required for generating that willingness and ability. For workers, their needs and desires are for elaboration of their lives, beyond their employers' need for labor-power. At subsistence levels of wages (minimal necessary labor) this is obvious, when workers' needs include better food, clothing, housing, medical services, and more free time for life-beyond-work. But the last of these remains true no matter a worker's income, no matter one's place in the

---

labor that must be expended in producing the means of subsistence, it increases surplus labor and surplus value, raising the rate of exploitation, *s/v*, and the rate of profit, s/(c+v). Therefore, as with successful waged struggles against work on the job, successful struggles against the work of producing and repairing labor power also undermine surplus value and amount to resistance to exploitation, even though the effect is indirect.

23 See, especially, his detailing of injuries to workers in Chapter 10, Section 3 of Volume 1 of *Capital*.

24 This did not change in the period following Marx and Engels' time. Nick Holdren in his book *Injury Impoverished: Workplace Accidents, Capitalism, and Laws in the Progressive Era* (Cambridge: Cambridge University Press, 2020), details the struggles of workers injured on the job in the first decades of the twentieth century employed by capitalists unwilling to take responsibility for workers' injuries.

unwaged/waged/salaried income hierarchy. The subordination of life to work defines capitalist domination and everyone who suffers it is deprived of the free time necessary for the flourishing of their life, as individuals and in their social relationships. Except for those we call "workaholics," individuals who have bought into the capitalist reduction of life to work and can no longer see or imagine life beyond their tools or offices, most workers not only imagine life-beyond-work but also struggle for it, either overtly or covertly, with greater or lesser consciousness of the class forces at work. Thus, the long struggle to shorten the working day (and later the working week, year and life).[25] Thus, individuals are predisposed to work *less* on the job, to *withdraw* their energy, imagination and creativity from what the boss wants and to apply them instead to meeting their own wants, along with whatever their wage or salary can purchase and their limited free time permits.[26] This is especially true because, as Marx recognized in his analysis of reproduction but didn't study deeply,

25 This struggle was partially successful in Marx and Engel's time, as analyzed in Chapter 10, Section 6, and even more successful later – reducing the average working week to roughly 40 hours for many, creating the weekend, freeing days for annual vacations and winning earlier retirement. Unfortunately, as Juliet Schor documented in her book *The Overworked American: The Unexpected Decline of Leisure* (1992), published ten years after this essay was first written, during this last period of neoliberalism capitalists have had considerable success on the terrain of absolute surplus value. The imposition of neoliberal policies of union busting, safety deregulation, lowering wages, cutting social services and raising unemployment have put sufficient pressure on workers to force many to accept, even demand, longer working hours. Downward pressure on wages and salaries, combined with a shift by employers to more part-time, precarious jobs, has forced many workers to seek out second jobs – often part-time. Every increase in work time strengthens accumulation and augments absolute surplus value.

26 The heterodox economist Thorstein Veblen (1857–1929) was spot-on when he defined sabotage as "the conscientious withdrawal of efficiency" in *On the Nature and Uses of Sabotage* (1919) (New York: Oriole Chapbooks, n.d.). Although this was a concept I understood intellectually, it was not until I spent time in the Soviet Union that I observed it in the behavior of virtually everyone I met. Art Linklater may have filmed *Slacker* (1990) in Austin, Texas, but he could have filmed it anywhere in the USSR at any time before or after 1989 when workers finally brought the regime down. I am not speaking just of those with make-work jobs, through which the Politburo kept everyone employed, such as those of the *babushkas* sitting in every room of every museum in the country, but of those with jobs that required serious physical or mental labor. Time and again, I saw how little they managed to do and how much time and energy they freed to pursue their own self-valorization, e.g., classical Russian literature for a secretary, personal artwork for professional artist, participation in the Russian orthodox church for a gardener, getting drunk for far too many. Unable to resist openly in that police state, workers' struggles went underground, where they channeled their creativity into diverse daily practices – all sorts of self-determined activities, including covert but clearly political resistance such as the production of *samizdat* – twentieth century versions of the subversive anonymous

so-called free time off-the-job is often taken up by the requirements of the job, the unwaged work of reproducing labor-power required to return to the job.[27]

But the individual, Marx repeatedly insists, is always a *social* individual, one who is reared and grows up as part of a larger society, so the wants and desires of social individuals – just like their skills and abilities – are shaped by others, those around them. Humans are "social animals."[28] Workers' imaginations, needs and desires are always social, overlapping and interrelated with those of others and, as a result, give birth to *collective struggles* against the common experience of exploitation and capital's domination of their lives. "As the number of the co-operating workers increases, so too does their resistance to the domination of capital."[29] While capitalists learned to draw workers together, to incarcerate them in factories to better tap the power of cooperation by controlling them directly (real subordination), Marx pointed out how such incarceration also resulted in workers recognizing their common lot and organizing together to change it. This has been true not only in factories but wherever workers mass as part of their work, e.g., train depots for railway workers, ports for dockers and sailors, hiring halls for others.[30] Echoing early statements in the *German Ideology*, Marx concludes: "There also grows the revolt of the working class, a class constantly increasing in numbers, and trained, united and organized by the very mechanism of the capitalist process of production . . . the

---

tracts produced by workers in early capitalism. On the latter See, E. P. Thompson, "The Crime of Anonymity," in Hay, et. al., *Albion's Fatal Tree*, 255–344.

27 Because of this, to the degree that workers are predisposed to resist work *on* the job, so too does it follow that they are also predisposed to resist work *for* the job done at home or, in anticipation of a future jobs, in schools. Unfortunately, neither Marx nor Engels appear to have either recognized or analyzed such struggles or their implications.

28 *Capital, Vol. 1*, p. 444, or *MECW*, *Vol. 35*, p. 331.

29 Ibid., p. 449, or *MECW*, *Vol. 35*, p. 336.

30 The same has been true in schools (edu-factories) and other juvenile detention facilities, where unwaged children have been incarcerated to be trained and disciplined for future jobs. Like waged workers, their common experience – of being conditioned to accept being exploited and alienated – have resulted in collective revolt. Similarly, in prisons for workers who have violated capitalist laws and rehabilitation is defined as accepting to be exploited in a job. Not for nothing did Malcom X call prisons "the universities of the working class" where methods of resistance are learned alongside whatever "job training" is imposed. NB: even though, as I discuss in Chapter 6, workers have succeeded in obtaining laws to restrict capitalists in various ways, few are ever convicted of so-called "white collar" crime and the few that are inevitably wind up in "low security" facilities far different from the hell-hole prisons filled with "blue collar" workers from the lower rungs of the waged hierarchy.

socialization of labour reaches a point at which they become incompatible with their capitalist integument."[31]

2.1.1.2 *Predispositions to Resist Alienation*

Workers, moreover, are predisposed to rebel not only against the *amount* of work imposed, the subordination of their lives to work, but also against the *kind* of work imposed on them. That work, Marx argued most fully in the *Manuscripts of 1844* but illustrated repeatedly in *Capital*, is alienated in four different ways.[32] First, workers are alienated from the work imposed on them because they are not acting freely, but doing what their bosses want, the way they are told to do it, producing what those bosses want produced for sale and profit. Second, they are alienated from the products of their labors because capitalists have arranged laws so that they own the products, and the only way workers can get their hands on them is by buying them and the only way for most to be able to legally get the money to buy is to work for some capitalist. So, their own products are wielded as weapons to coerce them into the labor market. Third, they are alienated from each other because their bosses organize their work to pit them against each other – to undermine and stave off collective resistance. Fourth, by being deprived of their individual and collective free activity, they are deprived of what makes them human, their "species being."[33] All these things have been characteristics of the subordination of workers to capitalist control, first formal, then real, as their work has been reorganized to enhance control.

31 This common experience of the industrial proletariat Marx juxtaposed to the situation of isolated peasants, whose dispersion and differing circumstances weakened their ability to unite as a class in common struggle. "Small holding peasants form a vast mass, the members of which live in similar conditions but without entering into manifold relations with one another. . . the isolation is increased by France's bad means of communication . . . they do not form a class. They are consequently incapable of enforcing their class interests in their own name." "The Eighteenth Brumaire of Louis Bonaparte," MECW, *Vol. 11*, p. 187. History has shown how important that "bad means of communication" was in limiting peasant abilities to collaborate. Modern means of communication, beginning in the twentieth century, have facilitated the self-organization of French (and other European) peasants to the point where they have been able to collectively resist the kind of enclosure that has virtually wiped-out small farmers in the United States – not only at the national level but also at that of the European Union. See the section on "The Attack on Agricultural Labor" in H. Cleaver, "Food, Famine and International Crisis," *Zerowork #2*, 1977, pp. 42–43.

32 See, the section on "Estranged Labor" in the "Manuscripts," MECW, *Vol. 3*, pp. 270–279.

33 For both Marx and Hegel, humans were the unique species – *homo sapiens* – having a will, i.e., being sapient. Today, we know better, although the nature of various species' sapience may differ.

Although these forms of alienation are structural, in the sense that they are characteristics of how work is organized, Marx did see a relationship between them and workers' discontent with their jobs. Against such work, he saw them predisposed to resist, to struggle, to rebel. Too much work, and of the wrong kind: that is the quality of the life sentence to hard labor handed out not just by courts but by the capitalist organization of society.

These two characteristics of work within capitalism explain why there is a predisposition for those condemned to it to struggle against it. That predisposition is a fundamental source of crisis for capitalists because every reduction in the length or intensity of work reduces absolute surplus value, the rate of exploitation s/v, the rate of profit $s/(c + v)$, and thus the capitalist ability to invest and impose more work, or even the same amount of work, in the future. Work reduction strikes at the heart of the capitalist system.[34]

2.1.2 Predisposition to Harm from Nature

In Chapter 4, I discussed the possibilities for workers, as well as the means of production, to suffer the vagaries of Nature. Unfortunately, how capitalists organize production often makes the impact worse and predisposes workers to more suffering than might otherwise be the case. How? Primarily by prioritizing profitability rather than the well-being of workers, capitalists make choices that increase the likelihood of harm to their employees and other workers.

First, in the nineteenth century, the profitability of the textile industry meant a prioritization of the production of fibers over food production. Early examples were the enclosures that Marx describes in Chapter 27 of *Capital*, Volume 1, which turned local food production into "sheep walks" for wool production. Marx cites, as prototypical, the "clearings" made by the Dutchess of Sutherland in Scotland. "Between 1814 and 1820, these 15,000 inhabitants about 3,000 families were systematically hunted and rooted out."[35] I've also mentioned how the diversion of land from the production of food to that of flax contributed to the Great Famine in Ireland. The same choice was made in colonies where the colonizers usurped the best land to produce raw materials for export, e.g., cotton in India destined for British cotton mills, plantation sugar in the West Indies shipped for New England distilleries. As a result, food produced for local consumption on poorer land was more vulnerable to bad weather, with workers suffering the consequences. Under these conditions,

---

34 And, as feminist Marxists have shown, this is also true of work reductions in the sphere of reproduction that subvert the reduction of life to labor-power.

35 K. Marx, *Capital*, Vol. 1, p. 891-92, or *MECW, Vol 35*, pp. 719-20.

bad weather = lower yields = less food = higher prices = lower real wages = greater malnutrition, susceptibility to disease, and starvation.[36]

Second, cost-minimization to maximize profits has often made workers more vulnerable to natural phenomena such as floods, storms, fires, and earthquakes because the factories in which they work and the homes in which they live have been cheaply and poorly built. Marx's research into the reports of government appointed Public Health and Factory inspectors revealed a full awareness of the dangers of leaving both factories and housing to the cost-minimizing practices of capitalists. In the colonies, where there was even less oversight and probably greater corruption due to the lack of colonizer concern with worker well-being, the situation was likely worse.[37]

The same choice to minimize costs has resulted in harm due to what economists call "negative externalities", e.g., the pollution of air, land and water, which harms not only employees but all workers. Capitalist lack of concern with dumping wastes into the surrounding environment undermines the health of humans (as well as animals and plants). Capitalist mine owners have had their workers dump mine tailings, willy-nilly, into the surrounding environment, regardless of its negative effect on the miners or people living nearby.[38] The mills of Manchester were called "satanic" not only because of the horrible working conditions but also because they operated with steam power. Fueled by coal, the factories produced prodigious quantities of smoke and waste coal ash, polluting both air and water. Engels has some nice, graphic descriptions in this book *The Condition of the English Working Class*. All these

36 The modern capitalist tendency in agricultural production to monoculture has increased the vulnerability of crops – both *MS* and *MP* - to bad weather. Replacing traditional, ecologically stable practices of growing many varieties of a given crop or breeds of animal with a single variety or the same breed makes production vulnerable to disease or parasites. See, H. Cleaver, "The Contradictions of the Green Revolution," *Monthly Review*, Vol. 24, no. 2 (June 1972): 80–111. The same cost minimization has produced what detractors call "factory farms" with very large numbers of enslaved animals herded into tightly packed confinement, such as feedlots for cattle or sheep or cruelly tight cages for individual pigs or chickens instead of allowing these animals to feed on open range.

37 Even in the post-colonial era, the perpetuation of capitalist practices with little effective regulation has produced some of the most devastating consequences, as in the case of the Rama Plaza building in Dhaka, Bangladesh that contained several garment factories. It collapsed in 2013, killing over a thousand workers.

38 With the modern development of strip-mining and mountain top removal to make ore veins accessible to strip-mining equipment, this devastation has become far worse. Patrick McGinley, "From Pick and Shovel to Mountaintop Removal: Environmental Injustice in the Appalachian Coalfields," *Environmental Law* 34, no. 1 (Winter 2004): 21–106.

were augmented in the nineteenth century by the absence of industrial regulations to limit both the phenomena and their effects.[39]

In all this, the vulnerability of workers to natural disasters at home and abroad was increased by 1) the almost universal capitalist effort to hold down wages to bare subsistence to maximize profits and 2) workers being forced to live in and pay rent for barely habitable huts near mines and construction sites and for slum flats in cities. The combination of low wages and miserable living conditions meant a great many workers were chronically malnourished, ill-clothed, living in ill-heated, over-crowded housing and therefore more susceptible to epidemic and pandemic diseases than they would be if instead they were paid wages that could buy more and better food, clothing, and housing.

2.2 *Predispositions to Breakdowns in the Means of Production, MP*

Most of the means of production are produced, even raw materials extracted from the earth, so their rate of depreciation and waste – integral aspects of their quality – are determined by the production processes of their extraction as well as by their physical nature and how they are handled in transportation from where they are produced to where they are used to produce other commodities.

2.2.1 Due to Workers' Actions

The production of the means of production are as susceptible to breakdown as any other production process. All of the factors mentioned in the previous section can have an impact on the quality of the means of production and thus on the production processes in which they are deployed. Central to my concerns are those actions taken by workers, which undermine the quality of the *MP* they are producing. Exploited and alienated mine, agricultural or machine workers can sabotage, to a greater or lesser degree, their products, reducing their quality. They can do this in revenge for how they are being exploited, or they may do so to enhance their income. When workers are paid on the basis of piecework, they can sabotage the pieces on the basis of which they are paid. Miners, for instance, when paid by the ton of ore, can mix easier-to-obtain

39 Although in recent decades environmentalists and popular pressure have resulted in government regulators forcing coal-fired plants to take some measures to scrub and reduce their pollution of the air, and the resulting acid rain that kills forests and fish in rivers and streams, the so-called Environmental Protection Agency in the US still refuses to recognize the dangers of coal ash or regulate its disposal. The result has been horrendous for both workers and communities. See, https://www.nrdc.org/stories/coal-ash-hazardous-coal-ash-waste-according-epa-coal-ash-not-hazardous-waste (accessed 7-13-2024).

rock with harder-to-obtain ore to increase their tonnage and wage. But doing so reduces the quality of their product. In the case of coal, it decreases the available BTU's per ton and in the case of other ores, it increases the costs of extracting desired minerals. Similarly, agricultural workers can be careless with cultivation or weeding (decreasing available nutrients and harvest) or with fruits and vegetables (damaging them, reducing their desirability and shelf life).[40] Machine operators can intentionally turn out flawed or broken parts. As I have already mentioned, leather, silk or boat building workers produced excess scrap. All such sabotage can increase the rate of depreciation or waste of the means of production, raising the costs of repair and replacement, undermining the profitability of their use. On a large enough scale, defects in *MP* can disrupt production, even bring it to a halt.

Interacting with worker struggles, failures in capitalist organization of production can also diminish the quality and quantity of the means of production being produced. Failure, for example, to mobilize enough labor at harvest time can leave crops rotting in the field, with the result being products of very poor quality – making them hard to process and therefore more costly. One example of poor quality, which Marx cites, was cotton from Surat, India, obtained by the British to replace that made unavailable from the Confederacy during the American Civil War. Surat cotton was of lesser quality partly due to its inherent qualities, e.g., shorter fibers and the unavoidable fragility of thread made from it. But according to reports Marx cites, it also arrived in Britain so filthy that handling it made workers sick and increased the costs of its processing.[41] To what degree that quality was due to worker resistance, mishandling, or sabotage is unclear because Marx provides no account of the conditions of either its production or its shipping. In the same passage, however, he does mention the use by textile manufacturers of "unsuitable machinery," which certainly indicates either incompetence or the inability to afford proper machinery.[42]

Yet another mixed example from the same period can be found in imported raw silk from China. Already uneven because of variations in the quality of peasant production, as soon as the reeling of silk from cocoons was industrialized

40 On the fruit farm where I worked in France, how fruits such as peaches and plums were handled was critical because they could only be sold at full value if there were no bruises on peaches and the grey surface dust of plums was intact. The French habit (at that time) of packing and selling fruit in trays where the condition of each piece was clearly visible meant sellers checked the quality of the fruit being picked because buyers did the same during sale.

41 *Capital, Vol. 1*, pp. 585–6, or *MECW, Vol. 35*, pp. 459–460.

42 Both reasons could cause small capitalists to be unable to compete, go bankrupt and out of business – hastening the centralization of capital.

and no longer in the hands of those producing them, their producers "paid less attention to the cocoon's quality" likely causing their quality to decline and making the processing of resulting silk more difficult, raising costs.[43]

2.2.2 Due to Nature

Leaving aside worker struggles and their interactions with capitalist incompetence, in Chapter 4 we saw there are also unforeseeable fluctuations and tendencies in "nature" that can lead to breakdown – especially changes in weather, soil fertility, the richness of mineral deposits and so on. The irregular recurrence of these changes, which make agriculture vulnerable, also predispose it to unplanned crises:

> It is particularly agricultural products, whose raw materials derive from organic nature, which are the most subject to these fluctuations of value, as a result of variations in the harvest, etc .... The same quantity of labour may here be expressed in very diverse amounts of use-values, depending on uncontrollable natural conditions, the seasons of the year, etc., and a particular quantity of these use-values will accordingly have very different prices.[44]

Along with variations in the *amounts* of use-values, so too may uncontrollable variations in weather cause substantial variations in their *quality*. For example, either too much or two little rain at the wrong time can seriously reduce the quality of many crops, undermining their value as *MP* and reducing the price at which they can be sold.

Given that these kinds of interruptions occur within an expanding system, the natural time constraints of agriculture also cause problems for investors.

> In the nature of the case, plant and animal products, whose growth and production are subject to certain organic laws involving naturally determined periods of time, cannot suddenly be increased in the same degree as, say, machines and other fixed capital, coal, ore, etc., ... It is possible, therefore, and indeed unavoidable when capitalist production is fully developed, that the production and increase of the portion of constant capital that consists of fixed capital, machinery, etc., may run significantly ahead of the portion consisting of organic raw materials, so that

43 Ma, "The Modern Silk Road," 334.

44 *Manuscript of 1864–1865*, p. 226, *Capital, Vol. 3*, p. 213, or MECW, *Vol. 37*, p. 119.

> the demand for these raw materials grows more rapidly than their supply, and their price therefore rises.[45]

Such differential ability to expand some elements of *MP* independently of others causes all the problems discussed above. Marx goes on to note that these tendencies are accentuated during periods of rapid expansion.

> … the more rapid the accumulation (particularly in times of prosperity), the greater is the relative over-production of machinery and other fixed capital, the more frequent the relative underproduction of vegetable and animal raw materials, and so more marked the previously described rise in their price and the corresponding reaction. The more frequent, therefore, are those revulsions which have their basis in this violent price fluctuation, and are a major element in the reproduction process.[46]

Again, the natural limits to the rate of expansion of one process can lead to problems of realizing the proper proportion between *LP* and *MP* in *M* – *C* and thus in … *P* ….

Beyond natural hazards that have always existed in agriculture (or in hunting and gathering for that matter), Marx also noted a tendency within *capitalist* agriculture that undermines expanded reproduction. Even when it is efficient and management is competent, it separates town and country, concentrating manufacturing and population in cities and reducing the countryside to the production of raw materials, *MS* or *MP*. In the process, it disrupts human interaction with nature, e.g., the return of waste to the soil and by so doing it accelerates its impoverishment with negative effects on agricultural productivity.

> Capitalist production collects the population together in great centers … it disturbs the metabolic interaction between man and the earth, i.e., it prevents the return to the soil of its constituent elements consumed by man in the form of food and clothing; hence it hinders the operation of the eternal natural condition for the lasting fertility of the soil … all progress in capitalist agriculture is a progress in the art, not only of robbing the worker, but of robbing the soil.[47]

---

45 *Manuscript of 1864–1865*, pp. 226–227, *Capital, Vol. 3*, p. 213, or MECW, *Vol. 37*, pp. 119–120.

46 *Manuscript of 1864–1865*, p. 227, *Capital, Vol. 3*, p. 214, or MECW, *Vol. 37*, p. 120.

47 *Capital, Vol. 1*, Chap. 15, pp. 637–638, or MECW, *Vol. 35*, pp. 506–507. This was written at a time when the fibers out of which clothing was made were natural, e.g., cotton, linen, wool, and therefore biodegradable. The advent of synthetic fibers has made return to the

Capitalists have counter-argued that their investments in things like fertilizer have enhanced the soil. Even then Marx saw how such investment could make things worse in the long run.

> all progress in increasing the fertility of the soil for a given time, is a progress toward ruining the more long-lasting sources of that fertility....[48]

The "more long-lasting" sources derive from the return not only of human waste but also of vegetable matter from plowing under crop residues and barnyard manure – a mixture of animal droppings and straw, what the French call "fumier" – a traditional byproduct on small farms that practice both horticulture and husbandry. Capitalist agribusinesses has replaced such balances with monoculture – in fields and in factory farms – and manure with synthetic chemical fertilizers derived from petroleum (thus no biological material to replenish the soil). Another soil-restoring practice generally abandoned by profit-greedy agribusiness is crop rotation that involves replacing harvestable (and profitable) *MS* or *MP* crops in one growing season with some nitrogen-fixing crop like clover or alfalfa in the next season.[49]

---

soil impossible. Today, due to regular overproduction on the part of the clothing industry and the short life span of modern "fast fashion," huge amounts of produced clothing are either never worn and discarded by firms that can't sell them profitably or worn but quickly discarded because either they are poorly made and wear out quickly or they are replaced by the "latest thing." The result is that "one garbage truck of textiles is landfilled or incinerated every second." Landfills are NOT what Marx had in mind by "returning to the soil" – which was the destiny of most clothing throughout human history until capitalism. Most clothing did biodegrade and replenish the soil. See, Ellen MacArthur Foundation, *A new textiles economy: Redesigning fashion's future*, 2017.

Marx's concept of a rupture in the metabolism between humans and nature, has recently become central to many Marxists' thinking about ecological crisis. See, John Foster, "Marx's theory of metabolic rift," *American Journal of Sociology* 105, no. 2 (September 1999): 366–405. Jason Moore, "Transcending the metabolic rift: a theory of crises in the capitalist world-ecology," *The Journal of Peasant Studies* 38, no. 1 (January 2011): 1–46, and references therein.

48 Ibid., p. 638, or *MECW*, *Vol. 35*, p. 507. Marx here, in a footnote, draws on the work of Justus von Liebig (1803–1873). Today, we know far more about these long-lasting effects, especially the use by capitalist agribusiness of artificial fertilizers derived from petroleum that, unlike traditional manuring and crop rotation, fail to return vegetable matter to the soil, gradually sterilizing it to a mere physical carrier of plants and whatever chemicals are used on them.

49 In the area of Ohio where I grew up, soil was rich and deep – the product of 10,000 years of untrammeled forest growing on a countryside scoured of rock by the glacier of the last ice age. The European settlers who took the land from the indigenous tribes, cut the forests, and created family farms using technologies which replenished the soil. Most raised

In Part Six of both the *Manuscript of 1864–65* and *Capital, Vol. 3*, on ground rent, Marx offered further discussion of capitalist progress in "increasing the fertility of the soil" through the introduction of those new technologies associated with the "agricultural revolution" of the time, e.g., investments in drainage, crop rotation, and fertilization. He gave enough importance to this investment and to the declining role of "natural" fertility (fertility that was not the outgrowth of such investment) that he accorded a far lesser role to diminishing returns in agriculture as a source of breakdown than had, for example, Ricardo. The latter saw therein (via rising rent) the source of capitalist decline and the origin of stagnation.

All of this allows us to see how Marx saw the occurrence of "natural" catastrophes in production, especially in agricultural production, as only partly exogenous to the system. The causes of disruptions in accumulation have fluctuated as the system has grown and efforts to achieve greater control over nature, have, sometimes, had the contradictory consequence of undermining the fertility of the soil or rendering cultivation more susceptible to disruption. Although farmers have been "selecting" both seeds and breeds long before capitalism, the risks involved in monoculture grew as profit-maximizing capitalist agribusiness has brought more resources to bear on raising the immediate productivity of crops and animals, without regard to long-term consequences.[50]

As early as his discussion in the *Grundrisse*, Marx recognized the intrinsic connections between local disruptions and international ones. (For more on the circulation of disruption, see Section 4 below.)

> This distinction between domestic and foreign, incidentally, is altogether illusory. The relation between the nation which suffers a crop failure and another nation where the former makes purchases is like that between every individual of the nation and the farmer or grain merchant. The surplus sum which it must expend in purchasing grain is a direct subtraction from its capital, from its disposable means.[51]

---

both crops and animals, rotated crops and had a manure spreader, usually a trailer with rotating prongs that flung the manure widely as it was towed across fields.

50 The dangers of monoculture became dramatically apparent in 1970 when the American corn crop was decimated by Southern corn leaf blight. The extent of the damage was due to the widespread use of a single breed of corn, peddled by seed companies but susceptible to the disease. The breed was vulnerable because the seed companies had introduced a detasseling gene to cut production costs – thus its widespread adoption by cost minimizing agribusiness – but one that increased vulnerability to the disease. The seed companies took their profits, while the losses were born by those who bought and planted the seed.

51 *Grundrisse*, pp. 128–129; *MECW*, *Vol. 28*, p. 67.

In the *Manuscript of 1864–1865* and in Volume 3 of *Capital,* in Chapter 6 on "The Effect of Changes in Price," he analyzed at length the role of agricultural production failures in causing crises both at home and abroad.

2.3 *Predispositions to Increasing the Organic Composition of Capital*

Because defeats on the terrain of absolute surplus value have been recurrent, so too has been the predisposition of capitalists to substitute less troublesome, more productive machinery for workers. When faced with a declining workday and thus less work, value and surplus value, capital has been forced to find some way to redistribute value to itself, that is, from v to s. The substitution of productivity-raising constant fixed capital for labor achieves this result. As early as 1843, Engels recognized this consequence of a capitalist inability to hire enough workers for long enough to generate profits.

> In the struggle of capital and land against labor, the first two elements enjoy yet another special advantage over labor – the assistance of science, for in present conditions science, too, is directed against labor. Almost all mechanical inventions for instance, have been occasioned by the lack of labour-power; in particular Hargreaves', Crompton's and Arkwright's cotton-spinning machines. There has never been an intense demand for labor which did not result in an invention that increased labor productivity considerably, thus diverting demand away from human labor. The history of England from 1770 until now is a continuous demonstration of this. The last great invention in cotton-spinning, the self-acting mule, was occasioned solely by the demand for labor, and rising wages. It doubled machine-labor, and thereby cut down hand-labor by half; it threw half the workers out of employment, and thereby reduced the wages of the other half; it crushed a plot of the workers against the factory owners, and destroyed the last vestige of strength with which labor had still held out in the unequal struggle against capital.[52]

Twenty-four years later, Marx described a similar response – albeit on a larger scale – to workers' success in getting laws passed to shorten the working day.

> As soon as the gradual upsurge of working class revolt had compelled Parliament compulsorily to shorten the hours of labor, and to begin by imposing a normal working-day on factories properly so called, i.e., from

---

52 "Outline of a Critique of Political Economy," *MECW*, *Vol. 3*, pp. 442–443.

> the moment that it was made impossible once and for all to increase the production of surplus value by prolonging the working day, capital threw itself with all its might and in full awareness of the situation, into the production of relative surplus value, by speeding up the development of the machine system.[53]

For individual capitalists, the introduction of machinery makes it possible for them to increase surplus value and profits in three ways. First, by controlling the speed and rhythm of machines, they can force workers to work more intensely, increasing work, and if there is no compensating increase in v, s will rise, as will s/v and $s/(c + v)$. Second, the higher productivity (product per unit of labor input) of the new machine technology results in products having a lower per unit cost than those of competitors, and hence enables them to sell at a lower price that redistributes surplus value to them, again raising s, reducing v relatively and thus raising s/v and $s/(c + v)$. Third, unless and until they are constrained by struggles, e.g., new legal limits on working hours, the introduction of machines provides an excuse to extend working hours. To avoid the extra costs of starting up, shutting down or having machines stand idle, capitalists try to run them continuously 24 hours a day wherever and whenever possible, with the fewest number of workers, e.g., two 12-hour shifts rather than three 8-hour shifts.

As the use of the new technique is generalized, the average per unit value of output declines. Where that output is either *MS*, or contributes to the production of *MS*, the result is a decline in the value of labor-power, which can be reproduced with less labor.[54] Thus, of the total $v + s$ being extracted from all workers, the capitalists get a relatively higher share; the rate of exploitation, s/v, and the rate of profit $s/(c + v)$ rise for one and all (*ceteris paribus*).

This strategy of substituting machines for labor Marx represents symbolically as a rise in the *technical composition of capital*: *MP/LP* – which is not a real ratio, because *MP*, *LP*, and their relationships to each other are heterogeneous and so a rise in *MP/LP* simply represents more machinery per worker.

---

53 *Capital, Vol. 1*, pp. 533–534, or *MECW*, *Vol. 35*, pp. 412–413.

54 This decline in the *waged* labor of producing commodities may, or may not, be accompanied by changes in the amount of *unwaged* labor involved directly in the production (gestation and birthing) and reproduction (caring labor) of labor-power. To the degree that this decline results in rising real wages and greater commodity consumption by workers, it may well result in more unwaged labor involved in managing consumption, e.g., more time washing an expanded wardrobe or preparing meals with a greater amount or variety of foods. For those displaced by machinery, loss of wages means more work of reproduction to compensate where possible.

Because this capitalist strategy is aimed at increasing profits, Marx analyzes the change in terms of the ratio of the (homogeneous) *value* invested in *MP* to that invested in *LP*, i.e., the *organic composition of capital*: c_o/v_o. It changes only "in so far as" the technical composition changes.[55] This constraint is important because it is also possible for the *value composition,* taken simply as the ratio of the value of *MP* to value of *LP*, or *c/v*, to change without any alteration in the technical composition. For example, with a sudden drop in the value of *MS*, *v* could fall and hence *c/v* could rise, but with no change in *MP/LP*. In Volume 1 Marx uses very precise language to explain this. He writes:

> I call the *value-composition* of capital, in so far as it is determined by its technical composition and mirrors the changes of the latter, the *organic composition* of capital.[56]

And then, referring to the above in a footnote, Engels repeats this point in Volume 3:

> The organic composition of capital is the name we give to its value composition, *in so far as* this is determined by its technical composition and reflects it.[57] [Emphasis added]

Now for the most important consequence, or predisposition, which follows from this recurrent increase in the organic composition of capital.

---

55 *Capital, Vol. 1*, p. 762, or MECW, *Vol. 35*, p. 608. Recent study of the *Manuscript of 1864–1865*, out of which Engels' fashioned Volume 3 of *Capital* has revealed that there are textual moments – left aside by Engels – in which Marx wrote of the organic composition of capital changing as a result of changes in the value composition. See, Fred Moseley's introduction to *Marx's Economic Manuscript of 1864–1865*, 16–18. That would appear to obliterate the distinction between the organic and value compositions upon which he insisted in other places, e.g., Volume 1 of *Capital*, where he tied the former but not the latter to the technical composition. If, however, what Marx meant was that a rise in the value of labor-power vis-à-vis that of fixed capital would encourage the substitution of the latter for the former, i.e., a rise in the technical composition and thus the organic composition, then there is no contradiction.

56 *Capital, Vol. 1*, p. 762, or MECW, *Vol. 35*, p. 608

57 *Capital, Vol. 3*, p. 245, or MECW, *Vol. 37*, p. 145. This sentence is Engels' version of what Marx writes in the *Manuscript of 1864–1865*, 253: "The proportion just mentioned constitutes the actual basis of the organic composition of capital." The proportion just mentioned is "A definite *number of workers* corresponds to a *definite quantity of the means of production* and thus a *definite amount of living labour* corresponds to a definite amount of *labour already realized in the means of production*." In other words, the *technical* composition.

2.4 *Predispositions to a Falling Rate of Profit Tendency and Its Crises*

The essential thing to understand about this much-disputed "tendency" is that Marx's analysis is not about the *monetary* rate of profit but rather about the *value* ratio $s/(c + v)$, i.e., the amount of surplus labor/value that can be extracted for a given investment in current (v) and in past (c) labor. With the secular rise in the organic composition, c_o/v_o, it is increasingly difficult (requires more and more $c + v$) to convert the time freed from production by the rise in labor productivity, into work and the social control (value) it provides. On the one hand:

> It is thus, despite itself, instrumental in creating the means of social disposable time, in order to reduce labor time for the whole society to a diminishing minimum, … But its [capital's] tendency always, on the one side, *to create disposable time, on the other, to convert it into surplus labor*.[58]

The manifestation of the failure to make that conversion is an increase in the proportion of workers who cannot be employed despite their ability, willingness, and availability to work. Marx clearly thought that the development of this tendency, which went with the growth of production, would lead the working class to overthrow a system for which it was increasingly obvious (because less and less work was required to produce wealth) they no longer needed:

> Forces of production and social relations – two different sides of the development of the social individual – appear to capital as mere means, and are merely means for it to produce on its limited foundation. In fact, however, they are the material conditions to *blow this foundation sky-high*.[59] (Emphasis added)

Which is to say, the dynamics of class struggle within capitalism creates the material foundations for the overthrow of the system by progressively reducing the need for work in society:

> The more this contradiction develops, the more does it become evident that the growth of the forces of production can no longer be bound up with the appropriation of alien labor, but that the mass of workers must themselves appropriate their own surplus labor. Once they have done so – and *disposable time* thereby ceases to have an *antithetical*

58 *Grundrisse*, p. 708, or MECW, *Vol.* 29, p. 94.
59 Ibid., p. 706, or MECW, *Vol.* 29, p. 92.

> existence – then on one side necessary labor time will be measured by the needs of the social individual, and, on the other the development of the power of social production will grow so rapidly that, even though production is now calculated for the wealth of all, *disposable time* will grow for all ... The measure of wealth is then not any longer, in any way, labor-time, but rather disposable time.[60]

In other words, once freed from the need to develop production in such a way that labor and surplus labor are necessary for keeping control of society, production can be developed so as to minimize work; and the tendency toward infinite work, dictated by capital's need for control, can be replaced by the working class' tendency toward Zerowork and free time for the "full development of the individual." By pointing out how that development "reacts back upon the productive power of labour," we see him recognizing how work can be only one among many forms of human self-valorization. The fully developed human life is more than work, not defined by it.[61] Thus the paradox that the end of capital will mean both the expansion of production and the reduction of work. It will mean the end of "the positing of an individual's entire time as labor time, and his degradation therefore to mere worker ..."[62]

This contradiction, Marx emphasizes, is a fundamental one in the system:

> To express this contradiction in the most general terms, it consists in the fact that capitalist mode of production tends towards an *absolute development of the productive forces* irrespective of value and the surplus-value it contains, and even irrespective of the social conditions within which capitalist production takes place; while on the other hand, its purpose is to *maintain the existing capital value and to valorize it* to the utmost extent possible ...[63] (Emphasis added)

And it leads directly to interruption of the smooth reproduction process:

> At certain points the conflict of contending agencies breaks through in crises. Crises are never more than momentary, violent solutions for the existing contradictions ...[64]

60 Ibid., p. 708, or *MECW*, *Vol. 29*, p. 94.
61 Ibid., p. 711, or *MECW*, *Vol. 29*, p. 97.
62 Ibid., p. 708, or *MECW*, *Vol. 29*, p. 94.
63 *Capital, Vol. 3*, p. 357, or *MECW*, *Vol. 37*, p. 248.
64 *Capital, Vol. 3*, pp. 357–358; *MECW*, *Vol. 37*, p.248.

It is worth noting how Marx's analysis, worked out in the *Grundrisse* notebooks, provided new foundations for the insight articulated by Engels in his 1843 "Outline" and in his 1845 speeches at Elberfeld, discussed in my Chapter 2 survey of their work in the 1840s. Based on observing the forces at work in English industry, Engels had projected how the development of productive power under capitalism would make possible escape from its efforts to condemn all of humankind to life sentences of labor. After a decade of work, Marx elaborated a theory providing theoretical grounds for believing Engels' projection had been correct. Over the following decade he would then give virtually every aspect of that theory a richer theoretical amplification and historical illustration as he reworked the ideas finally embodied in the first volume of *Capital*.

3 Predispositions in the Third Stage of the Circuit: Sales

Let us now turn to the *third stage* of the circuit of capital and examine Marx's discussion of the predispositions to crisis that lie therein. As in the previous analyses of the forces that predispose production to crisis, Marx always assumes that the other stages of the circuit are completed without difficulty unless otherwise indicated. In the present case, he takes as given both the first stage (that *MP* and *LP* have been obtained at profitable prices – given the expected price at which *C′* can be sold) and the second stage (successful production of *C′*). In the third stage *C′* – *M′*, capitalists must return to the sphere of exchange and find buyers for their products at profitable prices. Failure occurs and some degree of crisis ensues if the seller of *C′* fails to discover buyers with both the desire and the money (*M′*) necessary to purchase *C′* at prices that will realize its full value, and thus realize the surplus value (s) over the cost-price ($c + v$) incurred in its production.

The possible hindrances associated with this situation (discussed in Chapter 4, Section 5) include: (1) that either the working class or other capitalists may directly appropriate *C′*, thus undermining its exchange for *M′* – the working class mainly in the case of *MS* and capital mainly in the case of *MP*; (2) the possibility that a *C′* may be produced that has no use-value perceptible or desired by so many targeted customers that there are not enough buyers; (3) the possibility that those for whom *C′* is a potential use-value fail to have or be willing to spend an equivalent (money) equal to its value. This includes the possibility that the proportion of *MP* and *MS* produced and the distribution of the monetary equivalent *M′* between buyers of *MP* and *MS* may not be in the same proportion. In that case, some buyers will hoard their money and some sellers will fail to complete $C' - M'$. In each of these cases, the question is: are there forces at work which predispose these merely possible problems to become a concrete crises?

Although predispositions to crisis in the market for slaves, might reasonably be grouped either under the market for *MP* (viewing slaves as means of production) or, less frequently under the market for *MS* (viewing slaves as satisfying desires for status or the pleasures of control), I treat predispositions in this market separately because, from the point of view of the slaves, the motives of buyers are secondary to being subjected to the injustice of being sold as slaves at all. With respect to other commodity markets, as in Chapter 4 on the possibilities of crisis, I organize my discussion of Marx's analysis by "department," looking first at those forces which cause crises in the sale of the means of subsistence, $C(MS)'$, and then at those causing problems in the sale of the means of production, $C(MP)'$.

3.1 *Predispositions to Crises in Selling Slaves, $C(LP) - M'$*

The most obvious predispositions to disruptions in the selling of slaves derive from the nature of slavery itself. Because slavery involves reducing humans (and other animals) to sellable commodities, whose bodies and lives are totally subordinated to the will of first the seller and then the buyer, slaves resist. Differing from wage-slavery only in the degree of subordination, many of the modes of slave resistance are similar, including revolt and flight.

In the slave trade, revolt against being reduced to a commodity could occur at any time after capture, both before and after being sold initially. This included while being transported to the slave markets, e.g., whether by land or by ship, as across the Atlantic to the Western Hemisphere. Resistance could take forms as diverse as suicide, self-affirmation (singing and dance during periods of exercise) and revolt. All forms of resistance had the potential to deprive the would-be seller of their commodity. The predisposition of slaves to resist while being transported, is made clear in Marcus Rediker's book *The Slave Ship: A Human History* (2007), which includes a collection of narratives that well illustrate both the horrors of the ships and the resistance of their cargo. In *The Amistad Rebellion: An Atlantic Odyssey of Slavery and Rebellion* (2013) Rediker retells this famous story from the perspective of rebelling slaves who successfully took control over the ship transporting them and ultimately won their freedom in court.

Ultimately, the greatest crises in selling slaves have come with the success of slave struggles and abolitionists in getting new laws passed ending the legality first of importing slaves (Virginia in 1777, US and Britain in 1807), then of the international slave trade (US in 1794, Britain in 1807) and then of chattel slavery itself (Britain in 1833, US in 1863). Passed in countries where slavery had been legal, laws outlawing the slave trade reduced the demand for slaves; laws outlawing slavery per se reduced it even more. How much depended on the degree of enforcement. In the case of the Atlantic slave trade, it took the active intervention of government naval forces to bring the trade to a halt, e.g., the British Navy's West African Squadron. Unfortunately, even as enforcement increased, slavery did not disappear. It survived either in the legal form of forced prison labor or moved underground into the hands of so-called "organized crime", differing from regular capitalists only in the illegality of their businesses.

3.2 *Predisposition to Crises in Markets for* C(MS)' *or* C(MP)'

In Chapter 4, I noted that both capitalists trying to sell *C(MS)'* and those trying to sell *C(MP)'*, being unable to directly control either the output of their competitors nor the demand for their product, have the common problem of gauging production to the demand for their products and failure can mean crisis. Marx and Engels' usually assume that (1) individual producers and potential customers operate entirely separately with communication occurring only via the markets they share, (2) information flows in those markets are seriously lagged, and (3) the lack of accurate information about the exact state of others' production and of available demand predisposes over eager producers to bring more product to the market than it can bear, and thus predisposes capital to overproduction, glut, falling prices, falling profits, and crisis.

Logically, the same uncertainty driving overproduction can result in the opposite situation, underproduction, which can raise prices as buyers bid for scarce commodities, increase profits and spur increased production. Eventually, the increased profits can also draw in new producers, undermine existing producers' share of the market, cut their profits and cause a crisis for individual firms that can't compete. But on Marx and Engels' usual assumption that capitalists are almost always trying to increase production, they seem to think that such problems would be short lived and would not produce general crises on the same scale as overproduction, gluts, and the inability to service debts resulting in bankruptcies.

3.2.1 Predispositions to Crises Selling Consumer Goods, *C(MS)'* (Underconsumption)

Not surprisingly, the most important tendency, analyzed by Marx, which establishes a predisposition to a realization problem in *C(MS)'*–*M'*, is directly related to the relation between the classes, namely the general tendency for capitalists to overproduce *MS* relative to worker demand. In other words, Department II production of *C(MS)'* is predisposed to exceed the demand made up of the wages, $v_1 + v_2$, from both Department I and Department II. So, just as there is a predisposition to overproduction, glut and crisis at the level of the whole, so too is there *a predisposition to underconsumption* vis-à-vis the production of *C*(*MS*)'.

At the level of the whole, because workers produce both *C*(*MS*)' and *C*(*MP*)', their wages can never buy back everything they produce. On this general tendency, Marx approvingly quotes Malthus and Sismondi against Ricardo:

> Malthus and Sismondi have likewise correctly remarked that (e.g.) the workers' consumption is in no way in itself a sufficient consumption for the capitalist.[65]
>
> The demand created by the productive laborer himself [v_1] can never be an adequate demand, because it does not go to the full extent of what he produces. If it did, there would be no profit ... The very existence of a profit upon any commodity presupposes a demand exterior to that of the laborer who has produced it.[66]

Although it is true that the exchange of *M*, or *v*, for *LP* in the first stage of the circuit creates new points of exchange, the total new value created which must find an equivalent is not *v* but rather *v* + *s*. Worker expenditures of *v* on *C*(*MS*)' must be complemented by capitalist expenditures of *s* on *LP* and *MP*. Moreover, Marx argues, capitalists who produce consumer goods (*MS*) do so under an illusion: each capitalist sees that the working class as a whole constitutes a large consuming class, and: "would like the workers of other capitalists to be the greatest consumers possible ... the whole remaining working class confronts him as consumer." At the same time: "Every capitalist knows this about *his* workers, that he does not relate to them as producer to consumer and (he therefore) wishes to restrict their consumption, i.e., their ability to exchange, as much as possible."[67] To the degree that each capitalist does this, capital does it collectively – minimizing wages and working-class demand while expanding output to realize more profit.

These two tendencies clearly contradict each other, the first gives rise to the illusion that the working class is mainly a consumer: "It seems to the individual capital that the demand of the working class posited by production itself is 'adequate' demand,"[68] and so production is driven forward by this illusion.

---

65 *Grundrisse*, p. 413; *MECW*, *Vol. 28*, pp. 339–340.

66 *Grundrisse*, p. 418; *MECW*, *Vol. 28*, p. 344.

67 *Grundrisse*, p. 420; *MECW*, *Vol. 28*, p. 346.

68 *Grundrisse*, p. 420; *MECW*, *Vol. 28*, p. 349.

It "must drive it forward beyond the proportion in which it would have to produce with regard to the workers."[69] Results? Often *C*(*MS*)*'* is greater than *v* and markets for *MS* are glutted.

This contradiction and this tendency is accentuated by the dynamic of relative surplus value, in which the value of labor-power is driven down at the same time that production is expanded through productivity raising investments in constant capital. "By its nature therefore, it (capital) posits a barrier to labor and value creation in contradiction to its tendency to expand them boundlessly."[70] That barrier is constituted by the limitations on "the power of consumption within a given framework of antagonistic conditions of distribution, which reduce the consumption of the vast majority of society to a minimum level only capable of varying within more or less narrow limits."[71]

Marx's analysis of the tendency to worker underconsumption that undermines *C*(*MS*)*'* – *M'* is, at first, carried on purely in reference to those producing *MS* but he also recognizes how those workers who produce *MP* obviously add their demand for consumption goods to that of workers who produce *MS*.

LP_2 producing MS_2 demand MS_2
LP_1 producing MP_1 demand MS_1
Total demand for $MS = MS_2 + MS_1$

However, recognizing that total consumption demand is that of all workers, be their payment high or low and no matter what they produce, doesn't change the tendency to underconsumption created by the predisposition to hold down wages (and salaries) to maximize profits.

3.2.1.1 *The Predisposition to Reverse Enclosure*

Given the success of capitalists in imposing enclosures on small farmers and peasants, at home and abroad in colonies, throughout its first few centuries, 1600 – 1900's, it's understandable why Marx focused on their efforts and results. Resistance, however, never ceased. And, as mentioned in Chapter 4, resistance included efforts to take back what had been lost. But why? Why did many who had been expropriated not just give up and accept looking for waged jobs, in agriculture or in manufacturing? The reasons are two-fold.

The obvious one, the one that stands out in Marx and Engels' accounts, was the poverty of the new way of life being imposed. Even if successful at finding

69 Ibid.

70 *Grundrisse*, p. 421; MECW, *Vol. 28*, p. 350.

71 *Manuscript of 1864–1865*, p. 347, *Capital, Vol. 3*, p. 352; or MECW, *Vol. 37*, p. 243.

a waged job, the pay was low and the life it bought uncertain and often desperate. Instead of emphasizing the "push" factor of enclosure as Marx does, some modern theorists of rural-urban migration emphasize the "pull" of cities, not only their jobs, but their bright lights, diversity of amusements, etc. But in the nineteenth century, when Marx and Engels were writing, there were only dim gas-lit streets and few amusements for those earning subsistence-level wages. For those thrown off their land and headlong into the reserve army, city life was brutal – as Engels described at length in his book on the condition of the English working class. So, holding on to land, or reclaiming it to work in familiar ways that could provide essential means of subsistence often appeared to be worth a shot.

The other reason for holding on to or trying to regain land, less obvious to our two city boys, was a deep attachment to land and to the sense of place and unity with nature that comes with working it, not as waged labor, doing what others tell you to do, but as stewards of the land, working with it, year round, through all its changing seasons, colors, textures, smells and weather, year after year. One must look to those who have loved working the land to understand. While several middle- or upper-class poets wrote pastoral verses idealizing a vanishing world they knew only as tourists, lamenting its passing through enclosure, a handful of those who actually worked the land also wrote, chronicling the destruction of their world. One of them was John Clare (1793–1864), an agricultural laborer whose poems sang the beauty of the open commons and the ugliness of its reduction to "little parcels little minds to please / With men and flocks imprisoned ill at ease."[72] In the ever more urbanized capitalist world, in which most people are only able to shape the inside of the their little dwelling places, but otherwise live in a world shaped by capital for its purposes of control and profit, it has taken folklorists, anthropologists, and environmentalists to seek out and try to understand the bonds between humans and the rest of nature now so foreign to city folk.[73] But whether the desire for land has been motivated by the avoidance of worse fates or by attachment to it, "the long land war" as Jo Guldi calls it has repeatedly threatened the ability of

72 John Clare, *Selected Poems*, (New York: Penguin Classics, 2004).

73 Gustavo Esteva, "Mexico: Creating Your Own Path at the Grassroots", in Veronika Bennholdt-Thomsen, Nicolas Faraclas and Claudia Von Werlhof (eds.), *There Is an Alternative: Subsistence and Worldwide Resistance to Corporate Globalization.* (New York: Zed Books, 2001). See the report on the 4th International Indigenous Peoples Corn Conference in 2019, Avexnim Cojti, Cesar Gomez, and Bia'ni Madsa' Juárez López, *United in Tradition as Peoples of the Corn*, Cultural Survival Website, https://www.culturalsurvival.org/publications/cultural-survival-quarterly/united-tradition-peoples-corn (accessed 11-5-2023).

capitalists to maintain its monopoly of the means of subsistence, the means of producing them and thus of markets for them.[74] Every rural acre regained and every abandoned city lot taken over for autonomous "gardening" results in less demand for commercial agricultural products (and, moreover, less incentive to enter labor market).

3.2.1.2 *Predispositions to the Direct Appropriation of Consumer Goods and Services, C(MS)'*

What predisposes workers to disrupt *C(MS)' – M'* through the direct appropriation of *MS*? For Marx and Engels, the obvious answers were poverty and dire need! When wages are at or near subsistence, even workers with jobs earn barely enough to live. In such situations, many are tempted to take what they need to live, whether on-the-job or off, and many have done so. In Chapter 4, Section 3.3.3.1, I drew on Peter Linebaugh's research to point to direct appropriation on-the-job by silk and leather workers, so common as to constitute a regular source of income. More generally, exploitation and alienation within the income and power hierarchies, which capital creates to pit workers against workers, can lead some to appropriate use-values on-the-job, whether they really need them or not.[75] When the use-values appropriated would otherwise be sold, *C(MS)' – M'* is reduced (unless resold,) and *MS* remain use-values rather than commodities.

For the large number of unwaged in the "reserve army" – those with no jobs and little or no income – the temptation to directly appropriate *C(MS)'* must be even greater. And indeed, we know that "Albion's Fatal Tree" (the gallows) at Tyburn never lacked for those sentenced to death for such direct appropriation.[76] Whether those dispossessed from the English countryside, or ex-slaves freed from plantations in the post-Civil War United States but denied forty acres and a mule, or peasants deprived of their land in colonies, how could such people not be predisposed to directly appropriating what

74 Jo Guldi, *The Long Land War: The Global Struggle for Occupancy Rights* (New Haven: Yale University Press, 2021).

75 One report claims US businesses collectively lose 7 percent of their annual revenue to employee "theft." Given the widespread nature of such direct appropriation, it's not surprising that capitalists have complemented human guards with high tech surveillance systems to spot, and by their existence thwart, appropriation by their own workers or by others. Of course, both guards and those who operate surveillance systems may participate in precisely the activities they are hired to prevent.

76 See, Hay, et. al., *Albion's Fatal Tree* (1975) and Linebaugh, *The London Hanged* (1991). Nor are many contemporary jails and prisons, whether public or private, wanting inmates sentenced for "theft."

they need to survive? In the countryside, they could poach animals and pilfer crops. In cities – steadily growing and containing an ever-larger proportion of both industry and population – individuals can rob, and groups of workers can organize the self-reduction of prices or their complete elimination via the collective looting of shops, warehouses, and the homes of the wealthy to obtain what they need. While individual appropriation may mainly cause marginal increases in the cost of doing business, perhaps passed along to buyers through higher prices, large scale "looting," which often includes destruction of fixed capital, constitutes a much more serious disruption of multiple capitalist circuits. Marx wrote of several such uprisings.[77]

3.2.1.3 *Does C(MS)' have Use-value?*

While for consumers, the *use-values* of goods determine whether they meet their needs and desires, those are entirely secondary to capitalist sellers who are primarily interested in the *exchange-value* of their goods, i.e., the price at which they can be sold, because they are out to maximize profits.[78] Given this situation, in which the interests of consumers and of producer/sellers may conflict, there are at least two ways in which problems with use-value may emerge to cause a crisis in the ability of capitalists to sell their goods. First, in one way or another, consumers may discover that the goods or services don't live up their sellers' sales pitch and stop buying them. Second, even if those goods and services do provide the use-values touted by their sellers, sales may drop anyway. Let's look at these in turn.

Although the term "snake oil" comes down to us from the once-common practice in the eighteenth and nineteenth centuries for ineffective medical

77 See, Marx, "Political Movements – Scarcity of Bread in Europe," (Sept. 13, 1853) *MECW*, *Vol. 12*, pp. 301–308 and Marx to Engels, 12 Oct. 1853, *MECW*, *Vol. 39*, pp. 387–388. Today, it is more common on TV and in films to see portrayals of the bored middle- or upper-class shoplifters than it is to see scenes of food riots, whether inner-city explosions in the Global North or the innumerable uprisings in response to austerity imposed by repressive governments and international financial organizations such as the International Monetary Fund. But from the Watts Rebellion in 1965, through the food riots during the international debt crisis of the 1980s and 1990s to the risings of immigrant workers in French suburbs in 2005, poverty has repeatedly moved untold thousands to cry "Enough!" and take what they need to survive.

78 As I pointed out and elaborated in Cleaver, *Reading* Capital *Politically*, Chapter 3, p. 99: "Most fundamentally, the view of the commodity as use-value is the perspective of the working class. It sees commodities (e.g., food or energy) primarily as objects of appropriation and consumption, things to be used to satisfy its needs. Capital sees these same commodities primarily as exchange-values – mere means toward the end of increasing itself and its social control via the realization of surplus value and profit."

remedies to be sold as "snake oil liniment", it has long been applied more generally to denounce fraudulently marketed goods. Where, for example, capitalists hold a monopoly in a market, or collude in establishing an oligopoly, they have often sold inferior quality – or downright harmful – goods and at the price of higher quality items to make an extra profit. Marx gives many examples of such goods, such as adulterated bread, made with inferior and cheaper wheat and "bakers' stuff," i.e., "alum, either finely powdered or mixed with salt."[79] In this example, Marx draws on *Adulterations Detected* (2nd Ed., 1861) by the British chemist Arthur Hassall (1817–1894). Forty years earlier, a German chemist living in London, Frederick Accum (1769–1838) had revealed how bakers used alum to disguise inferior flour by bleaching it white, said to be a condition for successful sale in London at that time.[80] Very much in the spirit with which Marx writes, Accum complained in the Preface to his book, "The eager and insatiable thirst for gain, is proof against prohibitions and penalties; and the possible sacrifice of a fellow creature's life, is a secondary consideration among unprincipled dealers."[81] Such disregard for consumers reinforces the common capitalist practice of minimizing costs in order to maximize profits, regardless of the consequences.

However, as Accum and Hassall demonstrated, this manner of minimizing costs proved discoverable and when made public galvanized outrage and demands for governments to intervene to protect consumers from unscrupulous capitalists. When such revelations and the resulting outrage was sufficient to force regulation by the government, the effect on the targeted businesses varied. Faced with the regulation of the ingredients of bread, for example, bakers without enough resources to switch to higher quality flour were forced out of business. Others with more resources could adapt. In the case of demonstrable toxic or dangerous commodities their production has sometimes been banned and curtailed completely.[82] The primary pressure for the regulation of the quality of use-values via legislation are, of course, the buyers who demand acceptable quality in the goods and services they purchase. In the market for *MS* those buyers are mainly workers. As employees, they fight for better wages;

---

79 *Capital, Vol. 1*, p. 358, fn 42, or *MECW, Vol. 35*, p. 256, fn 1. Two footnotes on, Marx cites the French chemist Alphonse Chevalier (1793–1879) as having identified 20 different adulterations of bread as well as a great many adulterations in other foodstuffs.

80 Frederick Accum, *Treatise on Adulterations of Food and Culinary Poisons*, 2nd ed. (London: Longman, Hurst, Rees, Orme and Brown, 1820) 127–132.

81 Ibid., p. v.

82 Although not always. In some cases, with both *MS* and *MP*, when banned in one place their capitalist producers have simply sold them where they have not been banned, e.g., in other countries with fewer regulations.

as consumers, they fight to ensure that what their wages can buy meets their needs. This second terrain of struggle is a whole new front in the class war.[83]

This "front" was partially a legal one over the degree to which laws would give, or deny, worker/consumers the ability to challenge, even punish capitalists for producing and selling adulterated, often toxic or worthless commodities, i.e., tort and contract laws became terrains for worker/consumers could sue for damages caused by harmful products, false advertising or breaches of contracts.

Another way in which the quality of the use-values of any commodity can limit the ability of capitalists to sell them, derives simply from individuals' limited need or desire for them. One may enjoy a tart green apple, but after two or three, the enjoyment is likely to be replaced by a stomachache! A small amount of a drug may relieve pain or give pleasure, e.g., opium, but too much can kill.

> Use-value in itself does not have the boundlessness of value as such. Given objects can be consumed as objects of needs only up to a certain point.[84]

In other words, even if its quality is up to snuff (satisfies expectations) every specific product has a limited market – "as *use value* the product contains a

83 Thanks to consumer advocates and whistleblowers we know that such practices have continued. Probably best known are the crimes of the meatpacking industry revealed by Upton Sinclair in *The Jungle* (1906) and those of the tobacco industry that adulterated its products to increase addiction. One wonders if Sinclair read Marx's comment on a government report that it "roused not the heart of the public but its stomach," *Capital, Vol.1*, p. 361, or *MECW, Vol. 35*, p. 257, because in commenting on the reaction to his own book Sinclair stated "I aimed at the public's heart [sympathy for immigrant workers], and by accident I hit it in the stomach." Upton Sinclair, "What Life Means to Me" *The Cosmopolitan: A Monthly Illustrated Magazine* 41, no. 6 (October 1906). (Proquest ID: 124715199) In both cases, the revelations, court cases and legislation finally put some limit on the ability of meatpackers and the tobacco industry to sell toxic goods. Repeated revelations, such as those in *The Chemical Feast: The Ralph Nader Study Group Report on Food Protection and the Food and Drug Administration* (New York: Viking Press, 1970), have fomented the creation of a considerable number of collective endeavors to curb capitalist efforts to maximize profit by foisting off on consumers commodities with dubious or downright dangerous qualities. As the *Chemical Feast* demonstrated, even the creation of governmental regulatory agencies has had limited effectiveness in curbing capitalist crimes against consumers. Conflict over the degree to which the FDA protects and fails to protect food supplies continues today. See, the work and campaigns of the Environmental Working Group.

84 *Grundrisse*, p. 405; *MECW, Vol. 28*, p. 332.

barrier."[85] It may be impossible to sell ever increasing quantities of even high-quality products at their value because the need or desire and – when money is available – the demand for it is limited.[86]

For Marx, this limitation had two implications. First, the limited demand for any given use-value helps explain how markets often come to be glutted. Second, every product has a "life cycle"; some are longer, some are shorter. "Today the product satisfies a social need. Tomorrow it may perhaps be expelled partly or completely from its place by a similar product."[87] This is a well-known phenomenon: commodities are "born" via invention or innovation, then follows industrial design, production, marketing and sales. "Death" comes when the inability to sell renders production unprofitable and is terminated. None of these phases are guaranteed. Before many new products and services can be sold, people need to be convinced of their need. Failure results in abortion or infanticide and the abandonment of the production of the unwanted commodity. Thus, the commonplace heavy expenditures on initial marketing test groups and advertisements.

Life cycles are also "prematurely" shortened as new technologies render old ones obsolete. For example, like many before them, homes in the early capitalist era were lit with candles and with oil lamps. But with the development of first the coal and then the oil industry came the invention of new forms of illumination.[88] As a result, the development of gas lighting in homes dramati-

---

85 Ibid.

86 In modern economic analysis, the demand for commodities is commonly represented by demand curves, each point indicating how much individuals will want to buy at each price. Most such curves are assumed to be downward sloping, indicating that increasing quantities of use-values will only be bought at lower prices. Although no longer essential to the derivation of demand curves, textbooks continue to present the late nineteenth century theory of utility, which replaced the labor theory of value, and the concept of diminishing marginal utility that recognizes how increased consumption of any good or service eventually results in declining satisfaction and reduced demand.

87 *Capital, Vol. 1*, p. 201, or *MECW*, *Vol. 35*, p. 116.

88 The desire of oil companies to sell oil for home illumination prompted the marketing ploy of inventing lamps especially designed for the oil commodity. Standard Oil became famous for its efforts, in the late nineteenth century, to sell kerosene in China by giving away Mei Foo lamps specially designed to burn kerosene. In his memoirs, John Rockefeller (1839–1937) wrote, "In many countries, we had to teach the people…to burn oil by making lamps for them; we packed the oil to be carried by camels or on the backs of runners in the most remote portions of the world; we adapted the trade to the needs of strange folk." The Chinese, of course, had been burning oil in lamps for thousands of years, what Rockefellers' hucksters had to teach was the use of their new lamps for their new kind of oil. This marketing experience was made famous in Alice Hobart's novel *Oil for the Lamps of China* (1933) – itself made into a movie two years later. The marketing ploy itself became

cally reduced the demand for candles or for oil for lamps; the development of electricity did the same for gas lighting.[89]

When a decline in sales of some commodity occurs unexpectedly, it creates problems first for its sellers and then for its producers. The degree to which such sudden deaths result in crisis depends on the structure of both production and markets. For the small capitalist producing one or very few commodities, the commodity's death may mean that of the enterprise as a whole, but not for others with greater capacity to compensate for the decline by producing and selling more profitable alternatives. However, even in large businesses, with greater resources and flexibility, the collapse of a product line may still shock the company's bottom line – with reverberations in both supply chains and financial markets.[90] Sometimes for whole industries, adjustment may come only through crisis and reorganization via centralization as the stronger take over and absorb the weaker.[91]

---

widely used, e.g., polaroid cameras were sold cheaply but required expensive film. John Rockefeller, *Random Reminiscences of Men and Events* (New York: Sleepy Hollow Press, 1984).

89 These examples also illustrate how consumers must sometimes be convinced to replace old technologies with new ones. The TV series Downton Abbey illustrated two different responses to the replacement of candles in this upper-class mansion. While their servants were happy for the improved illumination that facilitated their work, some of the owning family were annoyed by the kind of light produced, preferring the softer, more familiar light provided by candles. The recognition of such resistance, and such desires led to different fuel mixes in the case of gas lighting and to the development of different kinds of electrical bulbs and dimmer switches to control the amount of light provided.

90 An infamous modern example was the Ford Edsel – an overhyped automobile that few wanted to buy (many thought it looked funny, like it had just eaten a lemon) and whose failure to sell cost the Ford Motor Company huge loses as many of the cars produced could not be sold. The production processes specific to that model had to be shut down. See, Peter Carlson, "The Flop Heard Round the World," *Washington Post*, September 4, 2007. In Francis Ford Coppola's film *Peggy Sue Got Married* (1986) there is a funny scene in which Peggy Sue, who has been thrown back in time to her high school years, bursts out laughing when her father shows off his newly purchased Edsel. Being from the future, she, but not him, knows how the car of which he is so proud will shortly be the object of laughter and derision.

91 Marx differentiated between *concentration* in industry, achieved through investment creating new means of production and *centralization*, resulting from some capitalists either squeezing out or taking over the operations of others, e.g., bankruptcies, takeovers, and mergers. Although such centralization has been common in moments of crisis when some capitalists prove incapable of coping, it also occurs during periods of expansion as some just prove more competent than others.

3.2.2 Predispositions to Crises in Selling the Means of Production, *C(MP)'*

In the market for *MP*, the buyers are other capitalists, who must decide if the quality of the means of production on offer meets their needs. Do the *MP* have the use-values required in the production processes into which they will be inserted. Where buyers are trying to cut costs, they may purchase inferior quality *MP*, often at workers' expense (as in the case of sub-standard cotton or poor building materials).[92]

The same forces which may predispose the marketing of *C(MS)'* to failure, may also disrupt that of *C(MP)'*. I highlight two: 1) those situations in which their *MP*'s are directly appropriated by others and 2) those situations in which they find themselves, like their counterparts in Department II, faced with having overproduced vis-à-vis the market.

3.2.2.1 *Predispositions to the Appropriation of C(MP)'*

In Chapter 4, Section 3.3.3, I sketched the possibilities of the direct appropriation of *MP* by workers or capitalists. The motivations have differed according to class.

3.2.2.1.1 Why Direct Appropriation of *MP* by Workers?

In the case of worker appropriation, what predisposes some to such acts? Poverty for some or simple anger at wages and working conditions for others may move individuals, or groups of individuals, to directly appropriate those elements of *MP*, susceptible to consumption e.g., basic food stuffs, such as grain, which can be processed at home as well as in factories. But workers have also found ways to adapt all kinds of *MP* for personal use, e.g., tools for home repair, coal and gas for home heating or cooking, or electrical lines tapped for diverse family consumption. As described in the *London Hanged*, "scraps" of cloth by tailors, wood by shipwrights or tobacco by those transporting it, all can be refashioned into either consumable forms or sellable products, both of which supplement money income.

---

92 Unfortunately, corruption is so rampant in some industries, such as construction, that the use of inferior materials is only discovered through structural failures that result from their use. In the "Degüello" episode (2019) of the British police procedural *Endeavor*, a building collapse is caused by the corrupt use of cheap, unwashed sea sand in concrete whose use rusts the structural steel. The episode is reminiscent of the collapse of dozens of apartment building in Mexico City that "pancaked" during the 1985 earthquake – later discovered to have been built with Styrofoam replacing some structural steel! Finally, the *Endeavor* episode also echoes the 2017 Grenfell Tower fire in London due to the use of dangerous materials in its construction.

3.2.2.1.2 Why Theft of *MP* by Capitalists?

As a general rule, capitalists hire workers to do the dirty work of stealing from competitors, an arrangement which allows the former to elude guilt and makes the hired workers run all the risks. Some are hired to steal simply to resell. When either means of production, *MP*, or final products *C*(*MP*)' are stolen merely to resell them, via hijacking or piracy, the thieves are effectively acting as *agents of rogue merchant capitalists* engaged in illegal activity. When raw materials stolen by hired workers are integrated into a firm's supply chain, they are acting as *agents of rogue industrial capitalists*. Although in both cases some investment (paying workers) may be required, if the net result of the theft of *MP* cuts costs, the motivation is nothing more than an illegal application of the omnipresent capitalist propensity to minimize costs to maximize profits.

The same motivation has predisposed capitalists to stealing secret information about production methods or products. This holds regardless of whether the theft is from individual worker inventors or industrial competitors, i.e., industrial espionage. In the case of in-house employees, it's just another case of exploitation – of the labor of thinking rather than of manual labor on the shop floor. In the case of competitors, it's an effort to benefit from the labor being exploited by other capitalists. Whether theft is better than the alternatives, i.e., hiring inventors away from competitors or buying rights, depends on the relative costs. As usual, it's just a matter of judging cost-effectiveness and the impact on profits.

3.3 *Predispositions to Credit Crises*

Credit crises result from the defaulting of debtors on repayment. With merchant and industrial capitalists, along with the government, being the primary borrowers in the nineteenth century, it was in the sources of *their* difficulties that Marx and Engels perceived the greatest threats of credit crises. As I've indicated in the foregoing discussion, those sources were many and by wreaking havoc in any stage of the circuits of capital, they could so reduce borrowers' profits to make it impossible to repay enough of outstanding debt to stave off crisis. So, to a substantial degree credit crises are derivative of industrial or commercial crises. The same is true for governments, as taxes are their source of the means of repaying debt, so any industrial or commercial crisis (whether domestic or international) that reduces taxes undercuts their ability to repay.

But why borrow at all, why take on debt? In the case of capitalist firms, Marx's circuits show available cash deriving exclusively from retained earnings and profits, *M'* – *M*, whether used today to finance new investment, or held over to cover tomorrow's expenditures. They borrow when that available cash is inadequate for what they want to spend it on, and they are unwilling or unable to wait. Unwilling, say, to postpone investment because of the perception of likely profits. Unable to wait when wages must be paid, more raw materials purchased, or repayment of debt comes due. With governments, the situation is similar; they borrow when tax revenues fall short of what are judged to be necessary expenditures. In both cases, borrowing other people's money allows the borrowers to proceed with their plans without waiting for sales, profits, or taxes to rise.

Among capitalist practices – often financed by borrowing – those most likely to provoke credit crises were speculative expenditures, which diverted capital from real investment, undermining the very foundations of many speculative ventures.[93] As Engels observed in 1890 (See, Chapter 2, Section 3.12), speculative investments have their own risky dynamics of "excitement" / "bubbles" and then spectacular collapses. As the forms of credit multiplied, so did the possibilities of speculation and associated crises. With the rise of joint stock companies and the spread of land-based mortgage lending, where the associated financial assets could themselves be traded, often in ways that raised their exchange value far above the value ostensibly represented, speculation against the value of such debt soared – often, as Marx showed in the case of the Crédit Mobilier through conscious manipulation and stock-jobbing. The attraction of all such speculation should be clear: buying some paper asset whose value is expected to rise, and then selling it when it does, is a lot easier than the requirements of real investment, i.e., purchasing *LP* and *MP* and then managing ...*P*... and $C' - M'$.

Apparently left out of such speculative games were waged workers. Because of their low wages and poverty, most had no access to bank credit because they had little wealth to serve as collateral. Nor did their wages pay them enough money to buy bonds or shares and speculate in the new financial markets. They tended to turn to their few sources of limited, local credit only in extremis, when they lost their job and wages or had sudden unexpected expenses, such as a marriage, an illness, or a funeral. Their options were few: 1) pawning their few things for cash, 2) borrowing from local money lenders, or 3) begging credit from the shopkeepers from whom they normally purchased consumer goods with their wages. Unfortunately, failure to find new jobs and wages meant 1) the loss of pawned objects, when unable to buy them back within a given time frame, and the risk of becoming ever more deeply indebted to moneylenders or retail shopkeepers. The Marx family was among those forced to

93 Engels, "The Prussian Constitution," February 1847, *MECW, Vol. 6*, pp. 66–69.

pawn their belongs (albeit often bailed out by Engels),[94] and in *Capital*, Marx cites the risks of workers becoming "almost of the slaves of the tradesman to whom they owe money."[95] None of this, per se, had much effect on the booms and busts resulting from capitalist speculations.[96]

At the same time, because business speculation is sensitive to perceptions of risks and sudden increases in risk can undermine the often-fragile optimism on the basis of which speculation is soaring, the negative impact on speculators of workers' struggles have often been far greater than the extent of rupture might otherwise warrant. A quite limited rupture, but noteworthy enough to come to public attention in newspapers or the business press, can undermine speculator confidence, bring on a crash, the end of a bubble, with ripple effects spreading crisis. So, as workers have often ruptured the best laid plans of their bosses (undermining those bosses' ability to pay back borrowings), those same struggles have sometimes triggered wider crises.[97]

3.3.2 Predisposition to the "Overproduction" or "Underconsumption" of *MP*

Although economists imagine equilibrating mechanisms automatically bring supply into alignment with demand, i.e., marginal adjustments in production in response to changes in prices or inventories, it is precisely how markets often fail to do this smoothly that preoccupies Marx and Engels. The key predisposition to failure, they saw to be the propensity of individual capitalists producing either *MS* or *MP* to expand production despite their ignorance of both short-term demand and the inevitable long-term limit to the social use-value of their

94 So well-known is the penury of the Marx family that reference to it shows up in popular music, e.g. The Clash: "Marx was skint, but he had sense / Engels lent him the necessary pence!" in "The Magnificent Seven" (1981).

95 Marx quoting Henry Fawcett, *The Economic Condition of the British Labourer* (1865), in *Capital, Vol. 1*, p. 807, or *MECW, Vol. 35*, p. 647.

96 That changed, of course, in the twentieth century as workers were more successful at raising wages, accumulating some wealth (collateral), and gaining access to many more sources of credit, from banks to credit cards issued by financial, commercial and industrial companies. Increased wages and credit made working-class expenditures even more central to the economy than before. Paul Volcker's attack on consumer credit in the early 1980s was one sign of its importance. The impact of the collapse of housing speculation – by banks and hedge funds – has become a major factor in recent credit crises and resulting recessions.

97 A modern example was the "Peso Crisis" triggered by the Zapatista uprising in Mexico in 1994 (discussed in a footnote to Section 5.1.1.). Although its effect on the local economy was limited and that on the national economy even less, it triggered the flight of hot money from speculative investment in the Bolsa, the Mexican stock market and caused a collapse in the value of the peso.

product. The check to that expansion is often dramatic discrepancies between supply and demand and resulting crises.

Marx integrated his discussion of the realization problems of both consumer goods and industrial goods with his reproduction schemes. Recall that the division of production into two departments, or the regrouping and aggregation of individual capitalists' production of *MP* and *MS*, gives as a condition of equilibrium in expanded reproduction:

$$\text{Department I: total product value } C' = C_1 + C_2 + C_1' + C_2'$$
$$\text{Department II: total product value } C' = V_1 + V_2 + V_1' + V_2'$$

The condition of equilibrium shows only that there *must be* a proper distribution of production according to demand if $C' - M'$ is to be realized completely in both sectors. However, this does not provide any reason to expect that this will happen. In the schemes, we see Marx explicitly recognizing how the consumption demands of the workers in Department II, which are necessarily less than the total value of *MS*, are complemented by the demands of the workers in Department I; similarly with capital's demand for *MP*. This is the desired equilibrium that capital needs to achieve, but which it often *does not* because capitalists act independently and in ignorance.

Are there any forces tending toward *dis*equilibrium? Marx rejects Ricardo's assertion that while there may be overproduction in one branch of production (or departments), there can be no general overproduction, but agrees that "if one branch of production does not realize itself then capital withdraws from it to a certain degree and throws itself on another point where it is needed."[98] He discusses the role of this important adjustment process in the formation of the general rate of profit, as capital is reallocated across profit differentials. But this adjustment, this "evening up,"

> presupposes the unevenness, the disharmony and hence the contradiction … between capital as directly involved in the production process and capital as money existing (relatively) outside of it. Finally, proportionate production … only when it is capital's tendency to distribute itself in correct proportions, but equally its necessary tendency – since it strives limitlessly for surplus labor, surplus productivity, surplus consumption etc. – to drive beyond the proportion.[99]

98 *Grundrisse*, p. 413; MECW, *Vol. 28*, p. 340
99 Ibid.

Also:

> Capital is just as much the constant positing as the suspension of proportionate production. The existing proportion always has to be suspended by the creation of surplus values and the increase of productive forces. But this demand that production should be expanded simultaneously and at once in the same proportion, makes external demands upon capital which in no way arise out of it itself.[100]

Again, attacking Ricardo:

> Thus allegedly there is no general overproduction but merely overproduction of one or a few articles, as against underproduction of others. This again forgets what the reproducing capital demands is not a specific use-value, but value itself, i.e., money … as a general form of wealth.[101]

In other words, overproduction in one sector is not compensated for by underproduction in another. All overproduction is "production which cannot be transformed into money, into value, production which does not pass the test of circulation."[102] As such, it is an interruption in the circuit of capital and a divergence between production and realization.

Elsewhere Marx also speaks of such partial interruption – of some circuits – and of the process of adjustment which overcomes crisis:

> It goes without saying that, in the whole of this observation, it is not denied that too much may be produced in individual spheres and *therefore* too little in others; partial crisis can thus arise from disproportionate production (proportionate production is, however, always only the result of disproportionate production on the basis of competition.[103]

> … the rise or fall of market-value which is caused by this disproportion results in the transfer or withdrawal of capital from one trade to another, the migration of capital from one trade to another. This equalization itself however already implies as a precondition the opposite of equalization

100 *Grundrisse*, p. 414; MECW, *Vol. 28*, p.341.
101 *Grundrisse*, p. 412; MECW, *Vol. 28*, p. 339.
102 Ibid.
103 MECW, *Vol. 32*, p. 150.

> and may therefore comprise crisis; the crisis itself may be a form of equalization.[104] (more on this in Chapter 7)

One can only speak, Marx insisted repeatedly, of the equilibrium tendencies in capital, the adjustments by which proportionality is restored, by recognizing that these tendencies are correctives to other tendencies to disequilibrium or disproportionality. These he located in the fundamental tendency of the system and all its parts (individual capitals) to drive production forward without regard to demand. "It is thus in the nature of capitalist production to produce without regard to the limits of the market."[105] This is because of both the illusions produced by the system and the associated inability of capital to plan the total distribution of production and demand. These tendencies constitute basic predispositions towards overproduction, which occur concretely only in particular circuits.

This last point leads to the question of the effects of the appearance of overproduction in a given circuit. On the one hand, Marx agreed with Ricardo that capital will respond to a substantial drop in profits by reorienting investment to other lines. But does the breakdown stop there? Is the crisis limited to these scattered interruptions if first one, then another unit of capital drives production beyond either need or demand? Marx argued that it is not. On the contrary, he showed how the breakdown of $C' - M'$ can reverberate, or circulate, through the system, causing other breakdowns, and how it may become generalized causing a "general overproduction."

4 The Circulation of Breakdown

Keeping in mind that the circuits represent a sequence, each step of which capitalists must successfully complete, Marx's theory of crisis includes analysis of the *circulation* of breakdown, of how failure at one point can result in failure at others. The very dependency of each stage on the viability of the others predisposes breakdown to circulate no matter where it begins. The most important sources of such circulation, for me, and I think for Marx, as suggested in each of the previous three Sections, 1 – 3, are workers' struggles. Therefore, what interests me the most is how Marx's analysis of the circulation of breakdown can help us see, understand, and perhaps contribute to the *circulation of struggle*. Unfortunately, focused as he was on analyzing capitalist accumulation, his

104 Ibid., p. 151.
105 Ibid.

treatment of the circulation of crisis often ignores the causes of a breakdown that circulates – despite having often identified them elsewhere. So, in the account below, as I follow his analysis of the *circulation of breakdown*, I remind my readers of some of those causes, especially those involving workers' struggles. I will then turn more directly to the circulation of struggle, how it happens and how it can cause the spread of crisis from one point in capitalism to others.

4.1 *Quantitative and Qualitative Change*

First, however, I'd like to point out that in the cases of both breakdown and struggle, the term "circulation" designates phenomena quite different from the circulation/metamorphoses of value through the circuits of capital. As I have shown, when capitalists have been successful in organizing and bringing all stages of the circuit to completion, they are back where they started, ready to begin again, albeit on a larger scale, a mere *quantitative* change. But crises are *ruptures* in that circularity and when ruptures circulate, when one rupture leads to another, one failure to another, they disrupt capitalist planning on an ever-larger scale.[106] If the disruption is serious enough, even if a circuit is successfully completed in part, its managers are rarely back where they started, but somewhere else, forced to adopt new plans. This is particularly true when the circulation of crisis is the result of the circulation of workers' struggles.[107] To the degree that workers succeed in their objectives and recompose their relationships of power with capital they force *qualitative* changes in the class relationship. An increase in wages or a decrease in working hours can shift the balance of class power in favor of workers, undermine the profitability of a particular organization of the circuit, and so on, forcing capitalists to change their *modus operandi*.

106 Although Marx juxtaposes capitalists' despotic planning on the shop floor with the "anarchy" of the market, the ever-expanding circuits of capital, reaching across markets, industries and international borders have required capital to extend its planning. Today's multinational corporations engage in a degree and scope of planning far beyond even that managed by their predecessors such as the East India Company (1600–1874). See, Raniero Panzieri, "Surplus Value and Planning: Notes on the Reading of Capital," in *The Labour Process and Class Strategies*, CSE Pamphlet, No. 1, (London: Stage 1, 1976) 4–25. Originally in *Quaderni Rossi* 4 (1964): 257–288. Reprinted as Chapter 25 in R. Panzieri, *La Ripresa del Marxismo Leninismo in Italia* (Milan: Sapere Ed., 1975) 329–365. And to this we must add the planning of national governments through "industrial policies" and those of international institutions such as the International Monetary Fund that imposes capital's rules of the game on national governments and blocks of capitalists.

107 The parallels and differences between the circuits of capital and those of workers' struggles are discussed more thoroughly in H. Cleaver, "Circuits of Struggle," *The Political Economy of Communication*, Vol. 4, no. 1 (2016): 3–34.

Marx illustrated this at length in showing how workers' success at reducing working hours, caused a crisis for their bosses and forced them to invest more in relative surplus value strategies involving more controllable machines and fewer troublesome workers, changing their interrelationships. In such cases, workers' struggles and the crises to which they give rise force *qualitative* changes in capitalist society. Whereas the expanded reproduction of capital, per se, involves merely *quantitative* change, the spiraling outward of more and more work, more and more production, more and more sales, etc., workers' struggles and the crises to which they give rise are propulsive forces imposing *qualitative* change on capitalism, pushing it into the future, and preparing the way, Marx and Engels believed, for its transcendence.

Marx sometimes portrays this phenomenon as one aspect of the dynamic unfolding of the relationship between the *living labor* of workers – both mental and physical – and the *dead labor* (means of production) controlled by capital. He argues that it is only living labor that creates something new, which in capitalism takes the form of a commodity (whether a scientific breakthrough, a new technology, a new machine, or a new final product). "Living labour must seize on these things, awaken them from the dead, change them from merely possible into real and effective use-values."[108] But what is true of living labor within the labor process, is also true of the relationship between the classes. Capital imposes sameness in its efforts to accumulate: more work, more means of production, more commodities. But creative living labor refuses mere quantitative expansion and infuses newness, new ideas, new theories, new products, new ways of making things, new ways of providing services.

Again and again, living labour ruptures the constraints capital imposes and not only breaks loose, creating freely but also organizes the power to create a crisis for capital and force it to adapt. Workers in a plant, for example, may strike to force their employer to adopt some recomposition of the labor process that makes it safer. Workers at the level of class relationships may organize a movement that forces recalcitrant, capitalist-dominated governments to enact laws imposing safer methods on a whole industry, e.g., laws requiring ventilation shafts and breathing masks for coal miners, or ventilators in factories to remove toxic fumes, cotton dust, etc. Whether in the case of individual circuits or at the level of capital as a whole, living labor imposes *qualitative* change on capitalism.[109]

---

108 *Capital, Vol. 1*, p. 289, *MECW*, *Vol. 35*, p. 193.

109 Given Marx's recognition that there is more to life than labor, we must also keep in mind that the qualitative changes workers impose often derive from life beyond work. New ideas on-the-job often derive from activities/life off-the-job. Unfortunately, some see in

4.2 *Circulation of Crisis within Individual Circuits*

How crisis can circulate *within* individual circuits is easy to see, obvious from all I have presented so far. Any breakdown, at any stage, will disrupt the subsequent stages. This includes disruptions in sequential circuits, e.g., the same circuit in the next period.

1. *M*. The inability to generate or borrow enough money to hire all the labor-power and to buy whatever means of production are required for any investment project will at least reduce the scale of operations (*...P...*, *C′*, *C′ – M′*) and at worst, nip it in the bud, ending the circuit before it begins. If the cost of *M* is high, net profits after repayment will be lower. Everything that raises the costs of production undermines the generation of surplus value, *s*, and profits. Everything that raises the cost of loans reduces the ability to compensate low *s* by borrowing.
2. *M – LP*. The inability to hire enough workers will cut planned production, *C′* and *C′ – M′*. If wages are too high, profits, *M′ – M*, will be reduced. These problems can be the result of many things. Emigration, reduced immigration, wars, epidemics and falling birth rates can all reduce the availability of labor and raise wages. The common refusal of subsistence peasants or those in the urban informal sector to enter the labor market also reduces the supply of labor-power and raises its price. The refusal of some workers to accept jobs that involve crossing picket lines to break strikes, strengthens demands for higher wages by workers on strike. And so on.
3. *M – MP*. Even with plenty of workers hired at profitable wages, any reduction in the availability of *MP* that decreases their supply and raises their price, limits *...P...*, *C′* and *C′ – M′*, or makes them impossible. Worker uprisings, crop failures due to natural disasters, export restrictions, disease, direct appropriation, and wars were all cited by Marx as sources of crises in the supply of *MP* and thus in the industries dependent on them for production.
4. *...P...* Breakdowns in production, which reduce *C′*, also reduce the possibilities of *C′ – M′* and any *M′* > *M*. True for the production of both the means of production, *MP*, and final consumer goods, *MS*. Strikes bring production to a halt. Sabotage may slow production, undermine it completely, raise costs or reduce the quality of products, all decreasing the profitability of *C′ – M′*.

---

this only capital's instrumentalization rather than appreciate how creativity often springs from non-work activities and is as often applied to projects of self-valorization rather than capitalist production.

5. *C′ – M′*. Miscalculations involving overproduction of C′ vis-à-vis available M result in buildups of unwanted inventory in the hands of either original producers or commercial intermediaries. For producers, the excessive inventories add to costs and reduce monies available the next round of investment. For merchants handling transportation and sales, excess merchandise must often be disposed of at less than profitable prices, reducing what they can buy the next time round.

This last is a kind of feedback within the circuit, wherein a disruption in a later stage, the inability to sell, *C′ – M′* has an impact on a previous one: investment, *M – (LP, MP)*. There are others. For example, a breakdown in *C′ – M′* may also result in cutbacks in production, shortened work time, wage cuts or layoffs of workers in ...*P*... and reduce or halt hiring, *M – LP*, and purchases and buildup of stocks of *MP*.

> If *C′ – M′* comes to a halt in the case of one portion, for example, if the commodity is unsaleable, then the circuit of this part is interrupted ... the successive parts that emerge from the production process as *C′* find their change of function barred by their predecessors. If this continues for some time, production is restricted and the whole process brought to a standstill. Every delay in the succession brings the co-existence into disarray, every delay in one stage causes a greater or lesser delay in the entire circuit ..."[110]

Or, workers going out on strike in ...*P*... may result in other workers, however dire their need, refusing to be pulled into the labor market, *LP – M*, as scabs by capitalists trying to replace striking workers.[111] Unlike the ongoing refusal of peasants or urban "marginals" to enter the labor market, this refusal – an act of solidarity – reinforces the impact of the strike by prolonging it and increasing the likelihood of the workers winning changes, e.g., higher wages, shorter working hours or better working conditions, that may cause other kinds of disruption.

---

110 *Capital, Vol.* 2, p. 183, or *MECW, Vol. 36*, p. 109.

111 There is a scene in John Sayles' film *Matewan* (1987) in which mine owners bring in Italian immigrant workers to break a coal miner strike in Appalachia. The Italians, all too familiar with such capitalist strategies, refuse to replace the striking miners. There's also an instructive scene where a wife of one of the Italians reacts with disgust to learning that there will be no job, no wage, no money to put food on the table, etc. One surmises that she does the housework, while her husband works for a wage, and she now faces more work than ever in sustaining the family.

4.3 *Circulation of Crisis among Interconnected Circuits*

As capitalism develops, as its functionaries reach out across the face of the earth (and now into space) creating new markets and putting people to work at new points of production, the growing complexity and time required for interconnection predisposes the system to a circulation of crisis from one circuit to others.

> Further, since the circulation process of capital ... extends over a fairly long period ... great upheavals take place in the market ... it is quite clear, that between the starting point, the prerequisite of capital, and the time of its return at the end of one of these periods, great catastrophes must occur and *elements of crises must have gathered and develop*.[112] (my emphasis)

Marx did not elaborate his evocation of elements "gathering and developing", but they clearly involve a chain of events across circuits – a circulation of interruption (the "must occur" is a predisposition). How that circulation happens depends upon the nature of the connections.

Among the *direct* connections between separate (not sequential) circuits of capital, through which crisis can circulate, are (1) *M*, the relationship between borrowers in one circuit and the lenders in another, and (2) *M – MP*, where one capitalist purchases means of production from another capitalist (or from a subsidiary). Among the *indirect* connections through which crisis in one circuit may circulate to another, are (3) *M – LP*, hirings, firings, and wage and benefit increases or decreases in one circuit affect the wages and benefits paid in other circuits, (4) *...P...C(MS)′ – M′*, increases or decreases in the production and price of the means of subsistence have an impact on the real wages being paid to workers in other circuits, and thus on their relationships with their employers, (5) Overproduction and gluts in major markets can ripple through other circuits. Let's examine these pathways through which crisis can circulate, one by one.

1. The most obvious way functionaries of capital who must borrow *M* to supplement their retained earnings may face crisis is because of an increase in the cost of borrowing sufficient to undermine their planned investment, forcing them to cut back – or even cancel – expenditures on *LP* and *MP*, and thus on the scale of *...P...*, *C′*, and *C′ – M′*. Such increases can be enterprise-specific or general. The former can be a response to

112 *MECW*, *Vol. 32*, p. 126.

lenders' doubts about the creditworthiness of the borrowing firm – say due to recent or current worker struggles, or to declining profit margins, either announced or anticipated. A general rise in the rate of interest, or lender wariness, is often the result of a widespread crisis in which many capitalists are facing difficulties, competing to borrow, and pushing up rates, or of action on the part of central banks or governments raising rates for some reason, e.g., to stem outflows of gold due to rising rates in other countries or crop failures requiring increased imports.[113]

Where, instead, capitalists have placed surplus value in excess of their immediate spending needs into financial institutions or into interest-bearing assets such as stocks or bonds, the bankruptcy of such institutions or the collapse in the value of their assets can also cause a crisis by dramatically reducing their access to cash and their ability to meet current debt obligations, payment for *MP*, meeting *LP* payrolls, or investing any time soon.

2. Where one capitalist buys the means of production from another, *M* – *MP*, the most likely source of crisis circulating from producers of *MP* to buyers are crises in the availability of *MP* and resulting increases in its price. Marx often mentions crises in the availability of *MP* from agriculture, e.g., grains, whether they are caused by blockades, as we saw during the Napoleonic Wars (see Chapter 4, Section 1.3.6) or poor harvests (see Chapter 4, Section 3.3.5). Both create crises for producers of *MP* and raise its price to buyers. Blocked exports and poor harvests reduce producers' ability to sell, *C′* – *M′*, and the increased price of grain can, in turn, raise the price of flour and thus of bread, or, in the case of feed grains, the price of meat. Such "supply-chain" crises, as they are known today, raise the costs of production and lower profits for those buyers unable to pass increased costs along to consumers. The increases in the price of *MP*, besides raising costs for buyers also reduces the amount of money, *M*, those buyers have left over to spend on *LP*. More money spent on *MP* means less money available to hire the workers required to process the now more expensive *MP* into *C′*, e.g., increases in the price of fertilizer reduces the money available to hire farm labor to spread it (resulting in less or wasteful spread and lower yields). If the effect is great enough it can mean cutbacks in production, less *C′* – *M′* and lower profits.
3. *M* – *LP*, crises in the labor markets, although originating in other circuits, may cause a crisis for all those drawing workers from the same source.

113 Marx to Engels, February 3, 1851, *MECW*, *Vol. 38*, pp. 273–278 and Engels to Marx, February 25, 1851, *MECW*, *Vol. 38*, pp. 299–300.

For example, the success of those working for other capitalists in the same industry in forming unions and raising wages can put pressure on those capitalists who have been able, so far, to stave off such problems, to follow suit. Or, some capitalists buying and installing new machines and laying off workers to improve productivity, to cut costs and to get a competitive edge, puts pressure on others in the same industry to do the same. But if, as with the Luddites, workers mount angry opposition to bearing the costs of such changes, following suit will bring that anger and disruption to their own factory gates (see Chapter 4, Section 4.2.1).

4. *...P...C(MS)' – M'*, any crisis in the production of *MS*, which reduces their availability and increases their costs, cuts real wages for all workers, and in turn, reduces the demand for other consumption goods, regardless of the circuit in which they are employed. In *The Manuscript of 1861–1863*, Marx explained in detail how such circulation of interruption may occur. He gave an example of how a breakdown in *C' – M'* in one circuit, that resulted in reduced production and the laying off of workers, would reduce the money in the hands of the laid off workers and hence their demand for consumer goods, both the ones they produce (if they do) and for those produced in other circuits. Not surprisingly he drew his examples from the textile industry – the leading sector of manufacturing in British industry and one that produced clothes for workers.

Now let us return to our example of calico.[114]

> The stagnation in the market, which is glutted with calicos, hampers the reproduction process of the weaver. This disturbance first affects his [laid-off] workers. Thus they are now to a smaller extent, or not at all, consumers of his commodity – cottons – and of other commodities which entered into their consumption. It is true, that they need cottons, but they cannot buy it because they have not the means, and they have not the means because they cannot continue to produce because too much has been produced, too many cottons glut the market ... They now form a part of the temporary surplus population.[115]

114 Calico = "a plain-woven textile made from unbleached and often not fully processed cotton." Originally from India.

115 *MECW*, *Vol. 32*, p. 152. "Temporary," i.e., part of the *floating* reserve army, IF their employer survives the crisis and they are rehired, or, if he does not, if they are hired by a similar producer. Otherwise, they may be pitched into the *stagnant* reserve.

Here Marx points to the circulation of breakdown from the industrial circuit that produces calico cottons to the "little circuit" *LP – M – C*(*MS*). Laying off workers breaks *LP – M* (no wages), which undermines *M – C*(*MS*) in the same and other circuits and thus accentuates the rupture of *C*(*MS*)′ – *M*′. All workers laid off in these industries have their income reduced. Thus, aggregate *LP – M – C*(*MS*) is restricted, the collapse in calico sales spreads further causing problems for other consumer goods producers who are also trying to achieve *C*(*MS*)′ – *M*′.

> Their means for buying calico and other articles of consumption shrink, contract, because there is too much calico on the market. This also affects other commodities (articles of consumption). They are now, all of a sudden *relatively* overproduced, because the means with which to buy them and therefore the demand for them, have contracted. Even if there has been no overproduction in these spheres, now they are overproducing.[116]

In these ways, he demonstrated how the interruption of *C*′ – *M*′ could not only move from the sphere of circulation to the sphere of production within a single circuit, but also to other circuits, and thus circulate the interruptions and generalize crisis. Moreover…

> If overproduction has taken place not only in calicoes, but also in linens, silks and woolens, then it can be understood how overproduction in these few, but leading articles, calls forth a more or less general (*relative*) overproduction on the whole market. On the one hand, there is a superabundance of all the means of reproduction and a superabundance of all kinds of unsold commodities on the market. On the other hand, bankrupt capitalists and destitute, starving workers.[117]

The same can result from suddenly reduced imports of *MS*, as during the Napoleonic Wars. Both situations can result in increased worker unrest, strikes, union formation and protests among those affected and well enough organized to act in self-defense, regardless of their employer. Such was the anger capitalists tried to mobilize in opposition to the Corn Laws, to shift worker disruption

116 Ibid., pp. 152–153.
117 Ibid., p. 153.

from themselves to landlords profiting from higher grain prices (as sketched in Chapter 2, pp. 35-37) and raising the price of bread to workers.[118]

5) Gluts in markets for major commodities, which reduce $C' - M'$ and force down prices can circulate to other markets bringing on crises for producers of both *MS* and *MP*. The most common cause cited by Marx and Engels was, as I've previously noted, overproduction vis-à-vis the size of actual demand – a problem unremoved, even by the advent of new electronic means of communication such as the telegraph, which dramatically sped up the flow of information (as discussed above in Chapter 4, Section 3.3.4).[119]

While some explain this predisposition to expansion purely by capitalists' lust for sales and profit, we have also seen how increased production in search of increased sales can be driven by the need to offset increased costs – often brought about by workers' struggles for less work, safer work or higher wages and by expensive responses to them, e.g., paying for safety equipment or relative surplus value strategies of investing in new, productivity-raising equipment.[120]

In such cases of overproduction, Marx and Engels saw crises in sales result in cutbacks in production, which in turn meant reduced purchasing of *MP* and layoffs of *LP*. Reduced purchasing of *MP* circulated crisis to suppliers of *MP* and layoffs of workers, the associated reduction of wages and the inability of workers to compensate by assess to credit, all cut consumer demand for all sorts of commodities.[121]

---

118 In the early 1970s, the government-engineered food crisis sketched in footnote 13, p. 103 resulted in dock worker strikes against loading grain to the USSR and a beef boycott in the US by workers against the increased cost of beef caused by the increased cost of feed grain.

119 This problem continues, even with more modern methods of communication, e.g., telephone and Internet, simply because fluctuations in demand have proved unplannable and unpredictable despite capitalists' best efforts to adapt, e.g., "lean" and "just-in-time" production.

120 In recent times, we must add the pressure from workers qua consumers qua human beings to force capitalists to spend money to avoid, or correct, production processes which cause ecological destruction, pollution, contribute to global warming and so on, e.g., selective rather than clear cutting by timber companies, scrubbers on industrial smoke stacks, capturing previously vented methane from oil wells.

121 When in the twentieth century workers were successful in raising wages enough to own property and gain access to credit beyond pawn shops and loan sharks, that access made it possible to offset any reduction or loss of wages by borrowing to sustain consumption, at least in the short term. The dangers of such recourse were recently glaringly obvious in the wake of the widespread successful attacks on unions, workers' protections, pensions, and wages in the early 1980s and subsequent decades. The longer it takes workers to find new jobs and new income the greater the number of worker bankruptcies, defaults

In turn, deficient demand in one market often results in the dumping of excess supply in other markets, disrupting circuits there. Writing of a crisis in Prussia, Engels argued:

> Every glut in the English market threw large quantities of English goods into the Zollverein, where they were sold at prices more ruinous to the Germans than to the English, because these latter made, during the times of flourishing trade, large profits in the American and other markets, while the Prussians could never sell their produce anywhere but within the circle of their own line of customs.[122]

Other outlets for excess production were established by force through colonialism. Not surprisingly, resistance to the imperialist imposition of markets was often recurrent, involving the refusal of labor-displacing foreign goods with $C' - M'$ interrupted by workers' struggles.[123] Widespread uprisings, on a sufficiently large scale ("riots" or revolutions) can bring markets for more than one commodity to a standstill. Chinese resistance to the importation of British opium from India limited both that market and others. It took two wars (1839–1842) and 1856–1860) to fully open China to that particularly poisonous British commodity and to its other exports via treaty ports.[124]

Under such conditions of global trade, circulation of stagnation and interruption is accentuated by the way production and circulation, (*...P...* and $C' - M'$) are often carried out by different people, often far removed from one another. When, for example, sale has been taken over by a commercial intermediary engaged in $M - C' - M'$, a breakdown in $C' - M'$ and a buildup of unsold

on borrowed money and the loss of homes and apartments. Repayment problems were accentuated by fraudulent bank practices of peddling "sub-prime" mortgages to workers whose limited income almost guaranteed their ultimate inability to repay.

122 Frederick Engels, "The Prussian Constitution," (*The Northern Star,* No. 489, Mar. 6, 1847) February 1847, *MECW, Vol. 6,* p. 66.

123 In the film *Gandhi* (1982) there is a poignant scene of Indians burning cheap English cloth in protest against its importation, the associated destruction of local textile industry and the resulting misery of displaced workers.

124 Karl Marx, "History of the Opium Trade," August 31 and September 3, 1858, *MECW, Vol. 16,* pp. 13–20. I write *poison* because the expanding market for opium in China was not due to increased medicinal uses but to spreading addiction. The story of the first opium war is told in the 1997 Chinese film *The Opium War,* released to critical acclaim in the West but now rarely screened. A rare film touching on opium production by the East India Company is *Sharpe's Peril* (2008).

inventory in some distant country may not be immediately apparent to those managing production (…*P*…), making the likelihood of overproduction worse:

> if *C′* circulates further, e.g., in the hands of the merchant who has bought the yarn, this in no way disturbs – initially at least – the continuation of the circuit of the individual capital that produced the yarn and sold it to the merchant … This point is an important one in considering crises … a great part of the commodities have only apparently gone into consumption, and are actually lying unsold in the hands of retail traders … One stream of commodities now follows another, and it finally emerges that the earlier stream had only seemed to be swallowed up by consumption. Commodity-capitals now vie with each other for space in the market. The latecomers sell below the price in order to sell at all … At this point the crisis breaks out.[125]

If glutted markets in Britain wreaked havoc on textile workers there, it paled in comparison with impact on Indian textile workers as a result of the British colonial imposition of cheap cloth from British mills. The Indian textile industry, which had been a major exporter of textiles for a thousand years, was destroyed by the British to make way for cloth produced in the British Isles for export to India. The Indian weavers were thus forced out of their traditional trade and into the production of the raw material for British mills. In other words, British industrialization (or development) was based, in part, on the de-industrialization (or underdevelopment) of India. Then, as it had done at home, British exports glutted markets in India. This whole sordid colonial history pitched Indian textile workers into desperate poverty.

> In India, on the other hand, the English cotton machinery produced an acute effect. The Governor General [of that British colony] reported as follows in 1834–35: 'The misery hardly finds a parallel in the history of commerce. The bones of the cotton weavers are bleaching the plains of India.'[126]

125 *Capital, Vol. 2*, pp. 155–156; *MECW, Vol. 36*, pp. 81–83.

126 *Capital, Vol. 1*, p. 558, or *MECW, Vol. 35*, p. 435. For a recent evaluation of the role of British textile exports to India in contributing to the de-industrialization and underdevelopment of that country, See, David Clingingsmith and Jeffery Williamson, "India's De-industrialization Under British Rule: New Ideas, New Evidence," NBER Working Paper, 2004 and its references. On the forcible suppression of Indian production. See, William Bolt, *Consideration on Indian Affairs, Particularly Respecting the Present State of Bengal and its Dependencies*, London, 1772. It was against this colonial suppression of traditional

The breakdown in $C' - M'$ can mean not only a reduction in $M - LP$ and hence in $LP - M - C(MS)$, but also a reduction in the demand for the *MP* required for production and thus a reduction in the ability of the suppliers of *MP* to convert their product C' into M'. In the "Manuscript of 1861–63," Marx writes:

> But apart from the workers who are directly employed by the capital invested in cotton weaving, a large number of other producers are hit by this interruption in the reproduction process of cotton; spinners, cotton dealers (or cotton cultivators), mechanics (producers of spindles and looms, etc.) iron, coal producers, etc. Reproduction in all these spheres would also be impeded because the reproduction of cottons is a condition for their own reproduction. This would happen even if they had not *overproduced* in their own spheres ...[127]

But this is not the only way in which the circulation of breakdown can take place. Breakdowns in production caused by "nature" (for example, crop failures) cause interruptions not by making C' greater than M', but by reducing C'. This can cause crisis in two ways. First, and most immediately, the M' earned is not large enough to give an average profit causing a crisis for the producers of C'. Second, if C' is an *MP*, (intermediate or producer good) the reduction in its production will have a negative impact on all the circuits that employ that commodity as a means of production because its buyers will be faced with either absolute or relative unavailability, a possibility which I discussed with respect to $M - C(MP)$, and thus a shortage of *MP*, and a reduction in profits as the price of *MP* rises.

> There are, however, also cases where the overproduction of non-leading articles is not the result of overproduction, but where, on the contrary,

Indian artisanal production of cloth, that Mahatma Gandhi (1869–1948) promoted the hand-crafted spinning, weaving and wearing of traditional cloth.

More recently, a version of this history (of no longer "primitive" accumulation) has been imposed in China. Where the British destroyed the Indian cotton industry, the Chinese government destroyed local production of both cotton and cotton textiles in Xinjiang. Where the British forced Indian weavers into cotton production, the Chinese government has imposed forced labor on the Uyghur people in both growing and processing of cotton into textiles and clothing. Where British control resulted in production of cotton cloth for export, Chinese control has resulted in huge exports of cotton, cotton cloth and cotton clothing – often in collaboration with Western capitalist corporations. Awareness of this has led to efforts to limit the importation of all those products *because* their production has been based on forced labor.

127 *MECW*, *Vol.* 32, p. 152.

> *underproduction* is the cause of overproduction, as for instance when there has been a failure in the grain crop or the cotton crop, etc.[128]

Earlier, he had pointed to the spreading ramifications of crop failures during the crisis of 1855.

> The surplus used to purchase [extra] grain [due to the crop failure] must correspond to a deficit in the purchase of all other products and hence already a decline in their prices … the nation would find itself in a crisis not confined to grain, but extending to all other branches of production … Quite apart from the role of money, the nation would thus find itself in a general crisis …[129]

5 Linkages among Tendencies

Having examined several of the tendencies that produce crises, we can identify certain linkages and common sources of their dynamic unfolding.

The first, and most fundamental, characteristic that links these tendencies to crisis, which I have been emphasizing, is their *common source in workers' struggles*. Among those tendencies, this essay has highlighted those most touted by Marxists as being the primary cause of crisis and key to the revolutionary overthrow of capitalism, e.g., underconsumption, overproduction, the tendency of the rate of profit to fall, and disproportionality. That assigning of primacy has resulted in endless debates among those who embrace one tendency or another. In each case, disruptions in individual circuits have been seen as multiplying to the point of crisis for the system as a whole. Where this essay differs from most formulations of these tendencies is that rather than seeing them as distinct, and perhaps rank-ordered, "laws of capitalist development," inevitable and unavoidable, I postulate that they are all observable realities rooted in workers' struggles and can be understood in terms of the unfolding dynamics of those struggles and capitalist responses. Moreover, because of this common root, these tendencies are not separate and distinct but intricately linked.

Perhaps the most obvious linkage or commonality among these tendencies to crisis is how they involve and unfold within the tendency of capital to expand – as much as possible and potentially endlessly. We can see this tendency in terms of both the profit-maximizing, repeatedly investing individual

128 Ibid., p. 160.

129 *Grundrisse*, p. 129, or *MECW*, *Vol. 28*, p. 67.

capital and the aggregate process of accumulation, i.e., the expanded reproduction of capitalist society as a whole. After all, crisis in one circuit can circulate to others potentially bringing on rupture at the aggregate level. In the case of underconsumption, the production of the means of subsistence outgrows the ability of workers to buy consumer goods. In the case of overproduction, the production of both consumer goods and producer goods outstrips the market for them. In the case of the tendency for the rate of profit to fall, the driving force is the rise in the organic composition of capital designed to increase productivity and, as a general rule, to increase output. In the case of disproportionality, both Departments I and II expand, but at unequal rates.

But what is the source of this tendency to expand? Most Marxists have located it in both the greed of individual capitalists trying to maximize their investment and profits and the dynamics of competition which push each capitalist to do so – whether greedy or not – under threat of being out-competed and displaced by those more successful at doing the same thing. In short, a story about the behavior of capitalists without regard to workers. I'm arguing instead that within the tendency to expand, both the strategies used by capitalists in their investments and search for profits and the resulting dynamics of competition must be understood as ways of coping with the problem of maintaining control over those exploited, alienated, and resisting the capitalist imposition of endless work.

Ways of coping with what? With the struggles of workers for higher wages, for less work, for safer work, for less alienating work, for cooperating in ways that escape their bosses' control. While all unfolding within the framework of capitalism, these struggles emerge from the autonomous desires of workers for better lives, to be gained by the lessening or freeing of their lives from the subordination, formal or real, to work-for-capital, within its global work-machine combined with better conditions of life off-the-job that make possible not merely the reproduction of their labor-power but of lives worth living. So, for example, to the degree that they are successful, struggles for higher wages and for less or safer work raise costs and reduce the rate of surplus value, s/v, and absolute surplus value. Such success is usually based on cooperation/collaboration among workers, e.g., informal or formal (secret societies, unions or COBAS), that escapes their employers' control.[130]

130 COBAS = Comitati di Base or Rank & File Committees; S. I. Cobas = Sindicati Interaziendali Comitati di Base or Cross-firm Rank & File Committees. These and similar alliances have been formed outside official unions that are recognized in law and that all too often collaborate in capitalist development.

Capitalists cope with all this, not only by calling on repressive forces (company goons, the police or military) but also by resorting to either an increase in the number of workers put to work using the same technology, or, shifting to or accentuating, the relative surplus value strategy of raising the organic composition of capital, i.e., raising productivity through the introduction of new technology and expanding output. (While it is technically possible to raise productivity while maintaining the same level of output, given the ability to increase production, capitalists usually try to do so, to increase revenue, profits and their share of the market.)

As they do this, capitalists try to use the reorganization of production that accompanies the change in technology to break-up and re-divided the work force and thus the pattern of workers hired and fired – irrespective of any change in the absolute number. In this way, the organization of workers based on a certain composition of the work force is undermined through re-division. Marx was adamant about the capitalist use of technological change in breaking the power of labor.

> But machinery does not just act as a superior competitor to the worker, always on the point of making him superfluous. It is a power inimical to him, and capital proclaims this fact loudly and deliberately, as well as making use of it. It is the most powerful weapon for suppressing strikes, those periodic revolts of the working class against the autocracy of capital.[131]

The same is true with respect to divisions among units of capital and among branches and departments of production. The expansion of capital takes place unevenly, with new branches arising and old ones declining with the life-cycle of products and changes in technology. In the process, the overall pattern of the division of labor is changed and any organization of workers based on it undermined. Looking at the same phenomenon from the workers' point of view, we can see that the tendencies that Marx describes in the production process: the reduced requirement for labor and the increasing difficulty for capitalists of converting disposable time into surplus labor time, clarifies for workers their lack of need for the system and often increases the time available for organizing.

Within Department II the result of such efforts to increase productivity and production will be an increase in the supply of the means of

131 *Capital, Vol. 1*, p. 562, or *MECW*, *Vol. 35*, p. 438.

subsistence – possibly outstripping any increase in the ability of workers in both Departments to buy, hence "underconsumption." With the same dynamic unfolding within both Departments, the increase in the production of both the means of subsistence and the means of production may exceed the ability of both workers and capitalists to buy the increased output, hence "overproduction" and widely glutted markets. With only inefficient markets to modulate increased production in both Departments so that they meet the requirements of both for expanded reproduction, the same dynamics can result in "disproportionality" between departments.

This same ever-increasing resort to raising the organic composition of capital in response to workers' struggles, in order to increase productivity and production, results in the constant production of a redundant population and ever greater investment requirements for imposing work, resulting in the tendency of the rate of profit to fall that undermines this work-based system.

These tendencies – to under consumption, to overproduction, for the rate of profit to fall and to disproportionality – may unfold separately or in conjunction with each other. They all stem from the same sources: workers' struggles and capitalist efforts to compensate via the expansion of production irrespective of circulation, that is, the expansion of the "substance" of value (work-as-social-control), irrespective of the "form" of value (exchange value). Both are thus aspects of a "plethora of capital" or an "overproduction of capital."

> The so-called plethora of capital is always basically reducible to a plethora of capital for which the fall in the profit rate is not outweighed by its mass … This plethora of capital arises from the same causes that produce a relative surplus population and is therefore a phenomenon that complements this latter, even though the two things stand at opposite poles – unoccupied capital on the one hand and an unemployed working population on the other … Over production of capital, not of individual commodities – although this overproduction of capital always involves overproduction of commodities – is nothing more than over-accumulation of capital.[132]
>
> Over-production of capital never means anything other than over-production of means of production – of means of labor and means of subsistence – that can function as capital …[133]

132 *Manuscript of 1864–1865*, p. 360, *Capital, Vol. 3*, p. 359, or MECW, *Vol. 37*, pp. 249–250.
133 *Manuscript of 1864–1865*, p. 364, *Capital, Vol. 3*, p. 364, or MECW, *Vol. 37*, p. 254.

Indeed, to be comprehensive, Marx might well have said that overproduction of capital inevitably includes overproduction of all of its elements: money capital, labor-power, commodities, and means of production. The common source of the tendency for the rate of profit to fall, and of C' to outstrip M', thus lies in the boundless expansion of production, driven on by the dynamic of class confrontation.

At the same time, we can see how the relative surplus value strategy, which can accelerate this expansion of production, affects the first stage of the circuit by the particular way in which it achieves that expansion. Because it is based on both a replacement of *LP* by *MP* and a cheapening of the *MS* required for the reproduction of *LP*, the struggles of capital and labor in the sphere of exchange ($M - LP$) are directly affected. If the *value* of *LP* is going down, then it is possible for capital to lower *wages* without undermining the reproduction of labor-power. Whether it can actually do this, depends on the ability of workers to resist such reductions. That ability is directly affected by the growth in the unemployed, redundant population that divides workers against each other and increases pressure on those who are still waged. In this way the expansion of production has an impact on circulation both fore and aft, both in stage I and stage III.

We can see not only how the motivation for a certain kind of capitalist accumulation is generated within the class struggle but also how the working out of that accumulation process, and its resultant tendencies, are also integral to the struggle. They are shaped by the pattern of relative power between the classes in various circuits, sectors, branches, and departments. Where working class pressure is strongest, and yet capitals' flexibility is sufficient to allow it to develop and adopt new productivity-raising technologies, the expansion will proceed rapidly. Where either the working class is weak, providing no motivation to capital to innovate, or it is strong and capital fails to do so, expansion will be slower.

This is the underlying dynamic to the process of *competition* to which Marx has often referred as allocating the various tendencies and effects. Competition is based on profit, and profit for Marx was basically determined by the organic composition of capital and the rate of exploitation – both of which are determined within the struggle between the classes. Managers of capital who prove their ability to control their workers and to keep profits up – win the competitive battle, expand, and take over more managerial responsibility for a larger number of workers. Managers who prove less able tend to lose their jobs.[134]

134 A recent example has occurred in the much-noted struggle of Amazon workers to unionize – very much against the desires and machinations of their managers. When

This ability to maintain profits involves both the ability to manage the rise in productivity (increase in c/v) and the ability to expand markets necessary to sell the increased product. Given the various predispositions for this expansion of production at average profit to break down, then the success of the competitive capitalist (as of capital in general in maintaining growth), is dependent on finding ways to offset these tendencies, with or without crisis.

---

workers at an Amazon warehouse in Staten Island voted to unionize, despite being force-fed anti-union messages by their managers, those same managers were fired by the company. See, Karen Weise and Noam Scheiber, "Amazon Abruptly Fires Senior Managers Tied to Unionized Warehouse," *New York Times*, May 6, 2022, accessed May 9, 2022.

CHAPTER 6

Offsetting Strategies and Their Contradictions

What Marx calls "Counteracting Factors," the title of Chapter 14 of Volume 3 of *Capital*, includes everything capitalists do to counter and minimize the impact of all those forces tending to rupture accumulation and create crises for their efforts to complete their circuits, achieve expanded reproduction and renew their control over society on an even larger scale. This chapter elaborates beyond the six "factors" Marx analyzes in Volume 3 of *Capital*[1] – both by bringing in material discussed elsewhere by Marx and Engels and by working systematically through the various stages of accumulation represented in the circuits and the forces that shape them. As in Chapters 4 and 5, the main focus is on capitalist efforts to deal with all those struggles by workers that rupture either individual circuits or circulate from circuit to circuit threatening the system more broadly. Looking back at the struggles already mentioned, it should be clear that because capital invades and attempts to subordinate every social activity, conflicts unfold throughout society and therefore capitalists have had to respond with a wide variety of strategies and related tactics. As a prelude to working through each stage of the circuit and their interconnections, I classify the methods capitalists use into four rough categories: force, law, ideology, and structural change. In varying degrees and mixtures, they have been deployed throughout the history of capitalist accumulation, and, as I then show in Sections 7, 8 and 9, at every stage of every circuit and elsewhere within society.

1 Force

For those of us who have learned to despise capitalism, by studying its way-too-long history of exploitation, alienation, and crimes against humanity and the rest of nature, its frequent use of force is often the first thing that comes to mind when considering the ways capitalists respond to crises. From its beginning, as Marx shows in his analysis of primitive accumulation, force was essential to the birth of capitalism. With no midwife to help, the birth of capitalism, described by Marx as coming into the world "dripping from head to toe, from every pore, with blood and dirt," metaphorically resembles

1 In the *Manuscript of 1864–1865*, discussion of these factors begins on p. 336.

the chest-bursting emergence of H. R. Giger's alien.[2] Born in blood, like every ruling class before them, capitalists have maintained their rule through force whenever they have judged it necessary to prevent or overcome crises in their organization of society.

They have deployed force to enforce laws created to codify and protect their order, from the sanctity of property to the regulation of their labor force – from putting down slave revolts and breaking up banned unions and strikes through the beating or assassination of organizers in the sphere of production, to terrorizing working class and immigrant communities in the sphere of reproduction.[3] They have used force to repress ideas subversive of their rule, from the jailing, execution or assassination of dissidents to the shutting down of critical publications and the banning of books – as Marx and Engels experienced repeatedly.[4] Many capitalist companies either maintain their own goons to violently repress worker organizing or hire them from independent security firms.[5] Every capitalist government maintains police, military, judges, jails and prisons to maintain their law and their order, including the "order" of ethnic, gender and racial discrimination and the repression of protests against it.[6] They also use force to impose structural change, e.g., colonialism, the enclosure of still-existing commons, eminent domain against individual private property to facilitate capitalist development, including the kind of slum clearance Engels

---

2 *Capital, Vol. 1*, p. 926, or *MECW*, *Vol. 35*, p. 748. Giger's creature first appeared in the sci-fi film *Alien* (1979), which was popular enough to spawn a whole series. Like capital, which Marx often referred to a "vampire-like", the creature in the film feeds off the workers in the freighter that discovers it. Like capital, its self-reproduction leaves dead bodies in its wake.

3 Despite some workers having won the legalization of unions in some places, the repression of other efforts has been widespread and even where they have been legalized, they have often been subject to such restrictions as to virtually neutralize their ability to fight for workers goals, e.g., the banning of strikes or closed shops and cooptation into collaboration with industry (see below). The terrorizing of immigrant communities has been recurrent and widespread throughout the capitalist world.

4 In recent years, it should suffice to evoke Vladimir Putin's repeated jailing and assassination of political opponents, Saudi Crown Prince Mohammed bin Salman's assassination and dismemberment of Jamal Khashoggi and the overt censorship of media by authoritarian forms of capitalism all over the world. While book banning has long been associated with Nazism, it has been increasingly deployed in the US as part of current right-wing attacks on the teaching of the history and nature of systemic racism and gender discrimination within capitalism.

5 The most familiar such firm in the US was the Pinkerton detective agency established in 1850 and, as previously noted, renowned for union busting. Such security firms – such as Blackwater/Academi – have evolved into providing private military forces, professional mercenaries, to anyone willing to pay, but most often to capitalist corporations and governments.

6 Most recently demonstrated in the US since the murder of George Floyd by multiple videos of white police killing unarmed Blacks and the repression of worldwide Black Lives Matter protests against just such racial discrimination .

describes in *The Condition of the English Working Class* and Marx analyzes in *Capital*.[7]

2 Laws: Writing and Enforcing

Laws, we are generally taught, are the set of rules which regulate social conduct and separate civilization from barbarism.[8] "We are a nation of laws, not men," Americans like to assert – in contradistinction not only to barbarism but also to rule by a monarch or some other kind of dictator. So, in childhood we are taught that like the rules laid down by our parents, societal laws are to be followed or obeyed. With time, study, and experience, however, we discover that not everyone has been in on writing the laws, that they have often been written to benefit some at the expense of others. Laws – subject to interpretation within the judicial system – often encode unjust relationships as well as just ones. "Law and order," the long-running TV show, takes its title from the much longer running practice of writing and enforcing *laws* to maintain the existing *order* – in our case, the capitalist one.[9] Once we realize how the laws in most civilizations we know about – including our own – have mostly been composed to organize and maintain domination over society by some ruling class, it is easy to see how considerations of justice have repeatedly provoked 1) the violation of laws viewed as unjust, 2) legal challenges to those laws, and

7 All of these continue, albeit sometimes under different rubrics. Formal colonialism has often been replaced by neocolonialism that has maintained essentially the same relationships created prior to "liberation." Settler colonialism in places like the US, Australia or Siberia, of course, has rarely been recognized as such except by its victims. Slum clearance is now called "urban renewal." Enclosure of commons in the US is managed by the federal government through the "leasing" of public lands for private exploitation. The seizure of private lands is called the exercise of "imminent domain" for the "greater," i.e., capitalist, good.

8 But then who qualifies as a barbarian and what behavior qualifies as barbaric have always been defined by those who call themselves "civilized," from at least the Ancient Greeks to the present. It is worth remembering that the origin of the Greek word for barbarian, βάρβαρος, simply referred to languages the Greeks could not understand. In other words, the word derived from ignorance and was used to deride and demean others – including those with longstanding and highly literate cultures, even other Greeks – a practice that simply glossed over the ignorance. Ignorance, not only of other peoples' languages but also of the rules and laws of their societies.

9 In the September 11, 2022 episode of John Oliver's TV show "Last Week Tonight" he dissects exactly how TV cop shows, especially "Law & Order" glorify police and prosecutors while demeaning defense attorneys. By juxtaposing their representation on TV to actual data on police and prosecutorial behavior and results, he shows how this iconic TV show grossly misrepresents how both police and judiciary actually function in New York City and elsewhere, thus perpetrating myths about their role within capitalism.

3) sometimes acts of civil disobedience to contest and force the abolition of, or changes to, existing laws in order to remove or reduce injustice.[10]

Over time, laws have been written, contested, rewritten or set aside and replaced to regulate virtually every aspect of capitalist society, including each stage of the circuit of individual capitals and their interactions. There are laws that concern markets for labor, the means of production and consumer goods. There are laws about the conditions of work in fields, mines, factories, offices, brothels, banks, retail sales outlets, schools, homes, and public places. So ubiquitous are laws that some tend think of passing a new law every time they confront some behavior they don't like. This assumption of law-as-remedy has been so widespread that a syndicated cartoon strip titled "There Oughta Be a Law" ran in newspapers for four decades (1945–1985).

Enforcing of all these laws in capitalism has always involved the use of *force* – from forcibly stopping their violation through immediate extra-judicial violence or through judicial procedures followed by punishment, from fines through incarceration and the quasi-slavery of prison labor to the imposition of the death penalty. Inevitably, both the content of laws and the pattern of their enforcement have both been terrains of class struggle. Their very scope makes consideration of their role in relation to crises of the relationships they are designed to regulate daunting. What follows barely scratches the surface.

A considerable amount of Marx's writing is concerned with this terrain. As mentioned in Chapter 2, Section 1, he recognized the importance of law as early as 1842, in the case of the laws outlawing the direct appropriation of wood in Prussia – a case that soon had him returning to and critiquing Hegel's treatment of law and civil society. That return produced "Contribution to the Critique of Hegel's Philosophy of Law" (1843–44), an essay containing a critique of various sections of Hegel's *Philosophy of Right* (1820).[11] Although in passing Marx quotes Hegel (§306) on "the uncertainty of business" and "the fluctuations in possessions," neither Hegel in his book nor Marx in this essay take up the role of law vis-à-vis crisis.[12]

---

10 In the wake of the Supreme Court attack on the right to abortion by overthrowing Roe vs Wade, we are seeing these conflicts play out on a massive scale all across the US. With some Supreme Court justices already discussing the possibility of banning contraception, that attack has clearly been only a first step aimed at rolling back women's rights more generally and decomposing the power of women in the labor force as well as in society at large.

11 *MECW*, *Vol. 3*, pp. 3–129, 175–187.

12 Ibid., pp. 74, 102. Samuel Dyde's translation is "the uncertainty of trade," *Philosophy of Right* (Mineola, NY: Dover, 2005), 162.

Arriving in England that same year, Engels observed the struggle of the Chartists to change the laws of suffrage to gain increased leverage over the writing of laws that shaped their lives. The Chartists were fighting for a law guaranteeing the right of adult males to vote; later suffragette movements demanded a law that would extend that right to women. Abolitionists were fighting for a law ending slavery and according ex-slaves all citizen rights, including suffrage.[13] *Rights* written into laws define what one is legally justified in doing. Laws also specify what you cannot do, thus defining *crimes*. The few rights workers have won have 1) taken the informal form of custom, 2) have been spelled out formally in Charters and Constitutions or 3) defined in specific laws. The many crimes which capitalists have defined – above all the violation of property rights – are spelled out in voluminous legal codes. Again and again, in every country in which capitalism has emerged (or taken over), concepts of property, exchange and the role of laws have been recast to form and reform legal systems. As Marx's analysis of the battles over laws governing the length of the working day shows, that recasting and the structure of laws at any given moment reflect the balance of class power, between capitalist efforts to maintain its order and repeated resistance and demands by workers.[14] Sometimes changes in law have codified capitalist concessions; sometimes they have legalized increased exploitation.

Despite his recognition that capitalists have dominated the writing of laws within their social system, Marx very much embraced workers fighting for the writing of at least a few laws that would benefit them. In his analysis of the battle over the length of the working day, in light of the coercive power of poverty achieved by capitalists in the labor market, which drove both adult workers and their children into wage-slavery, he wrote, "workers have to put their heads together and, as a class, compel the passing of a law, an all-powerful social barrier by which they can be prevented from selling themselves and their families

13 All these struggles, for equal rights for women, for the ending of slavery and for the rights of the descendants of ex-slaves, are still going on. In the United States, for example, attempts to deny citizen rights – to vote, to health care, etc. – to the descendants of ex-slaves and other "minorities" are currently rampant. The recent abolition of the Constitutional right to abortion – a right won by long struggles – by a US Supreme Court newly dominated by right-wing judges is an example of how all legal rights won by workers are never guaranteed but subject to cancellation when the balance of power changes against them.

14 The most obvious recent case is the right to abortion in the United States. For roughly fifty years it was a "constitutional" right, decided by the Supreme Court as a result of widespread demand. Then, after corrupt changes in court membership leading to its being dominated by reactionary, "conservative" justices, it was stricken from the books and abortion once again outlawed. The struggle has continued, partly around changes in both state and federal laws, partly in the streets in mass protests.

into slavery and death by voluntary contract with capital."[15] Thus, there was, from early on, a class struggle over the writing of laws and the degree to which they would serve the capitalist purpose of staving off or countering crisis and the degree to which they would make workers' lives less miserable, reduce exploitation and strengthen workers in their struggles.

Of course, the existence of laws favorable to workers has never guaranteed their enforcement. Whether and to what degree pro-worker laws have been enforced has, like the passing of the laws themselves, been a question of the balance of class power. Failing to finance the enforcement of laws constitutes a ploy used again and again, as Marx amply demonstrates and continues to this day.[16] Even when legislators do vote money for enforcement, those newly elected to the executive branch, or appointed by them, have often refused to continue spending the money, gutting enforcement, and thwarting the intent of the laws. But even where "the necessary official personnel" have been funded – as in the case of the English Factory Acts – the laws themselves have often been written in ways that have created so many loopholes that the factory inspectors or later regulators have found their job almost impossible. The combination of loopholes and capitalist deviousness led to repeated legal challenges by the factory inspectors themselves, by worker-hired attorneys and barristers as well as collective protests and uprisings against unjust or unenforced laws. Thus, alongside the struggle over the writing of laws was another, which played out in courts and in the streets, over their enforcement.

Such class conflict in the judicial arena has been heavily stacked against workers in two ways. First, because the laws often reflected capitalists' power and were written in ways that made it hard for workers to win any relief from their exploitation and second, because capitalists have largely controlled the appointment of magistrates and judges who heard most cases concerning labor, or, where judges were elected, they have dominated the selection of candidates and financing of their campaigns. So, where workers' struggles unfolded in courts, they have been subjected, in Nate Holdren's words, to the "tyranny of the trial."[17]

---

15 *Capital, Vol. 1*, p. 416, or MECW, *Vol. 35*, p. 306.

16 The *Manuscript of 1864–1865* contains a great many examples, beyond those included by Engels in Volume 3 of *Capital*, many drawn from factory inspector reports of the resistance of capitalists to implementing changes workers and reformers have succeeded in getting written into law and the paltry fines levied on them by their friends on the bench. Contemporary examples abound as well, as illustrated in footnotes to Sections 7, 8 and 9 below.

17 See Holdren, *Injury Impoverished*, which analyzes the various dimensions of that tyranny. His analysis shows how once workers and reformers succeeded in getting laws passed

Despite the ways capitalists have been able to shape the terrain of law in their favor, the ability of workers to pool their limited resources and hire attorneys has turned the legal system into a true terrain of class struggle. In Britain, losses before capitalist magistrates were often appealed to the Court of Queen's Bench on technical grounds and frequently overturned.[18] As working-class newspapers, such as the *Northern Star* to which Engels and Marx contributed, reported on these legal battles, their often-biased outcomes provoked worker outrage, protests and even violent uprisings, shaping the labor market, behavior on work sites and thus accumulation and crisis.

3 Ideology: Ideas, Institutions and Behavior

If the scope and roles of laws governing all aspects of capitalist society makes considering their various roles vis-à-vis crises daunting, I have found accounting for the role of ideology even more so. All laws, especially those that legalize exploitation and aim to repress resistance, require both careful aiming – to facilitate or curb some activity – and, if they are to be accepted, justification. The term *idéologie,* coined by the French philosopher Destutt de Tracy (1754–1836) as part of his response to the French Revolution that challenged virtually all existing laws and the class structures on which they had been based, literally means "science of ideas." From the point of view of Marx and Engels' analysis of the antagonistic class structure of capitalist society, the concept of ideology can be applied to both *strategic* and *apologetic* ideas. Certainly, down through the ages, laws have been crafted and justified by both rulers who benefit from them and their apologists. Although Marxists have tended to use the term

---

to provide workers some compensation for injuries on the job, they were written and enforced in ways which ignored the full extent of injury, reducing the calculation of their losses to monetary measurements of income lost. This Holdren called the "tyranny of the table" because courts relied on tables setting out the monetary value of lost body parts, lost waged income, etc., while largely ignoring the full range of personal, psychological, and social costs to injured workers and their families.

18 Against any tendency to view the judiciary as just one part of the state as a one-sided "organ of [capitalist] class rule," a large literature goes well beyond Marx's analysis in Chapter 10 to reveal in great historical detail how workers' challenges not only won victories against this stacked system but also forced changes in both laws and the judiciary itself. See the essays in Douglas Hay and Paul Craven, eds., *Masters, Servants, and Magistrates in Britain and the Empire,* and Christopher Frank, "'Let But One of the Them Come before Me, and I'll Commit Him': Trade Unions, Magistrates and the Law in Mid-Nineteenth-Century Staffordshire," *Journal of British Studies* 44, no. 1 (January 2005): 64–91, and the materials cited therein.

primarily in the sense of rigid dogma and apologetics, already in *The German Ideology* we can see Marx's recognition of how "systematic systems of ideas" play both roles. Marx certainly paid close attention to both; here too.

Understanding ideology in capitalism to include both ideas about strategies for managing class relationships and those justifying those relationships implies a breadth of definition that englobes virtually the entirety of ideas that take capitalism as a given to be propagated and supported. Trained as an economist and having only ventured beyond my field out of curiosity and political commitment, I decline the temptation to take on that whole and, for the most part, confine my comments about the role of capitalist ideology in countering the forces that rupture various aspects of the system and throw it into crisis, to the ideas of economists, as they evolved from mercantilism through the political economy of Marx and Engels' time.[19]

A preliminary note: there are ideas, and there are institutions devoted to promulgating them. They do so in at least two ways. First, they support the generation and repetition of useful ideas. Second, within capitalism in their very form they embody its paradigmatic structures and, by so doing, reinforce the inculcation and acceptance of those ideas and modes of behavior consistent with them (what some call the construction of "subjectivity"). Obvious examples are all those institutions that replicate the very capitalist mode of organizing labor: incarceration within factory-like structures and the changes in ideas and behavior that result – both intended changes, such as the internalization of disciplinary regimes and unintended changes, such as mutual recognition and rebellion. The latter, of course, was Marx's emphasis about the consequences of capitalists herding workers into factories to better impose work but where they discover their common exploitation and organize against it. Such is also the case, as Michel Foucault (1926 – 1984) has demonstrated, not only with prisons and their regimes of legal incarceration but also with institutions as diverse as hospitals, schools, and workhouses.[20] In the capitalist epoch, many traditional institutions were gradually transformed from purveyors of ideas and behaviors useful to earlier ruling classes into ones elaborating and spreading those useful to capitalists. I touch briefly on only four: schools, religion, the press, and the judicial system.

---

19 And to a lesser degree, in footnotes, to their evolution in neoclassical and neoliberal economics.

20 Michel Foucault, *Surveiller et punir: Naissance de la prison* (1975), (*Discipline and Punish: Birth of the Prison*). *Naissance de la clinique: une archéologie du regard médical* (1963), (*The Birth of the Clinic: An Archaeology of Medical Perception*).

Schools, colleges, and universities are the institutions most familiar to those of us trained in an academic field. During Marx and Engels' lifetimes, until the 1870 Elementary Education Act, which created a system of public education in England and Wales, schools were, for the most part, private and accessible only to the privileged few, future participants in the ruling class.[21] Workers'

21 In the early twentieth century, as workers began to free their children from waged labor, through the passage of restrictions on the use of child labor, the combination of working-class pressure and a growing capitalist need to find an alternative way to manage the young and to condition/discipline them for future entry into its labor force resulted first in widespread public schooling and later in the access of working-class children to universities. Integral to this expansion of institutions of so-called "education" was their gradual restructuring – in a division of academic labor, differentiated and organized to meet the needs of capitalists. See, Raymond Callahan, *Education and the Cult of Efficiency: A Study of the Social Forces that have Shaped the Administration of the Public Schools* (Chicago: University of Chicago Press, 1962).

Those needs have included the instrumentalization of criticisms of capitalism. Parallel to how capitalists have often been able to use labor unions to regulate and harness workers' struggles, has been the limited acceptance of oppositional thought within capitalist schooling. Allowing workers to contest the existing organization of production reveals weaknesses and the opportunity to overcome those weakness; allowing limited critique of capitalism within schools serves the same purpose – as well as keeping dissidents off the streets and away from other anti-capitalist organizing. (Recently, the pressures on and the exploitation of students have driven more and more of them to recognize their "schools," at all levels, as nothing more than edu-factories designed to transform them into useful workers.) Beyond the "repressive tolerance" highlighted by Herbert Marcuse (1898–1979) has been the real service to capital provided by critics in revealing weaknesses in both capitalist strategies and apologetics. Thus, at every level, these institutions have become bastions of capitalist ideology, institutions no longer designed to reproduce a narrowly defined ruling class but rather to produce both ideologues – dedicated to solving capitalists' problems and justifying their solutions – and a whole range of technically trained and ideologically indoctrinated workers, from technicians, engineers and scientists in factories and research laboratories to mid-level bureaucrats and high-level managers working in offices, both small and large, from those on the shop-floor to those managing whole cities, national and international policy formation and implementation. See Marcuse's essay, "Repressive Tolerance" in Robert Wolff , Barrington Moore, Jr. and Herbert Marcuse, *A Critique of Pure Tolerance* (1965).

In this manner, for example, the field of economics has sometimes tolerated not only criticisms of existing institutional arrangements and policies by those proposing alternative solutions but also by those opposed to any "solution" other than the overthrow of capitalism. This can be seen in the openness of some economists and some pro-business ideologues to assessing, rather than simply dismissing, the relevance of the work of Marx, Engels, and other anti-capitalists to the understanding of crisis. Two well-known examples from the first half of the twentieth century are the works of Joseph Schumpeter (1883–1950) and Wassily Leontief. The partial opening of university departments of economics to "radical," "Marxist" or "heterodox" ideas in the wake of the social movements of the 1960s and the crisis of Keynesianism provides more recent examples as student

"education" was mostly restricted to either on-the-job training, in workshops, factories and farms, or in workhouses.[22] The exceptions, such as the schools created by Robert Owen for his workers, were, like the later public school system as a whole, aimed at producing a peaceful, productive work force, both on the job and off. Owen's description:

> The children were taught reading, writing, and arithmetic, during five years, that is, from five to ten, in the village school, without expense to their parents … the children are taught to read in such books as inculcate those precepts of the Christian religion, which are common to all denominations.[23]

And, of course, precepts consistent with dutiful, non-antagonistic relations with their employer.

The ideas taught the privileged, beyond basic skills, were those judged appropriate to rulers and managers, from ideas about how to govern to those justifying the exercise of such power. In the West, the later included, for a long time, education in the classical literature of Greece and Rome and the associated languages – Greek and Latin. Knowledge of these languages set the educated apart from and above the masses. Workers were to be awed by and accept the authority of clergymen, lawyers and physicians who conversed in

---

radicals were allowed jobs in academia. It is worth noting that one of the great weaknesses in Soviet-style state capitalism is the intolerance of both worker and intellectual dissent and protest. By repressing such dissent with police state methods, those regimes cut themselves off from information flows they could use to better manage class relationships. That weakness is currently being demonstrated in reactionary governments in Eastern Europe, e.g., the regime of Viktor Orbán (1963 -) in Hungary – currently a darling of and exemplar for right-wing ideologues in the US and Western Europe.

22 John Locke, apologist and strategist of capitalism, wrote a whole book about the best ways to educate the children of his wealthy friends, but he thought the workhouse would do very well for workers' children, workers-in-formation. Compare his *Some Thoughts Concerning Education* (1693) with his "On the Poor Law and Working Schools" (1697).

23 Robert Owen, *A New View of Society, or, Essays on the Principle of the Formation of Human Character, and the Application of the Principle to Practice*,(1813–16). Besides creating schools for his workers, Owen also improved both housing and access to consumer goods in the village, with the objective of improving worker-employer relations. "Those employed became industrious, temperate, healthy, faithful to their employers, and kind to each other. while the proprietors were deriving services from their attachment, almost without inspection, far beyond those which could be obtained by any other means than those of mutual confidence and kindness."

these languages, especially in Latin.[24] The same objective was sought by other "well-educated" managers, politicians and academics who could draw upon classical history and literature to justify their policies.

In all cases, from private, then public schools for workers to more elite schools and universities for the few, the structure of schools and teaching more or less replicates the structure of capitalist industry. While those institutions incarcerate both teachers and students, the latter have no control either over what is taught or how it is taught. Laws often set subjects and standards, but the day-to-day power relationships between teachers and students mirrored those in industry, effectively subordinating learning to discipline. As Friedrich Nietzsche would describe such structures in Germany in 1872: "One speaking mouth, with many ears, and half as many writing hands ... the proprietor of this one mouth is severed from and independent of the owners of the many ears; and this double independence is enthusiastically designated as 'academical freedom'."[25] In other words, one overseer and many workers following orders in the production of labor-power and, at the level of many universities, the production of research and publications.[26]

A second set of well-known institutions that purvey pro-capitalist ideology are churches, institutionalized religions. Once primary managers and beneficiaries of pre-capitalist cultures, such as feudalism in Europe, they adapted to become handmaidens of capitalism. Like schools, in their makeup and operations most churches conveniently mirror the top-down power structure of capitalism, with clergy doing most of the talking and teaching and congregants for the most part just listening to instructions about how to behave. In those parts of the world where the Christian church has held sway, the Reformation and the rise and proliferation of Protestant sects brought new doctrines that replaced older ones. The divine right of kings was replaced by the idea that success in business revealed God's approval and grace.[27] The Catholic condemnation of

24 There are some very nice representations of such awe – by both officers and seamen – for Latin-speaking physicians in the novels of Patrick O'Brian (1914–2000) portraying relationships in the British Navy during the Napoleonic Wars. Even today, when most discourses in these fields are carried out in vernacular languages, e.g., in church liturgies, legal briefs and prescriptions, so many Latin terms are still in use as to be taught in special classes to students training to be clergymen, lawyers, doctors, nurses and pharmacists.

25 Friedrich Nietzsche, "The Future of Our Educational Institutions" (1872), or "Lecture v" in Paul Reitter and Chad Wellmon, eds., *Anti-Education: On the Future of Our Educational Institutions* (New York: New York Review of Books, 2016), 75.

26 This dual production is the subject of Krystian Szadkowski's *Capital in Higher Education* (London: Palgrave/Macmillan, 2023).

27 Marx and Engels addressed the role of religion in numerous works, including from The *1844 Manuscript* and *Critique of Hegel's Philosophy of Right* to Engels' *Socialism: Utopian*

usury was replaced by its acceptance. Similar transformations took place in other parts of the world where other religions, such as Islam, or Hinduism or Buddhism, dominated. With their "schoolbooks" limited to sacred texts, clergy of all sorts play an essential role in providing interpretations consistent with the capitalist rules of the game.[28]

A third set of institutions purveying pro-capitalist ideology came with the rapid rise and spread of printing and the production of widely available books, journals, newspapers, and sheet music in the nineteenth century. This dramatically widened old terrains of class struggle. Capitalist investment largely dominated the production and sale of the printed word and musical notation, making the dissemination of ideas supportive of its rule easier and easier.[29] Those ideas included not just justifications for capitalist economic policies, but also those propagating a wide range of social norms compatible with capitalist accumulation – such as acceptance of the myths of its origins, schooling as training for jobs, the value and payoffs of hard work, deference to authority, appropriate behavior for women, whether as wives and mothers working in the home to maintain and reproduce the labor force or working for a wage, either at home (taking in sewing) or in some garment shop or textile factory, and so on.[30]

---

and Scientific (see the 1892 Introduction to the English edition). The classic post-Marxian work is Max Weber (1864–1920), *The Protestant Ethic and the Spirit of Capitalism* (1904–5).

28 Once again, there are exceptions. Among the best known are those orders and sects which reject the consumerism of capitalism, e.g., the Amish, and those who critique capitalism directly, e.g., Liberation Theologists preaching among the poor in the US, Latin America and the Indian Subcontinent. Of course, they too tend to replicate the hierarchy of initiated teachers and passive students even as their ideas foment resistance.

29 So too, in the twentieth century, have radio, television and film technology provided capitalists with new media for the communication and indoctrination of ideas they find useful – such as spreading interpretations of crisis that fit capitalist needs for acceptance and acquiescence to the policies they adopt. The space and resources won by workers in these media have been limited. There is some "community" access to the production facilities of local television and some pirate radio stations. As the cost of video equipment has steadily declined, bottom-up film making, both imaginative and documentary has grown and the Internet has made it possible to share the results widely.

30 All these norms, of course, have changed over time as a function of capitalist needs and workers' struggles. An obvious example has been the norms for women's behavior. Although derived, historically, from both secular and religious "codes" of household organization, their application depended upon circumstances. When needed in industry – to undercut men's wages or during war time to replace men sent off to battle, women were drawn out of the home, into the waged labor force, and their labor valorized. When needed to boost the growth of that labor force their labor as wives and mothers was valued more highly – buttressed by pro-natalist laws and subsidies encouraging large families. Most recently, capitalist reaction to women's struggles successfully expanding their

But as workers' self-organization proceeded apace, challenging and shaping capitalist development, their access to those technologies also grew, making it possible to replace handwritten complaints or demands with typeset tracts, pamphlets and eventually books.[31] As small, independent "Left" publishers emerged, such as those to which Marx and Engels contributed, anti-capitalist writings have also been printed and distributed by capitalist publishers. Nowhere was the old saw that "capitalists would sell you the rope to hang them with if they could make a profit from the sale" truer than in the realm of publishing. The combination of increasingly comprehensive self-organization by workers and their ability to reduce work time and raise wages beyond subsistence created a growing market for printed words, some that critiqued capitalism, its crimes, and its ideological justifications, some that looked beyond it. The evolution I sketched of Marx and Engels' publications, from articles in liberal newspapers and journals to books such as *The Condition of the English Working Class*, *The Communist Manifesto* and *Capital*, were an important but very small part of a proliferating anti-capitalist literature throughout the nineteenth century.[32]

A fourth, and last, set of institutions with great responsibility for both controlling workers and convincing them of the reasonableness of that control were those of the judiciary. While force was widespread in imposing the capitalist rules of the game, punishing directly, or incarcerating or transporting workers who violated those rules, the judiciary – staffed as we have seen throughout the nineteenth century primarily by members of the ruling class – provided

rights, over property, access to jobs, participation in government, and control of their own bodies, have varied. Some have adapted, integrating new social norms into accumulation. Others, reactionary capitalists and their politicians, have launched a wide-ranging counterattack – starting with reversing the right to abortion – aimed at re-establishing a vicious patriarchal hierarchy.

31 Collectors of even "folk music" – that diverse array of chants, songs and ballads composed by workers and long circulated primarily by oral emulation or handwritten music notation – could take advantage of the same techniques of mechanical printing that were, at first, only used for liturgical, "classical" or "popular" music acceptable within bourgeois culture. Eventually, the same would be true with the music of twentieth and twenty-first century rebels, such as Acid Rock, Punk and Hip-hop.

32 Within capitalist-dominated radio and television, programs are sometimes subverted by critics and opponents of capitalism, but the arrival of the Internet has vastly facilitated the dissemination of the fruits of autonomous efforts at critique and the exploration of alternatives – a vast subversion of a physical infrastructure built for capitalist purposes of war and computer time sharing. See the original draft of H. Cleaver, "The Zapatistas and the Electronic Fabric of Struggle," a revision of which was published in John Holloway and Eloína Peláez. eds., *Zapatista! Reinventing Revolution in Mexico* (London: Pluto Press, 1998).

the means and justifications for enforcement. The long history of jurisprudence, dating back to the ancient Greeks in the West and even further back in some other cultures, such as those of India and China, has been one of seeking theoretical (ideological) justifications both for the setting out of laws and for their specific contents. Usually deeply rooted in some philosophical stance concerning such normative ideas as "the good" and "truth," judicial judgements have often been rendered in terms of "justice," whether for individuals, corporations, or society as a whole. Indeed, the judiciary as a whole is often referred to as "the justice system," or, by its critics as "the injustice system."

Just or unjust, that system operates in periods of crisis as well as in those of steady accumulation. The kinds of interventions mentioned above – countering workers' struggles through the enforcement of existing laws and contracts – have been even more important in moments of crisis. Whether the crisis has been caused by those struggles or upsurges in struggle are responses to crises imposing hardship on workers and their families, the judicial system has been wielded against workers with the aim of quelling upheaval and re-establishing profitable labor relations. Sometimes this is direct, as in imposing labor laws; sometimes it's indirect, as in sanctioning the takeover of businesses with insufficient control over their workers to ride out a crisis by those with greater control.

4 Strategic Ideas

Formulated within the context of antagonistic class struggle, capitalists and their strategists have fostered the development of exploitation within concrete historical moments, changing and adapting strategies in response to workers' successes in countering those efforts and imposing their own needs on the system. Nowhere has this been clearer than in the realm of economics. From before Marx and Engels' lifetimes to the present, economists have peddled their ideas to ruling elites primarily in the form of policy advice. Mercantilists, often merchant capitalists themselves, provided advice to kings who wanted gold, as to how best to manipulate trade to achieve that goal. Where agriculture still dominated the economy, the physiocrats also advised kings – as to the best methods of extracting wealth from that sector.

As industrial capitalism herded workers from fields and villages into factories and subordinated the role of commerce and agriculture, political economists like Adam Smith and David Ricardo appropriated some elements of the strategic reasoning of their forerunners but resituated them within a wider understanding. The political economists argued that while still essential, *trade*, which the mercantilists held up as the main source of wealth, existed only because *labor* had produced the goods being traded. While recognizing the agricultural labor that Quesnay thought to be the source of all wealth, they insisted it was rapidly being surpassed in importance by the ever more sophisticated division of labor in manufactories. All labor that produced commodities upon whose sale a profit could be realized, they argued, produced value and the surplus value necessary for the expansion of the system. So, for policy makers, be they kings or parliaments, who wanted to favor employment and the production of wealth, the political economists' "labor theory of value" provided a basis for their recommendations of investment and trade policies that favored the development of industrial capitalism.

5 Apologetic Ideas

Ideology, in the form of apologetic rationalization, has long played a key role in justifying laws to those being exploited, to those benefiting from that exploitation and to those enforcing the laws. The point of ideological justification, of course, has never been a purely intellectual endeavor, but has been aimed at achieving compliance with laws at the lowest cost possible, e.g., with minimal use of force. If you can persuade people that laws are just, they are more likely to obey them. While lawyers and university students may study Locke's *Treatises*, Hegel's *Philosophy of Right* or Adam Smith's *Lectures on Jurisprudence*, ideological acceptance/respect for law (including the fear of the consequences of violating it) has mainly been promulgated through capitalist influence on academia and popular culture. In one of Marx and Engels' most cited passages they characterize such apologists as a faction of the capitalist ruling class.

> The ideas of the ruling class are in every epoch the ruling ideas, i.e., the class which is the ruling *material* force of society is at the same time its ruling *intellectual* force. The class which has the means of material production at its disposal, consequently also controls the means of mental production, so that the ideas of those who lack the means of mental production are on the whole subject to it ... The division of labour ... manifests itself also in the ruling class as the division of mental and material labour, so that inside this class one part appears as the thinkers of the class (its active, conceptive ideologists, who make the formation of the illusions of the class about itself their chief source of livelihood) ...[33]

33 "The German Ideology", *MECW*, *Vol. 5*, pp. 59–60.

If we understand one's "class" within capitalism to be determined by the degree to which one's actions function to preserve or attack the system, then it is quite immaterial from which income or wealth strata those "conceptive ideologists" have come. They may, in general, have come from those strata able to afford a lot of education and the leisure to write.[34] But they may also come from working-class families with little access to such amenities.[35]

As indicated, my greatest familiarity is with the work of political economists and how they have crafted their ideas not only to figure out strategies to facilitate wealth accumulation but also to justify the policies they have recommended. As capitalist development increasingly found itself confronted by the autonomous self-organization of workers, the history of economic thought provides ample evidence of how political economists modified their theory to cope.

To take an early example, John Locke's 1690 justification for "property," namely that people deserved to "own" what they have produced with their own hands, while suitable for artisans and independent farmers, clearly was inadequate for an industrial capitalism in which what workers produced wound up being owned by their employers.[36] So apologists came up with new

34 Given how capitalism embraced, maintained, and promulgated both patriarchy and racism, those with the most access to education and the leisure to write have been white men. Men's monopoly of that access was pointed out by Jane Austen (1775–1817) in her novel *Persuasion* (1818) through the voice of Anne Elliot in a debate with Captain Harville (Chapter 23). Later, Virginia Woolf (1882–1941) in *A Room of Her Own* (1929) makes the same point, adding that education and leisure must be accompanied by the physical setting necessary for creative thought. After uprisings led by literate slaves, such as Cato's Rebellion (1739) in South Carolina or the Rebellion of Nat Turner (1831) in Virginia, most slave owners forbad teaching their black slaves to read and write. In the wake of such uprisings, laws were passed forbidding the teaching of slaves. After slavery, Jim Crow laws dictating segregation, including in schools, guaranteed that most black children would receive less training in reading and writing than their white counterparts. The horrors experienced by Native American children forced into boarding schools and deprived of their own languages and culture were even worse! See, David Adams, *Education for Extinction: American Indians and the Boarding School Experience, 1875–1928* (Lawrence: University of Kansas Press, 1995, 2020).

35 A modern example of the latter case is Eric Hoffer (1898–1983). Although from a working-class background, his writings were so beloved by President Ronald Reagan – infamous for his anti-working-class policies like union-busting and the imposition of unemployment so high as to force down nominal wages for the first time in decades – that he awarded Hoffer the Presidential Medal of Freedom.

36 See, Chapter v "Of Property" in Locke's *Second Treatise on Government*, "The 'labour' of his body and the 'work' of his hands, we may say, are properly his. Whatsoever, then, he

justifications for the capitalist appropriation of products produced by workers' hands. One such has clearly been legalistic, namely that if employers own the raw materials being transformed in production, own the tools and machines used in production *and* own the labor purchased from workers, then as owners of every element that goes into the product, they own the product itself; it is their property, not that of those who produce it.

But, as workers grasped the classical political economic theory that all value stemmed from labor, they began to argue that regardless of the laws – obviously crafted by capitalists and their representatives – the fruits of labor should belong not to capitalists but to those who labor, themselves. Basing themselves on the political economists' own reasoning, they challenged both capitalist property ownership and the laws that legalized it. In so doing, they undermined the usefulness of that theory for gaining acceptance of capitalist ownership. As a result, economists abandoned the labor theory of value and replaced it – via the "marginalist revolution" – by rebasing their theory of value from labor to "utility," thus undercutting workers' arguments while providing a new rationale and new, more precise tools for managing both production (of *C′*) and markets (for *LP*, *MP* and *C′*).[37]

The creation of pro-capitalist, apologetic ideas, however, have never been a monopoly of economists, but were created and spread by many of those full and part-time journalists, novelists, poets and playwrights throughout the nineteenth century who took on the "great transformation" being engineered by the capitalist class.[38] In the words of Elaine Freedgood, the hope of such writers was to "quiet the growing unease of members of the middle and upper classes and the growing unrest of the laboring classes as they experienced the increasingly de-regulated and industrialized market economy."[39]

One such author was Harriet Martineau (1802–1872), daughter of a textile manufacturer, who wrote a great many short stories and books with the

---

removes out of the state that Nature hath provided and left it in, he hath mixed his labour with it, and joined to it something that is his own, and thereby makes it his property."

37 A similar fate would befall utility theory in the twentieth century as workers used the theory of "marginal utility" to argue for the redistribution of income from the rich to the poor. Economists, once again, modified their theory; this time by replacing "utility" by individual "preference." More puzzling has been the abandonment of Marx's labor theory of value by some Marxists. See, Part 1 of Cleaver, *Rupturing the Dialectic*, on both these abandonments.

38 I like Karl Polanyi's sweeping title even if in his account it is the "market" rather than capitalist subordination of life to work that subsumes and transforms society. See, *The Great Transformation* (New York: Farrar & Rinehart, 1944).

39 Elaine Freedgood, "Harriet Martineau and the Popularization of Political Economy," *Victorian Studies* 39, no. 1 (Autumn, 1995): 33.

self-conscious objective of teaching "the principles of political economy," i.e., the capitalist rules of the game, through fiction to gain their acceptance.[40] While her tales were dismissed by Marx as "nursery stories," her *Illustrations of Political Economy*, published in nine pocket-sized volumes in 1832–1834 were widely read.[41] So too were the novels of other contributors to the "industrial novels" of the period, such as Benjamin Disraeli (*Sybil, Or the Two Nations*, 1845), son of a literary critic and historian, or Elizabeth Gaskell (*Mary Barton*, 1848, *North and South*, 1854), daughter of a Unitarian minister, or George Eliot (*Felix Holt, the Radical*, 1866), daughter of an estate manager. Such "fiction" contributed to "the ideas of the ruling classes" becoming "the ruling ideas."[42]

Maintaining what Gramsci called the "hegemony" of such capitalist ideology, however, has often been sought not just with ideas – bought and paid for by the capitalist class – but through both laws and force when ideas fail. I sketched some of Marx and Engels' own experience with this use of force in Chapter 2. The response to their writings that challenged others' justifications of exploitation or argued for democracy against authoritarian rule included writing, or reinterpreting, laws to criminalize their activity, forcibly shutting down of their newspapers and journals, banning their books and the forcibly deporting them from country after country.

Force, Law and Ideology have long been primary weapons of class rule. Which weapon is wielded varies. Where capitalism has resorted to slavery – in both the past and the present – Force dominates because slaves resist, and few accept either laws that legalize it or ideas that justify it.[43] Ever since workers succeeded in getting laws passed criminalizing chattel slavery, Law and Ideology have been front line weapons in organizing and justifying capital's system of generalized economic coercion. But in the class war, Force is still mustered

40 Beyond the obvious, often didactic, content of her stories, she made her intentions clear in her autobiography. Maria Chapman, ed., *Harriet Martineau's Autobiography* (Boston: James R. Osgood & Co., 1877).

41 *Capital, Vol. 1*, p. 999, or MECW, *Vol. 35*, p. 406. As I suggested in *33 Lessons on* Capital (2019) 454–5, Marx's dismissal of Martineau "was unfortunate because despite her role as an apologist for capitalism, a great many of Martineau's writings called attention to and provided analyses of various aspects of the work of the unwaged. Indeed, in recent years she has been celebrated not only as the first woman sociologist but also as an early analyst of the domestic labor of reproduction." – an essential aspect of labor to which Marx gave short shrift.

42 See too, Patrick Brantlinger, "The Case Against Trade Unions in Early Victorian Fiction," *Victorian Studies*, Vol. 13, no. 1 (September 1969): 37–52. All this before the spread of public schooling and the systematic indoctrination of children from an early age into "the ruling ideas" – not just in literature but in every scholastic field.

43 Even less in the contemporary world where slavery is mostly illegal, yet still practiced.

in the rear, of course, and its legions are marched forth whenever Law and Ideology fail.

6 Structural Changes

Beyond resorting to force, crafting and enforcing laws and reshaping ideology to meet new challenges to its rule, capital and its functionaries have often found themselves having to figure out new structures of production, reproduction and trade in order to maintain or regain control.

Within production, faced with workers' success in gaining reductions in working hours – a crisis in capital's *absolute* surplus value strategy – they have restructured the mix of machines, workers and raw materials, i.e., the technical composition of capital, to raise productivity, increasing *relative* surplus value to make up for the fall in absolute surplus value. Such structural changes within factories have also required extensive changes within the whole "supply chain" that supplies the means of production and within hiring practices as new technologies have required new worker abilities.

An example in the sphere of reproduction, has been the "education" of workers. Faced with workers' growing success in extricating their children from fields, mines, mills and factories, capitalists adapted by developing public school systems to re-incarcerate and control the young. That control, of course, has included the inculcation of ideological illusions about the nature of capitalism and acceptance of its rules, with both aimed at instilling the obedience and discipline desired by future employers.[44]

In the realm of trade, of commerce, an example of "structural adjustment" were capitalists' efforts to offset concessions extracted by workers' struggles at home through increasing reliance on the imperialist annexation of cheap foreign labor through colonialism and the subsequent importation of the cheap raw materials produced by that labor.[45] The first of these required either the

44 Since the early twentieth century "progressive" period in the US, which saw the spread of public schooling, respect/acceptance of law and capitalism has been drummed into the heads of most children by the enforcement of rules (governing behavior, often dress and even hair styles), by a single high school "civics" course and by whatever cultural artifacts are served up in courses on history, or literature, etc.

45 The revealing term "structural adjustment" has been a late twentieth-century byword in the conditions imposed by the International Monetary Fund and the World Bank to overcome the resistance of workers in countries applying for financial support. See, H. Cleaver, "Close the IMF, Abolish Debt and End Development: a Class Analysis of the International Debt Crisis," op. cit., and Silvia Federici, George Caffentzis and Ousseina Alidon,

forceful enslavement of the local population or the creation of labor markets and compulsions (such as taxes) to force participation. The second inevitably required the expansion of fleets transporting such raw materials and sometimes the creation of entirely new routes for their transportation, e.g., canals, railroads. A prototypical example in the case of railroads were those built by the British in India as they began to turn that country into a source of raw materials, e.g., cotton, opium, tea, and an outlet for British manufactures, e.g., cloth.[46] Where the supply chains have proved fragile, e.g., piracy or attacks by bandits or enemy nations' militaries, armed force has been mobilized for protection (in private or through the government).[47]

7 Offsets in the First Stage of the Circuit: Investment

Let us begin with an examination of responses to difficulties surrounding the acquisition of enough money to finance investment, which I identified as a potential source of crisis in the effort to launch or renew a circuit of capital.

7.1 *Getting Enough Money*

Although the problem of coming up with enough money to profitably engage in trade has been faced by merchants for millennia – as well as by governments seeking to finance their various projects, from palaces to wars – Marx and Engels were focused on the specific problems facing *industrial* capitalists, with the problems of merchants and governments analyzed as subsumed to the dynamics of developing capitalism. They analyzed how capitalists tried to cope with this problem of insufficiently available money, both during the rise of industrial capitalism as it sought to impose its new organization of life and during the much fuller developments of their times.

During the rise, would-be industrialists included skilled crafters bent on expanding their operations beyond guild limits and merchants extending their operations from commerce into production. Crafters usually hired workers for wages (or acquired slaves), but merchants often tapped labor using other

eds., *A Thousand Flowers: Social Struggles Against Structural Adjustment in African Universities* (Asmara: Africa World Press, 2000).

46 See, Christian Wolmar, *Railways & the Raj: How the Age of Steam Transformed India*, (London: Atlantic Books, 2017) and John Hurd and Ian Kerr, *India's Railway History: A Research Handbook*, (Boston: Brill, 2012).

47 Most recently against the Houthi attacks on capitalist shipping in protest against Zionist genocide in Gaza and the complicity of Western governments. Before that along the coast of Somalia against the seizure of ships then held for ransom.

methods, e.g., the "putting out" system in which they would buy the means of production, e.g., wool or cotton, and then put them out to independent spinners or weavers for processing, on the understanding that they would then pay them by buying the produced thread or cloth. Both sorts of investors required money to initiate, renew or expand such efforts.[48]

Within fully developed capitalism, Marx's circuits of money capital always portray the source of money for investment as deriving from sales resulting from previous investment. In other words, M' from past sales provides the money M to finance the next round of production. Not included in the circuits, but analyzed elsewhere, are what capitalists do with profits, $M' - M$, realized in the previous period but not immediately invested in expanding operations. They are usually hoarded as either cash-on-hand or in the form of readily available, highly liquid financial assets. Both methods keep the money available as reserves, for emergencies (such as unexpected increases in the cost of *LP*, *MP*, or borrowing) or for combining with future profits to finance future expansions.[49]

But, because of the very real possibilities of, and predispositions to not generating enough money through sales or having saved enough to either renew or expand their operations, capitalists have had to develop alternative sources of money to offset shortages. Their primary outside sources have been governments, financial institutions, and individuals.

7.1.1 With the Help of Governments

With respect to governments, industrial capitalists learned from their merchant forerunners to appeal to governments' self-interest. Merchants had long solicited local (or national) governments for financial support for their ventures. Such support took two forms: those that put money directly into the hands of merchants (and later industrial capitalists) and those that subsidized their operations. One iconic example of the former, often taught to American school children, was the successful appeal of Christopher Columbus (1451–1506) to the Iberian monarchs – Ferdinand of Aragon and Isabella of Castile – for financial support in his project to discover a shorter, and more

48 Today the putting-out system has largely been replaced by contracts between producers who finance their own operations and other firms who buy from them. A common example are farmers contracted to supply local supermarkets.

49 Such reserves count as part of Keynes' "precautionary" demand for money, mentioned in Chapter 4, footnote 15. Marx and Engels noted such unanticipated increases in interest rates due to government or central bank action to stem gold outflows. Marx to Engels, February 3, 1851, *MECW*, *Vol. 38*, pp. 273–278 and Engels to Marx, February 25, 1851, *MECW*, *Vol. 38*, pp. 299–300.

profitable trade route to the spice markets of the East Indies than either the Silk Road across the Middle East and Central Asia or sailing around the Horn of Africa. Eventually, those monarchs signed a commercial agreement to help finance his venture, i.e., pay for equipping two ships and hiring their crews, and eventually sharing ten percent of any profits with him.[50]

As it turned out with Columbus and others, the exploration of trade routes often involved conquest and colonialism. Where these made possible the looting of existing wealth, especially gold and silver, stocks of the precious metals were extracted from the colonized by force, bolstering the stock of metal money. This was primarily possible for the Spanish and Portuguese colonialists in Latin America who, in violently conquering the indigenous, discovered already refined gold and silver (and the mines for producing more). While most of such loot went to sponsoring governments, it eventually became available to other investors as it was spent and circulated.[51]

Where colonial efforts discovered neither existing hoards of precious metals to steal, nor mines to exploit, as was the case for a long time in the colonies in North America,[52] two alternative strategies emerged to counter this dearth. In one, both colonists and their governments engaged in letters of marque and privateering, sanctioning the seizure of the Spanish or Portuguese treasure ships. These practices were sometimes celebrated – as in the famous case of the English privateer Francis Drake (1540–1596) – and sometimes, if it got out of hand, condemned as piracy.[53]

As an alternative to the seizure of existing mineral wealth, merchant capitalists pushed government policies encouraging *trade surpluses*, i.e., those

---

50 Edward Hale, *The Life of Christopher Columbus, from his own letters and journals and other documents of the time* (Chicago: Howe, 1891), Chapter 2.

51 For some cliometric assessments of how much these thefts increased the money supply of Spain, see, Yao Chen, et. al., "Reconstruction of the Spanish money supply, 1492–1810" *Explorations in Economic History* 81 (July 2021): 2-26. Naturally, the fleets also repatriated all kinds of other "exotic" goods from the colonies, a practice which established the pattern of trans-Atlantic trade characteristic of the centuries of colonialism.

52 For a long time, but not forever, because as the colonial frontier in North America was pushed West, at the expense of the indigenous populations, new sources of precious metals were discovered. For example, the increase in money supplies resulting from the "gold rush" in California was duly noted by Marx, along with the incentives it gave to trade and investment. Karl Marx and Friedrich Engels. "Review: May to Oct. 1850," November 1, 1850, *MECW*, *Vol. 10*, pp. 504–505.

53 See, Kris Lane and Robert Levine, *Pillaging the Empire: Piracy in the Americas, 1500–1750* (Armonk, NY: M. E. Sharpe, 1998) and its sources. Drake and similar privateers have been repeatedly celebrated in novels, film and TV, e.g., Rafael Sabatini's novel *The Sea Hawk* (1915), the 1924 film of the same name, Errol Flynn in a second *The Sea Hawk* (1940) and the TV series *Sir Francis Drake* (1961–62).

favoring exports over imports. The sales pitch was the following: when exports pull in more gold and silver than is spent on imports, governments could tap the excess metal money through taxes. Such were the arguments of both the early "bullionists" and later, the more sophisticated mercantilists who understood that the path to more exports required more production at home, which required, in turn, money for investment and more imposed work in domestic production.[54] In this, they effectively supported the rise of industrial capitalism, whose spokespersons – the political economists – were shifting the emphasis on wealth generation from trade to the exploitation of labor in production.

Support for such trade policies inevitably involved government spending for the military colonization of foreign lands, for defending expanding trade on the open seas or on land, and for whatever infrastructure was needed by increased trade – all of which subsidized capitalist operations. Buying guns and ships obviously put money into the industries building them. Paying the costs of mobilizing and maintaining military forces put more money into circulation. Besides spending on military training facilities and fortifications, increased trade and colonialism also required new or improved social infrastructure, such as roads, canals, railroads, ports, etc., both for governments to rule and for business to thrive.[55] With the development of industry, government investment in social infrastructure came to include the kind of

54 See, the critique of the bullionists by Thomas Mun (1571–1641) in his "Englands Treasure by Forraign Trade, Or The Balance of our Forraign Trade is the Rule of our Treasure" (1664) in Thomas Mun, *The Complete Works: Economics and Trade* (Newton Page, 2013) and Adam Smith's assessment of his mercantilist predecessors in *The Wealth of Nations*, Book IV, Chapters I–VIII.

55 While cutting business transportation costs, government/taxpayer-financed road construction also makes it possible for police and military to move quickly to put down unrest or rebellion – as they did in the US during the urban uprisings of the mid-1960s. That was facilitated by the earlier development of the Interstate Highway System in the US, pushed by President Dwight Eisenhower. In urban areas, those highways were often driven through "slum" areas, disrupting or destroying working class communities. In the Global South in the 1960s, roads pushed into remote areas were justified as promoting farm-to-market commerce, but they were actually part of counterinsurgency efforts to put down peasant unrest and revolt. Such methods have continued right up to the present, e.g., the Mexican government began building new roads in direct response to the Zapatista uprising in 1994 to facilitate the military repression of their more remote communities. The current "Tren Maya" megaproject is a continuation of the practice. Peddled as an effort to bring more tourism to southern Mexico, regardless of the ecological cost, it is also clearly aimed at disrupting autonomous indigenous communities. See, Gerard Soler, "Tren Maya, the Mexican megaproject threatening the ecosystems of the Yucatan Peninsula," *Equal Times*, March 18, 2022.

subsidies to the development of science and technology familiar today, in the agricultural, medical, energy and military industries. For example, in the US, the Morrill Acts of 1862 and 1890 granted federal lands to fund the creation of universities "to teach such branches of learning as are related to agriculture and the mechanic arts ... to promote the liberal and practical education of the industrial classes."[56] Through teaching, research, and outreach, these "land-grant" institutions reduced costs to business of both training labor-power and acquiring technological knowledge in agribusiness and manufacturing.[57]

Among other policies indirectly increasing the monies available for business investment, we can include efforts to expand the supply of coin in circulation through the hiring of alchemists to conjure up precious from base metal (not successful),[58] the debasement – by mixing in non-precious metals – of government-issued metal monies (frequent),[59] and eventually central bank efforts to reduce interest rates and reserve requirements during periods of commercial and industrial crisis – both of which free up money for loans.[60] Although the first two were soon abandoned, the third and fourth of these methods became frequent practices as governments subsidized their suppliers and repeatedly bailed out capitalists during periods of crisis, when their own efforts to generate profits came up short.

7.1.2 *With the Help of Financial Institutions*

Supposedly originating as merely guarded storage facilities for valuables, banks developed into what economists call "financial intermediaries", taking

---

56 (July 2, 1862, ch. 130, § 4, 12 Stat. 504)

57 Struggles over the legitimate purposes and curriculum of the resulting institutions are detailed in Nathan Sorber, *Land-Grant Colleges and Popular Revolt: The Origins of the Morrill Act and the Reform of Higher Education* (Cornell: Cornell University Press, 2018).

58 See, "Chapter 2: The Alchemical Foundations of Credit" in Carl Wennerlind, *Casualties of Credit: The English Financial Revolution, 1620–1720* (Cambridge, MA: Harvard University Press, 2011).

59 Marx writes of debasement in *Capital, Vol. 1*, p. 194, or *MECW*, *Vol. 35*, p. 109. In Section I of Chapter 10 of that volume, he also refers in a footnote, to "the little shilling men," who he had previously identified in his *Contribution to the Critique of Political Economy* as those who advocated repayment of debt in debased shillings as a solution to currency problems. *Capital, Vol. 1*, p. 342, or *MECW*, *Vol. 35*, p. 241, Note 175, p. 778.

60 Until recently, we have been much more familiar with the opposite policies, i.e., tight money, high interest rates and augmented reserve requirements, all ostensibly designed to "fight inflation" but actually aimed at reducing investment, raising unemployment and putting downward pressure on wages and benefits. These policies have been all too familiar since the Carter-Volcker-Reagan attack on the world's working classes in the early 1980s via "supply-side economics", a global depression and an international monetary crisis.

in money (deposits) and loaning it out, in other words channeling money from those with money to spare to those wanting to borrow, while profiting from differences in the interest rates paid for deposits and those charged on loans. Although like money lenders, banks could loan to individuals, it was their loans to governments and to merchants that set the stage for loaning to industrial capitalists.

Banks first grew fat loaning money to governments for desired purchases beyond those which could be paid for out of tax revenues. In Chapter 31 of Volume 1 of *Capital*, Marx pointed to such "deficit financing" as key to capitalists amassing enough money to invest. Banks profit from governments repaying loans with money extracted through taxes.[61] In that chapter, he only points out how this source of money *can* finance industrial investment, but he ignores the history of the changing practices of bankers, who gradually made more and more loans to industrial capitalists. Elsewhere, however, he did trace such changes, especially in the case of the Crédit Mobilier, an early French bank that made itself famous by claiming to be at the forefront of such change, and reported on its evolution in his journalism.

In three articles, published in 1856, Marx describes the Crédit Mobilier's speculative manipulations. He details the various enterprises in which the Crédit Mobilier holds an interest as well as the high rate of profit being reported on these investments. The Crédit Mobilier, he claims, buys up shares in an enterprise, hypes them, and because it has done this, others buy, their prices rise, at which point it sells them off for a nice profit. In short, it engaged in manipulative "stockjobbing."[62] It was not alone.

The availability of loans from banks (or subsidies from governments) may depend on the degree to which the causes of the reduced profits that provoked the effort to get help are seen by potential sources as being countered. Banks and governments rarely act blindly but generally take into account the reasons why would-be supplicants are having problems coming up with enough money.[63] If, for example, the source is workers' struggles and banks

61 See, *Capital*, *Vol. 1*, Chapter 31, or *MECW*, *Vol. 35*, Chapter XXXI.

62 See his articles for the *New York Daily Tribune*, written in June 1856: Karl Marx, "The French Crédit Mobilier," *MECW*, *Vol. 15*, pp. 8–13, 14–18, 19–24.

63 Banks usually have specialists devoted to "risk assessment" who evaluate the situation of potential borrowers and provide their findings to those making the final decision as to whether to grant loans. There have, however, been times when such findings have been ignored, to the subsequent chagrin of bank administrators. Such apparently happened during the run up to the international financial crisis of the 1980s and 1990s when negative risk assessments were ignored, loans were made, and the banks found their borrowers threatening default – deepening the spreading debt crisis. One result involved

have leverage, they may demand repression of those struggles as a condition of loans. Marx and Engels observed just such pressure in the case of the Commune of Paris (see Chapter 2, Section 3.3).[64] From governments, the same may be true and, as in the case of the Commune, they may provide the military force necessary for suppression. If the business needing help is a state enterprise, its managers may be able to call on the police forces of the state even more easily than those in the "private sector."[65]

7.1.3 With the Help of Individuals

For a long time, there were only two ways for capitalists to tap the money of individuals. One mediated way was borrowing from banks, as mentioned above, whose funds were based on deposits by individuals. The other was personal gifts or loans, of cash or property or facilities, more common in early capitalism when most businesses were owned and run by individuals. But the rise of the joint-stock company made it possible for businesses to issue shares of proposed or ongoing business ventures in a completely impersonal manner. When needed and feasible, businesses can craft initial public offerings (IPOs) of stocks or bonds to raise money for investment, or they can sell holdings of such securities already in existence to individual "investors."[66] At the same time, with buyers having little direct knowledge of the viability of the enterprise issuing stocks or bonds, and with institutions such as the Crédit

---

private financial institutions turning to international supranational institutions, such as the International Monetary Fund and the World Banks for both assessment of risks and the specification of the conditions which would have to be met by borrowers for roll-over loans to be granted.

64 This has also been true for bank loans to both local and national governments, as demonstrated in the mid-1970s in New York City when banks would only roll over its loans if the city cut city-worker wages and benefits, in the 1980s-90s when the IMF demanded cutbacks in imports of consumption goods as one condition for granting "structural adjustment" loans, or in 1994 when Chase Manhattan Bank called on the government of Mexico to "eliminate" the Zapatistas whose uprising had contributed to stock market jitters and the associated Peso Crisis.

65 Indeed, as we have seen in the case of the USSR and similar regimes, police-state power has been wielded regularly to limit workers' overt struggles. The primary result, however, was to force resistance underground where it became covert but still disruptive – an important source of the notoriously low productivity in Soviet industry.

66 "Investors" is in quotation marks because most individuals buying stocks or bonds gain no control over businesses' whose shares or bonds they are buying. For buyers, purchasing stocks and bonds is usually either a form of savings or a means of speculation (betting on a rise in the value of the asset). Even if a purchaser buys a sufficient majority to give them control over the issuing business, the purchases are separate from decisions about running the company. Thus, economists call the investment Marx analyzes, $M - C(LP, MP)$, *real* investment to differentiate it from the money spent by purchasers of financial assets.

Mobilier hyping the value of some assets, huge amounts of ready money have been channeled into pure speculation, merely buying and selling financial assets, rather than being made available for real business investment of the sort represented by Marx's circuits of capital. When such speculation became manic, as it often did in the nineteenth century, and then collapsed, both the individuals who speculated and the businesses issuing the assets could go bankrupt.[67]

7.2 *Fixing the Supply of Labor-Power*

Given the widespread and varied resistance of people to having their lives subsumed by imposed work, capitalists have used every means at their disposal – ranging from the brutally repressive to the seductive – to obtain and maintain an exploitable labor force in the face of all kinds of problems interfering with their smooth management of the supply and demand for labor, and hence its costs and profitability. In Chapter 4, Section 3, I noted how those problems included the unwillingness of many to enter the labor market, workers fleeing oppressive labor markets, and reductions in the size of the labor force making labor too expensive due to such causes as disease, starvation, military drains and reductions in birth rates and the size of families. In Chapter 5, Section 1.2, I sketched some of the reasons why the labor market is predisposed to such problems. So, how do capitalists try to offset these difficulties?

7.2.1 Countering Avoidance of the Labor Market

In Chapter 4, Sections 3.2.2.1 and Chapter 5, Section 1.2.1, I discussed avoidance of the labor market in terms of the periods of people's lives: among children and youths, among mature adults and among adults nearing the end of their lives. Given the propensity of so many people, at different stages of life, to avoid the labor market, capitalists have deployed measure after measure to herd people into that market.

In the early centuries when capitalists began to impose their new organization of society on the world, the young, adults and aged were all treated with the same brutal methods Marx sketches in his chapters on "primitive accumulation" in Volume 1 of *Capital*. In Chapters 27 and 28 of *Capital* he describes the primary method by which capitalism imposed itself: violent force, enslaving some and expropriating the land and tools of others. Because even expropriated

67 See the classic early account by Charles Mackay, *Extraordinary Popular Delusions and the Madness of Crowds* (London: Bentley, 1841) and Robert Aliber and Charles Kindleberger, *Manias, Panics, and Crashes: A History of Financial Crises*, 7th ed., (New York: Palgrave Macmillan, 2015).

people – deprived of all material resources – resisted, capitalists followed up, he shows, with quite "bloody" measures against the unwaged. Although in *Capital* there's no parallel discussion of the violence used in acquiring, transporting and employing slaves, to his list of brutal punishments inflicted on those trying to avoid wage-slavery, we can add the even more vicious measures deployed against fugitive slaves, from slave patrols hunting runaways to efforts to seek out and eradicate maroon colonies. Although such methods as chattel slavery, branding, cutting off ears and public whipping have largely come to be replaced by jail sentences and forced labor, the repression of those in the streets has continued to be deployed against the dispossessed.[68]

Many of the expropriated were simply expelled from the countryside, reducing the rural population. Some took jobs with the emerging class of agrarian capitalists whose rise Marx analyzes in Chapter 29. In Britain, those capitalists did their best to transform a countryside hitherto characterized by landed gentry, rent-paying tenants, yeoman farmers, and commons (fields and forests accessible to all), into an agricultural industry employing waged farm workers. These expropriations and the structural transformation did not happen all at once but proceeded piece-meal (making collective resistance difficult) and continued, Marx argues, right through the nineteenth century.

As the transformation neared completion in Britain, capitalists exported their violence to colonial areas seizing ever more lands of local populations. Keeping in mind that before capitalism all peoples lived within some different kind of culture, a few with similarities (guilds paying wages to apprentices and journeymen), some radically different (in foreign colonies and among indigenous peoples on the "frontiers" of capitalist expansion), one part of transforming the world into the new capitalist order was wiping out and replacing cultures in any way inimical to the reproduction of capitalist social relationships, especially acceptance of the labor market and living by working for a wage or salary.

While these new relationships have been forced onto many adults in colonies, there have also been attempts to condition children into accepting the new order. The brainwashing of children into cultural assimilation began early with Christian missionaries, the main shock troops of cultural genocide. An early taste of this came with the rolls played by Catholic priests in Latin America. Along with their systematic theft or destruction of local cultural artifacts, e.g., pre-Columbian literature, they participated with their secular

68 Exceptions include countries like Saudia Arabia, Indonesia, Iran and Singapore where public flogging continues. Violence also continues within some schools and families where adults administer corporal punishment to children.

counterparts in the enslavement of the indigenous. They put the natives to work for them, building and sustaining various missions, while also undertaking their cultural conversion both through the work of converting to Christianity and through teaching the invaders' language and cultural values.[69] But the Catholics were not alone; throughout North America all kinds of religious sects, including Methodists, Baptists and even Mennonites, joined the crusade to transform Native Americans into pliable workers who accepted capitalist ways of organizing life around work, including the labor market.

While the systematic expropriation of Native American lands and their ultimate internment on "reservations" made their previous ways of life materially impossible, the theft of land was accompanied by the theft of children. In well-thought out efforts to wipe out their entire cultural heritage, children were forcibly stolen and incarcerated in boarding schools. There, they were forbidden to speak their own languages, to wear traditional clothes or to practice the spiritual rituals of their tribe. They were forced to cut their hair, speak the language of their jailors, dress in uniforms and learn elements of their alien culture – including the "naturalness" of the labor market.[70] All this was imposed by violence but sustained by more sophisticated methods, which were formalized by the use of laws, from treaties (soon betrayed) to those of private property – to put the stamp of legality on new structures.[71]

---

69 This cultural genocide through the imposition of language began in Spain with the imposition of Castilian Spanish in places where it was not spoken, e.g., Catalonia, Galicia, Basque, to help consolidate Castilian rule on the peninsula. See Ivan Illich's account of Elio Antonio de Nebrija, with his Castilian grammar in hand, arguing to the Queen, "Language has always been the consort of empire, and forever shall remain its mate. Together they come into being, together they grow and flower, and together they decline." *Shadow Work* (London: Marion Boyars, 1981) Chapter II: Vernacular Values.

70 David Adams, *Education for Extinction: American Indians and the Boarding School Experience, 1875–1928*. 2nd edition (Lawrence, KS: University Press of Kansas, 1995, 2020). The myth of assimilation hid its impossibility within a thoroughly racist culture that had enslaved both Native Americans and Africans and would continue to discriminate against both even after the end of slavery. NB: the Russians are currently following this pattern by abducting Ukrainian children, presumably to brainwash them into accepting a conquered Ukraine as an inevitable, integral part of Russia. This repeats the practice in the USSR of imposing Russian as a common language on all nationalities.

71 This process of enclosure continued to be deployed, throughout the colonial era and ever since to strip millions of peasants of their access to land and to frustrate most efforts to take it back. However, so too has resistance and repeated efforts to repeal enclosure through seizure, like the Diggers, or through formal legal land reform. Because of the role of peasants in anti-colonial struggles, new governments of national liberation have often been under great pressure to seize large estates and redistribute the land to peasants. In Mexico, repeated peasant uprisings, including their role in the Revolution of 1910–1920,

In other colonial areas, instead of trying to entirely wipe out indigenous cultures the invaders took what land they could use – for plantations, mines, etc. – and imposed new legal structures, usually reproducing the property laws of their home countries, but otherwise leaving much of local culture and languages intact. This facilitated pitting different cultural and linguistic groups against each other while extracting labor-power from all, a divide and conquer tactic widely used in European colonies.[72]

To justify all these efforts to transform the world, capitalists and their apologists have kept up the association of "freedom" with the "free markets" of capitalism, including the labor market. Doing so has required the development and promulgation of ideas, of ideologies, *legitimizing* the labor market as the most natural and only moral way of surviving in capitalist society. After all, if you can convince people that entering the labor market is normal and expected of everyone, you can avoid the more expensive use of force. Central to this effort have been the ideas of economists – from the mercantilists through the classical political economists of the eighteenth and nineteenth centuries to the neoclassical economists of the late nineteenth (and twentieth) century who followed them.[73] They have all denounced the preference for self-determined activity, instead of working and being exploited by some employer, as time "mis-spent" in "Idleness and Pleasure" or as "sloth" and mostly presented the labor market as an encounter of equals, in which capitalist buyers and worker sellers are free to negotiate terms.[74] With no coercion involved, people should enter the labor market willingly and negotiate their wages just like the price of any other good.

Marx, of course, excoriates this representation of the labor market as apologetic myth, as hiding its real nature, the history of its imposition, and the coercive factors which have given capitalists more power than workers in that

forced a series of partial reforms but culminated in President Lázaro Cárdenas redistributing some forty-five million acres of land. In other places, such as India, Egypt and the Philippines, such reform was only partial and quickly abandoned. These struggles continue in many places today.

72 This strategy was carried over by post-independence elites in places such as India. They have maintained patchworks of varied cultures, often playing one against others, as in the case of the current Modi government's promulgation of Hindu-nationalism against the many other cultures in India.

73 And the neoliberal economists of the late twentieth and twenty-first centuries.

74 For Thomas Mun 's denunciation of "Idleness and Pleasure" see his *Englands Treasure by Forraign Trade* (1664), op. cit. For Adam Smith's view of every "country workman" as "almost always slothful and lazy" see his *Wealth of Nations* (1776), op. cit., Book 1, Chapter 1.

pretended free exchange.[75] This ideological cloaking of reality, he points out, begins with the presentation of the labor market as one in which – as its name suggests – what is being bought and sold is *labor*. The money expended on wages and salaries, *M – LP*, economists have argued, buys *labor*, one factor of production alongside others, such as tools, machines or land, *MP*. Against this representation, Marx argues, in Chapter 6 of Volume I of *Capital* and then later in Chapter 19 on "wages," that this portrayal falsely misrepresents and hides what is actually bought and sold. As I explained in Chapter 3 on accumulation, he maintains that what capitalists buy is not labor, which only comes into existence when workers exercise their skills; instead, employers buy *labor-power*, i.e., the ability and willingness to work. So, *M – LP* and *LP – M* do not constitute the "labor market" but rather the "market for labor-power."

Moreover, the pretense of paying for *labor* performed, hides the extraction of surplus labor, i.e., exploitation, beyond what must be paid workers to reproduce their labor-power.[76] Marx points out how recognizing this distinction between labor and labor-power reveals that the labor market is a portal to exploitation, alienation and the wastage of lives – a passage to be abolished along with the whole wage-system.

A corollary of the myth of free labor markets, also aimed at overcoming reluctance to enter them, has been the pretense that they have always provided a path to upward mobility, to the bettering of one's life. Central to this pretense has been the myth of capitalist origins.

> Long, long ago there were two sorts of people; one, the diligent, intelligent and above all frugal elite; the other lazy rascals, spending their substance, and more, in riotous living ... Thus it came to pass that the former sort accumulated wealth, and the latter sort finally had nothing to sell except their own skins.[77]

---

75 In his *Wealth of Nations*, Adam Smith did recognize that because they are better organized, capitalists can exercise somewhat greater power in labor markets. As a result, he accepted workers self-organizing to counter that power. Eventually, neoclassical economists would treat such labor markets as "imperfect", in contrast to mythical "perfectly competitive" labor markets, with many buyers and many sellers.

76 The only *exploitation* recognized in neoclassical microeconomic theory is a wage smaller than the monetary value of a workers' marginal product. However, in so-called "growth theory" – which partly emerged out of industrialization efforts in the USSR – the production of a *surplus* as the only means to expand investment and accumulation is explicitly recognized and valorized. See, Evsey Domar, *Essays in the Theory of Economic Growth* (New York: Oxford University Press, 1957).

77 *Capital, Vol. 1*, p. 873, or *MECW, Vol. 35*, p. 704.

The moral of the story is that anyone who works hard (is diligent), saves their money (is frugal) and invests, can move up the wage/salary hierarchy, even become a capitalist. Those who do not do these things, have only themselves to blame for their poverty. So, in providing jobs (the demand side of labor markets) capitalists are supposedly offering a gift to people – the opportunity to improve their lives.[78] This myth of upward mobility – which parallels the myth of assimilation force fed to Native American children – has been propagated in literature by pro-capitalist writers as well as by economists. In the wake of the tales of Harriet Martineau, mentioned above, came those of Horatio Alger (1832–1899) about poor boys rising out of poverty through hard work and saving their wages.[79]

This myth, however, like others central to pro-capitalist apologetics, has long been contested, not only by Marx and other anti-capitalist revolutionaries but also by social reformers seeking to make capitalism less brutal. One such was Charles Dickens (1812–1870), whose novels often mocked the mythical character of this pretense of upward mobility. A good example can be found in his *Hard Times* (1854) where the claims of the central capitalist – Josiah Bounderby – to have risen from an impoverished working-class background to mill owner through hard work and self-sacrifice are eventually revealed to be false.[80]

---

78 Among the many places where this is spelled out clearly is Irving Kristol's *Two Cheers for Capitalism* (New York: Basic Books, 1978). The same argument has also been used to justify *racial* disparities in "upward mobility," namely that poor Blacks and other impoverished minorities have failed to mimic the behaviors of more successful whites and have only their own choices to blame for their poverty. See, Dinesh De Souza's *The End of Racism* (1995) and other writings.

79 The same myth has been repeatedly perpetuated in contemporary popular culture, e.g., films such as *The Secret of My Success* (1987) and *Working Girl* (1988) about individuals who work hard and scheme their way up the hierarchy. The myth lies in the pretense that what a few can accomplish is possible for all.

80 Universally, in the public schools of the twentieth century and today, from kindergarten through elementary to high school, children (and their parents) have been told, semester after semester, that if only they work hard, they will gain access to higher education and better jobs. Of course, in schools as in waged and salaried employment this promise has been a myth because it is only true for a tiny minority. No matter how hard they work the vast majority are tracked into labor markets for jobs devoid of the possibility of advancement. Indeed, as capitalists have replaced one "job ladder" after another with temporary and precarious jobs, what little mobility used to be available has been fast disappearing. With only footstools in sight, the job ladder myth has been partially replaced by that of entrepreneurship and quick advancement through creative "startups" to riches and wealth. Of course, most startups, like most small businesses before them, soon go belly up, dumping their owners back into waged employment.

While all these myths have been perpetrated against adults as well as children in schools, what is sometimes called "manpower planning" by capitalists – the conscious manipulation of labor markets to provide employers with the labor-power they require – has encompassed many policies designed to directly counter the efforts by some workers to avoid the labor market. Besides making avoidance as unpleasant and difficult as possible, those policies have included pretty much all efforts to expand the pool of available labor in order to pit the less reluctant against the more reluctant. For that, we find the attacks on women's efforts to limit childbearing, discussed in Section 7.2.3.3 below, and support for immigration policies to facilitate an influx of new workers – often from colonies (like Ireland).[81] Such immigrant workers are generally looking for work and can be easily pitted against locals, not just as scabs during strikes but by being brought in for less desirable jobs and at lower wages, they add a useful division in the hierarchy of waged and salaried workers. They are generally easier to lay off when either demand and the need for workers drops or they collaborate with locals and become troublesome. This is true not only for the individual firm but also for capital in general through national policies. Thus, the frequent replacement of pro-immigration policies with more restrictive ones and even mass deportations.[82]

At the same time, as we saw in the discussion of industrial espionage in Chapters 4 and 5, for skilled workers possessing specialized and desired knowledge, capitalists have not merely opened the door to immigrants but deployed more positive, even seductive measures to woe such workers. Besides offering higher wages than those available in immigrants' countries of origin – albeit often low from locals' point of view – some capitalists' recruitment methods have played up the attractions of the jobs they offer, both nature of the work

81 Or, since liberation from colonialism, from ex- or neo-colonies. Thus, the post-WWII influx of workers to Great Britain from both the West Indies and South Asia. Thus, a parallel influx to France from North Africa. In both cases, immigrant workers have been pitted against locals and the enmity of locals encouraged by flagrant racism and xenophobia.

82 Analyses which emphasize how immigration policies have been changed, positive to negative and back again, according to the needs of capitalist employers are provided by Rodolfo Acuña, *Occupied America: A History of Chicanos*, New York: Harper & Row, 1981 and Manuel Castells, "Immigrant Workers and Class Struggles in Advanced Capitalism: The Western European Experience," *Politics and Society*, Vol. 5, no. 1 (March 1975): 33-66. Those which emphasize how the struggles of immigrant workers provoke the shift from positive to negative include Mariarosa Dalla Costa, "Riproduzione e emigrazione" in A. Serafini, et al., *"L'Operaio multinazionale in Europa*, 1974 (in English) and Yann Moulier and Pierre Ewenzyck, ""Immigration: le blocage de la mobilité autour du bassin méditerranéen,"", *Critique de l'Economie Politique*, Nouvelle Serie, no. 3 (Septembre 1978) (in English).

for which they are trying to hire and the quality of communities where the jobs are located.[83]

As for those still avoiding the labor market by clinging to land, capitalists continued to support any and all measures designed to favor the development of agrarian capitalism rather than small family farms or peasant communities with collectively owned land. The processes Marx describes in Chapter 30 of *Capital*, on the rise of agrarian capitalism, continued to haunt the countryside, forced to follow basically the same path as manufacturing industry, i.e., ever greater concentration of the control of required resources, in this case land. Concentration was hastened by the spread of banking to rural areas, not to provide aid to small farmers but rather to finance the investments of emerging agribusiness (big, more credit-worthy farmers). And when they did make loans to small farmers, with the latter's only collateral being land, such loans took the form of mortgages. As a result, recurrent bad times provided the banks with opportunities to take over the lands of small farmers and resell them to more profitable and creditworthy agrarian capitalists, further expelling the rural population from the land and bolstering the "manpower" available to labor markets.

Given the importance of agricultural production, both to feed workers being herded into urban labor markets and for many countries a major source of gold from exports and thus – through taxation – of revenue to governments, the latter increasingly began to encourage and subsidize agrarian capitalism at the expense of small farmers and the indigenous.[84] One early form of subsidy in the US was the formation of the Land Grant universities following the Morrill Act of 1862, mentioned in Section 7.1.1. Those universities were financed by and sometimes located on the roughly 11 million acres of land stolen from some 250 Native American tribes.[85] These institutions developed research capabilities aimed at hastening the technological development of agriculture. As might

83 Today, such methods are common, as witnessed by high tech corporations creating landscaped "factories", designed to be attractive places to work, often surrounded by grass, trees, bushes and flowers – a far cry from the dank, polluted, satanic mills of the nineteenth century.

84 On the importance of agricultural exports to the US government and the impact of that importance on US imperialism, see William Appleman Williams, *The Tragedy of American Diplomacy*, (Cleveland: World Publishing Company, 1969). For how that has evolved in more recent times, see, NACLA, "U.S. Grain Arsenal," *Latin America and Empire Report*, October 1975.

85 See, Robert Lee and Tristan Ahtone, "Land-grab universities: Expropriated Indigenous land is the foundation of the land-grant university system" High Country News, March 30, 2020. (Accessed 7/15/2024.)

have been expected, the benefits of both teaching and research were mainly directed at agribusiness rather than family farms.[86] By so doing they hastened the faster development of the former and decline of the latter. In the process, they contributed in the countryside to the same dynamic of labor-displacing technological development Marx analyzed within manufacturing factories, adding to the refilling of the "reserve army" of unwaged workers competing in the labor market. In the process, the resulting rural-urban migration steadily reduced access to land as a means to avoid the labor market and the migrants became available as substitutes for recalcitrant city-dwellers.

Against the almost universal desire of worn-out workers to escape both work and the labor market as they have neared the end of their lives, capitalists' primary countermeasures have been two: one intentional, one a byproduct. The intentional measure has been keeping wages and salaries so low that saving enough to live on after quitting work has been very difficult or impossible, forcing people to work until they drop. The byproduct has been that aforementioned breakup of extended families that for millennia provided people with support in old age. (See Chapter 4, Section 3.3.3.2) What we now know as "pensions" – where ex-employers or governments provide post-wage income to support workers no longer earning either wages or salaries – were scarce to nonexistent for most workers until very late in the nineteenth century. The only group of workers to receive pensions early on were soldiers, which in the US began shortly after Independence in 1799 and expanded in the wake of the Revolutionary and Civil wars. Then came pensions for the guardians of capitalist property, the police, with New York City setting up a pension plan in 1857. The first private pension funds in the US came only in 1875 (American Express) and 1880 (Baltimore and Ohio Railroad), financed by both worker and employer contributions.[87] As might be expected these plans were mainly aimed at the embarrassingly visible disabled and could be canceled at the employer's whim. And, at least in the case of the Baltimore and Ohio Railroad Company, their plan came in response to the great Railroad Workers' strike of 1877. The velvet glove of a limited pension plan followed up the more brutal use of force during the strike.[88]

86 See, Grant McConnell, *The Decline of Agrarian Democracy* (Berkeley: University of California Press, 1953).

87 Patrick Seburn, "Evolution of employer-provided defined benefit pensions" *Monthly Labor Review* 114, no. 12 (December 1991): 16–23.

88 Robert Ovetz, *When Workers Shot Back: Class Conflict from 1877 to 1921* (Chicago: Haymarket Books, 2019), Part 1.

Also created under pressure – from the growing social democratic movement in Germany, supported by Marx and Engels – was the first serious old-age pension system implemented by Bismarck. It came in 1889, six years after Marx had died and almost as a direct counter to the Second International, founded that same year. (See, Chapter 2, Section 3.11) The English counterpart, the Old Age Pensions Act came only in 1908. To make a long, painful story short: trying to exploit workers until they dropped, capitalists refused to concede any post-job benefits until they came under extreme pressure from workers' struggles.[89]

7.2.2 Stemming Flight from the Labor Market

So many workers have fled labor markets through which they were previously employed – discussed in Chapters 4 and 5 – that capitalists have repeatedly tried to stem the resulting reduction in available labor-power.[90] In Chapter 4, Section 3.2.2.2, I distinguished between motivations based on conditions in labor markets and jobs that might provoke workers to flee and those that might attract them elsewhere. How have capitalists responded to those very different kinds of motivations?

In the case of both low wages and lousy working conditions, obviously capitalists *could* reduce flight by paying higher wages, shortening working hours and spending money to make work safer. While common enough for managers, they have, however, always been loath to do so for poorly paid manual workers. For the most part they have only raised those workers' wages when forced to do so, either by a dearth of workers or by laws.[91] It has been the same with both shorter working hours and working conditions. Resistance to shortening the one and spending money on the second seems to have been virtually universal. For each capitalist firm, fewer hours of work reduce output, sales and profits. Thus, their enthusiastic embrace of Senior's argument that a single hour's reduction would wipe out all profit (See, Section 8.1.1.1). Money spent on safety equipment increases costs and reduces profits. It's cheaper to tell workers to "just be careful." This resistance has been just one part of the capitalist

89 In the US, it took a whole wave of strikes by industrial workers and massive protests by the unemployed during the Great Depression to win general government managed pensions with the Social Security Act of 1935.

90 Slaves, of course, have fled wherever possible, into the hinterland to form maroon colonies or to merge with indigenous populations or to slave-free zones, sometimes through "underground railroads", be they on land or sea. I discuss capitalist countermeasures in Section 9.1 on crises in $C(LP) - M$.

91 Marx argued that in 1853 wages only rose because of prosperity (increased demand) and large-scale emigration of workers out of England that reduced labor supply. Marx to F. Lassalle, January 23, 1855, *MECW*, *Vol. 39*, pp. 511–514.

preoccupation with minimizing costs, analyzed in Volume 3 of *Capital*.[92] Thus, the long struggle Marx describes in Chapter 10, where the shortening of working hours is only achieved when workers and reformers succeed in blocking further increases and then forcing a reduction by law. In short, until compelled to make concessions on all these fronts, capitalists preferred to use *repression* to prevent workers from fleeing exploitative and alienating jobs and their associated labor markets. (See Sections 8.1.1.1 and 8.1.1.2 below.)

A typically repressive capitalist move to stem worker flight has been the passage of laws restricting the ability of workers to change employers anywhere within the law's reach. This amounted to an adaptation of traditional guild restrictions placed on apprentices and journeymen that *tried* to tie them to those who had trained them.[93] This tendency to restrict movement was opposed by Adam Smith, one of those few cases where his arguments didn't sit well with many capitalists. He wrote: "The statute of apprenticeship obstructs the free circulation of labour from one employment to another, even in the same place."[94] Recognizing and accepting how workers would naturally move from low wage to higher wage jobs, Smith thought this labor market dynamic facilitates capitalist development by allowing labor to move where capitalists need it most (and therefore pay higher wages). So many capitalists disagreed, putting their own corporate interests above any concern with the economy as a whole, that they were able to get laws passed blocking such flight.

A common contract imposed on individual industrial workers has bound them to the contracting employer yet provided no obligation on the part of the employer to provide either regular employment or steady payment for work performed.[95] Contractual clauses making withdrawal from employment difficult – no matter how dangerous and exploitative the conditions of work – have combined with statutes making it easy for employers to bring charges against workers. These laws, which have allowed for summary enforcement by local

---

92 Specifically, Chapter 5, Section 2: "Saving on the Conditions of Work at the Workers' Expense", where he presents a disgusting array of evidence from several industries, or *MECW, Vol. 37*, Chapter V, Section II.

93 The emphasis on "tried" is because journeymen – like later waged industrial workers – often migrated despite such restrictions. See, Stephan Epstein, "Labour mobility, journeymen organizations and markets in skilled labour in Europe, 14th-18th centuries," in Mathieu Arnoux and Pierre Monnet (eds) *Le technician dans la cité en Europe occidentale, 1250–1650* (École française de Rome, 2004) 251–269.

94 *The Wealth of Nations*, Chapter X, Part II: "Inequalities occasioned by the Policy of Europe" (New York: The Modern Library, 1937) 134. Smith clearly understood the need for a "malleable" labor force.

95 See, Christopher Frank, "'Let But One of the Them Come before Me, and I'll Commit Him': Trade Unions, Magistrates and the Law in Mid-Nineteenth-Century Staffordshire," op. cit.

justices of the peace and other magistrates (often employers themselves) have pre-tipped the scales of justice against workers. For workers to bring charges against employers has been much more difficult. Not only have low wages made hiring attorneys and paying court costs (if they lose) difficult, but local magistrates, even if they are not employers themselves, have almost uniformly been biased against workers.[96]

Of early labor laws in Britain, Douglas Hay recounts that between 1720 and 1792, Parliament passed ten different statutes providing for *imprisonment for workers* who "breached their contracts."[97] As with earlier Master and Servant laws, these statutes were systematically enforced, with few exceptions. Of later laws more favorable to workers, written under pressure, Marx wrote, "Parliament passed five Labour Laws between 1802 and 1833, but was shrewd enough not to vote a penny for their compulsory implementation, for the necessary official personnel, etc. They remained a dead letter."[98] Typical result: in the two years of 1854 and 1855, "5,560 workmen and women [were] summarily convicted and imprisoned in England, Wales and Ireland."[99] A similar situation obtained in France, during the regime (1830–1848) of the "bourgeois king" Louis Philippe I: "the one Factory Act passed during his reign, that of 22 March 1841 [limiting working hours for children], was never put into force … Only since 1853 and in a single department – the Nord – has a paid government inspector been appointed."[100] Eventually, despite such rigged legal systems, workers' collective formation of both covert and overt organizations, e.g., secret pacts or public unions in which they pooled some of their meager wages, dramatically increased their ability to organize resistance, such as strikes, to fight for higher wages, shorter hours and better working conditions. On capitalist responses to the threat posed to production by such self-organization, see Section 8.1.1 below.

96 Shockingly, such clauses are still common today under the rubric of "noncompete" clauses in contracts. See, Eric Posner, *How Antitrust Failed Workers* (Oxford: Oxford University Press, 2021).

97 Douglas Hay, "Patronate, Paternalism, and Welfare: Masters, Workers, and Magistrates in Eighteenth-Century England," *International Labor and Working-Class History* 53 (Spring 1998): 29. See also, Douglas Hay, "England 1562–1875: The Law and Its Uses," in Douglas Hay and Paul Craven, (eds), *Masters, Servants, and Magistrates in Britain and the Empire, 1562–1955* (Chapel Hill, NC: North Carolina University Press, 2004), 59–116.

98 *Capital, Vol. 1*, p. 390, or *MECW, Vol. 35*, pp. 283–284.

99 Hay, "England 1562–1875: The Law and its Uses," 60.

100 *Capital, Vol. 1*, p. 390, fn. 99, or *MECW, Vol. 35*, pp. 283, fn 3.

Along with restrictions on the movement of the waged, similar obstacles to movement were long applied to unemployed workers by the British Poor Laws and Settlement Acts written to deal with them. Those laws – whose formulation differed from parish to parish – generally made it difficult for a worker to move away from a local parish where some relief was available. As might be expected, Adam Smith was as opposed to these restrictions as he was to those on the employed, he considered both kinds incompatible with capitalist needs for labor-power.[101] As always, when economists' ideas coincide with capitalists' perceptions of their own interests they are accepted and put to use; in those rare cases where they don't, they are ignored.

When it came to unemployed workers, whether they were fleeing the labor market or failed to find a job in it, the economist whose ideas appealed to and were appropriated by capitalists most fervently was Thomas Malthus, especially his arguments aimed at making life for the unemployed as hard as possible by reducing or eliminating charity, e.g., Poor Law relief.[102] The objective, of course, was and has always been to drive workers off relief, out of workhouses and into the labor market as quickly as possible.[103] Workers, of course, have sought more relief and better conditions – but with little success in Marx and Engels' time – so being out of a job was truly a hardship.[104]

---

101 *The Wealth of Nations*, op. cit., pp. 137–138.

102 Reducing or eliminating poor relief for the unemployed also weakens employed workers' ability to negotiate wage increases – or resist wage decreases – by removing what was essentially a floor under the wage hierarchy. The same strategy has motivated opposition to, and efforts to reduce, modern welfare support for those without jobs, e.g., during the Covid pandemic and virtually every negotiation of the US Federal budget in recent decades.

103 The contemporary business resistance to unemployment compensation during the Covid-19 pandemic has been shaped by exactly the same sentiments. Trump and his cronies have objected to income relief for workers who have lost jobs through no fault of their own because the availability of that income might make them less inclined to look for jobs (whether old jobs still in existence, or new jobs because the old ones have disappeared completely). In the US several conservative-dominated state governments have explicitly cited that rationale for refusing federal funds and cutting off support for workers. Often, as in the cases of Texas, Georgia, and Florida, these are the same state governments that refused Federal funds for Medicaid expansion, which also benefits lower-income workers. The cut-offs, however, have NOT resulted in appreciably more workers returning to the labor market. See, Ben Casselman, "Cutoff of Jobless Benefits Is Found to Get Few Back to Work," *New York Times*, August 20, 2021. Given the long history of capitalist ideology – from Malthus on – that views ANY help to the poor as dangerous, the actual effects of cutting social safety net programs are less important to many capitalists than satisfying their lust for any policy that might make workers more compliant with capitalist needs.

104 Contemporary counterparts of these efforts can be found in the battles that have shaped laws of the "welfare state," i.e., who gets what money and under what circumstances.

The most dramatic flights from the labor market, at least in terms of scale, have occurred during those moments of emigration when very large numbers of unemployed workers, with no independent means of support and unable to find jobs, have decided their survival required not only fleeing local labor markets but leaving the country in which they are living to seek opportunities abroad. In the first few decades of the nineteenth century, when continuing enclosures and inability of early industrialization to absorb the displaced population, the presence of large numbers of unemployed and troublesome workers was met with Malthusian beliefs about overpopulation and capitalist support for emigration to mitigate problems at home. Channeling workers viewed as surplus to the colonies, especially to Australia and North America was thought to reduce costs (of Poor Law relief) and trouble in Britain while contributing to the expansion of the British empire. As manufacturing developed, the situation intensified. Marx writes,

> By constantly turning workers into "supernumeraries", large-scale industry, in all countries where it has taken root, spurs on rapid increases in emigration and the colonization of foreign lands, which are thereby converted into settlements for growing the raw material of the mother country, just as Australia, for example, was converted into a colony for growing wool.[105]

As a result of capitalist support for emigration the British state gradually evolved various administrative agencies for overseeing emigration and passed laws such as the Passenger Acts which regulated conditions of transporting emigrants oversees. When and where emigrants were desired, recipient colonial governments supported loose enforcement of protections for emigrants and cheap passage. Where the influx became too great and caused problems, they demanded restrictions. Similarly, attitudes within the British government at home depended on perceptions of the relative importance of various needs, which were often contradictory. The need to export what were viewed as an excess population of unwanted, troublesome workers vied with protests about the conditions of transportation (unseaworthy ships, fraud and

In the US, some programs are federal, e.g., Social Security and Medicare; in others, e.g., unemployment compensation and welfare, the laws are at the level of individual states and vary from one to another. Today, as a rule, unemployment compensation has been kept low enough to be a hardship for families, but sufficient to tempt some young, single workers to take a break from being exploited and have some fun for a while. (Much the way some take jobs, save up enough for a vacation and then quit!)

105 *Capital, Vol. 1*, p. 579, or *MECW, Vol. 35*, p. 454.

exploitation of emigrants) and sometimes with the opposed views from colonial administrators.[106]

As views of state officials varied, so did those of capitalists but always in line with their interests in having a manageable, exploitable supply of labor. For example, when crises in demand for goods caused the expelling of workers from employment, adding to those displaced by machinery, employers feared emigration of the "supernumeraries" would deprive them of workers when demand rebounded and they needed them. One such case, which Marx analyzes in Volume 1 of *Capital*, was during the crisis in the British cotton industry resulting from the American Civil War and the "cotton famine" when hundreds of thousands of "hands" were laid off. So bleak was the situation that workers organized themselves to emigrate. In Chapter 15, Section 8, Marx quotes from a "proclamation issued in 1853 by some cotton workers, for the purpose of forming an emigration society", which points out not only how millions have already emigrated but how, even in the most "prosperous" of times, "a large percentage of the male adults ... find it impossible to obtain work in factories on any condition whatsoever."[107]

The response of the cotton mill owners was predictable: they vociferously opposed any emigration, demanding that the unemployed and destitute workers be kept around for "one, two or three years" until the industry revives! Letting all that "mental and trained [labor] power" leave would cripple the industry because they could not be replaced "for a generation." In this, as Marx points out in Chapter 25, Section 3, they were backed by their economist apologists, with both Herman Merivale (1806–1874) and Thomas Malthus providing arguments in support of preventing emigration in order to keep workers in reserve for employers' eventual need.[108]

And how did Parliament respond? Although in earlier times it had subsidized emigration, in this case it did "not vote a single farthing in aid of emigration, but simply passed some Act empowering the municipal corporations to keep the workers in a state of semi-starvation."[109] As a result of this blockage of emigration by laid-off industrial workers, Marx found that most English emigrants were from agriculture, most often "tenant-farmers' sons, etc." and their

106 See Peter Dunkley, "Emigration and the State, 1803–1842: The Nineteenth-Century Revolution in Government Reconsidered," *The Historical Journal* 23, no. 2 (June 1980): 353–380.

107 *Capital, Vol. 1*, p. 588, fn. 67, or *MECW, Vol. 35*, p. 462, fn. 1.

108 *Capital, Vol. 1*, pp. 786–787, or *MECW, Vol. 35*, p. 628.

109 *Capital, Vol. 1*, p. 722–723, or *MECW, Vol. 35*, pp. 574–577. See also the contemporary account of workers' collective efforts to emigrate at that time and the opposition of the manufacturers in Arthur Arnold, *The Cotton Famine: From the Fall of Sumter to the Passing of the Public Works Act* (London: Saunders, Otley, and Co., 1864) 367–371.

emigration was offset by Irish immigration preventing any substantial decline in the exploitable population.[110]

As I discussed in Chapter 4, Section 3.2.2.2, among the "mental and trained [labor] power" sometimes fleeing through emigration were not only "hands", but highly skilled workers – critical to the operation of specialized new equipment. Such workers capitalists were even more loath to lose because they might carry their knowledge to competitors. So, adding to opposition to the departure of less skilled labor-power, capitalists demanded and obtained laws to punish both those who sought to entice such workers away, and any enticed workers who dared to leave.[111] In short, just as capitalists supported immigration when they wanted more workers, they opposed emigration when they were afraid of losing those they needed.

In the case of individual workers fleeing the labor market to set up small businesses or of collective flight to cooperatives, besides the various restrictions mentioned above, capitalists have countered in two main ways. First, setting up small businesses or cooperatives requires financing, usually beyond the resources of individuals or even small groups. The initiators of such projects must therefore often have recourse to banks or other financial resources. Taking on debt means accepting the capitalist mandate of profit-making, merely to repay loans and interest on them. Regardless of how a small business or cooperative is organized internally, it must meet this very capitalist criterion to survive. So, the labor of those escaping exploitation and alienation in waged jobs is recuperated via debt.

Second, some capitalists encourage "start-ups", even by ex-employees, because it amounts to an out-sourcing of risk. If they are successful, larger corporations with more resources can absorb them via mergers and takeovers or outcompete them in the marketplace. In all cases, they effectively neutralize their otherness and those who fled are forced back into the labor market and recuperated. These dynamics result in an increase in what Marx called the "centralization" of capital, which enhances the power of the more successful competitors.[112]

110 *Capital, Vol. 1*, p. 1080, or *MECW*, *Vol. 34*, pp. 467–468. "Tenant-farmer sons", of course, like daughters, are workers, just in the field of agriculture rather than manufacturing. While part of the *industrial* latent reserve army, both have always been integral participants in the *active* army of agricultural labor.

111 John Harris, "Industrial Espionage in the Eighteenth Century," *Industrial Archaeology Review* 7, no. 2 (1984–1985): 129.

112 *Capital, Vol. I*, pp. 777–780, or *MECW*, Vol. 35, pp. 621–622.

7.2.3 Offsetting Other Sources of a Shortage of Labor-Power

Well aware of all those forces cutting into their supply of labor, capitalists and their strategists developed measures to either counteract the effects or ward them off.

7.2.3.1 *Countering Disease and Starvation*

With the development of theories of disease that recognized not only potential causes but the existence of transmission and circulation, governments, often spurred by capitalists, began to take more preventive steps. They ranged from the simple, traditional quarantining of ships from infected ports or of hospital patients to the inspection of places suspected of harboring disease or facilitating its transmission, such as working conditions or horrible housing.

Capitalists generally tried to deny any causal relationship between working conditions and diseases such as black lung disease, which crippled coal miners or byssinosis, which crippled workers in textile factories. They were also resistant to the work of doctors who revealed how the low wages they were paying resulted in malnutrition and greater susceptibility to disease. They were more supportive of the work of public health inspectors against pandemic diseases such as the bubonic plague, cholera, typhus, measles, tuberculosis, malaria, yellow fever, smallpox, influenza, all of which periodically resulted in serious reductions in the available workforce, increased costs (of maintenance or turnover) and reduced profits. For the most part, while the functionaries of capital who could fled disease-ridden cities, they got government (taxpayers) to foot the bill for dealing with and preventing such diseases, such as the bubonic plague, which was endemic to London but once again reached epidemic proportions in 1665–66.

In the absence of government expenditures, say in imperialist investments abroad, they even spent their own money to save money. A notable example was United Fruit Company's actions in Central America. As explained by one company vice president:

> The work that has been done was done for a very practical hard-headed reason – that of self-interest ... sick people cannot work ... It may have been an enlightened self-interest but it was largely done because they [American Companies] could not get out the ore, or raise the bananas or pump the oil unless these fundamentals were taken care of.[113]

113 Quoted in John McClintock, "Responsibilities of Industry for Health of Local Populations Abroad," *Industry and Tropical Health*, II, 4–20–22, (1954): 39–42. Capitalist demands for public health measures also originated from their private foundations pushing "manpower

Many of the large-scale efforts to improve sanitation, however, took forms which hurt workers as much as the diseases themselves. In industrial cities, as Engels and Marx pointed out, sanitation measures such as the creation of sewage systems often involved tearing down worker housing – pushing them into even less desirable neighborhoods.

> The 'improvement' of towns that the sheer fear of contagious diseases, which do not spare even 'respectable people', brought into existence from 1847 to 1864 no less than ten Acts of Parliament on sanitation ... all the measures for the improvement of public health ... by demolishing uninhabitable houses, driven the workers out of some districts only to crowd them into still more closely in other districts.[114]

Where capitalist philanthropies have funded initial public health efforts, the usual objective has been to first demonstrate feasibility and then foist the costs of preventing disruption caused by disease onto the government and taxpaying workers.[115] While some capitalists may profit directly from the required expenditures of taxpayer money, for example in building or operating sanitation infrastructure or developing new medical treatments, the primary benefit to most capitalists derives from a healthier and more stable workforce.[116]

In colonial areas of the nineteenth century, where disease or fluctuations in weather have caused widespread suffering through drought or flooding, obvious countermeasures – such as the delivery of food and medical aid to local,

---

planning" on a larger scale. Examples of both direct business interest and indirect philanthropic efforts are cited in H. Cleaver, "Malaria, the Politics of Public Health and the International Crisis", *Review of Radical Political Economics* 9, no. 1 (April 1977): 81-103. The latter is analyzed in much greater detail in H. Cleaver, "The Origins of the Green Revolution" (PhD diss., Stanford University, 1974), Chapters III and V dealing with Rockefeller's anti-hookworm campaign in the American South in the early twentieth century and the later campaign against malaria during the Cold War.

114 *Capital, Vol. 1*, p. 812–14, or *MECW, Vol. 35*, p. 651–54.

115 An early example in the twentieth century were the efforts of the Rockefeller Sanitary Commission that financed a campaign from 1909 to 1915 to eradicate hookworm disease and its debilitating effects on workers in the American South. A more recent example has been the Bill and Melinda Gates Foundation's Water, Sanitation and Hygiene program to develop and promulgate better sanitation practices in areas not served by public infrastructure.

116 Our most recent illustration of this dynamic of public monies and private profits has been the Covid pandemic in which governments have spent vast sums of taxpayer money on research, the development of vaccines and the public distribution of vaccines, preventive masks, etc. to the benefit not only of those who have received the vaccines but the medical industry which received the money. Since declaring the pandemic over, that same industry is now charging for the vaccines developed with public money.

starving populations – have often been either lackluster or completely absent. Why? Where capitalist investment was limited in scope and largely confined to particular industries, the welfare, life or death, of the rest of the population, untapped for exploitation, proved of little concern to colonial authorities. How else to explain, say, the widespread starvation of millions on the South Asian subcontinent during the heyday of British colonialism? Given widespread resistance to foreign rule, not acting to counter famine amounted to a repressive policy of letting starve those portions of the population useless to British capitalists as sources of profits or troublesome in their resistance.[117]

7.2.3.2 *Countering the Military Poaching of Workers*

With military recruitment geared to the needs of capitalists rather than workers, both at home and abroad and with workers serving as cannon fodder in wars, the primary source of resistance has naturally been among workers.

But the "needs of capitalists" have never been uniform and have often been contradictory. While I have highlighted conflicts between capitalists in different countries, there have also been conflicts at home, over the priority of needs in the allocation of the labor force. Whereas some capitalists have needed the military, and thus recruitment and conscription, to help control either domestic or colonized workers and protect trade, other capitalists – such as the agrarian capitalists during the Crimean War, mentioned by Marx in Chapter 4, Section 3.2.2.3.2 – have resisted having their workers drawn off because it reduces their supply of labor, raises wages and sometimes forces them to invest in labor-saving technology. In this, the interests of workers resisting conscription and their employers coincided. While Marx's example mentions only farmers "howling" in protest, the influence of many capitalists in government has long been sufficient to achieve "exemptions" (*dispenses* in France) from military recruitment.

To more traditional excuses, such as infirmity, capitalists claimed not only the essentiality of some workers to the national interest but also the impossibility of replacing them. The rationale for some exemptions have been obvious enough not to ruffle the feathers of supporters of recruitment, e.g., workers in war-related industries who crank out the instruments of war. But capitalists also deemed others basic to the stability of the economy, such as coal miners or sailors on ships carrying coal whose work was vital to the emerging age of steam-driven machinery in manufacturing. By one account in Britain "by mid-[nineteenth] century over 50,000 protections were in circulation."[118]

117 Such policies of what we can call "repressive neglect" have continued ever since.

118 Nicolas Rogers, "British impressment and its discontents," *The International Journal of Maritime History* 30, no. 1 (2018): 60.

The existence of such exemptions provided the opportunity for all kinds of capitalist challenges to impressment including writs of habeas corpus taken out against seizures of individuals. When their immediate interests were at stake, many capitalists were more than happy to take up both legal and moral objections to impressment. Legal grounds included challenging the constitutionality of the practice. Moral objections harkened back to the supposed proverbial "freedom" of Englishmen since the Magna Carta, etc. For example, David Hume, writing in 1752, saw in the "pressing of seamen" – carried out with "great violence and disorder" and "impunity" – a worrisome encroachment on "the rights and privileges, which the law grants, without distinction, to all English subjects."[119] As with more traditional excuses, often subject to fraud and corruption, recent historical research has revealed all kinds of tricks and methods deployed by capitalists to avoid having their workers snatched for military duty, whether they cared for "rights and privileges" or not.[120]

7.2.3.3 *Managing Family Size*

With increasing income, and its potential to reduce families' need for children, having little effect in the nineteenth century, by far the greater threat to the capitalist management of the labor supply through the family, was resistance by women to being broodmares. It was certainly to forestall or counter such resistance that capitalists deployed every weapon at their disposal, including ideology, law, and force.

With patriarchy long pre-dating capitalism, its functionaries found many ideological weapons ready to hand and only requiring adaptation. For example, capitalists readily embraced long-standing church doctrines, such as those "domestic codes" that have given husbands dominion over wives and children. For example, Christian marriage rituals have often clearly stated that the objective of marriage is to breed children – more sheep for the church's tithed flock – and, conveniently, more workers for capitalists' labor force. So too, have marriage vows often demanded that women, but not men, obey their spouse.[121] All these have sanctified the role of men as mediating overseers of

119 David Hume, "Of Some Remarkable Customs" in *Political Discourses* (Edinburgh: Kincaid and Donalson, 1852) 152–154. As George Caffentzis has suggested, Hume may have become aware of this issue as early as 1834 during a visit to Bristol. See, Caffentzis, *Civilizing Money: Hume, his Monetary Project and the Scottish Enlightenment* (London: Pluto Press, 2021) 86.

120 See, for example, Nicholas Rogers, "British impressment and its discontents," op. cit., and Kevin Costello, "Habeas Corpus and Military and Naval Impressment, 1756–1816," *The Journal of Legal History 29, no. 2* (2008): 215–251.

121 From the Church of England's Book of Common Prayer's prescription for the ceremony of marriage: "First, it was ordained for the procreation of children, to be brought up in the

women, their childbearing, and their offspring. Indeed, in their critique of these power relationships within marriage, Marx and Engels mocked this very unequal application of a supposed moral principle.

Consistent with this, capitalist legal codes and laws have been written to legalize this gender domination, granting more rights to men, e.g., adult male suffrage years before that of women, husband control over their wives' property. Until fairly recently married women had zero property rights and any property acquired before marriage became their husband's. Men could rape their wives with impunity, even have them locked up at will. Both religious and secular ideas were deployed to justify these injustices. While social codes worked against middle-class women finding independence through waged work, for working-class women they were often means of survival.[122] This family hierarchy also served to justify gender inequality in the labor market where men's wages were presumed to provide the main support of families, whereas women's wages were treated as supplemental, less needed, and less well paid. Complementing laws codifying marriages between men and women, were those outlawing not only gay marriage but all forms of "sodomy" – assumed unproductive of children/workers – and demanding the punishment of transgressions with imprisonment or death. Of all this, Marx and Engels were undoubtedly aware, but said little.

As discussed in Chapter 5, the inevitable result of how women have been treated has been their continuing struggle against their subordination. Against day-to-day domination by men, often including violence, women have often had little recourse except escape, either psychological or physical; counterviolence, of course, has never been tolerated. Against the expectation that women should be wives and wives should breed children, women could refuse or delay marriage and, married or not, they have had recourse to various forms of birth

---

fear and nurture of the Lord, and to the praise of his holy Name." Under pressure from fed up women, in 1922 the Episcopal Church removed the word "obey" from the bride's wedding vows.

122 These differences show up in many novels of the nineteenth century. Compare the situation of the central women characters in Jane Austen's novels – those daughters of "gentlemen" who never even consider the possibility of working for a wage – with the main working-class character in Elizabeth Gaskell's *Mary Barton* (1848) who follows her father into the mills of Manchester, or the title character in Margaret Oliphant's *Kirsteen* (1890), who escapes her father's patriarchal effort to trade her for a parcel of land to become a needlewoman.

control, usually condemned by men, law, religion, and the portrayal of proper "womanly" behavior by capitalist authors and public media.[123]

As Silvia Federici has shown, in considerable, nauseating detail, in her book *Caliban and the Witch* (2004), the capitalist repression of women's abilities to control their birth rates started early during the first period of "primitive accumulation." That repression included not only attacks on birth control but on women's power more generally, especially when exercised autonomously in ways which ran counter to capitalist needs. So, in the wake of dramatic reductions in population such as that caused by the Black Death, and thus in the number of workers available to employers, repression of women's ability to control their own bodies and reproduction took the violent form of witch hunts, sanctioned by complicit capitalists, government officials and clergy.[124] Although the methods of repression changed over time, efforts to limit women' access to various methods of birth control continued throughout the nineteenth century. Although they were undoubtedly aware of these conflicts, I've found no evidence of either Marx or Engels analyzing them, in either published writings or correspondence.[125]

7.2.4 Offsetting Overzealous Investment

When zealous investment and speculation result in the demand for labor outstripping its supply and workers take advantage of competition among capitalists and the leverage it gives them to force wages up enough to cut into

---

123 As women have gained power against these modes of subordination, not only have some succeeded in telling their side of the story through novels, theatre, song and social media, but many capitalists have adapted and, as with other successful struggles by workers, sought to instrumentalize their voices in the service of profit, publishing and otherwise promoting women's voices and stories that in earlier times were repressed and silenced. The same has been true for other previously repressed minorities such as gays, lesbians, trans, etc. Of course, other capitalists have refused adaptation and have been funding and organizing a neofascist counteroffensive aimed at silencing all these groups, forcing women back into their roles as handmaidens and broodmares.

124 The current neofascist counteroffensive embraces just such violence, pushing laws mandating severe punishment for both women and doctors engaging in abortion – with the repression of birth control next on the agenda.

125 When capitalist needs for labor have been great, they have resorted not only to the stick of repressing contraception and abortion, but the carrot of incentives to women to procreate. Pro-natalist laws and policies – including "family allocations", which pay women money for having more children, to increase the supply of labor. Explicitly pro-natalist laws, both banning contraception and rewarding having children, have been most prominent in response to wartime losses in the labor force, e.g., after WWI and WWII. Naturally, the overturning of anti-contraception and anti-abortion laws have been mainly the result of women's struggles. Recent reactionary efforts at reversal are obviously aimed at re-subordinating women.

profits, the obvious capitalist countermeasures (besides going on strike, laying off workers, and cutting investment) are repressing workers' struggles and bringing in more workers. Repression, however, at best reduces or eliminates the disruptions of struggles but it doesn't resolve the problem of demand outstripping supply. Only the mobilization of more labor-power can do that. But how?

Partly, the increases in wages may help with the supply of labor-power by drawing more workers into the labor force, i.e., drawing workers out of the "latent" or "stagnant" reserve and into the "floating" reserve to look for jobs that now pay more. But Marx and Engels describe many other ways that capitalists try to control and manipulate the labor market in their own interest. Prominent have been strategies to maintain *an excess supply of labor* that will keep downward pressure on wages, countering workers' struggles for higher wages or salaries. Having plenty of workers looking for jobs also makes it easier to get rid of militant workers, e.g., activists, unionizers, and replace them. Capitalist strategies for obtaining such an excess include those processes of primitive accumulation that strip people of alternatives to the labor market and penalize resistance to entering it – processes that continue to this day.[126] Excess supply in the form of an unwaged reserve army has generally been maintained by annexing ever-greater sources of labor and by replenishing the reserves through population growth and the introduction of labor displacing machinery.[127]

But when such measures fail, and demand does outstrip supply, capitalists have some alternatives. Although in Marx's analysis, the labor market lies in the realm of circulation/exchange, as in the case of transportation the labor market also involves work – that by workers seeking out employment, but also by workers hired by capitalists to go out and find workers. As a general rule, capitalists prefer labor markets to be so well stocked that paying someone to find workers is not needed because workers are doing the unwaged work of looking for work, knocking on factory gates or office doors, engaging in what economists today call "job search."[128] Nevertheless, where desperate

126 *Capital, Vol. 1*, Pt. Eight, or MECW, *Vol. 35*, pp. 704–761. Besides capitalist penetration into its peripheries, we must include its tendencies toward centralization that involve, among other methods, big businesses driving small businesses and farmers bankrupt (well known cases of Standard Oil, of agribusiness, of Walmart in the US, now followed by Amazon) and precipitating their owners into the labor market.

127 *Capital, Vol. 1*, Chapter 25, or MECW, *Vol. 35*, pp. 607–703.

128 In modern times, despite laid off workers having won "unemployment compensation" from the government, to obtain aid the state usually puts the onus on workers to actively search for jobs and show evidence of having solicited and obtained interviews with employers.

workers are in short supply, businesses have spent money to find and hire more workers, sometimes directly, sometimes through intermediaries. In *Capital*, for example, Marx points to "gang-masters" who organize subcontracted agricultural labor.[129] The search can be local, within a region, within a country or from much further away, across borders. When it can, capital likes to impose the costs of bringing workers from a distance on its hires. One case Marx discusses is of agricultural laborers who were forced to walk many miles from "nearby" villages, the only places they could find shelter.[130] Such efforts, when they work, are clearly preferable to capitalists as opposed to responding to the decrease in profits by laying off workers and imposing higher unemployment.

Where there is constant pressure for immigration into the labor force and governments are playing a role in either blocking or facilitating the inflow of immigrant or migrant labor, they can obviously ease or tighten restrictions to regulate the flow and the resultant supply. As in the case of Irish workers, such inflows, from whatever source, can increase competition and counter pressures

129 *Capital, Vol. 1*, pp. 850–3. Such subcontracting has re-emerged with a vengeance in this neoliberal period as capitalists have sought to reduce labor costs by outsourcing to avoid providing benefits as well as good wages to in-house workers. The work of "headhunters," personnel workers who seek out higher level, salaried employees are probably better known than that of those employed to find cheap manual labor, or, these days cheap programmers and other digital laborers, often for temporary, precarious jobs. For some types of jobs, enough capitalists have found difficulty obtaining workers that Marx's "gang-masters" have been largely replaced by independent – "temp agencies" – businesses whose profits derive from charging workers and capitalists for their service bringing job seeker and employer together. These are often specialized in everything from office staff to traditional sex-workers. In some cases, e.g., the market for maritime workers, unions play this role, maintaining "hiring halls" where workers can get help looking for jobs, but, like temp agencies, they also serve employers by playing the role of Maxwell's daemon, weeding out high entropy workers (troublemakers) from low entropy ones (those whose energy is reliably available for work). See, George Caffentzis, "The Work/Energy Crisis and the Apocalypse," op. cit., Section G. The Manifold of Work: Anti-Entropy Qua Information.

130 *Capital, Vol. 1*, 838–840. The costs of obtaining extra labor-power may increase because of outlays on transportation or training – the former when recruiters must hire workers who live further away, the latter when workers must be retrained for new jobs. Two examples of the former that I have recently observed: when new factories were opened in Poznań, Poland, company buses had to be dispatched daily to bring newly hired workers from outlying villages. Another: as the cost of housing in San Francisco has risen so high that many workers must move out of the city, the value of their labor-power rises with their increased costs of commuting – an old story given the history of suburban sprawl. When factories are placed in areas of cheap labor lacking skilled workers, investment must be made in training. Where turnover is frequent, such expenditures become a permanent part of the costs of production.

to raise wages and reduce profits. Marx was acutely aware of various methods of increasing supplies of labor-power. Until reformers succeeded in abolishing slavery in 1833, the British government allowed capitalists to pillage Africa and import slaves, especially in its colonies, to create a massive black labor force in addition to existing waged and indentured workers. It also helped by "transporting" criminals and militant workers to colonies where they were forced into the labor market.[131] The form of the labor force has varied but the principle is the same. As Marx says in the chapter on the working day: "For slave trade, read labor-market, for Kentucky and Virginia, Ireland and the agricultural districts of England, Scotland and Wales, for Africa, Germany."[132]

7.3 *Offsetting Crises in Buying the Means of Production, M – MP*

Buyer strategies for offsetting shortages of *MP* or deficiencies in their quality have taken several forms depending on the source of the problem. An obvious strategy to offset cutoffs in supply from one seller is to diversify sources, whether they are domestic or foreign. This was apparently the response of Irish flax growers when imports of flax seed from the colonies were cut off by the American Revolution.[133] Another response to such dependence on foreign seeds, has been to maintain local production by preserving seed from one crop for the next.[134] As discussed in Chapter 4, Section 3.3.6, British textile manufacturers also switched suppliers in response to the Cotton Famine during the American Civil War. They replaced American with Egyptian and Indian cotton.

Clearly, the history of colonialism shows that one of its objectives and results was to create new sources of raw materials for the industries of the colonizing countries. Not only new sources, but cheaper sources as Marx analyzes

131 Some labor was directly forced, but as Marx points out in Chapter 33, Edward Wakefield (1796–1862) offered another solution: putting a price on hitherto free land so that workers had to work for a wage in order to accumulate enough money to buy it. *Capital, Vol. 1*, p. 938–39, or *MECW, Vol. 35*, p. 758–59.

132 *Capital, Vol. 1*, p. 378, or *MECW, Vol. 35*, p. 272. Replace "colonialism" with "globalization" and you have comparable phenomena today.

133 See, F. W. Smith, *The Irish Linen Trade Handbook and Directory* (Belfast: W. H. Greer, 1876), 46.

134 In modern times seed companies have acted to forestall such farmer self-reproduction by getting laws passed to force famers to buy their seeds. The most notorious case of attempted monopolization of seed production is Monsanto. Its scientists genetically engineered seeds whose plants produce sterile seeds that cannot produce new crops. The outrage by farmers, ecologists, etc., at these "terminator" seeds was so great that such seeds were apparently never commercially marketed. See, Genetic Literacy Project, "What's-the-controversy-over-terminator-seeds?" online. (Accessed 7/15/2024)

in Section 3 of Chapter 14 of Volume 3.[135] I have already mentioned Ireland, one of England's first colonies, which was reduced to being "merely an agricultural district of England … which provides corn, wool, cattle and industrial and military recruits."[136] So too with other colonies. Where they already produced desired raw materials, that production could be tapped, especially after local industry was destroyed, as in the case of India. Where they did not, colonialists often forced changes in land use, converting from local food production to the production of raw materials for export.[137] In some cases, the local population could be forced by taxes, to change production.[138] In others, colonial land seizures were followed by direct investment, e.g., the creation of plantations to produce crops.

While Marx draws principally on the colonial experience of England for his examples, the same was true for all colonial powers. Every population colonized was forced to produce raw materials for the colonizers' home industries, whether those materials came from agriculture or from mining. Nowhere did colonialists favor the development of local sites of manufacturing production that could compete with their own industries.[139]

---

135 *Manuscript of 1864–1865*, p. 340, "3. Cheapening of the Elements of Constant Capital," and *Capital, Vol. 3*, pp. 342–343, or *MECW*, *Vol. 37*, p. 234.

136 *Capital, Vol. 1*, p. 860, or *MECW*, *Vol. 35*, p. 694. Which raw materials could be imported from distant colonies was often determined by local producers in the colonizing country. So, in the case of Ireland, the owners of sheep walks in England soon put a stop to imports of Irish wool for the British textile industry with the Wool Act of 1699. Instead of wool, that industry wanted flax, so to earn cash to supplement their meager domestic production and pay taxes Irish peasants were forced to replace sheep with flax for the market.

137 The long-run effect of these land seizures, pushing local peasants onto marginal land, was to dramatically increase the risk of famine in times of drought or flood. In such manner did colonialism convert minor natural fluctuations in weather into major crises for the colonized. This problem has persisted in post-colonial times because seized land has rarely been returned to the locals via land reform.

138 Two examples were Ireland and Prussia where peasants were forced to grow flax – to pay taxes – providing raw or partially processed material to the linen textile industry. "… when the direct taxes fall due, he [the German peasant] would find himself incapable of paying them without his spinning wheel . . .," quoted by Marx from Mirabeaux's *De la monarchie prussienne sous Frédéric le Grand* (1788). *Capital, Vol. 1*, p. 894, fn 33, or *MECW*, *Vol. 35*, p. 722.

139 This was the reason why as people in the Global South freed themselves of colonial domination in the twentieth century, the new elites who took over, often schooled, and trained in the colonial countries, made industrialization an essential part of "national liberation" to escape their status as pure raw material producers. Increasing manufacturing to process local raw materials instead of exporting them became a central objective of national economic policy. See for example, the sequence of plans for post-colonial Indian development. The Prebisch-Singer hypothesis that raw materials producers are condemned to

7.3.1 Offsetting Crises in Barter Trade

The standard economist counter to problems in barter trade has long been replacing barter with trade using money – Marx's "universal equivalent." However, as mentioned in Chapter 4, Section 3.3.1, that has not always been possible because some folks, from whom capitalists have wanted to obtain goods, have historically had no use for money.

In the case of the North American fur trade, I mentioned possibilities of crisis in both the supply and demand for furs. From early on the counter to inadequate supply was two-fold. (1) European traders pushed ever deeper into the continent, developing relations with more and more tribes, elaborating a complex of trade progressively diverse in sources and therefore not only increasing total supply but making it more stable. (2) Contesting colonial powers, e.g., the French and English, allied with different tribes and, often playing on pre-existing antagonisms, pitted them against each other, not only over the fur trade but over the control of whole territories.

Unfortunately for trappers and capitalists buying their furs, the only counter to the long-run problem of depletion was the eventual option of "farming" fur-bearing animals, breeding them for their fur, e.g., mink farming, which began in 1860s. That industry marginalized trappers. It would not be until the end of the nineteenth century that governments began to worry about "conservation", e.g., President Theodore Roosevelt who established the first National Parks and National Forests in the United States. The regulated preservation of wilderness areas could protect species within them, but by that time fur production was largely industrialized.[140] Like hunting more generally, trapping was largely reduced to a bloodlust hobby, rather than a commercial source of fur. Barter no longer played a role.

Similarly, trappers and merchants had no control over the primary source of demand for fur: fashion. So, for example when the felt hats made from beaver fur went out of fashion, the demand for that kind of fur disappeared with the demand for the hats. The only possible response was to switch to trapping or

---

suffer inevitably from declining terms of trade with manufacturing good producers also grounded "dependency theory".

140 This industrialization of fur bearing animals has come to be condemned by animal rights activists for much the same reasons they have condemned the raising of animals for meat, hides, feathers, chemical testing, or even for pets (Puppy mills) – namely the cruelty of methods and the failure to recognize other animals as sentient beings worthy of respect and protection. See the abundant literature by groups such as People for the Ethical Treatment of Animals (PETA). The resulting *consumer* opposition to the use of fur, combined with the development of artificial substitutes, has caused a crisis for the fur industry not unlike previous drops in demand due to changing fashion.

hunting other sources of fur for which demand still existed, e.g., bearskins for military hats – common in the nineteenth century for several sorts of soldiers.[141]

7.3.2 Countering Workers' Struggles that Reduce the Availability of *MP*

In Chapter 4, Section 3.3.2, on workers' struggles that might cause a crisis in the supply of *MP*, I mentioned only how job actions such as strikes, slowdowns, etc., could have two effects. First, shutting down production stops additions to supply, while demand continues to grow. When whole industries are involved, the result can be serious shortages. Second, when such actions have proved successful, they have raised wages or other benefits increasing the costs of production, reducing profits for both producers of *MP* and for buyers who are forced to pay higher prices.

Until they were forced to negotiate with worker-organized collectives such as unions, the primary response of capitalists was repression: laws outlawing such actions, bringing in scabs from the reserve army and deploying violent force, by company goons, local militias or the military. That was largely the scene discovered by Marx and Engels when they turned their attention to investigating the class struggles of their time.

An alternative managerial response to *anticipated* strikes has been to ramp up production, with the objective of building up inventories that they could continue to sell even if strikes or other job actions shut down production. This has been particularly effective when inventories are not subject to deterioration. So, for example, coal mining companies have built up huge piles of coal and grain traders have filled silos to the brim to sell from during shortages, whereas before refrigeration neither fruits nor vegetables could withstand long delays in sales.

7.3.3 Countering the Direct Appropriation of *MP*

As indicated in section Chapter 4, Section 3.3.3, both workers and other capitalists sometimes directly appropriate means of production. Because capitalist laws accord ownership of those *MP* to the capitalist firms whose workers produce them, direct appropriation is treated as "theft" in both cases, with the appropriators subject to arrest and prosecution if they are caught. The obvious counters are all those means which either thwart or result in the apprehension of the "thieves." Let's start with direct appropriation by workers.

141 And still in use for ceremonial purposes in several countries' militaries. There is also an international campaign by PETA to replace bearskins with artificial substitutes, which has been done in some countries but not others. See, https://support.peta.org/page/35880/action/1 (Accessed 7/16/2024.)

Workers tend to directly appropriate either for consumption or for resale. In the case of the former, they are essentially supplementing their wages or salaries with things they would otherwise have to buy or do without. Examples: the peasants cited by Marx who collected fallen wood from enclosed forests, other peasants "poaching" animals for their dinner, or the many kinds of workers cited by Peter Linebaugh who took tobacco, somewhere between its production and its eventual purchase by consumers. In the cases of appropriation for resale, acting alone, it's merely another way to supplement their income. Acting in gangs, say hijacking trucks or raiding warehouses, participants are acting as rogue merchant capitalists aiming to take a cut of the value of the *MP* seized.

Among the countermeasures taken by capitalists have been surveillance and efforts to secure *C*(*MP*)*'* from direct appropriation. In the case of poachers, surveillance was by forest and game wardens. In that of the "socking" of tobacco, all along its material circuit, surveillance was by overseers at each work location. Watching out for direct appropriation complemented the more general purpose of surveillance: making sure workers are doing what they have been told to do, the way they have been told to do it, using only the tools provided, in the time specified by management and not doing anything else!

An early example of capitalist thinking about surveillance was the concept of the panopticon developed by the economist Jeremy Bentham (1747–1748) – physical arrangements to maximize surveillance while minimizing its cost by requiring fewer overseers.[142] Although Bentham was focused on organizing prisons to control prisoner behavior, it turned out to be an inspiring example for organizing surveillance to control workers, whether in a prison, a factory, an office, or a school and has been applied in all those workplaces. It obviously serves to thwart direct appropriation as well as putting psychological pressure on workers to keep working.[143]

Where they have been able to do so, capitalists have developed a variety of means to *physically* secure their *C*(*MP*)*'* from direct appropriation. Indeed, the threat has often been a goad to innovation. Whereas it's hard to "secure" a forest, except by fences or walls generally too expensive to be worth the effort, experimentation has led capitalists to secure many *MP* commodities in a variety of ways, from marking them, e.g., branding livestock, to packing

142 See Jeremy Bentham's *Panopticon, or The Inspection House* (1791) on his mode of organizing prison to control prisoner behavior – a major reference point for Foucault.

143 The panopticon approach is easily observable today, not only in factories with large numbers organized to be under the eye of single overseers, but also in office buildings where each office is enclosed in glass, or where work sites are arranged in "cubicles" making it easy for supervisors to see what workers are doing, while burdening workers with awareness of constant oversight.

them in sealed containers. In Linebaugh's example of tobacco, the container found to be most useful was the "hogshead", a large, wooden barrel.[144] Packed when ready for shipment, such containerization made "socking" (direct appropriation) by waggoneers, sailors, etc., more difficult. But, as Linebaugh points out, with such direct appropriation rampant in ports, the expense of building brick walls around docks, with protected gates to thwart potential thieves, was judged worthwhile and such walls were built.[145]

7.3.4 Reducing Time Lags

The inevitable capitalist response to the problem of time lags in the flow of information about the degree to which the quantity supplied to the market for *MP* matches the quantity demanded for the same *MP* has been to embrace every new technology that sped up that flow. As Marx's extended analysis of "turnover" in Part Two of Volume 2 of *Capital* showed, the greater the speed at which each stage and the whole circuit of capital is completed, the greater the profit. Therefore, built-in to the capitalist mindset is a general desire to speed up operations – indeed, it is precisely the tendency to increase production as fast as possible – in the absence of good information about demand – that contributes to excess inventory and glut. So, while capitalists have quickly adopted new technologies of transportation for gaining more rapid access to *MP* and sales of output, they have also embraced faster communication. In the nineteenth century, that also encouraged replacing wagons and canal boats by railroads, sailing vessels by steam-powered ones, traditional mail by optical and then electric telegraph. The first successful cable from Britain to France was laid in 1850. The first transatlantic cable and the first cable from England to India were laid in 1866, dramatically increasing the speed of information flows about market conditions among several of the world's largest markets. In the process, the quicker flow of information meant less likelihood of crisis-level mismatches between supply and demand.

Unfortunately, as Marx noted with respect to the telegraph, the development of new technologies while reducing the problem of time lags, increased the possibilities for speculation – another source of crisis. Both he and Engels

144 Linebaugh, *The London Hanged*, Chapter Five: Socking, the Hogshead and Excise. Today, the hogshead, handled manually by workers, has been replaced by massive steel containers, ubiquitous at ports, handled by cranes for transfers to and from ships, trucks, and railway cars.

145 Ibid., Chapter Eleven. Today, with relatively cheap steel fences, razor wire and electrification, it's hard to find a port or factory of any sort which is not surrounded by such, with guarded gate entryways, designed to keep appropriators out or to make it hard for those inside to get out with what they have taken.

saw speculation in railroads leading to numerous crises as did that in the creation of new networks of telegraph communication. In the case of railroads, Engels saw this as early as 1847,

> ... railway speculation, which, within the last eight years, were started in Prussia. These speculations, by raising the value of ready money, increased the depreciation of stock in trade, and were themselves, on an average not very profitable, on account of the comparatively thin population and trade of the greater part of the country. They offered, however, a still better chance of profit than other industrial investments; and thus everyone who could dispose of some capital engaged in them. Very soon these speculations assumed, as usual, a feverish character and ended in a crisis ... [146]

Thus, not only does the increased speed of information flows encourage speculation by tapping those flows, but the very industries that speed up the flows become themselves the targets of speculation.[147]

7.3.5 Offsetting Crises for Buyers of *MP* Caused by Nature

Where buyers of *MP* have no control or influence over their sources of *MP*, in the short term the best they can do is hedge against Nature-caused shortages and resulting high prices by diversifying their sources, so that not all would be hit by the same catastrophe at the same time. In the longer term, they have often taken over those sources, which has given them greater ability to anticipate and counter the hazards of Nature. Where the sources are domestic, this has usually been done by buying out producers or gaining control over them via contracts.[148] Where the sources have been foreign, they have been taken

146 Engels, "The Prussian Constitution," (Feb. 1847) *MECW, Vol. 6,* pp. 66–69. See also, Marx, "The State of Trade," (Mar. 6, 1849) *MECW, Vol. 9,* pp. 3–8; Marx and Engels, "Review: May to October 1850," (November 1, 1850) *MECW, Vol. 10,* pp. 492–3; Engels, "The Socialism of Mr. Bismarck," (February 1880) *MECW, Vol. 24,* pp. 272–280. This phenomenon, of capitalist money being diverted from real investment into speculation became rampant after the financial deregulation of the early 1980s, leading to the collapse of the Savings & Loan Industry in 1987 and many subsequent crises.

147 Competition among communications companies have been fierce because of the continuing massive amount of speculation in today's financial markets. See, Jenny Strasburg, "On Your Mark, Get Set…" *The Wall Street Journal,* October 10, 2011. (Accessed 7/15/2024).

148 These days, this is common as big grocery store chains have subsumed local farmer production – especially so-called "organic' farms – in contracts which allow the chains to control what contracted farmers produce and how, as conditions of continued purchasing.

over forcibly through colonialism or less violently through direct investment (buying a controlling interest). Where firms have gained control over the production of *MP*, creating "vertically integrated" businesses that produce their own raw materials as well as processing them, they have taken the kind of steps sketched in Section 8.1.2 below on countering harm from nature in the stage of production.

Securing lines of supply of *MP* has also involved obtaining support from the government, in everything from colonialization through armed protection for shipping to the creation of infrastructure both at home and abroad. The rail lines built across the United States that provided the means to bring grain from the "Corn Belt" to Eastern markets and livestock from Western ranches to Midwest and East Coast slaughterhouses were financed by vast land grants and secured bonds from governments, both national and local.[149] Pretty much the same obtained in the case of rail lines in colonies designed to speed the export of raw materials to home industry as well as to facilitate the movement of troops to quell local uprisings against the colonizing power.[150]

7.3.6 Circumventing Blockades

Besides prevailing on governments – through legal action or lobbying – to reduce or remove legal obstacles to the circulation of technology or goods and services, capitalists have used industrial espionage to circumvent them, as discussed in Chapter 4, Section 3.3.3.2 on the theft of technology by capitalists.

Both capitalists and governments have used smuggling to break both legal and physical blockades. Smuggling by capitalists has been endemic wherever the imposition of customs duties or other kinds of taxes on imported goods have been put in place. Because taxes raise the prices of taxed goods, there have been markets for cheaper, contraband goods, whether they be *MS* or *MP*.[151] The same methods, used to avoid expensive taxes, have been used to circumvent physical blockades put in place by governments for political reasons, usually of diplomatic enemies in times of war as during the Napoleonic Wars or the American Civil war.

A legal method of circumventing blockades was diversification of foreign markets (for exporters) and sources (for importers). Thus, besides smuggling

149 They also, of course, provided the means of moving both troops to the Western frontier to complete the genocide of the indigenous population and industrial goods to take advantage of growing markets among settlers.

150 See, Wolmar, *Railways & the Raj*, op. cit.

151 See, Andrew Cohen, *Contraband: Smuggling and the Birth of the American Century* (New York: W. W. Norton & Company: 2015).

during the Napoleonic Wars, British merchants (backed by the British Navy) responded to blockades to trade with Continental Europe by developing export markets in South America.

8 Offsets in the Second Stage of the Circuit: Production, ... *P* ...

Turning to the point of production, the job place, where capitalists own the means of production, factories, fields, mines, offices, machines, raw materials, etc., and organize workers with the objective of producing as much as they judge profitable, I have already touched on the many conflicts that arise and threaten the realization of that objective. As in the labor market, the methods capitalists deploy depend on the nature of the crisis they face, whether in the actions of the workers they have hired or in the supply or quality of their means of production.

8.1 *Countering Breakdowns in Labor-Power*

In Chapter 5, Section 2.1, I identified several forces acting to disrupt the extraction of work from labor-power, including the struggles of workers and apparently exogenous forces such as violent acts of nature which can harm workers. Capitalists have had to confront both of these disruptive threats and have taken action at both the level of individual firms, collectively through non-governmental organizations (such as the Chamber of Commerce in the US), and through the state. Let's begin by examining their responses to workers' struggles and then turn to threats from Nature.

8.1.1 Countering Predispositions of Workers to Work Less

As Marx has pointed out, workers struggle against both exploitation due to overwork (by fighting for less work) and alienation (by subverting other characteristics of jobs). To the various forms of struggle, capitalists have deployed responses on several of the levels mentioned above: force, law, ideology and structural change. Often, they have been deployed simultaneously, on two or more fronts in this class war. Which have been chosen has depended on the nature of workers' struggles.

8.1.1.1 *Countering Resistance to Exploitation*

Exploitation – the extraction of surplus labor and surplus value in commodity production – is undermined by successful struggles to raise wages, those to reduce working time, and those to work less intensely. These struggles may be individual or collective, with the latter being far more effective. Obviously, capitalists could reduce exploitation and resistance to it by increasing wages, but the only situation in which they have been inclined to raise wages is in *response* to a shortage of labor-power, when they have had to compete with others to attract workers. Throughout most of the nineteenth century, the only evidence of capitalists voluntarily raising wages to *avoid* shortages before they happen, can be found in the wage hierarchy. Besides accentuating competition between workers, higher pay for some, e.g., those with specialized skills, reduced the risk of losing them to some other employer.

All success in reducing work time directly reduces absolute surplus value and, if on a large enough scale, causes a crisis for capital. The importance Marx ascribed to the struggle over work time is amply demonstrated by Chapter 10 of Volume 1 of *Capital* being among the longest in the book. In that chapter, he traced the nature of the struggle between waged workers and their employers: right vs right, force vs force and its secular dynamics.

But this struggle has also taken place between capitalists and other kinds of workers, e.g., indentured servants, slaves, workhouse inmates and prison labor.[152] Wherever capitalists have been able to employ these kinds of workers to produce commodities, they have sought to impose as much work as necessary to gain surplus value. All these workers have resisted and their employers have had to counter their resistance. The main effort analyzed in Chapter 10 involved increasing extracted work by pushing for a longer working day, whether by informal "nibbling and cribbling" – a few more minutes here, a few more there – or by extending the formal, contracted hours of labor.[153] However, in the case of unwaged or marginally waged workers, there has often been no formal working day and the amount of work extracted has simply been the byproduct of struggle.[154]

In the case of waged workers, as Marx showed in Chapter 10, capitalists, their apologists, and the state have used various methods to overcome or undermine workers' resistance to long or intense labor. From early on, during the rise of capitalism, when workers were weak, we saw how capitalists were able

152 Even unwaged workers in homes and schools have struggled against the work of producing labor-power, although those struggles were ones that Marx and Engels largely ignored. As women and children were expelled from the waged labor force and re-confined within households and schools the amount of this kind of labor grew but so too did struggles to reduce it.

153 *Capital, Vol. 1*, Section 5.

154 Common, but only recognized thanks to feminist authors, is the work of "homemakers", usually housewives. Their "working day" has no set limits but starts with preparing breakfast and ends when nighttime feeding of infants, the provision of sexual services, or care of the sick or elderly is over.

to write *master and servant laws* governing labor contracts that gave them considerable power in both the labor market and within production. Supported by monarchies or by dominated parliaments, capitalist success at getting laws passed outlawing "breaches of contract" not only limited workers' access to alternative jobs in the labor market (as illustrated in Section 7.2.2 above) but bound them to existing jobs, making resistance through flight difficult. But, by so doing forced resistance onto the immediate shop floor.[155]

With respect to struggles to work less, capitalists have promulgated laws facilitating countermeasures. When and where laws permitted chattel slavery, they also sanctioned whatever violence slave-owning capitalists felt required to use. Once legal slavery was abolished, laws concerning indentured, waged and salaried workers only permitted less violent countermeasures. While imposing no constraints as to how employers organize production, no matter how exploitative and alienating, they legalized the power to respond to workers' roles in crises of production (from accidents to struggle) not only by dismissal but also by bringing charges in court that could result in fines, corporal punishment, imprisonment, or transportation.[156]

But, over time, as capitalists have gathered more and more workers together at various sites of production, and as workers have recognized their common situation and organized collectively, they have more effectively threatened absolute surplus value through collective sabotage on the job, strikes, and lobbying for laws, such as the Factory Acts, to mandate shorter working days.

The initial response by capitalists to this new threat was to stiffen oversight and to get laws written and passed that *banned worker attempts to organize collectively* to bargain with their employers. "All combinations contracts, oaths, etc. by which masons and carpenters reciprocally bound themselves were declared null and void. Workers' combinations were treated as heinous crimes from the fourteenth century until 1825."[157] The charge was usually conspiracy – whether the objective was raising wages, shortening the hours of work or improving working conditions. Such laws included the Le Chapelier Law of 1791 in France banning "coalitions" of workers and strikes and the Combination Acts of 1799 and 1800 in Britain banning both trade unions and collective bargaining.

---

155 Although "shop floor" usually refers to factory workspaces, it should be understood here to mean any point of production, whether in a factory, or an agricultural field, mine shaft, ship deck, loading dock, school classroom, home kitchen, etc.

156 In the example of railroad accidents despite being caused by overwork, it was (and continues to be) workers who were charged and convicted of manslaughter rather than the bosses who had forced them to work to exhaustion.

157 *Capital, Vol. 1*, p. 901, or MECW, *Vol. 35*, p. 728.

In response, workers took their struggles underground causing even more disruption.[158] That militant response led Parliament to pass another Act in 1824 legalizing unions. But when that resulted in struggles coming to the surface and spreading quickly, Parliament reversed itself again with the Combination Act of 1825, whose loosely worded prohibition against "threats, intimidation, obstruction and molestation" of strike breakers, made effective collective strike action difficult because biased magistrates would interpret even peaceful informational picketing as "obstruction."

This was the legal situation which the Chartist demands for voting rights were aimed at correcting through electoral politics. The failure of their protests and petitions, however, resulted in unions not being legalized in Britain until the Trade Union Act of 1871.[159] The French Law of 1791 was only partially overturned in 1864 by the Loi Olivier, and not completely replaced until 1884 by the Waldeck-Rousseau Law legalizing collective organizations of workers (and of businesses!).[160]

---

158 This response seems almost universal and has been widespread in regimes that repress overt worker resistance – including colonial, Soviet-style state capitalist and other authoritarian regimes. For colonial regimes, see the work of South Asian subaltern historians and that of James Scott, *Weapons of the Weak: Everyday Forms of Peasant Resistance* (1985) and *Domination and the Arts of Resistance: Hidden Transcripts* (1990). On the USSR, see Raya Dunayevskaya, *Marxism and Freedom* (1958). For covert resistance in communist Hungary, see Mkilós Haraszti, *A Worker in a Worker State* (1977).

159 Legalization came earlier in the United States, in 1842 with the decision in Commonwealth v. Hunt, but that decision was repeatedly circumvented for decades with all kinds of union activities being declared unlawful and frequently repressed with police and military force.

160 Once workers in the US gained the power in the 1930s to force the capitalists in some major industries, e.g., auto and mining, to recognize unions and to negotiate contracts, laws have specified how unions can be formed, among which workers (not all have been covered by such laws), the form, if not the content, of specific negotiated legal contracts between unions and employers, and the circumstances in which strikes are permitted (versus "wildcat" strikes for which unions can be fined for violating the terms of the contract), and so on. Some of these laws are federal and apply to all workers; many are state laws and differ radically, e.g., accepting or banning "closed shops" – where once a union is formed all workers must participate.

In the US, capitalists returned to full-scale assault on labor unions during the first Reagan Administration in the early 1980s. One of its first acts was to crush the Professional Air Controllers Organization (PATCO). By firing over 11,000 workers, Reagan sent a message to business, whose managers took up the attack. Those actions were followed by deregulation that facilitated the ploy of using debt and "Chapter 11 bankruptcy" to undercut union contracts and the removal of, or refusal to enforce, safety regulations that had protected workers in many industries. The success of these attacks, never reversed under Democratic administrations, contributed to a steady decline on the percentage of

Once legalized, unions renewed workers' long-standing demand for less work, fighting for an "8-hour day" – an advance over the 10-hour day established by Robert Owen in 1810 and then won by British workers through the Factory Act of 1847, or the 12-hour day won by French workers after 1848. Owen had coined the slogan which became the mantra of workers' struggles for less work: "Eight hours' labour, Eight hours' recreation, Eight hours' rest", or, the common American version: "Eight hours of work, eight hours of sleep and eight hours for what we will!"

As Marx detailed in Chapter 10, capitalists resisted every demand for less work, fighting against the Factory Acts in Parliament and the Press. Their efforts were buttressed by their apologists – especially economists – who provided arguments as to why less work would have devastating effects on the economy and thus on the welfare of society as a whole. Among those whose arguments Marx addressed directly was Nassau Senior (1790–1864). He argued against the Factory Act of 1839 limiting the use of child labor and the Factory Act of 1847, which granted the 10-hour day. His argument that reducing the working day would wipe out capitalist profits was thoroughly debunked by Marx in Chapter 9, Section 3, of Volume 1 of *Capital*. Senior was not, however, alone among economists in providing arguments about how much work should be forthcoming from workers.

Worker success at forcing their employers to recognize unions and bargain collectively, while forcing some capitalists to grant wage increases, reducing exploitation, has also given other capitalists a new incentive to raise wages: warding off efforts by their own workers to unionize. Higher wages, equal to or even exceeding those won by unionized workers became a price some employers have become willing to pay to avoid all the other annoyances caused by unions, e.g., conflict over working conditions, working hours, etc.

On the ideological front, economists have contributed to this new phase in the class war by providing arguments about the kinds of deals that might be cut, granting some concessions to workers but without seriously impeding the realization of surplus value and profits. As we saw in Chapter 2, Engels recognized and analyzed this shift in his 1885 update to *The Condition of the Working Class in England*.[161] His assertion that labor unions had come to be seen as "perfectly legitimate institutions and as useful means of spreading sound economical doctrines amongst the workers" is amply illustrated by the case of William

---

workers organized in unions and capable of collective bargaining – a trend only recently showing signs of reversal.

161 Engels, F., "England in 1845 and in 1885," MECW, *Vol. 26*, p. 297.

Stanley Jevons (1835–1882), one of the main contributors to the "marginalist revolution" that turned political economy into neoclassical economics.

In a lecture on "The importance of Diffusing Knowledge of Political Economy," originally delivered to public primary school teachers in 1866, Jevons argued for the instruction of workers to begin at a very early age – "almost as soon, in fact, as a boy [sic!] has acquired the power of reading with facility."[162] The urgency Jevons saw for such education was two-fold, first it was aimed at reducing future strife such as strikes and violence, and second, the prospect of the working classes of England obtaining the right to vote raised the specter of workers successfully imposing laws such as "minimum wage" or "living wage" laws that would violate the "natural laws that govern the relations of capital and labor" and disrupt the economy, undermine liberty and drive capitalists to invest abroad.

In that lecture, and in a subsequent invited lecture given two years later to Trades Unionists' Political Association in Manchester, Jevons spelled out in some detail which kinds of struggles he thought legitimate for union actions and which were not.[163] Among those actions he felt were legitimate were: the mutual aid activities of "friendly societies," demands for greater safety, sanitation, etc., in working conditions, and *the demands for shorter working hours*. In the case of working hours, Jevons clearly thought that workers were perfectly justified in wanting to take part of the fruits of rising productivity in less work. This was a major shift from Senior's absolute opposition to any reduction in the working day.

His position on this subject was based on his marginalist theory. Although he didn't recognize it, his position was consistent with Marx's theory of relative surplus value via rising productivity. In both cases, the possibilities of combining increased profits with less work were endless. The only issue is how much of the gains do workers get (and in what form) and how much do capitalists get. Only capitalist greed, demanding 100 percent of productivity gains in the form of surplus value precludes any reduction in work. When Marx was writing in the 1860s, capitalists were generally holding out for that 100 percent. But by the 1880s, under pressure from unions and with the help of marginalist theory, some were beginning to see alternatives. Jevons' only caveats were

162 In R. D. Collison Black, ed., *Papers and Correspondence of William Stanley Jevons, Vol. VII: Papers on Political Economy* (London: MacMillan Press, 1981).

163 In W. Stanley Jevons, *Methods of Social Reform and other Papers* (London: MacMillan & Company, 1883) reprinted (New York: Augustus M. Kelley Publisher, 1965), 101–121. See too, in the same collection, his essay on "Industrial Partnerships" in which Jevons supports profit sharing to stabilize capital-labor relationships and avoid conflict, strikes and political turmoil.

first, that reductions in work time should not exceed the rise in productivity, which would have the effect of cutting into profits, capital investment and future accumulation and second, that workers should be educated to improve their character and make better use of their free time.[164] Recognizing how rising productivity and wages can lead to the desire for more leisure would become common among neoclassical economists in the years that followed.[165]

Despite such efforts, workers taking time away from work for themselves has continued to be so prevalent on the job that whole industries of surveillance and legal prosecution have grown up to identify and minimize "time theft."[166]

8.1.1.2 Countering Resistance to Alienation

Although the term "alienation" has only recently been added to the vocabulary of those capitalists have hired to study and help control their workers, e.g., managers and industrial sociologists and psychologists, the existence of worker discontent with various aspects of their jobs has always been known and dealt with by bosses in various ways. Marx's breakdown of alienation into four kinds can serve to organize how functionaries of capital have responded to discontent. Efforts to turn alienated workers into happy ones who "whistle while they work," like the dwarves in Disney's film *Snow White* (1937), have sometimes been a joke, sometime serious.[167]

---

164 Jevon's racism and class bias against workers is sketched in Michael White, "Bridging the Natural and the Social Science and Character in Jevon's Political Economy" *Economic Inquiry* XXXII, no. 3 (July 1994): 429–444.

165 But not among capitalists. Resistance continued, theory be damned, until waves of workers' struggles, in the wake of the Russian Revolution in 1917 and then by industrial unions during the Great Depression of the 1930s, imposed the long-sought 8-hour day and 40-hour week, at least for well-organized union workers.

166 While portraying the simple, over-long cigarette break in his film *Modern Times* (1936), Chaplin provides a glimpse of future electronic surveillance when the boss, who has been spying on Charlie's break, suddenly appears on a screen screaming at him to get back to work! While the scene in Chaplin's film and George Orwell's omnipresent state surveillance in his novel *1984* (1949) were based on imaginary projections of the physical surveillance long deployed by capitalists, their prophetic quality has been borne out in contemporary electronic surveillance of workers while they are working. An early TV advertisement for America Online (AOL) zoomed in on an office worker sitting in a cubicle who turns, looks at the camera and says "The boss thinks I'm working; but I'm really browsing the web with America Online! Heh, heh." Not only did the ad soon disappear, but capitalists were soon putting limits on such employee use of computers for their own purposes. See, for example, the website of Epay Systems, its variety of employee surveillance software and download its e-book *How to Prevent Workforce Time Theft*. (Accessed 7/16/2024.)

167 Screened in a time of militant worker mobilizations during the Great Depression, Disney's depiction of miners as cute, lovable and happy workers must have struck members of

First, in the case of alienation from work due to a lack of control – being forced to follow others' orders as to what to do, how to do it, with what tools, etc., capitalists have complemented their hierarchies of income (and access to wealth) with a parallel hierarchy of degrees of supervision and control. At the bottom, among waged workers in fields, mines or factories, capitalists have often sought to exert absolute control over every detail of the work. It has been the objective of imposing de-skilling and a finely organized division of labor – the kind of thing described by Adam Smith in his analysis of pin production that opens his *Wealth of Nations* and by Marx in *Capital*. Both authors saw and critiqued how such meticulous control over every moment of work was debilitating for workers and conducive to dissatisfaction. Smith, writing in 1776, was concerned with manufacturing – workers using tools to make things, or parts of things, by hand. Such work requires close supervision to keep workers working and minimize their opportunities to use their knowledge of their tools to work less. Marx, writing decades later, was preoccupied with how capitalists used machines to control workers, subordinating their physical labor to the rhythms of mechanical devices. In both cases, the main managerial responses to worker discontent have been repressive: close supervision and threats of firing and replacement.[168] An exception, which Marx explored in Chapter 21 of *Capital*, has been the imposition of piecework and the replacement of annoying direct supervision with quality control. Where piece rates are set low enough to motivate intense work, that method, of course, only intensifies alienation rather than alleviating it.[169]

But, as you move up the income/control hierarchy, the degree to which managers try to impose detailed control is reduced and workers are allowed greater latitude in exactly how they utilize their tools or operate their machines. At

---

the United Mine Workers, who had only gained collective bargaining rights in 1933, as grotesque, perhaps designed to divert the general public's attention from the stark realities of their struggles. Recent criticism has emphasized its stereotypical treatment of dwarves but not its misrepresentation of workers' attitudes.

168 Eventually, as sociologists were mobilized to study discontent in rote work on assembly lines and such, other responses were suggested. One was to rotate jobs, shift individual workers from one narrow activity to another. Another was to reorganize the work into teams. Both approaches seek to avoid boredom and to give workers a sense of the whole production process in which each worker plays only one small part. See, for example, Robert Blauner, *Alienation and Freedom: The Factory Worker and His Industry* (Chicago: University of Chicago Press, 1964).

169 Harry Braverman's book *Labor and Monopoly Capital: the Degradation of Work in the Twentieth Century* (1974) provides nice examples of the extension of such detailed control into the various new methods of work that developed in the decades following Marx and Engels' time.

higher levels, say among scientists and engineers, capitalists only exercise control by setting frameworks, e.g., defining the kind of research needed or the new applications needing design, but leaving the choice of tools and how they are used to the workers involved. The more capitalists require creativity in a job, the greater the likelihood of workers being granted the freedom to use their imagination. This is apparent in those industries devoted to entertainment – the diversion of worker attention from struggle to passive reception of crafted spectacles, from traditional theatre, concerts, and sports to the film industry – just emerging as Engels died in 1895. Clearly, the more control workers have over their work, the less discontent they are likely to feel, even though the overall framework within which they are working is set by others. Alienation remains but is felt less keenly.

The alienation of workers from their products, owned by their bosses (or corporate entities) and only legally appropriable by workers through purchase, is built-in to the system and, as previously discussed, conducive to direct appropriation or sabotage. Besides surveillance to minimize such actions, some managers have also sought to foster worker identification with the company in which they are employed and its products. Two methods have been used: profit sharing and identification with the company's "brand." With profit-sharing, workers get a personal stake in the success of "their" company, with sales of "their" products.[170] With attachment to "brand" workers are encouraged to *feel* like the products of their labors are "theirs," at least in the sense of being the products of their work. As capitalist efforts to sell usually involve salespersons touting the good qualities of "their" products, it is with those qualities that managers would like their workers to identify – even to the point of being willing to testify in advertisements about those good qualities to which they are "proud" to have contributed! The rare exceptions to absolute alienation of the product have been when workers have been paid, in part, with some small portion of their product, e.g., farm workers getting part of the harvest as payment or Linebaugh's silk workers getting excess cloth.

Because the alienation of workers from each other has always been a mainstay of capitalist management, "divide and conquer" being the name of the game, ostensible efforts to foster things such as "teamwork" have been either superficial (and mocked by workers) or risk contributing to anti-management bonding and collective resistance – of the sort Marx thought inherent in bringing workers together under similar circumstances of exploitation and

170 Sometimes employers encourage workers to buy their company's products by giving them employee discounts. Their own use of "their" products serves as both motivation and advertising.

alienation. So, the wage/salary/income/control hierarchies have continued to be vital to stimulating worker against worker competition wherever promotion or some kind of reward for extra work has been possible. So too, have been the use of every identifiable (gender, age, race, ethnicity, language, etc.) difference to pit workers against each other.

Although capitalists sometimes give lip-service to "respecting and treating their workers as human beings" with wills of their own, what Marx considers the essential "being" of the human species, managers' need for control over what workers are doing requires carefully setting limits to whatever freedom workers are granted to exercise their collective will – to make sure workers' "choices" remain within those limits. So, even where teams in factories, mines, or fields are allowed to organize who does what when, their choices are limited by both manager-set objectives and available tools and methods. The same is true even where workers seem to have the greatest freedom, e.g., in academic laboratories. By controlling research funds and requiring the designation of "principal investigator" (PI) in grant applications, capitalists are able to determine what gets researched, by which team of collaborating scientists, and who is held to account.

As for life outside their waged or salaried jobs, already in Marx and Engels time, capitalists were beginning to infringe on workers' self-determination, both individual and collective, to make sure their choices would shape that life to reproduce labor-power rather than undermine it. As previously indicated, that shaping has become ever more detailed and intrusive, in families, in communities, in schools, in everyday experiences throughout the social factory.[171]

8.1.2 Countering Harm from Nature

Given 1) the demonstrated proclivity of nineteenth century capitalists to impose poverty-level wages and horrible living conditions on workers, 2) their equally demonstrated lack of action when millions were dying in colonies, and 3) how little they regularly allowed to be spent on "relief," their only apparent motives for doing anything at all to counter harm to workers from natural phenomena were two-fold: threats to their needed supply of labor-power and threat of angry uprisings by suffering workers.

171 Examine the endless contemporary blather about "work/life balance" and you will see how the ideal "balance" keeps you "productive" on the job, avoiding any physical or mental breakdown that might impair work performance. This view is closely related to the identification of "mental health" with the ability to hold down a job, whether waged or unwaged.

The reaction of capitalists – either individual firms or through their collective influence with governments – whose labor force (and the costs of its maintenance) were plagued by disease, I've already discussed in Section 7.2.3.1 Here I want to address how the poor quality of both factories and worker housing made workers vulnerable to other "natural" threats and how their bosses responded.

Along with low wages and miserable "relief", cost-minimizing capitalists tended to spend as little as possible building factories and even less on shoddy, working-class housing, making both kinds of constructions vulnerable to fire, flood and earthquakes. (Discussed in Chapter 5 section 2.1.2) Painful experience of the dangers posed by these practices did lead to widespread protests by workers from all parts of the wage/wealth hierarchy and the creation of building codes to counter the worst results of such behavior. For example, the Great Fire of London in 1666 that decimated timber-based buildings and fear of "rebellion amongst the dispossessed refugees" led to the Rebuilding of London Act requiring some fire resistance in construction.[172] Continued vulnerabilities eventually led to national standards in Britain with the Building Act of 1844 regulating many aspects of building design and construction. However, given what Engels observed and Marx found in the reports of Public Health and Factory Inspectors, it seems those standards were poorly enforced, workers continued to suffer from that failure, and labor shortages were recurrent.

Natural threats to poor construction, of course, have varied according to the geographies of empire. While earthquakes strong enough to cause serious damage to factories and human habitations were relatively rare in nineteenth century Great Britain, they were far more common and devastating in other areas, e.g., Venezuela (1812), Palestine (1837), Japan (1847, 1854, 1896), Italy (1857, 1887), Iran (1893), striking not only on land but also offshore, promulgating tsunamis that have wreaked havoc on coastal cities and communities. The same has been true with flooding due to heavy monsoons or violent storms, far more destructive along rivers and in low lying deltas than further inland. To reduce damage from flooding, dams and levees have been built – usually by capitalists under contract to governments, and paid for by tax-paying workers. When such constructions have been poorly executed and subsequently given way, the results have been even more devastating, e.g., the Great Sheffield Flood of 1864 brought on by the collapse of the Dale Kyke Dam upon its very

172 See, Thomas Reddaway, *The Rebuilding of London after the Great Fire* (1940) and the review by A. H. Thomas in *History* 25, no. 98 (September 1940): 97–112, which compares it to earlier studies. See too, John Schofield, "Buildings in the City of London after the Great Fire of 1666" *International Journal of Historical Archaeology* 26, no. 2 (June 2022): 401–433.

first filling! Once again, catastrophe led to revision of the design and building of such structures.[173] To reduce the damage from earthquakes, building codes have been upgraded where the problem has been recurrent, although corruption has guaranteed limited enforcement.[174]

8.2 *Countering Breakdowns in the Means of Production*

Breakdowns in the means of production can be caused either by deficient quantity or by deficient quality. Difficulties with the quality of the means of production can happen in both their production and in their utilization. With the quality of the means of production, *MP*, being key to the costs of production of those who buy them, and thus to their bottom line, those purchasing *MP* pay close attention to the quality of what they buy. Knowing this, the producers of *MP* must pay just as close attention to the quality of the *MP* they are bringing to market. Once purchased, once *M* – *C*(*MP*) is completed and *MP* are fed into the production process their quality and how they are handled or miss-handled, will determine their effective costs and thus profits.

8.2.1 Countering Workers' Actions vis-à-vis *MP*

As in the case of *C*(*MS*), the recognition by bosses of the threat of exploited and alienated mine, agricultural or machine workers sabotaging, to a greater or lesser degree, their production of *C*(*MP*) and reducing their quality has motivated many means of surveillance. Some methods of surveillance have been direct, e.g., overseers watching workers while they work; some have been indirect, e.g., the exercise of quality control to catch the results of any sabotage and to identify those responsible. In Chapter 5, Section 2.2.1, I mentioned the example of miners adding rock to the ore they cut when its weight determines their wage. Until outlawed, mine companies would employ children, "breaker boys", sitting next to conveyor belts carrying the new ore, with the job of spotting and removing such rocks and other "impurities." When workers are paid by the piece and piece-rates are kept low to encourage more intense labor, the same dynamic also encourages carelessness with the potential for damaging the pieces being produced. In fruit harvesting, for example, fast but rough

173 Even today, the limits to such efforts have been clear in such catastrophes as that suffered in 2005 by New Orleans as a result of Hurricane Katrina. Rebuilding the most devastated part of the city (the Black working class Lower Ninth Ward) has largely depended on grassroots efforts such as lowernine.org. (Accessed 7/16/2024.)

174 This has continued to the present day. See in Chapter 5, the example of the 2013 collapse of the Rama Plaza building in Dhaka, Bangladesh (footnote 37) and the treatment of corruption in the TV Show *Endeavor* (footnote 92).

handling can produce bruised and hard to sell fruit. Even tiny variations in machine tool manufacturing can make pieces unusable and thus either unsellable or requiring expensive replacement. Thus, the importance of quality control to assure the quality of work as measured by the quality of the product.

While consulting with cannery workers in South Texas, I observed an assembly line of women forking cooked spinach into cans which were then placed on a conveyer at the end of which they were weighed to make sure just enough spinach was in each can. Because each worker's supply of cans was marked to identify the individual worker, the quality control operator checking the weight of the cans could identify any woman whose weight was either too low or too high. Similar modes of quality control have been utilized by capitalist bosses throughout every domain of production.

In the two cases Marx noted, of Surat cotton and Chinese silkworm cocoons, the filth of the first and the irregularity of the second suggest serious failure on the part of those managing their production to exert effective quality control. We don't know exactly who was responsible, only that there was a breakdown in the production of these two *MP* used in the production of textiles.

8.2.2 Countering Harm from Nature

Just as capitalists try to organize and control workers to minimize disruptions they may cause, either in the production of *MP* or in their utilization, so too do they try to protect their production of commodities from the vagaries of Nature. Levees along rivers are raised to protect crops from flooding. Dams can do the same, but also provide controlled flows of water for irrigation or to drive machinery (or later for hydroelectric power). Typically, capitalists try to get governments to finance such infrastructure projects. When sufficient ground water is available, from dams or wells, irrigation nourishes crops in dry lands. By also protecting them from drought or flood, these measures prevent dramatic variations in the quantity and quality of crops and associated changes in price and profitability – to both *MP* producers and *MP* consumers.

Irrigation also facilitates multi-cropping in the tropics, which evens out the production of *MP* over the growing seasons and helps counter the problem Marx noted of capitalists finding it easier to quickly increase their machines than their supplies of raw materials. In temperate climates, capitalists complement irrigation with "hot houses", essentially moving production inside to protect crops from variations in the weather.

Similar to artificially supplying steady amounts of water to plants (and animals) has been the practice of countering both soil depletion (as plants suck up nutrients) and any original lack of nutrients (poor soils) with fertilization, either through rotating crops, or by adding nutrients, from animal wastes or manufactured fertilizers. As Marx pointed out, the capitalist separation of rural agricultural production from urban manufacturing (and the concentration of population in cities) makes this harder because, it makes the return to soil of processed agricultural products more difficult.

The agribusiness practice of short-term profit maximization through monoculture, which makes the crop more vulnerable to any disease or parasite to which the one chosen strain proves susceptible, has forced capitalists to turn to poisons (pesticides or fungicides) to counter infestations of bugs or fungi feasting on crops. As parasites develop tolerance to such poisons, dosage is increased over time, and eventually operators are forced to have recourse to new poisons. The develop of ever new poisons is, of course, costly, so capitalists have done their best to shift the cost onto taxpayers (government subsidies) or to invest in their development by the chemical industry.[175] So, profiting from monoculture opens the door to profits from the ever-greater amount (or type) of chemicals required to protect crops.

While all the measures listed above are taken to avoid natural erratic fluctuations in particular processes of commodity production, capitalists in many industries also use the quite different but common strategy: diversifying their sources of *MP*. So, if, for example, a disease ravages crops or animals in one place, or a political blockade cuts off sources from another place, access to multiple sources reduces disruption and the degree of crisis for buyers of *MP*. Sometimes diversification has been forced, as in the sudden cut-off of grain from the continent during the Napoleonic Wars or that of cotton during the American Civil War. But repeated experience with the dangers of having a single source has taught capitalists to diversify to avoid such moments.[176]

Against all these threats to the quality and quantity of their means of production, capitalists have invested in the insurance industry – both in the sense

175 This tendency has accelerated with modern methods of hybridization and genetic modification – as illustrated by the case of corn leaf blight mentioned earlier in Chapter 5, footnote 50. Within husbandry, "factory farming," has resulted in a dramatically high propensity to circulate disease within dense populations of animals. To counteract that threat, capitalists have had recourse to extensive use of antibiotics and other drugs to prevent or contain disease – a measure which, in turn, has led to new resistant strains of disease that threaten both the animals and their human consumers, e.g., mad cow disease, or the new H_5N_1 bird flu.

176 This has become such a standard practice among capitalists that it has been used as an argument against blockades of sources for political reasons. Cutting off one source will have little effect when multiple alternative sources are available.

of elaborating the industry itself and in that of buying insurance against risks from various disasters, both natural and man-made. Pre-dating the age of industrial capitalism, the insurance industry developed in reaction to risks to property, including mercantile trade and long-distance shipping. Given risks to ships, cargo, and personnel from storms to piracy, insurance buys some compensation for loss.

8.3 *Offsets to Crises Due to Rising Organic Composition of Capital*

Because raising the organic composition of capital is based on increasing the technical composition, *MP/LP*, primarily by substituting labor-displacing machines for workers, this strategy creates two kinds of problems for capitalists. First, because it always involves a reorganization of production and has often been aimed at undercutting workers' power, they resist – with slowdowns and strikes or the destruction of machinery, even whole factories. How capitalists have chosen to cope with that resistance has varied. Second, because this strategy has tended to be adopted in sector after sector, from manufacturing through agriculture to finance, the spreading displacement of workers undermines capital's need to find jobs to keep the vast majority of the population under control – either in jobs, preparing for jobs or rearing and repairing those condemned to jobs. Let's see how capitalists have responded to these two tendencies to crisis.

With respect to worker resistance, many have had recourse to the immediate use of force by mobilizing their goons to take out activists, or calling in the cops or militia or army to put down strikes, etc. Other capitalist managers have tried to convince workers that bringing in machinery is being imposed by competition and is therefore unavoidable. This argument was portrayed by Charlotte Brontë in her novel *Shirley* in which a capitalist, Mr. Moore, appeals to competition in refusing to even slow down the installation of new frames and shears into his mill.

> ... if I stopped by the way an instant, while others are rushing on, I should be trodden down. If I did as you wish me to do, I should be bankrupt in a month: and would my bankruptcy put bread into your hungry children's mouths?[177]

Failing to convince his workers to accept his planned investment, Mr. Moore switches to the more common response in Marx and Engels' time: appeals to

177 Charlotte Brontë, *Shirley, A Tale* (New York: Penguin Classics, 1985) 157.

law and force, the government, its troops and judiciary to pursue, prosecute and punish (through transportation to Australia) those workers who would destroy his machines and attack his mill. In this fictional case and in many actual ones the competition is local. But as capitalism has globalized the capitalist appeal to competition to get workers to accept increases in the organic composition of capital has come to evoke foreign as well as local competition – including either threatening to move production abroad to cheaper, more compliant labor forces or actually doing so with some operations in order to threaten others.[178]

As workers have won the legalization of unions and collective bargaining, along with reduced working hours and higher wages, some capitalists have found themselves forced to negotiate with workers. However much they might appeal to "managerial prerogative", workers have forced "shopfloor" issues, such as changes in technology onto the negotiating agenda, alongside wages, hours, benefits, etc. In these situations, thanks to economists who have shown how the increased productivity achieved by investing in new technology can finance both higher wages and more profits, some capitalists have cut deals with workers by offering higher wages in exchange for collaboration with labor-displacing changes in technology. More money to quell worker resistance to the loss of jobs with new technologies.[179]

With respect to the second problem – that of creating enough jobs to keep people working (both waged and unwaged) – where letting the unemployed starve is not an option (as it sometimes has been), capitalists have found several options. The primary counter has been the creation of new jobs, either through the expansion of existing industries, at home or abroad, or the creation of new ones. In the long term, although only beginning in Marx and Engels' time, the primary source of new industries has been in the creation of services, of all sorts. Along the way, of course, The solution to unemployed workers refusing

178 In the twentieth century, the rapid development and deployment of the multinational corporation with production and sales located in several countries has complemented more traditional threats of competition from foreign based firms. Both kinds of threat continue to be used by capital to obtain worker concessions to desired, labor-displacing changes. One vivid portrayal of such methods can be found in Michael Moore's film *Roger & Me* (1989) about General Motors closing down auto plants in Flint Michigan and outsourcing the jobs to cheaper labor in Mexico. (Accessed 7/16/2024.)

179 A dramatic example of such deals was that struck between the United Mine Workers union and mine owners in the 1950 National Bituminous Coal and Wage Agreement. The results included a doubling of productivity over the next decade along with a halving of the labor force and increased wages for those who retained their jobs. See, William Cleaver, "Wildcats in the Appalachian Coal Fields" *Zerowork 1* (1975): 113–127.

to play by the rules – searching quietly for jobs – has been prison or transportation and forced labor. The solution for children whose employment has been made illegal thanks to worker struggles: workhouses then schools, i.e., incarceration and the unwaged work of accepting discipline and a modicum of training for future employment. Similarly, with women when and where they have been excluded from the work force: the unwaged labor of reproducing labor-power. Sometimes governments have created make-work projects, hiring the unemployed with taxpayer money, in response to economic crises, e.g., the National Workshops created in 1848 in response to demands from unemployed workers.[180] Finally, in the absence of the means to implement such organized solutions, tolerance for letting people create their own modes of survival: the so-called "informal" economy discussed in Chapter 3, footnote 56.

8.4 *Offsets to the Falling Rate of Profit Tendency*

Marx's most detailed assessment of offsets or counters to the tendency of the rate of profit to fall identifies five factors. His discussions of these five Engels collects in Chapter 13 on "Counteracting Factors" in Volume 3 of *Capital*.

The first of the five factors is the "More Intense Exploitation of Labour." Greater intensity means working harder, working faster in a given time. The primary way capitalists achieve this, Marx shows, is through their use of machinery. For one thing, many machines can be speeded up, forcing workers to keep up by working faster.[181] For another, where work on machines is reduced to mere tending (see above), workers can be forced to tend or take care of two or more machines. The classic case in the textile industry is the tending of looms, which, once set up, mostly require only the quick repair of broken threads. So, workers, often children in the nineteenth century, can be set to watching and fixing breaks in more than one loom, shuffling from one

180 More recent examples have included the Civilian Conservation Corps created by the Roosevelt Administration during the Great Depression of the 1930s and Food-for-Work, famine relief programs run by national governments, international institutions such as the UN or private charities. Although originating during the early, tumultuous years of the Soviet Union, state maintenance of employment became permanent as that state-capitalist government effectively guaranteed employment for all who wanted it.

181 The most familiar modern example is the assembly line whose speed is controlled not by workers but by management – mentioned previously in a footnote to Chapter 3. But the same dynamic exists for many other kinds of machines, such as those used in agribusiness. How fast machines like the early McCormick reapers or modern harvesting rigs are towed determines the work speed of the farm workers who collect cut grain or cut produce.

to another as required and, in the process, overseeing the transformation of much more thread into cloth.

An entirely different kind of offset deriving from the deployment of machinery has been its use in providing excuses for prolonging the working day – fighting efforts of workers to shorten it. Where machines are inside and lighting is available, machines can be run 24 hours a day, with multiple shifts of workers. Where set-up time (when no raw material is being processed) is substantial, employers try to minimize costs by keeping machines running as long as possible. All these methods are aimed at increasing the rate of exploitation, s/v, and total surplus value, s, where possible. Finally, Marx points out how the use of machines facilitates the employment of women and children and thus the extraction of more surplus labor from working-class families.

The second factor is the "Reduction of Wages Below Their Value." Although only mentioned in Chapter 13, by evoking "competition", he clearly has in mind anything that increases competition among workers for jobs and by so doing forces them to accept lower wages, v, which lowers $(v + c)$, raising profits, $s/(v + c)$. This could, for example, be true for any influx of migrant or immigrant labor. Both phenomena increase the likelihood that employers are able to drive down wages, even below levels required to reproduce employed workers at their existing level of skill and endurance. Result: malnutrition, illness, more accidents, shorter lives. The frequency of this in the nineteenth century leads Marx to call it "one of the most important factors in stemming the tendency for the rate of profit to fall."[182]

The third factor is the "Cheapening of the Elements of Constant Capital." Cheapening "c" clearly complements cheapening "v" with the similar result of lowering $(v + c)$ and raising the rate of profit. With most of Chapter 5 in Volume 3 devoted to this subject, it is only mentioned here. Unlike some of his later followers, he does NOT conclude that this contradicts his argument about the tendency of the rate of profit to fall.[183] It doesn't because no fall in the value of constant capital *unconnected* to a change in *ML/LP* will change the organic composition of capital, c_o/v_o.

The fourth factor is "The Relative Surplus Population", the growth of which is accelerated by the substitution of machinery for labor. That growth

182 *Capital, Vol. 3*, p. 342, or *MECW, Vol. 37*, p. 234.

183 Such was the conclusion of Paul Sweezy who thought this observation invalidated the "Tendency." See, Paul Sweezy, *The Theory of Capitalist Development* (New York: Monthly Review Press, 1942), Chapter VI.

contributes to the cheapening of labor, v, which 1) by itself raises s/v, lowers $(c + v)$ and raises $s/(c + v)$ and 2) facilitates the development of new industries which by drawing on that cheap labor often have rates of profit higher than average and help offset the tendency for the average to fall. Given how capitalists have repeatedly turned worker creativity to account by creating new products and new very profitable industries, over the long term this factor has proved extremely important.[184]

The fifth factor is "Foreign Trade." Here Marx notes its contradictory effects. When it brings in cheaper *MP* and *MS*, this will increase profits by reducing the value of c and v, that increase in profits will accelerate accumulation and therefore the tendencies for the organic composition of capital to rise and the rate of profit to fall. But he also notes how "investment in foreign trade can yield a higher rate of profit", indeed, a "surplus profit", much like early investors in new technology who are able to sell their goods above their value because their competitors have lower productivity. Foreign trade, of course, is often accompanied by direct foreign investment (taking over production) that, he points out, can also earn a higher rate of profit, partly because of cheaper labor ("slaves and coolies").[185] The advantages of more developed countries, which can sell their products to lesser developed ones at lower prices ("battering down the walls of China"), can, however, result in overproduction in the latter – another kind of crisis all together.[186]

The sixth and last of Marx's "other factors" is "The Increase in Share Capital." From the point of view of the company that *sells* "shares", say initial stock offerings to raise money for real investment, *M* – *C*(*MP, LP*), the money raised is money borrowed and will have to be paid back with interest, a deduction from its profits or surplus value. For Marx, "interest", no matter who gets it, is, like rent, paid out of surplus value.[187] Stock issuance, like the financial intermediation of banks that take in deposits and loan out money for real investment, is a way of channeling money that might otherwise be spent on consumption into real investment. However, from the point of view of whoever *buys* the shares, whether from the issuing company or on the open market, they are making

184 As mentioned in Chapter 3, the rise of the service sector in the post-WWII period was every bit as striking as the earlier rise of manufacturing against the backdrop of mostly agrarian economies. As worker success in raising wages and consumer demand made it possible for capitalists to convert one human activity after another into the production of service commodities, many of those industries that Marx had dismissed as negligible became quite important for capitalist development as a whole.

185 *Capital, Vol. 3*, p. 345, *MECW, Vol. 37*, p. 236.

186 Ibid., p. 346.

187 Part 5 of Volume 3 is devoted to this question.

an "investment" only in the limited sense that shares are claims on the issuing company's earnings out of which they will receive income. Although in his short comment, Marx does not make clear how an increase in share capital constitutes a "counteracting factor", we can postulate two contradictory effects. First, when issuing companies plow the money gained into real investment, it will hasten accumulation and, as assumed elsewhere in this chapter, this may hasten the *fall* in the rate of profit. But second, we also know that the rapid growth of the "joint-stock" company, owned by many but managed by few, resulted in a booming stock market rife with speculation, i.e., buying and selling shares on the basis of changes in their expected value rather than on the basis of whatever profit was gained from the investment their issuance made possible. Such speculative buying and selling diverts money away from real investment, slows accumulation and thus counteracts the tendency of the rate of profit to fall.[188]

Once we understand that at the heart of "the tendency of the rate of profit to fall" lies the increasing difficulty of putting people to work, resulting from the steady increase in technical and organic compositions of capital, then pretty much everything that creates new jobs has the short-run ability to offset the tendency even if, in the long-run, such new employment proves profitable, accelerates accumulation, and "hastens the tendency."

9 Offsets in the Third Stage of the Circuit: Sales

Having identified the possibilities and predispositions to crisis in three different kinds of markets, for slave labor-power, for the means of subsistence and for the means of production, let's turn to the strategies used to offset, prevent or respond to these crises.

9.1 *Dealing with Crises in Selling Slaves, C(LP) – M′*

Given the way force has always been involved in some humans enslaving others, the resistance by slaves, whether daily slacking, sabotage, or efforts to escape or revolt have also generally been met by force. The brutality of many

188 In the wake of the Great Depression of the 1930s, various financial regulations were imposed precisely to reduce such speculation and encourage real investment. The financial *de*regulation imposed in the early 1980s had precisely the opposite effect and contributed to a whole series of financial and economic crises in the following decades, e.g., the collapse of the American Saving & Loan Industry in 1987, the "dot.com" bubble and bust in the 1990s, the housing bubble in 2006–2008 and resulting crash.

slave owners has been well documented in their acquisition, transportation (the slave trade) and deployment in production. Where slave owners have had the power, laws were written – such as the Fugitive Slave Act of 1850 – to protect their rights over their human property and spur local authorities to help recapture runaways. The formation of slave patrols to hunt down slaves trying to escape and forcibly return them to their masters was common. Those authorities were usually local but in response to large-scale slave revolt, such as the insurrection in the French colony of Saint-Domingue (1791–1804) led by Toussaint Louverture or Nat Turner's revolt in Virginia in 1831 or in reaction to the Emancipation Proclamation (1863), all pro-slavery authorities coalesced to crush such efforts. In Saint-Dominque, local then French troops sought and failed to defeat the insurrection, followed by intervening British forces that also failed, resulting in the success of those slave revolutionaries spreading fear among slave owners everywhere. In Virginia, state militia and federal troops were used to put down Nat Turner's Rebellion. In response to the Emancipation Proclamation, the slave owning southern states created the Confederacy to form a breakaway independent slave-owning nation and reorganized state militias into the Confederate army to fight a war of succession to preserve slavery.

Despite and partly in reaction to all this repression, the struggles of slaves, ex-slaves, and abolitionists to outlaw slavery and all its brutality went on, year after year, decade after decade, in the public arena, in the courts and in parliaments. Slavers and pro-slavery ideologs, of course, fought back in what proved, eventually, a losing battle.

The spread of anti-slavery and abolitionist ideas forced slavers and their apologists to come up with justifications for slavery. A central rationale – unsupported by scientific evidence and derided by most scientists – was that negroes are an inferior "race," another form of primate with brains inferior to those of white humans of European descent. It was an idea that paralleled similar arguments about the inherent inferiority of women that made them, it was argued, unfit for higher level jobs. The pseudo-scientific argument that essentially classified negroes as sub-human animals, made their enslavement as reasonable as that of other non-humans, such as horses or cattle. This ideology, which would later mutate into eugenics, was often complemented by the Christian beliefs that God gave humans dominion over all of nature to use for their own purposes. However, interpretations of religion to justified slavery was not limited to Christianity but could also be found in Judaism, Islam, Hinduism and Buddhism.

Others rejected such interpretations and argued against them on either theological grounds or differing philosophies, so conflicts over the legitimacy of slavery unfolded within all these religions alongside those in secular institutions such as mass media, the courts, and parliaments with some offering defenses of slavery and others attacking it. Despite the slave *trade* being made illegal in the United States by the Slave Trade Act of 1794, in Britain by the Act for the Abolition of the Slave Trade in 1807 and throughout the British Empire by the Slavery Abolition Act of 1833, these arguments continued.

One famous debate was between Thomas Carlisle (1795–1881) and John Stuart Mill (1806–1873). The discovery that slavery effectively continued in the West Indies led to renewed abolitionist efforts to suppress it. Against those efforts, Carlisle, a racist who believed that Anglo-Saxons constituted a superior race, published a vicious essay in 1849 supporting the official relegalization of slavery. John Stuart Mill responded with a counter essay. Carlisle's belief that labor was a virtue and work should be imposed on any who resisted, both the waged and unwaged, was countered by Mill's utilitarian understanding that while work was necessary and should be adequately compensated, its shirking was understandable.[189]

Another, albeit less prevalent pro-slavery idea was that while ownership of slaves was justified, it also involved as much responsibility for the welfare of slaves as for the welfare of other animals. This role was largely ignored by more brutal owners but embraced by those with a feudal-like sense of "*noblesse oblige*" toward their inferiors. Those who drew rationales for slavery from the Christian Bible, argued parallels between the divine right of husbands (men) over wives (women) and children.[190] Not surprisingly, the idea more often guided the behavior of slave owners toward slaves working within their homes than toward field hands. This idea was consistent with Christian ideas that emphasized human "stewardship" over the rest of nature, not merely the right to exploitation.[191] In the US, Christian justifications of slavery outlived emancipation.[192]

Although slavery was outlawed in most of the British Empire by 1833, it took almost thirty more years before the Emancipation Proclamation in 1863

189 The two essays are available together as *The Nigger Question and the Negro Question* (Whitefish, MT: Kessinger Publishing Reprints, 2010).

190 See, Elizabeth Jemison, "Proslavery Christianity After the Emancipation," *Tennessee Historical Quarterly*, Vol. 72, no. 4 (Winter 2013): 255–268.

191 This racist idea would mutate in the post-Civil War South into the paternalistic attitudes of whites toward legally free but employed black servants – right up to the present day.

192 See, Jemison, "Proslavery Christianity After the Emancipation," op. cit.

outlawed slavery in the United States.[193] It is worth noting that even with the abolition of slavery, its replacement with indenture or some variation of the "master and servant" laws succeeded for many years in legalizing what amounted to alternative forms of unfree labor, especially in colonies. And in the United States, as previously noted, the propagation of Jim Crow Laws and Constitutional Amendment No. 13, which permits forced labor in prisons, aimed at the same objective.

Yet, despite these adjustments through which some capitalists succeeded in limiting the freedom of supposedly "free" labor, many other capitalists have been able to maintain out-and-out slavery, albeit illegal. In some cases, slavers have been able to do this through corruption, i.e., buying complicity from the government or its agents. Other capitalists have moved their slaves into the shadows, out of public view, sequestering them in homes, orphanages, brothels, sweat shops, remote farms, or fishing vessels at sea where they are put to work and exploited, or sold off to other capitalists for similar purposes.[194]

9.2 *Dealing with Crises in Selling C(MS)' or C(MP)'*

As noted in Chapter 4, Section 5.2, the common, everyday problem facing producers of both consumer goods and the means of production is producing exactly the amount that, when marketed, will just equal the quantity demanded at profitable prices. If they produce too much, more than the market can bear, costly inventories will build up, prices will fall and profits along with them. When the discrepancy is great, the result can be crisis. For Marx and Engels, this possible problem periodically became a real one because of the predisposition of all capitalists to produce as much as possible, as fast as possible, despite often not having good information about either the level of their competitors' production or current market demand (see Chapter 5 section 3.2).

Capitalists have tried to counter these problems by taking measures to better control both supply (production) and demand. On the supply side, they have sought better control by either taking over or negotiating agreements with competitors to reduce or eliminate competition. The former is one route to that "centralization" of capital Marx analyzes in Chapter 25 of Volume I of

193 Eventually, chattel slavery was almost universally criminalized throughout the capitalist world. Actually ending slavery, however, has required both the discovery of slavery – in all its various forms, both overt and covert, hidden behind legal ruses, such as indenture mentioned above – and its prosecution. The struggle against it has continued to the present.

194 Today, such "selling off", along with the capturing and transportation of slaves, falls under the rubric of "Human trafficking." All illegal but immensely profitable to the capitalists who control it.

Capital and whose advanced form of "trusts" Engels denounced in *Socialism: Utopian and Scientific*. (See, Chapter 2, Section 3.8.) Capitalists have negotiated agreed-upon prices, production quotes, or dividing the market among themselves. Monopolistic or oligopolistic price-setting removes competitive price reductions, quotas reduce the likelihood of overproduction and dividing up markets eliminates competition in each one. Such practices were already common enough in the eighteenth century to draw Adam Smith's attention and his denunciation in his *Wealth of Nations*, arguing the benefits of competition (lower prices, more innovation) to consumers of both *MS* and *MP*. Marx and Engels' general opposition to capitalism included the added disadvantages to workers (higher prices, lower real wages) resulting from such collaboration among capitalists.

In the absence of such arrangements, individual capitalist firms try to expand demand by using lower prices, advertising, and product innovation to draw in new customers, some from competitors, which expands their share of the market. Sometimes, capitalists in the same industry have acted collectively, investing in generic advertising for their kind of product, e.g., milk, eggs, natural gas, and supported policies which expand the market for that product, a boon to all producers.

The most obvious counter to poor information is better information. When the low quality of information is due to time lags, as Marx and Engels thought, the counter is speeding up information flows. (See, Section 7.3.4). For a long time, the only way to speed up information flows was to speed up the travel of those with the needed information. Thus, an understandable interest by both industrial capitalists and merchants in the replacement of roads or canals with railroads and of sailing or paddlewheel vessels with faster steamers. These new technologies would speed up the flow of information as well as that of commodities (reduce turnover time), essentially by speeding up the movement of people or of correspondence with knowledge of market conditions.

The development of the telegraph, Marx and Engels clearly saw as dramatically improving the speed of transmission of information about markets. But, as Marx wrote in 1855, despite transforming "the whole of Europe into one big commodity exchange", the problems of overproduction, glut and crisis persisted.[195] When transatlantic telegraph cables were laid in 1858 and then, more successfully in 1866, the increased flow of information replicated the earlier acceleration in Europe. Once again, however, it did not eliminate

195 Karl Marx, "The Crisis in Trade and Industry," (Jan. 8–22, 1855) *MECW*, *Vol. 13*, pp. 571–578.

the problems of overproduction and crisis which continued to plague capital throughout the rest of the century. On the contrary, it may have accelerated the circulation of crisis.

How firms selling $C(MS)'$ have dealt with such problems has differed somewhat from those selling $C(MP)'$, so I deal with them separately below.

9.2.1 Countering Crises in Selling the Means of Subsistence, $C(MS)' - M'$

Obviously, first and foremost, capitalists try to *avoid* crises in selling consumer goods. They do this with strategies aimed at ensuring adequate demand for their products and gearing production to available markets.

On the demand side, as Marx showed in his analysis of primitive accumulation, by expropriating and enclosing most land and other means of production, capitalists have done their best to monopolize the production of consumer goods and by so doing *force* people who need or want them to *buy* them – which, in turn forces them to seek jobs with wages or salaries to have the wherewithal to do so. To maintain this situation, they have needed to thwart any and all efforts to reverse enclosure and prevent direct appropriation, both of which decrease demand. At the same time, they have also done what they can to increase demand by trying to get people to buy whatever they are producing. Except at the lowest level of income, capitalist sellers of $C(MS)'$ are well aware that workers can hold on to their money rather than spend it. Thus, their investments in marketing, advertising, and face-to-face selling in retail outlets. (See, Chapter 3, Section 3)

On the supply side, producers try to minimize their costs of production while producing goods consumers will want to buy. While some producers of consumer goods may simply add to the supply of existing goods delivered to known markets, others try to draw on the creativity of their workers to develop and market new products, create new demand, new markets, and new opportunities to realize profits. In both cases, as we have seen, the quality of consumer goods have often been revealed to be deficient, even dangerous, causing crises for capitalists trying to sell them.

Let's look at these in turn.

9.2.1.1 *Countering Struggles to Reverse Enclosure*

Against efforts to reverse enclosure and escape subordination to capital, capitalists have wielded ideology, laws, and force. Ideologically, the key concept has always been the sanctity of "private property" with land seizures treated as akin to stealing personal valuables. Laws protecting property have treated both as "theft," with the only issue being the monetary value of what is stolen and the implications for punishment. The higher the estimated market value, the more severe the punishment.[196] To impose both the laws and punishment, force has been the main vehicle, whether by landlord goons, local police, or military intervention.

The two early examples of attempts by the dispossessed to reverse enclosure cited in Chapter 4 section 5.2.2.1 were the German peasant uprisings in the sixteenth century and the campaign of the Diggers in the 1840s. In both cases, the response was dishonest negotiations followed by violent repression. Here's Engels describing the end of one peasant uprising in 1525,

> [Georg "Bauernjörg" Truchsess] cut off their supply routes and tried to demoralise them by burning about 200 villages in the vicinity. Hunger and the sight of their burning homes finally brought the peasants to their knees (July 25). More than twenty were immediately executed.[197]

When the Diggers seized St George's Hill in 1649, just outside London, the owners moved against them.

> … parson Platt and other Lords of manors in Surrey organized raids on the colony and an economic boycott; they harassed the Diggers with legal actions … Even after the Diggers moved to Cobham Heath a few miles away the raids continued, and by April 1650 the colony had been forcibly dispersed, huts and furniture burnt, the Diggers chased away from the area.[198]

When the Diggers tried similar seizures elsewhere, the response was always the same violence.

That violence, however, was limited compared to the genocide inflicted on the indigenous peoples of the Americas, throughout the hemisphere, when and where they resisted enclosure or tried to reverse it. In the British Isles and continental Europe, the conflicts were mostly among landlords, agrarian capitalists, and desperate members of the reserve army of labor over private

---

196 In the United States, stealing a little is deemed a "misdemeanor" and punishment is relatively light; stealing a lot is a "felony" and the punishment is more severe. As vividly illustrated by recent NYC indictment of Trump and his organization, capitalists often inflate or deflate the value of their property for their own purposes. There are no unquestionable "market values," yet folks are jailed on the say-so of those whose property has been stolen or directly appropriated.

197 F. Engels, "The Peasant War in Germany" (October 1850) *MECW, Vol. 10*, p. 468.

198 Christopher Hill, *The World Turned Upside Down: Radical Ideas During the English Revolution* (London: Penguin, 1984) 107–124.

property. But in the Western Hemisphere, European settlers and their governments portrayed the conflict over land as one between primitive savages and representatives of a higher civilization who, in consequence, had greater rights.[199] Many of these so-called "savages" responded to their expropriation more like the armed German peasants than the peaceful Diggers; they fought back against losing their land and their way of life, generally preferring death or retreating deeper into the hinterland to accepting subordination.

Where resistance was fierce, the invading settler forces sometimes negotiated, even signing treaties promising to leave some land to the natives. But as with the German peasants, again and again the negotiations and treaties merely delayed enclosure and were violated to take more land. With the laws and the courts controlled by the invaders, indigenous efforts to defend their land legally proved fruitless. Over time, European settlers and their descendants took all the best land for themselves and herded the remnants of the indigenous population into "reservations" with poor land and limited resources. Although the names changed, throughout the colonial world the same story was repeated with minor variations.[200]

All these rationales and laws mobilized to block the reversal of enclosure, however, have been repeatedly undermined by government seizures of privately owned land. By rationalizing such seizures as in the "public interest" and legalizing them as exercises in "eminent domain", they have twisted the usual anti-enclosure argument that commons benefit society as a whole into a justification for new enclosures. The imposition of eminent domain for purposes of public infrastructure, e.g., roads, railroads and ports, has usually been peddled as benefiting everyone, despite being primarily of value to capital to move troops and cut the costs and time of transporting *C*(*MS*)′ and *C*(*MP*)′. Moreover, as Marx and Engels pointed out, those displaced have mostly been workers. In some cases, small farmers have been pushed off land granted to railroads or highways in rural areas. In others, urban infrastructure has been

199 There was some of this attitude even within Europe, toward indigenous groups such as the Laplanders (Sámi) in northern Scandinavia or ethnic minorities in Eastern Europe. See Engels' attitudes quoted in Appendix I "Note to Polish Readers."

200 Some "land reform" measures in the post-colonial, post-WWII era, formed modern apparent exceptions to capitalist opposition to reversing enclosures. In a number of countries, where demands for reform were fierce, capitalist policy makers granted some reversal of enclosure by breaking up large estates and distributing parcels of land to landless peasants. In retrospect, they were half-hearted measures designed more as temporary palliatives to ward off more rural unrest, counterinsurgency holding actions to stabilize the rural population until it was needed as active *LP* for capitalist development. See, Harry Cleaver, "Food, Famine and the International Crisis," *Zerowork*, no. 2, (Fall 1977): 7–69.

driven through poor neighborhoods of tenements rented by workers. Where it has been exercised for the benefit of particular capitalists, such as private railroads or toll roads operated as private capitalist businesses, the hypocrisy of pretending to be in the interests of the "public" is obvious.

9.2.1.2 *Countering the Direct Appropriation of C(MS)'*

Besides pervasive ideology extolling the sanctity of private property and the myriad laws protecting it – mostly enforced by police and the judiciary to protect *capitalist* private property rather than the much-evoked *personal* property – the primary counters to the direct appropriation of consumer goods have been surveillance and the use of force to prevent, stop, or punish.

In the case of surveillance, in Marx and Engels' time, within spaces of production it was the work of shopkeepers, company goons, or hired guards. In society at large, it was the work of sheriffs, constables, police and, in some cases the military.[201] Surveillance was required all along the material circuit of production and transportation, and everywhere workers were supposed to spend their hard-earned wages to buy *MS* but might choose instead to take what they need or want.[202]

The need for the deployment of force against direct appropriation, to get finished goods to market, and to get them sold, grew with the expansion of production and markets, both at home and abroad. The police force created in Paris in 1667 was designed primarily to "procure abundance" – of goods in shops – by protecting businesses, not individuals. In England, in 1797, merchants created a police force to prevent direct appropriation from ships handling consumer goods and from the docks along the Thames in London. That private force would eventually merge with the Metropolitan Police Service, created in 1829. A similar evolution took place in other places in response

201 Still true. It is said that during the big city uprisings in the US in the mid-1960s, e.g., Watts and Newark, the informal slogan was "Always loot before you burn!" The burning, that is, of stores judged to be screwing local workers with unacceptably high prices and practices. It seems likely the same attitude was prevalent in the world-wide "food riot" uprisings against International Monetary Fund imposed austerity during the debt crises of the 1980s and 1990s. See, David Seddon, *Riot and Rebellion: Political Responses to Economic Crisis in North Africa (Tunisa, Morocco and Sudan)* Discussion Paper No. 196, School of Development Studies, University of East Anglia, October 1986. The pattern has continued: Ray Bush, "Food Riots: Poverty, Power and Protest," *Journal of Agrarian Change* 10, no. 1 (January 2010): 119–129.

202 In modern times, surveillance has become even more pervasive through the use of alarm-triggering gadgets attached to consumer goods, video cameras watching and recording potential appropriators and computer programs tracking the use of online digital consumer goods, such as video and TV streaming.

to both worker uprisings and their disruptions in the ability of capitalists to move their commodities to market. As Robert Ovetz has pointed out, the great railroad strike of 1877 in the United States – which ruptured the circulation of both people and commodities – provoked major reforms in the organization of police, speeding up the conversion of volunteer and state militias into a National Guard and the reorganization of local police in the image of the military.[203]

Besides policing day to day markets, capitalists have also had to contend with major, collective uprisings that have included the direct appropriation of goods by outraged and angry workers. To such revolt, capitalists have responded in two ways: 1) with violence – using police and military to put down workers and protect property – and 2) with various forms of "poor relief" to avoid future revolt.[204] In the nineteenth century, minimal subsistence was doled out, mainly through "Parish relief" and "workhouses" in England and Wales ("poorhouses" in Scotland), where those without jobs or income were fed, housed and in the case of children, sometimes provided some modicum of "education" – but only in exchange for make-work, i.e., unskilled labor, such as breaking stones, crushing bones for fertilizer or picking oakum.[205] Though their inmates had

203 Robert Ovetz, *When Workers Shot Back,* op. cit. This militarization of the police has become obvious since massive transfers of military equipment to local police has made a great many of the latter almost indistinguishable from military forces in terms of armored clothing and equipment, e.g., "swat" teams and those aimed at "crowd control." Such have also been deployed not just to stop looting and burning rioters but also to suppress peacefully demonstrating protestors – as we have seen around the world in reaction to anti-Zionist, pro-Palestinian protests.

204 The central city uprisings in the US in the 1960s – beginning with Watts in 1965 – were dubbed, ex-post, "commodity riots" by social scientists and one federal response, to ward off the recurrence of widespread looting, was a vast expansion of food stamps. See, the McCone Commission Report, *Violence in the City—An End or a Beginning?* (1965), most of whose recommendations went unheeded, and Tim Reynolds, *The Food Stamp Explosion*, University of Texas at Austin, M.A. Thesis, 1980.

205 See, the Wikipedia for a brief history of these "houses". The same kind of work has been common in prisons, far beyond and long after Victorian Britain. The phrase "making little ones out of big ones" has often referred to the prison labor of breaking stones into small pieces to be used in roadways. While some of this make-work has disappeared, e.g., picking oakum (because ships are now made of steel, not wood whose cracks needed caulking), others continue, in or out of the modern equivalent of workhouses. See, Akachi Adimora-Ezeigbo, *Hands that Crush Stones* (Ibadan: University Press, 2010), a play about women doing this work in Nigeria and their struggle for higher wages. On the other hand, penal forced labor in the United States has evolved into a multibillion-dollar industry, both private and public, in which prisoners work for pennies – a situation which has resulted in numerous strikes by prison workers and a

no money to spend, the monies channeled through such institutions at least partially replaced the absence of $M - C(MS)$ among inmates.[206]

As the export trade in consumer goods grew along with their production, so too did the need for armed protection of shipping, on land, canals, and rivers against hijacking, on the high seas against mutiny, piracy, and foreign powers. Guards were ubiquitous in freight shipping, not only on the stagecoaches and railroad freight cars often portrayed in Western films, but around the world defending commodities carried in camel trains, freight wagons, flatboats, keelboats, canal boats, sailing vessels and eventually steamboats. Seagoing commercial vessels were armed, both to maintain control of their crews and to repel pirates, or, during wartime, foreign warships. They often sailed in convoys for mutual protection, escorted by warships of their nation of origin.[207]

Obviously, force played a central role in colonialism, both in annexing land and labor for the production of raw materials for factories back home, and in opening new markets for *MS*. Chinese (or Indian, or Indonesian, or African) walls were hammered down, not only by the "cheap goods" noted in the *Communist Manifesto*, but by gunboats and troops deployed for conquest, pacification, destruction of local competition or, as in the case of the opium trade, simply forcing foreign governments to accept particular goods.

Finally, besides guards, police, and the military, where practical, physical measures have been taken to avoid losses of $C(MS)'$ due to direct appropriation or theft. In Section 7.3.3, I mentioned the enclosure of tobacco leaf in hogsheads during shipment. Walls were built around factories and other workplaces, e.g., shipyards. The capitalists who organized a police force to protect their goods on the London docks also built walls around those docks. Like those around manufacturing factories, they served a double purpose: making

---

movement against such forced labor. See, the Wikipedia article on Penal Labor in the US. (Both accessed 7/17/2024.)

206 Eventually, in the 1930s and 1940s, capitalists replaced such institutions with alternatives ranging from concentration camps and prisons to various welfare programs. Capitalist recognition of the sharp distinction between "need" and "ability to pay" has also been recognized in periods of drought and flood when famine relief has taken the form of the distribution of cash rather than food, where scarce food has been hoarded, sold only to those with money, with those without left to starve.

207 This has continued through WWII, where allied ship convoys needed protection from German U-boats (submarines), and more recently where US warships have fended off efforts by the Iranian government to disrupt oil tankers, and a Combined Task Force of national naval forces are defending ships against pirates in the Gulf of Aden and along the coast of Somalia and against Houthi in Yemen protesting genocide in Gaza.

it hard for dock and lighter workers to get directly appropriated commodities out and hard for others to get in with the same objective.[208]

9.2.1.3 *Countering Problems with the Use-Values of C(MS)'*

Capitalists' first line of defence against questions about the use-values of their commodities has always been proactive: efforts to convince potential buyers of their goods' glowing, spectacular qualities. In the nineteenth century, those efforts were mainly verbal assurances given by sellers directly to consumers and advertising in print, mostly in handbills, magazines, and newspapers. Until the mid-1800's, in Britain and the United States there was virtually no government regulation of the quality of consumer goods or advertising, so "Snake Oil" of all sorts could be sold with all the advertising lies their producers could come up with.

Under the circumstances, as mentioned in Chapter 5 section 3.2.1.3, revelations of the poor or dangerous quality of products came primarily from independent sources such as Arthur Hassall in Britain, whom Marx cites about poor quality bread, or Frederick Accum who revealed the same practices decades earlier. Against such revelations, capitalists not only renewed their lies by denying claims but were not above harassing those exposing the dangers of their products. Short of expensive lawsuits against defamation few could afford, there was little or no protection for those journalists or scientists who exposed producer lies and crimes. Accum, who exposed faulty products in several industries, was so systematically harassed for his revelations that he was forced to flee England back to his native Germany.[209] Hassall was luckier.

His work was discovered by Thomas Wakley, founder in 1823 and editor of *The Lancet*, an English medical journal. Already interested in the issue of adulteration, Wakley created the Analytical Sanitary Commission in 1851, invited Hassall to be the Commission's chief analyst, write its reports – reports which ultimately identified companies producing adulterated products – and

---

208 These days physical walls continue to be used, often topped with razor wire and complemented by security cameras. Since the onset of the computer era "firewalls" form digital walls to keep hackers *out*. However, keeping software secrets *in* has required other means such as legal barriers to the "theft" of "intellectual property" by the workers producing it, by competing capitalists, or by directly appropriating consumers, e.g., P2P, Peer-to-peer sharing of digital media. See, Brett Caraway, "Survey of File-Sharing Culture", *International Journal of Communication* 6, (2012): 564–584.

209 At least he wasn't murdered, as many believe Karen Silkwood was in 1974, because of her revelations of the dangers at the Kerr-McGee Cimarron Fuel Fabrication Site plant where she worked creating plutonium fuel pellets.

promised to cover any court costs caused by company legal actions.[210] Hassall's reports, published week after week in the manner of Charles Dicken's novels, led to a Parliamentary Committee of Inquiry and then to the creation of the First Adulteration Act in 1860, which made it illegal "To sell any article of food or drink with which, to the knowledge of the seller, any ingredient or material injurious to health has been mixed."[211] Needless to say, phrases like "to the knowledge of the seller" provided loopholes for capitalists to such a degree that Marx called it "an inoperative law."[212] Nevertheless, countering attacks on the quality of the use-values of their commodities became more difficult for capitalists as the terrain moved from charge and denial to the courts. While laws passed by Parliament and the courts became terrains for injured consumers to seek redress, it was also one where capitalists sought to escape accountability for their crimes. With more resources and pull with legislators and judges, capitalists have sought to limit their liability through "tort reform", creating procedural limits on class action lawsuits and caps on damages.

But how to counter limits on the demand for even unadulterated, high-quality goods, i.e., those annoying limits eventually portrayed by economists as downward sloping demand curves, because buyers become scarce as expanding supply pushes prices below profitable levels? There have long been two obvious responses. The first has been to seek out new buyers for existing products (expand demand), often in new places, first domestically, then abroad, say in colonies where new markets were often created by destroying local production – a common dimension of imperialism. The second response has been attempts to manage demand. One way has been controlling the life cycle of commodities through "planned obsolescence" wherein products are designed to fail so more or newer ones can be sold, or the moment is planned at which they are no longer serviced and must be replaced. This avoids crisis because "death" has been factored into product development, with replacements ready for sale.[213] Another way has been to diversify. Just as buyers of *MP* have often diversified their sources to respond to or as a hedge against possible

210 John Forrester, "The Lancet's Analytical Sanitary Commission" *The Lancet* 322, no. 8364 (December 10, 1978): 1360–1362.

211 Arthur Hassall, "The Adulteration of Food and Drink Act" *The Lancet* 76, no. 1933 (September 15, 1860): 272–273.

212 *Capital, Vol. 1*, p. 358, or *MECW, Vol. 35*, p. 256.

213 Today this is obvious in the fashion, automotive, computer hardware and software industries. Even when a given combination of hardware and software still serve the purposes for which they were purchased, computer companies force their abandonment by refusing to continue to provide technical updates and assistance, e.g., parts for hardware or defense against malware.

disruptions (See, Section 7.3 above) so too have producers and sellers of *MS* responded to markets drying up, or to their production exceeding market demand, by producing and marketing other commodities meeting the same or similar needs and desires, e.g., clothing made from some new fabric might replace those made with older ones, or create new products catering to new markets alongside those no-longer expanding. Even before industrialization, clothiers – from tailors to "needle women" – essentially annexed the cultural fad of "fashion" to peddle new designs – touted as more attractive and more up-to-date, more "modern" than outmoded ones. Thus, new products, new markets, and new profits, even as the market for the outmoded dwindles or disappears. By making a fetish of "newness", treated as the equivalent of "progress" in many dimensions of their ideology, not just advertising, capitalists have created a culture supportive not only of more consumption but of the consumption of *new* products of all sorts.

9.3 *Dealing with Crises in Selling the Means of Production, C(MP)' – M'*

Given the objective of sellers of *C(MP)'*, like that of sellers of *C(MS)'*, is to maximize profits, the most obvious sources of crisis have been forces that reduce 1) the known *quality* of the *MP*, and thus the price at which they can be sold, 2) the *quantity* of *MP*, and thus the revenue obtainable from their sale, or 3) demand for the *MP* on offer.

9.3.1 Countering Crises due to Deterioration of the Quality of *MP*

Leaving aside measures taken in the production of *MP* to assure sufficient quality to sell, the primary sources of deterioration in quality during the effort to sell *MP* are in their storage or transportation. As indicated in Chapter 4, Section 5.2.3.3, the degree to which this can be a problem, and therefore countermeasures required, depends on the perishability of the *MP*. For *MP* such as coal or metal ores, neither storage nor shipment has any impact on their quality. On the other hand, *MP* such as tobacco, grains, lumber, or fibers are very much subject to deterioration; either in storage or during shipment from place of production to place of use. To counter this problem and thus preserve the value of their goods, capitalists have tried both to protect perishable goods and to shorten the time during which the *MP* lay in storage or the time of their transportation.

Protection during storage and transportation depends on the nature of the goods stored. The primary threats to the quality of grains, for example, endemic since long before capitalism, are weather (water), insects and rodents, so capitalists both continued the use of old, proven methods, such as tightly sealed containers, from large grain bins and storage barns to transportable barrels and sought to improve them. Shipped tobacco, for example, may have been packed in hogsheads to avoid pilfering, as Peter Linebaugh has argued, see above, Section 7.3.3, but those containers may also have been used because they have traditionally been made water-tight (to hold liquids) and thus could preserve the leaves from deterioration on leaky ships. Commercial sailing ships also had built-in pumps to daily remove infiltrated bilge water to protect vulnerable cargoes.[214]

As agribusiness displaced small-scale farming and the quantity of grain being produced, stored, and transported for commerce increased, along with the distances transported, new technologies were developed to handle and protect the increased amounts. For example, more traditional storage structures of wood or brick were replaced with metal silos, easier to seal and providing better protection. Wagons were replaced with specialized railroad cars, as were wooden ships and barges with dedicated metal ones. For some perishable foods, such as meat, which could only be sold locally or shipped during winter months, the development of refrigeration technology for trucks, railroad cars and "reefer ships" toward the end of the nineteenth century made year-round shipping possible. For a while, capitalists could use insulation and ice in trucks and railroad cars, but they had to wait for the development of new refrigeration technologies to make long-distance, trans-oceanic shipping of perishable goods possible.

Capitalists have also sought to preserve the quality of their *MP* during transportation by making use of faster transportation, whether by truck, rail, or ship. Faster transportation not only reduces the time of transportation, a quickening of turnover profitable to all capitalists, but for sellers of perishable *MP* it reduces the dangers of deterioration and the costs of transport, while increasing the number of potential markets.

9.3.2 Countering Reductions in the Supply of *C*(*MP*)*'* for Sale

I've delineated several forces that potentially threaten reductions in the quantity of *MP* available for sale. These have included losses due to natural catastrophes and the direct appropriation of *MP* by workers and theft by other capitalists. Whether chronic or episodic, they have all required countermeasures by capitalists who want to avoid losses of their product and subsequent sales, revenue, and profits. On counters to natural catastrophes, see Section 8.1.2.

---

214 See, Charles Bendig, "Ships' Pumps: From Antiquity to the Early Modern Era," *Journal of Maritime Archaeology 15, no. 2* (June 2020): 185–207.

9.3.2.1 *Countering Direct Appropriation of MP or C(MP)' by Workers and Theft by Capitalists*

Whether at the original point of production or during transportation, capitalists have long taken the same kinds of measures to thwart losses of *C*(*MP*)' that have been used to avoid losses of *C*(*MS*)'. As sketched in Section 9.2.1.2, these have included: 1) internal surveillance by overseers, supervisors and guards to make sure not only that workers do the work they've been assigned but that neither they nor anyone else take either *MP* on the job or produced *MP* waiting to be sold as *C*(*MP*)' and 2) the mobilization of force through the state, justified ideologically as the protection of private property, in the form of police and even the military. To some degree, the nature of the *C*(*MP*)' determines the measures used to prevent losses. While for high-value items in small numbers, guards at factories and on trucks or trains might suffice, lower-value bulk *C*(*MP*)' being shipped long distances might require not only armed guards but military protection from privateers, pirates, or hostile foreign powers.

Along with all these measures to protect physical commodities have been those to protect less tangible ones, such as "proprietary" secret knowledge about methods used in production or embodied in commodities, whether goods or services. Just as early capitalists sought and obtained exclusive rights (later patents) to the use of specific production methods, to prevent others from appropriating the creations and innovations made by their workers,[215] so too were copyright laws written against the appropriation of written materials.[216]

Given the centrality of competition in Marx's analysis of the diffusion of technology, and his attention to protectionist measures blocking trade, I have been surprised to be unable to find any discussion by either him or Engels of either of these legal restrictions. Although ideologically rationalized to spur creativity, to the degree they have been enforced, both have slowed the diffusion of new creations to the profit of the owners of copyrights and patents and increased the cost to consumers or competitors. At the same time, they

215 NB: scientific and technological innovation are accomplished by *workers*, sometimes by operatives, more often by engineers and scientists. Most remain hirelings, like manual workers, but when they spin off from employers and link up with financial capitalists to implement their ideas on their own, they are called "entrepreneurs." Such was Thomas Edison (1847–1931) who set up his first laboratory in 1876. Such too, in more recent years was Steven Jobs (1955–2011) who incorporated Apple Computer Company in 1977.

216 See, Joanna Kostylo, "From Gunpowder to Print: The Common Origins of Copyright and Patent," in Ronan Deazley et al., *Privilege and Property: Essays on the history of Copyright* (Cambridge: Open Book, 2010) 21–50. Copyrights were extended from print to audio and visual materials as they were developed.

undoubtedly encouraged that industrial espionage discussed in Chapter 4, Section 3.3.3.2.[217]

9.3.2.2 *Countering Reductions in Demand for C′(MP)′*

There are several kinds of reductions in demand for *MP* to which their sellers have sought counters. Most common have been 1) foreseeable fluctuations in demand due to things such as changes in seasons. More dramatic have been 2) unforeseeable drops in the demand for *MP* or for the final products made using a given *MP*, and 3) the imposition of tariffs or other protectionist trade measures that cut off the ability to export to some markets.

In the case of foreseeable fluctuations in demand, e.g., less demand for feed grains and silage in the summer where livestock is let out to pasture, and thus fewer sales at lower prices and profits, normal capitalist business practice to avoid crisis is to adjust accordingly. When demand and prices drop, they hold on to their *C*(*MP*)*'*, albeit bearing the cost of accumulating inventories. When demand and prices rise, they sell more, drawing first on inventories then on new production.

Being able to do so requires planning ahead for adequate storage for their inventory of *C*(*MP*)*'* and financing when prices, sales and revenue are low. Among obvious, visible, examples of such storage are grain bins and silos for temporarily storing silage, coal, sawdust, cement, etc. Such storage facilities may be small, e.g., located on individual farms or other local businesses, or huge, e.g., the rows of towering grain elevators owned by grain trading companies, located along railroads or rivers with gear designed for loading the stored material into rail cars or barges.[218] In the case of grain or silage because they are perishable, storage requires specialized technologies, to maintain adequate

217 Today, when so much industrial and commercial information is digitized and communicated within corporations electronically, much industrial and commercial espionage is conducted by hackers, either hired or freelance. In response, security firms – such as Securitas USA, which absorbed the Pinkerton detective agency, once the biggest private security operation in the world and notorious for its union-busting activities – have complemented their physical protective services with electronic ones. Well-connected corporations, of course, also benefit from the help of national security agencies in thwarting both domestic and foreign industrial espionage – as exemplified by both sides of the Cold War and in recent years by the US government crackdown on Chinese industrial espionage.

218 It was just such huge storage capacity of the grain trading companies that made it possible for them, but not the farmers from whom they had bought grain to profit from the notorious giant grain deal negotiated between the US and the Soviet Union in 1972. See, James Trager, *Amber Waves of Grain: The Secret Russian Wheat Sales that Sent American Food Prices Soaring* (New York: Arthur Fields Books, 1972).

air circulation to avoid the spoilage of grain or air-tight sealing to maintain low-oxygen conditions for silage, both of which lengthen the period these *MP* can be held without serious deterioration.

One counter to unexpected drops in the demand for some *MP*, or for the products for which *MP* is an input, has been to shift investment to the production of alternative products. In the case of the fur trade, the drop in the demand for the kinds of hats made from beaver-derived felt resulted in a drop in the demand for beaver fur. For trappers, whether Native American or Europeans, the only short-run counter was shifting their trapping/production to other kinds of animals to obtain other kinds of fur still desired by producers of other, still fashionable clothing.[219] However, the demand for *trapped* furs of any kind also dropped with the development of "fur farming", the industrialization of fur production by raising fur-bearing animals and then skinning them. As I pointed out in Chapter 4, Section 5.2.3.1, the development of this alternative source of furs reduced the demand for trapped furs, forcing many to abandon trapping and seek alternative sources of income.

Counters to unforeseen reductions in demand have varied depending on the source. Where markets have been cut off completely, producers have sought alternative markets for their *MP*, whether domestic or foreign, whether legal or illegal.[220] Such was the problem facing grain producers in Napoleon's empire when exports to Great Britain were outlawed by the French government and cut off by British blockades of French ports. The same problem faced wheat producers in the Czarist empire during the Crimean War when Anglo-French fleets cut off exports through the Black Sea and from St. Petersburg in the Baltic. Faced with legal and military obstacles to trade, smuggling and blockade running provided capitalists only risky and dangerous counters.

219 The rise of the animal rights movement's attacks on the use of fur has reduced demand for fur as clothing producers under pressure from both activists and consumers have switched to synthetic imitations. Parallel attacks on the use of leather in clothing, briefcases, handbags, etc., on the use of feathers in down jackets, comforters, pillows, etc., and, of course, the consumption of animal flesh have also either slowed the growth of, or reduced the demand for those all those *MP*. In several countries, such as Austria, the UK, Croatia, the Czech Republic, Norway and Italy, fur farming has been banned entirely. However, increased demand in countries such China and Russia has offset the reduction in demand in those countries.

220 When the US government cut imports of sugar from Cuba in 1960, the leaders of that country increased exports to Europe and the USSR. But when the USSR collapsed in 1991, Cuban exports were again dramatically reduced, forcing a new search for markets beyond the reach of US sanctions. In recent years, Cuba, Russia, Iran, and North Korea have all be the subject of US sanctions and have all had to find importers willing to buy their products despite those sanctions.

Against the imposition of steep tariffs or quotas on imports to "protect" non-competitive, local industries – a function of both the lobbying power of the protected industrialists and the nationalist motivations of governments – in both European countries and the United States in the nineteenth century (see Chapter 2, Section 1), exporters have had recourse to both the ideology of "free trade" and the various theories put forward by economists as to how the fewer the obstacles, the greater the benefits to trading countries, e.g., Ricardo's theory of "comparative advantage." They have also, at times, sought retaliatory measures against such obstacles, counter tariffs, subsidies, and so on, to protect their profits if not their markets.

9.4 *Countering Credit and Commercial Crises*

Risk-averse, conservative managers of individual capitalist firms engaged in real investment, i.e., building or expanding production facilities, hiring new workers and arranging for increased sales, try to avoid the dangers of defaulting on debt by 1) minimizing borrowing by relying mainly on internally generated profits, 2) maximizing those profits to facilitate repayment of any necessary debt, 3) avoiding investment in what are obviously speculative adventures, and 4) maintaining reserves to cover any shortfalls in profits. Such caution is often the result of previous experience of losses when undertaking risky investments. Risk-taking managers, on the contrary, are more likely to borrow whatever is necessary for their investment schemes, including questionable ones that carry substantial risk – if they seem likely to bring high rates of profit.

The steady growth of credit instruments (securities) and markets for their sale and resale created whole new options for financial speculation, adding to those existing within the realm of real investment. As indicated in Chapter 5, Section 3.3, the temptation for risk-takers, whether capitalist managers deciding how to use their available monies or individuals deciding how to "invest" their savings, are obvious.

So, how to minimize the chances of default, resulting credit crises and their consequences? And how to counter those crises and consequences when avoidance fails?

For individual investors, the surest path is the conservative, risk-adverse one: just avoid speculative ventures of all sorts. For risk-takers who eschew such an approach, they often hedge their bets in two ways: 1) diversifying their "investments" so risky ones are offset by more secure ventures, and 2) taking a page from the risk-adverse playbook by maintaining reserves to cover potential losses. They also, frequently, count on government bailouts if things go sour.

While governments have much the same options with respect to their own debts, repeated experience with speculative booms and busts has also provoked the creation of regulatory rules and agencies for their enforcement to counter potentially costly risky behavior, not just costly for speculators but for the economy as a whole, including the government's ability to cover its obligations through taxation. Thus, the passage of laws creating central banks and banking regulations that seek to limit speculation and prepare for potential losses, e.g., requirements for bank reserves as protection against loan defaults or runs on the bank by depositors. Thus, also, the creation of securities regulation – often tightened in the wake of speculative crashes.

So limited and so ineffective were regulations in the eighteenth and nineteenth centuries that Marx and Engels were often dismissive of such efforts. They watched again and again how the Bank of England would raise or lower its "bank rate" (interest rate), trying to stem developing crises, often in reaction to inflows and outflows of gold.[221] Their skepticism was based partly on observation of how regulations, such as the Bank Act of 1844, were often set aside in crises.[222] Marx's theory of endogenous money also explained how Bank of England's belief that it could control the amount of money in circulation – based on the quantity theory – was illusory and resulted in such failures.[223] All of which convinced Marx and Engels that ultimately neither the efforts of private capitalists nor those of their stalwarts in government would prove effective in stemming the return of crises.

10 Offsets to the Circulation of Breakdown

Capitalists have always been aware of how crises in circuits at one point can circulate to other points, making everything worse. As I sketched in Chapter 5, Section 4, such circulation can occur *within* individual circuits of capital or *from* one circuit to another. With some ruptures capitalists have responded by trying to restore the way things were, simple reproduction, but with others, capitalists have been forced to accept and adapt to qualitative changes, e.g., the introduction of machines that displace labor, or the replacement of some machines with newer and more productive ones, altering the technology of production

221 See, for example, Marx, "The State of Trade," March 6, 1849, *MECW, Vol. 9*, pp. 3–8.

222 See, among others, Marx and Engels, "Review: May to Oct. 1850," November 1, 1850, *MECW, Vol. 10*, pp. 490–532, Marx, "The Vienna Note – The US and Europe – Letters from Shumla – Peel's Bank Act," September 9, 1853, *MECW, Vol. 12*, pp. 292–300, Marx, "The Bank Act of 1844 and the Monetary Crisis in England," November 6, 1857, *MECW, Vol. 15*, pp. 379–84, Marx, "The English Bank Act of 1844," August 6, 1858, *MECW, Vol. 16*, pp. 3–7.

223 See, Marx's critique of the quantity theory in *Capital, Vol. 1*, Chapter 3, pp. 213–20, or *MECW, Vol. 35*, pp. 127–34.

and the relationships among workers, machines, and management. New technologies as well as changes in labor-management relations, e.g., new labor laws or changes in immigration, can also force qualitative changes in labor markets. Similarly, unexpected changes in trade relations can force qualitative changes in $C' - M'$, domestic or foreign. Figuring out how to manage such changes in ways that either restore or enhance their control and profits has been a recurrent problem for the managers of capital throughout its history. Many of such changes have ripple effects, circulating through circuits or from one to another, so before turning to offsets to circulation, let's look briefly at such qualitative changes and capitalist responses.

10.1 *Dealing with Qualitative Change*

When capitalists fail to either forestall ruptures or "nip them in the bud", they are often forced to cope with qualitative changes imposed by workers or other "outside" forces. As I noted in Chapter 5, Section 4.1., the source of qualitative changes within capitalist society is almost always, "in the final instance", the self-activity of workers, often seeking creatively to break through the constraints imposed by capitalist efforts to always be in control and to maximize work and profits.

From the point of view of individual capitalists, one force that appears to be "outside" – to which Marx and Engels often pointed – was competition from other capitalists. The successful (profitable) implementation of change by others puts pressure on latecomers to make the same or similar changes. But that "outside" is only from the point of view of individual capitalists or firms, the class dynamics bringing change are "internal" to capital as a whole, lying within the antagonistic relationships between capitalists and workers. Even when workers have organized sufficiently to impose industry-wide or economy-wide changes, such as Factory Acts shortening working hours or limiting the use of child labor, dealing with such imposed changes takes place within individual firms.

Given how change always, inevitably, involves *uncertainty*, when faced with new contingencies, capitalists can either attempt to avoid change by clinging to familiar ways or adapt to a greater or lesser degree. When the source is worker self-activity, adaptation means harnessing this power-beyond-itself, taming and channeling worker creativity to its own objectives.[224] So, when workers dream up new things they can make, capitalists only facilitate that making

224 One aspect of workers' power that capitalists try to harness is *cooperation*. Its autonomy and how capital tries to harness it, is discussed at length in Chapter 13 of Volume 1 of *Capital*. Had he followed up with a chapter on workers' creativity and imagination and how

(modify their product lines) to the degree that those things take the form of commodities that can be sold for a profit. When workers figure out safer ways to work, capitalists only adopt them voluntarily if they enhance control, cut costs, and increase profits. This means that new creations which do not meet those criteria are ignored or shelved and remain unadopted. This is one way capitalism blunts creativity, by subordinating it to its own quantitative expansion.[225] It is the reason why scientists have had to struggle to convince capitalist-dominated governments to invest in basic research as well as applied research, i.e., research applied to enhancing capitalist operations and profits.

Resistance to change, to adaptation, has also provided a common argument against protectionist trade measures. While supposedly buying time for improved productivity to make local production competitive, critics have often pointed to protected industries merely profiting from protectionist measures without making significant changes to increase productivity. Which capitalists choose – avoidance or adaptation – almost always depends on their evaluation of the impact of proposed changes on their control and what it does to their bottom line, estimated future profits.

With respect to control, the attachment of many bosses to "managerial prerogative" has often resulted in them ignoring suggestions by line workers that would require substantial (costly) changes and responding only to suggestions by workers trained as engineers or scientists. The latter are conditioned and trained to channel their creativity to solving only problems identified by management. But the effect of ignoring suggestions by other workers is to quash some ideas and by so doing discourage others.[226] The obvious fear is of giving workers the sense of being more knowledgeable about and more in control

capital tries to harness them, there would be less fascination these days with the idea of "immaterial" labor.

225 There are many other ways as well, such as the way capitalists organize education to produce mostly disciplined, obedient workers rather than creative ones – so institutionalized as to frustrate even the most gifted teachers who, against the grain, cultivate creativity. See, for example, the experience of one such teacher in Herbert Kohl's classic *36 Children* (New York: New American Library, 1967).

226 In Bill Watkin's "Counterplanning on the Shopfloor," besides worker-planned breaks and play on the job, he also cites such refusal of managers to listen to suggestions by blue collar workers. More recently "neo-Schumpeterians" among both economists and managers have recognized how a far greater proportion of the labor force can contribute to innovation, given proper incentives and managerial openness to new ideas from a diverse array of workers. See, Horst Hanusch and Andreas Pyka, eds., *Elgar Companion to Neo-Schumpeterian Economics* (Cheltenham: Edward Elgar Publishing, 2007).

of their tools than their bosses – steps towards recognizing bosses as unnecessary.[227] Despite Marx and Engels' recognition of the need for coordination of complex processes, they and many who have followed in their footsteps have also understood that coordination can be achieved without recourse to capitalists.[228]

The greater the amount of new investment – say, in the reorganization of production or distribution – the more difficult it is to evaluate the impact of any given change, especially when both production and distribution are spread out over great distances and multiple markets – as they began to be in the Imperialist age of colonialism. In such cases, even the acceptance of some proposed change may result in only tentative, limited alterations, with the degree of follow-up being determined by initial results. Certainly, the failure of some new products to gain sufficient buyers to be profitable has provided some capitalists with reason for caution. See the discussion of product life cycles in Chapter 5, Section 3.2.1.3.

Even the recognition of new ideas as useful by capitalists who quickly have them patented or copyrighted, is no guarantee of their implementation, of actual change. The purpose of such legal protections, after all, is to ensure monopoly to their owners. But when and under what circumstances the protected ideas might be implemented is always contingent upon calculations of their effects and profitability. Inventors who sell patent rights to capitalists or writers who sign away copyright to journal or book editors may or may not see their creations materialize, depending on the new owners' estimates of profitability.

10.2 *Blunting Circulation within Individual Circuits*

Having demonstrated in Chapter 5, Section 4, how crises can disrupt each stage of the circuit of individual capitals and circulate to other stages, let's now look at what capitalists have done to counter the immediate spread of such disruption through the circuit in which they are investing. The measures they have taken have depended on both the originating cause and the mode of circulation. Continuing the pattern set out in Chapter 5, Section 4.2, let's examine strategies

---

227 This absence of necessity has long been in the minds of many anarchists for whom self-management is a central tenent of their politics. Today, if you do an Internet search for "Who needs bosses?" you quickly discover a whole series of articles in business magazines setting out reasons why bosses ARE needed. Clearly, the fear of being recognized as unnecessary parasites haunts the capitalist class, e.g., Steve Tobak, "Why We Still Need Bosses", *Fortune*, June 24, 2016.

228 *Capital*, Vol. I, pp. 448–449 , or *MECW, Vol. 35*, pp. 335–336, and F. Engels, "On Authority" in *MECW, Vol. 23*, pp. 422–425. Also, see *33 Lessons on Capital* (2019) 283–290.

deployed in each moment of a circuit: 1) *M*, 2) *M – LP*, 3) *M – MP*, 4) …*P*…*C′*, and 5) *C′* – *M′*.

1) "*M*"? In Section 7.1 I sketched the many ways capitalists have sought to offset shortages in the monies they need for the investment required to initiate each circuit, whether starting from scratch or renewing their operations. Because many of those take considerable time to bring to fruition, e.g., the looting of newly colonized peoples, they cannot provide immediate relief to capitalists and prevent the effects of shortages from rippling through their circuits. The only ones that can are those providing immediate access to ready cash or credit.

Against the real possibility of failures in the previous circuit to generate enough surplus value to renew the required investment, capitalists who are able maintain reserves in the form of cash or highly liquid assets that they can draw upon to cover shortfalls. The primary alternative for those who are unable to maintain adequate reserves is credit, e.g., from financial institutions, individuals, or governments. From banks – whether private or government operated – they can try to borrow; from individuals they can try to peddle stocks and bonds; from governments they can seek subsidies in the form of transfers of money (usually easier for state enterprises). They can also lobby for policy changes – such as protectionist measures that by reducing outside competition allow them to sell at higher prices and realize higher profits. If successful in obtaining outside money and such protection, both *M – LP* and *M – MP* can be realized, preventing any circulation of interruption.

2) In the case of crises in *M – LP* due to shortages in available labor, caused by workers' refusal to enter the labor market or their escape from it, the classic capitalist counter, Marx argues in Chapter 25 of Volume 1 of *Capital* has been the maintenance of a reserve army of desperate workers large enough to offset any such defections. Tapping that reserve, of course, has often required outlays in recruitment expenses, in both money and time (finding and evaluating possible hires). Much less preferred, and resisted where possible, is the obvious tactic of increasing wages or some other benefits to attract needed workers quickly enough to prevent any reduction in …*P*… or *C′* – *M′* – only possible without reducing other investment expenses (*MP*) if sufficient reserves are available. Such methods are more common for skilled jobs higher up the wage/salary hierarchy than for those lower down.

3) Capitalists often try to avoid crises in *M – MP* due to shortages in available *MP*, by buying more than is immediately needed and maintaining inventories to cover such shortfalls. To free themselves from dependence on suppliers of *MP*, one approach has been to take over the production of the needed *MP*, e.g., companies producing steel buy up and then operate iron or coal mines. Such "vertical integration" doesn't eliminate possible shortfalls – mines can

suffer cave-in's, ore veins can dwindle – but in the absence of such problems it frees the supply of *MP* from the vagaries of the market. In effect, such capitalists adopt, to a limited degree, precisely the planning that Marx and Engels repeatedly argued was superior to markets as a way of matching production to needs.[229]

Alternatively, shortages from one supplier, domestic or foreign, are countered by seeking and maintaining more than one source of supply. The history sketched in Chapter 2 demonstrated multiple occasions when capitalists have learned the hard way about the necessity of such diversity. Early in the nineteenth century, during the Napoleonic Wars and naval blockades, bread makers in England found themselves facing shortages of flour and forced to pay higher prices to local landlords/agribusiness. Decades later, English cotton textile manufacturers suddenly faced the need for optional sources when the American Civil War cut off supplies from what had been their main source. Assuming normal supplies of *MP* are always bought at the lowest price, buying from alternative suppliers may cost a bit more, but avoids any absolute shortfall whose effects would reverberate through the circuit, limiting ...*P*..., C', and $C' - M'$, and causing a more serious crisis.

4) Turning to the production stage of the circuit, ...*P*..., assuming no shortage of *LP* or *MP*, clearly the biggest threat facing the functionaries of capital are disruptions caused by workers' struggles, or, in the case of agriculture, bad weather. By reducing or completely stopping production, strikes that stop ...*P*... also limit $C' - M'$, revenue, profit, and investment in the next period. The effects of bad weather depend, of course, on its severity, from merely reducing production to wiping it out completely, Experience has taught capitalists about such ripple effects, so management has long tried to either forestall or end any and all such disruptions as quickly as possible. Let's look at these two kinds of counters.

First, with respect to workers' struggles, forestalling means managing things with sticks and carrots so that workers don't sabotage production or strike and shut it down completely. The threat of the stick for a long time, when strikes were illegal, was violence by company goons, local police, and the military and then by judicial prosecution. Even when and where workers have won the legal right to strike, the law hasn't always been enforced and violence has been deployed. Where workers have won sufficient power for their legal rights to be enforced, capitalists have been more inclined to use carrots.

---

229 Not, in this case, to the needs of workers, but to those of capitalists trying to avoid crisis. Today, multinational corporations manage vertically integrated subsidiaries all over the world.

One obvious way of avoiding strikes, of course, is to remove causes that might motivate them, e.g., pay living rather than subsistence wages, create safe working conditions, cultivate and appreciate workers' contributions, and encourage identification with the "company's" success. From all evidence, such efforts to reconcile worker and capitalist relationships were rare in the nineteenth century despite reformers' suggestions that such measures would ultimately prove profitable. Adam Smith's recommendation to educate workers to better understand market forces largely fell on deaf ears. An exceptional, real-world example of efforts to not only educate but make life better – to avoid strife, strikes, and improve productivity – were Robert Owen's actions, first among his own workers then in his recommendations to the government and other capitalists. As previously noted, his recommendations – like Smith's – were almost unanimously ignored by both capitalists and policy makers in government. Countering worker unrest by improving their conditions of work and life was simply not on the agenda of most capitalists for most of Marx and Engels' lives. Only late in the nineteenth century, as Engels noted in his 1885 update on the *Condition of the English Working Class*, did capitalists begin to adopt improvements rather than the repression of workers as a serious option, e.g., the 1870 Elementary Education Act, creating a system of public education in England and Wales, the acceptance of unions, and negotiations with workers.

Failing to forestall strikes, capitalist countermeasures were usually violently repressive, attempts to nip such actions in the bud by immediately crushing them to prevent their effects from circulating. As illustrated in Chapter 2, Marx and Engels saw this repeatedly during the decades in which worker organizing was outlawed. Bringing in the police or the military to attack workers could and often has driven striking workers from factory gates or off the streets. But successfully restoring production requires either getting striking workers back to work or bringing in substitutes, i.e., strike breakers. But getting those out of work to "scab" on those on strike has required, along with the usual threat of poverty and starvation, success in turning some workers against others, undermining solidarity. Such success Marx and Engels saw in the capitalist cultivation of ethnic differences.

For example, during Marx's time in Paris he observed, through direct contact, how different groups of workers could be played off against each other when organized separately, divided by language, culture, and history. This lack of communication, he saw, made solidarity between German and French workers difficult. He and Engels saw similar situations everywhere they went. In England, they saw how Irish workers were pitted against English ones in a fashion that made the latter hate the former.

> All industrial and commercial centres in England now have a working class *divided* into two *hostile* camps, English proletarians and Irish proletarians… This antagonism is kept artificially alive and intensified by the press, the pulpit, the comic papers, in short, by all the means at the disposal of the ruling class. *This antagonism* is the *secret of the English working class's impotence*, despite its organization.[230]

Such methods undermined the potential for collaboration and lay the groundwork for using the Irish as strike breakers against English workers. Of course, given the opposition of striking workers to their replacement, armed and violent force has often been used to suppress strikers' efforts to prevent scabs from getting into factories and restoring production. However, where replacement workers refuse to be used, such methods fail.

Second, with respect to bad weather, countermeasures by capitalists have, per force, been limited to those aimed at mitigating the negative effects, often adapting traditional indigenous methods. For example, in response to drought, capitalists have continued the use of wells to provide water for irrigation but have also orchestrated the building of giant dams with the same purpose. In response to flooding by monsoon or typhoon rainfall in the floodplains of South Asia, agriculturalists have chosen "deep water" rice varieties capable of thriving even with flooding. Elsewhere, they have built dams on rivers and levies alongside them to prevent the flooding of more sensitive crops. But alongside such technological measures in production, capitalist ability to invest in expanded storage of some crops, such as grains, has facilitated speculation against bad weather, made it even more profitable than traditional hoarding by merchants, and likely responsible for some of the extensive starvation that occurred in the colonial period. (see Chapter 4, Section 3.2.2.3.1.)

The results of all such efforts have been mixed; sometimes production has been quickly restored, sometimes not. The longer the delay, the deeper the rupture and the wider the ramifications elsewhere.

---

230 *MECW, Vol. 43*, pp. 471–476. Once slavery was abolished in the United States, American capitalists supported the immigration of workers from the Europe and Asia, then from the Caribbean, Mexico, and Central America. Continental European capitalists brought in workers from the Iberian Peninsula and then from colonies and ex-colonies in Africa, the Middle East and elsewhere. Those in England drew workers mainly from their ex-colonies in the West Indies and South Asia. These patterns persist to this day – augmented by workers from post-Cold War Eastern Europe and refugees from wars in Africa and the Middle East. In all these cases, capitalists and their minions have encouraged discrimination against each new wave of "interlopers" among local workers and in their communities.

5) Assuming success in initial investment, *M – C*(*LP, MP*), and in orchestrating production, ...*P*..., crises in the final stage of the circuit, selling what has been produced, *C′ – M′*, can cause a negative feedback loop on previous stages that plays out in the next iteration of the circuit. It may result in cutbacks in production, shortened work time, wage cuts or layoffs of workers and reduce or halt hiring, *M – LP*, and purchases and buildup of stocks of *MP*.

> If *C′ – M′* comes to a halt in the case of one portion, for example, if the commodity is unsaleable, then the circuit of this part is interrupted ... the successive parts that emerge from the production process as *C′* find their change of function barred by their predecessors. If this continues for some time, production is restricted and the whole process brought to a standstill. Every delay in the succession brings the co-existence into disarray, every delay in one stage causes a greater or lesser delay in the entire circuit.[231]

As noted in Chapter 4, Section 5.2.1, not only can this problem arise for producers of both *MS* and *MP*, but conjuring new markets out of thin air is not an option. The only immediate or short-term solution for those who have overproduced for the available market demand is to lower their prices to sell, which means less revenue, lower profits, and reduced investment in the next circuit, i.e., the circulation of crisis.

Therefore, the only way capitalists in this situation can avoid the current crisis in *C′ – M′* causing a crisis in the next period, e.g., bankruptcy, is to borrow money to replace their losses due to inadequate sales. Such interim financing or "bridge" borrowing essentially buys the time required to wait out temporary downturns in demand, to find new markets for current products, or shift production to new products for which markets are available. Being able to borrow in such circumstances usually requires such a past pattern of successful borrowing and repayment, as to reassure lenders and improve a firm's credit rating. When the crisis is general, a large-scale commercial crisis, competition for available funds can be fierce. So, establishing such a pattern today provides a counter to potential failures in *C′ – M′* tomorrow. Given the frequent recurrence of crisis throughout the nineteenth century, establishing good credit with commercial and industrial banks was often key to both short and long-term corporate survival.

---

231 *Capital, Vol. II*, p. 183; *MECW, Vol. 36*, p. 109.

Because one source of overproduction is poor or late information about market conditions, to ward off over- or under-production capitalists have created both in-house specialists to gather needed information and gotten governments to create whole wings of its bureaucracy to do the same. Some such wings have been created to track and supply general information about market conditions, others have been much more specialized, e.g., those tracking agricultural markets.[232] Similarly, financial institutions have done the same, both for their own use and for that of their customers. Subscribing to such sources provides businesses with better information and reduces the likelihood of overproduction and crisis.

10.3 *Blunting Circulation among Interconnected Circuits*

In Chapter 5, Section 4.3, I identified a number of connections among circuits of capital, through which crisis can circulate, the question now is what measures do capitalists take to avoid or blunt such circulation. Their preoccupation, of course, is offsetting the negative impact of the circulation of crises on their own operations, present and future, and only peripherally with how circulation affects workers.

1) *M*. When, in the midst of crisis, *M* must be borrowed from financial circuits, lenders are wary of the ability of borrowers to repay and tend to raise interest rates and toughen conditions for borrowers. They do this because if borrowers default on their loans, lenders' assets shrink and they may also fail. To offset lender's worries and increase their chances of getting loan money when they need it, capitalists try a) to have made as much profit as possible to demonstrate their creditworthiness, b) have maintained backup cash or liquid reserves for emergencies, c) take action to counter whatever difficulties they might have that trouble lenders, e.g., worker agitation, possible shortages of *MP*, and d) enlist government support when necessary for such counters, e.g., to put down worker strikes, to protect shipping lanes for imported *MP*. Where there is intense competition in borrowing, with rising interest rates and tougher conditions, businesses hope both their past and present actions will get them loans (at "prime" rates of interest) when others are turned down.

232 Given the centrality of agriculture in the US economy, in 1862 the Morill Act created the Department of Agriculture (along with land grant colleges) and a year later a Division of Statistics (later the Economic Research Service, ERS) was created in to compile data needed for both agribusiness and policy makers. The ERS publishes "Situation and Outlook Reports" that track the production and stocks of various agricultural commodities both at home and abroad – to help producers decide how much of what crop to plant or bring to market and to inform government policy making. See, *Sowing Seeds of Change: Informing Public Policy in the Economic Research Service of USDA* (1999), Chapter 3.

Lenders' perception of increased risk of default also drives them to hold onto their assets to cover losses, which reduces monies available for lending. The degree to which governments, increasingly via central banks, bailout both lenders and borrowers has usually depended on a host of factors specified in regulations plus whatever "pull" those institutions have via their political contacts.

2) *M – MP*. Against potential reductions in either the producing or purchasing of *MP*, which would at least raise prices and cut profits, capitalists try to build up inventories that are greater than immediately needed. This Marx observed in the runup to the cotton crisis brought on by the Civil War in the United States. Textile industrialists in Britain also sought to influence government policies they believed would protect their supply lines, e.g., supporting the cotton-producing Confederacy. They failed but they did try. Such efforts are typical on the part of industries facing supply problems.

3) *M – LP*. Because disruption in *M – LP* in one circuit can cause disruption in others, capitalists have often tried to unite in a common front to limit such circulation, e.g., in fixing wages, opposing unions, or getting laws passed setting maximum wages or outlawing unions. This was just what Adam Smith observed and was the reason he supported counter self-organization on the part of workers. Marx and Engels, of course, also supported such self-organization, indeed did what they could to foster it, including its circulation from circuit to circuit, across ethnic and linguistic barriers. Because capitalists tended to fire militants, they also "blacklisted" them so others wouldn't hire them. Blacklisting works where the labor pool is local and capitalists know each other. Absent such immediate connections, capitalists resort to careful evaluation in recruitment to avoid hiring potential activists. Accomplishing this often involved the use of the government, first in putting down worker actions, such as strikes or sabotage, followed by judicial repression and punishment: jail or transportation, e.g., to Australia.

4) *...P...C(MS)′ – M′*. How to counter crises in the production of the means of subsistence, which raises their prices, cuts real wages, and stirs up discontent, depends on the source of the crisis. When the breakdown is localized, one counter is diversifying sources, e.g., while drought or disease in one food producing area can be eventually be countered by irrigation or public health measures, immediate relief can be obtained by importing food from other, unaffected areas. (Precisely what Britain failed to do in Ireland and then in its colonies in South Asia, see Section 7.2.3.1.) Because crop failures are known to result in higher prices, both producers and merchants often hoard their supplies to further drive up prices. Capitalists faced with starving or upset workers have pressured governments to intervene against such price-gouging

and force the selling of food stuffs at lower prices. In extremis, e.g., during wars, governments have resorted to rationing to distribute limited supplies, maintaining at least the illusion of fairness in times of crisis.[233]

5) *C′ – M′* gluts. Countering the oversupply of commodities, which can involve either too much *MS* or too much *MP*, or both, is a problem, first and foremost for suppliers who, trying to sell their products in the face of inadequate demand, see their prices fall and with them revenues and profits. Buyers, of course, profit from the reduced costs. When the problem is only local producers can counter by holding on to inventory, withholding it from markets – but at the cost of storage. But where costs prove too great, one recourse is to destroy some of the excess, removing it permanently from the market and eliminating storage costs. During widespread and deep crises, where no immediate improvement in demand is expected, this solution has been far more frequent than commonly recognized.[234] But even in more normal times, the recognition of excess supply has sometimes triggered collective destruction.[235] Both situations contradict economists' endless praise of the "efficiency" of capitalism.

Another counter has been for governments to intervene in either production or markets. In the former, they sometimes mandate cutbacks in production to reduce the excess of supply over demand. In the latter, they buy up excess production, supporting the price of the product being bought up and producer revenues and profits. Both methods have been used to manage the production and prices of grain destined for both consumer (cereal, bread, etc.) and producer (feed grain, seed) markets. The latter has also been used to create "strategic reserves" of *MP* judged essential, e.g., setting aside forests reserved for wooden ship building, or supplies of sources of energy such as coal or later oil. Such reserves keep prices up during gluts (and can be released to lower prices to offset unexpected reductions in supply).

---

233 Rationing was extensive in WWII, covering most basic consumer goods, from food to fuel. Complications in managing rationing, e.g., countering corrupt practices, have been portrayed in films such as Foyle's War, most episodes (2002–2010) unfolding on the southern coast of England. More recently governments have overseen some rationing of medical equipment (masks, test kits) during the Covid-19 pandemic.

234 During the Great Depression of the 1930s when both local and international markets collapsed, vast quantities of produced goods were destroyed. One dramatic example was the burning of over 10 billion pounds of coffee beans in Brazil. See: Jonas Ferraresso, "90 Years Ago, Seeking Salvation, Brazil Burned Billions of Pounds of Coffee", *Daily Coffee News*, September 22, 2021. (Accessed 7/18/2024.)

235 One modern example is discussed in Chapter 5, footnote 47: the fashion industry which regularly destroys vast quantities of unsellable cheap clothing.

CHAPTER 7

Crises as Solutions to the Contradictions of Accumulation

Although contradictions, inherent in the antagonistic social relationships of capitalism, cause crises in accumulation, i.e., *problems* for capitalists, the latter have repeatedly been able to convert such crises into *solutions* to those problems in ways which have permitted the restoration of continued expansion. In other words, the crises or ruptures imposed on capital (the "first moment" of crisis) by workers' struggles or some other cause, get turned into the means of relaunching accumulation. As solution-for-capital, those means constitute the "second moment" of crisis, this time crisis-for-workers, either because their struggles have been defeated or simply because capital has emerged strengthened from *its* crisis. This is the phenomenon to which Marx is referring when he calls crises "momentary, violent solutions for the existing contradictions, violent eruptions that re-establish the disturbed equilibrium for the time being."[1] Because the contradictions are, above all, those between capitalists and workers; re-established equilibrium is a new balance of power that allows accumulation, i.e., the continued imposition of work and the perpetuation of the capitalist social order.

But how do capitalists accomplish this feat? Partially by actions taken in the private sector, in the direct relations between workers and capitalists or among capitalists, and partially by mobilizing the state, especially the government, to act on their behalf. In the private sector, one action that is taken when profits drop and crisis circulates, becoming widespread, is cutting back investment, laying off workers, and cutting wages. Imposing greater suffering on workers creates excellent opportunities to deploy the various offsetting strategies that I have outlined above. Indeed, increased unemployment is not just a symptom of crisis, it is often the first counter strategy deployed. Which other strategies are used depends on the source of the crisis. As for government interventions, they are usually designed to complement and reinforce whatever measures are being undertaken by private capitalists. For example, layoffs and rising unemployment, which increase worker poverty, have been accompanied by contractionary changes in fiscal and monetary policies and

1 *Manuscript of 1864–1865*, p. 358, *Capital, Vol. 3*, p. 357, or *MECW*, *Vol. 37*, p. 248.

reductions in government support for the poor, which further deepen that poverty, putting more pressure on workers to bow to capitalist demands.

An essential element in how such scenarios play out is the differential ability among capitalists to successfully deploy whichever strategies are chosen. Some have more resources and are better able; others have fewer and are less able. At the level of worker-management relations, greater ability means some are better able to obtain whatever concessions from workers are required to re-establish profitability. With some better able to cope and others less so, the competitive position of the latter deteriorates and, in extremis, they either go bankrupt and out of business or are taken over by those better able, with more resources, resulting in an increased "centralization" of capital, i.e., more capital in fewer hands. Along the way capital assets are devalued and, in the end, the power of capitalists as a class is strengthened vis-a-vis workers.

Whatever the methods used, where capital as a whole is successful in finding a solution to crisis, the dynamic of crisis/solution forms a moment of accumulation. The recurrent historical pattern of ruptured and successfully restored accumulation, of periodical bust and renewed boom, explains both economists' preference for the concept of business-cycle over that of crisis and their optimism about the adaptability and longevity of the system. The optimism of Marx's analysis, on the contrary, derives from the inability of capitalist solutions to eliminate the fundamental sources of antagonism that are inherent in the system. So, their solutions forever renew the contradictions and struggles that challenge their very survival – no matter how many times capitalists and their economists succeed in converting crisis into solution.

Let's examine some examples of how these two moments of crisis unfold.

1 In the First Stage of the Circuit: *LP – M/M – LP*

We have seen how successful struggles for higher wages may increase them more than productivity gains such that the rate of exploitation and the rate of profit fall – undermining relative surplus value and causing a crisis for capitalists. How capitalists respond to turn their crisis into one for workers depends upon just how workers have achieved the increase in wages. For example, workers may have taken advantage of tightening labor markets during a period of rapid accumulation in which capitalists have been forced to bid up the price of labor-power, a situation which gives workers increased leverage, not just in one, but in many circuits. Workers may also have achieved increased leverage by organizing successfully to overcome divisions and competition among themselves, say between local workers and cheaper foreign workers. In both cases, repressive force – by either private goons or government agencies – was long used to break up workers' self-organization. But whether such force is available or not, capitalists, both singly and collectively, have had another strategy to attack wages: cutting back on investment and current production, effectively going on strike. Workers go on strike when they refuse to work, walking away from both production and the labor market; capitalists go on strike when they refuse to invest, stop hiring new workers and lay off presently employed ones.[2] Layoffs immediately end workers' wages, reduces their ability to eat or pay rent and thus increases evictions and their exposure to the extreme poverty of starvation, susceptibility to disease and homelessness. Such action in the private sector, is often complemented by government cutbacks in support for the wageless and homeless, i.e., poor rates and workhouses in Marx's time, "social safety net" support in ours.[3] The first to be fired, of course, would be those workers identified as most militant, as organizers. Reduced expenditures in investment and wages reduces aggregate demand in both departments, further increasing unemployment, loosening labor markets, and bringing pressure to bear on those still employed to accept either a reduction in increases or an absolute drop in wages (common in Marx's time):

> ... accumulation slackens as a result of the rise in the price of labor, because the stimulus of gain is blunted. The rate of accumulation lessens; but this means that the primary cause of that lessening itself vanishes, i.e., the disproportion between capital and exploitable power-power. The mechanism of the capitalist production process removes the very obstacles it temporarily creates. The price of labor falls again to a level corresponding with capital's requirements for self-valorization.[4]

---

2 In his *On the Nature and Uses of Sabotage* (1919), Veblen draws a parallel between worker attacks on equipment and such capitalist "strikes," calling them both "sabotage" of industrial production.

3 This double whammy was precisely what happened in the early 1980s when Jimmy Carter and Ronald Reagan unleased Fed chairman Paul Volcker to attack wages by driving up interest rates and plunging first the United States and then the rest of the world into crisis, including the biggest increases in unemployment since the Great Depression of the 1930s. Reagan complemented this attack on wages by simultaneous attacking food stamps, expelling veterans and others from mental hospitals, trying to privatize Social Security, breaking unions (starting with the firing of PATCO workers) and rolling back regulations protecting those workers still employed. The same pattern was repeated after the financial crisis of 2006–8 when millions lost their jobs and hundreds of thousands their homes. The recent indulgence of hedge fund capitalists in speculation in the housing market has only worsened these phenomena by pricing both houses and rent beyond what existing wages can afford.

4 *Capital, Vol. 1*, p. 770, or *MECW*, *Vol. 35*, p. 614.

Marx felt that capital was able to dominate workers' wage struggles repeatedly through this use of crisis. He notes several times that the downturn in accumulation can control the upward movement of wages. Any reduction of surplus value caused by rising wages can cause crises but never go so far as to threaten the system itself.

> The rise of wages is therefore confined within limits that not only leave intact the foundations of the capitalist system, but also secure its reproduction on an increasing scale … the very nature of accumulation excludes … every rise in the price of labor, which could seriously imperil the continual reproduction, on an ever enlarging scale, of the capital-relation.[5]

This pessimistic assessment includes a statement that appears to strip the proletariat of its subjectivity and revolutionary potential:

> It is these absolute movements of the accumulation of capital which are reflected as relative movements of the mass of exploitable power-power, and therefore seem produced by the latter's own independent movement. To put it mathematically: the rate of accumulation is the independent, not the dependent, variable; the rate of wages is the dependent, not the independent variable."[6]

While repeatedly cited by orthodox Marxists as limiting the potential power of wage struggles (which for them rationalized the priority of the Party's leadership of "political" struggles), this passage seems totally one-sided. Capital accumulates and sometimes the pace of that accumulation induces increases in the demand for labor and hence increases in wages, sometimes the pace slows and induces their fall. In contemporary terms, this way of looking at the situation sees the rise and fall of wages as determined only by the changing industrial demand for labor.[7]

But, compare this with the discussion in Section II of *Value, Price and Profit* (1865). In those two lectures attacking the arguments of Owenite John Weston, Marx argued vigorously in favor of wage struggles, during both periods of

---

5 *Capital, Vol. 1*, pp. 771–772, or *MECW, Vol. 35*, p. 616.

6 *Capital, Vol. 1*, p. 770, or *MECW, Vol. 35*, p. 615.

7 Whatever its limitations, this argument was wielded by Marx against Malthus who was arguing the exact opposite, namely that the rise and fall of wages was due to changes in the *supply* of labor.

expansion and those of contraction. Although he agreed that capitalist crisis would set a limit to the upward movement of wages, workers could still push their wages up higher than they would otherwise rise during an expansion and prevent them from falling as low as they otherwise would during a contraction. Wage struggles could rupture capitalist development, at least periodically. Furthermore, because Marx's theory allowed for the possibility of secular increases in real wages,[8] and thus a secular increase in the wealth and power of the proletariat, the recurrent crises were expected to get worse and worse. This prognosis was one he held with Engels from the early 1840s on. It thus appears wrong to interpret the foregoing passage, as many have done, as a denial of the subjectivity of the working class, or of the autonomy of its struggles. What is really at issue is the assessment of class power and the relative effectiveness of wage struggle and capitalist strategy under varying circumstances.

Furthermore, an objectivist interpretation of the passage on dependent and independent variables depends on a narrow interpretation of the meaning of accumulation. In the usual interpretation, accumulation is thought of one-sidedly as the reinvestment of surplus value – an act undertaken by capitalists – and any resulting growth in output. Yet only pages earlier Marx goes out of his way to emphasize that accumulation is above all the expanded reproduction of the class relation. In this light, accumulation is the expanded reproduction of all the elements of the class relation. To say that changes in wages are dependent upon accumulation is, therefore, to say that those changes are dependent on a whole complex of antagonistic class forces. Read this way, the objectivist interpretation is too narrow. Once "accumulation" is not reduced to the notion of capitalist reinvestment and growth narrowly defined, with its effect on labor demand, we retain the whole complexity of class struggle as an analytical framework for investigating both the first moment of crisis (when, for example, the working class pushes wages up faster than productivity, or otherwise disrupts the circuits) and the second moment (when capital strikes back by, for instance, wielding low investment and higher unemployment to reduce wages and restore profitable conditions).

2 In the Second Stage of the Circuit: *...P...*

When the causes of crisis are to be found in struggles within production – about work and the conditions of work – then the offsetting strategies capitalists

8 Remember, as both Marx and eventually marginalist, neoclassical economists recognized, increases in productivity make possible simultaneous increases in both profits and wages.

use as a solution can involve more than just unemployment. Such struggles have included both resistance to the introduction of technologies perceived as threatening to workers and demands for better working conditions, e.g., shorter and safer working hours. Classic examples of the former were worker attacks on labor-displacing power looms (Luddites, etc.) and of the latter were those demanding legal limitations on working hours and investment in safety equipment (Factory Acts). In response, capitalists have sought to restructure the organization of production in ways that fragment workers' organizations and alliances, undermining their collective strength. This restructuring can occur at any level of the division of labor.

In his extended discussion of relative surplus value, Marx showed repeatedly how technological innovation, embodied in new machinery and new work organization, has been used by capital against workers' struggles. The substitution of steam for waterpower facilitated the building of factories to enclose and control the hitherto dispersed labor of the putting-out system. Power looms not only displaced labor but also deskilled it – undermining workers' control over the process of production and facilitating their replacement by less skilled women and children.[9] This kind of reorganization, which decomposes the power of workers has also been accomplished by introducing immigrant workers, setting them against local ones, partly by paying them lower wages, partly by playing on ethnic differences (as in the case of Irish and English workers discussed in Chapter 6 above).

Similar reorganizations were carried out in both agriculture and mining, e.g., the introduction of mechanical for human reapers in fields and of steam-powered drills in mines in the nineteenth century replaced skills and reduced both the bargaining power of workers and the demand for their labor-power.[10] In the United States, such moves, especially in mining, was accompanied by widespread hiring of immigrant labor – a strategy that lay the basis for the later "Red Scare" attacks on miners and widespread deportation. Such moves can occur during periods of expansion, but downturns, when existing capital is devalued, production reduced and workers laid off, provide capitalists with opportunities at precisely the same moment that workers are weakest.

9 Besides Marx's analysis in Chapters 12–15 on relative surplus value, see Raniero Panzieri, "Sull'uso capitalistico delle macchine nel neocapitalismo," *Quaderni Rossi* 1, (1961): 53–72. In English as, "The Capitalist Use of Machinery: Marx Versus the 'Objectivists,'" in Phil Slater, ed., *Outlines of a Critique of Technology* (Atlantic Highlands: Humanities Press, 1980).

10 The pitting of steam-power drills against workers was immortalized in American folklore legends and songs about "steel-driving man" John Henry. See, too: Doreen Chaky, "John Henry v. Charles Burleigh's Drill," *Mining History Journal 1* (1994): 104–108.

Such restructuring of industrial production may also involve geographic reorganization as well as that of shopfloors, plants, mines, or fields. As I pointed out in Chapter 6, direct overseas investment in areas of lower wages (a weaker proletariat) and higher profits is one option. Colonialism, by dramatically enhancing the ability of capitalists to impose work – whether in mines, fields, or factories – in other geographic areas, provided new possibilities for outflanking the growing strength of workers self-organization at home, e.g., in England as the enforcement of the Factory Acts improved their bargaining power, by investing in areas where workers were substantially weaker. Production shut down in one area during a crisis can be started up, or expanded, in another area where the balance of class forces is more favorable to capital. Such reorganization can impose a massive restructuring of global labor-power as one group of workers is substituted for another, either partially or totally.

A final way in which crises in production may be used by capital as an opportunity to reorganize itself to raise average profitability and restore accumulation, is the kind of industrial reorganization at the level of individual firms that Marx termed the *centralization* of capital. Crisis affects different firms to different degrees; some go bankrupt and disappear, others weaken, are taken over and absorbed by stronger companies. Competition, Marx says, "always ends in the ruin of many small capitalists, whose capitals partly pass into the hands of their conquerors, and partly vanish completely." It is the "expropriation of capitalist by capitalist, transformation of many small into few large capitals."[11]

When capital is able to collectively take advantage of crisis in this way, through the centralization of capital, Engels added the observation, in the fourth German edition, that it "intensifies and accelerates the effects of accumulation, it simultaneously extends and speeds up those revolutions in the technical composition of capital which raise its constant portion at the expense of this variable portion, thus diminishing the relative demand for labor."[12] This in turn accentuates other contradictions of accumulation, especially the tendency of the rate of profit to fall.

This tendency, brought on by the rising organic composition of capital, which requires a larger and larger proportionate investment to put the same number of people to work, appears to capital mainly in the form of unemployment aggravated by automation. The only possible industrial responses to this problem are either the slowing down of labor displacing innovation – and this can only be temporary – or creating new opportunities to put people to work

11 *Capital, Vol. 1*, p. 777, or MECW, *Vol. 35*, p. 621.

12 *Capital, Vol. 1*, p. 780, or MECW, *Vol. 35*, p. 622.

through investment in new industries producing new products, which speeds up accumulation.

3 In the Third Stage of the Circuit: $C' - M'$

Faced with crises in their ability to sell C' at prices equivalent to their value M' capitalists have found various ways to convert crises into solutions to restore accumulation. Some solutions are found in the "private sector," i.e., relations between workers and capitalists and those among capitalists, and some by mobilizing state intervention. Which solution is tried depends on the reasons why production exceeds market demand. The excess can arise from either production accelerating faster than the expansion of demand, by a contraction of the latter or some combination of both.

Let's look first at solutions that emerge in the private sector. Where excess production is marginal and limited to a single product and market – the usual assumption of both classical and neoclassical economists – the solution comes with a fall in price that leads capitalist managers to reduce production to levels consistent with existing demand. But reduced production generates less surplus value, less investment and slows accumulation. The more general the overproduction for existing markets, the more general the crisis and the less such marginal adjustment can resolve the problem – the point made by both Malthus and Marx against Ricardo and Say.

In the eighteenth and nineteenth centuries, when industrialization and accumulation were based on a small number of industries, e.g., textiles, a crisis in those few major industries had widespread negative ramifications for all those connected to it. With textile production reduced, so too would agricultural production of raw materials for those industries, e.g., flax, wool, cotton, be forced to contract. Moreover, the financing, transportation, and sale of products, from cloth to everything made from cloth, would all be reduced. This is one reason Marx paid so much attention to the textile industry and its crises.[13]

13 Although the diversification of production discussed in the last section has rendered capitalist production less susceptible to the vagaries of a single industry, as recently as the "automobile age," and the "computer" or "information" age, crises in those industries have rippled far more strongly across the economy as a whole than those in unrelated secondary industries. Some have argued that the military-industrial complex, with its array of industries building bases all over the world and churning out weapons to supply them has played a similar central role. See, James Flink, *The Automobile Age* (1988), Manuel Castells, *The Information Age: economy, society and culture* (1996), Marcel van der Linden, "Edward Sard (1913–99), Theorist of the Permanent War Economy," *Critique 46, no. 1* (January 2018): 117–130, and Michael Kidron, *Western Capitalism Since the War* (1970).

When a crisis in $C' - M'$ becomes general, part of the solution derives from how the fall in prices devalues not only existing commodity capital – sold under value or destroyed outright – but also once productive, now rusting fixed capital of the producers. The "dumping" of excess production on markets, either domestic or foreign, at lower prices is a well-known feature of crises. Dumping from foreign sources may undermine local producers unable to compete but create future markets for those doing the dumping, helping resolve their crisis. (Thus, the demand for protectionist measures by local producers.) In extremis, final products, instead of being sold for their ostensible use-value may also be dumped as even lower value raw materials for other industries, e.g., clothing, unsellable as such, is sold below its value to the paper industry. When even those markets are unavailable or prices so low as to make even such sales not worthwhile, products are simply destroyed. This has been true for clothing, as well as harvested crops of raw materials and animals. The destruction reduces supply but also often results in the bankruptcy of producers unable to survive the loss of revenue.[14]

In other words, the solution to overproduction involves precisely that weeding out discussed above, in which some capitalists fail and their assets are redistributed to others, with a resulting centralization of control over production. Centralization can increase oligopolistic power in that industry and convey greater control over markets – especially if a small number of oligopolists collude to form a cartel with monopolistic power to determine both prices and market shares. Regardless of how production is brought into line with market demand, capitalists are forced to adjust the other components of their circuits to the new scale of circulation. In such crises, although initially involving a reduction in surplus value, industrial reorganization provides a solution that recreates the equilibrium conditions for renewed expansion. This is true for surviving individual circuits of capital and true for the aggregate – at the level of whole industries and of the balance among industrial departments, where new arrangements reduce disproportionalities.[15]

---

14 The most vulnerable are small farmers or peasants whose production, both for domestic consumption and for sale, has merely supported survival, never generating surplus value beyond that required for the repayment of debt. Unlike larger agribusinesses who experience these difficulties as falling profits, the bankruptcy of small farmers and peasants becomes a mechanism of renewed not-so primitive accumulation, foreclosure/enclosure and proletarianization, facilitated by the financial institutions that hitherto sucked out what little surplus value was generated in the form of interest.

15 Marx's skepticism of the ability of markets to bring about smooth adjustment, as opposed to traumatic, system-wide adjustment at great human cost, was shared by state capitalists who developed planning at the aggregate level to avoid such trauma and resulting social upheaval.

Beyond such readjustments in the private sector, capitalists have made use of the state, especially of national governments, to overcome crises of overproduction and inadequate demand and to reestablish conditions of renewed accumulation. Two uses, mentioned above, particularly obvious at the international level were laws enacted to facilitate trade and the deployment of force to both create and protect it.

Mercantilists obtained from their sovereigns laws in support of expanding export markets for domestic production. The bullionists argued for net exports to bring in gold, but others understood that properly done, invested gold could bring in more gold through trade. After them, governments drew on the ideas of political economists like Adam Smith to support both export and import trade, as well as the use of force and laws to facilitate colonialization to widen markets for *C′*. Equally obvious have been those laws allowing the chartering of corporations such as the East India and Royal African Companies to facilitate colonial expansion and all those laws helping to protect and regulate financial services in support of trade. I have also mentioned the deployment of armies of colonial conquest and national warships to accompany convoys of merchant ships from the same country and to protect/maintain home markets, e.g., the blockade of French ports and repression of smuggling during the Napoleonic Wars. Then, once again, the Corn Laws were passed in its wake to sustain domestic grain markets – to the benefit of producers and at the expense of workers whose real wages were undermined by the higher cost of bread.

All of these efforts by the state have been financed either by borrowing – to the profit of lenders – or by taxes. This made fiscal policy as much a terrain of class struggle as monetary policy. Capitalists have sought expenditures that benefited them, and taxes mostly levied on workers where possible, e.g., customs tariffs on consumer goods, sales taxes, and income taxes, despite their negative effects on aggregate consumption demand. On the other side, workers and social reformers have pushed for state expenditures to benefit workers, e.g., Factory Acts, while seeking to make capitalists share the burden of taxation – share via progressive income taxes, e.g., the British Tax Act of 1798 that imposed higher taxes on higher income and the American Revenue Acts of 1861 and 1862 to finance the Civil War. Repealed in 1872, a progressive federal income tax in the US was reborn through the Sixteenth Amendment to the Constitution in 1909.

As for the failure of capitalist price mediation through direct appropriation, although Marx discussed the phenomenon of crime in a number of places, including working class direct appropriation, and considered it a spur to capitalist development, he never (to my knowledge) integrated these discussions with the general topic of crisis. Clearly crime can rupture the circulation of capital – perhaps contributing to the creation of crisis – as amply demonstrated by repeated urban and even regionwide "rioting" by workers.[16] When capitalist price mediation fails in circumstances of direct appropriation, then capital responds with violence to forcibly re-impose the price form in order to ensure that C' not only reaches the market but its monetary value is also realized as M'.

To summarize, just as the most fundamental contradiction of capitalism is between the classes, so the most fundamental role of crisis-as-solution is restoring the balance of class forces so that capital can resume its growth – that is, growth in its control over the working class and society. The predispositions to crisis show how the fundamental antagonism between the classes over each element of the class relation and each stage of the circuit of capital predisposes the system to rupture. Capital must fight in each case to maintain its control, which is never guaranteed and is repeatedly challenged. Aspects of capitalist crisis that do not appear immediately as questions of class relations, I have nevertheless revealed to be forms of those relations and their development to be a function of class struggle. For example, competition that appears solely as a relation between individual capitals, thus internal to capital and separate from the working class, we see to be an organizational form through which collective capital selects the best of its managers and discards the rest. The pattern of class struggle is reflected in the uneven success of firms, expansion or closure being two ways capital responds to working class pressure during periods of crisis.

---

16 In more recent times, "commodity riots" – involving widespread direct appropriation – have periodically shaken American cities, from the 1960s through the 1990s and uprisings exploded in many countries in reaction to increases in food prices imposed by International Monetary Fund's "structural adjustment programs" during the international debt crisis of the 1980s and 1990s. Direct appropriation also deepened the crisis caused by Hurricane Katrina in 2005 along the US Gulf Coast in response to the failure of local and federal governments to either prepare for or respond to the disaster in ways benefiting workers.

CHAPTER 8

Crisis and Revolution

The relationship between crisis and revolution has loomed large in the thinking of both Marx and Engels and in that of many of their followers. The reasons are obvious enough. Looking back, I showed in my historical sketch in Chapter 2, how both men perceived a relationship between the two phenomena, mainly in the likelihood that a crisis involving high levels of unemployment and widespread suffering among workers had, in the past, and would probably continue to provoke uprisings, revolts and ultimately revolutions. Their world, after all had already experienced a whole series of revolutions before these two young men turned their attention to the study of the possibilities in the world around them.

The rise and spread of capitalism throughout the world in the sixteenth to nineteenth centuries – whose imposition Marx eventually analyzed in terms of primitive accumulation – provoked resistance, sometimes passive but often involving violent rebellion and revolution. A very short list, all of which were known to them, includes Germany in 1524, England in 1549, England, Portugal and Spain in 1640, Jamaica in 1728, America in 1775, France in 1789, Haiti in 1791, France, Belgium, Poland and Switzerland in 1830.[1] Moreover, the one revolution in which they directly participated – that in Germany in 1848 – exploded in the wake of the crisis of 1847, providing another confirmation that crisis could lead to revolution. As we saw, their subsequent analysis of that revolution (and the others which broke out in country after country that same year) examined the relationship between that crisis and these upheavals on the Continent. That analysis was one reason why, ten years later, as the crisis of 1857 deepened, Marx anticipated another revolution and set to work night after night pulling his thoughts together in the *Grundrisse* notebooks.

Their analyses, as interpreted by many of their followers in both the nineteenth and twentieth centuries, tended to be simplified into a cause-and-effect relationship: crises can give rise to uprisings, large-scale breakdowns can give rise to revolutions. Among those whose analyses of crisis focused purely on the "laws" emanating from intra-capitalist dynamics, such as the anarchy of competition, tendencies to overproduction and the exhaustion of markets, the

1 This list includes only a few of the many, many rebellions and revolutions. A more comprehensive list is provided by Wikipedia.

 | DOI:10.1163/9789004708631_009

corollary to this perception of cause and effect sometimes led to a politics of simply waiting for the system to breakdown and the subsequent, inevitable revolution. In the worst case, it involved "la politique du pire," i.e., embracing whatever makes the suffering of workers worse, and thus, supposedly, their revolt more likely. Less passive responses involved efforts to organize workers – through strikes that Marx and Engels had seen as training grounds – and to build organizations prepared to lead other workers in the revolutionary overthrow of the system when the crisis occurs.

1 Revolution: Another Amoebic Term

I have devoted most of this essay to analyzing Marx and Engels' writings on crisis and the meanings they gave to the concept, but before assessing their analysis of the relationship between crisis and revolution, I think it worthwhile to pause and consider the meanings of the term "revolution." It has become one of those amoebic terms whose meanings change from usage to usage. From a word evoking massive social upheavals with the potential to change society, its use has devolved so much as to warrant some dissection.

In day-to-day life, except for historians and lefties who have absorbed Marxist or anarchist traditions, the term has become trivialized. In the onslaught of advertising with which capitalists bombard us endlessly, every small new variation in some commodity is declared "revolutionary" – supposedly warranting immediate purchase by anyone who usually buys "the next big thing." On such use of the term, I know no better commentary/parody than Tom Waits' song "Step Right Up" in his album *Small Change* (1976).

Unfortunately, intellectuals are also prone to declaring each new formulation in concept or theory "revolutionary." For example, in economics, the substitution of utility for labor as the source of value and the use of the calculus in formulating economic theories in the late nineteenth century is called the "Marginalist Revolution." Similarly, the reworking of Adam Smith's eighteenth-century preoccupation with the aggregate "Wealth of Nations" by John Maynard Keynes in the mid-twentieth century into what came to be called "macroeconomics" is dubbed the "Keynesian Revolution."

The use of such terminology by economists, of course, amounts to mimicry of its use by historians of science. The discovery in the sixteenth century by Nicolaus Copernicus (1473–1543) that the earth revolves around the sun, instead of the reverse, is celebrated as the "Copernican Revolution." Then came the seventeenth century Newtonian Revolution in which the capitalist machine age gave birth to Isaac Newton's mechanics, and the twentieth century Einstein Revolution[2] in which his theory of relativity eclipsed Newton's mechanics which by then had become "classical," and so on.[3]

The term "revolution" is also used in less promotional, more mundane ways denoting not some supposedly earth-shaking radical change but merely repetition, a "going-around" in which some moving object returns to its original position. This is the case when scientists talk about celestial revolutions (and their duration) – of the earth around the sun (one year), or of the moon around the earth (a sidereal or synodic month), or of the rotation of the earth on its axis (a sidereal or stellar day). It is also the case when engineers who design, or industrial workers who use, machines talk about aspects of their operations that involve simple mechanical revolutions, such as those of a drill press or a lathe. Among those who can afford them, some cars sport tachometers, which monitor engine rpm's, revolutions per minute.

2 "Revolution" as Used by Marx and Engels

In Marx's analysis of capitalism, the closest analogy to such scientific and engineering uses are his concepts of "circuits" and of "reproduction." As capitalists successfully complete a circuit, they wind up back where they started, and ready to start over. They have reproduced their operations, albeit, if as successfully as hoped, on a larger scale. Although these are biological, rather than mechanical metaphors, the concept of reproduction nevertheless denotes processes in which the combined effect of all circuits merely recreates the original situation. In "simple" reproduction, the values of all the components – means of production, labor power, commodities and money – remain the same; in "expanded" reproduction there is also a return to the beginning, qualitatively speaking, but on a larger scale. When ruptured in some way, this hoped for eternal return is not realized, in either quality or quantity, thus crisis.

When the forces at work that repeatedly disrupt circuits and reproduction – especially antagonistic class forces – not only disrupt capitalist plans but also impose more profound shakeups in the way reproduction is organized there is no true "return," regardless of the scale. The overall pattern remains, e.g., $M - C - M'$, but the whole set of relationships is reshaped into something new. Such

2 For those with a sense of humor, Einsteins Revolution is also the name of a $2 million dollar quarter horse available for stud.

3 Thomas Kuhn's concept of paradigm shifts in the evolution of science has provided support for viewing such shifts as "revolutions."

reshaping often includes changes in technology for which Marx (and many historians) did use the term "revolutions."[4] The use of the term "revolutions" for such changes is closer to its use in designating major social upheavals, not only because major technological changes alter the technical class relations but because Marx judged that even those introduced against workers' struggles ultimately advanced the class conflict toward more profound revolutions. Such was the introduction of steam engines and the power looms they made possible – looms that were introduced to destroy the power of handicraft, handloom weavers but contributed to the creation of an industrial proletariat.[5] Such changes/revolutions do not immediately threaten the existence of capitalism but result in new processes of worker self-organization, on an ever-broader basis. Factories and their power looms gave capitalists more immediate control over workers, by subjecting every minute of work to supervision. But by bringing workers together in one place they facilitated the collective formation of unions – a whole new organization of workers' power, which renewed their struggles on a new basis. For Marx and Engels such limited "revolutions" and their results were steps toward the kind that interested them most: those that threatened to overthrow the whole system.

It was that kind of revolution which inspired them, whether they succeeded or failed. In Germany in 1848, Marx and Engels saw themselves fighting in support of the replacement of an absolutist regime by a more liberal one, which they expected would provide more scope for workers' struggles. They had seen, of course, how the American Revolution in 1775, the one in France in 1789 and those in Haiti in 1791 all succeeded in overthrowing the existing *political* organization of capitalism, even if not the system itself. They also knew the one in France in 1830 and those in Europe in 1848 failed even in that limited goal. Yet they called them all Revolutions. Why? Because those fighting in the streets

4 Such was the "Green Revolution" in agricultural technology of the 1950s and 1960s – the development of high yielding varieties of wheat and rice – financed by capitalist philanthropies (the Ford and Rockefeller foundations) in response to peasant revolt in the Global South. Although, understood politically, those technological changes might more properly be described as a "Green Counter-Revolution," they were, nevertheless, modern versions of those changes Marx saw as "the most powerful weapon for suppressing strikes" (*Capital, Vol. 1*, p. 562, MECW, *Vol. 35*, p. 438). See H. Cleaver, "The Contradictions of the Green Revolution," op. cit.

5 This pattern of reorganizing production to increase control over skilled workers through deskilling was repeated, years later, by Frederick Taylor, whose "principles of scientific management" were developed to extract more work and increase productivity. His first paper on "A Piece Rate System" was published in 1895, the year Engels died. In the decades that have followed, historians have identified a whole series of "revolutions" including that of electricity, of the automobile, of nuclear power, and most recently the computer or informational "revolution."

were demanding fundamental changes in society. The Americans, the French and Haitians wanted independence from monarchy and a chance to form a new system of government and, in Haiti an end to slavery. The French in 1789 wanted to overthrow the monarchy and establish a new system of government with greater "rights of man."

Win or lose, they saw that struggles against capitalism itself are inevitably renewed – along with the crises they induce and at least the possibility of fundamental change. Why? Because the capitalist way of life for most people means the endless subordination of life to work, exploitation and alienation. By pitting people against each other, capitalists against workers and workers against each other, this system has fundamental, inescapable antagonisms that make crisis permanently imminent in the system. By reducing the lives of most people to that of mere worker, it has effectively created and maintained a class division, between a capitalist class imposing work and a working class resisting it. This working class has developed from a capitalist-defined "class-in-itself" to a self-defined "class-for-itself," a class that has developed its subjectivity from that of living labor to that of a potentially revolutionary class subject. Marx's writings show how capitalist crises are often, from the point of view of workers, moments not of breakdown but of breakthrough, opening new opportunities. Where crises for capital result from its loss of control (direct or indirect) over workers, they are simultaneously moments of eruptions of working-class subjectivity rejecting the way things are and demanding something new.

The rupture of accumulation by workers' struggles is a moment of conquest. It is the opening of a breach in the enemy lines in the class war. When struggle circulates rapidly, the breach is widened and whole lines may give way, widening the scope for workers' own self-organization and mobilization. The circulation of struggle to more and more sectors of the class and the increasing of the space, time, and resources available for organizing further struggle, strengthens the ability to resist. Even if the struggles that produce and grow out of a crisis are ultimately crushed by capital, they are still important experiences in the development of the working class as revolutionary subject. As Engels wrote in 1845, they are still "the military school of the working-men in which they prepare themselves for the great struggle which cannot be avoided."[6]

Marx repeated this theme almost two decades later in *Value, Price and Profit* where he saw each and every struggle as a conditioning prelude to revolution. He also took up this theme in *Capital*, Volume 1, where he not only chronicled the growth of working-class struggle and capitalist crisis (for example, in

6 "The Condition of the Working Class in England" (1845), *MECW*, *Vol. 4*, p. 512.

Chapter 10 on the working day) but also outlined the "historical tendency of capitalist accumulation" (in Chapter 32). There, he argued that along with the growth of accumulation, centralization and monopoly went, hand in hand, "the revolt of the working class" – a revolt which could ultimately lead to the final rupture of the "integument" of capitalist control and the expropriation of the expropriators.[7]

But what do "expropriation," and "revolution," mean? This can only be answered with reference to our understanding of the nature of capitalist control. I have argued that the central characteristic of the capitalist organization and control of society is the generalized imposition of commodity producing work, which includes both the production of goods and services upon which it can earn a profit and its efforts to organize the rest of society so that its activities contribute to the reproduction of human life as the capacity and willingness to work, i.e., as labor-power. If this is the central substance of capitalist control, then in class terms, *revolution against capitalism must be defined in terms of the overthrow of capitalist-imposed work and of the subordination of life to that work.*

This essay has shown how Marx's analysis of crisis can be interpreted in a non-objectivist way. How we can understand the value concepts, accumulation, and its interruption in terms of the class struggle over work. How, therefore, the pattern of development of capitalist society (including its crises) is the outcome of the confrontation of two active class subjects and involves the growth of the working class along with the expansion of capital. From this perspective, struggles become revolutions which succeed when they throw capital into a crisis to which it is unable to fashion a solution, when there is no "second moment" of crisis, or that second moment fails. The rupture of capitalist control spreads and grows, overthrowing more and more of the social relations that capital created to reinforce its imposition of work. The capitalist "integument is burst asunder," when the entire capitalist social system shaped around imposed labor is ripped apart and people build something new out of its ruins.

The expropriation of the capitalists is not simply the expropriation of their "property" in any usual sense, it is rather the appropriation of the whole of society. Moreover, it is clear enough in Marx and Engels' writings that expropriation means freeing society from capitalist organization in such a way that wholly new kinds of social relationships can be elaborated. Thus, it means the end of the commodity form and money, of the fetishism of production, of the

7 *Capital, Vol. 1*, p. 929, or MECW, *Vol. 35*, p. 750.

hierarchy of work, of the alienation of labor, through the transformation of relationships both among humans and between humans and the rest of nature.

Marx and Engels' observations of the pattern and content of working-class struggle led them again and again to emphasize how the revolutionary destruction of capital would involve, in a fundamental way, the liberation of people from a life sentence of hard labor. I already noted how Engels argued in his "Outline of a Critique of Political Economy" how the development of productivity during the capitalist period would create the possibility of reducing "to a minimum the labor falling to the share of mankind."[8] And how he argued at Elberfeld, in detail, that providing the unemployed with jobs and liberating people from many wasteful activities, would cut in half the amount each person needs to work.[9]

This early insight received extensive theoretical elaboration by Marx in the *Grundrisse*. He saw how the growing use of machinery and the associated productivity of labor reduced the need for work, making its imposition more and more difficult. This creates a problem only for capital. For workers, on the other hand, it is a continual expansion of the potential for reducing the labor required to meet their needs and desires to a minimum while freeing more and more time and energy for non-work activities. Revolution must involve the creation of a new historical situation in which, as Marx wrote in the *Grundrisse*, "disposable time will grow for all ... The measure of wealth is then not any longer, in any way, labor-time, but rather disposable time."[10] Of the content of this time, Marx spoke only of the "free development of individualities," of the expansion of the multidimensional, self-defined needs and activities of ex-members of the working class.

Ultimately, what defines people as revolutionary subjects is not only their *negative power* to abolish capital, exploitation, alienation, and their own status as members of a class of "mere workers." It is their *positive power* to increasingly define their own needs and desires, to carve out expanding spheres of their own autonomy and to create new worlds in the place of capitalism. New worlds? While, to the end of their days, Marx and Engels refused to offer their own outlines of post-capitalist utopias, I have already mentioned in Chapter 2 how they did see – alongside the reduction of necessary work time – some steps being taken in the creation of alternatives to the capitalist organization

8 MECW, *Vol. 3*, p. 436.

9 "... the present customary labor time of the individual will be reduced by half simply by making use of the labor which is either not used at all or used disadvantageously," MECW, *Vol. 4*, p. 251.

10 *Grundrisse*, p. 708; or MECW, *Vol. 28*, p. 94.

of society. The most obvious examples were co-operatives created by workers from the bottom up.

In his 1864 Inaugural Address to the First International, after recounting workers' successes in reducing the hours of labor, Marx turned to their positive power.

> But there was in store a still greater victory of the political economy of labour over the political economy of property. We speak of the co-operative movement, especially the co-operative factories raised by the unassisted efforts of a few "bold hands". The value of these great social experiments cannot be over-rated. By deed, instead of by argument, they have shown that production on a large scale, and in accord with the behests of modern science, may be carried on without the existence of a class of masters employing a class of hands; that to bear fruit, the means of labour need not be monopolized as a means of domination over, and of extortion against, the labouring man himself; and that, like slave labour, like serf labour, hired labour is but a transitory and inferior form, destined to disappear before associated labour plying its toil with a willing hand, a ready mind, and a joyous heart.[11]

Three years later in the newly published Volume 1 of *Capital*, Marx inscribed a whole chapter (13) on "Co-operation" arguing that despite its usurpation by capitalists, co-operation is an inherent power of collective human beings as "social animals."[12] "When the worker co-operates in a planned way with others, he strips off the fetters of his individuality, and develops the capabilities of his species."[13] This is a power that long predated capitalism, too often commanded by some ruling class but one that workers take back into their own hands when and where they can. While modern co-operation depends on large numbers of workers being brought together and coordinated, when that is forced by capital for purposes of "the greatest possible exploitation of labour-power," the inevitable, "unavoidable antagonism" generates resistance and struggle.[14] Marx noted that workers had already demonstrated how, once in control, they could take over and ordinate co-operation among themselves. He noted with

11 Marx, "Inaugural Address of the Working Men's International Association," October 21–27, 1864, *MECW*, *Vol. 20*, p.11.

12 *Capital*, *Vol. 1*, p. 444, "man, if not as Aristotle thought a political animal, is at all events a social animal." Or, *MECW*, *Vol. 35*, p. 331.

13 Ibid., p. 447, or *MECW*, *Vol. 35*, p. 334.

14 Ibid., p. 449, or *MECW*, *Vol. 35*, p. 336.

humor how capitalists knew this full well and feared the obvious implication: the end of any justification for capitalist control.

As evidence, he cited an article from "the philistine English periodical, the *Spectator*" lamenting how this was being revealed in the success of an Owen-inspired co-operative in Rochdale, a town in the Manchester industrial region. The Rochdale Equitable Pioneers Society began as a consumer co-operative but soon laid down general principles, including for the organization of production. The danger of this example of worker self-organization, the paper lamented was that it "showed that associations of workmen could manage shops, mills and almost all forms of industry with success, and they immediately improved the condition of the men, but then they did not leave a clear place for masters." "*Quelle horreur!*" Marx quips.[15] A nightmarish horror for capitalists, but a promise for workers as this example demonstrated how workers could do just fine without capitalists in organizing both production and distribution to meet their needs. While the Rochdale co-operative turned out to be fundamental in the development of the co-operative movement in England (and beyond), for Marx its importance lay not just in its practical success but in its demonstration of how workers could do away with capitalism and manage society on their own.

Thirteen years later, in his *Socialism: Utopian and Scientific*, Engels echoed this theme. Amplifying his critique of Dühring's ignorant criticism, Engels not only praised Owen for his perception of how "co-operative societies for retail trade and production" could be "transition measures to the complete communistic organization of society," but also pointed out how such actual societies "have since that time, at least given practical proof that the merchant and the manufacturer are socially quite unnecessary."[16] What the Utopians had imagined, workers were putting into practice based on their evolving material circumstances. As those circumstances changed, Marx and Engels argued, so would the nature of the revolutionary changes necessary to move beyond capitalism, its exploitation, and its crises.

So, how to get from here to there, where "there" is defined as the replacement of capitalist society, in all its aspects? As the historical sketch of Chapter 2 showed, Marx and Engels' ideas about the solution to this problem changed over time. In 1848 they thought workers needed to support bourgeois revolutions against absolutism because it would facilitate subsequent worker efforts to replace capitalism with communism. In the wake of their experience with the failure of the uprising in Germany and elsewhere in Europe, having seen

15 Ibid., p. 449, fn., or *MECW*, *Vol. 35*, pp. 336–37, fn.

16 *MECW*, *Vol. 24*, p. 296.

how the liberals they supported sold out workers' interests, they argued that from the get-go workers needed to fight for their own goals, independently of those of capitalists and their liberal supporters. But how to do that?

Their basic principle, reiterated many times, was that workers had to carve out the path from here to there through their own initiatives. Workers, they saw, were progressively organizing themselves along two lines. One was the formation of workers' autonomous organizations in and around their direct relationships with capitalists. The primary and most obvious such organization was the union – formal collective self-organization by workers to fight with their bosses over relationships both in the labor market and in production. While battles in production involved waged workers, those in the labor market also involved the unwaged, i.e., those in the reserve army who mobilized against the suffering imposed by the capitalist practice of only providing meaningful income to those working for them directly. The inclusion of conditions off-the-job, in the larger society, meant unions were always under pressure from workers to fight for the needs of both waged and unwaged. So naturally both men supported these kinds of struggles.

The other line of worker self-activity, which was growing fast in Marx and Engels' later years and in which they participated, was the formation of worker organizations fighting for access to roles in government, i.e., the ballot box and through elected representatives, influence in the formation of laws which would help them in their daily lives and in their struggles. Here too, Marx and Engels supported such "political" engagement, from the Chartist Movement through the formation of working-class political parties to elect representatives. As previously discussed, in this they differed from those anarchists, such as Bakunin, who dismissed such activity as hopeless drains on energy better channeled into struggles for the things workers wanted changed in their lives. Of this these critics of working-class political parties were never able to convince either Marx or Engels. Instead, the two men studied the rise of such parties and the different tendencies among those organizing them. They critiqued directions they found counterproductive – such as the failure to be inclusive of different kinds of workers – and embraced those they judged working in more effective directions.

Question: "All in all, what are we left with?" Answer: Marx and Engels left us legacies of both methodology and commitment. They showed us how to study workers' struggles, their circulation, their relation to crises, and the possibilities of overthrowing capitalism and getting beyond it. But they also demonstrated by their own actions how the point of all this study and effort to understand the world was to participate in the struggle to change it.

APPENDIX 1

Note to Polish Readers (2016)

This essay contains a systematic reinterpretation of Karl Marx and Frederick Engels' writings on various kinds of crises that were common in the capitalism of the nineteenth century. In their writings, they set out both political commentary on contemporary upheavals and, over time, developed and offered various theories to explain both the possibilities of crisis and the forces generating them. In this prefatory note, I want to add to the essay, briefly, two sets of considerations that I think might be of interest to Polish readers. The first concerns what I have discovered about Marx and Engels' thinking about the partitioned Poland of their time. The second concerns the relevance of these ancient texts to contemporary struggles in Poland. The analysis that follows, in both sections, is based on my reading of materials available in English – and to a lesser degree in French – but has been formulated without my being able to read materials in German and in Polish. Because some of the materials upon which I have drawn have made use of sources in those languages, I am aware of the limitations of my reading, and therefore, that my analysis might change with access to those sources. However, one does what one can and I offer my thoughts for your consideration, dissection, and critique.

Marx, Engels, and Poland: Then

As part of their work on crises, and on the prospects for revolutionary change, Marx and Engels followed, sought to understand, and respond to events and crises in Poland. They saw the unfolding of conflicts in Poland as important for Europe more generally, but they also saw Poland, and the other countries of central and eastern Europe, as harboring a barely developed capitalism, far behind that of England. In England, they observed the great textile mills of Manchester feeding on expropriated labor from the countryside and raw materials from the New World and pumping out an endless stream of commodities that British ships and troops were carrying to the far reaches of an expanding colonial empire. But in Poland, they saw capitalist development restricted to a few cities and mostly limited to commerce and small-scale industry, often monopolized by Germans who had colonized the Western edge of the country since the first partition in 1772. While conceding that those invaders had "brought to

DOI:10.1163/9789004708631_010

Poland culture, education and science ... retail trade and guild crafts,"[1] Engels also argued that their efforts:

> ... remained at the lowest stage of industrial development; they did not accumulate large capitals; they were neither able to set up large-scale industry nor control any extensive commercial networks .... The entire activity of the German Poles was restricted to retail trade, the handicrafts and at most the corn trade and manufacture (weaving, etc.) on the smallest scale.[2]

Years later, Rosa Luxemburg (1871–1919) concluded from her study of the industrial development of Poland that the first typical capitalist crisis in Poland didn't occur until 1884.[3] Therefore, for their studies of the kinds of periodic booms, busts, and associated upheavals characteristic of industrial capitalism, Britain, and to a lesser degree France and the United States, provided Marx and Engels with their main fields of research upon which to base their theories of crisis. In other words, the limited capitalist development in Poland, they perceived to be enclaves surrounded by a countryside organized in a feudal manner with the vast majority of the population being peasant serfs subordinated to big landowners – the *szlachta*, or traditional Polish nobility. In the period 1850–1870, grain produced by those peasants was being exported, but the proceeds only financed industry on a very small-scale.[4]

Therefore, Marx and Engels assessed crises in Poland to be primarily political ones involving two kinds of conflicts. First were the struggles of Poles for national independence from the Holy Alliance of Germany, Russia and Austria that had repeatedly seized their lands, ultimately obliterating their country as an independent nation with the Third Partition of 1794. Second, were struggles within Poland for democracy via agrarian reform against the country's still dominant patriarchal feudalism. They saw these two kinds of struggles as closely connected. In 1848, Marx wrote: "The men who led the Kraców revolutionary movement were deeply convinced that only a democratic Poland could be independent, and a democratic Poland was impossible without the abolition of feudal rights, without the agrarian movement which would transform

1 Frederick Engels, "The Frankfort Assembly Debates the Polish Question," MECW, *Vol. 7*, p. 339. For inclusion in this book, I have converted what were Endnotes in the Polish original into footnotes – the same format employed elsewhere in this book. In a few cases, I have amplified the footnotes, providing a bit more information.

2 Ibid., p. 340.

3 Rosa Luxemburg, "The Industrial Development of Poland," *The Complete Works of Rosa Luxemburg, Volume I: Economic Writings I*, Peter Hudis (ed.), (London: Verso, 2013) 32.

4 Jean Batou, *Between Development and Underdevelopment: the precocious attempts at industrialization of the periphery, 1800–1870* (Genève: Librairie Droz, 1991), 130.

the tied peasants into free proprietors, modern proprietors."[5] In the *Communist Manifesto* (1848)[6] they affirmed their support for "the party [in Poland] that insists on an agrarian revolution as the prime condition for national emancipation, that party which fomented the insurrection of Kraców in 1846."[7]

But if the abolition of serfdom and of the rights of the *szlachta* were prerequisites for a broad-based democratic struggle for Polish independence, that objective was controversial among European revolutionaries who shared an internationalist perspective and opposed the way ruling elites used nationalism to divide and conquer. For example, in his 1861 book *La Guerre et la Paix*, Pierre J. Proudhon portrayed the demand for Polish independence as nothing more than the old nobility's desire to take back their estates and their power from Holy Alliance interlopers.[8] The restoration of Poland, he argued, would do nothing for the mass of the population who would find themselves saddled with and exploited by local rather than foreign masters. He argued that history had spoken, that the Holy Alliance's partition of Poland had given Europe peace, that "the Poles have no right" to independence and sovereignty and that partition amounted to "deliverance for the working classes"; it was literally their "emancipation."[9] He was referring to how serfdom had been formally abolished in Prussia in 1807, in Austria in 1848 and in Russia in 1861.

Let us be clear, Marx and Engels had long denounced the reactionary character of the Polish nobility, as exemplified by their condemnation of the *szlachta*'s refusal to accept the social reforms put forward by Joachim Lelewel (1786–1861) during the "Cadet Revolution" in 1830.

> What did the Polish aristocracy want in 1830? To safeguard its own acquired rights with regard to the Emperor [Nicholas I]. It limited the insurrection to the little country which the Congress of Vienna was pleased to call the Kingdom of

5 "Speech by Mr. Karl Marx" [On the Polish Question] *MECW, Vol. 6*, p. 549.

6 *MECW, Vol. 6*, pp. 477–519.

7 Ibid., p. 518.

8 Pierre J. Proudhon, *La Guerre et la Paix, Recherches sur le principe et la constitution du droit des gens*, (Paris: Michel Lévy Frères Libraires, Tome II, 1861) 228–9. The question of Polish nationalism, he argued, was only « une question d'aristocratie polonaise » and therefore of no revolutionary interest to the French people. « Existe-t-il une idée polonaise ? La Pologne n'a toujours à offrir au monde que son catholicisme et sa noblesse. » Eventually, perhaps, « la Pologne entrerait dans la phase revolutionnaire ; elle proclamerait, comme la France de 1789, le droit de l'homme et du citoyen ; elle reconnaitrait, comme la France de 1848, le droit au travail. » Until then « Qu'est-ce que le monde a perdu, en laissant perir la Pologne ? »

9 Pierre J. Proudhon, *Si les traités de 1815 ont cessé d'exister? Actes du future congrès*, 3rd ed., (Paris: E. Dentu, Libraire-Editeur, 1864) 68. « Non, les Polonais ne sont pas en droit. » 86. "Le partage, pour la plebe polonaise, ç'a été l'émancipation."

> Poland;[10] it restrained the uprising in the other Polish provinces; it left intact the degrading serfdom of the peasants and the infamous condition of the Jews... But within the conservative revolution, within the national government itself, there was one man who vigorously attacked the narrow views of the ruling class. He proposed really revolutionary measures before whose boldness the aristocrats of the Diet recoiled. By calling the whole of ancient Poland to arms, by thus making the war for Polish independence a European war, by emancipating the Jews and the peasants, by making the latter share in landed property, by reconstructing Poland on the basis of democracy and equality, he wanted to make the national cause the cause of freedom; he wanted to identify the interest of all peoples with that of the Polish people. Need I name the genius who conceived this plan, at once so vast and so simple? It was Lelewel.[11]

When, in 1866, Proudhon's followers within the First International attacked support for Polish independence as being of no interest to the working class, Engels wrote a series of articles on "What have the working classes to do with Poland?"[12] In those articles he made two arguments as to why workers elsewhere should support, not dismiss, Polish struggles for independence. His first was that workers in places such as Germany and Austria had an interest in limiting the expanding power of the Russian Czar – whose power he and Marx saw as the most powerful reactionary force on the continent. After sketching the history of Czarist annexations and efforts to subordinate various parts of central Europe, the "restoration of Poland," he argued, would amount to the emancipation of not just Poles, but also Germans "from Russian vassalage."[13]

His second argument was to remind the Proudhonists of the long history of workers' support for the right of self-determination of people living within historically identifiable *nations*, i.e., large "bodies of undoubted vitality."[14] This he juxtaposed to the Czar's "principle of nationalities" used to divide and conquer, used, for example, to

10 The Congress of Vienna in 1814–15 liquidated the so-called duchy of Warsaw which depended on Napoleonic France. It was formed by Napoleon in 1807, after the defeat of Prussia, on the Polish territory seized by Prussia as a result of the three partitions of Poland. The Congress repartitioned the duchy between Prussia, Austria, and Russia with the exception of the free city of Kraców, which was under the joint protection of the three powers up to 1846. The part incorporated into Russia was called the Kingdom of Poland with Warsaw as its capital.

11 "The Frankfort Assembly Debates the Polish Question," *MECW*, *Vol. 7*, pp. 550–551.

12 *The Commonwealth*, Nos. 159 (March 24), 160 March 31) and 165 (May 5) in *MECW*, *Vol. 20*, pp. 152–54, 155–58, 158–61.

13 Ibid., p. 154, "Restoration of Poland, to them, is emancipation of their own country from Russian vassalage."

14 Ibid., p. 156.

justify the seizure of territory in Eastern Poland.[15] (Both Putin's seizure of the Crimean Peninsula and his interventions in Eastern Ukraine are strikingly similar to the actions of the Czar in Marx and Engel's time and have been justified using the same logic.)

Yet, Engels' manner of framing this argument was also dismissive of the rights of then sub-national, but culturally and linguistically coherent bodies of people to independent nation-state status, i.e., Laplanders in Scandinavia, or "Serbians, Croats, Ruthenes [Ukrainians], Slovaks, Czechs, and other remnants of bygone Slavonian peoples in Turkey, Hungary, and Germany."[16] This disdainful attitude toward those lacking "civilization" must appear retrograde today when many of those peoples have indeed achieved independent nationhood. Equally unappealing is his scornful mocking of Laplanders as "nomadic savages" and of their resistance to cultural assimilation and the loss of their "own barbaric, half Esquimaux idiom."[17] Today, not only have well-organized indigenous people all over the world been fighting for autonomous self-determination, but they have also inspired peoples of many nations to join together in precisely the kind of anti-capitalist, alter-globalization movement dreamed of in the First International.[18]

Early the following year in a speech in London, Marx reiterated Engels' argument of the need for an independent Polish buffer to check the Czar's imperial ambitions.[19] It was the Poles, he reminded his listeners, whose insurrection prevented Czarist troops from marching on France to put down the uprising in Paris of 1830 against Charles X. "The uprising of Warsaw saved Europe from a second Anti-Jacobin war."[20] It was why the revolutionary Berliners of 1848 called for the restoration of Poland.[21] After describing in some detail the expansion and growing strength of the Czarist Empire, he concluded,

> There is only one alternative left for Europe, Asiatic barbarism under Muscovite leadership will burst over her head like an avalanche, or she must restore Poland, thus placing between herself and Asia 20 millions of heroes, and gaining breathing time for the accomplishment of her social regeneration."[22]

15 Ibid., p. 157, "The principle of nationalities … is nothing but a *Russian invention concocted to destroy Poland.*"

16 Ibid.

17 Ibid., pp. 157–158.

18 Harry Cleaver, "Trayectorias de autonomía," in Claudio Albertani, et al., eds., *La autonomía possible: Reinvención de la política y emancipación* (México: Universidad Autónoma de la Ciudad de México, 2009), 25–65. (In English.) (Accessed 7/18/2024.)

19 "Speech at the Polish Meeting in London" (1857), *MECW, Vol. 20*, pp. 196–201.

20 Ibid., p. 196.

21 Ibid., p. 197.

22 Ibid., p. 201.

At the same time, Marx and Engels insisted, the struggle by Poles against foreign domination was the only possible path to social development *within* Poland. Against those who deprecated Polish struggles for national independence, they affirmed:

> As long as a viable people is fettered by a foreign conqueror, it must necessarily apply all its strength, all its efforts, all its energy against the enemy from without; for this length of time, then, its inner life remains paralyzed, it remains unable to work for social emancipation. Ireland, Russia under Mongolian rule, etc., provide striking proof of this thesis.[23]

As for the Czarist emancipation of the serfs in Poland, celebrated by Proudhon and his followers, Marx and Engels argued that it had only been done with the objective of undermining the local nobility and making peasants available for Russia exploitation and for induction into the Czar's armies.

But beyond their sympathy for the struggles of a subjugated people, Marx and Engels had tremendous respect for those Polish revolutionaries in exile who fought alongside others throughout Europe and even in America. As early as 1858 Marx and Engels co-authored an article praising Józef Bem (1794–1850), a Polish military leader who had fought with Napoleon against the Prussians and Russians, during the 1830 uprising against the Russians, and in Austria and Hungary on the side of the revolutionaries of 1848.[24] Looking back, almost 20 years later, Marx wrote that the Poles were:

> the only European people that has fought and is fighting as the *cosmopolitan soldier of the revolution.* Poland shed its blood during the American War of Independence; its legions fought under the banner of the first French Republic; by its revolution of 1830 it prevented the invasion of France that had been decided by the partitioners of Poland; in 1846 in Kraców it was the first in Europe to plant the banner of social revolution; in 1848 it played an outstanding part in the revolutionary struggle in Hungary, Germany and Italy; finally, in 1871 it supplied the Paris Commune with its best generals and most heroic soldiers.[25]

For those unfamiliar with the history, these examples are worth explaining. The participation of Polish exiles in the American Revolutionary War included Tadeusz Kościuszko (1746–1817) and Kazimierz Pułaski (1745–1779). Kosciuszko, a skilled engineer, served as a colonel in the Continental Army, designed and oversaw the construction of various fortifications, including those at West Point – services for which he was

---

23 "For Poland" (1875), MECW, *Vol. 24*, p. 57.

24 "BEM" (1857), MECW, *Vol. 18*, pp. 130–133.

25 "For Poland" (1875), MECW, *Vol. 24*, p. 57–58.

promoted to brigadier general. He returned to Poland to join the Polish-Lithuanian Commonwealth Army's fight against Russia and was commander-in-chief of the uprising of 1794 against Russian occupation.[26] Pułaski, after fighting in the failed Bar Confederation war against the Russians, also came to America and joined the Continental Army, reformed the Army's cavalry, and created the Pułaski Cavalry Legion. It was his blood that was shed while leading a cavalry charge against the British at the Battle of Savannah.[27]

What Marx here calls "the Polish revolution" of 1830, was the Cadet Revolution referred to above, that blocked Russian plans to use Polish draftees against uprisings in France and Belgium. Besides the role of Józef Bem, Marx and Engels were, as previously noted, particularly impressed by the agrarian reform plans of the historian and politician Joachim Lelewel put forward in the midst of the uprising. When the uprising was crushed, Lelewel fled into exile in France and then Belgium. He continued to write and agitate for reform in Poland and collaborated with Marx and Engels in 1847 to found the *Demokratische Gesellschaft zur Einigung und Verbrüderung aller Völker* (Democratic Society for Unity and Brotherhood of All Peoples).[28]

The Kraców Uprising of 1846 only lasted nine days but its leaders not only fought for national liberation but also put forth the kinds of demands made by Lelewel sixteen years before.

> The men at the head of the revolutionary movement in Krakow were most deeply convinced that only a democratic Poland could be independent, and that a Polish democracy was impossible without an abolition of feudal rights, without an agrarian movement that would transform the feudally obligated peasants into modern owners.[29]

That same year, in the wake of the economic crisis of 1847 that caused unemployment to soar, there were revolutionary uprisings in many countries of Europe. Marx and Engels returned to the continent, first to Paris during the February Revolution and then to Cologne in Germany where revolution began in March. There, Marx published the *Neue Reinische Zeitung* and Engels helped out on the barricades. Among the many

---

26 Monica Gardiner, *Kościuszko: A Biography* (London: George Allen & Unwin LTD, 1920). (Online by Project Gutenberg)

27 Douglas Shores, *Kazimierz Pułaski: General of Two Nations* (San Diego: Create Space, 2014).

28 Monika Barr, *Historians and Nationalism: East-Central Europe in the Nineteenth Century* (Oxford: Oxford University Press, 2010). Joan Skurnowicz, "Lelewel in Polish Historiography in People's Poland," *The Polish Review* XXXVI, no. 3, (1991): 269–82.

29 Karl Marx, "On the Polish Question," *MECW*, *Vol. 6*, p. 549, or, Karl Marx, *The Revolutions of 1848, Political Writings: Volume I* (London: Penguin Classics, 1973), 104.

uprisings was one in Poznań against the Prussian occupiers of that part of Poland. But everywhere, Marx and Engels saw Poles joining revolutionary risings. Engels later wrote, "In Paris, Vienna, Berlin, Italy, Hungary, the Poles shared the fighting in all the revolutions and revolutionary wars, regardless whether they were fighting against Germans, against Slavs, against Magyars, or even against *Poles*."[30]

In 1871, when in response to Emperor Napoleon III surrendering to the Prussian Chancellor Bismarck, all of Paris rose and created the Paris Commune, Jarosław Żądło-Dąbrowski (1836–1871), who had fought in the 1863 Polish uprising against the Russian Empire, was elected to the Commune's Council. As counterattack by the exiled French government and by Prussian troops that had surrounded and laid siege to the city loomed, Dąbrowski was appointed Commander-in-Chief and organized the defence of Paris. He was killed in the fighting, five days before the Commune was crushed and the massacres of the Communards began. Another Pole, Walery Wróblewski (1836–1908), who had commanded rebel detachments during the Polish Uprising of 1863–64, also joined the Parisian Communards as a general who organized the southern defence of the city. Unlike Dąbrowski, Wróblewski survived the defeat of the Commune and emigrated to London. In 1872 he became a member of the General Council of the First International supporting Marx and Engels in their conflicts with Bakunin. These are but a few of the Polish émigrés whose participation in uprisings at home and organizational work abroad inspired Marx and Engels' solidarity with Polish revolutionaries.[31]

Between Then and Now

Between Marx and Engels' writings and the present lay long and tumultuous decades. They include the years of the Second International (1889–1914), of World War I (1914–1918), of the Second Polish Republic (1918–1939), World War II (1939–1945), of the Polish People's Republic (1945–1989) and of the Third Polish Republic (1989-present). During those years, capitalism continued to develop in Poland, and with it connections between crises within Poland and those unfolding in the wider capitalist world. The character and extent of those connections, of course, varied enormously, differing in periods of relative independence from those when Poland was subjected to foreign domination of one sort or another. From once-again-partitioned neo-colonial subordination during World War II, through domination by the Soviet Union in the post-WWII era, the development of capitalism within Poland took place within constraints imposed from without. Most obviously, perhaps, was the imposition of Soviet-style

30 Frederick Engels, "Democratic Pan-Slavism," *MECW*, *Vol. 8*, p. 375.

31 Adam Ciołkosz, "Karl Marx and the Polish Insurrection of 1863," *The Polish Review* 10, no. 4 (Autumn, 1965): 8–51.

state capitalism in the period of the Polish People's Republic. Despite its self-representation as socialist, and its more common designation as communist, the Soviet regime's institutions merely reorganized capitalism rather than progressively substituting something new and different. Like capitalists elsewhere, the regime's planners focused on organizing life around work and extracting the greatest amount of surplus labor possible. These objectives were replicated by its client government in Poland. Since regaining nominal national independence in 1989, the organizers of capitalism in Poland have found Soviet influence replaced by that of contemporary supra-national capitalist institutions such as the European Union, the European Central Bank, the International Monetary Fund and the World Bank.

Throughout those decades, a wide variety of Marxists, both Polish and foreign, have undertaken to analyze the development of capitalism in Poland, the struggles of Polish workers and episodes of crisis. However, the period is far too long and the number of such analyses far too great for us to even sketch an outline. Some such analyses, such as those of Rosa Luxemburg, probably Poland's most famous Marxist, have been subjected to numerous close studies and critiques. Those studies have involved an assessment of both the similarities and differences between her analyses and Marx and Engels' own work, e.g., her opposition to Polish independence or her use of Marx's reproduction schemes to ground her theories of crisis and imperialism. Obviously, the reinterpretation offered here could provide one point of departure for studying her work – and I have had occasion to make some brief comments on her theory of crisis.[32] I have not, however, undertaken re-evaluations of Marxist writings on Poland in any great depth. Therefore, I leave to others an assessment of the relevance of my work here to such efforts. What I do offer are a few reflections on that relevance in the present period – in the hope of provoking *militant* readings of my essay.

Marx, Engels, and Poland: Now

Peter Bell and I have insisted, repeatedly, that our interest in Marx and Engels' writings is not philological but political. We have not intended our reinterpretation to be just another contribution to the analysis of the history of thought, but rather one that uncovers how, and in what ways, these old ideas can help us cope with new problems, especially the constraints imposed on our lives by contemporary capitalism. Today, we are over a decade into the twenty-first century. Obviously, a lot has changed since our two authors wrote. Yet, despite many changes, crises of all sorts are still very much with us. Are Marx and Engels' thoughts from so long ago still relevant? Are the sorts

32 Harry Cleaver, "Karl Marx: Economist or Revolutionary?" in Suzanne W. Helburn and David F. Bramhall, eds., *Marx, Schumpeter & Keynes* (M.E. Sharpe, Armonk, 1986), 124–26.

of crises they addressed similar to the crises that you face today and to what degree, if any, do their analyses illuminate your present problems and can usefully inform your strategies of struggle?

When it comes to judging the relevance of these old writings to struggles in contemporary Poland, I am acutely aware of the limitations of my distance and knowledge. If, as I have maintained, the value of any socio-political theory depends upon its ability to provide weapons in the struggle against capitalism, then the evaluation of the practical usefulness of any theoretical understanding must be carried out in the light of, and with concrete knowledge of, particular real-world situations. Theory is always general; the world is always specific. So, I repeatedly query whether my theory draws my attention to phenomena that I think are important and whether it illuminates specific circumstances, particular concrete sets of relationships. Yet, I also recognize that what I have been able to study has been limited and my knowledge bounded. So, when an opportunity arises, such as this one, for my writing to be translated into another language and published in another country, I hope that you, my new readers, will do the same, i.e., carefully evaluate the contemporary relevance to your own circumstances of the interpretation I offer, as well as of the original writings that have been my object of study.

The obvious question is "What is involved in such an evaluation? How to proceed?" Useful answers to such questions do, I think, depend upon the theory in question. The abstract propositions theories set forth are usually framed, by their authors, with some real-world reference. Newton explained the inspiration for his theory of gravity with a story about a falling apple. In Marx and Engels' case, as you will see in the body of our essay, their proposals of abstract generalizations about the nature of crises were usually offered with illustrations drawn from observations made during their own time. So, for example, when highlighting the way in which limitations on the demand for consumption goods (or means of subsistence) could cause a crisis in the realization of capitalist plans, they could point to examples both of capitalists doing their best to hold down wages and of recurrent situations in which such limitations on buying power forced capitalists to lower prices, undermining their profits. An evaluation of the relevance of that aspect of their theory of crisis to any given historical period would thus involve an examination of the effects of capitalist policies on wages, salaries and other forms of income on consumer demand and any evidence of those policies limiting demand to such a degree as to cause problems in sales and the realization of profits.

Our reinterpretation of Marx and Engels' theory of crisis presented in this essay does not privilege, *a priori*, any particular moment of their theorization over others. Instead of joining one of the traditional Marxist schools of thought, such as that which has privileged underconsumption or that which has privileged the tendency of the rate of profit to fall, Peter and I sought out, in their writings, all the possibilities of crisis and all the forces at work tending to turn those possibilities into realities that they identified and analyzed. Which forces have been at work and which possibilities have been realized, we argue, has varied in particular historical periods. And yet, we do argue that at the heart of all of those possibilities and forces at play, there is a common element that unifies that diversity, or, rather, that they are all manifestations of a common conflict: the struggle between capitalist attempts to impose its way of organizing society around work and resistance by those of us who seek out and craft alternatives.

Importantly, the particular forms through which crises have played out have been shaped by local, national and international institutions, both those of capital and those created by those of us who resist. Those Marx called the functionaries of capital, with capital understood as a particular way of organizing social relationships, have always devised and sought to implement policies to promulgate their system and solve whatever problems that have arisen, including crises. Those of us who have resisted have also devised tactics and strategies, sometimes as individuals, more fruitfully in collaboration with one another, collectively. So, for example, the policies and associated institutions that capital developed and deployed for the use of commodity money (e.g., gold and silver) against us differed from those created and utilized for the management of paper and credit money. The former involved alchemy, coinage, recoinage, debasement, bank vaults and torture; the latter have involved a whole array of policies to control the quality and quantity of money that has mainly existed only as entries on balance sheets. Similarly, the tactics and strategies the rest of us have used in confronting money have varied according to the kind of money with which we have had to deal. Against commodity money, individuals used clipping, direct appropriation, and counterfeiting, while collective working-class efforts focused on the formation of unions and wage struggles, sometimes local, sometimes with international connections. But with the capitalist substitution of national fiat money and bank credit for commodity money, direct appropriation and counterfeiting have become more difficult and struggles have tended to focus more on efforts to increase income, to shape access to and terms of credit or to escape money altogether.[33]

Today, as I see it, if from afar, those of you in Poland find yourselves in a country whose capitalism, although bearing scars from its earlier subordination to Soviet-style state capitalism, has been forcefully integrated into the global capitalist system. Since rejoining the International Monetary Fund and the World Bank in 1986, since gaining national independence in 1989, since the imposition of "shock therapy" on Poland after 1989, since joining the OECD in 1996, NATO in 1999, the European Union in 2004, and Schengen in 2007, Polish capitalism and, perforce, all of you, have benefited or

33 Wennerlind, *Casualties of Credit*. Caffentzis, *Clipped Coins, Abused Words and Civil Government*. Anitra Nelson and Frans Timmerman, eds., *Life without Money: Building Fair and Sustainable Economies* (London: Pluto Press, 2011). "Potential Strategies and Tactics for Rupturing the Dialectics of Money" in Cleaver, *Rupturing the Dialectic*, 235–64.

suffered the consequences of government policies aimed at integration with Western European capitalism and with multinational capitalism more generally.

That history of integration suggests to me that today a much more straightforward evaluation of the relevance of Marx and Engels's theory of crisis to Poland is possible than they, or many of their followers, believed. As in the rest of our contemporary capitalist world, we need only examine the relevance of various aspects of their abstract analysis to the specifics of the situations in which Polish workers find themselves exploited, alienated and often in resistance. The systematic manner in which this essay lays out our study of Marx and Engels' theory allows for an equally systematic examination of relevance. As you will find, we organized our study around their representation of the "circuit" that capital must complete in order to realize its self-reproduction. In other words, the sequential steps that it must successfully organize in order to be able, once again, in the next period, to impose its peculiar organization of society on an expanded scale. The relevance and character of the various steps of the circuit – that begins with the mobilization of resources, both human and material, through various markets, continues through the combining of those resources in the production of some commodity and ending (this round) with the sale of the commodity and the realization of enough profit to permit starting all over again on a larger scale – to particular, concrete moments of capitalism, e.g., in Poland and its connections with the rest of the world, can be examined one by one in sequential order and in relation to each other.

Before proceeding with some illustrations, I would like to point out that the above procedure reverses the more general method that I usually employ in examining the dynamics of social conflict within capitalism. I prefer to start with the struggles themselves, with our own self-activity, and then see how both our actions and capital's reactions are shaping the present, or have shaped the past (if we are looking backward).[34] When studying Marx and Engels' writings, however, I recognize that *the* focal point of their *theoretical* work was capital, as is manifest in the title of Marx's most complete theoretical work: *Das Kapital*.[35] Yet, precisely because their theory was a socio-political one that understood capital as an antagonistic social relationship, they formulated it in terms of the labor theory of value, i.e., a theory of value of labor to capital, every aspect of which, from the beginning, was challenged, contested and often ruptured

34 Mario Tronti, "Lenin in England" in *Working Class Autonomy and the Crisis* (London: Red Notes and CSE, 1979), 1–6. Originally in *Classe Operaio* 1 (January 1964): 18–20. Republished in Mario Tronti, *Operai e Capitale* (Torino: Einaudi Editore, 1966) as "Lenin in Inghilterra," 89–95 and "A New Type of Political Experiment: Lenin in England" in Mario Tronti, *Workers and Capital* (New York: Verso, 2019), 65–72. "Introduction," *Zerowork: Political Materials 1*, 1975, pp. 1–6.

35 Marx, *Capital: A Critique of Political Economy, Volume 1*, trans. Ben Fowkes (New York: Pelican Books, 1976, London: Penguin Classics, 1990)

by those upon whom the functionaries of capital have sought to impose labor as the core of their mode of organizing society.[36] Therefore, whether we start from our own struggles, or, as in the case of this essay we follow Marx and Engel's lead and start from the relationships capital seeks to impose and re-impose, we wind up at the same place, namely an analysis of the dynamics of struggle over the present and the future.

As I explain in the essay, Marx and Engels' circuit-of-capital has three steps; (1) the organization of what economists call input markets, symbolically $M - C(LP, MP)$, where M = money for investment, LP = labor-power, MP = means of production, (2) the sphere of production ... P ... C', where LP and MP are combined to produce a new commodity C', and (3) the organization of the sale of the new commodity for money, $C' - M'$. Already in Marx and Engels' time, each of these steps were complicated affairs with many different actors and each of these three steps involved quite distinct operations, both within capitalist firms and among them. Today, they are even more complex and spread out over an even more diverse, often multinational, geography of markets and of production. Given that complexity, I want to do no more here than offer some suggestive examples of where and how their analysis may be applicable to social conflict in Poland.

Let's start with just one part of step #1: $M - C(LP)$. The labor market has always been a terrain of conflict, both for those trying to hire labor and for those who might be hired. As much as capitalists might desire it, individuals do not enter the labor market automatically. Throughout the history of capitalism many have resisted prostituting themselves in labor markets. As Marx showed in his analysis of "primitive" accumulation, capital has had to use considerable force and violence merely to create labor markets.[37] We also know that the obstacles that capitalists had to overcome in those days have continued ever since. Time and again, across the globe people have found ways to survive *without* entering the labor market. From hanging on to land affording subsistence, through direct appropriation and emigration, millions have done their best to avoid being pushed through this doorway to exploitation and alienation.

For many years in the nineteenth century, Marx and Engels saw the attachment to land in places such as Poland as something forced, through laws and practices of serfdom. Later, study of the Russian *mir* and other agrarian peoples revealed to them how attachment could be a source not only of resistance to the depredations of capitalism but of alternatives to it.[38] Such was the resistance faced by Soviet state-capitalist planners who, when they were able, imposed collectivization to maximize the imposition

36 Harry Cleaver, *Polityczne czytanie Kapitału* (Posnań: Oficyna Bractwa Trojka, 2011). Originally, *Reading* Capital *Politically*.

37 *Capital, Vol. 1*, Chapters 27–28.

38 Theodore Shanin, ed., *Late Marx and the Russian Road: Marx and the Peripheries of Capitalism* (New York: Monthly Review Press, 1983).

of work and the collection of a surplus to finance industrialization. Where they, and their client administrations, were less successful – because of fierce resistance, as in Hungary and East Germany in 1953 and Poland in 1956 – large numbers of peasants succeeded in avoiding the labor market.

This continues to be the case in Poland, to some degree, as evidenced by two phenomena. The first is the difficulty some employers have in recruiting workers from the countryside. During a visit to Poznań in 2012, I heard stories about how employers had to provide daily bus service to distant villages to obtain workers. The stories reminded me of the situation in Detroit after the uprisings in 1967 and 1968 when the auto companies of that Motor City sent out buses each morning to make sure rebellious young workers actually showed up for their jobs. (They did, but they carried their struggles with them from the streets to become the cutting edge of resistance inside the factories.)[39] The second phenomenon is the effort to get farmers to leave the land, especially in Eastern Poland, what capitalist policy makers like to call "structural reform." There, where the concentration of land holding and the conversion of family farming to capitalist agribusiness is less advanced than in the Western part of the country, policy makers both within Poland and those associated with organizations such as the European Union, the OECD and IMF lament Polish government policies that facilitate staying on the land and call for them to be changed. In a recent interview, for example, Daria Zakharova, IMF mission chief for Poland, argued that the Polish government should "phase out taxation incentives and retirement privileges that encourage people to continue small-scale farming." Such policies, he argued in IMF-speak would "help workers' transition out of agriculture and into higher productivity sectors, such as manufacturing and services."[40]

Resistance to labor markets, as the example of Detroit makes clear, has continued even among people successfully forced off their land. One form of resistance was emigration from available rural and urban jobs to new lands open to settlement. Such emigration from Europe, including Poland, constituted much of the history of the American frontiers, from Canada, through the United States to the Pampas of Argentina. But also, constituting less of an escape, has been emigration from one labor market to another. Just as capitalists have long sought to play emigrating workers against local workers, e.g., Germans against Poles in the eighteenth and nineteenth centuries, Poles against Germans today, so have workers used mobility to resist bad labor market conditions, e.g., low wages, scanty benefits, and dangerous working conditions, to take advantage of better ones, with higher compensation, better benefits, and less danger.

---

39 Dan Georgakas and Marvin Surkin, *Detroit, I do Mind Dying: A Study in Urban Revolution* (New York: St. Martin's Press, 1975).

40 "Poland Strong Institutions a Must for Steady Growth," *IMF Survey* interview with Zakharova, July 5, 2016.

As noted in the first part of this note, Marx and Engels were well aware of how Polish emigrants carried their militancy into other countries. More recently, between 2004 and 2007, 1.27 million workers left Poland, most moving West to more attractive labor markets.[41] Today, we find resistance among Polish workers in England on YouTube, where the group Slav Squad mocks the Brexit vote.

Within cities, amongst diverse markets for many different kinds of labor, resistance to labor markets has continued. This has been obvious in the so-called labor movement, where workers have organized unions to fight for recognition, collective bargaining, and then better contracts. Resistance has been less obvious, but no less persistent in such phenomena as individual young people dropping out of schools – organized mainly to prepare them for the labor market – and into the streets and by squatters who have seized abandoned buildings and organized their living arrangements so only some hold waged jobs while others arrange their collective lives outside the labor market. Such struggles are widespread and have formed an important tactic among the young (and sometimes among the old) in resisting labor markets and other aspects of contemporary capitalism. In Italy they are known as "social centers," and where the squatters have been numerous enough and well enough organized to hold on to properties they have seized, they have created pirate radio stations, e.g., Radio Alicia, and computer networks, e.g., the European Counter-Network, linking such efforts across the country and to the wider world. During the previously mentioned visit to Poland in 2012, I visited such "squats" in both Warsaw and Poznań. In many cases, various forms of government-provided income have been used to support such resistance, e.g., student stipends, social security, unemployment compensation or welfare payments.

This kind of resistance has forced capital, again and again, to make such modes of living outside the labor market difficult. Misrepresented as delinquency or criminal trespass, such refusals have been outlawed by the state via laws against truancy, vagabondage, and squatting. The state has also withheld or reduced sources of unwaged income such as unemployment compensation or welfare. Marx and Engels' analysis suggests that such contemporary reductions, just like attacks on the Poor Laws in England in the nineteenth century are aimed, like the anti-farmer policy changes called for by Zakharova, at increasing pressure on people to enter the labor market. In recent years, according to IndexMundi, such has been the case in Poland where "the total transfer amount received by the population participating in unemployment benefits and active labor market programs" as a share of their total income was lowered from 2005 to 2007 and has been kept low ever since.[42] This has been particularly true for young workers, where the already low percentage of those eligible for unemployment

---

41 Pawel Gajewski, *Labour Market Measures in Poland 2008–13: The Crisis and Beyond* (Geneva: International Labor Office, 2015) 6.

42 IndexMundi, online.

benefits has dropped almost continuously after 2009.[43] Those who have taken care of themselves by putting otherwise abandoned buildings to good use have been confronted by increased state efforts to evict them from their refuges.

With the imposition of work being the most basic vehicle for organizing capitalist society, policy makers have a difficult task balancing their need to impose work versus the need for a sufficient number of unemployed workers to keep the employed in line with the threat of job loss and poverty. Thus, in Poland, we find the usual careful measuring of the "unemployment rate" and "labor force participation" by government agencies and the same, equally careful, assessment of the relationship between those numbers and changes in wages and degrees of unrest, both on the job and off. Capitalist policy makers must constantly adjust policies in response to challenges from both employed and unemployed that disrupt their planned modes of expanded reproduction. At times, for example, they pursue policies that increase unemployment. Before learning from John Maynard Keynes (1883–1946) how to use state fiscal and monetary policies to manipulate the demand for labor, individual capitalists responded to worker threats to their profits and control by cutting back existing operations, by laying off workers, and by refusing to invest – all of which raised unemployment. They responded to more profitable conditions by expanding investment and expanding employment. Since grasping Keynesian methods, the state has acted at all levels, from the local to the supranational, to "fine tune" the demand for labor and to manipulate levels of employment and unemployment and with them the growth of wages. We can call the active pursuit of higher levels of employment a "development" strategy, and one that fosters more unemployment an "underdevelopment" strategy. In the current neoliberal period, underdevelopment-as-strategy has been deployed not only in so-called "underdeveloped" capitalist countries, but also in so-called "developed" ones, such as the United States and Europe. In country after country in recent years, policy makers have seized upon crises in debt to impose austerity, high unemployment, and falling living standards as punitive measures against workers, seeking to force them to accept ever lower wages and ever more onerous working conditions.

However, keeping in mind that those policy makers usually restrict their definition of the "unemployed" to those actively looking for jobs, Marx and Engels provided us with a more accurate characterization of all of those not currently employed for wages (or salaries) in their definition of "the reserve army of labor." That definition included those looking for jobs (the "floating" part of the reserve), but also those who might look (the "latent," e.g., subsistence peasants, housewives, children) and those who would probably never look ("stagnant" and "lumpen" parts, e.g., the crippled, the

43 Gajewski, *Labour Market Measures in Poland 2008–13*, p. 16.

aged, criminals).[44] All of the people included in those three categories were, in nineteenth century terms, *unwaged* (the wage being the dominant form of payment for labor power).

The unwaged, just like the waged, have always had to be *managed*. Why? Not only because they could be troublesome – protesting their poverty – but to make sure of their availability, either immediately or at some future date when they were needed. In other words, capital has tried to ensure that their various methods of unwaged survival produce and reproduce labor-power, i.e., their ability and willingness to work. In the nineteenth century, besides the kind of anti-vagabondage laws mentioned above, such management was accomplished with a modicum of poor laws (parish relief) complemented, when necessary, by force. In boom times, Marx argued that for the most part capital left the reproduction of labor-power to the workers themselves.[45] In periods of crisis, however, in an era in which rising unemployment often meant starvation or death by untreated illness, guns and the gibbet were required to contain working class uprisings.

In years since their writings, when and where workers have succeeded in freeing children and many women from dangerous waged labor, capital has been forced to intervene more systematically. Capitalists have sought to retain control over unwaged workers through mass schooling, the family, and the welfare state – all of which provide the means of "management" primarily through the structuring of schools, homes and access to unwaged income in ways designed to turn daily activities into the unwaged work of producing labor-power – thus paralleling the production of other commodities.

Although methods have changed and new institutions have been built, resistance has persisted. When students have been able to organize effectively, they have been able to change the school curriculum from job training to better meet their own needs instead of those of future employers. When women have been able to organize effectively, they have achieved greater independence, more control over their work and less of it. They have, for example, been able to reduce their workload by gaining access to contraception and to compensation for childbearing and child rearing. For example, in Poland, despite bans on some kinds of abortion, women have been successful in reducing the fertility rate from roughly 2 in 1989 to 1.29 in 2014. Those gains have been won against capitalist-imposed restriction of access to contraception (often backed by the church – ever greedy to add to its tithable flocks) and in making use of pro-natalist laws designed to induce women to have more children, with all the work that entails. In the case of welfare recipients, localized high levels of chronic unemployment and poverty have resulted in collective urban rebellions that capital has only been able to

44 *Capital, Vol. 1*, Chapter 25.

45 *Capital, Vol. 1*, Chapter 24.

put down by armed force – as in the central city uprisings of the 1960s in the United States, the Brixton "riots" of the 1980s in London, the "révolte des banlieues" in France in 2005 or the more recent protests in the US, spear-headed by the Black Lives Matter movement. Where the revolts have been powerful enough, armed repression has sometimes been followed by concessions aimed at preventing future uprisings, e.g., a dramatic expansion of food stamps in the US in the late 1960s.

But, over time, where gains have been won, capitalist counterattacks to re-impose more work have not been long in coming. Where students won changes in curriculum, academic structures of rewards worked to turn once radical courses into tame, tolerable and optional elements of degree programs. In the US, although the central city risings of the 1960s won a vast expansion in food stamps that fed millions, the decades since have witnessed recurrent efforts, often barely fended off by renewed protest, to cut back those subsidies to the consumption and well-being of their recipients. Where women in the US won access to contraception, social conservative "pro-life" groups (often rooted in some church) immediately launched counterattacks to reverse those gains. In the United States struggles around these issues continue to be waged in state after state. As I am writing these lines, I am reading reports of a church-backed Polish government plan to extend its bans on abortion to almost all cases of unwanted pregnancy, including incest and rape. Fortunately, I am also reading of the "Black Monday" protests by tens of thousands of Polish women dressed in black, boycotting work, shutting down offices, universities, and schools in 90 cities and taking to the street in protest to block that plan. (At last report, the protests were successful in forcing the Polish government to set aside its plan. One can only hope that the momentum of protest will succeed in eliminating existing bans.)[46]

I have also noted contradictions in capitalist policies being put forward for Poland. From the point of view of capitalist policy makers, there is a serious long run "demographic" problem haunting the Polish labor market: a below-replacement fertility rate combined with outmigration means a shrinking labor force and an aging population. Labor supply growing more slowly than the demand puts upward pressure on wages and downward pressure on profits, strengthens labor and undermines capital. Within this context, banning abortions might be rationalized as an encouragement to increased fertility and increased labor supply. But while bans certainly result in more work for women outside the waged labor force – either it increases the costs, time and risks involved in getting an illegal abortion or travel for a foreign one, or, if it results in more children, it makes for more work in the home – it also makes women less able to participate in the labor market. Dropping unemployment in recent years has already

---

46 Joanna Berendt, "Protestors in Poland Rally against Proposal for Total Abortion Ban," *New York Times*, October 3, 2016. Rick Lyman and Joanna Berendt, "Poland Steps Back from Stricter Anti-Abortion Law," *New York Times*, October 6, 2016.

put upward pressure on wages, making capitalist policy makers anxious to increase the labor force participation rate of Polish women. As a result, they have been recommending reducing ineffective pro-natalist policies, such as family cash benefits under the new "Family 500+" program that began in April 2016, that encourage women to stay home and replacing them with increased child care (that, it is hoped, will also raise fertility), *not* reducing the statutory retirement and pension age for women and lowering marginal tax rates for second earners in families, usually women.[47] Given that Polish women are as well educated as men, and "have a longer potential working lifespan," they are seen as "an important underutilized source of qualified labor." In other words, they are seen as a significant part of the "latent" reserve army that policy changes would shift into the "active" part of the reserve and hence into directly exploitable additions to the waged labor force.[48]

A more general assessment of contestation of these kinds of relationships in Poland I leave to you, my readers. Just scanning the European Union's 2013 document on *Your social security rights in Poland*, suggests that the terrains of likely conflict over the imposition and conditions of unwaged work are multiple. I do note that there is no mention, whatsoever, of access to contraception and abortion – an obvious, present terrain of struggle. At any rate, it seems clear to me that not only are the possibilities of crisis in *M – C*(*LP*) and the forces that tended to bring on such crises that Marx and Engels identified still with us, but with the growth in the strength and organizational abilities of workers, with the concessions won from capital – both in the private sector and from the state – those possibilities and forces have multiplied, making crisis even more likely than before.

Turning now to step #2, … P … C′, let us evaluate, once again, the possible usefulness of one aspect of Marx and Engels' theory of crises – this time in production – and my reinterpretation of it: the struggle against work. I see the avoidance of the labor market discussed above as one form of the refusal of work, of waged work anyway. But there are two other great domains where this is a recurrent issue: (1) Marx and Engels' primary concern: points of production (*P*) of saleable, and potentially profitable, commodities (*C′*), which capital has multiplied far beyond the factories, mines, fields and sailing vessels of the nineteenth century to include all of those places employing workers who provide services to both businesses and consumers, and (2) a set of work places they largely ignored, namely all of those where people's activities were organized to produce the singular commodity labor-power.

---

47 OECD, *OECD Economic Surveys: Poland* (March 2016): 17–20. IMF, *Republic of Poland, Selected Issues*, IMF Country Report No. 16/211, (July 10, 2016). IMF, "IMF Executive Board Concludes Article IV Consultation with the Republic of Poland," July 5, 2016.

48 IMF, *Republic of Poland, Selected Issues*, IMF Country Report No. 16/211 (July 10, 2016): 21–36.

Given the exploitation and alienation unavoidably produced by what Marx called capital's vampire-like thirst for ever more labor, the struggle against work plays out in multiple dimensions. Struggles to minimize the amount of one's time and energy given up to employers were of central concern to Marx in Chapter 10 of Volume 1 of *Capital* on the "working day." There, he analyzed how workers were ultimately able to block capital's efforts to make them work longer and begin to hammer down their hours of work. Those blows struck at the heart of absolute surplus value and profit. Failing to impose more work by lengthening hours, capital turned to the substitution of machines, whose rhythms they could control, to make workers toil more intensely. Workers, of course, resisted – from the out-and-out tool breaking of the Luddites to covert sabotage and collective slow-downs. All forms of sabotage, whether undertaken by individuals or by collaborating groups, reduce the amount of work imposed, increase the costs of production and harm profits. Whether the use of machines succeeds in making workers work faster, the reorganization that usually accompanies their introduction has also been used to undercut workers' self-organization by providing new opportunities to pit workers against each other – a long-standing ploy to divert frustration and antagonism into intra-class conflict, e.g., creating competition through which workers are induced to work harder. When they can, workers subvert such tactics by forming new alliances across whatever differences capital has tried to play upon and collaborate in collective resistance to more work. Some mix of the above forms of resistance are virtually universal. Few are those who are paid enough or find work that they love enough – regardless of being overseen by an employer – to throw themselves whole-heartedly into their jobs.

In such circumstances, Marx and Engels supported workers' demands for access to the vote, through the People's Charter, which would help them get laws passed limiting work, such as the Factory Acts, and for the recognition of unions through which they could negotiate hours and conditions of work directly with their employers. The battle for the Charter (1838–1858) failed and for a long time unions were outlawed. Eventually, through the Reform Act of 1867, some British workers did obtain suffrage and in 1871 unions were decriminalized. Faced with unions – first mostly craft unions, later industrial unions acting as a collective force demanding, among other things, less work – the functionaries of capital developed several ways to neutralize them. First, despite legal recognition, they often deployed paramilitary, police and military forces to crush strikes and protests. Second, they sought to instrumentalize them through legal contracts. Third, they used the government to directly take over and control a union's organizational apparatus, turning it into an arm of the state. This last was the dominant mode of control deployed by Soviet-style state capitalist regimes such as the Polish People's Republic and has been widely used in other kinds of dictatorial regimes that have severely punished overt worker protests.

Under such circumstances, Polish workers' struggles against work, like that of workers in similar circumstances elsewhere, were generally organized covertly. Although underground, such struggles have often been surprisingly effective at subverting capitalist attempts to impose work. This was true throughout the Soviet Union and its East European satellites and was a major source of the low levels of productivity in both agriculture and manufacturing, long cited by Western critics. Reports of the negative impact on agricultural production were common.[49] Concrete examples of work refusal and sabotage circulated in *samizdat* literature, in a few exceptional reports such as Miklós Haraszti's account of the subversive struggles of piece workers in Hungary,[50] and, after Glasnost, more openly in magazines such as *Ogonyuk*. Such invisible resistance fermented the discontent that repeatedly blew up in the face of Soviet-style state capitalist planners, exploding in upheavals such as those in East Germany in 1953, Hungary and Poland in 1956, Czechoslovakia in 1968, Poland in 1970, 1976, 1980, gestated *Solidarność* in both the cities and countryside of Poland and ultimately brought down the whole state-capitalist system in 1989. The profound impact of such resistance on labor productivity became apparent once those countries were opened to competition from foreign corporations that had found more sophisticated ways of imposing work and extracting surplus labor from their workers. The upshot, especially after the imposition of shock therapy in Poland, are well known: myriad plant closings, deindustrialization, massive layoffs and high unemployment – all of which constituted global capitalist revenge on the resistance of Polish workers. In the midst of these multi-pronged efforts to regain control over the Polish working class, the functionaries of capital – acting within Poland and from the offices of those supranational state institutions overseeing the "transition," i.e., a change in the mix of planning and markets – sought to revamp the role of unions using the more sophisticated capitalist methods of instrumentalization through laws and collective bargaining contracts.

In the wake of 1989 despite such attacks, Polish workers retained enough power of resistance to force capitalists and the state to concede some protections and put some limits on exploitation. Three places where this would seem to have been the case are (1) the enactment of a Polish Labor Code in 1974, (2) union recognition and collective bargaining for about 20% of the waged labor force and (3) the creation at the national level of the Tripartite Commission for Social and Economic Affairs in 1994 and at the voivodship level of "social dialogue commissions" created in 2002, where employers are forced to sit down with union leaders and government officials to negotiate capital/labor relations. Let's look briefly at these three phenomena.

1) The Labor Code, despite repeated amendments, has been a continuing source of irritation for capitalists, both domestic and foreign, who find labor and employment

49 See, Cleaver, "Food, Famine and the International Crisis," *Zerowork*, no. 2, (Fall 1977): 29–32.

50 Miklós Haraszti, *A Worker in a Worker's State*, London, Penguin 1977,

laws far too rigid for their tastes. The Code contains clear cut limits to the hours of work that can be imposed and mandates equally clear periods without work. This is, of course, true throughout Europe because, despite their best efforts, capitalists operating in the area have never been able to achieve the freedom of corporations in the US to rig work schedules to fit corporate needs, or to fire workers at will, for whatever reason, including slacking on the job. Capitalist response to these limitations, however, has tended to eliminate jobs subject to such rigidities and increase the number of precarious jobs providing them with greater flexibility in imposing work. Moreover, in the wake of the economic crisis of 2006–2008, a so-called "Anti-crisis package" was enacted into law – including changes in the Labor Code – with considerable union connivance, that gave employers even greater power to alter and control both the contractual framework and the amount of work being imposed.[51] As a result, in Poland the proportion of unstable, precarious jobs, e.g., temporary, under "civil contract," and with few or no benefits, have risen to over 25%.[52] Such enhanced control undoubtedly helped capitalists limit the local impact on their profits of the global crisis of the time – while imposing costs on workers of greater subordination of their time and energy and of all the psychological uncertainty and stress that accompany such changes. Conflicts and struggles over worktime, and hence over capitalist efforts to extract ever more absolute surplus value have continued in Poland and can be expected to be an important factor in future crises.

2) The trade union "connivance" mentioned in the last paragraph refers to the flip side of recognition. On the one hand, the legal recognition of trade unions and trade union alliances, and their presence in negotiations over employment and social issues is a measure of workers' power. On the other hand, they function like formal political parties that limit their partisans' activities to periodic voting, sapping energy from more direct action. Both provide means for taming, even harnessing working-class struggles. Such means have been widely deployed in the United States and Western Europe. For example, although arrangements vary from country to country, carefully structured labor contracts between employers and unions limit legal worker struggles to periods of contract negotiations. The rest of the time, under the terms of the contract, trade union bureaucrats are obligated to help managers impose the terms of the contract on their own members – even as employers are doing their best to renege on their own contractual obligations.[53] (It was no surprise that the Nobel Prize in Economics in

51 Gajewski, *Labour Market Measures in Poland 2008–13*, 2015, pp. 33–34.

52 Piotr Arak, Piotr Lewandowski, and Piotr Zakowiecki, "Dual Labor Market in Poland – Proposals for Overcoming the Deadlock," Instytut Badań Strukturalnych Policy Paper 01, 2014, p. 4.

53 Martin Glaberman, *Punching Out* (Detroit: Correspondence Publishing Committee, 1952). Martin Glaberman, *Union Committeemen and Wildcat Strikes* (Detroit: Correspondence Publishing Committee, 1955).

2016 was awarded to economists working on "contract" theory – because, the awarding committee claims, "contracts help us to be cooperative and trusting.")[54] Despite being representative of only about a fifth of the Polish Labor force, the main trade unions have gone along with amendments to the Labor Code and other changes in social policy that have made it easier to impose work and harder for workers to resist.

3) The thing that has struck me most in official representations of the purposes of the Tripartite Commission (TC) and the voivodship social dialogue commissions (VSDC) has been the way in which they have been explicitly given the mandate to limit social conflict. In the case of the TC, I find it stated that the forum was created "in order to conciliate the interests of employees, the interests of employers and public welfare. The aim of the Commission's activity is to achieve and maintain social peace." In the case of the VSDC, I find that they are intended to help "to solve many problems on the territorial level in the situation of threats connected with existence of possible socio-economic conflicts in the region."[55] Agreement with these motivations among trade union members has been manifested not only by continued participation but by judgements on the organizations' effectiveness. In one report, *NSZZ Solidarność* judged only the work teams of the TC to have been useful. Useful at doing what? In "defusing tensions within specific industries."[56] In principle, the trade unions whose representatives sit on these forums, are not only "obliged to communicate agreed regulations to [their] members ... but also to guarantee their support"[57] Such a structure parallels the kind of co-optation of trade unions as contract enforcers cited above. At least one analysis of the actual functioning of the TC – its role in the creation of the "Anti-Crisis Package" – suggests that because there is nothing in the acts creating the TC that compels the government to follow its suggestions, the "social dialogue" organized by these institutions is an illusion hiding actual government monopoly over decision making.[58]

Finally, let us examine step #3: C′ – M′. In the body of my text, I examine the array of possibilities, identified by Marx and Engels, that capitalist attempts to sell their commodities might fail, and then those forces tending to turn potential failure into reality. The possibilities and forces were many in the nineteenth century and continue to be numerous in our twenty-first century. Which, I ask myself, and to what degree, have the many possible sources of failure-to-sell been a source of crisis for Polish capitalism in recent years? I want to differentiate here between chronic problems, such as limited

54 Tore Ellingsen, et. al., "Contract Theory: The Prize in Economic Theory 2016," Popular Science Background, (The Royal Swedish Academy of Sciences, 2016).

55 Ministry of Labor and Social Policy, n.d.

56 Jan Czarzasty, *Capacity building for social dialogue in Poland*, European Foundation for the Improvement of Living and Working Conditions, 2006, p. 16.

57 Piotr Sula, "Role of social dialogue institution in the time of crisis. The case of Poland," Research Papers of Wroclaw University of Economics, 136, no. 9 (January 2010): 211.

58 Ibid., p. 218.

consumption demand due to wages, salaries and other forms of working-class income being held down by capitalist efforts to maximize profits, and those whose dimensions swelled during or in the wake of the global crisis of the late 2000s.

On the whole, by all reports, Polish capitalists were more successful than most other parts of Europe in fending off crisis, keeping output and employment growing. Despite a brief slowdown in 2012–2014, GDP growth has averaged about 3% since 2008 reaching 3.6 in 2015.[59] The obvious question about sales is "for what markets?" The main answers are (1) domestic investment and consumption markets whose growth offset declining foreign demand due to the wider economic crisis in Europe and (2) monetary policies that offset financial instability in the EU and allowed a continued expansion of credit that supported the expansion of both investment and consumption demand.

Investment demand continued to grow because of accommodating monetary policies, credit expansion and an inflow of funds from the European Union, the IMF and private investment. Domestic consumption demand grew because of expanded hiring (even if much of that hiring involved low-paid workers in temporary, low- or no-benefit jobs), increases in government transfer and subsidy programs (such as the "Family 500+" and "Home for the Young" programs), and minimum wage hikes.[60] (Average real wages and real consumption grew even faster because of deflation.) So, although more full-time, higher wage employment would have benefited the working class more, there was enough improvement to overall income to keep up consumption demand, i.e., the market for $C(MS)'$.

With respect to monetary policy, the Polish government, with support from the EU and the IMF, took steps to insulate financial markets in Poland from instability in the rest of Europe. Domestically, the Polish government held down inflation then moved against deflation, imposed increased supervision on banks, floated the zloty, implemented counter-cyclically, stimulating monetary policy in response to slowdowns in exports due to the crises of its trading partners, and started cutting back expenditures to limit public debt while taking steps to increase tax receipts.[61] It also acted as lender-of-last-resort to banks, e.g., rescuing the SK Bank in 2015.[62]

Membership in the EU has resulted in substantial net capital flows into the country. In 2014, for example, EU spending in Poland amounted to €17.436 billion whereas Poland's contribution to the EU budget was only € 3,526 billion. The net inflow of

59 IMF, "Poland: Staff Concluding Statement of 2016 Article IV Mission, International Monetary Fund, (May 16, 2016)

60 IMF, Cross-Country Report on Minimum Wages: Selected Issues, IMF Country Report 16/151, (June 2016). Katarzina Kuniewicz, "Home for the Young scheme affects prices of dwellings and sales volumes," REAS, February 5, 2015. (No longer online)

61 IMF, Press release: IMF Executive Board Approves US$20.58 Billion Arrangement for Poland Under the Flexible Credit Line, (May 6, 2009).

62 Narodowy Bank Polski, *Financial Stability Report*, February 2016, pp. 51–52.

€13.9 billion made Poland the biggest recipient of the EU budget. As percentages of Polish gross national income, these amounts are small, but their net effect has been to dampen the circulation of negative shocks from crisis elsewhere in the Union and beyond. Contributions from five different EU funds, e.g., European Regional Development fund and the Cohesion Fund, have financed some 125 projects. The bulk of those projects, ranging from infrastructure development to tourist attractions, are aimed at so-called less developed areas, e.g., the Eastern voivodes. The second largest number of projects are aimed at "rural development," i.e., supporting farmer income and modernization, that is to say encouraging exodus from the land and the growth of capitalist agribusiness. Moreover, as Polish policy makers have progressively approached meeting the criteria for admission to the Eurozone, private investment income has flowed in from multinational corporations.

The IMF's support primarily took the form of a series of loans (2009, 2010, 2011, 2013, 2015) under its new Flexible Credit Line (FCL) created in response to the international financial crisis and intended primarily to provide an emergency source of financing if needed. Although the IMF touts FCL loans as being free of the usual conditionality clauses with which it has battered governments to make policy changes that impose the costs of crisis on workers, FCL loans must be applied for and are only granted if the applying governments "qualify," i.e., already manage class relations using methods of which the IMF approves. That the Polish government has qualified five times shows that the IMF finds its managerial methods quite acceptable.

Among policy makers, their greatest worries about potential crisis in Poland appear to be focused on continued economic and political instability in the EU and on their Eastern borders, e.g., conflict in the Ukraine and recession in Russia. Because Polish policy has been ever more closely tied to the EU, with the objective of fulfilling sufficient preparatory criteria to permit abandoning the zloty and joining the Eurozone, past success in avoiding the circulation of crisis is not assumed for the future. The perceived risks of crisis are thus the same as those of their European partners: financial instability and stagnation in the growth of industry and trade.[63] In class terms, which policy makers rarely use, the potential for crisis in Poland is closely tied to prospects for those class struggles elsewhere in Europe to circulate to Poland, as they have from Greece to Spain and Portugal. As I discuss in Chapter 5, Section 4 of my essay, Marx and Engels highlighted how crisis and class struggle could circulate through and across the circuits of capital. This was something they not only analyzed but participated in. The greatest potential threat to Polish capitalism, and to the circuits of capital in Europe more generally, would be a perfect storm of resistance and demands for alternatives

63 IMF, "Poland: Staff Concluding Statement" op. cit. IMF, "IMF Executive Board Concludes Article IV Consultation with the Republic of Poland," July 5, 2016, *OECD Economic Surveys: Poland* (March 2016).

akin to those that swept Europe in 1848 and 1968. As always, we would expect the forms of struggle and ideas for alternatives to change with the evolution of the class composition, but given the experiences of the last twenty years, such a storm is imaginable.

The storm has been gathering for a long time. From the point of view of Polish capital, they were, at first, dark clouds over the horizon. Anti-IMF/World-Bank demonstrations in Berlin in 1988 and the first counter-summit against the G7 in Paris in 1989 took place just as Poland was gaining independence from Soviet domination. In 1990, I participated in a massive gathering in Venice of young activists from all over Europe titled Europe Against the Bosses, another counter-summit to a meeting of the G7 in that city. In the wake of the Zapatista organized Continental and then Intercontinental Encounters in 1996, People's Global Action was formed and moved against the WTO in Geneva. Following that effort, a whole series of massive collective actions were undertaken beginning in 1999 with the June eighteenth Carnival against Capital (J18) organized in dozens of cities around Europe, as far East as Minsk and Prague, and the Battle of Seattle (N30) on November 30th in the US. The J18 slogan "Our Resistance is as Transnational as Capital" expressed not anti-globalization – as the movement was sometimes called – but *alter*-globalization, dedication to building a non-capitalist global community. For several years, the alter-globalization movement organized protest demonstrations against the meetings of capital's supranational coordinating bodies, especially the IMF, the World Bank, and the G7/8. The apex of those efforts were the demonstrations of over 100,000 against the G8 in Genoa, Italy in 2001. But two factors meant that apex also turned out to be the beginning of the end of that kind of transnational protest. The first factor was the violent police repression of the demonstration that led to two days of bloody confrontation and the killing of one protestor. The second was the realization that while the years of protest had built international networks of solidarity and cooperation, they had failed to change the neoliberal policies being foisted on the world's working class.

Although there have been scattered protests, gathering activists from many nations, in the years since 2001, both capital's tactics and workers' reactions have shifted. The widespread financial crisis of 2007–2009, subsequent general crisis throughout the circuit of capital, especially in many OECD countries, and the resultant crisis of debt repayment in Greece, Spain and Portugal, provided capital with an opportunity to impose on those in the Global North the same neoliberal austerity methods it had deployed against workers in the Global South during the international debt crisis of the 1980s and 1990s. Differential degrees of imposition have allowed capitalist policy makers to divide and, so far, to undermine the development of transnational resistance. While Occupy Wall Street burned brightly for a while – igniting other fires in other places – its fires have dimmed and the embers smolder. Workers hardest hit in places such as Greece have fought back fiercely, from the streets to the ballot box (SYRIZA), elsewhere less austere methods and anti-Greek propaganda have been mostly successful at dissuading workers from rising up in support of those on the cutting edge of resistance. Added to that divide and conquer tactic has been the strategy of pitting the tides of refugees from wars in the Mid-East against local workers – a strategy that resembles the efforts to pit East European workers against West European workers in the wake of 1989. While, therefore, multiple storms of struggle are disrupting capital accumulation, there will be no "perfect storm" until the transnational anti-capitalist movement discovers new and more effective methods to respond to and overcome current capitalist attacks.

Harry Cleaver
Austin, Texas
October 2016

APPENDIX 2

Annotated Bibliography of Marx and Engels' Writings on Crisis

1839

Engels, Friedrich. "Letters from Wuppertal," MECW, *Vol. 2*, pp. 7–25. (*Telegraph für Deutschland*, in March and April 1839.)

Articles describing the suffering of workers in the Wupper Valley of Prussia, foreshadowing his descriptions a couple of years later of similar suffering of workers in Manchester, England.

1842

Marx, Karl. "Proceedings of the Sixth Rhine Province Assembly, Third Article, Debates on the Law on Thefts of Wood," MECW, *Vol. 1*, pp. 224–63. (*Rheinische Zeitung*, October and November 1842.)

Marx's commentary on the persecution of peasants for directly appropriating fallen wood in now enclosed forests. Supports peasants against landlords' usurpation of the laws.

Engels, Friedrich. "The English View of the Internal Crisis," November 29, 1842, MECW, *Vol. 2*, pp. 368–69. (*Rheinische Zeitung*, No. 342, December 8, 1842) and "The Internal Crises," November 30, 1842, MECW, *Vol. 2*, pp. 370–74. (*Rheinische Zeitung*, Nos. 343, 344, December 9, 10, 1842.)

Articles on Chartist agitation in England. Engels notes that downturns in commerce raises unemployment and leaves workers "without bread." Although the demonstrations he is discussing failed, he predicts that further downturns will produce a "general lack of food among the workers" and then "fear of death from starvation will be stronger than fear of the law" and revolution will result.

1843

Engels, Friedrich. "Outline of a Critique of Political Economy," October - November 1843, MECW, *Vol. 3*, pp. 433–43. (*Deutsch-Franzosische Jahrbucher*, 1844.)

DOI:10.1163/9789004708631_011

Engels attributes trade crises to competition and the anarchy of supply and demand when supply is based on imperfect knowledge of market conditions. Supply is seen as driven by competition, especially that between capitalists. Law of competition is "purely a law of nature" that leads to recurrent overproduction and crisis on an ever more universal scale that leads to revolution. The alternative to competition is communal planning of production to meet needs and the replacement of selfishness with "the spirit of emulation grounded in human nature." Also: crisis leads to centralization of capital and decline of the middle class – thus polarization between "millionaires and paupers."

1844

Marx, Karl. "Economic and Philosophic Manuscripts of 1844," *MECW*, *Vol. 3*, pp. 229–346.

"Finally, as the amassing of capital increases the amount of industry and therefore the number of workers, it causes the same amount of industry to manufacture a larger amount of products, which leads to over-production ..." (p. 238) Whilst labour brings about the accumulation of capital and with this the increasing prosperity of society, it renders the worker ever more dependent on the capitalist, leads him into competition of a new intensity, and drives him into the headlong rush of over-production, with its subsequent slump. (p. 240) Quoting Adam Smith about industry producing ever more output, he comments "Hence, over-production." (p.258) "Large landed property ... leads to crisis even more quickly than the partitioning of land." (p. 269) Marx's analysis of how the work imposed by capital is alienating in several ways, and thus workers' resist, is mostly in the section on "Estranged Labour." (pp. 270–82) On family, property and communism. (pp. 294–96)

1845

Engels, Friedrich. "Speeches in Elberfeld," February 8, 1845, *MECW*, *Vol. 4*, pp. 243–51. (*Rheinische Jahrbucher Zur Gesellshaftlichen Reform*, 1845.)

In this speech, Engels juxtaposes a "competitive," i.e., capitalist, society with a communist society. Included in his reason for rejecting competition in favor of communism is the tendency of competition to produce periodic commercial crises. These crises he attributes to the inability of producers to obtain adequate information about their markets. There are middlemen and time lags, even in prices, which lead to production being continued despite markets becoming glutted. Communism, he argues would do away with such crises by planning production to meet peoples' needs.

Engels, Friedrich. "Speeches in Elberfeld," February 15, 1845, *MECW, Vol. 4,* pp. 256–64. (*Rheinische Jahrbucher Zur Gesellshaftlichen Reform,* 1845.)

In this second speech at Elberfeld, Engels extends his critique of competition to the conflict between national groups of capitalists. In the context of an analysis of the pros and cons of List's arguments for protective tariffs for Germany, Engels argues that with either free trade or with tariffs, the results will ultimately be the same: trade crises due to glutted markets, rising impoverishment of the working class and a bloody social revolution. The only alternative, he says, is "the peaceful introduction or at least preparation of communism."

Engels, Friedrich to Karl Marx, February 22 – March 7, 1845, *MECW, Vol. 38,* pp. 22–23.

Letter about his talks at Elberfeld: "Here in Elberfeld wondrous things are afoot. Yesterday we held our third communist meeting in the town's largest hall and leading inn." Etc.

Engels, Friedrich. "The Condition of the English Working Class," September 1844 - March 1845, *MECW, Vol. 4,* pp. 375–88, 397–99, 501–29; 579–83. (Leipzig, 1845) Chapters on competition and on labor movements.

In his description of competition: the "battle of all against all," Engels discusses how the capitalists set workers against workers as a means of control and of limiting wages. He also discusses "industrial competition" among capitalists and the "commercial crises which arise from it." He attributes the commercial crisis to overproduction resulting from inadequate information about the state of markets. In describing the pattern of economic cycles, he also mentions commercial, industrial and financial speculation which not only accentuates overproduction but also creates a system of credit which rapidly circulates collapse once a break occurs, i.e., someone must come up with money that cannot be had. His major contribution to crisis theory in this book is his analysis of the reserve army which grows during crisis and whose desperate plight can lead to revolt. In his discussion of workers' struggles, Engels notes how crises force reductions in wages and thus limit workers' power to raise or sustain wages. Yet he also argues that the struggles keep average wages higher than they would otherwise be and even if they fail, they constitute "military schools" for the workers that prepare them for revolution. In the chapter on labor movements, he also describes how the English capitalists tried to use working class militancy during the crisis of 1842 to attack the Corn Laws and their landlord backers.

Engels, Friedrich. "History of the English Corn Laws," Autumn 1845, *MECW, Vol. 4,* pp. 656–61. (*Telegraph Fur Deutschland,* Nos. 193, 194, December 1945.)

Brief account of how the Anti-Corn Law League sought and failed to use working class militancy engendered by the crisis of 1842 to overthrow the Corn Laws (essentially the same material as in *Condition of the English Working Class,* pp. 519–23).

Marx, Karl and Friedrich Engels. "The German Ideology," 1845–1846, *MECW, Vol. 5*, pp. 19–539.

An early, massive tome, mostly critiquing the Young Hegelians and Feuerbach on the basis of their materialist theory of history. "Thus all collisions [Crisis/revolution] in history have their origin … in the contradiction between the productive forces and the form of [social] intercourse." (p. 74) Also: "The ideas of the ruling class are in every epoch the ruling ideas, … The division of labour … manifests itself also in the ruling class as the division of mental and material labour, so that inside this class one part appears as the thinkers of the class (its active, conceptive ideologists, who make the formation of the illusions of the class about itself their chief source of livelihood) …" (pp. 59–60) "Herr Grun forgets that the over-production causes crisis only through the influence on the exchange value of products." (p. 518)

1846

Friedrich Engels, "Violation of the Prussian Constitution," May 1846, *MECW, Vol. 6*, pp. 52–53. (*The Northern Star*, No. 446, May 30, 1846.)

First of three articles on illegal Prussian state borrowing.

Friedrich Engels, "The Prussian Bank Question" June 1846, *MECW, Vol. 6*, p. 57. (*The Northern Star*, No. 451, July 4, 1846.)

Second of three articles on the King of Prussia's borrowing and manipulations of money.

Marx, Karl to P. V. Annenkov, December, 28 1846, *MECW*, *Vol. 38*, pp. 95–106, or *Marx Engels Selected Correspondence* (*MESC*) (Moscow: Progress Publishers, 3rd rev ed. 1975) 29–39.

In this long review of Proudhon's *Philosophie de la misère, ou Système des contradictions économiques* (1846), Marx critiques both method and specific moments of analysis. In repeatedly juxtaposing actual reality/history to Proudhon's sacred ideas, he emphasizes real conflicts within real historical social systems. Critiquing Proudhon's eternal concept of machinery, Marx argues "Up till 1825 – when the first general crisis occurred – it might be said that the requirements of consumption as a whole were growing more rapidly than production, and that the development of machinery was the necessary consequence of the needs of the market. Since 1825, the invention and use of machinery resulted solely from the war between masters and workmen." (*MESC*, p. 33, *MECW*, p. 99)

1847

Engels, Friedrich. "The Prussian Constitution," February 1847, *MECW, Vol. 6,* pp. 64–71. (*The Northern Star,* No. 489, Mar. 6, 1847.)

Third of three articles on Prussian state shenanigans. International circulation of crisis: English glut led to dumping of excess goods into German markets and depression/depreciation of German industry. Railroad speculation (speculative boom, then crash) involved diversion of money capital from manufacturing. In addition, potato harvest failure and increased corn prices led to crisis/famine. Crisis forced Prussian King to create a constitution and United Diet in 1847. Engels forecasts rise of industrial middle class, with constitutional rights, will be "the beginning of a new epoch … the downfall of absolutism and nobility …" (p. 71)

Marx, Karl. "Poverty of Philosophy," *MECW, Vol. 6,* pp. 137, 160. (Paris, Brussels, 1847).

"overproduction … [has its] explanation in this mode of evaluation [by minimum socially necessary labor time]" p.136. "With the birth of large-scale industry this correct proportion had to come to an end, and production is inevitably compelled to pass in continuous succession through vicissitudes of prosperity, depression, crisis, stagnation, renewed prosperity, and so on … What kept production in correct, or more or less correct, proportions? It was demand that dominated supply … Large-scale industry … can no longer wait for demand. Production precedes consumption, supply compels demand." (p. 137)

Engels, Friedrich. "The Commercial Crisis in England – The Chartist Movement – Ireland," October 23, 1847, *MECW, Vol. 6,* pp. 307–9. (*La Reforme,* Oct. 26, 1847.)

1. Crisis of 1847 more severe than 1837 or 1842; all branches of industry affected. Cotton textile workers, angry over unemployment and wage cuts, are threatening to join iron workers and miners in strike. This could lead to a general strike as in 1842. 2. In Ireland where famine rages, "hungry people gather in thousands to ransack the barns and cattle sheds of the farmers and even of Catholic priests." "It looks as though the Irish will not die of hunger as calmly next winter as they did last winter." Irish immigration to England will lead to increased "competition among the workers."

Engels, Friedrich. "Principles of Communism," October 1847, *MECW, Vol. 6,* pp. 347–48, 352–53.

Five to seven-year periodicity of overproduction crises and "general revolutionary ferment" during crises. Communist planning of production in accordance with social needs will eliminate crises.

Marx, Karl. "Wages," December 1847, *MECW*, *Vol. 6*, pp. 415–33. (*Sotsialisticheskoye Khozyaistvo*, 1924.)

In this set of lecture notes, Marx notes how wages fall with overproduction crises as demand for labor falls. Overproduction crises become more extensive and more violent with growth of world market and so too wage fluctuations. In addition, reserve army of unemployed prevents or limits rise in wages in booms.

Marx, Karl. "Wage Labor and Capital," December 1847, *MECW*, *Vol. 9*, p. 228. (*Neue Rheinische Zeitung*, Nos. 264–67, 269, April 5–8, 11, 1849.)

With continuous production across the world, "fewer and fewer [new] markets remain available" – fewer places to dump output.

1848

Marx, Karl. "Speech on the Question of Free Trade," February 1848, *MECW*, *Vol. 6*, pp. 458–63. (Brussels, Feb. 1848.)

Growth of capital and rise of world market accelerates overproduction crises. Within global capital overproduction is an international phenomenon, e.g., English textiles dumped on India destroy Indian textile manufacturing with lower prices based on more developed technology. Workers suffered the consequences of Free Trade, which accelerated the development of capital, but Marx supports it because he thinks that development will hasten the parallel development of worker's struggles and the overthrow of capitalism.

Engels, Friedrich. "The Situation in Belgium," March 18, 1848, *MECW*, *Vol. 6*, pp. 569–70. (Marx/Engels, *Gesamtausgabe*, Bd. 6, 1932.)

Engels mocks the Belgian bourgeoisie, which does not want to follow the French move to a Republic, but which cannot prevent the French crisis from circulating to Brussels and bringing: stock market panic, bankruptcies, increased unemployment and angry workers.

Marx, Karl and Friedrich Engels. *Manifesto of the Communist Party*, December 1847 - January 1848, *MECW*, *Vol. 6*, pp. 488–93, 508–9. (London, Feb. 1848.)

Mainly interesting for seeing periodical overproduction crises, caused by competition among capitalists, as a manifestation of the contradiction between productive forces and property relations. Mentions productive forces that "slumbered in the lap of social labor."

1849

Marx, Karl. "The State of Trade," March 6, 1849, *MECW*, *Vol. 9*, pp. 3–8. (*Neue Rheinische Zeitung*, No. 239, Mar. 7, 1849.)

On crisis of 1847 and Revolutions of 1848, crisis caused by overproduction and railroad speculation, which led Bank of England to raise bank rate and restrict credit. International circulation of crisis as declining demand led to declining imports, which led to crisis in other exporting countries. Also, German industrial prosperity dependent on English prosperity and imports (locomotive effect). "The revolutions," Marx wrote, "contribute to the fact that now and then trade stagnated, that sales became difficult and dangerous," BUT in Germany "with or without the revolution we would have had our bankruptcies." (p. 7)

Marx, Karl to Joseph Weydemeyer, 19 December 1849, *MECW*, *Vol. 38*, pp. 218–21.

"... just now, when trade is continuously expanding, neither the working masses in France, Germany, etc., nor the whole strata of shopkeepers, etc. are really in a revolutionary frame of mind" – no crisis, no revolution.

1850

Marx, Karl. "Class Struggles in France," January-November 1, 1850, *MECW*, *Vol. 10*, pp. 48–63, 74–75, 132–35. (*Neue Rheinische Zeitung P. - o. Revue*, Nos. 1, 2, 3, 5–6, 1850.)

This is an extremely important case study of the Provisional Government in France in 1848. It is not one of the role of money in the genesis of a commercial crisis as much as it is one of the utilization by capital of money against workers in the midst of both an economic and political crisis. The relevance to current debt problems in countries such as Argentina or Brazil is striking. Marx's analysis brings out a number of basic points: (1) Borrowing can be a way of buying time for capital to find ways of dealing with the working class. This is what the provisional government did to finance concessions to workers without raising taxes that would cause revolt. (2) The crisis of credit is a crisis of the capitalist order. Support for credit, for the repayment of debt to financial capitalist creditors eventually requires making workers and peasants pay – this is what Provisional Government in France ultimately did; it increased taxes on peasants, pitting them against the workers. The alternative was revolutionary destruction of debt and creditors. (3) Prosperity = no revolution. Revolution only possible when productive forces and forms of production are in collision, so revolution depends on crisis, but revolution can increase crisis as in 1848. (4) Circulation of crisis: England as demiurge.

Both crisis and prosperity originate in the center of capitalist world, but revolution is more likely in the periphery that has less ability to adjust.

Marx, Karl and Friedrich Engels. "Review: January-February 1850," January 31, 1850, *MECW*, Vol. 10, p. 257–67. (*Neue Rheinische Zeitung P. - o. Revue,* No. 2, 1850.)

Prosperity in England partly result of elimination of continental competitors by crisis and revolution. However, already some markets are glutted and crisis will come. They predict it will coincide with crisis on continent and "will mark the beginning of the modern English revolution" (It did not.) In addition, English trade undercut Chinese industry and brought on "social crisis" and talk of "abolition of private property."

Engels, Friedrich. "The Ten Hours Question," February 8–20, 1850, *MECW, Vol. 10*, pp. 271–76. (*The Democratic Review,* Mar. 1850.)

The virtual repeal of the 1847 Ten Hours Bill by juridical action would lead, Engels argued, to "such a rush at overtrading that revulsions upon revulsions will follow, so that … a revolution made inevitable …" "Production," he notes "cannot outdo existing markets" but "there are no new markets." He also mentions "better exploring" of existing markets, and the reduction of production costs via reducing wages as ways of overcoming crisis.

Engels, Friedrich. "The English Ten Hours Bill," March 1850, *MECW, Vol. 10*, pp. 289–300. (*Neue Rheinische Zeitung P. - o. Revue,* No. 4, 1850.)

Old Ten Hours Bill (1847) aimed by aristocracy against capitalists. Its fall will speed production, overproduction and crisis. Limits of markets means need to cut production costs via (1) "New and more highly perfected modes of production," (2) cutting profits, (3) cutting wages. However, #1 means more production and more problems. #2 profits already negative in crisis. #3 wage cuts possible by reducing prices of necessities of life. Hence, repeal of Corn Laws. In future workers' demand for less work "will be introduced quite of its own accord … the only solution to the ten hours question … lies in the proletarian revolution."

Marx, Karl and Friedrich Engels. "Review: Mar.-Apr. 1850," April 18, 1850, *MECW, Vol. 10*, pp. 338–41. (*Neue Rheinische Zeitung P. - o. Revue,* No. 4, 1850.)

Onset of English crisis delayed by usual spring upturn in markets plus improvements in East India. However, emerging gluts in industry is coinciding with crisis in agriculture so overall crisis still seems imminent and should come when American markets are glutted. Then crisis will create political openings for working class in English parliament.

Marx, Karl and Friedrich Engels. "Review: May to Oct. 1850," November 1, 1850, *MECW*, *Vol. 10*, pp. 490–532. (*Neue Rheinische Zeitung P. - o. Revue*, No. 5–6, 1850.)

Covers two major periods: crisis of 1847/48 and prosperity of 1848–1850. "Crisis first breaks out in the field(s) of speculation … overspeculation … a symptom of overproduction … appears to the superficial view as the cause of the crisis." In Britain, speculation was concentrated in railroads, cotton, corn and trade with East India and China. Collapse of railroads meant collapse of iron production. Overproduction for East India and China meant collapse of cotton industry. Outflow of gold and silver due to investment and speculative imports led to Bank of England raising discount rate to 5% in April 1848. This resulted in shut down of credit. Continued crisis again led Bank of England to raise discount to 5 and 1/2% in October. This resulted in collapse of banks and suspension of Bank Act of 1844. Crisis circulated to continent, gold flowed to UK and US which helped them and undercut Europe. Relation between crisis and revolution: "the commercial crisis contributed infinitely more to the revolution of 1848 than the revolution to the commercial crisis." Prosperity: lack of speculative outlets meant capital flowed into real investment. Output expanded with market at home and exports to US (especially California and Pacific). With increase in steamship line investment, New York would be the center of speculation on steamships. (Section on France included in *Class Struggles in France* – see above.)

On the discovery of gold in California, increase in money supply and stimulus to investment, not only locally but in the growth of trade across the Pacific Ocean. "The discovery of the California gold-mines set the seal on the prosperity of America." "positive effect on trade", "incentive which the mineral wealth of California gave to capital on the world market … continuing expansion of all the markets of the Pacific Ocean" (p. 504)

1851

Marx, Karl to Friedrich Engels, February 3, 1851, *MECW*, *Vol. 38*, pp. 273–78.

In the course of an attack on the "currency school's" naive quantity theory (species flow mechanism) Marx argues that when a crisis occurs and gold flows out of a country (e.g. M > X), bank practices may make things worse. For example, drain on bank reserves can lead it to raise the interest rate on loans and reduce loans (hence "pressure") to build up its reserves. However, the decline in commercial loans depresses business activity and accentuates the crisis.

Engels, Friedrich to Karl Marx, February 5, 1851, *MECW*, *Vol. 38*, pp. 278–81.

Comments on the Free Traders' "exploiting the prosperity" to "buy the proletariat" with free libraries, etc.

Engels, Friedrich to Karl Marx, February 25, 1851, *MECW*, *Vol. 38*, pp. 299–300.

Engel's response to Marx's of 3 Feb. '51: agreeing with Marx that crisis will reduce deposits and compel the bank to raise interest rates to bolster bullion reserves, thus reducing loans and dampening business activity.

Marx, Karl. «Reflections," March 1851, *MECW*, *Vol. 10*, pp. 584–92. (*Kommunist* [USSR] No. 1, Jan. 1977.)

Monetary crises are manifestations of commercial crises, i.e., inability sell commodities. Commercial crises begin with failure of dealers to sell overproduced items to consumers, then collapse in relations between dealers. But overproduction "must not be attributed solely to disproportionate production," it is ultimately due to the "relationship between the class of capitalists and that of workers." All class societies give rise to money systems and in capitalist society the split between commodities and money is the most developed. Greatest separation between commodities and money means greatest possibility of crisis of realization of capital, i.e., C' - M' and as result, greatest possibility of resulting monetary crises as forms of collapse of money capital.

Engels, Friedrich to Karl Marx, July 30, 1851, *MECW*, *Vol. 38*, pp. 395–96.

Note on how big cotton crop may coincide with collapse of overstocked East India trade to precipitate a trade crisis.

Engels, Friedrich to Karl Marx, circa August 11, 1851, *MECW*, *Vol. 38*, pp. 419–22.

During critique of Proudhon's plan to reduce interest, Engels notes that during crisis the part of interest charges "representing the guarantee of repayment" rises enormously.

Engels, Friedrich to Karl Marx, September 23, 1851, *MECW*, *Vol. 38*, pp. 458–62.

Observation of rapid increase in cotton textile production with no apparent new outlets – except maybe Australia because of recent discovery of gold – and therefore prediction of overproduction.

Engels, Friedrich to Karl Marx, October 15, 1851, *MECW*, *Vol. 38*, pp. 477–79.

Iron trade paralyzed. Prospect that an English crisis might coincide with the expected spring "convulsions on the Continent."

Marx, Karl to Ferdinand Freiligrath, December 27, 1851, *MECW*, *Vol. 38*, pp. 520–21.

"Since the latest events I am more convinced than ever that there will be no serious revolution without a trade crisis."

1852

Marx, Karl. "The Eighteenth Brumaire of Louis Bonaparte," December 1851 - May 1852, *MECW*, *Vol. 11*, pp. 99–197. (*Die Revolution*, New York, 1852.)

Description of the "minor trade crisis" in France prior to Louis Bonaparte's coup d'état in the fall of 1851. Marx attributes the crisis to (1) overproduction following prosperity in 1849 - 50, (2) rise in prices of raw materials (cotton, silk, wool), (3) English competition and circulation of commercial crisis from England to France which hit French industry harder than English, and (4) he argues that although political instability in France had "a depressing effect on some branches of industry in Paris and in the departments," the effect was "only local and inconsiderable" as evidenced by "the improvement of trade set in ... at the very moment when the political situation grew worse." (pp. 170–77) Also, his likening of French peasants to a "sack of potatoes", i.e., a class in-itself but not for-itself. (p. 187)

Engels, Friedrich. "England," January 23, 30, 1852, *MECW*, *Vol. 11*, pp. 198–209. (*Letopisi Marksizma* [USSR] V. IV, 1927.)

(1) "it is not continental political upheavals but world-wide trade crises, direct material blows calling into question the livelihood of each individual, which are the mainsprings of development in England." (2) How great the advantages of electoral reform will be to the proletariat will depend on whether it comes "before the trade crisis breaks or rather coincides with it; for the proletariat, for the time being, only plays an active part ... at great moments of decision ..."

Engels, Friedrich to Joseph Weydemeyer, February 27, 1852, *MECW*, *Vol. 39*, pp. 52–55.

Downturn in Indian and American markets suggest commercial crisis by May despite delay caused by English Free Trade measures, opening of Dutch colonies, lowered tariffs in Spain and drop in cotton prices.

Engels, Friedrich to Karl Marx, March 2, 1852, *MECW*, *Vol. 39*, pp. 55–58.

A month later Engels is still expecting crisis, which has been delayed, he says, by (1) California, (2) low cotton prices, and (3) timidity to speculate (even in gold and steamships). Crisis expected in fall - winter 1852–1853.

Engels, Friedrich to Karl Marx, April 20, 1852, *MECW*, *Vol. 39*, pp 81–83.

Crisis delayed by (1) resilience of Indian markets (based on crushing of native handicraft production), (2) confusion created by California and Australia, (3) cheap raw materials, and (4) absence of speculation. Maybe a crisis in spring of 1853.

Marx, Karl to J. Weydemeyer, April 30, 1852, *MECW*, *Vol. 39*, pp. 94–97.

Crisis postponed by California, Australia, India. Until crisis "there can be no thought of revolutionary convulsions."

Marx, Karl to Friedrich Engels, August 19, 1852, *MECW*, *Vol. 39*, pp. 159–63.

Crop failures in England and the continent plus wild speculation in London and New York leads him to say, "Is that not approaching crisis? The Revolution may come sooner than we would like. Nothing could be worse than the revolutionaries having to provide bread."

Engels, Friedrich to Karl Marx, August 24 1852, *MECW*, *Vol. 39*, pp. 164–65.

Engels is somewhat less optimistic than Marx about the likely onset of crisis. He writes, "harvests in N. E. Germany, Poland and Russia show signs of being passable," speculation in London is "evenly distributed" and "I don't believe that the crisis will this time be preceded by a regular rage for speculation ..." Also: "whether a revolution is immediately produced – immediately, i.e., in 6–8 months – very largely depends on the intensity of the crisis." He is also concerned with the unexpected effects of events in Australia which they had been following for some time: "Australia also does some harm ... her gold and the stoppage of all her other exports ... heavier imports ... and the fact that she is draining off the *surplus population* here *at the rate of 5,000 a week*. California and Australia are two cases which were not foreseen in the *Manifesto;* creation of large new markets out of nothing. They will have to be included."

Engels, Friedrich to Karl Marx, September 24, 1852, *MECW*, *Vol. 39*, pp. 196–98.

"The workers would appear *aprés tout* to have become utterly bourgeoisified as a result of the present prosperity and the prospect of *La Gloire de L'Empire*. They will have to be severely chastened by crises if they are to be good for anything again soon." He felt the next crisis would be serious due to the length of its development in production. "No crisis is worse than when over-speculation develops slowly in the sphere of production, so that its results take as many years to mature as they would months on the stock and commodity exchanges."

Engels, Friedrich. "Revolution and Counter-Revolution in Germany: XVIII: Petty Traders," *MECW*, *Vol. 11*, p. 90. (*New-York Daily Tribune*, No. 3576, October 2, 1852.)

An early, complementary comment on Bakunin and his role in the 1849 Dresden uprising, "The working men ... found *an able and cool-headed commander in the Russian refugee Michael Bakunin ...*"

Marx, Karl. "Pauperism and Free Trade - The Approaching Commercial Crisis," October 12, 1852, *MECW*, *Vol. 11*, pp. 357–63. (*N.Y. Daily Tribune,* No. 3601, Nov. 1, 1852.)

Periodical cycles of 5–7 years: stages: quiescence - improvement - growing confidence - activity - prosperity - excitement - overtrading - convulsion - pressure - stagnation - distress - quiescence. In the process of critiquing both Free Traders and anti-Free Traders on the impact of Free Trade on pauperism, Marx argues that pauperism rises and falls with the cycle. In comments similar to Engels' in his letter of Sept. 24th, Marx argues that the next crisis will be severe because capital is being invested in factories rather than commerce or financial speculation. The next crisis, he says "will take a far more dangerous character than in 1847, when it was more commercial and monetary than industrial. This time it will fall with its heaviest weight upon the manufacturing districts ... The more surplus capital concentrates itself in industrial production ... the more extensive, the more lasting, the more direct will the crisis fall upon the working masses and upon the very elite of the middle class." He goes on to note that a vast influx of gold due to exports outstripping imports is creating a situation of low interest rates and easy money which "regularly opens, in the commercial cycle, that phase where prosperity passes into excitement, where on the one hand over-trading in imports, on the other, wild speculations in all sorts of attractive bubbles .... Excitement is the highest apex of prosperity; it does not produce the crisis, but it provokes its outbreak."

Marx, Karl. "Political Consequences of the Commercial Excitement," October 12, 1852, *MECW*, *Vol. 11*, pp. 364–68. (*N.Y. Daily Tribune*, No. 3602, Nov. 2, 1852.)

Marx argues that during the prosperity, "The mass of the people is fully employed and more or less well off ... it is therefore not at present a very malleable material for political agitation." Also, the bourgeoisie is preoccupied with making money and not with supporting its representatives in Parliament. So, the Tories, he says are making hay while the sun shines in the political sphere: taxes to help farmers, attacking political opponents in the courts, limiting their opponents' efforts to get new electors, building a militia, etc.

Marx, Karl. "Attempts to Form a New Opposition Party," October 16, 1852, *MECW*, *Vol. 11*, pp. 376–77. (*N.Y. Daily Tribune*, No. 3622, Nov. 25, 1852.)

While analyzing various efforts to reorganize the opposition to the Tories, Marx argues that material prosperity has produced "political flaccidity and indifference" and that "the people are too indolent to create, for the moment, a movement of their own."

Engels, Friedrich to Karl Marx, November 29, 1852, *MECW*, *Vol. 39*, pp. 252–53.

"Fortunately, the only circumstance which might have brought over-production in the cotton industry to a premature end has now been eliminated; the new crop will be far in excess of 3 million bales, i.e., the biggest there has ever been, ... only let the corn harvest fail next year and we shall see a merry dance. But unless it does so, it is difficult to say whether anything decisive will happen as early as next year [1853], given the abnormal conditions, given the mushroom growth of markets in Australia and California ..., given the new market which the Calcutta houses are already exploiting in Burma ... "

1853

Marx, Karl to Friedrich Engels, January 29, 1853, *MECW, Vol. 39*, pp. 274–77.

Poor winter crops lead Marx to think "that the crisis will become due."

Marx, Karl to Friedrich Engels, March 10, 1853, *MECW, Vol. 39*, pp. 287–89.

Letter asking Engels to write some articles about the "Eastern Question"—the recurrence of conflict between Russia and Western Europe over Turkey, a recurrence which would soon lead to the Crimean War. Marx makes the appeal because "What is to become of the Turkish Empire is something I have no clue about. I cannot therefore present a general perspective." He then goes on, however, to suggest an outline of subject matter to Engels that includes: commercial interests, [those interests of Russia and England were in conflict]; "Turkey will compel England to come in on the revolutionary side, an Anglo-Russian clash being inevitable in such a case." [which is more or less what happened]; and "inevitable disintegration of Mussulman Empire [which] ... will fall into the hands of European civilization." [which is also what happened]

Engels, Friedrich. "The Real Issue in Turkey," between March 23 & 28, 1853, *MECW, Vol. 12*, pp. 13–17. (*New York Daily Tribune,* No. 3740, April 12, 1853.)

Engels' second article on the conflict in the Crimean. Here he traces the commercial rivalry between England and Russia, noting "The supreme necessity of a never-ceasing expansion of trade—this fatum which, specter-like, haunts modern England, and, if not appeased at once, brings on those terrible revulsions which vibrate from New York to Canton, and from St. Petersburg to Sidney—this inflexible necessity has caused the interior of Asia to be attacked from two sides by English trade." Thus, England needs to control the trade outlets of the Crimea to avoid economic crisis at home. Moreover, in the clash between Russia & Absolutism versus Revolution & Democracy, "let Russia get possession of Turkey, and her strength is increased nearly half, and she becomes superior to all the rest of Europe put together. Such an event would be an unspeakable calamity to the revolutionary cause ... In this instance the interests of the revolutionary Democracy and of England go hand in hand."

Engels, Friedrich. "What is to Become of Turkey in Europe?" April 1853, *MECW, Vol. 12*, pp. 32–36. (*New York Daily Tribune,* No. 3748, April 21, 1853.)

In this article Engels draws political conclusions from his analysis of the Crimean situation and argues for English support for Slavonian freedom from both Turkish and Russian rule via the creation of an "independent Christian state on the ruins of the Moslem Empire in Europe" which would "inaugurate the long-maturing conflict between Russian Absolutism and European Democracy." By European democracy, of course, what he means is the historical movement set in motion by the French Revolution and renewed in 1848.

Engels, Friedrich to Weydemeyer, April 12, 1853, *MECW*, *Vol. 39*, pp. 303–11.

Speculation in cotton, damaged winter and spring crops … "the present prosperity cannot last beyond the autumn."

Engels, Friedrich to Karl Marx, April 26, 1853, *MECW*, *Vol. 39*, pp. 319–20.

French commerce in trouble. Drop in cotton imports. Displacement of French exports by domestic manufactures in England and America.

Marx, Karl. "Russian Policy Against Turkey – The Labor Movement in England," July 1, 1853, *MECW*, *Vol. 12*, pp. 168–173. (*N.Y. Daily Tribune*, No. 3819, Jul. 14, 1853.)

Commentary on spread of strikes. "Without the great alternative phases of dullness, prosperity, over-excitement, crisis and distress, which modern industry traverses in periodically recurring cycles, with the up and down of wages and profits, the working classes of Great Britain, and all of Europe, would be a heart-broken, a weak-minded, a worn-out, unresisting mass, whose self-emancipation would prove as impossible as that of the slaves of Ancient Greece and Rome."

Marx, Karl. "The War Question—Doings of Parliament—India," July 19, 1853, *MECW*, *Vol. 12*, pp. 212–13. (*New York Daily Tribune*, No. 3838, August 5, 1853.)

Marx notes Tsar's actions partly prompted by "more dangerous symptoms of self-emancipation manifest amongst the Slavonians" as well as the connection between economic crisis and the conflict in the Crimea: "The approaching industrial crisis, also, is affected and accelerated quite as much by this semi-Eastern complication, as by the completely Eastern complication of China. While the prices of corn are rising, business in general is suspended, at the same time that the rate of Exchange is setting against England, and gold is beginning to flow to the Continent."

Marx, Karl. "The Vienna Note – The US and Europe – Letters from Shumla – Peel's Bank Act," September 9, 1853, *MECW*, *Vol. 12*, pp. 292–300. (*N.Y. Daily Tribune*, No. 3881, September 24, 1853.)

An analysis and attack on [Robert] Peel's Bank [Charter] Act of 1844. Based on the currency school's quantity theory, the Act tried to force the Bank of England to maintain a tie between its issuance of notes and its bullion reserves. In a crisis, when bullion drain occurs, the Act required the bank to limit note issue to available backing. This forced the Issue Department to reduce note issue (not replace returned notes). If there was a need for more notes in a crisis, the Issue Department could requisition bullion from the Banking Department. But this forces the Banking Department to raise interest rates and reduce loans. This reduction of accommodation to business needs can "aggravate the disasters of a commercial crisis ... may ... transform every commercial stagnation into a monetary peril." Thus in 1847 the Act forced the Banking Department to raise interest rates and to stop payment of deposits and dividends. "It created amidst the real crisis a series of money panics in April and October 1847." The Department was saved from bankruptcy only the suspension of the Act on 25 Oct. 1847.

Marx, Karl. "Political Movements – Scarcity of Bread in Europe," September 13, 1853, MECW, *Vol. 12*, pp. 301–8. (*N.Y. Daily Tribune*, No. 3886, Sept. 30, 1853.)

Bullion drain, rising interest rates and glutted markets presage crisis. "But it is the bad harvest which, above all, will drive the long accumulated elements of a great commercial and industrial crisis to eruption ... corn, as it becomes appreciated, is only the more eagerly sought for, drawing depreciation of all other commodities ... A general bad harvest is in itself a general contraction of markets, at home and abroad ... the consequences of the dearth are already appearing ... bread riots" (in Italy and Belgium), problems in France, Austria and Prussia. "There are economical disasters and social convulsions which must be the sure forerunners of European revolution."

Marx, Karl. "The Western Powers and Turkey – Imminent Economic Crisis – Railway Construction in India," September 20, 1853, MECW, *Vol. 12*, pp. 309–17. (*N.Y. Daily Tribune*, No. 3889, October 4, 1853.)

Tight money, glutted markets, manufacturers are combining to cut production by lockout.

Marx, Karl. "The Western Powers and Turkey – Symptoms of Economic Crisis," September 23, 1853, MECW, *Vol. 12*, pp. 318–28. (*N.Y. Daily Tribune*, No. 3892, Oct. 7, 1853.)

Prosperity has been rolling along but signs of trouble are frequent. Short crops and rising prices of provisions will undercut demand for manufactured goods in the home market. "The demand for goods is decidedly falling off, while the supply increases every day." The coming on line of new factories now opening will, by spring, bring to bear on the market "new and stupendous" productive power that will dramatically add to overproduction. Marx notes that the impact of the Crimean conflict is still limited: "The fact is that the right sunshine of prosperity is for the moment hidden by gloomy clouds. No doubt the altered aspect of the Eastern dispute has contributed a good deal; but that affects the home, American and Colonial trade very little."

Marx, Karl. "Panic on the London Stock Exchange – Strikes," September 27, 1853, *MECW*, *Vol. 12*, pp. 329–34. (*N.Y. Daily Tribune*, No. 3900, Oct. 17, 1853.)

Falling stock prices due to rumors of war and of commercial difficulties. Sub-average crops, rising prices and increased imports. Widespread successful strikes for higher wages show changes in supply and demand favor workers. But, "the (negative) change in the general commercial prospects must change the relative position of the workpeople and their employers … should, as I suppose, the depression prove lasting, the workpeople will soon get the worst of it … But then their activity will soon be carried over to the political field and the new organization of trades, gained in the strikes, will be of immense value to them."

Engels, Friedrich to Karl Marx, September 29, 1853, *MECW*, *Vol. 39*, pp. 374–75.

Yarns and cotton down. "Over speculation in the Australian trade … In 4 weeks time the Australian crash should be well under way." "Manufactured goods are also coming down smartly, and here stocks are far more catastrophic than in the case of yarn. The manufacturers' decision to stop work thus kills two birds with one stone: 1. it disarms the workers, 2. it cuts down production."

Marx, Karl to Friedrich Engels, September 30, 1853, *MECW*, *Vol. 39*, pp. 375–76.

Marx tells Engels that in his strike articles, he has depicted the lockouts at Preston "as an attempt by the manufacturers to use the operatives, whose demands are forcing closure of the mills, to cover their retreat from overproduction" as well as "an attempt to starve the operatives into submission."

Marx, Karl to Friedrich Engels, October 12, 1853, *MECW*, *Vol. 39*, pp. 387–88.

Expectation of crisis in France. Failure of corn and grape harvests. Falling wages in Paris. Bread riots in Alsace-Lorraine. Falling demand. Closing of workshops beginning. "Hollowness of the entire credit system, turned into nothing more or less than a colossal institutionalized racket … the court itself dangerously exploiting fluctuations in the stocks."

Marx, Karl. "The Turkish Manifesto – France's Economic Position," October 18, 1853, *MECW*, *Vol. 12*, pp. 416–20. (*N.Y. Daily Tribune*, no. 3912, Oct. 31, 1853.)

Bad harvests in France lead government to repeal the Navigation Laws, to reduce tonnage dues on food, prohibit food exports and to fix the price of bread.

Marx, Karl. "The Labor Question," November 11–12, 1853, *MECW*, *Vol. 12*, pp. 460–63. (*N.Y. Daily Tribune*, No. 3936, November 28, 1853.)

Sarcastic article on British press attacks on workers' efforts to raise wages during the current prosperity. Marx both notes that workers are simply taking advantage of a situation in which "capital turns out to be abundant and labor to be scarce" and rebuffs the absurd suggestion that workers should save their increased wages and become capitalists. He also notes that the suggestion that workers should be spending more time in school ignores how the expansion of the factories is employing more and more children and women.

Marx, Karl. "The Turkish Wars - Industrial Distress," December 2, 1853, MECW, *Vol. 12*, pp. 523–26. (*N.Y. Daily Tribune*, No. 3952, December 16, 1853.)

Marx argues lockouts are "a financial measure on the part of the masters, as a sort of antidote to an industrial over-production." However, the lockouts "have revolutionized the industrial proletariat, and, stirred up by dear food and cheap labor, the political consequences will show themselves in due time."

Marx, Karl. "The Russian Victory – Position of England and France," December 13, 1853, MECW, *Vol. 12*, pp. 536–542. (*N.Y. Daily Tribune*, No. 3961, December 21, 1853.)

Discussion of Bonaparte's troubles at home: high price of provisions, stagnation of trade, exhaustion of the Imperial Exchequer. The peasantry are angry because of dragonnades and famine. Incendiarism spreads. The middle classes have found that military despotism doesn't eliminate industrial crisis and does increase financial crises through lavish expenditure, so it too is ready for a change of power. The proletariat waits.

1855

Marx, Karl. "The Crisis in Trade and Industry," January 8–22, 1855, MECW, *Vol. 13*, pp. 571–78. (*Neue Oder-Zeitung*, Nos. 17, 19, 33, 41, Jan. 11, 12, 20, 25, 1855.)

Looking at reports of glutted markets and bankruptcies, Marx concludes that "once again one of the great British crises in trade and industry has broken out." "the commercial cycle has again reached the point where overproduction and over speculation turn into a crisis." He goes on to argue that "such glutting of the world market has been achieved in spite of the improvisation of two new golden markets – Australia and California, in spite of the electric telegraph which has transformed the whole of Europe into one big commodity exchange, in spite of railways and steamships which have improved communication and therefore commerce to an incredible degree." Moreover, the crisis would have come on sooner if workers had not been successful in legally limiting the hours of labor. Marx also argues that the Crimean war was not responsible for the crisis as some were claiming. If anything, the war stimulated the economy by increasing the demand for ships, steel, weapons, etc. Nor did the cession of corn imports from Russia hurt the economy because of an excellent harvest in 1854 and increased imports from other countries. Overproduction, not war, was the problem and cause of the crisis.

Marx, Karl. "The Commercial Crisis in Britain," January 11, 1855, *MECW*, *Vol. 13*, pp. 585–89. (*N.Y. Daily Tribune*, No. 4294, Jan. 26, 1855.)

A variant on the previous article. Marx again argues that the Crimean war was not the cause of the crisis, although it might "dangerously aggravate the severe ordeal" by leading to increased taxes which "are certainly no cure for diminished incomes." The crisis was rather caused by overproduction as usual. With respect to the international circulation of the crisis he says (more clearly than in the last article): "In 1837 the American crisis followed at the heels of the English crisis of 1836, while now the English crisis follows in the tracks of the American one; but in both instances, the crisis may be traced to the same source – the fatal working of the English industrial system which leads to overproduction in Great Britain and to over speculation in all other countries."

Marx, Karl to F. Lassalle, January 23, 1855, *MECW*, *Vol. 39*, pp. 511–14.

While discussing the relationship between Free Trade and wages, Marx argues that the temporary rise in wages in 1853 was not attributable to Free Trade but "corresponds wholly to the rise that takes place in all years of prosperity." In fact, he argues free trade, by lowering the cost of food, made it possible for manufacturers to refuse to raise wages in 1849–52. They only rose in 1853 because of prosperity and large-scale emigration of workers out of England that reduced labor supply.

Marx, Karl. "Herbert's Re-election - The First Measures of the New Ministry - News from India," February 16, 1853, *MECW*, *Vol. 14*, pp. 21–23. (*Neue Oder-Zeitung*, No. 85, Feb. 20, 1855.)

Note on Manchester factories going short-time because of overproduction. "*The Manchester Guardian*" admitted last Wednesday that there was overproduction not only of manufactured goods but also of factories."

Marx, Karl. "The British Constitution," March 2, 1855, *MECW*, *Vol. 14*, pp. 53–56. (*Neue Oder-Zeitung*, No. 109, Mar. 6, 1855.)

Glut in American and British markets led British merchants to re-route goods to India, China, Australia and California which were soon glutted as well. Then came the business failures: cotton printers, ship owners, Australian and Californian merchants, then Chinese houses, finally the Indian. Also silk manufacturers and already the cotton spinners and manufacturers are on short time. What will be the political effects? First, the crisis will hit the working classes and its movement "which has more or less been dormant ... over the past six years ... will spring up again. The conflict between the industrial proletariat and the bourgeoisie will flare up again." And second, at the same time that the conflict between the bourgeoisie and the aristocracy that still has effective control over the government will reach its climax.

Marx, Karl. "The Crisis in England," March 2, 1855, *MECW*, *Vol. 14*, pp. 59–62. (*N.Y. Daily Tribune*, No. 4346, Mar. 24, 1855.)

Commercial and industrial crisis since Sept. 1854. Aggravated by difficulties in America, glutted markets in India, China, California, and Australia. Goods which could not be sold at home were shipped to these last four countries and they caused gluts there. Breakdown for calico textile manufacturers, ship owners, Australian and California merchants, then China traders, then Indian houses. "A few more months and the crisis will be at a height … when its effects begin to be fully felt among the working classes, then will that political movement begin again, which has been dormant for six years. Then will the working-men of England rise anew …"

Marx, Karl. "The Buying of Commissions – News from Australia," March 3, 1855, *MECW*, *Vol. 14*, pp. 63–66. (*Neue Oder-Zeitung* No. 111, March 7, 1855.)

Armed worker revolt in Australian gold fields against gold digging license tax on free labor, and against property qualification for parliamentary membership.

Marx, Karl. "Questions of Finance," May 19, 1855, *MECW*, *Vol. 14*, pp. 198–200. (*Neue Oder-Zeitung*, No. 233, May 22, 1855.)

Decline in business indicated by a drop in discount rates, rise of idle capital held in vaults as gold and as bank notes.

Marx, Karl. "The Commercial and Financial Situation," September 24, 1855, *MECW*, *Vol. 14*, pp. 534–36. (*Neue Oder-Zeitung*, No. 453, Sept. 28, 1855.)

Speculation, debt financed government expenditures and grain import are draining bullion from Bank of France and forcing it to raise its discount rate – this together with note and bond issues that vastly exceed their capital base is creating danger of a panic.

Marx, Karl. "The Official Financial Report," October 2, 1855, *MECW*, *Vol. 14*, pp. 554–56. (*Neue Oder-Zeitung*, No. 467, Oct. 6, 1855.)

Tax revenues far less than expected. Public preoccupation with future of Crédit Mobilier.

Marx, K. "The Bank of France - Reinforcements to the Crimea - The New Field Marshals," October 4, 1855, *MECW*, *Vol. 14*, pp. 557–59. (*Neue Oder-Zeitung*, No. 469, Oct. 8, 1855.)

Bank of England raising discount rate to stem outflow of gold caused by Bank of France which is "heading towards a crisis" having been converted into an "inverted credit pyramid" under Louis Napoleon.

1856

Engels, Friedrich to Karl Marx, April 14, 1856, *MECW, Vol. 40*, pp. 34–36.

Speculation growing in Germany and Russia. "This time the crash will be quite unprecedented; all the ingredients are there: intensity, universal scope, and the involvement of all propertied and ruling social elements." Speculation in communications in England and rapid growth of textile industry on the continent imperil outlook in England. "it is in this enormous leap forward of industry on the Continent that the most viable embryo of English revolution lies."

Marx, Karl. "Prussia," April 15, 1856, *MECW, Vol. 14*, pp. 657–61. (*New York Daily Tribune,* No. 4694, May 5, 1856.)

Comments on the rapid spread of speculation in Germany where "every shopkeeper is turned into an alchemist." Marx notes that the basis of this speculation, which is leading to financial crisis, lies in the recent accumulation of wealth by the industrial middle classes – based on textiles, railroads and insurance – and by the landlords (profits from high wartime prices).

Marx, Karl. "Speech at the Anniversary of The People's Paper," April 18, 1856, *MECW, Vol. 14*, pp. 655–56. (*The People's Paper,* No. 207, Apr. 19, 1856.)

"The antagonism between modern industry and science on the one hand, modern misery and dissolution on the other hand; this antagonism between the productive powers and the social relations of our epoch is a fact, palpable, overwhelming and not to be controverted."

Marx, Karl. "The French Crédit Mobilier," June 6, 1856, *MECW, Vol. 15*, pp. 8–13. (*The People's Paper,* No. 214, June 7, 1856, and *New York Daily Tribune,* No. 4735, June 21, 1856.)

First of three articles that draw attention to this new French financial enterprise, which was receiving much acclaim in England. Marx mentions the various enterprises in which the *Crédit Mobilier* holds an interest as well as the high rate of profit being reported on these investments. He explains how the *Crédit Mobilier* presents its operations of "financial intermediation": as "the conversion of the different titles of various enterprises through the means of consolidating them in one common fund." He explains how this is done: "by buying up with its own titles the titles of the various industrial concerns." Given that the *Crédit Mobilier* is backed by Napoleon, Marx calls this takeover of French industry "Imperial Socialism."

Marx, Karl. "The French Crédit Mobilier," June 12, 1856, *MECW, Vol. 15*, pp. 14–18. (*New York Daily Tribune,* No. 4737, June 24, 1856.)

Continuing his discussion of the *Crédit Mobilier*, Marx notes its political role in bolstering Napoleon in his political struggles. He also notes its philosophical background: St. Simonism and Proudhon who thought to eliminate class antagonisms through the manipulation of credit. Marx, for his part, goes on to argue that the *Crédit Mobilier*, far from being the savior of France, operates in such a way as to precipitate financial crisis.

Marx, Karl. "The French Crédit Mobilier," late June 1856, *MECW*, *Vol. 15*, pp. 19–24. (*New York Daily Tribune*, No. 4751, July 11, 1856.)

Finally, in this third article on the *Crédit Mobilier*, Marx sketches its speculative dealings and situates them within the generalized spread of speculative manias in France at the time. The *Crédit Mobilier*, Marx claims, buys up shares in an enterprise, and because it has done this, their prices rise, at which point selling them off: in short, "stock jobbing." This is accentuated by the *Crédit Mobilier* being obliged to invest where the rate of return is highest, and thus in shares "subject to great fluctuations and alterations of price." Moreover, Marx argues, the *Crédit Mobilier* tends to invest in fixed capital but not to supply operating capital and thus undermines the viability of its investments. He gives a description of the joint stock company, noting the growing numbers of workers organized by this kind of capitalism, workers "who become more dangerous in direct ratio to the decreasing number of its [capital's] representatives.

Marx, Karl. "The Economic Crisis in Europe," circa September 26, 1856, *MECW*, *Vol. 15*, pp. 109–12. (*New York Daily Tribune*, No. 4828, October 9, 1856.)

In the place of past speculative manias focused on one or few activities, Marx claims the present is characterized by generalized speculation, e.g., the *Crédit Mobilier*, and originates largely in France, but is fed by English capital which flows across the Channel to take part in the great gambling craze. He then notes the coarser and primitive forms of fraud in England and gives some examples.

Marx, Karl to Friedrich Engels, September 26, 1856, *MECW*, *Vol. 40*, pp. 70–72.

Increases in the banks' discount rates probably reaction to withdrawals of silver (then appreciating against gold). Increases are "precipitating the downfall of the vast speculative transactions and more specifically of the grand pawningshop at Paris." (probably *Crédit Mobilier* and Bank of France)

Engels, Friedrich to Karl Marx, September 27, 1856, *MECW*, *Vol. 40*, pp. 72–74.

Expectation of crisis in 1857 (it did come then). Speculators somewhat restrained by high prices of raw materials. Bullion withdrawals. Silver vanished.

Marx, Karl. "The Monetary Crisis in Europe," circa October 3, 1856, *MECW*, *Vol. 15*, pp. 113–16. (*New York Daily Tribune*, October 15, 1856.)

The monetary crisis in Europe, Marx argues, originated this time in Germany and sweeping West to France and hence to England. Marx claims the ruling classes of Europe fear the return of crisis because they fear the return of the Revolutions of 1848 and he claims they can sense that this time it will not just be a political revolution but a social revolution – "brought on by the public contrivances of the Crédits Mobiliers of the ruling classes." The crisis originated in Germany, Marx claims, because the Germans learned the lessons of the Crédit Mobilier quickly and developed speculation to a high degree. "This is the immediate cause of the panic having made its first and most widely spread appearance in Germany."

Marx, Karl. "The Causes of the Monetary Crisis in Europe," circa October 14, 1856, *MECW*, *Vol. 15*, pp. 117–22. (*New York Daily Tribune,* No. 4843, October 27, 1856; reprinted as "The Coming Crash" in the *New York Weekly Tribune,* No. 791, November 8, 1856.)

Money panic and gold flight in Germany leads to an increase in interest rates which reverses gold flow, leading the Bank of France to increase its interest rates to achieve the same result which in turn forces the Bank of England to increase its own interest rate to reverse outflows to France. Marx then discusses depreciation of gold (due to cheap gold production in American and Australia and huge imports of it to Europe) relative to silver and the drain of bullion into hoard and of silver out of Europe into Arab hoard and trade with Russia, India and China. Behind the money panic, he argues, lies "all the elements of commercial and industrial revulsion [which are] ripe in Europe and aggravated in France [by crop failures, floods, etc. which have forced increased imports and silver outflow] ... "

Marx, Karl. "The Monetary Crisis in Europe – From the History of Money Circulation," circa October 17, 1856, *MECW*, *Vol. 15*, pp. 123–29. (*New York Daily Tribune,* No. No. 4848, November 1, 1856; reprinted as "*The Crisis in Europe*," in the *New York Weekly Tribune,* no. 793, November 22, 1856.)

The continuing decline in Bank of France reserves leads it to buy gold from England through the Rothschild Bank which causes problems for the Bank of England without solving those of the Bank of France. Marx argues that the later will lose its gold as fast as it gets it because it must pay off foreign debts; it will be absorbed in interior hoard; it must replace silver which is being drained by foreign trade (from China and India especially) and to finance the railroad companies which are in increasingly dire straits. He then examines the international trade in silver and the ebb and flow of Asian demand, distinguishing three periods: 1. –1830, when silver exports to Asia were increasing; 2. 1831 – 1848, when they were lessening as Britain exported more to India than it imported (overtrading with India contributed to crisis of 1847); 3. 1849 to the present when exports of silver accelerated, prompted in part by the Chinese rebellion and refusal to buy foreign manufactures while British imports of tea continued to increase. This tendency was accelerated by failure of European silk crops which led to increased silk imports from China and silver exports from Europe.

Marx, Karl. "The Economic Crisis in France," circa November 7, 1856, *MECW*, *Vol. 15*, pp. 130–35. (*New York Daily Tribune*, No. 4866, November 22, 1856.)

Conflict between speculative and productive business for increasingly scarce capital is forcing up interest rates. Added to this is the demand for finance from the railroad companies who want to issue new paper to raise money but this is resisted by the government. Moreover, capital has flowed out of the country further increasing pressure on interest rates just as silver has flowed out of France (and Spain) making it difficult for companies to come up with cash money to pay wages. The high price of Chinese silk has brought some mills to a halt and the high price of cotton and difficulty of selling fabric causing unemployment and falling income for workers in that industry. On top of all this, are harvest failures, the withdrawal of labor from agriculture (for the Crimean War and railways), the flight of capital from the countryside into speculation, increasing taxes on the peasantry. All this leads Marx to focus on rising discontent, strikes and "insurrectionary placards" in the cities, incendiary fires in the countryside and the "revolutionary disposition" of the peasantry. "In view of all these facts, it seems hardly possible that French commerce and industry should avoid a collapse, attended by political events more or less serious."

Engels, Friedrich to Karl Marx, November 17 1856, *MECW*, *Vol. 40*, pp. 82–84.

Bonaparte in trouble with growing worker unrest. Bankruptcies in France. "It looks as though the financial crisis will linger on through the winter, becoming gradually more acute …" "Never again, perhaps, will the revolution find such a fine TABULA RASA as now. All socialist dodges exhausted …"

Marx, Karl. "The European Crisis," circa November 21, 1856, *MECW*, *Vol. 15*, pp. 136–38. (*New York Daily Tribune*, No. 4878, December 6, 1856.)

Continued speculation keeps up demand for money and interest rates; Crédit Mobilier having to pay cash to Austrian government, 2000 laid off by Grand Central Railroad contractors; Bank of France keeps "severest restriction upon loans, advances, discounts and emission of notes" but outflow of gold continues. The "final collapse of speculation" cannot be far off."

1857

Marx, Karl to Friedrich Engels, January 23, 1857, *MECW*, *Vol. 40*, p. 98.

Marx complaining about working for piece-wages: "It's truly nauseating that one should be condemned to count it a blessing when taken aboard by a blotting paper vendor such as this [the Tribune]. To crush up bones, grind them and make them into soup like PAUPERS in the WORKHOUSE – that's what the political work to which one is condemned in such large measure in a CONCERN like this boils down to. I am aware I have been an ass in giving these ladies more than their money's worth – not just recently but for years past."

Marx, Karl. "Crédit Mobilier," May 12 and 15, 1857, *MECW*, *Vol. 15*, pp. 270–77. (*New York Daily Tribune,* Nos. 5027 and 5028, May 30, and June 1, 1857; reprinted in the *New York Semi-Weekly Tribune,* no. 1254, June 2, 1857.)

Commenting on a report of the president of the Crédit Mobilier (CM), Marx shows that its real profits (dividends over interest) had decreased by nearly one half in the last year for those who paid the original 500 francs, for late-comers who may have paid up to 1500 francs the rate was much lower. He goes on to show how its attempts to raise new money for speculation in the wake of the end of the Crimean War was checked by the government. Moreover, speculative capital began to flow away from the government regulated "Societés Anonymes" (such as the CM.) toward the unregulated Sociétés en Commandité (limited liability stock issuing companies).

The CM blames Bank of France (BoF) for the violence of the crisis because it turned down a) an effort by CM in 1855 to issue bonds, and b) an offer by CM to purchase public debt in such a way as to permit the BoF to continue loaning against public debt and railway shares (of which the CM held a vast amount). "The proposal amounted, therefore, in fact, to an invitation to the Bank to keep the [public debt] held by itself off the market, in order to make place for the railway shares held by the Crédit Mobilier." – thus helping the CM increase the value of its shares and its ability to make money through their sale. The CM also offered to buy up all French Railway Company loans, which would have made it their proprietor – this was rejected. In essence, Marx argues, all it is trying to do is borrow money from the public to lend to stock speculators while speculating itself on the increased prices produced by its loans!

Marx, Karl to Friedrich Engels, May 22, 1857, *MECW*, *Vol. 40*, pp. 132–34.

Commentary on the continuing problems of the Crédit Mobilier in France. Fall in profits. "the Crédit's business is still vastly disproportionate to its capital and … it has used the capital loaned by the public exclusively to further its gambles on the Bourse."

Marx, Karl. "The French Crédit Mobilier," September 8, 1857, *MECW*, *Vol. 15*, pp. 357–60. (*New York Daily Tribune,* No. 5128, September 8, 1857.)

Value of shares of CM falling (from about 950f to 850f lately) in response to revelations about bankruptcy of one of its directors. But, Marx argues there are reasons to think the whole company is on a long downhill slide, not only have its share values fallen steadily (though with oscillations) from their high of 1900f but some of the directors are bailing out.

Marx, Karl to Friedrich Engels, October 20, 1857, *MECW*, *Vol. 40*, pp. 191–95.

"The American crisis ... is beautiful and has had immediate repercussions on French industry, since silk goods are now being sold in New York more cheaply than they are produced in Lyons." Data on the growth of Crédit Mobilier debt.

Marx, Karl. "The Bank Act of 1844 and the Monetary Crisis in England," November 6, 1857, *MECW*, *Vol. 15*, pp. 379–84. (*New York Daily Tribune,* no. 5176, November 21, 1857.)

An account of the structure and workings of the Bank of England under the Bank Act of 1844. Marx shows how the workings of the bank aggravate crises, as in 1847, and suggests that as the American crisis of 1857 reduces English exports (as does the cut off in the Indian trade brought on by "insurrectionary convulsions" and the glut in Australia) the same kind of cycle will be repeated once more in England. "Insurrectionary convulsions" refers to the Indian Rebellion of 1857, that lasted from May 1857 to June 1858, against the British East India Company, that was begun by Indian soldiers (Sepoys) in the Company's army and then spread to civilians. The revolt was so widespread that it led to direct rule by the English government and Queen Victoria promising Indians rights equal to those of British citizens. Marx published a series of articles in 1857 and 1858 on the revolt. So, here Marx traces the "monetary crisis in England" to commercial crises.

Marx, Karl. "The British Revulsion," November 13, 1857, *MECW*, *Vol. 15*, pp. 385–91. (*New York Daily Tribune,* no. 5183, November 30, 1857.)

Title in Marx's notebook: "English Monetary Crisis, Suspension of Peel's Act." In this article, Marx deals with "three distinct forms" of crisis: (1) "pressure on the money and produce markets of London and Liverpool," (2) "a bank panic in Scotland," and (3) "an industrial breakdown in manufacturing."

(1) Marx documents how, prior to appealing to the government for suspension of Peel's Bank Act of 1844, the Bank of England had repeatedly raised its rate of discount – up to 10% – even faster than it had done in the crisis of 1847. He also notes the 10% is "merely nominal" and, citing business newspapers, that not only does "the interest really paid by first-class paper in London, greatly [exceed] that figure," but "second and third class paper" can obtain no accommodation whatsoever. The result: "firms are falling whose assets exceed their liabilities" – because they cannot borrow, for any purpose, including buying raw materials. This collapse of demand, coupled with increased imports from the US, has produced falling commodity prices.

(2) The monetary crisis of the Bank of England has been intensified by its need to transfer huge sums to banks in Scotland, and to a lesser degree in Ireland, to help them ward off collapse due to "a general run of depositors among the middle class and of note holders among the working classes." Among those threatened with collapse were the Western Bank of Scotland and the City of Glasgow Bank. The panic resulted in

"riotous disturbances" and the "aid of bayonets" to quiet them. Marx notes the "capital of these banks was to a large extent furnished in small sums by the agricultural population."

(3) The "industrial breakdown in manufacturing" – including large scale layoffs (short time) and mill closures – is due to the collapse of demand coupled with overstocked inventories from over-expanded production capacity.

Finally, Marx ends with some observations on the international circulation of the crisis (beyond that from the United States to England): from Sweden to Italy, from Madrid to Pesth and from England to France – as the Bank of France has increased its rates in response to the increases by the Bank of England and falling domestic demand has led the government to revoke prohibitions on the export of wheat. [In the case of circulation from the United States to England, Marx might also have mentioned (1) the failure of remittances to British banks in general and (2) the failure of some Scottish banking speculations in American, e.g., those of the Western Bank of Scotland.]

Engels, Friedrich to Karl Marx, November 15, 1857, MECW, *Vol. 40*, pp. 200–204.

Discussion of growing speculation in shares and raw materials; collapse of speculation in New York will hurt European investors who put money into New York markets; return of unsold English goods from America; spurt in Indian trade; expectation of long and big crisis after 10 years of prosperity. "A period of chronic pressure is needed to get the people's blood up. The proletariat will then fight better ... The long period of prosperity is bound to have made the masses damned lethargic."

Marx, Karl to Friedrich Engels, November 24, 1857, MECW, *Vol. 40*, pp. 208–10.

(1) Monetary panic in London has subsided. (2) Will begin again due to outflow of gold to France. (3) Suspension of Bank Act of 1844 will help (via increase circulation of notes). (4) Fall in prices of corn, sugar, etc. will cause bankruptcies. (5) Joint stock banks supporting money market by mobilizing small capitals at 1% less than Bank of England.

Marx, Karl. "The Trade Crisis in England," November 27, 1857, MECW, *Vol. 15*, pp. 400–3. (*New York Daily Tribune*, no. 5196, December 15, 1857.)

The "trade crisis" seems to have involved the bankruptcy of several merchant capitalists. In his commentary, Marx begins by mocking those journalists in *The London Times* who, after heralding free trade as the panacea for commercial crises, now lament, with moral indignation, "gangs of reckless speculators and fictitious bill drawers" characterizing them as new "Roman censors of modern money-lending. Against such efforts to blame the crisis on "the recklessness of single individuals" Marx argues that "it must not be forgotten that speculation itself was engendered in the previous phases ... and is therefore, itself a result ... instead of the final cause ..." While crisis in America at first "manifested itself [in Great Britain] as a monetary panic, he argues, now [1857] "the industrial crisis now stands at the top and the monetary difficulty at the bottom."

He goes on to argue that ups and downs in money markets can occur quite independently of the situation in industry – the value of "London paper" *rises* when the Bank of England buys more gold, while the value of "Manchester paper" *falls* in anticipation of an expected rise in interest rates and fall in the prices of manufacturing products. Or, while the Bank of England "recovers," the Northumberland & Durham District Bank goes bankrupt – which, he points out, will bring on the "stoppage of the great collieries and iron-works carried on by the advances of this bank."

Finally, Marx argues that it is "perfectly understood" that as the Bank of England has bought more gold, it has also "screwed up the rate of interest" with the following predictable effects: on the one hand, decreased imports and increased exports – which would presumably aid the merchants handling international trade – and, on the other hand, a reflux of British capital from abroad (thus a further increase in gold reserves). These results, he argues, can only be sustained as long as the Bank of England has the resources to keep up the "discount" [rate of interest which, he says, was "successively advanced to 6, 7 and 8 percent"]. The success of this policy, he predicts, will be short lived – not only because the Bank of England may not be able to sustain the higher rate of interest, but because foreign markets are becoming "overstocked" (glutted). One reason for the shrinkage of foreign markets, he notes, was "news of the Indian mutinies" that resulted in exports to India being diverted elsewhere.

Marx, Karl. "The Financial Crisis in Europe," December 4, 1857, *MECW*, *Vol. 15*, pp. 404–9. (*New York Daily Tribune*, no. 5202, December 22, 1857.)

"Hamburg still formed the center of the convulsion" with varying shocks to Prussia, Spain, Italy, Sweden, England and France. The financial crisis, i.e., inadequate money, resulted from a commercial crisis, i.e., drop in demand and inability to sell at profitable prices. In Hamburg, first a private effort – a Guaranteed Discount Association – then a government one sought to stem commercial panic, the first by guaranteeing some bills and notes and the second by issuing "securities bearing interest." Prussia followed by "authorizing the Berlin Bank to advance loans on goods deposited and by suspending the usury laws." None of this succeeded in restoring trade, so the inability to sell (commercial crisis) was spreading to industry. The result: "the palsy of industrial activity and the consequent distress of the laboring classes are rapidly spreading." About this government effort, Marx writes, "In other words, the fortune of the whole community, which the Government represents, ought to make good for the losses of private capitalists. This sort of communism, where the mutuality is all on one side, seems rather attractive to the European capitalists." True in 1857, true in 2008 as governments bailed out investors at the expense of everyone else.

Marx then turns to England – that has been relatively immune so far – and foresees commercial crisis in 1858 due to the repeal of the Corn Laws going into effect, new agricultural imports from France and the United States that are unlikely to be sufficiently offset by British exports to India resulting from the suppression of the rebellion in that country.

Engels, Friedrich to Karl Marx, December 7, 1857, *MECW*, *Vol. 40*, pp. 211–13.

(1) Corrects Marx (of 24 Nov. '57): drawees of bills cannot discount them, only pay them when due. (2) Falling commodity prices are producing bankruptcies. (3) Some big houses are saving themselves by borrowing from Bank of England. (4) Sales to India and Mid-East are helping some manufacturers. (5) Hamburg in panic collapse: "Everything is worthless, utterly worthless, save for silver and gold."

Marx, Karl to Friedrich Engels, December 8, 1857, *MECW*, *Vol. 40*, pp. 214–17.

(1) Marx makes fun of his own mistake. (2) Corn prices down, will fall even further with spring shipments from US and France – more bankruptcies, effects of repeal of corn laws will finally be felt. (3) His prediction of suspension of bank act and crisis laughed at, then vindicated! (4) French government trying to block gold, corn, silk and wine exports, but drain will come and with it crisis. (5) State capitalists can last longer than private capitalists. (6) "I am working like mad all night and every night collating my economic studies so that I at least get the outlines clear before the deluge."

Engels, Friedrich to Karl Marx, December 9, 1857, *MECW*, *Vol. 40*, pp. 218–19.

(1) Hamburg bills being discounted at 12 and 1/2 per cent! (2) Liverpool and London produce houses on verge of bankruptcy. (3) "monetary speculation was the least important factor in the crisis."

Engels, Friedrich to Karl Marx, December 11, 1857, *MECW*, *Vol. 40*, pp. 220–22.

Overproduction unusually general: colonial produce and corn, industry and agriculture. General overtrading based on expansion of credit, even paying interest not bills – leads to expansion of production beyond the rise of consumption. "This alone would be bound to precipitate a crisis." "The present crisis provides an opportunity for a detailed study of how overproduction is generated by the expansion of credit and by overtrading."

Engels, Friedrich to Karl Marx, December 17, 1857, *MECW*, *Vol. 40*, pp. 222–24.

Four distinct crises: (1) colonial produce, (2) corn, (3) spinners and manufacturers, (4) home trade. In Germany as in England "the temporary disruption of the money market has a less severe effect than the protracted period over which goods have been unsaleable." "There are as yet few signs of revolution, for the long period of prosperity has been fearfully demoralizing. The unemployed on the streets continue to beg and to idle away their time."

Marx, Karl to Friedrich Engels, December 18, 1857, *MECW*, *Vol. 40*, pp. 224–25.

"I am working enormously, as a rule until 4 o'clock in the morning. I am engaged in a twofold task: 1. elaborating the outlines of political economy ... 2. the present crisis ... all I do is keep records."

Marx, Karl. "The Crisis in Europe," December 18, 1857, *MECW*, *Vol. 15*, pp. 410–12. (*New York Daily Tribune,* No. 5213, January 5, 1858; reprinted in *New York Semi-Weekly Tribune,* No. 1316, January 5, 1858.)

A short survey of crisis – drawing information from Engels' letters above – in England, Germany, Sweden and Denmark emphasizes three aspects: (1) an easing of English money markets, (2) collapsing prices in English produce markets, (3) increasing failures of English textile manufacturing firms and (4) monetary crisis in Germany, Sweden and Denmark where no bills can be discounted.

Marx, Karl to Friedrich Engels, December 25, 1857, *MECW*, *Vol. 40*, pp. 228–32.

Summary of conclusions on French Crisis: (1) Crisis in England, N. Europe, US never produce bullion drain crises in France because France has a favorable balance of trade with them. But drain can come from capital exports to higher discount rates in those countries. (2) First phase of crisis has arrived. (3) In France the first effect of crisis is a decline in business and a decline in circulation of bank discounts. At the end of the year Louis Philippe ordered the bank to reduce bank rates to 4% to avoid political problems so things picked up a little. (4) Increased availability of capital buoys the bourse. (5) Crisis in Holland, Belgium, Italy, etc. where France has unfavorable trade balance will cause monetary panic in France. (6) In France biggest gambling and swindling is done by State through Crédit Mobilier, etc.

Marx, Karl. "The French Crisis," December 25, 1857, *MECW*, *Vol. 15*, pp. 413–18. (*New York Daily Tribune,* No. 5219, January 12, 1858.)

This article, which repeats much of what Marx wrote to Engels (see above), argues that while the crisis in France has so far been limited, it is getting worse and will get much worse. Despite trade surpluses with the US, the UK and the Hanseatic towns, demand elsewhere has been drying up causing reduced production (short time), increased unemployment to such a degree that the state has extended credit to help create jobs and appealed for increased private charity. But it has also "ordered military precautions to be taken in [hard-hit] Lyons." The commercial stagnation has been accompanied by a decrease in circulation and growing numbers of bankruptcies. The government has also failed to stem the precipitous fall in the prices of wheat and flour.

Crises elsewhere in Europe, e.g., within the Zollverein, the Black Sea and Levantine trade and in Italy risk bringing on a run on the French capital market as holders of French securities try to cash them in. The danger is augmented by way the government has forced the Bank of France to buy new bonds from railway whose values, in the case of a run, will collapse, endangering the bank itself.

Marx, Karl to Friedrich Engels, December 25, 1857, *MECW*, *Vol. 40*, pp. 228–32.

Summary of conclusions on French Crisis: (1) Crisis in England, N. Europe, US never produce bullion drain crises in France because France has a favorable balance of trade with them. But drain can come from capital exports to higher discount rates in those countries. (2) First phase of crisis has arrived. (3) In France the first effect of crisis is a decline in business and a decline in circulation of bank discounts. At the end of the year Louis Philippe ordered the bank to reduce bank rates to 4% to avoid political problems so things picked up a little. (4) Increased availability of capital buoys the bourse. (5) Crisis in Holland, Belgium, Italy, etc. where France has unfavorable trade balance will cause monetary panic in France. (6) In France biggest gambling and swindling is done by State through Crédit Mobilier, etc.

Engels, Friedrich to Karl Marx, December 31, 1857, *MECW*, *Vol. 40*, pp. 233–36.

"Just now people here are deluding themselves into thinking that the crisis is over because the first phase, the monetary crisis, … is over" But prices of commodities will fall and commercial crisis will come.

1858

Engels, Friedrich to Karl Marx, January 6, 1858, *MECW*, *Vol. 40*, pp. 239–40.

Crisis at stand-still, should blow up in February or March with spring shipments of raw materials and produce that will drop prices.

Marx, Karl. "British Commerce," circa January 7, 1858, *MECW*, *Vol. 15*, pp. 425–34. (*New York Daily Tribune*, No. 5238, February 3, 1858.)

Critiquing reports and debates over England's foreign trade deficit, Marx points out that the deficit is inevitable given the way in which England's capital has been increasingly loaned abroad, financed competitors to English manufacturers – especially in the woolen textile industry – and received its profits largely in the form of imported raw materials – often re-exported to those same foreign competitors. The result is a high price for wool, high costs for British manufacturers, increased foreign competition, a reduced ability to sell/export and crisis in the industry. Moreover, he points out, the manufacturers use their crisis to impose one on the working class: the "small margin of profit thus left to the British manufacturer … is then compensated for by curtailing the wages of the laboring classes and creating home misery on a rapidly-enlarging scale."

Engels, Friedrich to Karl Marx, January 25, 1858, *MECW, Vol. 40*, pp. 252–53.

Cotton business in Manchester shaky, low domestic demand. Irregular sales to Indian and Levantine buyers temporarily raise prices, which soon fall again.

Marx, Karl. "The Economic Crisis in France," February 12, 1858, *MECW, Vol. 15*, pp. 459–63. (*New York Daily Tribune*, No. 5270, March 12, 1858.)

Commenting on the economic crisis in France, Marx begins, and ends, by pointing to the precariousness of the position of Louis Napoleon and the threat of deepening crisis to political stability. He makes several interesting points. (1) The crisis in France is part of a wider economic crisis that has circulated internationally, having come closer to an end elsewhere, so "the crash [in France] is still impending." (2) The Bank of France has been having to pay higher premiums to keep up its gold stocks even as "the activity of trade has diminished." (3) The Bank, under pressure from the government, has twice renewed bills and loans that could not be paid, in order to ward off a fall in prices due to "depressed trade," high unemployment and reduced demand. "Thus," he writes, "more or less directly, the means of the French people, accumulated in bank vaults, have been employed to keep up inflated prices against that very people." (4) The result has been an "enormous accumulation of commodities in the Customs entrepots" that will inevitably have to be dumped on the market – an action that will produce a "violent self-adjustment of prices." This has already begun with bread-stuffs and the resulting drop in the price of wheat is causing a crisis for the French peasantry's ability to meet its mortgage payments. (5) Therefore, he concludes, the "agricultural distress, taken together with the depression of trade, the stagnation of industry, and the commercial catastrophe still in suspense, must tend to bring the French people into that state of mind in which they are wont to embark in fresh political ventures. With the disappearance of material prosperity and its regular appendage of political indifference, every pretext for the prolongation of the second Empire also disappears."

Marx, Karl to Friedrich Engels, February 22, 1858, *MECW, Vol. 40*, pp. 272–74.

Complementing his remarks on the "Economic Crisis in France" about the international crisis finally reaching its nadir in that country, Marx comments to Engels about the further circulation of crisis, "There is no doubt, there will be a crash in France, answered by crashes in Belgium, Holland, Rhenish Prussia etc." Optimistically, he ends the letter with "Taken all in all, the crisis has been burrowing away like the good old mole it is."

Marx, Karl to Friedrich Engels, March 5, 1858, *MECW*, *Vol. 40*, pp. 282–84.

Thirteen-year replacement cycle of machinery more or less "coincides with periodicity of crisis." "For me the important thing is to discover, in the immediate material postulates of big industry ONE factor that determines cycles."

Engels, Friedrich to Karl Marx, March 17, 1858, *MECW*, *Vol. 40*, pp. 289–93.

Rescheduling debt "to overcome a crisis can be of avail only if the resumption of business is a REAL one in industry too."

Marx, Karl. "The Financial State of France," April 13, 1858, *MECW*, *Vol. 15*, pp. 499–503. (*New York Daily Tribune*, No. 5312, April 30, 1858.)

Commenting on attempts to silence journalists blowing the whistle on the financial problems of various corporations supported by the government, Marx accuses the state of trying to cover-up the "impending breaking up of that monster imposture [the Crédit Mobilier]." The Crédit Mobilier's impending breakup, he suggests, is manifested in the falling value of its shares and an array of recently revealed speculations, embezzlements and frauds in several closely connected corporations. Moreover, he points out, the Bank of France – that had been forced by the government to finance various railway companies – is now stuck with railway bonds it is unable to sell because of the "continuous falling off in receipts" in those companies. All of which comes of Bonaparte "sinking capital in unproductive works" – unproductive in the sense of real returns on investment. This, however, was no barrier to the high profits made by insiders who sold initial shares at high prices, pawning eventual disaster off on those who bought them and then saw their value decline precipitously. In short, the state of both private and state finance is one of growing crisis. [This account should evoke the more recent story of how US banks pawned securities, based on bundled and fraudulently constructed sub-prime debt, off on unsuspecting buyers who then lost massively as the rate of default soared and the value of those securities plummeted.]

Marx, Karl. *Grundrisse,* October 1857 - May 1858, New York: Pelican Books, 1973, Baltimore: Penguin, 1993, pp. 115–134, 321–26, 401–50, 699–712, 745–67, or *MECW, Vol. 28* and *Vol. 29*.

This is the first of several very large works by Marx & Engels that contains so much material relevant to the issue of crisis that I have merely summarized what I take to be the most important passages and not tried to include all those germane to the essay. A few are included below but many others will be found within the text rather than here.

Chapter on Money: pp. 115–238, or *MECW, Vol. 28*, pp. 51–170.

Marx begins his notebooks with a reading/attack on Alfred Darimon, a follower of Proudhon. Darimon argued that the Banque de France's restrictive monetary policy of raising the discount rate was the cause of crisis in 1855. Marx points out that the Banque's actions (a response to a gold drain brought on by crop failures and increased imports, and also by the Crimean war's unproductive expenditures, Crédit Mobilier's foreign ventures and speculation in finance and trade) were normal practices. The central bank cannot, as Darimon seems to think, control the means of circulation.

The crop failures, by necessitating imports, diverted demand from other goods and would, by itself cause their prices to fall and a "general crisis." "The crisis reduces itself simply to the law of supply and demand, which, as is known, acts far more sharply and energetically within the sphere of primary needs – seen on a national scale – than in all other spheres. Exports of gold are not the cause of the grain crisis, but the grain crisis is the cause of gold exports." (p. 130, or MECW, *Vol. 28*, p. 68)

At the same time, Marx seizes on the occasion to attack the general Proudhonist position that crises can be avoided by changes in the money and credit system. "Can the existing relations of production and the relations of distribution which correspond to them be revolutionized by a change in the instrument of circulation, in the organization of circulation?" Marx asks rhetorically. His answer is, of course, no. "How to overcome the rise and fall (crisis) of prices. The way to do this: abolish prices. And how? By doing away with exchange value. But the problem arises: exchange corresponds to the bourgeois organization of society. Hence one last problem: to revolutionize bourgeois society economically." (p. 134, or MECW, *Vol. 28*, p. 72) Much of what follows in the Chapter on Money is an elaboration on the logic of this passage.

Darimon's, and Proudhon's, solutions that seek to destroy the special privileges of gold as money by making all commodities money ignore that "the bourgeois system of exchange itself *necessitates* a specific instrument of exchange." (p. 127) It is important to see the path of Marx's thought in these pages. From the critique of the Proudhonist economic analysis of crisis at the level of money and circulation – gold drain and Banque de France actions – Marx moves to the underlying crisis in production – crop failure – and argues that breakdown in production will produce crisis even without reference to money and circulation because of the need to divert resources from other pursuits. "The replacement of a sudden or chronic shortage of (grain, tea, cotton, flax, etc.) in the case of a domestic crop failure deprives the nation doubly. A part of its invested capital or labour is not reproduced – real loss of production. A part of that capital which has been reproduced has to be shifted to fill this gap ... A crisis caused by a failure in the grain crop is therefore not at all created by the drain of bullion ... Exports of gold are not the cause of the grain crisis, but the grain crisis is the cause of gold exports." (pp. 120, 127–130, or MECW, *Vol. 28*, pp. 58–59, 65–68. True locally, true internationally: "This distinction between domestic and foreign, incidentally, is altogether illusory. The relation between the nation which suffers a crop failure and another nation where the former makes purchases is like that between every individual of the nation and the farmer or grain merchant. The surplus sum which it must expend in purchasing grain is a direct subtraction from its capital, from its disposable means." (pp. 128–29; *MECW*, *Vol. 28*, p. 67.)

In the pages of the Chapter on Money that follow this section, Marx's path explores the result of exchange "necessitating" a general equivalent. In this exploration he goes from exchange and money to labor time and value and shows that money is the independent form of exchange value, and thus that it is impossible to abolish money without abolishing the system of commodity exchange.

In his analysis he explores the separations that appear in exchange, between the use-value and exchange value of a commodity, between the function of exchange for the merchant and its function for the consumer. The different functions have different laws, which can be in contradiction. It is in this separation that the "possibility of commercial crises is already contained." (p. 149, or *MECW*, *Vol. 28*, p. 86.) Indeed, crisis lurks in the very nature of commodities. "The simple fact that the commodity exists doubly, in one aspect as a specific product ... and in the other aspect as manifest exchange value (money) ... this double, differentiated existence must develop into a difference, and the difference into antithesis and contradiction ... this contradiction ... contains the possibility that these two separated forms in which the commodity exists are not convertible into one another ... the exchangeability of the commodity for money ... may or may not be present." (p. 147, or *MECW*, *Vol. 28*, p. 84–85.) And "Just as the exchange value of a commodity leads a double existence ... so does the act of exchange split into two mutually independent acts ... purchase and sale. Since these have now achieved spatially and temporally separate and mutually indifferent form of existence, their immediate identity ceases. They may correspond or not ... consonance may be reached only by passing through the most extreme dissonance." i.e., crisis. (p. 148, or *MECW*, *Vol. 28*, pp. 85–86.) "There are contradictions which are unpleasant for the apologists of bourgeois common sense, and must hence be covered up. In so far as purchase and sale ... are indifferent to each other and separated in time and space, they by no means need to coincide ... But in so far as they are both essential moments of the whole, there must come a moment when the independent form is violently broken and when the inner unity is established externally through a violent explosion ... in the splitting of exchange into two acts, there lies the germ of crises, or at least their possibility" (p. 198, or *MECW*, *Vol. 28*, p. 133.)

Money as the incarnation of exchange value represents exchange as a system and as such stands as a "social power" "alien" to and confronting and subordinating the worker - producers. (p. 157) This, of course, is money as capital standing against and over workers. Yet, Marx says within this situation "there arise (antithetical) relations of circulation as well as of production which are so many mines to explode it." (p. 159, or *MECW*, *Vol. 28*, p. 96) From crisis and money to production & class struggle, to revolution, such is Marx's initial path in the *Grundrisse*. Here is the great leap forward of the *Grundrisse*: the monetary and commercial and industrial crises of the nineteenth century which Marx had been studying for so long are shown to be rooted in the value relations of capitalist class relations with all its antithesis and violence. Proudhonist attempts to change the system by tinkering with its money forms are doomed to failure. The system cannot be reformed out of existence, only exploded.

Chapter on Capital: pp. 321–26, or *MECW, Vol. 28*, pp. 246–51

In this section which begins with a discussion of surplus value and the value of labor-power, Marx evokes the tendency of productivity to rise with the development of capitalism. While at this point, he treats this tendency only as the result of capital "whipping it onward with its unlimited mania for wealth" and of capital's "ceaseless striving," thus failing to deal with growth as integral to the class struggle, he does focus on the possibilities created by this process for the reduction of work. The development of the productive powers of labor, he argues, progresses to the stage "where the possession and preservation of general wealth require a *lesser labour time* of society as a whole ... hence where labour in which a human being does what a thing could do has ceased." (p. 325, or *MECW, Vol. 28*, p. 250.)

This progress creates new possibilities for post-capitalist communist society: "thus creates the material elements for the development of the rich individuality which is as all-sided in its production as in its consumption." (p. 325, or *MECW, Vol. 28*, p. 251.) Yet at the same time this process "encounters its barrier in capital itself" – a barrier which causes crisis. (p. 325, or *MECW, Vol. 28*, p. 251.) To illustrate this barrier, Marx draws on the remarks of a plantation owner quoted in the *The Times* who laments of the attitudes and behavior of the Quashees or free blacks of Jamaica, who "content themselves with producing only what is strictly necessary for their own consumption, and, alongside this 'use value', regard loafing (indulgence and idleness) as the real luxury good." (p. 325–26, or *MECW, Vol. 28*, p. 251.) Marx notes that these blacks have "ceased to be slaves, but not in order to become wage labourers, but, instead, self-sustaining peasants working for their own consumption." Here is the antagonistic barrier to capitalist development: people who would subordinate work to need rather than endlessly subordinating needs to a life based on work. As the development of productivity within capital proceeds the possibilities of the realization of more wealth for less work comes to conflict with the capitalist need to impose work as its source of value and social content.

Chapter on Capital: pp. 401–50, or *MECW, Vol. 28*, pp. 329–99.

This section begins with a theoretical discussion of what is called the "realization problem" or the need for capital to reinter the sphere of circulation from the sphere of production and regain the form of value, i.e., money, by being sold in the market. The flight from the money form creates the possibility that the form cannot be regained – that the produced commodity *C′* cannot be sold – and thus the possibility of a crisis of realization.

Overcoming the possibility of crisis means overcoming what appear as external *barriers*: (1) whether there is a need for the item produced and (2) whether that need has a money equivalent with which it can be effectively expressed in the market. The first of these barriers is implicit in the bodily form of the commodity "Use value in itself does not have the boundlessness of value as such. …as use value, the product contains a barrier." That is to say consumers only want limited amounts of it, regardless of the price. Marx calls this a contradiction between the commodity as use value and the commodity as value. The second barrier, the need for an equivalent, concerns the availability of money to potential consumers as well as their desire for the particular commodity. This need for equivalent, he notes, means the need for an equivalent that includes the surplus value embodied in the commodity. In modern terms these two barriers are those which constitute the downward sloping demand curve for any good. Thus, the realization of capital is not automatically given but is linked to "external" conditions.

However, as Marx goes on to discuss the "external conditions" required for realization to occur, specifically, the multiplication of points of exchange which result from the multiplication of points of production, we begin to see that "externality" is not so external after all, and "circulation …already appears as a moment of production itself." In fact, Marx discusses how in both absolute and relative surplus value, capital tends to create such multiplication and with it the world market which is "directly given in the concept of capital itself."

Yet this process is not automatic but contradictory and difficult for capital to manage. For example, in the case of relative surplus value the rise in productivity reduces necessary labor. If labor is set free (unemployed) then "a new, qualitatively different branch of production must be created, which brings forth and satisfies a new need." Hence the need to set people to work leads to the expansion of needs and the division of labor and industry – thus ultimately the "cultivation of all the qualities of the social human being" whose being will come to conflict with capital's own needs for endlessly imposed work.

Yet these are only possibilities for overcoming the barriers of demand, there is no guarantee that capital can actually carry out its intentions and achieve such a realization. Moreover, the contradictions and barriers are only displaced each time they are overcome. They are reposited in a new way by the character of the force which opposes it: the demand of the working class. "The universality towards which it irresistibly strives encounters barriers in its own nature, which will, at a certain stage of its development, allow it to be recognized as being itself the greatest barrier to this tendency and hence will drive towards its own suspension." i.e., the end of capital.

At this point (p. 410, or *MECW, Vol. 28*, p. 337) Marx confronts the issue of "overproduction" directly: seeing Ricardo one-sidedly emphasizing the infinite tendencies of capital while Sismondi one-sidedly emphasized the barriers. Ricardo and classical orthodoxy, especially Say, deny the possibility of "general overproduction," a position Marx characterizes as "childish." Marx points out that Ricardo's assertion that only overproduction of a few items is possible forgets that what is needed in exchange is money and the lack of money is the same as overproduction. In the case of a "*general crisis* of overproduction" he argues, "the contradiction is ...between industrial and loanable capital – between capital as directly involved in the production process and capital as money existing (relatively) outside of it." Most importantly, he goes on to argue, is the contradiction between the entire credit system and the monetary barriers to trade which it is aimed at overcoming – contradictions which are most obvious, he says at the level of relations among nations rather than among individuals., e.g., "the English forced to lend to foreign nations in order to have them as customers." This in response to the limitations of the local market.

Marx then goes on to discuss the forces which limit the local market – namely the relationship between the working class and capital. Whereas in the case of individual items he has stressed the limits of demand set by workers' limited desires for particular commodities, in the case of aggregate consumption demand he stresses the contradiction between capital's desire to hold down costs by limiting wages and the need for markets which can only expand as wages expand. Here he honors Malthus, for a change, who saw the limits of the market provided by workers for their product. This contradiction between the need for a market and the desire by capital to limit costs defines the forces at work to produce a disproportionality between consumption supply and consumption demand and thus overproduction.

Yet Marx is no mere underconsumptionist as some would have it, for parallel to this discussion is another of the possibilities of disproportionality in the supply and demand for investment goods. On page 421 (or, *MECW, Vol. 28*, p. 349) in a lengthy footnote, we find his recognition of the forces which can produce an overproduction of the means of production thus crisis from that source as well. In fact, Marx explicitly notes in the body of the text, that "if the demand exterior to the demand of the labourer himself disappears or shrinks up, then the collapse occurs." Such a collapse due to a drop in investment demand is as well known in the twentieth century as it was to Marx in the nineteenth.

Chapter on Capital: pp. 699–712, or *MECW, Vol. 29*, pp. 80–99.

Although not in the order of composition, this section should be read in connection with that on pages 321–326, for it is here that Marx most fully develops the contradiction between capital's ability to impose labor as value and the rise in productivity. In this section, sometimes known as the *Fragment on Machines*, Marx pushes the tendency to the limit: at which point labor ceases to be the well spring of wealth and can no longer play the key role of social control in capital. With the development of productivity, individual labor has "ceased altogether to appear as productive, is productive rather, only in these common labors which subordinate the forces of nature to themselves…social labor," but these "common labors" are embodied in fixed capital, in the machines of large industry, indeed in science as a whole. At this point, "labour no longer appears so much to be included within the production process; rather, the human being comes to relate more as watchman and regulator ….In this transformation, it is neither the direct human labor he himself performs, nor the time during which he works, but rather the appropriation of his own general productive power, his understanding of nature and his mastery over it by virtue of his presence as a social body…which appears as the great foundation stone of production and of wealth." With this development, he argues it becomes clear that the labor time must cease to be the measure of wealth and "hence exchange value [must cease to be the measure] of use value." This is the crisis of value, that is to say the crisis of capital's ability to impose work as the fundamental organizing form of social order. This is the crisis which Marx will later, in *Capital* Volume 3, call the most fundamental contradiction of capitalism.

At this point in his argument, he reiterates the earlier discussion of how high productivity will allow the "free development of individualities and hence … the general reduction of the necessary labor of society to a minimum." But this again conflicts with capital's nature as social organization founded on work, so rising productivity appears as the material condition to "blow this foundation sky-high." (p. 706, or *MECW, Vol. 29*, p. 92.)

The upshot of the explosion of the social antagonism of capital will be its overthrow and the creation of a new social order wherein not labor time but "disposable time" will "grow for all" and will become "the measure of wealth." (p. 708, or *MECW, Vol. 29*, p. 94.) This will be the end, Marx notes, of the "positing of an individual's entire time as labor time, and his degradation therefore to mere worker, subsumption under labor." (p. 708, or *MECW, Vol. 29*, p. 94.)

Marx, Karl to Friedrich Engels, April 2, 1858, *MECW, Vol. 40*, pp. 296–304.

Outline of first part of his economics, including "the lack of congruence of C – M and M – C is the most abstract and superficial form in which the *possibility* of crises is expressed." (p. 302) Also, money qua money important in times of crisis.

Marx, Karl. "The English Bank Act of 1844," August 6, 1858, *MECW, Vol. 16*, pp. 3–7. (*New York Daily Tribune*, no. 5409, Aug. 23, 1858.)

Marx attacks bullionist quantity theory arguing that "efflux and influx of bullion affect the state of the hoards (central or private), but not the state of the currency, and thus no action at all is exercised upon general prices." The object of the Bank Act of

1844 was to tie the amount of currency to the amount of bullion to allow the automatic price adjustment of the species flow mechanism. But in the crises of 1847 and 1857 the Act was suspended (Nov. 12, 1857) and notes were issued in excess of the amount prescribed by the act. For Marx this is not surprising because the amount of currency required is determined by circulation, not by bullion reserves and it was not only wrong to try to tie notes to gold reserves, but impossible to maintain without central bank bankruptcy in times of crisis when there is great demand for money qua money.

Marx, Karl. "Commercial Crises and Currency in Britain," August 10, 1858, *MECW, Vol. 16*, pp. 8–12. (*New York Daily Tribune,* no. 5414, Aug. 28, 1858.)

Demonstration that crisis was not a reaction to inflation based on an over-issue of bank notes. Marx shows with data that the number of notes declined as trade and prices rose (displaced by credit operations).

Marx, Karl. "History of the Opium Trade," August 31 and September 3, 1858, *MECW, Vol. 16*, pp. 13–20. (*New York Daily Tribune,* nos. 5433, 5438, Sept. 20, 25, 1858.)

A new treaty with China, in the wake of the second Opium War (1857–58), is likely – like the last one, imposed after the first Opium War (1841–42) – to conjure up "dreams of an inexhaustible market" and to foster "false speculations" which would prepare a new commercial crisis based on overproduction and the collapse of that speculation. The article contains a brief history of the British export of opium from India to China, of the resistance of the Chinese government as imports of opium drained its coffers of silver while poisoning its people.

Marx, Karl. "The Anglo-Chinese Treaty," September 10, 1858, *MECW, Vol. 16*, pp. 28–32. (*New York Daily Tribune,* no. 5446, Oct. 5, 1858.)

This follow-up to the previous article examines the collapse of exports to China in the years following the 1842 treaty through a critique of the analysis presented by the London *Economist.* He makes two main points, both supported by evidence. First, in the wake of the treaty of 1842, the Chinese market was excessively and speculatively overstocked, i.e., exports were far in excess of demand such that prices fell to the point "that scarcely realized their freight." This, he argues, was not unique to the China situation but such a "sudden expansion of commerce … followed by its violent contractions … is a standing feature in the history of the markets of the world." Second, evidence contradicts the *Economist*'s arguments that the demand for British exports was reduced by American competition and by the turbulence of the Taiping uprising. Thus, the essential cause of the collapse of exports to China was the result of British exporters having "greatly overestimated" the "consuming and paying powers" of the Chinese – and those "paying powers" were made worse by the "derangement" of

Chinese "finances and monetary circulation" caused by the import of opium imposed on China by England and France, and the consequent drainage of silver that left little ability to finance other kinds of imports.

Marx, Karl. "British Commerce and Finance," September 14, 1858, *MECW*, *Vol. 16*, pp. 33–36. (*New York Daily Tribune*, no. 5445, Oct. 4, 1858.)

Marx criticizes the House of Commons Committee on the Crisis' (1857) report for not recognizing the recurrent pattern of crisis. He agrees that the 1857 crisis was due, at least partly, to "excessive speculation and abuse of credit," but points out the periodicity of such behavior, that such "seasons of general self-delusion, of over speculation and fictitious credit" are inherent in the present system of production." Yes, the peculiarities of each crisis should be recognized, but so should "the aspects common to all of them." Marx also discusses that fictitious credit and its structure: it is created through accommodation bills discounted by joint-stock country banks, which rediscounted them with London bill brokers who mostly ignored the quality of the bills themselves and relied on the Bank of England. He gives examples of careless practices of joint stock companies which, while stimulating accumulation, had not yet developed a responsible "corporate conscience" to replace individual responsibility.

Engels, Friedrich to Karl Marx, October 7, 1858, *MECW*, *Vol. 40*, pp. 343–45.

Manchester cotton business very good. "If it goes on like this much longer there'll be movements for increased wages." "… the devil only knows how long it will last unless there is substantial overproduction with India and China in view …"

Marx, Karl to Friedrich Engels, October 8, 1858, *MECW*, *Vol. 40*, pp. 345–47.

"The proper task of bourgeois society is the creation of the world market … and of the production based on that market … For us the difficult question is this: on the continent the revolution is imminent … will it not necessarily be crushed in this little corner of the earth, since the movement of bourgeois society is still in the ascendant over a far greater area?"

Marx, Karl. "Project for the Regulation of the Price of Bread in France," November 19, 1858, *MECW*, *Vol. 16*, pp. 110–14. (*New York Daily Tribune*, no. 5507, December 15, 1858.)

Marx mocks Napoleon III's projects of stabilizing the price of bread by (1) forcing bakers and cities to maintain grain/flour reserves and (2) creating a Bakers' Bank to sustain baker income in the face of losses. The initial experiment in Paris, he argues, not only failed to stabilize the price of bread but resulted in massive municipal debts, increased excise taxes and a bail-out by the government. The extension of this approach to the main towns in the country would require immense granaries, whose financing, Marx claims, would merely enrich "the Crédit Mobilier and the other gambling companions of his Imperial Majesty" while failing to stabilize the price of bead. The political motive behind these schemes is the artificial enhancement of grain prices to "stop the mouth to agricultural France," i.e., stave off peasant unrest brought on by "ruinously low" grain prices. The result would be speculation and a higher price of bread for urban workers.

1859

Marx, Karl. "A Prussian View of the War," May 24, 1859, *MECW*, *Vol. 16*, pp. 341–45. (*New York Daily Tribune*, no. 5659, June 10, 1859.)

Austrian commercial crisis has circulated to rest of Germany with widespread bankruptcies. Government has refused to issue more inconvertible paper money and cut back public works for employment.

Marx, Karl. "Manufactures and Commerce," September 5, 1859, *MECW*, *Vol. 16*, pp. 492–96. (*New York Daily Tribune*, No. 5747, Sept. 23, 1859.)

(1) On the basis of data on export, Marx argues that there is a "law" of production concerning a secular upward trend: "That if, by over-production and over-speculation, a crisis has been brought about, still the productive powers of the nation and the faculty of absorption on the market of the world, have, in the meantime, so much expanded, that they will only temporarily recede from the highest point reached, and that after some oscillations spreading over some years, the scale of production which marked the highest point of prosperity in one period of the commercial cycle, becomes the starting point of the subsequent period."

Marx, Karl. "Trade with China," mid-November 1859, *MECW*, *Vol. 16*, pp. 536–39. (*New York Daily Tribune*, No. 5808, December 3, 1859.)

The inability of British merchants to expand exports of cotton and woolen goods to China – despite two wars and several treaties opening new areas to trade – Marx explains by the lack of demand, itself the result of self-sufficient domestic agriculture and industry. Evidence in government reports reveal, he points out, how both domestic needs and market demand is primarily met by Chinese farmers also producing cloth on their own looms, making their own clothes and selling any excess of either in towns and cities. Whereas in India the colonizing British were able to destroy such domestic manufactures, they have neither gained the power to do so in China, nor were they ever likely to.

1861

Marx, Karl. "The British Cotton Trade," September 21, 1861, *MECW*, *Vol. 19*, pp. 17–20. (*New York Daily Tribune,* No. 6405, Oct. 14, 1861.)

Commentary on the effects of rising cotton prices due to American Civil War blockade on Southern cotton exports to England: reduced profits and production of cotton textiles, speculation in cotton, oversupply to China and India after reduction of Northern imports. "The present American crisis forces them to enlarge their field of supply and emancipate cotton from slave breeding and slave-consuming oligarchies." England, Marx argues, won't attempt to break the blockade because of financial investments in Northern industries and the need for Northern corn.

Marx, Karl. "The Crisis in England," circa November 1861, *MECW*, *Vol. 19*, pp. 53–56. (*Die Presse,* November 6, 1861.)

Similar to *New York Daily Tribune* article of Oct. 14th. But Marx notes here that "it will be years before India can produce for export the requisite quantity of cotton." Also cotton speculation resembles railway speculation of 1845.

Marx, Karl. "British Commerce," November 2, 1861, *MECW*, *Vol. 19*, pp. 57–61. (*New York Daily Tribune,* No. 6440, Nov. 23, 1861.)

Marx analyzes recent British trade statistics, noting the "sudden contraction" of trade with the U.S. due to the "American crisis," i.e., the Civil War, and the resulting "feverish state of the Liverpool cotton market," which he likens to the railway mania in 1845. In other words, intense participation in speculation on cotton prices by all sorts of people. He also notes the opposition to any effort by the British government to intervene in support of the secessionists by speculators who were basing their buying and selling on current conditions. Marx also comments briefly on a crisis in French finance caused by bullion outflow to England, efforts to stem it by increasing the interest on French Treasury Bills and debates over other possible ways to counter it.

Marx, Karl. "Economic Notes," November 3, 1861, *MECW*, *Vol. 19*, pp. 62–65. (*Die Presse,* Nov. 9, 1861.)

French Monetary crisis – rate of interest rising, conflicts over future of Bank of France – cotton speculation, English trade deficit.

Marx, Karl. "French News Humbug, Economic Consequences of the War," December 31, 1861, *MECW*, *Vol. 19*, pp. 131–33. (*Die Presse,* January 4, 1862.)

Report of English arguments against war with US: need for US grain, UK investments in US, US privateers' threat to UK trade with Australia, India, etc., cheaper to feed cotton districts than go to war.

1862

Marx, Karl. "On the Cotton Crisis," early Feb. 1862, *MECW*, *Vol. 19*, pp. 160–62. (*Die Presse*, February 8, 1862.)

Chamber of Commerce of Manchester against intervention in American civil war, says current crisis mainly due to overproduction, not the war: "… since 1858 an unprecedented glutting of the Atlantic markets has taken place and that in consequence of steadily continuing overproduction on a mass scale the present stagnation was bound to occur, even without the American Civil War, the Morrill tariff and the blockade."

1863

Marx, Karl. "Manuscript of 1861–63," which includes *Theories of Surplus Value.*

This huge manuscript of 23 notebooks became available to us in English in two forms. The first was an English translation of the set of excerpts edited by Karl Kautsky (1854–1938) in 1862–63 and originally published in German in three volumes as *Theorien über den Mehrwert* in 1905–1910. That material was re-edited and translated into English and the three volumes were published sequentially by Progress Publishers (Moscow) as *Theories of Surplus Value: Volume 4 of Capital,* Pt. I in 1963, Pt. II in 1968 and Pt. III in 1971. The second form, this time of the entire Manuscript, become available in English in *MECW* in Volumes 30 (1988), 31–32 (1989), 33 (1991), and 34 (1994). The material constituting *Theories of Surplus Value* can be found in the second part of Vol. 30 and Vols 31–34. For more detailed history see the wiki and its references.

This is the second of Marx & Engels' works so large and so full of relevant material that I only give here a few examples from Marx's critique of Ricardo's Theory of Accumulation, *MECW, Vol. 32*, pp. 103–74. In the Progress Publisher's edition, from which I drew citations for the original version of this essay, this most important part of the manuscript with respect to crises can be found in Vol. 2 in Chapter XVIII, Sections 6–14, pp. 492–546 (Below I have included page numbers only for *MECW*.) "just as the examination of money … has shown that it contained the possibility of crisis, the examination of the general nature of capital … reveals this still more clearly." (p. 124) "If … market prices of the commodities … fall far below their cost prices, then reproduction of capital is curtailed as far as possible. Accumulation, however, stagnates even more … The same hold up could occur for the opposite reasons, if the real prerequisites of reproduction were missing … there occurs a stoppage in reproduction … purchase and sale get bogged down and unemployed capital appears in the form of idle money … the same phenomenon can appear when surplus capital is produced at a very rapid rate and … brings a rise in the prices of all commodities … the rate of interest falls sharply … leads to the most risky speculative ventures." (pp. 125–26) Because C′ – M′ can take a long time, "great upheavals and changes take place in the *market* … great changes take place in the productivity of labor and therefore also in the *real value* of commodities … great catastrophes must occur and elements of crisis must have gathered and develop." (p. 126) The destruction of capital = machinery not used, labor not exploited, commodities left to rot, "destruction of capital through crises means the depreciation of values," not use values. If profits fall, "old capitalists go bankrupt … [which] may expedite the new reproduction … fall in purely nominal capital, state bonds, shares, etc… . amounts only to the transfer of wealth … will, on the whole, act favorably upon reproduction, since the parvenus … are mostly more enterprising than their former owners." (p. 127) "In the crises of the world market, the contradictions and antagonisms of bourgeois production are strikingly revealed." (p. 131) "the possibility of crises, by no means explain their actual occurrence. They do not explain *why* the phases of the process come into such conflict." (p. 133) "The general nature of the metamorphosis of commodities … contains the possibility of a general glut." (p. 135)

1864

Marx, Karl. *Marx's Economic Manuscript of 1864–1865*, trans. Ben Fowkes (Brill, 2015, Haymarket Books, 2017).

Following the *Grundrisse* manuscripts of 1857 and the "Manuscript of 1861–63", this is the third large body of text containing far more material than can be annotated here. Footnotes to various quotations, however, also provide page references to the passages in the *Manuscript* as well as those to in Volume 3 and in *MECW*.

For some, the major value of this new translation is identifying changes Engels made in excerpting from it to prepare Volume 3 of *Capital*. A secondary issue concerns the proper translation of various words and passages. For studying Marx's writings on accumulation and its crises, its main value is the inclusion of material Engels left out – because that material often amplifies what he did include by providing more source material and Marx's own worked-out examples of the issues. This new edition contains an appendix listing the pages containing material Engels either left out or substantially changed. One example is in Marx's discussion of capitalist efforts to keep costs down and profits up by NOT spending money on measures which would safeguard workers and then resisting the implementation of regulations once workers and reformers have succeeded in getting them written into law. In the Manuscript we discover some 15 pages of evidence, mostly from factory inspector reports. (pp. 158–73)

Marx, Karl. "Inaugural Address of the Working Men's International Association," October 21–27, 1864, *MECW*, *Vol. 20*, p. 11.

In this address, Marx sketches what has been accomplished so far, including the reduction of working hours and praises bottom-up co-operatives as demonstrating how workers could run production and distribution on their own, effectively a demonstration of how they could move beyond capitalism without the capitalists. "Bottom up" cooperatives as opposed to the kind of government-aided cooperatives supported by Lasalle that he would latter denounce in his "Marginal Notes on the Programme of the German Workers' Party" (1875).

Marx, Karl to Friedrich Engels, November 4, 1864, *MECW*, *Vol. 42*, pp. 18–19.

"Bakunin sends his regards … I saw him yesterday for the first time in 16 years. I must say I liked him very much, more so than previously … On the whole, he is one of the few people whom after 16 years I find to have moved forwards and not backwards."

1865

Engels, Friedrich to F. A. Lange, March 29, 1865, *MECW*, *Vol. 42*, p. 137, or *Marx Engels Selected Correspondence,* 3rd rev. ed. (Moscow: Progress Publishers, 1975) 161.

"We start from the premise that the same forces which have created modern bourgeois society – the steam engine, modern machinery, mass colonization, railways, steamships, world trade – and which through the unending commercial crises are already now working towards its ruin and ultimate destruction …"

Marx, Karl to Frederich Engels, May 3, 1865, *MECW*, *Vol. 42*, p. 150.

"The great achievement of the 'International Association' is this: The Reform League, is our doing." That League's mobilizations contributed to the passage of a new Reform Act in 1867, granting adult male workers the right to vote.

Marx, Karl. "Value, Price and Profit," end of May and June 1865, *MECW*, *Vol. 20*, pp. 138–49. Section 13: "Main Cases of Attempts at Raising Wages or Resisting Their Fall" and Section 14: "The Struggle between Capital and Labour and its Results." (first published in 1898)

Report read by Marx to Central Council of the International on June 20 and 27, 1865. In this report Marx argues against the Owenite Weston that workers have to fight to raise their wages by as much as possible during business upturns and to limit their fall during the downswing of the business cycle. Partly the fight maximizes their income, partly it is training for future struggle.

1867

Marx, Karl. *Capital: A Critique of Political Economy, Volume 1*, trans. Ben Fowkes (New York: Pelican Books, 1976, London: Penguin Classics, 1990), *MECW, Vol. 35*.

For this volume, as well as for others as substantial, there are too many passages to cite them all, so I either summarize briefly or give a few examples.

Part 1: Commodities and Money. He highlights the *possibility* that one might sell but not buy, holding on to money instead, in such a manner that other commodities cannot be sold (and thus fail to realize either their exchange value or their use value). "These forms," he writes, "therefore imply the possibility of crises, though no more than the possibility." (*Capital, Vol. 1*, p. 209, or *MECW, Vol. 35*, p. 124.) His critique of the quantity theory of money (*Capital, Vol. 1*, pp. 213–20, or *MECW, Vol. 35*, pp. 127–34.) In his discussion of money as means of payment, or credit money, he also points out how being able to buy on credit in the present opens the possibility of not being able to pay later on. The development of the credit system leads to complicated credit relationships of interdependence, such that a few failures to pay (for whatever reason, and with whatever form of money) can lead to a wider collapse of credit and a more general crisis. "Such a [monetary] crisis [within an industrial or commercial crisis] occurs only where the ongoing chain of payments has been fully developed, along with an artificial system for settling them." (*Capital, Vol. 1*, p. 236, or *MECW, Vol. 35*, pp. 148–49).

Part 2: Money into Capital. *M-C-M′* no direct discussion of crisis, although there's the possibility that one may sell but then hoard money instead of spending/buying implies the possible rupture of the circuit. Also, possibilities of crisis in labor market due to the refusal of people to sell their labor power and in the failure of capitalists to buy, say, because they don't have enough money at going wages.

Part 3: Production of Absolute Surplus Value. In labor process: crisis implicit in possible refusal of workers, failure of tools or raw materials (drought, etc.) can = crisis. Reduction in working hours reduces surplus value and rate of profit. Successful struggle to reduce working day = crisis of absolute surplus value strategy.

Part 4: Production of Relative Surplus Value. Failure of individual or capitalists as a class to raise productivity enough to offset reduction in working hours = crisis. If workers succeed in realizing the technical possibilities of decreasing work with rise in productivity, the reduction in work undermines relative surplus value strategy. Competition among capitalists based on relative control over work force, crisis for those least able to control. Biggest threat to capitalists: workers turn cooperation against their employers, e.g., informal collaboration, formal unions, struggle for pro-worker laws, etc. Workers' resistance to being pitted against each other can cause crisis for capital. Capitalists use machines against workers but workers resist = crisis. In battles over safety, worker victories increase costs to capitalists, reduces surplus value = crisis. Capitalists seek to thwart Aristotle's dreams of replacing work with robots; workers seek to realize them; to the degree they succeed = crisis for capitalists. Factories incarcerate, concentrate workers but workers collaborate = crisis. Machinery accentuates pattern of crisis and recovery. Relative surplus value strategy raises technical composition of capital, thus organic composition of capital. Replacing workers by machines undermines imposition of work, increases struggles of reserve army. Struggles of latent, floating and stagnant differ, so too do effects on accumulation.

Part 5: Absolute & Relative Surplus Value. Review

Part 6: Wages. Builds on Chap. 6 on *M-LP*, focus on how wages hide exploitation. The "superintendence of labour becomes to a great extent superfluous." (*Capital, Vol. 1*, p. 695, or MECW, *Vol. 35*, p. 552). But wages also = power for workers, more wages, more power, including increased ability to struggle over other issues; hence class struggle, hence crisis. Workers can undermine time and piece wage reducing surplus value = crisis. Worker struggles can undermine national differences in wages = crisis. Critique of both "free trade" and "protectionism," two strategies vs workers, undermined by their struggles.

Part 7: Accumulation of Capital. "accumulation reproduces the capital-relation on an expanded scale, with more capitalists, or bigger capitalists, at one pole, and more wage labourers at the other pole ... Accumulation of capital is therefore multiplication of the proletariat." (*Capital, Vol. 1*, pp. 763–64, or MECW, *Vol. 35*, p. 609.) Simple reproduction requires replacing every element of production including labor-power, whether "left to workers" or shaped by capitalists. "the capitalist may safely leave this [reproduction] to the worker's drive for self-preservation and propagation" (*Capital, Vol. 1*, p. 718, or MECW, *Vol. 35*, pp. 572.) Failure = crisis. Diversion of surplus value from investment (to consumption, etc.) undermines reproduction, can create crisis. Critique of "abstinence" and "wages-fund" implies workers can fight for higher wages without necessarily causing crisis. Expanded reproduction requires expansion of all elements necessary to expanded imposition of work and production of commodities. Accumulation = accumulation of classes, of class struggle. Wage and general economic fluctuations mainly due to those in investment, but worker successes that undermine surplus value are crises for capitalists that can lead them to cut investment, raise unemployment, lower wages, and create crises for workers. Accumulation always includes both waged and unwaged (e.g., reserve army) thus class struggles include both waged and unwaged. "When this periodicity has once become consolidated, even political economy sees that the production of a relative surplus population ... is a necessary condition for modern industry." Same page, footnote, from the French edition, "But only after mechanical industry had struck root so deeply that it exerted a preponderant influence on the whole of national production; only after foreign trade began to predominate over internal trade, thanks to mechanical industry; only after the world market had successively annexed extensive areas of the new World, Asia and Australia; and finally only after a sufficient number of industrial nations had entered the arena – only after all this had happened can one date the repeated self-perpetuating cycles, whose successive phases embrace years, and always culminate in a general crisis, which is the end of one cycle and the starting point of another." (*Capital, Vol. 1.*, p. 786, or *MECW, Vol. 35*, pp. 627–28.) and *Le Capital: Livre 1,* (Paris: Garnier-Flammarion, 1969), 462. Concentration and centralization of capital accelerate fluctuations. Military poaching of workers causing crisis in agricultural labor supply. (*Capital, Vol. 1*, p. 791, or *MECW, Vol. 35*, p. 632.)

Part 8: Primitive Accumulation. Force, not differential frugality, expropriation of means of production, but resistance. Bloody legislation to force expropriated into labor market, force because of resistance, degree of force measures degree of resistance. Rise of agrarian capitalists, from landlords to production for profit. Expropriation + wages creates home market, expropriated forced to buy what they need. Resistance via direct appropriation. Rise of industrial capitalists, amassing of necessary investment monies via colonialism, state repayment of debt. Resistance of the would-be colonized; colonization driven by resistance and struggle of workers at home. As capitalists gain power, they draw more and more on the state, especially government, to impose changes advantageous to them, e.g., maximum wages, colonies, deployment of violence. Overall vision: capitalism not eternal, was born, will be killed. Final crisis, expropriation of expropriators, end of capitalism. Wakefield's strategies for imposing labor where lots of land provides alternative to labor market.

1868

Marx, Karl to Kugelmann, March 6, 1868, *MECW, Vol. 42*, p. 544.

"I must be grateful to the man [Dühring]," Marx wrote, "since he is the first expert who has said anything at all [about Volume 1 of *Capital*]." (p. 544) However, he also disdained how Dühring was setting "himself up as a revolutionary in political economy" (p. 544) Engels would take on the job of critiquing Dühring's work. (see below)

Marx, Karl to Friedrich Engels, April 30, 1868, *MECW, Vol. 43*, p. 24, or S. W. Ryazanskaya, ed. *Marx Engels Selected Correspondence,* 3rd rev. ed. (Moscow: Progress Publishers, 1975) 191–95.

Outline of Vol. III of *Capital* material including surplus value as profit on social capital and the tendency of the rate of profit to fall which "follows from what was developed in Book I [Volume 1] on the change in the composition of capital with the development of the social productive power. This is one of the greatest triumphs over the *pons asini* [bridges that the slow minds of classical political economists were unable to cross] of all previous political economy."

1870

Marx, Karl to Sigfrid Meyer and August Vogt, April 9, 1870, *MECW, Vol. 43*, pp. 471–76.

In this letter to members of the First International, Marx explains his views on the relationship between workers' struggles in Ireland and in England and how Irish workers and English workers are pitted against each other. "All industrial and commercial centres in England now have a working class *divided* into two *hostile* camps, English proletarians and Irish proletarians ... This antagonism is kept artificially alive and intensified by the press, the pulpit, the comic papers, in short, by all the means at the disposal of the ruling class. *This antagonism* is the *secret of the English working class's impotence*, despite its organization." So, he concludes that successful struggles in Ireland are essential to the success of struggles in England. Indeed, successful revolution in Ireland would circulate to England. "Thus, to hasten the social revolution in England is the most important object of the International Working Men's Association. The sole means of doing so is to make Ireland independent."

Marx, Karl. "To the Members of the International Working Men's Association in Europe and the United States," July 19–23, 1870, *MECW, Vol. 22*, pp. 3–8.

"Despotism at home and war abroad." Mainly about how both Napoleon and Bismark used war abroad against workers at home.

Engels, Friedrich. "Notes on the War – x," August 19, 1870, *MECW, Vol. 22*, pp. 52–55.

"... it is not intended to send the mass of the troops now in Paris to the front. Paris must be kept down." (p. 55)

Engels, Friedrich. "Notes on the War. – XIV," August 30 or 31, 1870, *MECW, Vol. 22*, pp. 74–77.

On war speculation, ""a set of adventurers who turned administration, government, army, navy – in fact, all France – into a source of pecuniary profit to themselves." (p. 77)

1871

Marx, Karl. "The Civil War in France, Address of the General Council of the International Working Men's Association," May 6–30, 1871, *MECW, Vol. 22*, pp. 307–59.

Marx's major account and analysis of the rise and fate of the Paris Commune. Preceded by two drafts: first draft, *MECW, Vol. 22*, pp. 437–514, and second draft, *MECW, Vol. 22*, pp. 515–551. Bourgeois "financial swindling celebrated cosmopolitan orgies, the misery of the masses was set off by a shameless display of gorgeous, meretricious and debased luxury," this "rottenness ... [was] laid bare by the bayonet of Prussia." (p. 330)

Engels, Friedrich. "On the Company Swindle in England," November 4, 1871, *MECW, Vol. 23*, pp. 34–36. (*Der Volksstaat,* No. 91, November 11, 1871.)

"... these people never learn anything, and even if they do, they are forced by the intrinsic law of capitalist production constantly to repeat the old, familiar cycle of boom, overproduction and crisis, and to repeat it on an ever-increasing scale until, finally, the proletariat rises and liberates society from enduring this absurd cycle."

1872

Marx, Karl to Maurice La Châtre, March 18, 1872, *MECW, Vol. 44*, p. 344.

"I applaud your idea of publishing the translation of *Das Kapital* in periodic installments. In this form the work will be more accessible to the working class and for me that consideration outweighs any other."

1873

Engels, Friedrich. "The Housing Question, Pt. II," May 1872 - January 1873, *MECW, Vol. 23*, pp. 340–41. (*Der Volksstaat,* Nos. 103-104, Dec. 25 and 28, 1872 and Nos. 2-3, Jan. 4 and 8, 1873.)

"Whence the housing shortage them? ... it is a necessary product of the bourgeois social order; ... in which improvements of the machinery, etc., continually throw masses of workers out of employment; in which violent and regularly recurring industrial fluctuations determine on the one hand the existence of a large reserve army of unemployed workers, and on the other hand drive the mass of the workers from time to time on to the streets in the big towns at a quicker rate than dwellings come into existence for them . ."

Marx, Karl. "Postface to Second German Edition of *Capital*," January 24, 1873, *Capital, Vol. 1*, p. 103, or *MECW, Vol. 35*, p. 20.

"The fact that the movement of capitalist society is full of contradictions impresses itself most strikingly on the practical bourgeois in the changes of the periodic cycle through which modern industry passes, the summit of which is the general crisis. That crisis is once again approaching..."

1875

Engels, Friedrich to August Babel, March 18–28, 1875, MECW, *Vol. 24*, pp. 67–73.

"Thirdly, ... the Lassallean 'iron law of wages' ... is exhaustively refuted by Marx in the section [of *Capital*] on 'Accumulation of Capital.'" (p. 69)

"Fifthly, there is absolutely no mention [in the draft] of the organization of the working class as a class through the medium of trade unions. And that is a point of the utmost importance, this being the proletariat's true class organization in which it fights its daily battles with capital, in which it trains itself ..." (p. 70)

Marx, Karl to Wilhelm Bracke, May 5, 1875, MECW, *Vol. 24*, pp. 77–78.

"It is my duty to refuse recognition ... to a programme which, I am convinced, is altogether deplorable as well as demoralizing for the Party." This letter included, separately, Marx's critique of that program, prepared for the forthcoming meeting in Gotha (see next).

Marx, Karl. "Marginal Notes on the Programme of the German Workers' Party" [Critique of the Gotha Program], MECW, *Vol. 24*, pp. 81–99.

The only aspect of crisis touched upon in this document is the final one, of workers taking over. Marx and Engels critiqued the Gotha Program because they differed with its proposed tactics and strategies for doing so, e.g., depending on the state to finance worker education and cooperatives, while ignoring the need for cross-border solidarity among workers in different countries.

"It is altogether self-evident that, to be able to fight at all, the working class must organize itself at home as a class ... To this extent its class struggle is national, not in substance, but, as the *Communist Manifesto* says, "in form." But the "framework of the present-day national state, for instance, the German Empire, is itself in turn economically 'within the framework of the world market'," politically "within the framework of the system of states." (pp. 89–90)

"In the place of the existing class struggle appears a newspaper scribbler's phrase: '*the* social *question*', for the '*solution*' of which one 'paves the way'," (p. 93).

"But as far as the present co-operative societies are concerned, they are of value only insofar as they are the independent creations of the workers and not protégés either of the governments or of the bourgeois." (p. 94)

"'*Education of the people by the state*' is altogether objectionable ... Government and Church should rather be excluded from any influence on the school. Particularly, indeed, in the Prusso-German Empire … the state has need, on the contrary, of a very stern education by the people." (p. 97)

Engels, Friedrich to P. L. Lavrov, November 12–17, 1875, *MECW*, *Vol. 45*, pp. 108–109, or *Marx Engels Selected Correspondence,* 3rd rev. ed (Moscow: Progress Publishers, 1975) 284–85.

In the context of an argument against the Darwinian overemphasis on struggle – that forgets cooperation – Engels outlines overproduction in the presence of underconsumption: "… production in its capitalist form produces means of subsistence and development far in excess of what can be consumed by capitalist society since it keeps the great mass of real producers artificially at a distance from these means of subsistence and development; if, by its own existential law, that society is compelled continually to raise what is, for its own purposes, an already excessive production and hence periodically, every ten years, gets to the point of destroying, not only huge quantities of products, but even the productive forces – what meaning still attaches to talk of 'struggle for existence'? For in that case the struggle for existence can consist only in this – that the producing class takes over the management of production and distribution from the class formerly entrusted with the task but now no longer capable of it, and this, in effect, is socialist revolution."

1876

Marx, Karl to Friedrich Engels, May 25, 1876, *MECW*, *Vol. 45*, pp. 119–21.

Marx decided that Dühring's ideas needed to be critiqued "without any compunction" (p. 119).

Engels, Friedrich to Karl Marx, May 28, 1876, *MECW*, *Vol. 45*, pp. 122–24.

"It's all very well for you to talk. You can lie in a warm bed – study Russian agrarian relations in particular and rent in general without anything to interrupt you – but I have to sit on a hard bench, drink cold wine, and all of a sudden drop everything else and break a lance with the tedious Dühring." (p. 122)

1877

Marx, Karl "Letter to [the editorial board of] *Otechestvenniye Zapiski,*" November 1877, *MECW*, *Vol. 24*, p. 200.

Marx's letter refuting Mikhailovski's interpretation of primitive accumulation as "a historico-philosophical theory of general development."

1878

Engels, Friedrich. "Herr Eugen Dühring's Revolution in Science" [*Anti-Dühring*], (1876–78), MECW, *Vol. 25*, pp. 1–309. (*Vorwörts* from January 3, 1877 to July 7, 1878. Published as a book in 1878.)

"Then it was seen that *all* past history was the history of class struggles; that these warring classes of society are always the products of the modes of production and of exchange – in a word, of the *economic* conditions of their time ..." (p. 26)

"We have seen that the ever-increasing perfectibility of modern machinery is, by the anarchy of production, turned into a compulsory law that forces the individual industrial capitalist always to improve his machinery, always to increase its productive force ... [However,] resistance is offered by consumption, by sales, by the markets for the products of modern industry ... The extension of the markets cannot keep pace with the extension of production. The collision becomes inevitable ... collisions become periodic ... since 1825, when the first general crisis broke out, the whole industrial and commercial world, production and exchange among all civilized people and their more or less barbaric hangers-on, are thrown out of joint about once every ten years .... the productive forces are in rebellion against the mode of exchange ..." (pp. 262–63)

"The fact that the socialized organization of production within the factory has developed so far that it has become incompatible with the anarchy of production in society, which exists side by side with and dominate it, is brought home to the capitalists themselves by the violent concentration of capital and occurs during crises, through the ruin of many large and a still greater number of small capitalists." (p. 264)

In the case of joint-stock companies, "all the social functions of the capitalist are now performed by salaried employees." (p. 265) Who Marx called the "functionaries of capital."

From joint-stock companies to the state: "this form also becomes insufficient: the official representative of capitalist society – the state – will ultimately have to undertake the direction of production." (p. 265)

These transformations in the form of management "either into joint-stock companies, or into state ownership, does not do away with the capitalistic nature of the productive forces ... The more [the state] proceeds to taking over the productive forces, the more does it actually becomes the national capitalist, the more citizens does it exploit. The workers remain wage-workers – proletarians. The capitalist relation is not done away with." (pp. 265–66)

The capitalists' "political and intellectual bankruptcy is scarcely any longer a secret to the bourgeoisie themselves. Their economic bankruptcy recurs regularly every ten years. In every crisis , society is suffocated beneath the weight of its own productive forces and products, which it cannot use, and stands helpless face to face with the absurd contradiction that the producers have nothing to consume, because consumers are wanting." (p. 269)

Marx, Karl. "X. From Kritische Geschichte," in "Herr Eugen Dühring's Revolution in Science" [*Anti-Dühring*], (1876–78), MECW, *Vol. 25*, pp. 211–43.

This chapter was written by Marx in 1877 as a contribution to Engels' vivisection of Dühring's writings. Here Marx crtiques Dühring's account of the history of political economy in his *Kritische Geschichte der Nationalökonomie und des Socialismus* (1871). He takes apart Dühring's comments on various writers one after the other and instead, gives credit where he thinks it is due. Among the latter is his long exposition of Quenay's *Tableau*, which Dühring admits to not understanding, but upon which Marx draws in his schemes of reproduction, central to his theory of accumulation and its crises.

1879

Marx, Karl to N. F. Danielson, April 10, 1879, MECW, *Vol. 45*, pp. 353–58, or *Marx Engels Selected Correspondence*, 3rd rev. ed (Moscow: Progress Publishers, 1975) 296–300.

Writing about the then current crisis, he suggested, "the phenomena are this time singular, in many respects different from what they were in the past, and this ... is easily accounted for by the fact that never before the *English crisis was preceded* by tremendous and now already 5 years lasting crisis in *the United States, South America, Germany, Austria*, etc.... . One of the singular aspects of the present state is this: there have, as you know been crashes of banks in Scotland in some of the English counties ... still the real *centre of the money-market* – not only of England but of the world – *London* has till now been little affected." This despite, he says, "the utter despair of the English commercial and industrial philistine of seeing ever better times again! I have not seen the like, I have never witnessed a similar moral dislocation although I was in London in 1857 and 1866." The London banks were being supported by influx of French "to buy securities momentarily depreciated ... and the quiet state of the banks of Lancashire and the other industrial districts." However, he adds, those banks have sunk a great part of their capital in the foundation of new fabrics ... [while] stocks, mainly of cotton produce are daily accumulation not only in Asia ... but at Manchester, etc.... How this state of things can pass away without a general crash among the manufactures, and, consequently, among the local banks reacting directly upon the London money market – is difficult to foresee.... .

However the course of this crisis may develop itself ... it will pass over, like its predecessors, and initiate a new 'industrial cycle' with all its diversified phases of prosperity, etc.

But under the cover of this 'apparently' solid English society, there lurks another crisis – *the agricultural* one which will work great and serious changes in its social structure." [His discussion continued in another letter to Danielson of September 12, 1880. See below.] He goes on to discuss the impact of railroad construction in various countries and of how they transform local production for consumption to commercial production, and how "the agricultural population was driven away." I.e., continuing enclosures of "primitive" accumulation.

1880

Engels, Friedrich. "The Socialism of Mr. Bismarck," February 1880, *MECW*, *Vol. 24*, pp. 272–80. (*L'Égalité*, Nos. 7 & 10, March 3 and 24, 1880.)

"What had happened in Paris in 1867, ... happened all over again in 1873 in Berlin: unbridled speculation terminated in a general collapse... . the public need [for railroads] which had served as a pretext had been outstripped by far ... After the railways . . speculation had been chiefly directed at the iron and steel industry. The mills had multiplied rapidly ... Unfortunately, on the day of the crisis it turned out that there were no consumers for this gigantic production."

Engels, Friedrich. "Socialism: Utopian and Scientific," January - March 1880, *MECW*, *Vol. 24*, pp. 281–325. (*La Revue Socialiste*, Nos. 3, 4 & 5, March 20, April 20 and as a pamphlet, May 5, 1880.)

"The extension of the markets cannot keep pace with the extension of production. The collision becomes inevitable ... As a matter of fact, since 1825, when the first general crisis broke out, the whole industrial and commercial world, production and exchange among all civilized peoples and their more or less barbaric hangers-on, are thrown out of joint about once every ten years... . The stagnation lasts for years ... until the accumulated mass of commodities finally filter off, more or less depreciated in value.... *The mode of production is in rebellion against the mode of exchange.*" (pp. 315–17)

"The producers on a large scale in a particular branch of industry in a particular country unite in a "Trust," a union for the purpose of regulating production. They determine the total amount to be produced, parcel it out among themselves, and thus enforce the selling price beforehand... The whole of the particular industry is turned into one gigantic joint-stock company; internal competition gives place to the internal monopoly of one company ... In trusts, ... production without any definite plan of capitalist society capitulates to the production upon a definite plan of the invading socialistic society." (pp. 317–18)

Marx, Karl to N. F. Danielson, September 12, 1880, *MECW*, *Vol. 46*, pp. 31–32.

"The present crisis was the greatest England has passed through with regard to duration, extent and intensiveness ... As to the agricultural crisis, it will gather strength, develop itself, and, by the bye, come to a head, carrying with it quite a revolution in the relations of landed property, - quite independent of the cycles of the commercial-industrial crises… . letters of farmers giving the items of their expenses in cultivating their farms, comparing them with their returns at present prices, and winding up with a positive *deficit*… . The farmers themselves … dare not yet assume attitudes of bold vitality, considering that they, on their part, are denounced by the rustic 'labouring class'. A nice pickle it is altogether."

1881

Marx, Karl to N. F. Danielson, February 19, 1881, MECW, *Vol. 46*, pp. 60–64, or *Marx Engels Selected Correspondence* (Moscow: Progress Publishers, 3rd Revised Edition, 1975) 316–17.

Comments on natural cyclical pattern of good and bad years in agriculture, checked only "by the modifying intervention of the agriculturalist himself."

Verification of 10 April 1879 assertion that absence of financial crash in London due to French gold.

Sketch of the games of "railroad magnates" with loans and debt which "must one day or another terminate in an ugly catastrophe."

Engels, Friedrich. "Trades Unions," May 20, 1881, MECW, *Vol. 24*, pp. 383–84. (*The Labour Standard*, Nos. 4 & 5, May 28 and June 4, 1881.)

"When the general peace, in 1815, re-established regularity of trade, the decennial panic began. Whatever advantages the workpeople had preserved from old prosperous times, and perhaps even increased during the period of frantic over-production, were now taken from them during the period of bad trade and panic . . But in the meantime the Trades Unions, legalized in 1824, had also stepped in … [to obtain] full value of the working power . . This, however is the utmost Trades Unions, as at present organized, can hope to obtain, and that by constant struggle only, by an immense waste of strength and money; and then the fluctuations of trade, once every ten years at least, break down for the moment what has been conquered, and the fight has to be fought over again."

1882

Engels, Friedrich to Eduard Bernstein, January 25 and 31, 1882, MECW, *Vol. 46*, pp. 186–90. Marx, Karl and Friederich Engels, *Letters on* Capital, trans. Andrew Drummond (London: New Park Publications, 1983) 209–210.

"The fact that these crises are one of the most powerful levers in political upheavals has already been stated in the *Communist Manifesto* and is explained in the review section of the *Neue Rheinische Zeitung* up to and including 1848, but it is also explained that returning prosperity also breaks revolutions and lays the foundations for the victory of reaction. A detailed proof of this would have to take into consideration the interim crises, which are partly of a local and partly of a special nature; we are at present undergoing such an interim crisis which can be traced to pure stock-exchange swindles; until 1847 these were regular connecting links ..."

Engels, Friedrich to Karl Kautsky, September 12, 1882, *MECW*, *Vol. 46*, pp. 320–23. Marx, Karl and Friederich Engels, *Letters on* Capital, trans. Andrew Drummond (London: New Park Publications, 1983) 213–14.

English workers, Engels argued, "eat happily thanks to England's monopoly of the world market and colonies." The colonies with large indigenous populations – India, Algeria, etc. – "will have to be taken over rapidly by the proletariat and will have to be led towards independence as rapidly as possible ... India will perhaps have a revolution ... this of course could not pass off without all kinds of destruction – but that is in any case inseparable from all revolutions."

Engels, Friedrich. "The Dialectics of Nature," 1873 to 1882, *MECW*, *Vol. 25*, pp. 584–85. (First published in full in *Marx-Engels Archives*, 1925.)

"... under a capitalist mode of production, production reaches such a high level that society can no longer consume the means of subsistence, enjoyment and development that have been produced, because for the great mass of producers access to these means is artificially and forcibly barred; and therefore every ten years a crisis restores the equilibrium by destroying not only the means of subsistence enjoyment and development that have been produced, but also a great part of the productive forces themselves. Hence the so-called struggle for existence assumes the form: to protect the products and productive forces produced by bourgeois capitalist society against the destructive, ravaging effect of this capitalist social order, by taking control ... out of the hands of the ruling capitalist class, which has become incapable of this function, and transferring it to the producing masses – and that is the socialist revolution."

1884

Engels, Friedrich. "Preface to the First German Edition [of Marx, K. *The Poverty of Philosophy*]," October 23, 1884, *MECW*, *Vol. 26*, pp. 278–91.

This preface, also published in *Die Neue Zeit*, No. 1, 1885 under the title "Marx and Rodbertus," consists primarily of a critique of Rodbertus' criticisms of Marx and the relationship of his ideas to those of Proudhon and other socialists who had offered schemes for overcoming exploitation and achieving utopia by making exchange based on labor values. Engels argues that Rodbertus fails to understand how the "industrial and commercial crises," which he would like to abolish, play an essential role in the "evening out" of miscalculations by individual producers who can never be certain as to whether their production is appropriate to the current level of demand. Eliminating competition, as Rodbertus suggests would remove those fluctuations in prices that guide producers to adjust production to demand and make crises even worse. In a footnote, he qualifies this argument by saying "this was the case until recently." "Since England's monopoly of the world market is being shattered by the participation of France, Germany and, above all, of America in world trade, a new form of evening-out appears to be in operation." That new form, he suggests, involves the failure to achieve expansion after crises resulting in "chronic stagnation" becoming "the normal condition of modern industry."

1885

Marx, Karl. *Capital, Vol. 2*, (1860s) New York: Penguin Books, 1978, *MECW*, *Vol. 36*.

In a letter to Engels, Marx points out how Vol. II goes beyond Vol. I by investigating "the conditions under which these elements [*s, v, c*] are to be found in existence, that is to say the social intertwining of the different capitals, of parts of capital and of *revenue* (= surplus value)" (April 30, 1868, *MECW*, *Vol. 43*, p. 21) "Found in existence" or NOT found and thus resulting in crisis! Although Mandell, in his introduction to Vol. II, interprets this investigation as only concerning "a movement of commodities and of money" (*Capital, Vol. 1*, p. 12), for me the "social intertwining" is among moments of the antagonistic relations of class in which commodity and money are only elements. Mandell agrees with Engels' that the text has "little in the way of agitation" (Engels to Sorge, June 3, 1885, *MECW*, *Vol. 47*, p. 296) and Harvey says "Class struggle disappears, as do active class relations" (David Harvey, *A Companion to Marx's Capital, Volume 2*, (New York: Verso, 2013), p. 8.) Such interpretations are only possible to those who fail to see in every element/category of Marx's analysis moments of class struggle. As with previous long texts with lots of material relevant to crises, below I only give examples from each part of the book.

Part I, Chaps 1–6: on metamorphoses and circuits of capital. All elements of the circuits of money, productive and commodity capital must be reproduced, and on an expanded scale, for accumulation to be successful. Any interruption at any point can be a crisis, e.g., "If the second metamorphosis M-C comes up against obstacles, (e.g., if the means of production are unobtainable on the market) then the circular flow of the reproduction process is interrupted." (*Capital, Vol. 2*, p. 154, *MECW*, *Vol. 36*, p. 80.).

Part II, Chaps 7–17: on turnover, concerns the speed of accumulation, how quickly capital is able to successfully achieve the stages of its circuits. The faster the turnover, the more output, sales and profits. So, all disruptions that slow down any step have the potential to cause crisis, both in one stage but also in those with which it is "intertwined." "the cycle of related turnovers ... is one of the material foundations for the periodic cycle [crisis] in which business passes through successive periods of stagnation, moderate activity, over-excitement and crisis... . a crisis is always the starting point of a large volume of new investment. It is also, therefore, ... more or less a new material basis for the next turnover cycle." (*Capital, Vol. 2*, p. 264, MECW, *Vol. 36*, pp. 187–88.)

Part III, Chaps 18–21: on schemes of reproduction, the conditions of complementary interconnection between departments that have to obtain for either simple or expanded reproduction to be achieved. Any rupture in any of those conditions has potential to cause crisis. "It is pure tautology to say that crises are provoked by a lack of effective demand or effective consumption ... if the attempt is made to give this tautology the semblance of greater profundity, by the statement that the working class receives too small a portion of its own product, and that the evil would be remedied if it received a bigger share, i.e., if its wages rose, we need only note that crises are always prepared by a period in which wages generally rise, and the working class actually does receive a greater share in the part of the annual product destined for consumption." (*Capital, Vol. 2*, pp. 486–87, MECW, *Vol. 36*, pp. 409–10.)

Engels, Friedrich. "England in 1845 and in 1885," March 1885, MECW, *Vol. 26*, pp. 295–301.

An important piece providing a sketch and update on changes since *The Condition of the Working Class in England* was written in 1845. On the crisis of 1846, Engels wrote: "Forty years ago England stood face to face with a crisis, solvable to all appearances by force only. The immense and rapid development of manufactures had outstripped the extension of foreign markets and the increase of demand. Every ten years the march of industry was violently interrupted by a general commercial crash, followed, after a long period of chronic depression, by a few short years of prosperity, and always ending in feverish overproduction and consequent collapse." (p. 295).

And on changed class relations: "The Factory Acts, once the bugbear of all manufacturers, were not only willingly submitted to, but their expansion into acts regulating almost all trades, was tolerated. Trades Unions, lately considered inventions of the devil himself, were now petted and patronized as perfectly legitimate institutions and as useful means of spreading sound economical doctrines amongst the workers." (p. 297).

Then, on the mutation of crisis into stagnation: "We did not, indeed, pass through the full crisis at the time it was due, in 1877 or 1878; but we have had, ever since 1876, a chronic state of stagnation in all dominant branches of industry. Neither will the full crash come; nor will the period of longed for prosperity to which we used to be entitled before and after it. A dull depression, a chronic glut of all markets for all trades, that is what we have been living in for nearly ten years." (p. 299).

Engels, Friedrich to August Bebel, October 28, 1885, *MECW, Vol. 47*, p. 340, or S. W. Ryazanskaya, ed. *Marx Engels Selected Correspondence,* 3rd rev. ed. (Moscow: Progress Publishers, 1975) 364.

Engels notes "chronic pressure on all the crucial branches of industry" in England as well as in France and America. "It is an unprecedented state of affairs, for all that it is the inevitable consequence of the capitalist system: overproduction on such an enormous scale that it can't even manage to produce a crisis! The overproduction of disposable capital seeking investment is so great that the discount rate here actually fluctuates between 1 and 1 and 1/2 per cent per annum ... the very fact that the financial capitalist prefers to invest his money thus rather than in new industrial enterprises amounts to an admission that the economy is, in his eyes, rotten to the core. And this fear of new investments and any kind of speculation, already a feature of the 1867 crisis, is the main reason for the inability to bring about an acute crisis." He goes on to note that the crisis will destroy the skill-based trade unions which have been refusing admission to the growing numbers of unskilled manufacturing workers.

Engels, Friedrich to N. F. Danielson, November 13, 1885, *MECW, Vol. 47*, pp. 349–50, or S. W. Ryazanskaya, ed. *Marx Engels Selected Correspondence,* 3rd rev. ed. (Moscow: Progress Publishers, 1975) 367.

Referring to Marx's letter of 10 April 1879, Engels says: "That crisis of which the author speaks in his letter was indeed an exceptional one. The fact is it continues still, all Europe and America suffer under it to this day. The absence of the financial crash is one cause of it. But the principal cause is undoubtedly the totally changed state of the *Weltmarkt* [world market]. Since 1870, Germany and especially America have become England's rivals in modern industry, while most other European countries have so far developed their own manufactures as to cease to be dependent on England. The consequence has been the spreading of the process of overproduction over a far larger area than when it was mainly confined to England, and has taken – up to now – a chronic instead of an acute character. By thus delaying the thunderstorm which formerly cleared the atmosphere every ten years, this continued chronic depression must prepare a crash of a violence and extend such as we have never known before. And the more so as the agricultural crisis of which the author speaks, has also continued up to now, has been extended to almost all European countries; and must continue while the virgin черноземъ [black earth] of the Western American prairies remains unexhausted."

1886

Engels, Friedrich to Bebel, January 20–23, 1886, *MECW, Vol. 47*, pp. 386–92, or S. W. Ryazanskaya, ed. *Marx Engels Selected Correspondence,* 3rd rev. ed. (Moscow: Progress Publishers, 1975) 370–71.

"This is already the eighth year in which overproduction has exerted pressure on the markets and, instead of improving, the situation is getting steadily worse, nor can there be any doubt that it is essentially different from what it used to be. Since the arrival of serious rivals to Britain on the world market, the era of crises, in the old sense of the term, has come to an end. If from being acute, the crises become chronic yet lose nothing of their intensity, what is likely to happen? There is bound to be another, if brief, period of prosperity after the vast stocks of goods have been run down, but I am curious to see what will come of it all. Of two things, however, we may be sure: We have entered a period which poses a far greater threat to the existence of the old state of society than did the period of ten-year crises; and, secondly, prosperity, if it comes, will affect Britain to a much lesser extent than before, when it alone used to skim the cream off the world market. The day when this is clearly realized in this country will be the day when the socialist movement will begin here in real earnest – and not before." (p. 390)

Engels, Friedrich to Bebel, February 15, 1886, *MECW, Vol. 47*, pp. 406–10. *Correspondence 1846–1895*, (New York: International Publishers, 1935) 445–48.

"As a result of the collapse of Britain's monopoly of the world market, a state of crisis has persisted uninterruptedly since 1878 and is growing worse rather than better. Poverty, particularly in London's East End, is appalling. The winter, which since January, has been exceptionally severe, combined with the abysmal indifference of the propertied classes, has given rise to great unrest among the mass of the unemployed." (p. 407)

Engels, Friedrich to Bebel, March 18, 1886, *MECW, Vol. 47*, pp. 426–29.

He agrees with Bebel "that periods of prosperity of over 6 months will cease to occur" (p. 428) "Apart from destroying Britain's monopoly on the world market, the new methods of communication – the electric telegraph, the railways, the Suez Canal, and the supplanting of sail by steam – have gone some way towards breaking down the ten-year industrial cycle." (p. 428)

Engels, Friedrich. "Preface to the English Edition," November 5, 1886, in Marx, K. *Capital, Vol. 1*, pp. 109–13, or *MECW, Vol. 35*, pp. 30–36.

With foreign industry encroaching on England's markets, Engels predicts crisis and possible revolution. "While the productive power increases in geometric ratio, the extension of markets proceeds at best in an arithmetic one. The decennial cycle of stagnation, prosperity, overproduction and crisis, ever recurrent from 1825 to 1867, seems to have run its course, but only to land us in the slough of despond of a permanent and chronic depression." That depression, he notes, is bringing rising unemployment, so great that "we can almost calculate the moment when the unemployed, losing patience, will take their own fate into their own hands." Yet, he also writes that Marx thought that perhaps "England is the only country where the inevitable social revolution might be effected entirely by peaceful and legal means."

Engels, Friedrich to Danielson, November 13, 1886, *MECW*, *Vol. 47*, pp. 347–50.

"But the principal cause is undoubtedly the totally changed state of the *Welmarkt* [world market]. Since 1870, Germany and especially America have become England's rivals in modern industry, while most other European countries have so far developed their own manufactures as to cease being dependent on England. The consequence has been the spreading of the process of overproduction over a far larger area than when it was mainly confined to England, and has taken – up to now – a chronic instead of an acute character. By thus delaying the thunderstorm which formerly cleared the atmosphere every ten years, this continued chronic depression must prepare a crash of a violence and extend such as we have never known before." (p. 349)

1890

Engels, Friedrich. "Preface to the Fourth German Edition of the *Manifesto*," May 1, 1890, *MECW*, *Vol. 27*, pp. 53–60.

In this Preface, Engels spells out, in retrospect, how the objective of the First International, at least from his and Marx's point of view, was: "Its aim was to weld together into one huge army the whole militant working class of Europe and America." He goes on to explain how that couldn't happen at that time. But in 1890, the birth of the *Second* International encouraged him to write, optimistically, "today, as I write these lines, the European and American proletariat is reviewing its fighting forces, mobilized for the first time, mobilized as *one* army, under *one* flag, for *one* immediate aim: the standard eight-hour working day to be established by legal enactment ... today the working men of all countries are united indeed." (p. 60).

Engels, Friedrich. "May 4 in London," May 5–21, 1890, *MECW*, *Vol. 27*, p. 61.

Speaking of the first celebration of May Day by large numbers of unskilled workers, Engels wrote that "the *English proletariat*, rousing itself from forty years of hibernation, *rejoined the movement of its class.*" Those forty years he attributed to "the failure of the Chartist movement of 1836–50 and ... the colossal rise of industry between 1848 and

1880," during which time skilled workers had shared in increased creation of wealth by collaborating with their employers. That period of quietude, he declared, "has come to an end."

Engels, Friedrich to Conrad Schmidt, October 27, 1890, *MECW, Vol. 49*, pp. 57–65, or S. W. Ryazanskaya, ed. *Marx Engels Selected Correspondence,* 3rd rev. ed. (Moscow: Progress Publishers, 1975) 397–98.

Discussing various aspects of "historical materialism," Engels mentions that "in the forties" many tried to explain everything by crises in the money market. That was an error, he argued, because "Production is, in the final analysis, the decisive factor." (p. 58) However, he does argue that both commerce and "the money market" can also have their own crises, once they are developed enough that their internal dynamics separate to some degree from changes in production. "As soon as trade in products becomes independent of actual production, the former follows a trend of its own which is, by and large, undoubtedly dictated by production but, in specific cases and within the framework of that general dependence, does in turn obey laws of its own, laws inherent in the nature of this new factor; it is a trend having its own phases and reacting in turn on the trend of production… . It is the same with the money market. Once trade in money becomes divorced from trade in commodities, it will – uncertain circumstances determined by production and by the trade in commodities and within those limits – develop in its own way subject to the special laws and distinctive phases determined by its own nature." (pp. 58–59) He goes on to argue that if "trade in money expands to comprise trade in securities, the said securities being not simply government paper, but also the shares of industrial and commercial concerns … then the reaction of the trade in money on production will be even stronger and more complex. Traders in money own railways, mines, foundries, etc.… They must be run, now in accordance with the immediate interests of production, now in accordance with the needs of the shareholders …" (p. 59)

1891

Engels, Friedrich, "Preface to the Fourth Edition of *Socialism: Utopian and Scientific*," May 12, 1891, *MECW, Vol. 27*, p. 202.

Engels notes he added his comments on "trusts" to this edition because they have "become important." NB: this was just as the work of muckrakers was beginning to make the public aware of the "importance" of the trusts – through their monopoly powers in the economy and corruption of government.

Engels, Friedrich to Oppenheim, March 24, 1891, *MECW, Vol. 49*, p. 152. Marx, Karl and Friederich Engels, *Letters on* Capital, trans. Andrew Drummond (London: New Park Publications, 1983) 255–56.

"It is the old story: when business is good, demand compels the masters to be accommodating, when it is bad, they exploit the excessive supply of labor to contest all these concessions again." But, he goes on, on the whole, on the average, the wage "improves slightly and no crisis can lastingly drag the workers *down to* or *below* zero, the nadir of the previous crisis. But it would be difficult to say what would happen if at any time we were to experience a prolonged, chronic, *general* industrial crisis of 5 to 6 years' duration."

1892

Engels, Friedrich. "Preface [to the 1892 English Edition of *The Condition of the Working Class in England*]," January 11, 1892, *MECW*, *Vol. 27*, pp. 257–69.

In this Preface, Engels sketches how times changed after he wrote *The Condition of the Working Class in England* in 1845 – how England "has thus outgrown the juvenile state of capitalist exploitation described by me …" (p. 260) and how: "The revival of trade, after the crisis of 1847," he wrote "was the dawn of a new industrial epoch." (p. 258)

Engels also argues that the vulnerability of capitalism to crises caused by epidemics had been reduced because of public health measures taken: "… the repeated visitations of cholera, typhus, smallpox, and other epidemics have shown the British bourgeoisie the urgent necessity of sanitation in his towns and cities, if he wishes to save himself and family from falling victim to such diseases. Accordingly, … the most crying abuses … have either disappeared or have been made less conspicuous." (p. 260)

Engels, Friedrich to Bebel, March 8, 1892, *MECW, Vol. 49*, p. 373, or S.W. Ryazanskaya, ed. *Marx Engels Selected Correspondence,* 3rd rev. ed. (Moscow: Progress Publishers, 1975) 418–19.

Protectionism, like Free Trade, Engels argues, has had the effect of glutting individual national markets. "But in this country where we have come through two or three insidious little crises since 1867, we would at last seem to be heading for another acute one. The enormous cotton crops of the last 2 or 3 years, … have depressed prices to the same extent as in the worst days of the 1846 crisis, and are thus exerting tremendous pressure on production which means that the manufacturers here are having to overproduce because of overproduction by the American planters."

1893

Engels, Friedrich to Sorge, December 2, 1893, *MECW*, *Vol. 50*, p. 235. Marx, Karl and Friedrich Engels, *Letters on* Capital, trans. Andrew Drummond (London: New Park Publications, 1983) 280.

"The repeal [at the end of October 1893] of the silver purchase law [Sherman Silver Purchase Act] has saved America from a serious financial crisis and will help to promote an industrial recovery. But I am not sure whether it might not have been better had there really been a crash. The phrase 'cheap money' seems to be deeply engraved in the minds of your Western farmers. In the first place, when they suppose that, if there be ample means of circulation in a country, the rate of interest must fall, they are confusing means of circulation with disposable money capital, a matter upon which considerable light will be shed in Volume 3. And, secondly, all debtors find it convenient to incur debts in good currency and subsequently pay them off in depreciated currency. Hence every indebted Prussian Junker clamours for bimetallism that would rid him of his debts in disguised fashion." At the same time he muses that it might have been better if the crisis had occurred because it might have "dinned some sense into many a thick skull."

1894

Marx, Karl. *Capital 3*, (New York: Penguin, 1991), or *MECW*, *Vol. 37*, chapters 13–15, 25, 27, 30.

This is the last of the weighty tomes too long to give more than an outline and a few examples in what follows.

Engels' "Preface" of October 4, 1894 is mainly an explanation of how he constructed Volume 3 of *Capital* out of Marx's notes and critiques of several critics of Marx. The criticisms he addresses mainly concern the relationship between values and prices and are of interest mostly to those preoccupied with variations of the so-called "transformation problem."

Part One: Surplus-Value and Profit, character, rates, determinants. Effect of speeded up turnover: "The two major foci of crisis between 1825 and 1857, America and India, have been brought 70 to 90 per cent closer to the industrial countries of Europe by this revolution in the means of commerce, and have lost in this way a good deal of their explosive potential." (*Capital 3*, p. 164, or *MECW*, *Vol. 37*, p. 75.)

Part Two: Profit into Average Profit. "The organic composition of capital is the name we give to its value composition, in so far as this is determined by its technical composition and reflects it." (*Capital 3*, p. 245, or *MECW*, *Vol. 37*, p.145.)

Part Three: Law of tendential fall in rate of profit. "The progressive tendency for the general rate of profit to fall is thus simply the expression, peculiar to the capitalist mode of production, of the progressive development of the social productivity of labour." (*Capital 3*, p. 319, or *MECW*, *Vol. 47*, p. 211.)

Part Four: Commodity & money capital into commercial capital and money-dealing capital. The relative autonomy of commercial capital drives reproduction "beyond its own barriers. This inner dependence in combination with external autonomy drives commercial capital to a point where the inner connection is forcibly re-established by way of a crisis." (*Capital* 3, p. 419, or MECW, *Vol.* 37, p. 303.)

Part Five: Division of Profit into Interest and Profit. "If we consider the turnover cycles in which modern industry moves – inactivity, growing animation, prosperity or especially high profit, a rise in interest comes between prosperity and its collapse, while maximum interest up to extreme usury corresponds to a period of crisis." (*Capital* 3, p. 482, or MECW, *Vol.* 37, p. 358.)

Part Six: Surplus Profit into Ground-Rent. "… large landed property reduces the agricultural population to an ever decreasing minimum, and confronts it with an ever-growing industrial population crammed together in large towns; in this way it produces conditions that provoke an irreparable rift in the interdependent process of social metabolism, a metabolism prescribed by the natural laws of life itself … industrially pursued large-scale agriculture … [lays waste and ruins] the natural power of the soil." (*Capital* 3, pp. 949–50, or MECW, *Vol.* 37, pp. 799–800.)

Part Seven: Revenues and Sources. Critique of the Trinity Formula. "Freedom, in this sphere, can consist only in this, that socialized man, the associated producers, govern the human metabolism with nature in a rational way … accomplishing it with the least expenditure of energy and in conditions most worthy and appropriate for their human nature … the true realm of freedom, the development of human powers as an end in itself, begins beyond [the realm of necessity] … the reduction of the working day is the basic prerequisite." (*Capital* 3, p. 959, or MECW, *Vol.* 37, p. 807.)

1895

Engels, Friedrich to Conrad Schmidt, March 12, 1895, MECW, *Vol.* 50, pp. 463–65, or S. W. Ryazanskaya, ed. *Marx Engels Selected Correspondence,* 3rd rev. ed. (Moscow: Progress Publishers, 1975) 456–60.

After praising Schmidt for discovering on his own "why it is that the rate of profit tends to fall," Engels argues, at length and with examples not only from political economy (value, wages, general rate of profit) but from the natural sciences (evolution), that all conceptual "laws" never correspond exactly to the reality from which they are abstracted, but only manifest themselves as averages or tendencies, Engels notes "the total amount of surplus value from which, however, we must deduct that portion that is *presented to the buyer*, especially at times of crisis when overproduction is reduced to its true content of socially necessary labour."

Engels, Friedrich to Richard Fischer, April 15, 1895, *MECW*, *Vol.* 50, pp. 496–98.

A letter about possibly reprinting his and Marx's articles from "the old *Rheinische Zeitung*." Looking back: "Marx always used to tell me that it was precisely his preoccupation with the law on thefts of wood and the condition of the Mosel wine-growers that led him from politics pure and simple to economic conditions and thus to socialism."

Engels, Friedrich to Franz Mehring," End of April 1895, *MECW*, *Vol.* 50, p. 503.

On his first, "distinctly chilly" meeting with Marx" in 1842 in the offices of the *Rheinische Zeitung* in Cologne, Prussia.

Index

NB: to avoid redundancies 1) this Index does not cover the annotated bibliography (Appendix II), and 2) there are no entries under the rubric of either "crisis" or "class struggle", those being the subject of pretty much everything in this book.

www.ingramcontent.com/pod-product-compliance
Lightning Source LLC
Chambersburg PA
CBHW071232230926
51849CB00001B/77
* 9 7 8 9 0 0 4 7 0 8 3 6 5 *